PROJECT MANAGEMENT
Effective Scheduling

PROJECT MANAGEMENT
Effective Scheduling

J. Brian Dreger

The Boeing Company
Wichita, Kansas

VAN NOSTRAND REINHOLD
New York

Library of Congress Catalog Card Number 91-23958
ISBN 0442-00565-2

Printed in the United States of America.

Van Nostrand Reinhold
115 Fifth Avenue
New York, New York 10003

Chapman and Hall
2-6 Boundary Row
London, SE1 8HN, England

Thomas Nelson Australia
102 Dodds Street
South Melbourne 3205
Victoria, Australia

Nelson Canada
1120 Birchmount Road
Scarborough, Ontario MIK 5G4, Canada

16 15 14 13 12 11 10 9 8 7 6 5 4 3 2 1

Library of Congress Cataloging-in-Publication Data

Dreger, J. Brian
    Project management : effective scheduling / J. Brian
Dreger.
        p.   cm.
    Includes bibliographical references (p.   ) and index.
    ISBN 0-442-00565-2
    1. Industrial project management.   I. Title.
HD69.P75D74   1992
658.4′04--dc20   91-23958
                                                    CIP

To Barbara, Eddy, Susan, Barbara Jo, and Paul

Contents

Preface

YOU ARE A PROJECT MANAGER!

Everyone is a project manager because everyone manages projects.

Regardless of occupation or position within an organization, we are all project managers. We must plan and schedule activities. We have to coordinate our activities with those of others. We face time and budget constraints. And we face pressures for good quality.

So begins another, *complementary* (and outstanding) book on the subject (Alan Randolph and Barry Posner, *Effective Project Planning and Management*, Prentice Hall, 1988). They go on (p. 3) to ask if you:

- Must finish assignments by a specified deadline
- Have more than one task to accomplish during the day
- Must complete these tasks with limited *resources* (money, personnel, equipment, material, energy, or facility (other than time) required to complete a project)
- Need to work with other people to get your own work done
- Work for/with other people who change their mind about what they want.

Unless you answered "No" to all the above (or live in Peter Pan's Never-Land, "where time is never planned"), you are—whether you thought it before or not—a project manager. You may, at any point, be asked how a delay will affect this particular project or other projects. And you will be judged on the speed, accuracy, reliability, and completeness of your answer (Figure 1).

Please read on . . .

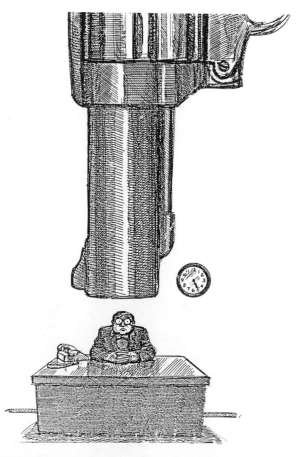

FIGURE 1. "Under the gun."

Acknowledgments

This book would not have been possible without the help of many people, to
whom I am very grateful:

Access Technology, Natick, Massachusetts:
Allan Kluchman, Founder
Carl Nelson, President
Ellen S. Dana, Beth A. Hennessy, and Chris Saulnier, Marketing Managers
Natalie Sciacca, training specialist.

Authors:
A.T. Armstrong-Wright, author and lecturer, United Kingdom
Professors Richard B. Chase, University of Southern California, and Nicholas J. Aquilano, University of Arizona
Professor Harold Kerzner, Baldwin-Wallace College
Harvey A. Levine, author, consultant, lecturer, professor, and former Project Management Institute President
Professors W. Alan Randolph, University of South Carolina, and Barry Z. Posner, Santa Clara University.

The Boeing Company, Wichita, Kansas:
Ernie R. Shoaf, Engineering Training Manager
Mary K. Bonebrake, Andrea E. Tolbert, and Phil T. White, *Primavera* Scheduling Specialists
C. Rodger Moran, Computing Strategic Planning Consultant
B. Lynn Wells, devoted and exceptionally competent associate
Several hundred quality project management students.

Comshare (formerly Execucom Systems)
Austin, Texas: Steve Stewart and Robert Welch, Consultants
Dallas, Texas: Kenneth Spalding, Regional Marketing Manager
Seattle, Washington: Kathie J. MacIndoe, Regional Marketing Manager
Washington, D.C.:   Grant Wheeler, Consultant.

Primavera Systems, Bala Cynwyd, Pennsylvania:
Joel M. Koppelman, Co-founder and President
Amy L. Abrams and Lou Sassano, Regional Marketing Managers.

Van Nostrand Reinhold, New York, New York:
Editorial: Bob Argentieri, Gene Dallaire, and Betty Sheehan
Marketing: Cindy Clearwater
Production: Ken Allen and Joy Aquilino.

My Wonderful Family—Barbara, Eddy, Susan, Barbara Jo, and Paul—all of whom gave up much of their time with
    Daddy while I wrote it. And Grandma, who again looked after them all while I did.

My sincere thanks and appreciation to all of you!

Comments, thoughts, criticisms, and advice are solely those of the author. They do not necessarily represent those of
The Boeing Company. No attempt should be made to imply otherwise.

1
Why Is Project Management So Important?

This is a book about time, money, resources, and performance. It discusses how each may best be used to manage activities and achieve a wide variety of objectives:

- On time—meet *schedule*
- On budget—meet *cost*
- Within specifications—meet *performance*
- While maintaining good human relations

It is a book about *project management*. Its primary focus is on project planning, scheduling, tracking, and control. These, along with human resource management (only summarized in this book), are absolutely crucial to project success. Together, they will enable *your* project, whatever its details and characteristics, to succeed, too. Your project will finish on time, on budget, on specification, and within the framework of good human relations. It will improve your contribution to the overall business process, and its financial success. It will get more things done better. It will conform to valid customer requirements. It will demonstrate your high level of professionalism and competence: Do it right, or don't do it at all!

Why is this so important? Spirer (p. 77) notes four challenges in the modern economic environment that can only be met by formal project management principles:

- Margins for error in performance, schedule, and cost have been reduced
- Competition has increased
- The cost of money has dramatically increased, making the consequences of overruns and late deliveries much more serious than when funds were cheap
- Project complexity and interrelationships have greatly increased

A similar view is shown in Fig. 1-1.

Project management, however, is an extremely complex and rigorous subject not very intuitive even to experienced project managers. For students new to the subject, the amount of detail involved may at times seem overwhelming. Why is there so much stuff to learn? Why so many examples and case studies? Each of these focuses on a different topic or condition you will likely confront and must learn to handle effectively. Since the human mind works best when guided by example, you will be better prepared to meet these challenges. Even successful project managers will find a wealth of knowledge with which to hone their skills and keep for later review.

Levine (p. 2) defines a *project* as "a group of tasks performed in a definable time period in order to meet a specific

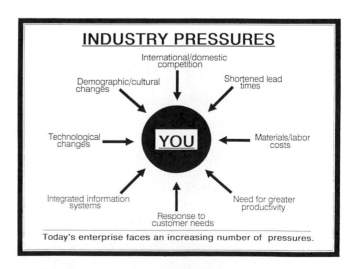

FIGURE 1-1. Today's enterprise faces an increasing number of pressures.

set of objectives." He then (p. 3) defines *project management* as "planning, organizing, directing, and controlling resources for a specific time period to meet a specific set of one-time objectives." We shall revisit these definitions.

BENEFITS

Now let's consider what various authors see to be the great advantages of project management.

Chase and Aquilano (p. 296): "Project management offers the best available technique to plan, operate, and control a firm's operation within this climate of short product cycles and rapid change," larger projects, increased competition, more expensive costs of capital, greater opportunity costs, increased risks of cost overruns, and more government regulation.

Cox (Digital News, p. 58): "For many companies, the competitive battle will be won by whomever has the sharpest pencil and the sharpest knife—the most careful project scheduling and the most exact cost controls. The instrument putting the point to the pencil and the edge to the knife is a new generation of project management software. Beating competitors calls for sharp pencils and sharp knives. Integrated software is the cutting edge."

Kerzner: "Executives will be facing increasingly complex challenges during the next decade. These challenges will be the result of high escalation factors for salaries and raw materials, increased union demands, pressure from stockholders, and the possibility of long-term, high inflation accompanied by a mild recession and a lack of borrowing power with financial institutions. These environmental conditions have existed before, but not to the degree that they do today.

"The solution to the majority of corporate problems involves obtaining better control and use of existing corporate resources. Emphasis is being placed on looking internally rather than externally for the solution to these problems. As part of the attempt to achieve an internal solution, executives are taking a hard look at the ways corporate activities are being managed.*

"To make better use of and to achieve greater control over resources, more and more executives [and employees at all corporate levels] are realizing the importance of adopting and implementing the project management approach. Today, project management has spread to almost every major industry in the world, on either a formal or informal basis." (p. vii, Kerzner)

Kerzner (p. 3) also lists as benefits the ability to:

- Identify responsibilities to ensure that all activities are accounted for
- Minimize need for continuous reporting
- Identify scheduling time limits
- Identify ways to trade time for money, and money for time
- Measure accomplishments against plans
- Identify problems early for follow-up corrective action

- Improve estimating capability for future planning
- Know when objectives cannot be met or will be exceeded

Other benefits include the ability to:

- Plan, monitor, and control *progress* (accomplished work) and costs
- Objectively evaluate project health
- Identify current or potential trouble spots
- Allow more timely warning in order to act, not react
- Identify when and where the project manager must act
- Indicate what he or she should do to reduce delays or cost
- Point out where extra effort would be wasted
- Catch people doing something right

This is true regardless of project size, length, complexity, industry, or deliverables.

Knowing the immense value of formal project management, many companies have issued directives similar to the following: "It shall be enforced company policy to apply project management principles to every funded project."

The Boeing Total Quality Commitment (TQC) summarized its benefits as follows: Getting the job done right the first time is a basic TQC premise. This can best be achieved by combining management by facts with teamwork, two-way communication, and respect for human worth and dignity. In a manufacturing environment, when these elements are introduced into a program, the results can be fewer engineering changes, less rework, less scrap, and fewer withhold tags. In turn, this can translate to a higher quality product, built ahead of schedule and under budget.

The recent explosion of interest in project management should be no surprise. If your competition has not already implemented project management methodologies, it will do so soon:

- To gain competitive advantage over you
- To take away your market share
- To enjoy profits that you could have enjoyed instead
- To try to drive you out of business

For they, not you, will now have:

- The "sharpest pencil"
- The "sharpest knife"
- The best income statement!

Project management is highly useful in all enterprises, but is absolutely mandatory in some. Those enterprises whose tasks are complex—especially those whose environment is dynamic—*must* employ project management methodologies today just to remain in business. Tomorrow would be too late. Other enterprises are strongly recommended to use the methodology for improved performance. This is summarized in Table 1-1.

---

*Kerzner, Harold. *Project Management For Executives;* and *Project Management: A Systems A Planning, Scheduling, and Controlling.* New York: Van Nostrand Reinhold.

Table 1-1   Why All Enterprises Can Benefit From Project Management

PRIORITY	TASK LEVEL	ENVIRONMENT	COMMENTS
HIGHEST	Complex	Dynamic	MANDATORY
2	Complex	Static	MANDATORY
3	Simple	Dynamic	STRONGLY RECOMMENDED
4	Simple	Static	USEFUL AND RECOMMENDED

Regardless of organization type or project nature, the current widespread use of project management techniques stems from growing shortages of:

• Time
• Money
• Human resources
• Materials
• Other resources

It is not just a saying: We *do* need to work smarter, not harder! This means we must utilize expensive plant, equipment, money, personnel, and other resources to maximum efficiency. It also means we need to plan and control our projects better than ever before—completely, precisely, professionally, and profitably. Without a plan, there can be no monitoring or control. A budget is an agreed-to allocation of resources; control is based on existing plans and their related budgets. One monitors to determine the "actual," which is then compared with the "budget" for control.

We need ample time to discover difficulties that may lie ahead, so we may take action to prevent—or at least mitigate—them. We need to call a time-out and draw up new plans if necessary. An effective method of project planning and control must, without exception, provide a clear picture of:

• Relationships among the activities making up the project
• Resources required to complete these activities
• Areas where resources are insufficient to do this

At the same time, we must also know how delays or other disruptions at any stage will affect the remainder of the project. In this way, resources may be reallocated well in advance, and last-minute panics and delays—which may be insurmountable or costly to overcome—are avoided.

But no control system can ever take corrective action or predict events that will require plan changes. The project manager must do this. Although it is easy to describe the above cycle, many project managers have not, putting it very politely, made this pattern part of their behavior. How very unfortunate. Control problems usually arise from one of the following:

• Failure to react to a variance, even if clearly signaled
• Excessive concern for and fussin' about past events, which diverts effort from the future and its success

Project management techniques are proven and clearly provide:

• The easiest—yet most effective—adaptation to an ever-changing environment and the best response to customer problems
• The only effective way by which a multidisciplinary set of activities may be handled within a specified period of time or given amount of money
• Easier identification of activity responsibilities
• Horizontal as well as vertical work flow for optimal efficiency
• Assistance in overcoming such executive-level obstacles as:
> Unstable economy
> Shortages
> Soaring costs
> Increased complexity
> Heightened competition
> Technological changes
> Societal concerns (consumerism, ecology, quality of work, and the like)

The need for flexibility is absolute and paramount, since no two projects are ever precisely alike. There are always differences in:

• Goals and deliverables
• Technology
• The client's approach to the project
• Geographic locations
• Contract time and conditions
• The schedule
• Financial approach to the project
• Resources
• People

Regardless of these differences, you finish projects by completing all activities in accordance with their dependency relationships. The activity *network,* about which we shall learn much more later, is the current method of choice for illustrating, presenting, and analyzing project dependencies, status, simulation results, and forecasts. When expressed verbally, dependency relationships can be ambiguous, but a network is unambiguous. It can be used to do creative sequencing and reduce the number of surprises.

In project management, the best surprise is no surprise!

In days of (project management) old, many desirable changes were rejected only because of the expense involved in recalculating the network. There were also temptations (often not resisted) to accept hasty decisions that proved costly.

Today, fortunately, we may ask unlimited "what if" questions and constantly update and optimize our schedule with only a few:

• Keystrokes
• Minutes
• Pieces of paper

Additionally, people can get timely, accurate answers to individual questions and concerns without the need to employ a hundred draftspersons. This results in a better, more optimal network for all. Still, the simplest model that helps project personnel do a better job is the best.

WHAT IS PROJECT MANAGEMENT?

People often:

• Understand project management to mean many different things
• *Mis*understand project management to mean many others

The average bear may know of ongoing (and frequently troubled) local projects and feel project management is used to plan and control these activities. Instead, it is usually project *mis*management that does *not* control these activities. Attempting to manage "on the fly"—which translates to "winging it"—cannot and will not meet your needs. The perception, however, remains. Listed below are some of the wide-ranging views people have on project management:

• A threat to established authority and top management
• A colorful, pretty-picture computer drawing tool
• A source for future general managers
• A cause of unwanted change in ongoing procedures
• A means to an end
• An end to a means
• A contradiction in terms
• Hard work
• A course in the School of Hard Knocks
• A way to build an empire
• A necessary evil to traditional management
• An opportunity for growth and advancement
• A better way to motivate people to work toward accomplishment of an objective
• A source of frustration
• A way of introducing controlled change
• An area of research
• A vehicle for introducing creativity
• A means of coordinating functional units
• A means of deep satisfaction
• A way of life
• A way to drive senior management nuts
• An unjustified panacea
• A scapegoat cause of world hunger and disease
• The art of creating the illusion that any outcome is the result of a series of predetermined, deliberate acts when, in fact, it was dumb luck
• The end of civilization

Rejecting the whimsical definitions and those born of fear and ignorance, we may define important terms, optimistic in outlook, as follows:
A *project:*

• Is a series of related jobs
• Is usually directed toward satisfactory completion of a major objective
• Must meet certain technical and performance specifications
• Requires a significant amount of time and resources to perform
• Must have defined start and end dates

The jobs must follow one another in a given sequence to ensure that prerequisite activities are completed and needed resources are available.

Kerzner (p. 4) defines *project management* as follows:

"Project management is the planning, organizing, directing, [sometimes staffing], and controlling of company resources for a relatively short-term objective that has been established to complete specific goals and objectives. Furthermore, project management utilizes the systems approach to management by having functional [line] personnel (the vertical hierarchy) assigned to a specific project (the horizontal hierarchy)."

Its objective is to complete a project:

• On time
• On budget
• At the desired performance level
• All with good customer and employee relations

It must conform to valid customer requirements and improve someone's life. How Kerzner (p. 5) presents this concept is shown in Fig. 1-2.

FIGURE 1-2.   Kerzner project management objectives.

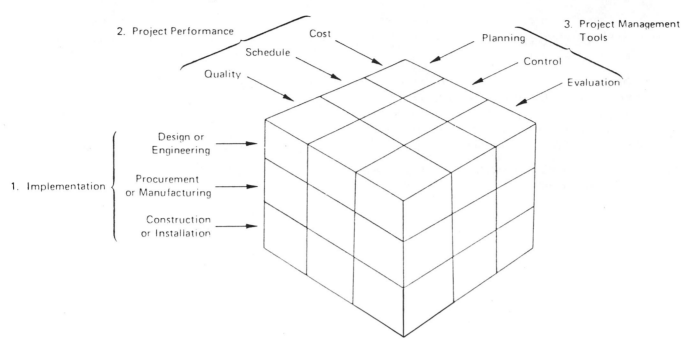

FIGURE 1-3. Dinsmore project management objectives. Reprinted by permission of the publisher, from *Human Factors in Project Management* by Paul Dinsmore, © 1990 AMACOM, a division of American Management Association, New York. All rights reserved.

Dinsmore (p. 26) presents a more complete depiction: the "Dinsmore Cube" is even harder to solve than Rubic's cube is (Fig. 1-3).

Project management is designed to manage the use of a company's resources on a given activity (or the entire project collection of activities) on time, within cost, and within performance expectations. Time, cost, and performance:

- Relate to each other
- Act as constraints on the project

If the project is for an outside customer, it must also be completed with good customer relations. A project may be managed internally within time, cost, and performance objectives but still so alienate the customer as to eliminate any future business.

The 3M Corporation, however, teaches a more progressive, thoughtful definition of customer: *Anyone* with whom the project or its members deals is a customer—to be accorded proper dignity and respect.

A Boeing project management student put it this way:

"I once enjoyed a 3M-developed seminar called "Customer Satisfaction." In this seminar, a customer was defined as *anyone* with whom I interact—including providing a product, service, response, or even a phone call. One never knows what future relationships he or she might have or what future business opportunities may be affected. A customer, therefore, may be my manager, employee, vendor, contractor, even janitor. All will provide better, more satisfying results if treated with dignity and respect and as if they were "the customer" on whom my bread and butter depended. Some day, our current relationship might change; their memory of our previous

encounter(s) could directly affect my business success and income."

Excellent thoughts and some very wise advice!

The *Critical Path Method* (*CPM*), the most enhanced version of which is fully discussed in this book, is an:

- Invaluable management tool for initial schedule planning
- Excellent means of project review and control

Network preparation and scheduling builds an acceptable plan. But—in project management, at least—nothing ever goes as planned. This is normal and should be expected. We must therefore have complete, accurate, useful, and timely information on when, where, and how management should act to restore schedule, cost, or project performance. We must also know why things go well so that we may continue doing them.

A project comes in several flavors, as you would expect:

- *Individual project*—a short-duration project assigned to one individual sometimes acting as both a project manager and functional manager.
- *Staff project*—a project that can be accomplished by one organizational unit, such as a department; a staff is developed from each section involved and works best if only one functional unit is involved
- *Special project*—a project that requires temporary reassignment to other individuals or units; "TDY" (Temporary Duty). Works best for short projects
- *Matrix of aggregate projects*—a series of interrelated projects that requires input from many functional units and usually controls vast resources

CHARACTERISTICS OF A PROJECT MANAGER

Project management is very goal-oriented. Success depends on the extent to which the manager understands the relationships among, and effective use of, people, time, money, and resources. The project manager must have management skills of highest quality. He or she must develop:

- Patience, in order to plan the project well (a project well planned is a project half completed)
- Wisdom to know the difference between effort and progress (wheels in motion may be wheels in reverse)

The project manager must be a complete manager, fully self-contained, reliable, capable, and confident. (You might even need to "toot your own horn" a little because no one will reach in and toot it for you!) There is often no one ready (or willing or able) to help him or her, other than line managers and perhaps top management. But, if these persons are the cause of the problem . . .

Above all, he or she must be able to manage and work effectively with people—customer, coworker, vendor, and others.

If a project is large, the project manager may take personnel on temporary full-time loan from functional areas to work directly for him or her. If, however, full-time help is not provided, then the project manager must compete with other jobs on that department's schedule—much the same as in the traditional organizational structure—as well as with other project managers to get his or her work done.

"Here is an area," write Chase and Aquilano (p. 300), "that truly requires the skills of a good project manager—the ability to get the work done while maintaining a good relationship with functional managers." He or she must be able to solve problems (see Fig. 1-4).

A good, even great, project manager does not ensure a successful project, but a mediocre or bad selection will often kill even a promising project before it can begin. The project manager is the heart, the mind, and the soul of the project management team; he or she alone is responsible for how this team performs.

The project manager is also responsible for coordinating and integrating activities across multiple functional lines. In order to do this, he or she:

- Requires strong communication and interpersonal skills
- Must be familiar with the operations of each contributing line organization
- Should have a general knowledge of the technology involved in the project.

Note well: The project manager need *not* be an expert in the technology under his or her control—even in the "home base" area. As with other management positions, promotion to project manager should not be just a reward for good performance. It should instead reflect senior management's confidence in the potential to do the job right—

on time, on budget, on specification, within the framework of good human relations, and in conformance to valid customer requirements.

Reward for performance, but promote on potential! Rather than being a hot-shot technician, it is more important for the project manager to:

Bring to the job a wide-ranging background and strong credentials in such subjects as:
    Human relations
    Accounting (cost and management)
    Engineering
    Environmental issues
    Finance
    International considerations (if applicable)
    Law
    Management
    Negotiation ("horse-trading")
    Operations
    Organizational structures and behaviors
    Planning—the major responsibility of the project manager
    Quantitative tools and techniques
    Regulatory agencies and policies
    Scheduling
    Vendor relations
Fully understand his or her own job description, and where authority and responsibility begin and end
Know customer and organizational requirements
Be able to gather information from across all functional lines on a systematic basis
Maintain good relations with all line organizations—even with those in political competition with each other

Ain't no doubt one of 'em's right, Clem, but ya can't get the other to admit it.

FIGURE 1-4. Why interdepartmental co-operation is crucial to your enterprise.

Maintain proper balance between technical and managerial project functions

Be able to cope with both risk and constraints

Be able to identify important issues

Ask appropriate questions and advice from proper personnel

Assimilate this information

Make a reasonable, business-like decision based on knowledge of all the facts and issues

Serve as a general manager who learns total company or organization operation

The major project manager responsibility is to plan—a project that is:

- On time
- On budget
- On specification
- Within the framework of good human relations.

The project must conform to valid customer requirements and improve people's lives. But nothing ever goes "as planned," says a corollary of Murphy's Law; so the project manager, always beset by changes and things not going according to plan, is not at all likely to plan himself or herself out of a job. Few projects are ever completed without some conflict that the project manager must resolve.

The project manager's job is not an easy one. It is not likely to become one. It makes up in criticality what it lacks in ease. Selection of a top-quality individual is crucial.

Providing the project manager with total, integrative responsibility results in:

- Total accountability being assumed by a single person
- Project, rather than functional, dedication
- A requirement for coordination across functional interfaces
- Proper utilization of integrated planning and control
- Authority and motivation to do the job right

THE NEED FOR PROJECT MANAGEMENT

Do you ever face these challenges?

- Executives do not understand what is really going on "in the trenches"
- Senior management allots less time than is needed to complete the project
- There is a lack of resources—not enough staff, money, equipment, and the like
- Customer needs are unclear and constantly changing
- There is a fear of initiating change
- There is a lack of ownership—accepting responsibility—when tackling a problem
- It is difficult to plan for the future
- It is difficult to forecast technology trends
- Vendor management can be hard to deal with

- Managing people is demanding
- Employee communication is frequently poor
- Organization goals are often placed above enterprise
- The corporation is too internalized in its thinking and insufficiently oriented to the outside world, especially competition
- Long-range corporate planning is sporadic and superficial
- Executives have inadequate financial information and control
- The time span between project initiation and completion is increasing
- Capital committed prior to the use of the deliverable is increasing
- Time and money commitments become less flexible with more advanced technology
- Technology requires more highly-specialized human resources
- Turf issues must be considered (Some people go to the office to do more politickin' than producin')

PURPOSE

Although most projects do have their own horror stories, project management in general need not be like the problems listed above. My own project management experiences have been wonderful—very rewarding and deeply satisfying. The foundations on which I successfully managed more than a dozen major projects over fifteen years are described at length in this book. These same principles have been used to schedule many thousands of activities, mostly by former students in both industry and at universities.

These ideas are both practical and proven. They have worked well for me, my clients, and my students. They can also work well for you. They are unlimited in promise except only by your ingenuity.

Welcome to my world!

The purpose of this book is to discuss useful, practical project management scheduling principles (and relevant examples) suitable for use in both classroom and industry. The featured projects are not "canned" exercises written on my Monday lunch hour, but instead are comprehensive examples, both of which are based on actual, successful projects:

- *Home:* housing construction
- *Cars:* plant expansion and modernization (presented in Appendix A)

Both projects may be easily understood by a wide range of readers. Other, less complex, examples illustrate important scheduling points. Solutions to both case studies and all examples are provided by *Primavera Project Planner* (*P3*), a high-end, integrated project management software tool that operates in MS-DOS and Digital VAX/VMS environments.

***But note well Table 1-2.

Table 1-2   What This Book Is Not

```
This is NOT a book about:

* Computers
* Computer software
* Primavera Project Planner.

It does NOT teach - or require the reader to know - how to:

* Like a computer
* Operate a computer
* Enter data
* Generate reports
* Push buttons
* Operate Primavera or any other software tool.

It is NOT a P3 user manual!
```

The reports shown throughout this book provide information that you need in your environment, manual or computerized, to do your job properly. This book applies to your project in your environment, be it:

• Manual
• Competitor software
• *Primavera Project Planner*

The highly respected Harvey A. Levine, former Project Management Institute president and a noted author and consultant, contends:

• Vendors are responsible for training on their particular tool
• *You* are responsible for learning the principles—both basic and advanced—in whatever environment you operate

To be considered a professional, you must do things like a professional. Proper education in project management concepts and methods will certainly help you gain the respect accorded a professional. Always be the best you can be, and do the best you can do. Nothing else is acceptable, nothing less will suffice, nothing more will be expected.

There is no substitute for "knowing what's going on." This book applies to both manual and electronic project management environments, *P3* and otherwise. In each, your objective is still the same—to complete your project:

• On time
• On budget
• Within specifications
• All within the context of good human relations

Your project must conform to valid customer requirements. Through it, you must improve people's lives.

BASIC PROCESS

Essentially, project management consists of:

• Defining what is to be done—and what is not to be done

• Dividing a project into more manageable, clearly defined activities
• Illustrating it as a network of boxes representing those activities and arrows showing work flow connecting them

Activities that follow each other are drawn as boxes in sequence. The direction of the connecting arrows indicates relationships and the direction of progress. Activities that can be carried out concurrently are drawn as parallel paths. A complex project will consist of many (thousands of) such sequences, some with variations on the above. Once the initial network has been completed, it is possible to assign additional details, such as *durations* (amount of time, often based on similar processes done in the past, needed to complete an activity), costs, resources, and so on. It will also be possible to schedule, evaluate, and control the rates of progress, costs, and resource allocation.

So that close control can be maintained, it is necessary to:

• Measure actual progress
• Compare this with planned progress (the target schedule)
• Evaluate the effect of any deviations from the plan
• Replan to meet the new circumstances

This should be a continuous, iterative process during the entire project life cycle. A complete step-by-step analysis would include activity:

• Sequences
• Timing
• Required *resources* (personnel, money, equipment, information, and the like)
• Interrelationships

In effect, the astute project manager comes very close to identifying, simulating in advance, and planning for most of the actual conditions that may arise during the course of the project. This will allow him or her to act, not react, when necessary. Your customer, whomever it may be, will also appreciate such attention to detail and efforts to optimize performance. The point is this: Replan when and as necessary. You are not doing your job if you do not. The frequency of each review cycle will depend on the type of project and the amount of control required.

The original schedule should be used as the target, or baseline, plan from which future progress and financial performance are measured. It also serves as a reference point from which simulation results may be measured. At any given time, *Primavera* allows two target plans in addition to the current schedule. This enables direct, easy comparison with both plan and forecast or simulation.

It also enables similar comparisons with project changes. For configuration control and audit trail purposes, all changes (who, what, when, where, and why) must be fully and formally documented. There must be some complete, formal record of what happened and why. You should also add summary information and comments to the affected activity records themselves; in *Primavera,* this may be added to the nine-line "scratchpad" log associated with every project activity or to the bottom right corner of every graphics plot.

This history should be retained well after project completion—at least several years. While extremely important to all project phases (and to future projects that depend on this experience), it is especially important in decisions regarding time–cost tradeoff, which will be studied in Chapter 9.

Regardless of the level of detail at which it is to be reported or used, a project must be broken down into manageable units before a plan or schedule can be prepared, or work begins. The degree necessary depends on the:

• Type of project
• Purpose for which the planning is being done
• Persons to whom reports will be made

As with all other aspects of project management, the project manager must strike a proper balance between the:

• Value of information produced
• Cost of producing it

Even though detailed planning is rarely wasted, too much detail—cutting things down to frog hairs—may be just as costly as too little. That will not suit your purpose, either.

Once the required level of detail has been decided, the project is divided into clearly-defined activities. Where possible, an activity should consist of only one type of work, so that responsibility may be exclusively assigned. This is particularly important if the network is later used for resource analysis or cost control. Similarly, the activity should be self-contained. If part of the activity depends on, or controls, another part of the same activity, it should be divided appropriately. Readers familiar with the data base normalization process may correctly consider activity descriptions to be at third, if not fourth, normal form. Activity designations should neither be too simple nor too complex, neither too general nor too detailed. Work carried out at different locations should be represented by activities corresponding to each.

Activity scheduling is the single most important tool for determining how to apply company resources to meet project objectives. Activity schedules:

• Forecast time-phased resource utilization requirements
• Provide a basis to track progress and performance effectively

Most projects begin, therefore, with schedule development—to estimate costs and resource requirements. Schedules serve as master plans from which both customer and team members have an up-to-date picture of project status.

In a nutshell: A *Forward Pass* (beginning to end) analysis of the network gives *Early Start* and *Early Finish* times for all activities, and for the whole project. Even before taking into account calendar and resource constraints, one can use this information to verify feasibility. Next, a *Backward Pass* gives *Late Start* and *Late Finish* times. One can then:

• Find the *Critical Path*(s), along which a day's delay means a day's delay in project completion
• Determine activity *float*—the difference between Early Start and Late Start and a measure of scheduling flexibility.

The start and finish of every project activity is an event worthy of tracking and careful management, but one does not always need to work closely with such a large number. A *milestone* is an activity that is of zero duration, uses no resources, and represents:

• A significant point in time
• A motivator toward which project staff can direct efforts
• Overall progress via a checkpoint
• A major accomplishment
• Notable deliverable result
• Critical event or approval/decision point in a time-logic network

Milestones can indicate the start or end of a series of related activities or an accomplishment in the course of a project. But the above purposes dictate a small set of milestones, usually no more than twenty at a high managerial level, or about three per month. Milestones are sometimes erroneously equated with resource-consuming activities.

We can now answer "what if" questions about the effects of relationships and efforts to reduce completion time or cost, or both. We must first estimate activity time durations (assuming unlimited resources and ignoring calendar constraints). The resulting analysis is a crucial input to incorporating calendar and resource constraints—usually by far the most difficult to handle effectively. Project planning is most effective when done iteratively, like any other design process—moving from first to second approximations, then to third, and so on, sharpening the design as you go. A computer with good project management tools is highly desirable if not absolutely essential.

The guidelines for effective project management include the following:

- The schedule must be both accurate and realistic
- All major activities and dates must be clearly defined, including constraints specified in the Statement of Work
- Schedules should relate directly to the Work Breakdown Structure (WBS) discussed in chapter 2 and should use the same numbering system in both
- The exact work sequence should be defined through a network of activities in which interrelationships can be readily identified
- Needed resources should be included for each activity
- Neither too few nor too many activities should be included

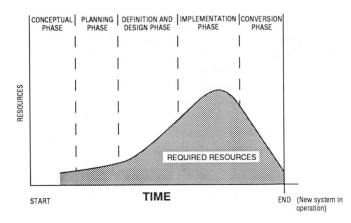

FIGURE 1-5.   Project life cycle as defined by Kerzner.

PROJECT PHASES

Every project has certain development stages, known as life-cycle phases, through which it proceeds. Hopefully, these phases are *not* the same as those detailed at the end of this chapter! Although the precise definitions and boundaries of these operational phases tend to vary by industry, by company, and by author—sometimes even by project within the same company—the basic idea remains the same. These phases often have names similar to those in Table 1-3 and Fig. 1-5.

These terms all describe nearly the same thing. As long as the underlying concept is understood, the differing terms should not be cause for concern. Cleland and King (pp. 187–90) include the following characteristics in their set of definitions. While software-oriented, these definitions nevertheless apply equally to other project types as well:

1. Conceptual
   Determine existing needs or potential deficiencies of existing systems
   Establish system concepts that provide initial strategic guidance

   Determine initial feasibility and practicability
   Examine alternative ways to accomplish objectives
   Provide initial answers to important questions:
     What will it cost?
     When will it be available?
     What will it do?
     How will it be integrated into existing systems?
   Estimate required human and nonhuman resources
   Select initial system designs that accomplish objectives
   Determine initial system interfaces
   Establish a system organization
2. Definition
   Identify required human and nonhuman resources
   Prepare detailed plans to support the system
   Determine final and realistic cost, schedule, and performance requirements
   Identify high-risk areas and plans to further evaluate these areas
   Determine final system interfaces

Table 1-3   Project Life Cycle as Defined by Various Authors

SHELLY/CASHMAN (pages 13-14)	UNISYS BURROUGHS (page PM2)
1. Initiation and preliminary investigation 2. Detailed investigation and analysis 3. Design 4. Development 5. Implementation/evaluation	1. Requirements definition 2. Conceptual design 3. Detail design 4. Development 5. Implementation 6. Post-implementation
CLELAND/KING (pages 187-190) 1. Conceptual 2. Definition 3. Production 4. Operational 5. Divestment	DINSMORE (page 24) 1. Conceptual 2. Planning 3. Execution 4. Termination

Table 1-4   Kliem's Ten-Point Guide to Project Success

```
 1. Publish project plans
 2. Use kickoff meetings
 3. Employ change control
 4. Do replanning sparingly
 5. Know project status
 6. Conduct useful meetings
 7. Make action items visible
 8. Know what to do
 9. Use a good project management software tool
10. Get out (of your office) and visit the team members' environment.
```

Determine necessary support subsystems and documentation

3. Production

    Update detailed plans

    Identify and manage required resources

    Verify performance specifications

    Begin project activities

    Prepare final documentation

    Perform final testing

    Develop plans to support system during operational phase

4. Operational

    Use the system

    Ensure that it meets performance requirements under operating conditions

    Integrate system into existing systems

    Provide necessary feedback (compare actual experience with plan)

    Evaluate adequacy of supporting systems

5. Divestment

    Commence phasedown

    Develop transfer plans

    Divest or transfer resources to other systems

    Determine "lessons learned" for use in later systems

    Customer image and perception

    Major problems and their solutions

    Technological advances

    Advancements in knowledge base

    New or improved managerial techniques

    Recommendations for future research and development

    Recommendations for future project management

    Other important lessons learned

ORGANIZATION

Much has been written about the human and organizational aspects of project management. Although crucially important to project success, they are beyond the scope of this book and will therefore only be summarized. For in-depth coverage of these topics, please read Dinsmore, Kerzner, Martin, Randolph/Posner, and other authors. Kliem gives a succinct ten-point guide to starting your project right and keeping it on track (Table 1-4).

The project management work approach is:

* Relatively modern
* A result of the failure of traditional organization methods to work well in the project-oriented environment
* Characterized by new organization structure methods and special managerial techniques

Traditional organization structures are unable to accommodate the wide variety of interrelated project tasks. Lower-level and middle managers often find it impossible to exercise effective resource control of the diverse activities within their line organizations. Kerzner (p. 5) shows how discrete management levels further divide, not unify, departmental arrangements to produce multiple "operational islands" that are not conducive to effective management (Fig. 1-6).

This is not really surprising since these managers will frequently feel the impact of a changing environment more than upper-level executives, whose planning horizon and perspective is much longer (up to twenty years). Once the need for change is identified:

Middle management must convince top management that such change is necessary and desirable

* Executives must be willing to listen to and support middle management when it identifies a resource-control crisis (precisely when the need for project management should first appear)

The final decision to implement formal project management rests with executive management. Project management will not be formally adopted if senior management:

* Cannot recognize these resource-control problems
* Fears change (and loss of power and ego)

But it will probably:

* Be done, at least informally, anyway
* Work very well

One does what one needs to do.

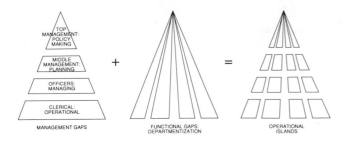

FIGURE 1-6. How operational islands reduce management effectiveness. *Source:* public domain.

Clearly, project management requires restructuring of the:

• Organization chart
• Traditional concept of how work is to be done

"How much" and "how long" cannot be uniformly advised here; there are no "cookbook answers" to questions like these. You must evaluate all the facts completely and systematically, then decide what is best for your particular situation. This may well be different from the last project, even if generally similar, since conditions have probably changed from then. A critical success factor is how well top management understands its changing role in a project management environment. They cannot operate as they did in a traditional organization structure. They must now expect different things from different people. In return, the expectations others now have of them are different. Let us compare these structures in greater detail.

A *traditional* or *classical organization* groups similar work and processes together by function—accounting, engineering, management information systems (MIS), marketing, personnel, production, quality control, and so on. An example is shown in Fig. 1-7.

Because this arrangement is so cohesive and similar in function:

• Group members share common knowledge, goals, and interests

• The work process is quite efficient
• Managing the group is relatively easy

However, a severe disadvantage is that no one in the group has any special interest in any given job flowing through it. Doing only their particular portion of the work at hand, they lack ownership of the situation. Many times, their contribution to the total effort is not even explained to them, which is certainly wrong and no proper way to treat employees.

In addition, the rapid rate of change in both technology and the marketplace has created enormous strains on existing organizational forms. The traditional structure is highly bureaucratic and cannot respond rapidly enough to a changing environment.

In project management situations, however, the project manager has a very special interest in getting his or her job done. If the job is only routed through the functional group with a "Please do ASAP" memo attached, the manager loses control. The job may not even get done on time because the line manager is not held accountable if it is not. Understandably, a line manager will give priority to those jobs for which he or she is held accountable. What gets monitored gets done.

On the other hand, the project management arrangement is much better able to respond to rapid changes in the competitive marketplace and in technology. This is true for developing situations both within and outside the company. Project management structures may capably integrate complex work efforts and reduce red tape and hassle.

For these reasons, the traditional organizational structure has often:

• Met with poor results in a changing or project environment
• Been replaced by the matrix organization

A *matrix organization* retains some of the efficiencies of the traditional functional grouping, while at the same time gives the project manager some input and control. An example is shown in Fig. 1-8.

Note how responsibility for functional performance is still shown vertically, but:

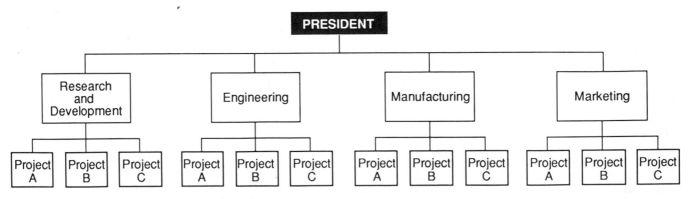

FIGURE 1-7. The traditional or classical organization structure. *Source:* public domain.

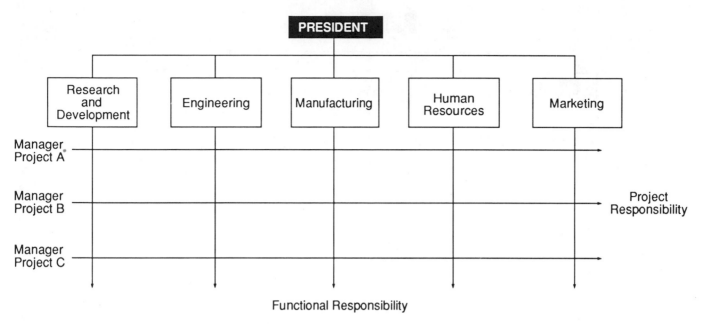

FIGURE 1-8.   The matrix organization. *Source:* public domain.

- Project responsibility is also formally shown—by horizontal lines intersecting the vertical
- Project managers must still utilize the services (including personnel administration) of the functional departments with which they interact

Project management arrangements make better use of existing resources by getting work to flow, and people to communicate, horizontally as well as vertically in the company. Note well that this does not destroy the vertical lines of authority, but simply requires that the same line organizations talk to one another:

- Horizontally, across lines
- Without going all the way to the first common manager and back down the line on the other side of the mountain (organization chart), so work will be accomplished more smoothly throughout the organization

The vertical flow of work is still the responsibility of the line managers; the horizontal work flow is the responsibility of the project managers, whose primary objective is to communicate and coordinate activities horizontally between the line organizations.

This arrangement has enabled organizations to complete:

- Tasks not effectively handled by the traditional structure
- One-time processes with minimum disruption of routine business

True, the matrix organization is the most difficult to manage—too many Chiefs and not enough Indians—but it is ideally suited to the team emphasis and does provide the best flexibility and payoff. The key to success with a matrix organization is to have line managers who understand their role, are cooperative, and are not possessive.

When a project is very large, it may be organized along traditional functional lines—much like a temporary department—to take advantage of efficiency and control. This is especially true when people work full time on the project over a long period. The project itself is the deliverable, the measurable output, with the project manager at the top of a traditional hierarchy—not off to the side as in a matrix organization. While duplication may cause some loss in functional-area utilization, the advantages of focus and control may well justify the structure. An example of this type of organization chart is shown in Fig. 1-9.

In most cases, the project manager provides detailed definitions of the work to be accomplished (what is to be done), but the line managers (the true experts) do the detailed planning—how it will be done. In particular, the project manager must provide appropriate line managers with:

- *Mandatory* training, for all managers and leads, so that they will:
    Know the methodology
    Understand the reports
    Provide help and support
- Complete activity definitions, both detail and summary
- Resource requirements
- Major milestones—especially intended start and finish dates
- Constraints and logic considerations

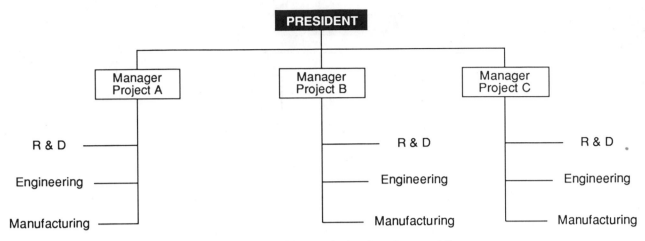

FIGURE 1-9.   When projects become permanent elements of the organization chart. *Source:* public domain.

- Definitions of end-item deliverables, quality, and reliability requirements
- A basis of performance measurement

Education and training are a crucial part of any project. Require this to be completed *before* project team members can start work on the project. Project success depends heavily on it.

This will ensure the following:

- Functional units will understand how their operation fits into "the big picture," and how their contributions help meet project objectives. When employees know they are a valued part of a process, they will:
    - Support that process
    - Identify improved ways to perform that process
    - Do a better job
- Problems arising from scheduling and resource-allocation conflicts are known far enough in advance that a workable, satisfactory solution may be determined and implemented: "The best surprise is no surprise!"
- Other problems likely to arise during the project are identified early enough, too, that they may be prevented or at least solved in timely manner

Although project managers usually cannot control or even assign line resources, they must still ensure that assigned personnel are adequate to do the job and are scheduled to meet project needs. Of course, line managers who fail to deliver quality resources when needed may get motivated to do so if top management provides a little encouragement. The project must not be:

- Allowed to drop to second-class status
- A stash job for bad apples
- Staffed by personnel whose highest priority is not the project

Project managers may not usurp responsibilities and authority that properly belong to the line managers (but may

and should provide feedback and guidance) concerning such matters as promotion, grade level, future work assignments, salary, bonus, and responsibilities after leaving the project. On the other hand, since the project manager is responsible for proper, effective project administration, he or she does have the right—so long as it does not conflict with higher authority—to establish certain policies, procedures, rules, guidelines, and directives. In organizations with mature, seasoned project management structures, the latitude in this regard is quite broad and allows the project manager considerable field command powers. But those companies with only recent implementation, or with less than satisfactory experience, usually keep the project manager on a short leash.

EXECUTIVE RELATIONS

Many project managers see the first critical planning step as getting support and commitment from top management. Not at all a bad idea. If the project manager has their support and backing, then he or she is much more likely to get needed support and resources from the line managers.

In *Project Management for Executives,* Kerzner discusses at length the role executives should, and should not, play in a project management environment. This new role involves three major changes.

First, executives must rely heavily on the project manager and the line manager to run the day-to-day company activities. Executives can then do what they are paid to do:

- Look out for long-range company growth through strategic planning
- Establish administrative policies

Unless an emergency arises, executives should not be as involved in the daily activities of the company as they once were. Executive interference ("meddling" or "tampering") can and often will destroy the project management environment. Many executives now involved with project management claim they work sixty (or more) hours each week and blame project management for the balance above forty. But this may be their own fault: They spend at least forty hours each week on executive duties, then try to run—or at least monkey around with—the daily activities of the various line and staff groups. The reason they do this is both simple and wrong: Executives refuse to surrender control of daily activities to the project and line managers. The effect on morale and authority can be devastating. How can a nonexecutive manager, whether line, staff, or project, ever gain self-confidence and respect from others if his or her work is always scrutinized to the finest detail and second-guessed by top management?

Although executive input is both needed and desirable during initial project phases, executives thereafter must:

- Have confidence in the ability of project and line managers to execute and implement the project
- Maintain only a monitoring presence except for:
  Conflict resolution
  Shifting of priorities
  Project redirection
  Other problems requiring executive-level attention

Kerzner supports a new trend in executive compensation: Pay year-end bonuses five years downstream based on how well their strategic plan has been achieved—not (as is common today) on profitability of only the last twelve months. This compensation treatment would more closely match performance to responsible time frame. When an executive realizes that bonuses are based on short-term profits, he or she, being only human, will:

- Neglect the primary (long-range) functions
- Meddle more in daily activities
- Window-dress operations for short-term expedient advantage (and higher bonus payment!) at the expense of long-term accumulation of corporate wealth, market share, and improved public perception

If a company adopts this new policy and executives separate themselves from daily activities, then who but the line and project managers are in better position to take over—as they should—daily operational control?

To summarize, executives interfere with project management because they:

- Are reluctant to delegate sufficient authority, accountability, and responsibility to the project managers—perhaps from a combination of fear (of loss of ego and power), lack of self confidence, or lack of confidence in the abilities of subordinates
- Want a more active role in this "new" concept called project management
- Are unfamiliar with their new responsibilities and relationships in a project management environment

A second major change in the way executives carry out their duties takes place in the chain of command—the lines of authority. As before, executives are responsible for monitoring the environment—that is, changes in law, societal values, economics, technology, and so on. A project manager must have the right to go immediately to any level—including executive—of management to obtain information needed to perform his or her duties. Time is often of the essence, and the project manager cannot wait until necessary information filters down (often being distorted in the process). Even one unnecessary level is too much. Worse still, in some organizations, gaining an audience with upper-level executives is harder than it was for Dorothy to see the Wizard of Oz!

Ideally, project managers are at the same level as people with whom they negotiate for resources. If project managers wish to meet with an executive in order to obtain necessary information (or resources), they should inform intermediate levels of management of their intentions, at least as a courtesy, in case they also want to attend.

The third major change involves the detrimental effects of "tunnel vision." Most good project managers will naturally focus on their own projects and exclude other concerns. They know they will be measured on whether or not they meet the deadline under budget and deliver a satisfactory product or service, and they accordingly direct all their efforts toward meeting these objectives. In this sense, it could be considered dedication. But project managers with tunnel vision will often make decisions that are:

- In the best interests only of the project
- Suboptimal solutions not in the best interests of the entire organization

If this can happen, who should provide a system of checks and balances to ensure that the project manager's decisions are in the company's best interests? Not an easy question to answer.

The first inclination might be to say the executive. But they should not meddle in daily activities. How about the line managers? Yes. Line managers must ensure that project demands and decisions are in the best interest of the enterprise as a whole. After all, it is they who provide personnel and other resources to support a project. What if they do not provide these needed personnel and resources, but instead save the best for their own operations—or empire? Well, they have supervisors, too. It should not come to this, but competition for a particular worker or resource has led to some great debates along "Mahogany Row." When an appeal on behalf of two or more critical long-term projects or operations is made, such decision-making is not meddling and is proper.

There is, however, another side to the issue. Time, budget, and performance notwithstanding, it often happens that other projects or organizations:

- Raid the project manager's people
- Plunder and steal his or her operating budget

The unfortunate project manager is still held responsible for the same performance objectives. And if the schedule, budget, or performance standards are not adhered to, executives should make absolutely sure that the project manager is informed as early as possible—preferably before his or her personnel and funds are applied elsewhere. It is only common sense and courtesy.

IMPLEMENTATION

Once the need for project management methodologies has been identified, the issue becomes how well implementation can be effected. Obviously, if the company mismanages this project, there will be a severe (and justified) loss of confidence as to how future projects will be managed. Project management implementation is itself a project and as such must be properly and professionally conducted. It must:

- Be well defined and organized
- Deserve the respect and support of the employees on whom successful implementation (and subsequent operation) will depend

The overall business environment must adapt to rapidly changing technology. In an ideal situation, the company organizational structure would adapt immediately. But people (especially) and traditional organization charts prevent this from happening. However, people can make even a mediocre organization chart work, if they believe in it and are willing to make it work. At the same time, if the consequences of reorganization are explained to them—how the changes will affect them and what benefits will accrue from the changes—people will no longer be an impediment. Quite understandably, they only wish not to be ill treated. Employees will be convinced of the benefits only after they see the new system in action, and this takes time. In general, it often requires two to three years to convert to the new system. Once implemented, the project management arrangement affords:

- Substantially faster response time to change
- More, not less, personnel stability

Sometimes, though, "executive insecurity" strikes hard and senior management, fearing "revolutionary" changes, hits the brakes when in reality it should press on the accelerator. The major problems seem to center around conflicts in authority and resources. Senior management often fears that it must surrender some of its authority, through delegation, to middle management. Middle management has sometimes even passed top management in available tactical power, although strategic power is still clearly the domain of senior management.

HUMAN RELATIONS

Managers at all levels must both insist on and promote positive working relationships—for the good of the organization, the project, and the individuals concerned. Both vertical and horizontal lines contribute to profits. Both must work together to continue this contribution. Arguing who contributes more is counterproductive and immature.

Line personnel who must report to a line manager and to a project manager for each project to which they are assigned must be given guidance on how to serve multiple managers. This is especially true if certain of these managers do not like each other and attempt to jerk the worker around in an attempt to get at the other boss.

Be careful not to get carried away with lines and boxes. Remember it is people primarily (and only secondarily equipment, money, resources, and methods) who do the work on your project. They substantially determine whether or not it is a success or failure. Certain efficiencies may be realized in the way people are organized, but the greatest efficiencies will always be realized by how they are managed. As is true with traditional management in particular and human relations in general: Take good care of your people, and they will take good care of you!

Never lose sight of the human dimension in this, or any other, endeavor. Ultimately, it is people who make a project succeed—or fail. The project manager who takes care of his or her people will in turn be well taken care of. Not that the project manager must necessarily win popularity contests. This only means that he or she must be:

- Respected
- Worthy of that respect

The project team must also be imbued with a "can-do" team attitude in which maximum authority and accountability rest with the project manager. This has consistently proven to be the most effective arrangement for many projects across many companies. What was yesterday's "Mission Impossible" is today's Management by Objectives (MBO) line item!

A 1986 *Computerworld* article on project management put it very well:

"Effective leaders, the kind whose organizations consistently perform up to standards of excellence, possess a clear vision—a strategy—that creates a focus for the organization. These leaders communicate this vision frequently and creatively, and position the organization for change. They also empower those who follow them by emphasizing accountability and reliability."

Two years later, a different author went on to say:

"Although it's possible for a team to succeed in spite of its leader, the leader makes or breaks the team in most cases.

"The people-oriented leader sets difficult goals and high standards, and demands excellence at all times—both in himself and the people who work for him. These leaders see people as the prime medium through which everything is accomplished. They have a tremendous respect for the potential of every individual.

"There are several things the leader must do for the team. They include providing and conveying a vision, ensuring that team and individual accomplishments are recognized, clearing away bureaucratic hurdles and other obstacles, providing the best tools and equipment, and establishing well-defined short-term goals.

"Train, train, train. Train for the development of broad-based skills. We want people to understand not only every aspect of their job, but also the jobs of every other team member. This increases our flexibility in personnel assignments and has resulted in some surprising innovations. Encourage innovation at all levels. Finally, do not try to tell [team] members how to accomplish their tasks—only what the tasks are."

Regardless of how much knowledge the project manager may have, his or her job is not to "be a hero" and do it all alone, but to get the work done, and the project satisfactorily completed, through the efforts of others—on time, on budget, and according to specifications. As with all other aspects of management, it is important to have the approval—if not support—of those responsible for actual implementation. Forcing a network, a schedule, a policy, or anything else onto the project team will cause the very people on whom you depend to look good:

- To resent you
- To do things their own way anyway
- To get mad, get even, or "get ahead"
- To make you look very, very bad

One way of taking care of everyone at the same time is to allow all persons involved in the project a voice as to how it should be done, how long activities should take, what resources will be needed, and so on.

Participative management works, and works well. No one knows your job better than you do, right? Similarly, no one knows another person's job better than he or she does. There is a gold mine of information out there—if only someone would invest a little time to ask people about their work! They would love to tell you about it, but do not want to unless you ask because they feel you might:

- Otherwise not be interested
- Think they were only trying to oil the wheels of self-promotion

It is not-so-amazing how much better your project will go if the methods and schedules are accepted, supported, and institutionalized by the project team. They must be accepted from the start, and people must be included from the start.

If the project consists of multiple categories with different groups responsible for each, it may be necessary to represent each group when the network is prepared and the schedule agreed to. Overall responsibility should be vested in a senior individual who is both competent and respected. Each group should thoroughly prepare its part of the project. Then, when the network is prepared, representatives from each group should work closely together while each person determines his or her group's individual portion. When it conflicts with the plan of another group, a decision must be made and, if necessary, a compromise reached. Later, we shall learn how such tradeoffs may be quantitatively evaluated. This is still a people problem that must be solved by people. The conflict must be eliminated, the compromise acceptable to all concerned. Otherwise, the project plan will be ineffective.

WHY PROJECTS FAIL

The major reason for project failure is human, not financial or technical. Failure results when people who should be:

- Respected
- Communicated with
- Included in all project phases
- Motivated and encouraged

are ignored, mistreated, and disrespected. Other reasons for failure include:

Frustrated, confused, demoralized work force

Insufficient attention paid to underlying business process improvement

Ongoing business processes are ineffective and obsolete

Insufficient interest, support, guidance, or commitment from top management to the methodology—or outright resistance from fearful, insecure "Mahogany Row" bureaucrats

Project did not support business goals and objectives

Project did not appear to provide "value added" contribution—even if it really does

Top management set unrealistic schedule, cost, or performance goals and forced compliance

Too much executive meddling

Employees unconvinced that executives were in total support

There was no need for project management, or it was attempted too soon

Top management did not properly plan for or supervise implementation of project management

Employees were not educated and trained on how project management should work

Executives did not select appropriate projects or project managers

The project manager did not understand his or her job description, responsibility, or authority

No one individual person was responsible for the total project

Integrated planning and control were not performed

Policies and procedures were inflexible and incapable of change

Insufficient functional input was provided in the planning phase

Project attempted to operate in a vacuum

People fought instead of cooperated

Too much was attempted with too little time, resources, experience, planning, coordination, or people; company resources were overcommitted

Plans were not critically reviewed

Junior staff members were assigned tasks planned for senior staff with no adjustment made in costs, schedules, or performance

Planning and review meetings were not scheduled

Suggestions made at review meetings (if held at all) were not incorporated

No attempt made to explain the effect of the project management organizational form on the wage and salary administration program—or how to work for multiple supervisors

Unrealistic, unprofessional planning and scheduling were performed

Unverified sources were used to provide status reporting

Status reporting techniques covered up problems to save face and exaggerated positives to induce false respect and confidence

If even honestly reported, these techniques were normally subjective (percent complete), not objective (earned value)

Conflicting project priorities assigned

Top management mishandled conflicts or did not resolve them early and fairly by establishing criteria for project priorities

Impossible (suicide-mission) schedule commitments were assigned (probably without adequate field input to check for reality and properly analyze risk)

Planned productivity levels (useful hours per day) were consistently unattainable

Level-of-effort estimates based solely on best-case assumptions

Design and customer changes were poorly controlled; the rate of change (and response) exploded to exceed the rate of progress

No one had project cost-accounting ability

Simple details overlooked, forgotten, or left to the last moment

Inadequate education and training

Corporate goals and objectives not understood at lower organizational levels (often at higher levels, too!)

Problems at lower organizational levels ignored or not understood at higher levels

Poor financial, time, staffing, resource, or risk estimates

Unsatisfactory definition of requirements

Insufficient data to produce a valid plan

Insufficient time, people, information, or support provided in the estimating process

Planning done willy-nilly without organization or systematic thinking

Commitments made without ensuring that adequate people, time, money, and resources were available

Project team members not told of current status

Project team members working on different specifications, schedules, and the like

People constantly shuffled in and out of the project

Original plan left unchanged after substantial change in requirements, constraints, or simply the passage of time

Project manager did too much alone, without developing any backup capability—then was transferred or incapacitated

"No one knew or cared what was going on!"

Somebody screwed up big-time

"Sooner or later," goes another version of Murphy's Law, "the ability of an organization to survive in spite of itself disappears!"

If these situations occur simultaneously on several projects, there could—and usually will—be much confusion throughout the organization. The resulting fear and panic will only make things worse. Most of these causes can occur in any type organizational structure, but they are most pronounced with project management. Therefore, executives must ensure that its implementation is correctly planned. Both executives and lower-level personnel (including nonmanagement) must also watch for the following effects that usually indicate current troubles bound only to get worse if not immediately corrected:

- Late activity completion
- Cost overruns
- Substandard performance
- Poor quality in deliverables
- More fights and hassles
- Loss of respect toward team members, to management, or to the company
- High turnover in project staff
- High turnover in functional line staff
- Two functional departments performing the same things on one project

WHY PROJECTS SUCCEED

Why do projects succeed? Because projects:

- Manage their people as instructed by Randolph and Posner
- Organize their processes and paperwork as suggested by Kerzner
- Schedule their activities as described throughout this book

Keep in mind the twelve Spirer-inspired guiding principles set forth in Table 1-5.

Do you get the feeling training is absolutely crucial to project success?

Project management is a continuing, iterative process. The above principles can—and should—be used throughout the project, not just at the beginning while doing initial planning, or during management status review. Even on a project progressing satisfactorily, planning and estimating "to completion" is an essential component of managing the project:

- On time
- On budget

Table 1-5   Twelve Rules of Effective Project Scheduling

OBJECTIVES

1. Clearly state project objectives, in terms of deliverable items, well before scheduling begins. Defective objectives are frequently the main cause of project difficulties. Include all features and deliverables; most project delays result from last-minute addition of new features, or by neglecting to include all essential work in the baseline schedule. "Don't tell me what you're going to do, or how - instead, tell me what you're going to give me - what tangible, measurable deliverables". *Train your staff and your management!*

WORK BREAKDOWN STRUCTURE

2. Establish a good WBS in *product* terms at higher levels and *process* terms (manageable work units) at the lower. *Train your staff and your management!*

ACTIVITY LISTS

3. List all activities needed to accomplish the project. Provide adequate detail to indicate what must be done and how long it should take. *Train your staff and your management!*

NETWORKS

4. Define the network - and keep it SIMPLE! - in the very best way possible to determine the Critical Path, calculate early and late schedule dates, and accomplish the activities. *Train your staff and your management!*

SCHEDULING

5. Let the project team make its own viable, easily-understood schedule that properly integrates network relationships, calendar deadlines, and resource constraints. Although they may not know exactly how long it takes to do the work, they will at least think through the entire project to ensure all pieces have been included in the baseline. *Train your staff and your management!*

6. Establish a baseline schedule against which to measure progress, cost, and slippage. Use resource loading summaries, histograms, and cumulative resource plots; ensure they make sense to team members. Status the schedule and recheck resource assignments every week. Track how long it really takes to do the identifiable work, and why; record actual hours for each resource by activity and compare with reported progress values. *Train your staff and your management!*

ESTIMATING

7. Estimate activity durations by using standards if available, analyzing similar activities, modifying estimates by differences, and using rational analytical methods; also, use more detailed networks. NEVER try to force duration estimates; measure performance against realistic baselines only. *Train your staff and your management!*

8. When useful, provide three estimates (pessimistic, most likely, optimistic) for time and other resources; summarize into a single value for CPM use. *Train your staff and your management!*

MILESTONES

9. Choose a set of milestones that will help you manage the project well. *Train your staff and your management!*

ACCOUNTABILITY

10. Assign accountability for every activity to one and only one person. Write that person's name on each activity. Meet regularly with the project team to ensure everyone knows what is expected of them, and to invite participation. Require the project manager to prepare complete, accurate weekly status reports that indicate: 1) what was accomplished last week; 2) what will be done next week; 3) slippages and variances; 4) what problems might cause what delays; and 5) what will be done about it - including a request for assistance, if appropriate. *Train your staff and your management!*

CONTROL

11. Control the project! Status projects based on remaining duration, not percent complete or resources used. *Train your staff and your management!*

EARNED VALUE

12. Know how and when to use earned value. Where activity work content can be clearly defined, one can get accurate, highly-useful information on cost and schedule status using only three values (ACWP, BCWP, BCWS), all expressed in monetary or work units. *Train your staff and your management!*

- On specification
- While maintaining good human relations

It will enable the project to conform to valid customer requirements, and to improve people's lives. These principles prove their value to the extent that they enable one to manage projects more successfully and effectively.

WHY PROJECTS END

All projects that start must end. Below are several reasons why:

"Mission accomplished!"—objectives achieved
"Mission scrubbed!"—poor initial planning
Better alternative found
Funding cancelled
Change in company (or customer) interest and strategy
Problem found to be too complex for available resources
Allocated time has been exceeded
Budgeted costs have been exceeded
Key people have left the organization
Personal whims of top management

Once the reasons for cancellation have been defined, the next step is to decide how to terminate the project. There are three major areas of concern:

- Employee morale
- Personnel reassignment
- Adequate documentation and project wrap up

Methods by which a project may be terminated include:

- Orderly, planned termination
- The hatchet (instant cutoff of funds and removal of personnel)
- Reassignment of personnel to higher-priority activities
- Draining too many resources from a successful project and applying them to an unsuccessful project so that both are mediocre at best and failures at worst
- Project redirection toward accomplishment of different objectives
- Slow, wither-on-the-vine death, or pocket veto—no official action

However it is terminated, ensure that your project goes out a winner!

Project scheduling begins with the Statement of Work (SOW) and the Work Breakdown Structure (WBS), the subjects of Chapter 2. But first:

PROJECT MANAGEMENT "LITE"— ONE-THIRD LESS SERIOUS

There is also a lighter side to project management, which sees things as follows:

Seven phases of a project:

1. Enthusiasm
2. FUBAR (Fouled Up Beyond All Repair) management
3. Disillusionment
4. Fear and panic
5. Search for the guilty
6. Punishment of the innocent
7. Praises and honors for the nonparticipants

There is but one universal truth about project management: There are no universal truths about project management!

Things go right so they can go wrong.

After things have gone from bad to worse, the cycle will repeat itself.

There are two universal things on earth—hydrogen and stupidity. One is commonly found in the atmosphere, the other in the boss's office.

Global human intelligence is a constant; the population is rapidly growing.

People will occasionally stumble over the truth, but will usually pick themselves up and continue on in the previous fashion.

Believing is seeing.

Complex problems have simple, easy-to-understand wrong solutions.

No major project is ever installed on time, within budget, or by the same staff that started it. Yours will not be the first!

The urgent is more important than the important is urgent.

A crisis is when you can't say, "Let's forget the whole thing."

Projects progress quickly until 90 percent complete, then remain that way (90 percent complete) forever.

Adding personnel to a late project makes it even later.

Measure with a micrometer, mark with a chalk, cut with an axe.

Never let facts get in the way of ignorance or blind stupidity; always talk in warm fuzzies—with a smile.

One great advantage of fuzzy project objectives is they let you avoid the embarrassment of estimating the corresponding costs or measuring progress.

Actual costs always exceed budgeted costs.

Disorder expands proportionately to the tolerance for it.

A project expands to consume the amount of time, money, and space available.

The project that pays the most will be offered when there is no time to deliver the services. If you have the time, you will not have the money; if you have the money, you will not have the time.

All rush jobs are due the same day.

When things are going well, something will go wrong. When things just can't get any worse, they will. When things appear to be going better, you have overlooked something.

Anything that begins well, ends badly; anything that begins badly, ends worse.

If you can keep your head when all about you are losing theirs, you just don't understand the problem.

If you are feeling good, don't worry—you'll get over it!

If it's good, duration is infinitesimal; if it's bad, duration is infinite.

Anything that can be changed will be changed until the rate of change exceeds the rate of progress and until ultimately there is no time left to change anything!

A carelessly planned project will take three times longer to complete than expected; a carefully planned project will take only twice as long.

The greater the cost of putting a plan into operation, the less chance there is of abandoning the plan—even if it subsequently becomes irrelevant.

If a series of events can go wrong, it will do so in the worst possible sequence.

Project teams detest progress reporting because it vividly manifests their lack of progress.

The length of a progress report is inversely proportional to the amount of progress.

A meeting is an event at which:

Minutes are kept

Hours are lost

The deadline is one week after the original deadline.

Procrastination reduces anxiety by reducing the expected project quality from the best of all efforts to the best that can be expected given the limited time; but project quality varies inversely with time remaining before the deadline.

Never postpone until tomorrow what you can:

Get someone else to do today

Do the day after

There are some things that are impossible to know; but it is impossible to know what these things are!

Anything is possible, if you don't know what you're talking about!

Nothing is impossible, if you don't have to do it yourself!

When it gets to be your turn, they change the rules.

The only time you come up with a great solution is after somebody else has solved the problem.

Never create a problem for which you do not have the answer; create problems for which *only* you have the answer.

When all is said and done, much more will be said than done.

If you're early, it will be cancelled. If you're on time, you'll have to wait. If you're late, you will be too late.

No matter how much you do, you'll never do enough; but what you don't do is always more important than what you do do.

A good slogan will stop all analysis for fifty years.

A conclusion is where you got tired of thinking.

The sooner you fall behind, the more time you have to catch up!

The only way to make up for being lost is to make record time while you are.

To estimate duration:

1. Guess the time you think it should take
2. Multiply by two
3. Change the unit of measure to the next higher unit.

Thus, allocate two days for a one-hour task.

After adding two weeks to the schedule for unexpected delays, add two more for unexpected unexpected delays, and still two more for unexpected unexpected unexpected delays.

What goes around, comes around.

Do right, no one notices; do wrong, no one misses. Do right, no one remembers; do wrong, no one forgets.

Whatever hits the fan will not be evenly distributed. The project manager will get most of it.

If it looks easy, it's tough; if it looks tough, it's damn well impossible.

Anyone can make a decision given enough facts. A good manager can make a decision without enough facts. A perfect manager can operate in total ignorance.

Whatever happens, look as if that was what you had intended. If you don't succeed, be sure to destroy all evidence you tried.

Doing it the hard way is always easier.

It is easy to make things hard, hard to make things easy.

The best-laid plans of mice and people are usually about equal.

The chances of anybody doing anything are inversely proportional to the number of other people who are in a position to do it instead. Never make a decision you can get someone else to make instead. But never trust anyone who would not lose more than you.

When success seems doubtful, delegate.

When the going gets tough, everyone leaves.

Confusion creates jobs. Jobs create confusion.

In case of doubt, make it sound convincing. If you cannot convince them, confuse them. If you cannot confuse them, make them doubt.

People in systems do not do what the system says they are doing.

Any system that depends on human reliability is by definition unreliable.

No person's life, liberty, property, or pursuit of happiness is safe while the legislature is in session.

To err is human. To blame it on someone else is even more human: The person who can smile when things go wrong has thought of someone to blame.

Blame the past for the present, others for yourself.

Your boss's job is to discover what his or her employees are doing, and stop them.

You may not know who's right, but you always know who's the boss.

With your boss, it is unreasonable to be reasonable, illogical to be logical.

Don't let your bosses know that you're better than they are.

No matter how well you do your work, the boss will:
      Not like it
      Try to "fix what ain't broke"
      Screw it up big-time

The words "boss" and "manager" have opposite meanings. The words "boss" and "leader" have opposite meanings. The words "boss" and "yahoo" have similar meanings.

Never take your vacation the same time as the boss.

Happiness is seeing your boss's picture on a milk carton.

The one time in the day you lean back and relax is the one time the boss walks through the office. Corollary: The one time in the day you visit the boss is the only time your boss actually does something worthwhile.

Will Rogers never met the boss.

What really matters is the name you succeed in imposing on the facts—not the facts themselves.

Offer a suggestion and the whole project gets dumped on you.

The amount of flak received on any subject is inversely proportional to the subject's true value.

Teamwork is essential: It allows you to blame someone else.

If you do something sure to meet with universal approval, somebody won't like it.

Where there's a will, there's a won't.

For every action, there is an equal and opposite criticism.

For every vision, there is an equal and opposite revision.

The supply of boo-birds substantially exceeds their demand.

Never conduct negotiations before 10:00am or after 4:00pm:

Before 10:00am, you appear too anxious
After 4:00pm, they think you are desperate

No matter how large the work space, if two projects must be done at the same time, they will always require the use of the same part of the work space.

If a project requires N components, there will be $(N - 1)$ units in stock.

Any time you try to do something, you find you must do something else first!

In any organization, there will be one person who knows what's going on. That person must be fired (for competence).

The squeaking wheel gets replaced, not the grease.

If you are right all the time, the boss will can you. If you are wrong any of the time, the boss will can you.

The inevitable result of improved and enlarged communications between different levels in a hierarchy is a vastly increased area of misunderstanding.

Any instruction that can be misunderstood will be misunderstood.

PROJECT "THUMBTACK"

PRELIMINARY DESIGN

RELIABILITY REVIEW

PROJECT REDIRECTION

SAFETY REVIEW

PRODUCTION

FIGURE 1-10.   Project "THUMBTACK."

Quality assurance doesn't.

No system is ever completely debugged. The process only introduces new bugs that are even harder to find.

Garbage in, garbage out! (Common MIS expression.)

If you screw things up at electronic speed, you only have human speed to fix it.

If you fail to plan, then plan to fail!

(Special note of thanks: Many of the above were taken from, or inspired by, my yearly purchases of "Murphy's Law Desk Calendar: 365 Reasons Why Things Continue to Go Wrong," Price Stern Sloan, Inc., Los Angeles, published annually since 1981.)

2
The Work Breakdown Structure (WBS)

THE NEED FOR EFFECTIVE PROJECT PLANNING

"Cheshire Cat," she began, rather timidly, "Would you please tell me, please, which way I ought to go from here?"

"That depends a good deal on where you want to get to," said the Cat.

"I don't much care where," said Alice.

"Then it doesn't matter which way you go," said the Cat.

"So long as I get somewhere," Alice added as an explanation.

"Oh, you're sure to do that," said the Cat, "if you only walk long enough!"

This famous example from *Alice in Wonderland* teaches this: If you don't know where you are going, any road will get you there!

Why manage your project and determine network status? If you do not, no road will get you anywhere: Your project will:

- Finish late, if at all
- Overrun budget or be cancelled
- Not meet satisfactory performance levels
- Strain or sever customer and employee relations.

People who do not manage their projects as they should usually get what they deserve (Fig. 2-1).

Consider the following two Randolph/Posner analogies:

1. An expert archer not told where the target is
2. A skilled jigsaw puzzle worker not shown the picture on the box (what if the project were to assemble a Boeing 747 without a bill of materials?)

Is either person likely to succeed? If they are expected to do "it" right the first time, how can they do this unless they know what *it* is? If their efforts are considered to be a project (as they may be), will either project finish:

- On time?
- On budget?
- On specification?
- With good human relations?

Will either project even finish? Randolph and Posner (p. 11) summarize their entire book in the ten "GO-CARTS DRIVER" rules (Table 2-1).

FIGURE 2-1.   "TURKEY OF THE YEAR AWARD".

Table 2-1   Randolph and Posner's "GO-CARTS DRIVER" Rules for Project Success

```
 1. Set a project Goal both clear and "smart":
    Specific
          Measurable
              Agreed upon
                   Realistic
                        Time-framed
    "What, exactly, do you want to do?"
 2. Determine project Objectives, expressed both clearly and concisely
 3. Establish Checkpoints, Activities, Relationships, and Time estimates
 4. Draw a picture of the project Schedule
 5. Direct people individually and as a project team
 6. Reinforce the commitment and excitement of the project team
 7. Keep everyone connected with the project Informed
 8. Build agreements that Vitalize team members
 9. Empower yourself and others on the project team
10. Encourage Risk taking and creativity.
```

An old Navy proverb (the "Five Ps") says: "Proper planning prevents poor performance." The first four rules in Table 2-1 pertain to project planning, the rest to management and control. Keep these in mind as we discuss the more quantitative aspects of effective project management.

- You must plan your project well if it is to succeed.
- You will fail if you do not plan your project well.

Spirer, in his project management seminars, gives simple goal-setting exercises. More than 85% (WOW!) of the multithousand participants produced objective statements that were "seriously deficient." They:

- Stated activities rather than deliverable end items
- Exceeded the scope of the defined project
- Failed to be specific
- Omitted important deliverables

A well-defined project objective might read: "Design and build 100 new-style widgets meeting current written customer quality standards. Complete project by 23 October 1992 and within allocated budget of $123,456.78."

If project objectives cannot be defined, how can they possibly be met?

A 1989 University of Arizona study discovered that unfounded optimism and excessive change were more likely to cause project failure than mere size or technical complexity. The findings are summarized (by percent) below and underscore the need for proper planning:

Planning begins with setting project goals and, from these, objectives. It defines what the project will—*and will not*—do. McLeod (p. 116) suggests the systems approach to determine project goals, objectives, and boundaries (Table 2-2).

This step forms the foundation for all processes to follow, and therefore molds the success—or failure—of the project. A house built on sand cannot last. No amount of subsequent estimating, scheduling, or just plain hard work will be of any avail, no matter how painstakingly or well done, if insufficient attention and care has been given to initial planning.

There is another important benefit as well: It not only begins to organize the project into manageable form, but also sets clear professional standards early under which people know they are expected to perform.

There is always a tendency to jump right into things and to solve "the problem" before anyone even really knows what "the problem" actually is—not just what it appears to be (Fig. 2-2).

Would you want airliners to be manufactured like this? Would the President wish *Air Force One* to be built like this? Of course, what might result is shown in Fig. 2-3.

Or, perhaps, what is shown in Fig. 2-4.

You have certainly seen at least one version of Fig. 2-5.

People who jump right in argue that they have no time to plan things correctly, that they only have enough time to get at it—now! Four thoughts come to mind:

```
CAUSE OF FAILURE            OVER BUDGET          LATE
Unfounded optimism              93                85
Excessive change                86                77
Size or complexity              71                71
```

Table 2-2   The Systems Approach, as Suggested by McLeod

1. <u>Define the true problem.</u>
    * Define what the problem is.
    * Define what the problem is not.
    * Where is the problem?
    * What is causing the problem?
    * Is this the true cause?
2. <u>Gather data and information describing the problem.</u>
    * What kind of data should be gathered?
    * How should it be measured?
    * Who will use this data?
    * Does new data need to be gathered, or does data already exist?
    * Who will gather the data? How?
3. <u>Identify alternate solutions.</u>
    * How many should be identified?
    * Are there any others not yet considered?
    * Are any of these feasible?
4. <u>Evaluate the alternatives.</u>
    * Which criteria should be used?
    * How does each alternative measure up to each criterion?
    * What weights should be applied to each criterion?
5. <u>Select the best alternative.</u>
    * Is there enough information to make a good decision?
    * Which alternative measures up best to the criteria?
    * Has the selection process been fair and unbiased?
    * Will the selected alternative be supported?
6. <u>Implement the solution.</u>
    * When should this solution be implemented?
    * How should it be implemented?
7. <u>Follow up to ensure the solution is effective.</u>
    * Who will perform the evaluation?
    * How well is the solution meeting the objectives?
    * Did the solution introduce any new problems needing correction?
    * ...and so on.

* They are rushed for time because they are fighting fires caused by earlier "jump right in and fix it" campaigns that began before anyone even knew what to fix
* If they are "too busy to do it right the first time," how will they find time to do it right the second time? Or the third? Or the fourth? Will they have adequate resources then? Will they even have a job?

* Proper planning prevents poor performance!
* A problem well defined is a problem half solved; a project well planned is a project half completed

The "wheels in motion" people (WIMPs) described above must instead realize:

FIGURE 2-2.   "Everyone get to work on the problem while I go find what it is!"

FIGURE 2-3.   How NOT to build airliners. *Source:* unknown.

FIGURE 2-4.   The Boss: "Oh, @#*^! You did it *just* like I told you!"

- They could not even benefit from the Cheshire Cat's advice
- Their wheels may actually be going in reverse or deeper into the mud!
- Effective, proper planning:
    Is necessary for project success
    Represents valuable progress every bit as much as production does

If they still cannot sleep at night unless they "have something to show for their work," simply provide them a timeline (representing project planning) on which they can record planning progress and get their daily fix of visual feedback.

FIGURE 2-5.   Compare what was wanted with what was received. *Source:* public domain.

For projects to be planned and controlled successfully, they must be divided into manageable portions. Tasks must be:

- Small enough to be understood and accomplished by those performing them
- Large enough not to become endless minor details lost in the jungle

This, in turn, will provide:

- Clarity of expected action
- Understanding
- Commitment
- Confidence to perform the work

Whenever work is thought out, organized, structured, understood, and within the capabilities of the individuals expected to perform the job, there will most always exist a high degree of "can-do" confidence that the objective can be achieved.

IMPORTANT DEFINITIONS

Keep Table 2-3 in mind as we define some important terms.

Regardless of particular format or deliverable, a project starts out as a written *Statement of Work* (*SOW*). This may be a (customer-provided) narrative description of:

- Project objectives
- The work to be done
- Performance expectations
- Funding considerations
- How and when progress will be measured
- Required reports (content, format, and frequency)
- Proposed start and completion dates
- Major milestones (important checkpoints)

If the proposed work is quite large, it is often referred to as a *program*. A program, which may take years to complete, is:

- Complex
- Comprised of several or many interrelated projects
- Part of the ongoing long-term business objectives: "the system"

A *project* is similar to a program, but is less complex and is of shorter duration. Often it represents a portion of a program, and always has a:

- Scheduled beginning
- Scheduled finish
- Primary purpose and objective
- Set of tangible, measurable, and deliverable end products

Even intangible things, like organizational change, can be managed well by project management principles if they:

- Meet the above four criteria
- Are defined in terms of deliverable results

Table 2-3   Project Breakdown

LEVEL	DESCRIPTION
1	Program
2	Project
3	Activity
4	Task/Subtask
5	Work Package

- Clearly and measurably, within a given time frame, increase the effectiveness of a function normally conceived to be an ongoing process

An *activity* is the basic project measurement unit. It varies in length from a few hours or days to several weeks or months, depending on project specifics. An activity always consumes time and often consumes other resources, too.

A *task* or *subtask* may be used if needed to further subdivide project activities into more meaningful pieces.

A *work package* is the smallest project measurement unit, distinguishable from all others. It is a group of related jobs, of relatively short duration, assigned to a single organizational unit. In this way, the work package assigns time, cost, and performance responsibility to one person; this facilitates tracking and control. The work package provides a specific, definable, and measurable output—and also includes descriptions of:

- What is to be done
- How it will be measured
- When it is to be started and completed
- Budgeted cost amounts
- The (single) cost account to charge
- Specific events to reach, or deliverables to provide, at specified milestones

Kerzner (p. 725) shows how the work package integrates project job descriptions with the organization chart and accounting systems (Fig. 2-6).

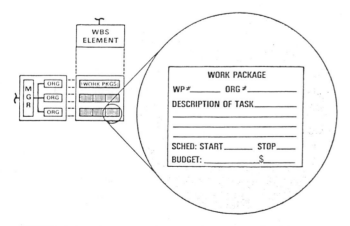

FIGURE 2-6.   How the work package integrates project job descriptions with the organization chart and accounting systems. *Source:* Kerzner p. 725.

We shall discuss the significance of this requirement many times throughout this book. Project planning, tracking, and control center on the work package.

Moder, Phillips, and Davis (p. 141) list these typical characteristics:

- Relates work costs to proper manager and charge number
- Represents work units at levels where work is performed
- Clearly distinguished from all other work packages
- Assignable to a single organizational element
- Scheduled start and completion dates
- Has a budget of assigned value expressed in terms of monetary units, person-hours, or other measurable resource units
- Limited duration—or subdivided by discrete milestones to facilitate objective measurement of work performed (progress)
- Integrated with detailed engineering, manufacturing, or other schedules

WORK BREAKDOWN STRUCTURE (WBS)

The *Work Breakdown Structure,* to which we have often alluded, is a hierarchical format (like an organization chart) to divide a project into:

- Succeedingly greater levels of detail
- Measurable and controllable activities that people can understand

The WBS is the heart and basic cornerstone of effective project management. It reflects the project manager's concept of the project as a whole. The lack of a clear and comprehensible WBS is a serious handicap to any project. Proper design is crucial to project success. Not only must it sufficiently identify and detail all project activities, it must also provide a complete and accurate mechanism by which work package consumables (time and resources) may be charged to the proper cost account for tracking and performance measurement purposes.

Major WBS purposes are:

- To define total project effort—what the project is
- To define project scope and limit—what the project is not
- To state project objectives as tangible, measurable deliverables

Table 2-4   WBS Breakdown

```
LEVEL       DESCRIPTION
  1         Project
  2             Area
  3                 Group
  4                     Activity
  5                         Work Package
```

- To reduce the tendency to confuse a deliverable with the activities, processes, and resources needed to produce it
- To structure the work into smaller, more detailed units that better define scope and deliverables

These smaller units must in turn be:

- *Manageable*—specific authority and responsibility can be assigned; lowest-level WBS elements usually represent 0.5—2.5 percent total project budget
- *Unique*—identifiable as a single, independent operation with minimum dependence on and interfacing with other activities
- *Measurable*—may be quantifiably evaluated to determine progress and performance
- *Integratable*—may be combined with other operations at the same level to provide the "big picture"

Kerzner (p. 553) feels the WBS to be "the single most important element" because it provides the common framework from which:

- The total project can be described as the sum of contributing elements
- Planning and forecasting may be performed
- Schedules and budgets can be established
- Time, cost, and performance can be tracked
- Objectives can be linked to company resources in a logical manner
- Schedules and status reporting procedures can be established
- Network construction and control planning can be initiated
- Responsibility assignments for each element can be established

By convention, increasing WBS detail levels are indented as shown Table 2-4.

The WBS is a hierarchical structure. It uses:

- Indented listings (Table 2-4), for textual representation
- Tree diagrams, such as we shall soon see, for graphical representation

These terms sometimes vary. The criteria or central WBS theme may also vary. Some possible yardsticks by which a WBS may be constructed include:

- Deliverables (most common and effective WBS arrangement)
- Systems and subsystems
- Technology
- Vendor deliverables
- Geographic area
- Organization

The very top level must list all major deliverables. The upper three levels:

- Are normally specified by the customer as required summary levels for reporting purposes
- Should reflect broad, integrated work efforts that cut across multiple departmental lines

For preliminary planning or proposal-writing purposes, this is as far as is necessary to go for now. Levels four and five are provided by the contractor for in-house planning and control. They might also be required under contract. Even if not, they are required under prudence. They should generally not contain any out-of-department work.

Certainly the most common WBS use is to produce and track a viable work schedule that reflects customer time and specifications objectives. Other possible uses include:

- Responsibility matrix
- Costing
- Risk analysis

Table 2-5   Project Purpose and Deliverables, by Level

LEVEL NUMBER	PURPOSE
1 (program)	Definition, authorization, and release of all work
2 (project)	Budgets and major deliverables
3 (activity)	Schedules and subsidiary/internal deliverables
4 (task/subtask)	Detail
5 (work package)	Integration with labor/resource/cost accounting systems

- Organizational structure
- Coordination of objectives
- Contract administration
- Project control

In addition, each level also serves its own vital purpose (Table 2-5).

STRUCTURED SYSTEMS ANALYSIS APPLIED TO PROJECT MANAGEMENT

How do we know what goes where? Readers familiar with structured systems analysis and top-down design techniques will find ready use for these tools. They work, and work well, on *all* projects—including yours—not just on software.

A complete treatment of the structured systems analysis methodology cannot be provided here. For an excellent discussion, read applicable portions (especially pp. 50–113 and the Sunrise Sportswear Company case study throughout) of Jerry and Ardra FitzGerald's classic *Fundamentals of Systems Analysis*. The essence of this methodology is first to define project limits and objectives, then systematically to provide the following:

- Overview of what must be done to meet these objectives
- Major processes necessary to do this
- Minor processes necessary to do this
- Process details for succeedingly lower levels

At each level, ask the question, "What do I need from the level just below?"

A person cannot be born before his or her parents! Neither should twigs and leaves be produced before the tree. Each level of greater detail is created only after its summary level. Otherwise, all you will have is randomly accumulated piles of stuff.

Beginning with a *context diagram,* which—like the SOW—shows what the project is (and is not), we identify operations and projects external to ours ("external entities") that provide information to and/or receive information from our particular project. The context diagram, again like the Statement of Work, is then broken down into succeedingly greater detail levels by identifying all activities necessary to carry out the summary activity under review. These subactivities can be connected to the parent activity or among each other with:

- Deliverables
- Data/information flows
- Control sequences
- Other applicable items

In turn they may be progressively broken down until no further decomposition is necessary, practical, or possible. An example of a context diagram (note again its similarity to the SOW) is shown in Fig. 2-7.

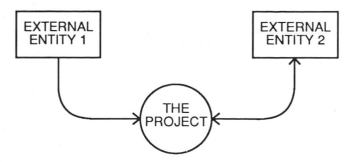

FIGURE 2-7.   Example of a context diagram.

FitzGerald and FitzGerald (p. 64) show the first detail level as Fig. 2-8.

In Fig. 2-8, External Entities 1 and 2 are the same as seen before; they are operations and projects external to our own project that, nevertheless, are important to our project because they:

- Provide information, deliverables, and the like *to* our project
- Receive information, deliverables, and the like *from* our project
- Both

The processes labeled 1.0, 2.0, and 3.0 are summary-level activities that together constitute "The Project," the context diagram "area under study." They also answer the question, What *major* activities must be accomplished in order to complete "The Project"? As such, they provide greater detail and more description to "The Project." In turn, they too may be broken down into greater detail to identify the following processes:

- 1.1, 1.2, and so on
- 2.1, 2.2, and so on
- 3.1, 3.2, and so on

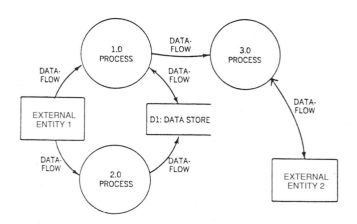

FIGURE 2-8.   Example of a Level-0 diagram.

Continue this procedure as long as necessary for each path produced by asking, What *major* activities must be accomplished in order to complete this particular process? Note that some paths will be longer, more complex, and more detailed than others. For example, it may be unnecessary to define 1.1 any further, whereas 1.2 may require definition to Level 7 (1.2.V.W.X.Y.Z) precision. It is not necessary or desirable to force all to come out even. Do you see how the technique can also apply to WBS construction?

HOW MUCH DETAIL DO YOU NEED?

Project personnel need a detailed listing of every activity needed to complete the project. How detailed must this be? Sometimes only experience can tell. The level of detail to which you plan your project must be sufficient for you to:

- Plan your work
- Work your plan
- Tell other team members what (but not how!) to do
- Summarize and combine information to tell others what you are doing

If the WBS does not contain enough levels, scheduling and activity integration may prove difficult. If it contains too many, then much:

- Time and effort will have been wasted
- Suspicion and resentment will arise from the perception that management is trying to run things too closely and "cut things down to frog hairs"

Note well: Not everyone requires the same detail level. Provide enough detail to accomplish the above, but resist the urge to show the whole world all you have done! Examine closely intended audience needs. As is true of schedule, cost, and resource utilization reports, planning reports must fit the purpose to which they will be put.

Senior management needs little detail; what they need more is easily understood summary information from which they can make strategic long-range planning or broad policy decisions. If they need more detail they will tell you. On the other hand, people "in the trenches" need much more detail so they can do their jobs on the basis of complete information (Fig. 2-9).

Top management is most interested in summary reports, workers and supervisors in detail reports. It depends on which end of the telescope you look through. The underlying detail base is still the same. Establishing sufficient detail early in the project enables people to:

- Do their jobs better
- Easily provide summary information as required

Hansen (p. 34) illustrates this, as shown in Fig. 2-10.

At higher levels, little in-depth detail is needed about many project activities; at lower levels, more in-depth detail

FIGURE 2-9.   "Good work, but I think we might need just a little more detail right here!"

is needed about fewer. This is no different from a typical organization chart. The need for multiple schedules is clear. Martin (p. 137) says why:

"In larger complicated projects, planning and status review by different echelons are facilitated by the use of detailed and summary networks. Higher levels of management can view the entire project and the interrelationships of major tasks without looking into the detail of the individual subtasks. Lower levels of management and supervision can examine their parts of the project in fine detail without being distracted by those parts of the project with which they have no interface."

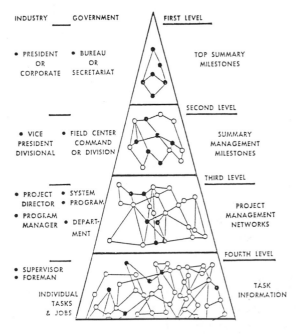

FIGURE 2-10.   Who needs what level of detail. In public domain.

As a rule of thumb, no manager should work—at close detail—with more than about fifty activities. The project manager summarizes project activities into ten to twenty "top-level" activities that he or she can analyze, plan, and control.

Question: But what if the project involves thousands of activities?

Answer: Establish and use a hierarchical structure, founded on organization-chart principles, that recognizes that most of the project manager's ten to fifty activities are projects for other managers, who themselves work with ten to fifty activities, and so on until all activities are properly accounted for.

NOW CHECK YOUR WORK

Now that project detail has been adequately established, check your work. This process ensures the following:

- All processes are properly defined and accounted for
- All processes relate to each other in proper manner
- No processes fall through the cracks to become a "missing item" indicated in an upper level but not actually performed anywhere in the lower
- No process takes a free ride into the work system as a "free item"; all activities must be known by their parent—just as a manager should know all of his or her employees by name and not have any phantoms in the organization.

Each work element must:

- Be assigned one and only one place
- Report to only one parent
- Represent the sum of all of its components

Again from the software world comes the concept of Leveling and Balancing, which—like structured analysis in general—applies to all projects, not just software development. We have just described *leveling* in decomposing the Statement of Work to form the Work Breakdown Structure and a more meaningful work representation. *Balancing* refers to the systematic summarization of all operations, from bottom up, to disclose:

- Inconsistencies
- Free and missing items
- Process validity

Clearly, the final result of this process should be a Statement of Work substantially equal to the original. It is common practice to include the original Statement of Work, along with other supporting documents, as the needed WBS description. This also:

- Ensures that all customer objectives have been adequately addressed
- Counteracts human tendency to subconsciously self-correct errors

Unless you made a mistake, there are probably some serious WBS construction errors if the two documents do not match. These deficiencies must be corrected now—not just be "blown off" as nuisances that will correct themselves later on. They will not. In fact, the hassle of "fixing things right" now is nothing compared with the disruption this could cause your project later, in actual production. If something seems hard to fix now, it may well indicate the extent of the disruption it might cause if left uncorrected.

WBS SUMMARY

We have learned the importance of the Work Breakdown Structure. A good WBS is essential to get your project off to a good start. Time, money, and effort spent to this end is time, money, and effort wisely invested. Unfortunately, many organizations and project managers do not learn this lesson until too late. Once the WBS is established and the project is kicked off, it becomes very costly to add, change, or delete activities or to deepen reporting levels. The cost is prohibitive. Dinsmore (p. 28) compares the WBS with spacecraft booster rockets: "Once their highly significant job is done, they fall by the wayside, retaining no residual value." Organizations that do not give careful attention and forethought to the importance of proper WBS development ultimately (probably sooner!) risk severe problems:

- Cost and schedule control problems in your current project
- Lack of a good information base for future proposals and project plans

Note again the second point. A very important WBS use is to provide time estimates and cost standards for any future activities that may:

- Follow from this project
- Be similar in nature, but are part of another proposal or project.

Either way, a good WBS is necessary for future needs as well as current. Improperly prepared now, it cannot be effectively utilized later.

YE HARVEST WHAT YE SOW!

The WBS and corresponding timetable should now be reviewed with your customer to:

- Show your customer that you:
  - Value their participation
  - Welcome their input
  - Are concerned their objectives will be met
- Verify that the schedule is complete, accurate, and meets their objectives
- Get things off to a surer start
- Increase confidence in the plan
- Reduce costs by minimizing the number of early revisions

To summarize, the keys to a good Work Breakdown Structure are:

To include all significant work activities required to complete the project on time, on budget, on specification—with good human relations

To make the above tasks manageable in size

To state all required deliverables—including report content and frequency

To state all deadlines, constraints, and other important considerations

To use structured analysis and top-down design techniques

To provide adequate but not excessive detail

To be flexible and require little additional paperwork

To establish meaningful cost accounts which will accurately match costs to progress

To relate costs to proper manager and charge number by work package

To represent no more than 0.5–2.5 percent of total project budget at the lowest detail level

To include line-manager risk assessments

To properly and clearly relate activities to others

To drive all schedules from the WBS

To grant authority commensurate with responsibility

To provide required resources

To measure and track project time, cost, and value of work accomplished

Preparation of a good, workable WBS:

- Is mandatory
- Is not easy
- Is well worth the effort

Once this is done, it is time to schedule these activities and apply these resources in the most cost-effective manner possible.

PROJECT HOME WBS EXAMPLES

Three short but complete Project HOME Work Breakdown Structures are provided in Fig. 2-11. The first diagram is based on primary work areas (deliverables) and is always needed. Other WBS diagrams, representing other project views, could also be drawn. The additional two examples shown here are based on craft and financial categories.

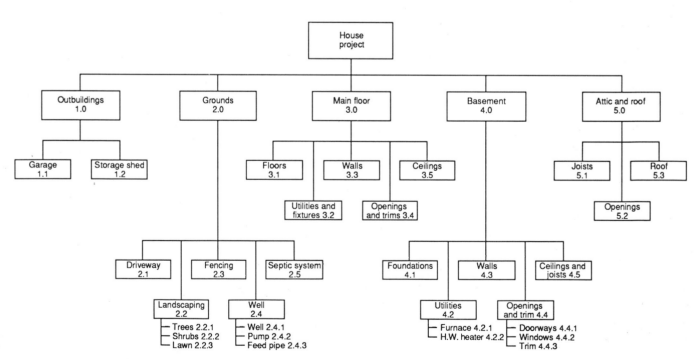

FIGURE 2-11A.   Project HOME WBS by major deliverables.

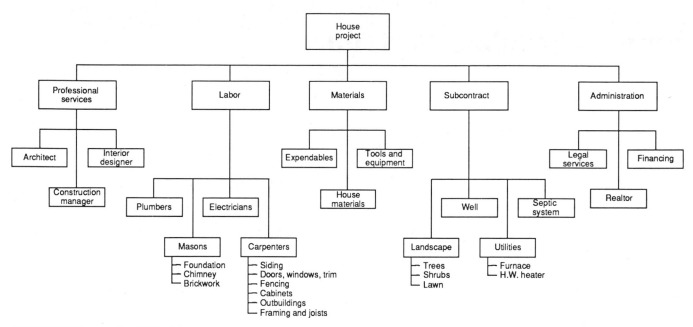

FIGURE 2-11B.   Project HOME WBS by major processes.

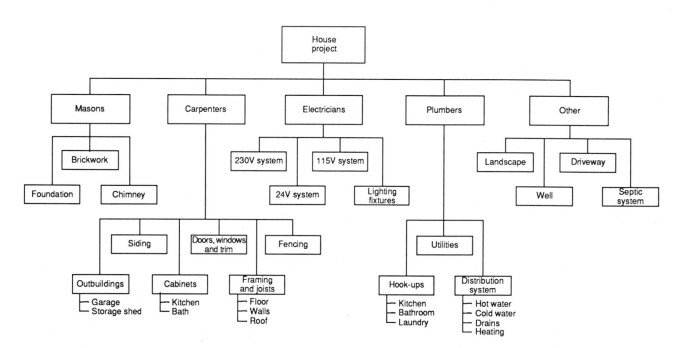

FIGURE 2-11C.   Project HOME WBS by major worker categories.

3
Basic Scheduling Procedures

This chapter introduces the Critical Path Method (CPM) five-step scheduling methodology:

Planning

Step 1: List each activity.
Step 2: Determine activity sequences and relationships.

Scheduling

Step 3: Determine activity time estimates and apply constraints.
    A. Date constraints.
    B. Time duration constraints.

Step 4: Determine the Critical Path.

Organization and Presentation

Step 5: Organize and present the schedule.

These topics will be presented in greater detail in Chapters 4 through 7.

In any project, there are three factors of concern:

- Time
- Cost
- Resource availability

The *Critical Path Method*, or *CPM*, may be used to plan and control each of these factors, as well as the project as a whole. It displays a project in related graphical form and emphasizes the activities crucial to project completion—on time and within budget. Together with an alternative approach called *PERT* (*Program Evaluation and Review Technique*), CPM has inspired a number of useful improvements on the plain-vanilla versions of old. The featured software

tool, *Primavera Project Planner,* supports an advanced version of the more popular CPM technique. This methodology finds wide application in such industries as manufacturing, software development, utilities, construction, and general business management. Necessary project characteristics include the following:

1. Well-defined jobs whose completion marks the end of the project
2. The jobs are independent in that they may be started, stopped, and conducted separately within a given sequence
3. The jobs or tasks are ordered in that they must follow each other in a given sequence

Both CPM and PERT find the longest time-consuming path through a network of activities as the basis for project planning and control. Originally, only minor differences distinguished the two methods; the only one of significance was that PERT calculates variance (and from this, probability) in its time estimates and CPM does not. However, difficulty in providing valid best-case and worst-case activity time estimates, required by PERT, has caused many project managers to abandon the three-value PERT in favor of the single-value CPM. And as we shall see, improvements made to CPM—especially how activities may relate to each other—did not transfer to PERT. Nevertheless, PERT is still used in industry and discussed in the literature, and so will be introduced in Chapter 8.

If such probabilities are desired in a CPM environment, activity time estimates may be computed by simulations, spreadsheet modeling, and other extensions to CPM. When it is necessary to do this—which is not often—one approach is to export project schedules into such tools as:

- Spreadsheet
- Decision support system
- Statistical analyzer

Throughout this book we shall see supplemental analyses provided by a top-quality electronic spreadsheet: *20/20* by Access Technology. (Please appreciate this fully: It is *not* necessary to know how to operate *20/20* or any other spreadsheet in order to understand these analyses.) If desired, the newly calculated activity times may then be reintroduced into the network and the resulting schedule recalculated.

Both techniques owe their development to serious defects inherent in their common predecessor, the Gantt Chart. The Gantt Chart, an example of which is shown in Fig. 3-1, is a graphic representation of a project schedule that shows each activity as a bar whose length is proportional to its duration; the bars appear in rows on a timeline representing the time frame in which the project occurs.

While from the outside things look pretty good, lift up the hood and—well, would you buy a car or fly in an airplane without an engine or powertrain?

Although the familiar Gantt Chart is able to relate activities to time and to display progress for all size projects, it is often relied on to do more than it is able. It does not, for example, show how activities relate to each other or what their resource requirements are. This is especially detrimental when the number of network activities exceeds twenty-five to thirty (a very small project and the approximate limit of human computational abilities). Even worse, it easily lends itself to "milestone manipulation"; that is, monkey business whose purpose is to window-dress the schedule and status reports to higher management. Without naming names, cheating is especially easy with some of the new GUI-based (Graphical User Interface) schedulers. Activities are often scheduled on a whim or a "Gotta-do-it-then-to-get-the-boss-off-my-back" feeling, whether or not realistic. Tasks perceived as urgent will frequently take precedence over important ones. In extreme cases, activities are positioned within the chart in such a way as to paint the prettiest or most unusual diagram. The impact of Gantt Chart's deficiencies is the following:

1. It cannot determine the Critical Path
2. It cannot evaluate the effects of change (either real or simulated) on the project plan
3. It cannot tell you how delays will affect the remainder of the project
4. It provides no help identifying resource availability or constraints. As a result, activities will be scheduled and commitments made that should not have been were it

known that adequate resources would not—and could not—be available
5. Similarly, it cannot identify the most cost-effective way by which available resources may be utilized. Inefficient resource usage will contribute to future shortages and, perhaps, constraints when they are needed elsewhere more
6. It provides false, usually overly optimistic, project status

Even with all these limitations, don't throw away all your Gantt Charts and put a curse on Henry Gantt's grave! Properly used, the Gantt Chart provides a simple and effective summary of project schedule and progress—but only if its foundation is built upon rock, not sand. We shall learn how to construct this necessary foundation.

OVERVIEW: CPM AND PERT HISTORY

Better, more effective planning and control tools were needed—and developed. In 1957, the DuPont Company—long an industry leader in many fields—developed the Critical Path Method (CPM) in conjunction with Remington Rand. The technique:

- Focused on the activities comprising a project
- Required relationships between activities to be identified
- Featured a single time estimate for each activity
- Allowed both a normal and an expediting cost to be associated with each activity duration
- Computed the shortest or most economical means to accomplish a project

While a great idea in theory, actual CPM usage was inhibited by the technical details of how project activities were represented. Later, we shall discuss why the AOA, or "activity-on-arrow" [also known as the "I-J" method or the *Arrow Diagram Method (ADM)*], approach fell short of idea potential.

Only one year later (in 1958), Professor John Fondahl of Stanford University proved that an alternative approach, in which activities were represented by nodes rather than arrows, could more effectively model network logic. Unfortunately, his work was all but forgotten until 1973, when it was modified to include the more complex activity relationships and came to be known as the *Precedence Diagram Method (PDM)*. This method is the most powerful, versatile, and realistic implementation of CPM. It will be used exclusively throughout this book, except in the brief Chapter 8 introduction of PERT.

Also in 1958, the United States Navy developed the Program Evaluation and Review Technique (PERT). Its first major use was to manage the Polaris Missile Program. PERT enabled this program to complete two years ahead of schedule. (CPM would have been equally successful.) Events were represented by nodes (or bubbles) and connected by arrows depicting both relationships and activity durations. As mentioned earlier, the probability of on-time project completion was also calculated.

FIGURE 3-1.   Project FUBAR Gantt Chart.

HOW TO DEVELOP A CPM NETWORK

Consistent with the required level of detail, we must divide the project into clearly defined activities that:

- Represent some specific and required action
- Logically relate to other defined activities
- Consume both time and resources (not necessarily without interruption, or "contiguous")
- Begin and end at well-defined times

An activity:

- Represents something that must be done to complete the project
- Consumes time and, perhaps, other resources

Usually, activities are roughly equivalent in detail. They vary widely in duration, needed resources, and other matters. Sometimes they even represent idle time during which nothing is actually done, such as when concrete is allowed to harden or paint to dry. It may seem incorrect to call such situations an "activity," but any function (or process) that occurs between specific points in time and also consumes time has generally been considered an activity.

On the other hand, this entire issue is probably moot because more advanced methods of representing activities (including PDM) are now available. These methods regard such situations merely as required lead or lag times within a more traditional activity that consumes resources other than only time.

The two general areas in which the Precedence Diagram Method is superior to other techniques are:

- Activity relationships
- Resource leads and lags

The featured software tool, *Primavera Project Planner,* fully supports PDM. The methodology will be used exclusively throughout this book, except in the brief Chapter 8 introduction to PERT.

Some (but by no means all) of the activities from our sample project, HOME, include:

- Layout
- Rough plumbing
- Excavation
- Rough electrical
- Pour foundation

The start of every activity is, in general, prompted by:

- Completion of a previous activity
- Project start

This means that an activity cannot start partway through the project without being initiated either by project start or by completion of an appropriate prior activity. There may be several activities that need to be completed for the next one to start. At the same time, all activities—even if completed—must relate to some later activity unless it is the final activity in the entire network.

Another way of saying this is that a properly-designed network must never have:

- Multiple start points
- Multiple end points
- Dangling activities

Suppose visitors to your residence entered only by way of the front door and departed only by way of the back. In this analogy, the front door would represent the start of the project and the back door would represent the end of the project. And just as visitors are not welcome to climb in or out of your windows, all project activities must be properly related to both the start and finish of the project. Within these two boundaries, there is often some latitude about how activities could occur. Some schedules will be better than others. Although there may be several viable schedules, there is usually only one optimal network. In Chapters 9 and 10, we shall learn how to compute the better, if not best, schedule.

The completion of every activity marks, in general, one of the following:

- Commencement of a later activity
- Project end

Therefore, every activity, without exception, must be connected to both project start and project finish. If not directly connected, it must be done through other activity sequences. Either way, there must never be any discontinuity at any point for any reason. If there is, the schedule is invalid and must be corrected. A good scheduling tool will find any errors in logic that you might have made. And *Primavera,* at least, is more polite than your boss would be!

There are two ways, as we indicated earlier, by which activities may be visually represented. The choice of style is *not* just one of personal preference. We shall learn why soon.

In the older and less capable activity-on-arrow, event-on-node (abbreviated as ADM, AOA, or "I-J") format, each arrow represents one activity and each node represents one event—either the start or the finish of an activity. Since an event is merely the start or finish of an activity and not the activity itself, it requires no time and consumes no resources. Events do, however, represent successive points in time. Except for project start and end events, each event represents both the completion of one activity and the start of another.

For example, "Write book" would be an activity because it takes both time and resources (and patience!). "Book completed" would be an event (and cause for much celebration!) because it represents the end of the activity just described.

Arrows connect the events and show the logical flow of the work. They represent the passage of time, and direction of progress, from left to right and as much as possible, from the top down. An activity in this format is always repre-

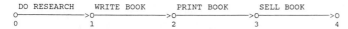

FIGURE 3-2.   Activity-on-arrow (AOA) representation.

sented by combining its tail number ("I") with its head ("J"), joining them with a hyphen. Each I-J identifier must be unique. An example will be given shortly.

In the simple network segment presented in Fig. 3-2, we have specified three events (other than 0 and 4) and four activities. Note as just discussed that each node actually signifies two events—the end of one activity and the beginning of another. That is, Event 1 marks not only the completion of research, but also the start of writing; Event 2 marks not only the end of writing, but also the start of printing, and so on.

The activities described on the arrow shafts would be called 0-1 for "Do research," 1-2 for "Write book," 2-3 for "Print book," 3-4 for "Sell book," and so on.

Recall that each I-J pair must be unique. One of many difficulties with this methodology (in diagrams more complex than this) arises when multiple paths with a common predecessor event converge on a single event node. Since each activity must be uniquely identified, the solution to this problem is to insert a *dummy activity* (which consumes no time or resources, but is not a synonym for "Congressional budget proceedings"!) into one or more of the paths to provide unique activity and path sequence numbers for each while maintaining proper relationship logic among all. When used, dummy activities are usually represented by dashed lines or thin arrows. Examples of dummy activities (Chase and Aquilano, p. 309) are shown in Fig. 3-3.

This additional and unnecessary complexity limits AOA value. Your project cannot be represented as accurately as it should be. This brief discussion of the AOA method is provided for historical purposes only, should the need arise to translate into PDM.

In the AON "activity-on-node" format, the format is reversed: Arrows denote only precedence; nodes denote activities. It can be said that nodes also include events. The left node wall represents the start of an activity and the right wall represents its finish. You are not required to think in these terms, but may do so if it helps. In any case, the AOA dummy-activity problem never occurs with this format. This is because an activity is designated only by a single, self-contained box rather than by an arrow connecting two events. Although this simpler, more flexible format does not by itself support the more complex relationships, it does not prevent that, as the AOA format does.

Recall that each project must have one and only one start and one finish. When multiple activities could independently commence at project start, it is usual to precede these with a synthetic milestone start activity of zero duration. Similarly, when multiple activities could independently end at

FIGURE 3-3.   Other activity-on-arrow representations. *Source:* Chase and Aquilano, page 309.

Implies A must be completely finished before B can start.

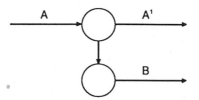

Indicates that B can start when A is partially completed.

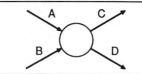

Implies that C and D are dependent on A and B.

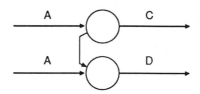

Indicates that D depends on A and B; C depends only on A.

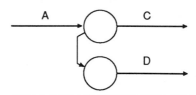

Indicates that C cannot start (in this case) until equipment becomes available from A.

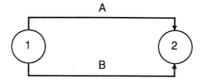

Conceptually correct but two activities have identical event numbers

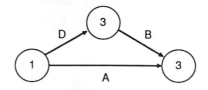

Enables separate activity designations; that is, for activity D, 1-3; A, 1-2; and B, 3-2.

project finish, it is usual to follow these with a synthetic milestone activity of zero duration.

This will prevent the situation in which multiple concurrent activities at either project start or project finish would otherwise:

- Produce a network with more than one start
- Produce a network with more than one finish
- Necessitate staggering the activities (and lengthening the project) only in order to accommodate the "rules of the game"

None of these options is acceptable. The purpose of start and finish activities is, therefore, to:

- Define clearly the start and the finish of the entire project for ready reference
- Provide but a single point to which are assigned scheduled start and finish dates

Employing the same network segment as above, we would have what is illustrated in Fig. 3-4.

Although activity representation is different in this simple example, the underlying relationships among activities are the same. In each, the end of one activity prompts the start of another, later activity. This is:

- By far the most common relationship
- Found in every project
- Not surprisingly called a *Finish-to-Start,* or *F/S,* relationship
- The only relationship supported by either AOA or AON
- One of four relationships supported by PDM

The activities described within the boxes in Fig. 3-4 are simply identified by a single number—1, 2, 3, 4, and so on—unlike the number pairs we saw earlier in the activity-on-arrow ("I-J") format. Events are not required; therefore they are not numbered. Each activity must complete before the next can, or should, start. Another way of saying this is that no activity (except 1) can start unless the activity before it has finished. Exceptions to this rule will be discussed later.

The following basic rules apply when constructing a network:

- Both time and progress flow from left to right, and from the top down
- Activities are uniquely identified
- Earlier activities are given lower numbers than later activities to help find loops and readily locate activities in the network

- So long as these rules are followed, activities need not be numbered in strict sequence. This would be difficult and is not necessary. Just as you should number your BASIC programs in multiples of ten, you should also allow plenty of room for your project to grow, too. Project HOME does precisely this. Its 58 activities are numbered from 1 to 146

Actually, in a production environment, you might also wish to label activities alphanumerically. In this way, you could easily combine subprojects into a master project schedule and still know the activity origins. Project CARS, for example, contains three subprojects coded within the activity identifier as *A, B,* and *C:*

- *A*: Automation system
- *B*: Building addition
- *C*: Conveyor system

Thus, activity A100 represents an activity from the automation system, B200 from the building addition, and C303 from the conveyor. All activities beginning with an *A* could be selected to focus on the automation system subproject, and so on. Since the identifying letter ensures that all activities will be uniquely identified, the subprojects may be combined for a more complete look at project status.

You could also explode a project into its component subprojects for further *drill-down* (working from the top downward) analysis. That is, you could separate all *ANNN* activities to investigate only the automation system, all *BNNN* activities to look at only the building addition, and all *CNNN* activities to look at only the conveyor system. Further levels of detail could also be coded into each subproject. For example:

- AD could represent design procedures for the automation system
- AI could represent installation procedures for the same system
- BD could represent design procedures for the building addition
- BI could represent installation procedures for the same system
- CD could represent design procedures for the conveyor system
- CI could represent installation procedures for the same system

Good project management software will allow you to formulate, say, a design subproject by selecting (in this example) all those activities whose second activity identifier letter is equal to *D*. This is especially useful when assigning resources. The process could continue until sufficient detail levels have been reached. Whether your project requires one or several such levels (probably no more than seven) depends on its unique requirements measured against the additional cost of greater detail. In any case, your activity identification scheme—and your software—should provide intelligent coding such as this.

FIGURE 3-4.   Activity-on-node (AON) representation.

(Step 1) Identify Each Activity to be Done in the Project

The result of this process is simply a list of all activities necessary to complete the project. It is an open question whether or not they should always be represented at the same level of detail.

Some people contend that the network should show the same level of detail throughout. For example, in building a house, an activity such as "nail down front steps" would not be shown on the same activity chart as "lay foundation." This is because the two activities represent substantially different levels of detail. But there is nothing that (within reason) requires them to be the same. If activity descriptions are forced to be equal in detail (but in what terms?), some will be more detailed than necessary and some will be less. The advantages must be found to outweigh the disadvantages. Different charges could be developed for each desired level, but this would be:

- Unnecessary excess work
- Error-prone
- Subject to updating inconsistencies
- Inadvisable

This author does not see the need for uniform detail levels. Include, as an activity, any time-consuming work process on which you wish to focus closer attention and control. One of the many advantages of CPM is its ability to identify trouble well in advance of actual occurrence. This makes it possible to amplify that part of the network in which trouble is indicated. This can be done at any stage of the project. It is, of course, preferable to do this before it starts, but it is still very useful once work is in progress.

If you use project management software, you should be able to:

- Explode any activity or series of activities into component parts
- Drill down into as many detail levels as desired
- Summarize ("roll up") any group of activities into any higher summary level
- Summarize any cost/resource group into any higher summary level
- Look ahead well into the future for such problems (*P3* allows one to look forward eighty-eight years!)

Alternatively, a desired collection of activities may be summarized in a pseudo-activity called a "hammock." This may be done as many times as necessary. "Hammock your hammocks" to provide succeedingly higher summary levels. Hammock activities, however, accurately represent underlying detail only if date constraints and special relationships, including out-of-sequence progress (to be defined later) are *not* present. If this happens, the hammock will only closely (but not precisely) represent its component parts. This slight offset will be carried throughout the entire summary, although its actual effect may be negated by other included activities that have been scheduled outside its range. "Hammocking your hammocks" is:

- Not always 100 percent precise
- Sometimes confusing to understand and explain
- Not supported by all software tools (*P3* does support this feature)

The most common usage of a hammock is to summarize similar operations on multiple like-items—for example, the steps necessary to build all columns on one (only!) floor of a new building. We shall study hammock activities in more detail in Chapter 6.

Activities are usually listed by corresponding WBS task. They should be listed before we concern ourselves with:

- Relationships with other activities
- Time durations
- Cost and resource requirements

For Project HOME, we list fifty-eight activities in their approximate starting order (Table 3-1).

(Step 2) Determine Activity Predecessor/Successor Relationships

This is a highly valuable process, but only if it is done correctly. It requires the project manager to:

- Carefully identify (not just "wing it") activity dependencies and interrelationships
- Present them in visual format

For each activity, the project manager must ask the following three questions:

- What other activities must be completed for this activity to start? (What are my predecessors?)
- What other activities can be done while this activity is being performed? (What are my parallel activities?)
- What activities cannot start until this activity has been completed? (What are my successors?)

This process is exactly like planning a school curriculum. Some courses must be taken before others. These prerequisites, therefore, are predecessors to other courses. For example, you should take accounting before you take finance. Some courses may be taken at the same time; these are parallel activities. You can, for instance, take finance at the same time as you take English. Others may be taken after one or more of these; they are the successors. Business policy would be an example.

Appreciate that it is both normal and common for some precedence relationships to change as activity data change. When reporting progress, you should review both predecessor and successor relationships, as well as activity durations. You should also look for activities that could be done in parallel. This can often significantly reduce the amount of time required to complete the project.

Report progress as often as necessary. Daily is prefera-

Table 3-1   Fifty-Eight Easy(?) Steps in Building Your Dream Home

```
Soil stabilization
Layout
Plumbing - street connection and underslab
Foundation excavation
Granular fill
Termite protection
Underslab electrical line
Underslab air conditioning freon line
Concrete slab on grade
Curing time
Set precast concrete panels
Grout precast panels
Frame interior walls
Install tub, stack out plumbing
Pull wire; rough in electric & telephone in walls
TV wire pulling
Plates, lintels, and roof trusses
Redwood fascia, soffit, and plywood decking
Dry sheeting
Stock bulk material inside building
Roof shingles
Set infill panel framing
Windows
Wood siding
Wall insulation
Exterior railings
Concrete stairs
Sheetrock walls
Tape and bed
Fur down for ceiling air conditioner
Blow on ceiling insulation
Air conditioning rough in
Sheetrock fur downs
Tape and bed fur downs
Texture walls and ceilings
Doors and trim
Bathroom tile
Painting
Vinyl wall covering
Hardware
Clean up
Resilient flooring and bases
Install cabinets
Paneling, finish carpentry and millwork
Install condensers and air conditioning trimout
TV trimout
Electrical connections and trimout
Plumbing connections and trimout
Set appliances
Bathroom accessories
Clean up
Paint touch up
Install carpeting
Install drapes
Install metal stairs
Clean up
Punch list
Building complete
```

ble, but weekly is mandatory. If your network is not current, it cannot be accurate and will not be reliable. When reporting progress, you must also:

- Ensure claimed values are reasonable
- Record actual start and finish times (both intermittent and final)
- Update precedence and successor relationships
- Note reasons for any unusual delays or better-than-average times
- Compute new network values

It is important to record these actual times as soon as possible. This is because:

- Incomplete activities (including finished activities not reported as complete) always affect the future schedule
- Completed activities no longer constrain the future schedule
- The actual dates can serve as historical data that may be useful when you plan another project, or when writing a proposal or bidding on future work

Remember, too, that there are relationships other than the common Finish-to-Start (F/S) relationship described earlier. The project manager must identify those activities that share:

- A common starting point (*Start-to-Start,* or *SS*)
- A common ending point (*Finish-to-Finish,* or *FF*)

He or she must also identify activities related by a *Start-to-Finish* arrangement. These three advanced relationships are supported by PDM only and will be discussed in great detail in Chapter 4. Table 3-2 lists the four activity relationships supported by PDM. It is strongly suggested that you not even think of settling for less! There is no compelling reason to do so. The numbers in parentheses represent the relative ease by which most people can understand and explain the relationship to others.

For Project HOME (Table 3-3), we add relationships to the fifty-eight activities that were listed in Table 3-1.

In Project HOME, for example, walls cannot be painted before they have been framed and sheetrocked. We cannot grout precast panels until five days after they have been set. Appliances must be set prior to the last five days of electrical trimout and connection work; they will be hooked up at that time.

(Step 3) Determine Time Estimates for Each Activity

We are now ready to begin steps 3 and 4, the schedule phase, in which we:

- Apply time estimates to each activity
- Determine the Critical Path

These two steps, along with schedule presentation, are every bit as crucial to the success of the project as were the previous (list activities and relationships). Even if the project manager went no further, he or she would—by thoroughly analyzing the project, breaking it down, and preparing the network logic—have a clear understanding of the work involved. This in itself would place the project manager in a substantially better position to manage than if it were not done.

Nevertheless, the greatest benefits will be achieved only from the remaining three steps. Simple arithmetic calculations, coupled with well-defined rules of logic, easily provide a wealth of information that remains highly valuable throughout all stages of a project. The introduction of the time element into project calculations enables the project manager to accurately determine the following:

- Overall project length
- What activity sequences control this length
- Timing of intermediate goals and deadlines

The unit of time used in computations will depend on the degree of detail necessary, as indicated by the WBS and the planning process. If the schedule is used for overall long-range planning, activity duration will probably be best measured in weeks or even months, while for a highly detailed project involving very close control and day-to-day timing, time measurement should be expressed in days or perhaps even hours. In Chapter 5 we shall learn how to provide good time estimates. For now, accept them as a given as they apply to Project HOME (Table 3-4):

Time governs all. The third scheduling step, therefore, is to:

- Assign a realistic duration to each activity (may be estimated)
- Compute starting times for each activity
- Compute finishing times for each activity

Scheduling depends very heavily on the earliest date on which an activity can start. This date depends on when required predecessor activities are completed, and if required resources are available. The idea is again exactly like a college curriculum: Certain courses may be taken only upon successful completion of prerequisites. Course length as well as order determines this. In the same way, some activities can start only when others have finished. When they can start depends on predecessor:

- Order
- Completion status
- Length

Not surprisingly, the earliest date on which an activity can start is known as the *Early Start* date (*ES*). It represents an activity's objective starting date. The earliest date on which an activity can finish is known as the *Early Finish*

Table 3-2   The Four PDM Relationships

PREDECESSOR \ SUCCESSOR	START	FINISH
START	SS (2)	SF (4)
FINISH	FS (1)	FF (3)

Table 3-3   Project HOME Activity List (With Relationships)

```
------------------------------------------------------------------------
SCHEDULE SETUP                              DATE: _____
------------------------------------------------------------------------
PROJECT NAME:  58-ACTIVITY "HOME" HOUSING PROJECT (DALLAS, TEXAS)_____
               PRIMAVERA SYSTEMS, INC., BALA CYNWYD, PENNSYLVANIA 19004
------------------------------------------------------------------------
```

ACT ID	PRED/ REL		SUCC/ REL		ACTIVITY DESCRIPTION
1	None		3	F/S	Layout
3	1	F/S	5	F/S	Soil stabilization
5	3	F/S	7	F/S	Plumbing - street connection and underslab
7	5	F/S	9	F/S	Foundation excavation
9	7	F/S	11	F/S	Granular fill
			12	F/S	
			13	F/S	
11	9	F/S	22	F/S	Underslab air conditioning freon line
12	9	F/S	22	F/S	Underslab electrical line
13	9	F/S	22	F/S	Termite protection
22	11	F/S	24	F/S	Concrete slab on grade
	12	F/S			
	13	F/S			
24	22	F/S	26	F/S	Curing time
26	24	F/S	27	SS5	Set precast concrete panels
			30	F/S	
			50	F/S	
27	26	SS5	30	F/S	Grout precast panels
			50	F/S	
30	26	F/S	32	F/S	Install metal stairs
	27	F/S			
32	30	F/S	34	F/S	Plates, lintels, and roof trusses
34	32	F/S	41	F/S	Redwood fascia, soffit, and plywood decking
41	34	F/S	43	F/S	Dry sheeting
			58	F/S	
43	41	F/S	45	F/S	Stock bulk material inside building
45	43	F/S	47	F/S	Set infill panel framing
47	45	F/S	49	F/S	Windows
49	47	F/S	66	F/S	Wood siding
50	26	F/S	52	F/S	Frame interior walls
	27	F/S	53	F/S	
			54	F/S	
52	50	F/S	58	F/S	Install tub, stack out plumbing
53	50	F/S	66	F/S	Pull wire; rough in electric & telephone
54	50	F/S	66	F/S	TV wire pulling
58	41	F/S	66	F/S	Roof shingles
	52	F/S			
66	49	F/S	67	SS2	Wall insulation
	53	F/S	68	SS3	
	54	F/S	70	F/S	
	58	F/S			
67	66	SS2	128	F/S	Concrete stairs
68	66	SS3	128	F/S	Exterior railings
70	66	F/S	72	F/S	Sheetrock walls
72	70	F/S	74	F/S	Tape and bed
			76	FF5	
74	72	F/S	128	F/S	Blow on ceiling insulation
76	72	FF5	78	F/S	Fur down for ceiling air conditioner
78	76	F/S	80	F/S	Air conditioning rough in
80	78	F/S	87	F/S	Sheetrock fur downs
87	80	F/S	89	F/S	Tape and bed fur downs
89	87	F/S	91	F/S	Texture walls and ceilings
			93	F/S	
91	89	F/S	95	F/S	Bathroom tile
93	89	F/S	95	F/S	Doors and trim

Table 3-3   Continued

```
------------------------------------------------------------------------
  ACT            PRED/          SUCC/
   ID             REL            REL      ACTIVITY DESCRIPTION
------------------------------------------------------------------------
   95      91    F/S      99    F/S      Painting
           93    F/S     100    F/S
   99      95    F/S     128    F/S      Hardware
  100      95    F/S     107    F/S      Vinyl wall covering
  107     100    F/S     109    F/S      Cleanup
  109     107    F/S     112    F/S      Resilient flooring and bases
                         113    F/S
                         114    F/S
                         115    F/S
  112     109    F/S     128    F/S      Paneling, finish carpentry, and millwork
  113     109    F/S     128    F/S      Install condensers & air conditioning trimout
  114     109    F/S     128    F/S      TV trimout
  115     109    F/S     117    F/S      Install cabinets
                         118    F/S
  117     115    F/S     119    FF5      Set appliances
                         128    F/S
  118     115    F/S     123    F/S      Plumbing connections and trimout
  119     117    FF5     128    F/S      Electrical connections and trimout
  123     118    F/S     128    F/S      Bathroom accessories
  128      67    F/S     136    F/S      Cleanup
           68    F/S
           74    F/S
           99    F/S
          112    F/S
          113    F/S
          114    F/S
          117    F/S
          119    F/S
          123    F/S
  136     128    F/S     138    F/S      Paint touchup
  138     136    F/S     140    F/S      Install carpeting
  140     138    F/S     142    F/S      Install drapes
  142     140    F/S     144    F/S      Cleanup
  144     142    F/S     146    F/S      Punch list
  146     144    F/S    None             Building complete
------------------------------------------------------------------------
```

date (*EF*). It represents the objective ending date for that particular activity.

The latest date on which an activity can start is known as the *Late Start* date (*LS*). It represents an activity's deadline starting date. The latest date on which an activity can finish is known as the *Late Finish* date (*LF*). It represents the deadline ending date for that particular activity. More formal definitions follow.

Early Start (ES)

Early Start is the earliest possible time an activity can begin. This depends on whether or not necessary predecessor activities have been completed and whether or not needed resources are available. It is also based on the cumulative length of time required to complete the chain of events that lead up to that activity. Where two or more chains of events lead up to an activity, the earliest time at which that activity can begin is when the chain taking the longest time to finish

is completed. Note well that "Early Start" does *not* mean "starting early" as in "Let's get an early start on that fishing trip!" (The term *out-of-sequence progress* refers to this condition, that is, work completed for an activity before it is logically scheduled to occur.) Neither does it refer to any of the following (or similar expressions):

- Fast start
- Good start
- Head start
- Quick start
- Strong start

It only means the earliest possible time that an activity can begin. For critical activities it also means the time by which an activity must begin so as not to delay project completion. Critical activities must begin on the Early Start date. Other activities should also start then if adequate resources are available. Consider this time to be your objective starting time.

Table 3-4   Project HOME Activity List (With Relationships and Durations)

```
-------------------------------------------------------------------------------
SCHEDULE SETUP                                    DATE: _____

PROJECT NAME:   58-ACTIVITY "HOME" HOUSING PROJECT (DALLAS, TEXAS)_____
                PRIMAVERA SYSTEMS, INC., BALA CYNWYD, PENNSYLVANIA 19004
-------------------------------------------------------------------------------
```

ACT ID	PRED/ REL		SUCC/ REL		ACTIVITY DESCRIPTION	DUR
1	None		3	F/S	Layout	5
3	1	F/S	5	F/S	Soil stabilization	15
5	3	F/S	7	F/S	Plumbing – street connection and underslab	8
7	5	F/S	9	F/S	Foundation excavation	5
9	7	F/S	11	F/S	Granular fill	7
			12	F/S		
			13	F/S		
11	9	F/S	22	F/S	Underslab air conditioning freon line	5
12	9	F/S	22	F/S	Underslab electrical line	7
13	9	F/S	22	F/S	Termite protection	13
22	11	F/S	24	F/S	Concrete slab on grade	5
	12	F/S				
	13	F/S				
24	22	F/S	26	F/S	Curing time	13
26	24	F/S	27	SS5	Set precast concrete panels	10
			30	F/S		
			50	F/S		
27	26	SS5	30	F/S	Grout precast panels	6
			50	F/S		
30	26	F/S	32	F/S	Install metal stairs	50
	27	F/S				
32	30	F/S	34	F/S	Plates, lintels, and roof trusses	23
34	32	F/S	41	F/S	Redwood fascia, soffit, & plywood decking	20
41	34	F/S	43	F/S	Dry sheeting	5
			58	F/S		
43	41	F/S	45	F/S	Stock bulk material inside building	4
45	43	F/S	47	F/S	Set infill panel framing	3
47	45	F/S	49	F/S	Windows	5
49	47	F/S	66	F/S	Wood siding	8
50	26	F/S	52	F/S	Frame interior walls	20
	27	F/S	53	F/S		
			54	F/S		
52	50	F/S	58	F/S	Install tub, stack out plumbing	4
53	50	F/S	66	F/S	Pull wire; rough in electric & telephone	15
54	50	F/S	66	F/S	TV wire pulling	8
58	41	F/S	66	F/S	Roof shingles	15
	52	F/S				
66	49	F/S	67	SS2	Wall insulation	5
	53	F/S	68	SS3		
	54	F/S	70	F/S		
	58	F/S				
67	66	SS2	128	F/S	Concrete stairs	5
68	66	SS3	128	F/S	Exterior railings	6
70	66	F/S	72	F/S	Sheetrock walls	25
72	70	F/S	74	F/S	Tape and bed	20
			76	FF5		
74	72	F/S	128	F/S	Blow on ceiling insulation	10
76	72	FF5	78	F/S	Fur down for ceiling air conditioner	5
78	76	F/S	80	F/S	Air conditioning rough in	10
80	78	F/S	87	F/S	Sheetrock fur downs	4
87	80	F/S	89	F/S	Tape and bed fur downs	15
89	87	F/S	91	F/S	Texture walls and ceilings	13
			93	F/S		
91	89	F/S	95	F/S	Bathroom tile	5
93	89	F/S	95	F/S	Doors and trim	10

Table 3-4 Continued

ACT ID	PRED/ REL		SUCC/ REL		ACTIVITY DESCRIPTION	DUR
95	91	F/S	99	F/S	Painting	20
	93	F/S	100	F/S		
99	95	F/S	128	F/S	Hardware	5
100	95	F/S	107	F/S	Vinyl wall covering	8
107	100	F/S	109	F/S	Cleanup	5
109	107	F/S	112	F/S	Resilient flooring and bases	10
			113	F/S		
			114	F/S		
			115	F/S		
112	109	F/S	128	F/S	Paneling, finish carpentry, and millwork	14
113	109	F/S	128	F/S	Install condensers and A/C trimout	10
114	109	F/S	128	F/S	TV trimout	5
115	109	F/S	117	F/S	Install cabinets	13
			118	F/S		
117	115	F/S	119	FF5	Set appliances	5
			128	F/S		
118	115	F/S	123	F/S	Plumbing connections and trimout	13
119	117	FF5	128	F/S	Electrical connections and trimout	12
123	118	F/S	128	F/S	Bathroom accessories	5
128	67	F/S	136	F/S	Cleanup	10
	68	F/S				
	74	F/S				
	99	F/S				
	112	F/S				
	113	F/S				
	114	F/S				
	117	F/S				
	119	F/S				
	123	F/S				
136	128	F/S	138	F/S	Paint touchup	5
138	136	F/S	140	F/S	Install carpeting	15
140	138	F/S	142	F/S	Install drapes	5
142	140	F/S	144	F/S	Cleanup	10
144	142	F/S	146	F/S	Punch list	10
146	144	F/S	None		Building complete	5
					*** TOTAL WORKDAYS ***	597

Early Finish (EF)

Early Finish is the earliest possible time an activity can finish. It is equal to the Early Start plus the time needed to complete the activity (activity duration). For the same reason as explained above, "Early Finish" does *not* mean "finishing early!" It only means the earliest possible time that an activity can finish. It also means, for critical activities, the time by which an activity must finish so as not to delay project completion. In any case, an activity must start no later than its ES time and take no longer than its expected duration in order to meet Early Finish. Consider this time to be your objective finishing time.

Late Start (LS)

Late Start is the latest an activity can begin without delaying the project. "Late Start" does *not* mean "starting late!" Nor does it refer to any of the following (or similar expressions):

- Bad start
- Poor start
- Slow start
- Weak start
- Delayed start

However, if no progress (on any activity) occurs before the Late Start:

- All activities turn critical
- You have most unwisely wasted all your scheduling flexibility (*float*)
- Your schedule will soon suffer havoc and disruption

Where two or more chains of events stem from one activity, then that activity—if the project time is not to be exceeded—must take place within sufficient time to allow the longest sequence of subsequent activities to take place.

Table 3-5   Activity List (With Relationships and Durations)

```
----------------------------------------------------------------------------
SCHEDULE SETUP                                  DATE: _____

PROJECT NAME:    FOUR-ACTIVITY CRITICAL PATH METHOD EXAMPLE_____
                 CHASE (USC) AND AQUILANO (ARIZONA)
----------------------------------------------------------------------------
  ACTIVITY     DUR      PREDECESSOR/    SUCCESSOR/
    ID        (DAYS)    RELATIONSHIP    RELATIONSHIP    ACTIVITY DESCRIPTION
--------     ------    ------------    ------------    -------------------
    A          2       None            B    F/S
                                       C    F/S
    B          5       A    F/S        D    F/S
    C          4       A    F/S        D    F/S
    D          3       B    F/S        None
                       C    F/S
----------------------------------------------------------------------------
```

Often, this time is not displayed on reports for fear that people will wait until the last minute to start an activity. Consider this time to be your deadline starting time.

Late Finish (LF)

Late Finish is the latest an activity can finish without delaying the project. It is equal to the activity Late Start plus duration. "Late Finish" does *not* mean "finishing late!" For the reasons discussed above, this time is often not displayed on reports. Consider this time to be your deadline finishing time.

How are these times computed? The process requires two passes through the network, one in each direction. Early times (both start and finish) are calculated on the forward pass and late times (both start and finish) are calculated on the backward pass. This is best explained by example (see Table 3-5).

The form illustrated in Table 3-5 is not a standard input form. A *Primavera* report served as the basis of this form. The basic *P3* input screen is presented in Fig. 3-5.

An alternative, graphics-based, interface paints activities

and relationships directly onto the screen. It is shown in Fig. 3-6.

These screens are presented as examples only. Since the purpose of this book is *not* to teach the reader how to "push buttons," on-line data entry procedures will not be discussed.

The abbreviated form provides all the information necessary to produce a basic time schedule for each activity and includes:

- Activity identifier
- Activity duration
- Activity predecessors, successors, and relationships
- Activity description

If useful, a blank example is presented in Table 3-6.

Let us now draw a diagram of this network (Fig. 3-7).

In Fig. 3-7, which is organized in PDM (or at least AON) format, letters represent activities and numbers indicate the duration of these activities. Assume the time unit to be days. Schedule computations always look for the longest trail through the network. This requires two passes, one forward

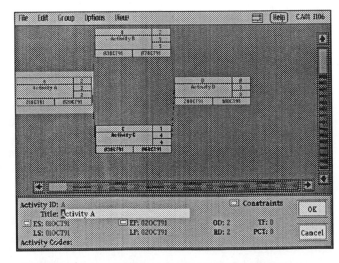

FIGURE 3-5.   *Primavera* basic input screen (Primavera Systems, Inc.).

FIGURE 3-6.   Sample *Primavera* PENGUIN screen painter (Primavera Systems, Inc.).

Table 3-6 Schedule Setup Form

ACTIVITY ID	DUR (DAYS)	PREDECESSOR/ RELATIONSHIP	SUCCESSOR/ RELATIONSHIP	ACTIVITY DESCRIPTION

SCHEDULE SETUP   DATE: _____

PROJECT NAME: _____

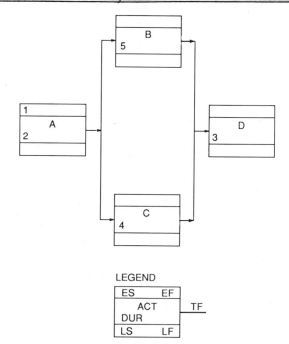

FIGURE 3-7. Network setup diagram.

and one backward. The following times are calculated in each:

• Early Start and Early Finish, using the latest ES times, in the forward pass
• Late Start and Late Finish, using the earliest LS times, in the backward pass

Intuitively obvious to the casual observer, wasn't it?

Let us take a step-by-step look at how we find these four values.

Calculate Early Start Times

For simplicity, assume the following:

• Project start is the first day of the month, say October 1991
• The workweek is seven days (the effects of nonworkdays will be discussed later)

To clarify a point of confusion: Some people set project start date equal to zero. Conceptually, "zero" (for our purposes) means "no progress." It represents the beginning of a day (the *Zero Hour*) on which "start-activity" progress begins to happen. Progress is reported at the end of this day. Since one day of progress has been recorded, this initial schedule day is properly referred to as Day 1. It began at 0 and ended at 1. This one-day offset is carried throughout the network.

But no month actually has a Day 0. If the schedule refers, as it should, to specific calendar days, this confusion will never arise if we remember:

• Early Start and Late Start are always measured at day's beginning
• Early Finish and Late Finish are always measured at day's end

The examples in this book will refer to the actual calendar.

Since it is the project start activity, *A* is assigned an Early Start value of 1. This represents the beginning of the 1 October 1991 workday, regardless of whether the actual time is midnight, 8 A.M., 4 P.M., or any other time of day. It only means when work that particular day is supposed to start.

To find Early Start for activity *B*, we need to add the duration of *A* (which is 2) to 1 (the ES for *A*) and obtain 3. Therefore, *B* is scheduled to start the beginning of the 3 October 1991 workday—again regardless of whether the actual time is midnight, 8 A.M., 4 P.M., or any other time of day. It will usually, but not necessarily, be the same time as the October 1 workday start. It will be different only if workdays are not uniform in their starting times. In all cases, however, it represents the normal start of business for that particular day. Activity *B* is scheduled to begin two complete workdays after *A* was supposed to start, regardless of when business actually starts on October 1, 2, or 3.

Likewise, the Early Start for activity *C* would also be 1 + 2, or 3. Both *B* and *C* are scheduled to begin at the same time on October 3, two days after *A* was supposed to start. We say that *B* and *C* are *parallel* activities.

If an activity, such as *D*, has more than one predecessor, Early Start must be computed as seen by each. To find Early Start for *D*, therefore, we must calculate and compare the two times as seen by each of its predecessors, *B* and *C*.

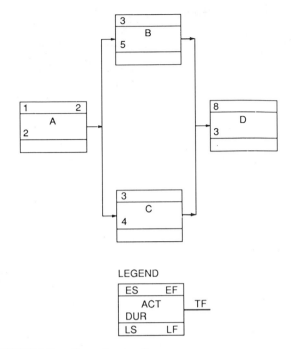

LEGEND

ES	EF
ACT	TF
DUR	
LS	LF

FIGURE 3-8.   Network setup diagram.

As seen by *B*: 3 + 5 = 8.
As seen by *C*: 3 + 4 = 7.

We always select the larger (later) of these two values, or 8. Therefore, Early Start for *D* is 8 October 1991. If both *B* and *C* have completed by then, *D* can begin at the start of the October 8 workday. Because it determined its successor's schedule, *B* is called a *driving predecessor* for *D*.

It is not necessary to trace the chain of events from project start each time we need to determine a later activity's Early Start. We only need to:

• Keep a running total of cumulative durations of all previous chains of events leading up to this activity
• Select the longest chain

This is why, in calculating Early Start for *D*, we needed to consider only *B* and *C*, not *A*. Applicable *B* and *C* times included those from *A*. These values are entered in the diagram, as seen in Fig. 3-8.

Table 3-7   Schedule Summary: Early Start

SCHEDULE SUMMARY   DATE: _____

PROJECT NAME: FOUR-ACTIVITY CRITICAL PATH METHOD EXAMPLE_____

ACTIVITY ID	ORIG DUR	REM DUR	% DONE	EARLY START	EARLY FINISH	LATE START	LATE FINISH	TOTAL FLOAT
A	2	2	0	1OCT91				
B	5	5	0	3OCT91				
C	4	4	0	3OCT91				
D	3	3	0	8OCT91				

Table 3-7 tells us what we now know.

Since no progress has been made on any activity, each activity is 0 percent done and remaining duration is equal to original duration.

Calculate Early Finish Times

Fortunately, activity finish times are not affected by how their start times are represented. Early Finish times are simply the sum of an activity's:

- Early Start (just calculated)
- Duration

Usually, Early Finish is calculated at the same time as Early Start. I have separated them here only for clarity. Also, remember that the Early Finish time represents the end of that particular workday whether the actual time is 8 A.M., 4 P.M., midnight, or any other time of day. Like Early Start, the time of day represented by Early Finish may vary by calendar day. In all cases, however, it represents the normal close of business for that particular day.

Early Finish for activity A is equal to its Early Start time plus its duration. But we cannot simply add these two numbers and get 3 (= 1 + 2) because they represent different measurement points in time:

- Early Start always represents the beginning of a workday
- Duration is always measured at the end of a workday

Therefore, A is scheduled to begin first thing October 1 (ES) and take two days to complete (duration). At the end of the October 1 workday, it should be half done and have one day left. It should continue progress beginning first thing October 2 and finish by the end of that same day. This would represent Early Finish for activity A. As a check, recall that B and C cannot start until A completes. Can they begin as scheduled October 3? Yes. Since A is due to finish by the end of the workday on October 2, B and C should be able to start as scheduled at the beginning of the workday on October 3.

The Early Finish for B is the October 3 Early Start plus the five-day duration, or October 7. Recall that C shares the same Early Start as B but takes one day less to complete. The Early Finish for C is the October 3 Early Start plus the

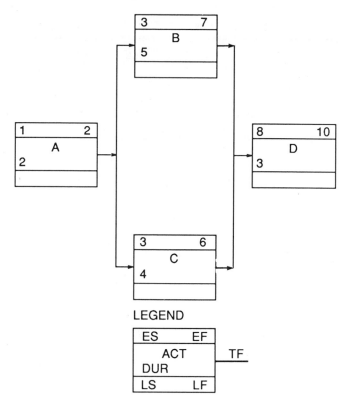

FIGURE 3-9. Network setup diagram.

four-day duration, or October 6. It is one day earlier than B because it takes one day less to complete. What about D? We do not need to revisit the "which path is longer?" issue; D should begin October 8. The Early Finish for D is the October 8 Early Start plus the three-day duration, or October 10.

Therefore, the soonest all four activities could be completed is ten days. If A began October 1, D should be finished by the end of October 10.

These values are entered on the diagram, as seen in Fig. 3-9.

Table 3-8 tells us what we now know. Table 3-9 summarizes the rules by which these dates were calculated.

Remember, if needed, to translate the zero-baseline Early Start into the actual calendar start date and compute accordingly. A more complete table, summarizing rules for advanced relationships, will be presented later.

Table 3-8 Schedule Summary: Early Start and Finish

```
----------------------------------------------------------------------------
SCHEDULE SUMMARY                                    DATE: _____

PROJECT NAME:  FOUR-ACTIVITY CRITICAL PATH METHOD EXAMPLE_____
----------------------------------------------------------------------------
```

ACTIVITY ID	ORIG DUR	REM DUR	% DONE	EARLY START	EARLY FINISH	LATE START	LATE FINISH	TOTAL FLOAT
A	2	2	0	1OCT91	2OCT91			
B	5	5	0	3OCT91	7OCT91			
C	4	4	0	3OCT91	6OCT91			
D	3	3	0	8OCT91	10OCT91			

Table 3-9   Calculation of Early Start and Early Finish Times (Forward Pass)

ACTIVITY	RELATIONSHIP	EARLY START (ES)	EARLY FINISH (EF)
First	Any	Zero (always)	Activity duration
All sub-sequent	F/S	EF of preceding activity	ES + activity duration

This concludes the forward pass. In this process we calculated Early Start and Early Finish times for each activity.

Calculate Late Start and Late Finish Times

Now put in the clutch, shift into reverse, and do the next step. By:

- Going from network end to network start
- Deducting activity durations along the way

you will next calculate Late Start and Late Finish for each activity.

There is generally no reason to extend a project beyond the earliest time it can be completed, that is, beyond its Early Finish date. As we shall see in Chapter 9, this only hogs resources and increases costs. And unless an earlier deadline has been set for the project, there is no reason to move this date up. We shall see why in Chapters 5 and 6.

Our sample project can finish as early as (the end of) October 10. Therefore, we set the Late Finish date equal to the Early in order not to delay the project. Now, for both end-activity *D* and the project as a whole, Early Finish and Late Finish are exactly the same—the end of the October 10 workday. We did this to avoid unnecessary delay and cost.

We must now do this: Working back from project finish to project start, one activity at a time, we determine how long the start of an activity may be delayed without affecting when its successor(s) can start. Where two or more chains of events (for example, *B* and *C*) branch from one activity (*A*), then the predecessor activity—if the project is not to be lengthened—must take place in sufficient time to allow the longest sequence of subsequent activities to take place.

We begin at project finish, where we have just set LF = EF, or October 10. The latest that *D* could possibly start without delaying project finish is Late Finish minus duration, or October 8 (three days duration prior to October 10). October 8 is, therefore, the Late Start time for activity *D*. If *D* begins first thing October 8 and takes no more than three days to complete, the project will finish before EF/LF (late) October 10. If it begins after this time, or takes longer to complete than three days, the project will definitely be delayed.

But *D* cannot begin until both *B* and *C* have finished. This means that both *B* and *C* Late Finish times must be at

the end of the prior workday, or October 7. What will be their Late Start times? For each, it will again be Late Finish minus duration:

- For *C*, October 4 (four days duration prior to October 7)
- For *B*, October 3 (five days duration prior to October 7)

October 4 is, therefore, the Late Start time for activity *C*. If *C* begins first thing on October 4 and takes no more than four days to complete, *D* will be able to start as scheduled on October 8. If it begins after this time, or takes longer than four days to complete, both *D* and the project will definitely be delayed. Similarly, October 3 is the Late Start time for activity *B*. If *B* begins first thing on October 3 and takes no more than five days to complete, *D* will be able to start as scheduled on October 8. If it begins after this time, or takes longer than five days to complete, both *D* and the project will definitely be delayed. Both *D* and the project will be delayed beyond October 10 if any of the following happen:

- *B* starts after October 3
- *C* starts after October 4
- *B* takes longer than five days
- *C* takes longer than four days (with an October 4 or later start)

Why might *B* or *C* begin late? Recall they both depend on *A* to finish before either activity can start. Therefore, *A* must finish no later than:

- October 3, so as not to delay *C* (also *D* and the project)
- October 2, so as not to delay *B* (also *D* and the project)

We compare these two possible Late Finish dates for *A* and always select the earlier, or October 2. If *A* completes by then, none of its successors—*B*, *C*, or *D*—will be delayed. Neither will the project. Had we selected October 3:

- *B* would start one day late and delay both *D* and the project
- *C* could still begin by October 4 LS and cause no delays

Clearly, *B*—not *C*—must determine the Late Finish for *A*. Finally, because *A* must finish by the end of October 2, it cannot start any later than first thing on October 1—which you will remember is also its Early Start time.

This is true for all plans: Both Early Start and Late Start for the start activity must always be identical, the activity always critical. A later start than ES (or LS) would definitely

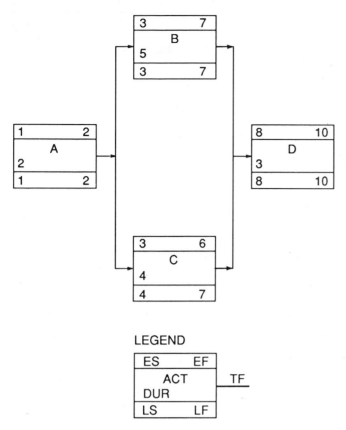

LEGEND

ES	EF
ACT	TF
DUR	
LS	LF

FIGURE 3-10.   Network setup diagram.

delay the project, but activity durations would still be the same along the way (assuming the same resource availability levels).

You have made an error if you find otherwise. This is because the procedure:

• Adds the longest-chain activity durations to obtain project EF
• Sets LF = EF
• Deducts the durations of the same activities (of obviously same value as when adding) to arrive at start-activity LS value
• Compares LS with ES to ensure that they are equal

This provides a valuable check that everything has been done correctly. If start activity Late Start does not equal start activity Early Start, find your error and correct it.

These values are entered on the diagram, as seen in Fig. 3-10. What we now know is shown in Table 3-10.

These Late Start and Late Finish values are entered in the network, activity by activity. As with their early-event counterparts, it is not necessary to trace the chain of events from project finish each time we need to determine an earlier activity's Late Start. We only need to:

• Keep a running total of cumulative durations of all successor chains of events leading from this activity
• Select the longest

These rules are summarized in Table 3-11. Remember that predecessor EF/LF is always measured at the end of the prior workday. Also remember to translate, if required, the zero-baseline Late Start into the actual calendar date and compare that with the intended Early Start to see if they are the same. A more complete table, summarizing rules for advanced relationships, will be presented later.

This concludes the backward pass. In this process we calculated Late Start and Late Finish times for each activity.

Now that we have done this, we may continue our project time analysis.

(Step 4) Determine the Critical Path

As we have just seen, project length depends on when it can start and how early it can finish. This, in turn, depends on which path, or chain of activities, requires the longest time to complete and is the most critical—thus the name *Critical Path*.

The Critical Path is anything but the Yellow Brick Road!

In fact, the wizard must be at the beginning of the path, not at its end, carefully managing each activity along the way (and those off the path as well) and fighting both schedule slippages and wicked witches! The *Critical Path*:

Table 3-10   Schedule Summary: Early and Late Dates

```
-----------------------------------------------------------------------------------
SCHEDULE SUMMARY                                          DATE: _____

PROJECT NAME:   FOUR-ACTIVITY CRITICAL PATH METHOD EXAMPLE_____
-----------------------------------------------------------------------------------
```

ACTIVITY ID	ORIG DUR	REM DUR	% DONE	EARLY START	EARLY FINISH	LATE START	LATE FINISH	TOTAL FLOAT
A	2	2	0	1OCT91	2OCT91	1OCT91	2OCT91	
B	5	5	0	3OCT91	7OCT91	3OCT91	7OCT91	
C	4	4	0	3OCT91	6OCT91	4OCT91	7OCT91	
D	3	3	0	8OCT91	10OCT91	8OCT91	10OCT91	

Table 3-11   Calculation of Late Start and Late Finish Times (Backward Pass)

ACTIVITY	RELATIONSHIP	LATE START (LS)	LATE FINISH (LF)
Last	Any	LF - activity duration	EF (always)
All prior:	F/S	LF - activity duration	LS of following activity
First	Any	Zero (always)	

- Is the longest (in time) sequence of connected activities
- Is the path with zero float, or slack (to be defined shortly)
- Represents project length

The significance of the Critical Path is this: If the time required for this series of activities can be shortened, then the entire project can be shortened. But if this sequence takes longer, so will the project. The time for this path is critical. So is the name. How to find and navigate the Critical Path is the subject of this step.

Associated with each activity is a float value that determines whether that activity is critical. *Float* (sometimes called "slack") is the difference between the following:

- Latest expected completion time (LF)
- Earliest expected completion time (EF)

It is also the difference between:

- Latest expected start time (LS)
- Earliest expected start time (ES)

In Fig. 3-11, the activity represented by the solid bar:

- Cannot start until the beginning of the third day
- Must be finished by the end of the thirteenth day
- Is expected to take two days to complete

This means the activity could finish:

- As early as the end of the fourth day
- As late as the end of the thirteenth
- Any time between these two extremes

Within this range, it will neither shorten nor delay the project. The total float for this activity is the difference between the two extremes, or nine days ($= 13 - 4$). Needed resources may be applied, consistent with other demands on them during the same period, to help this activity complete by then.

But it is *not* appropriate (even though often done) merely to push the activity willy-nilly down the line. The underlying assumption that sufficient resources will be available on those two particular days may in fact be—and often is—wrong.

If this happens and you had selected days 12 and 13, congratulations! You have just delayed your project accordingly! Float guarantees only the availability of time, not resources. It does, however, provide you with additional flexibility in using those resources. When used wisely, this flexibility increases the probability of satisfactory project completion. As we shall see in Chapter 10, float is sometimes best used to allocate scarce resources effectively. By performing an activity with float during a time period in which resource demand is lowest, proper resource balance may be maintained.

More formally, float is equal to:

- $(LS - ES)$, or
- $(LF - EF)$

Do not confuse float calculations with duration calculations. The latter are equal to $|(EF - ES)|$ or $|(LF - LS)|$. We shall learn later why the absolute value requirement. Fig. 3-12 may help.

For each activity, the difference between the two start times, and also between the two finish times, is always the same. It represents activity float.

If this is a positive number, it represents how long an activity may be delayed without delaying project completion. If this value is zero, the activity:

- Is critical (on the Critical Path)
- Cannot be delayed without delaying the rest of the project

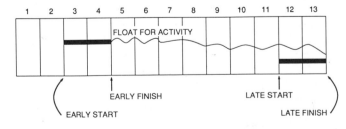

FIGURE 3-11.   Float equals (LF − EF) or (LS − ES).

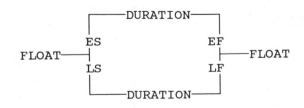

FIGURE 3-12.   How float, duration, and the "Big Four" times relate to each other.

Let us now return to our sample four-activity network. Does any activity contain float? Yes, only *C*. For activities *A*, *B*, and *D*, Early Start is equal to Late Start, and Early Finish is equal to Late Finish. There is, therefore:

- No difference between these times
- No float in these activities

For activity *C*, however, Early Start is not equal to Late Start, and Early Finish is not equal to Late Finish. Since there is a difference between these times, we know that *C* contains float. How much? One day, calculated as follows:

- For start dates, (October 4 − October 3) = 1 day
- For finish dates, (October 7 − October 6) = 1 day

We already knew that *C* could be delayed by one, but not more than one, day and not delay *D* or the project. We also knew that *A*, *B*, and *D* must not experience any delays whatsoever. The Critical Path through this network consists of activities *A*, *B*, and *D*. (The Critical Path does not pass through *C* because it contains float.) None of these activities may be delayed without delaying project completion beyond October 10. The Critical Path also determines our project length to be ten days. Table 3-12 summarizes this.

The two paths through the network may be compared as shown in Table 3-13.

Recall some of the Gantt Chart deficiencies listed earlier:

1. It cannot determine the Critical Path or project length
2. It cannot evaluate the effects of change (either real or simulated) on the project plan
3. It cannot tell you how delays will affect the remainder of the project

PDM scheduling eliminates these deficiencies. A properly developed Gantt Chart is the easiest way to display activities, completion dates, progress, and milestones, but it cannot replace the steps just completed. Even a good slide camera cannot replace a movie camera. Similarly, without underlying network logic, the Gantt Chart is unable to update as the following happen:

- Activities are added or deleted
- Relationships vary
- Constraints are applied or eliminated
- Durations change
- Delays occur

(Step 5) Organize and Present the Schedule

The time-scaled logic diagram, or time-logic plot, is the best way to display activities and their relationships. Both relationships (logic) and activity duration (time) determine its layout. It contrasts with the pure-logic plot, which contains only relationships but no time reference.

The "PENGUIN" screen seen earlier (Figure 3-6) was actually a pure-logic plot. The corresponding time-logic plot and Gantt Chart are presented in Fig. 3-13A and 3-13B.

Report presentation will be discussed more thoroughly in Chapter 7.

Note the timeline highlighting the "as of" or *data date* in the (properly developed) Gantt Chart and the time-logic plot. This could be either today's date or any project date of your choosing. That is, the data date can represent not only today's current status, but may also:

- Reconstruct past project status
- Forecast future project status

Project status will vary according to the time at which it is measured. The *data date* is the time at which a summary snapshot of project condition is taken. Progress, of course, should at least keep pace with the advancing data date. If it does not, your project is falling behind schedule. The data date also affects how PDM activities with lag are reported. This will be covered extensively in Chapter 4.

Appreciate, too, that this schedule is good only until the first deviation (of many, probably) occurs. When that happens, we should retain the original planned schedule as our baseline, from which to measure progress and identify trends. The revised schedule becomes our new target schedule until it, too, is revised, and so on. As mentioned earlier, all changes must be fully and formally documented to maintain configuration control and an audit trail—who, what, when, where, and why. There must be a complete, formal record of what happened and why. This history should be retained well after project completion—at least several years, longer if needed to comply with laws or regulations. This explanatory detail may conveniently be logged:

- For each activity in the nine-line "scratchpad" log
- For each *Primavera* plot in the Revisions Status miniform

In a more complex network than this, we would next ensure that other Critical Paths do not exist. Never assume there to be only one Critical Path. If you have found one, never assume you have found all. Expect and look for more. They would be, of course, every bit as important to identify and manage well as the one we just happened to find first.

As circumstances change, so can the Critical Path. It may shift, split, or both. Stay tuned—much more on this later. Keep project status current!

Let us now set up another network. Please study the activities listed in Table 3-14. Do these constitute a valid network?

It may help to sketch a figure of the network (Fig. 3-14).

You should agree that this is not a valid network. Activity 2 is neither connected to a previous activity nor to the start. Wrong! This example can be corrected in one way only. The only prior activity to which activity 2 could connect is also the start activity. Therefore, activity 1 now becomes a predecessor to 2, and activity 2 now becomes one of three successors to 1.

In most situations, dangling activities such as this may be connected to a variety of other activities—but, of course,

Table 3-12   Schedule Summary: Early and Late Dates With Float

```
------------------------------------------------------------------------
SCHEDULE SUMMARY                                    DATE: _____

PROJECT NAME:  FOUR-ACTIVITY CRITICAL PATH METHOD EXAMPLE_____
------------------------------------------------------------------------
```

ACTIVITY ID		ORIG DUR	REM DUR	% DONE	EARLY START	EARLY FINISH	LATE START	LATE FINISH	TOTAL FLOAT	
A	*	2	2	0	1OCT91	2OCT91	1OCT91	2OCT91	0	*
B	*	5	5	0	3OCT91	7OCT91	3OCT91	7OCT91	0	*
C		4	4	0	3OCT91	6OCT91	4OCT91	7OCT91	1	
D	*	3	3	0	8OCT91	10OCT91	8OCT91	10OCT91	0	*

Table 3-13   Paths Through the Network

	-------------------- PATH --------------------	
	A-B-D	A-C-D
CRITICAL?	YES	NO
LENGTH	10 days	9 days
TOTAL FLOAT	0 days	1 day
CAN BE DELAYED?	NO	1 day (C only)

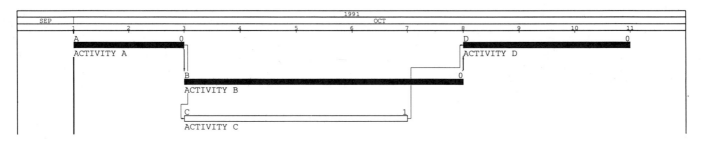

FIGURE 3-13A.   Time-logic plot.

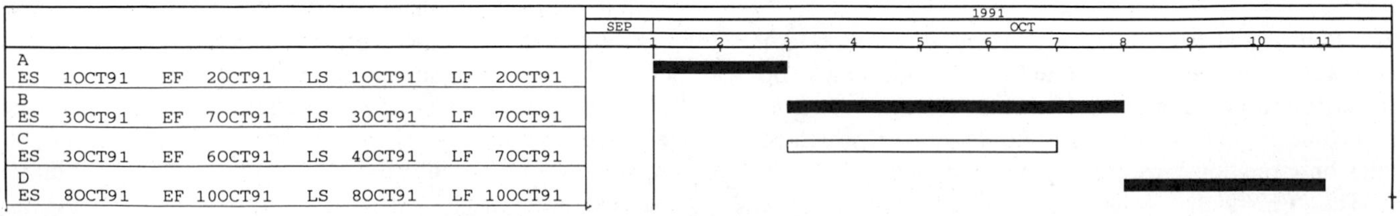

									1991		
			SEP						OCT		
				2	3	4	5	6	7	8	9	10	11
A	ES 1OCT91	EF 2OCT91	LS 1OCT91	LF 2OCT91							
B	ES 3OCT91	EF 7OCT91	LS 3OCT91	LF 7OCT91							
C	ES 3OCT91	EF 6OCT91	LS 4OCT91	LF 7OCT91							
D	ES 8OCT91	EF 10OCT91	LS 8OCT91	LF 10OCT91							

FIGURE 3-13B.   Gantt Chart.

Table 3-14   Schedule Setup

```
--------------------------------------------------------------------
SCHEDULE SETUP                              DATE: _____

PROJECT NAME:   SIX-ACTIVITY NETWORK SETUP EXAMPLE_____
--------------------------------------------------------------------
```

ACTIVITY ID	DUR (DAYS)	PREDECESSOR/ RELATIONSHIP	SUCCESSOR/ RELATIONSHIP	ACTIVITY DESCRIPTION
1		None	3 F/S	
			4 F/S	
2		None	5 F/S	
3		1 F/S	5 F/S	
4		1 F/S	5 F/S	
5		2 F/S	6 F/S	
		3 F/S		
		4 F/S		
6		5 F/S	None	

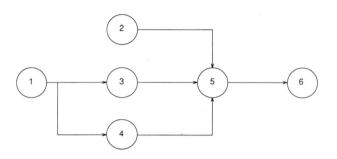

FIGURE 3-14.   Network setup diagram (initial).

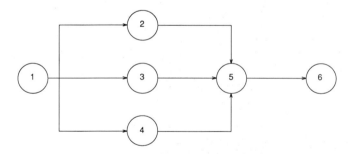

FIGURE 3-15.   Network setup diagram (corrected).

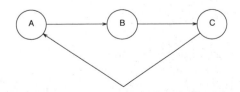

FIGURE 3-16.   Your project cannot turn back the hands of time.

should only be connected to the most logical one(s). This added connection may indicate a relationship previously overlooked.

A properly constructed network must not have more than:

- One activity with no predecessor (the start activity)
- One activity with no successor (the finish activity)

The corrected network is shown in Fig. 3-15.

Another scheduling "Gotcha!" is called the *closed loop*, or simply *loop*. In this situation, an activity is erroneously connected to an earlier activity on the same path. If, for example, A precedes B and B precedes C, it is impossible that C could ever precede A because this would represent a backward passage of time (Fig. 3-16).

Note from Fig. 3-16 that C doubles back and returns to A. But A has already been completed! If it had not, neither B nor C could have started. Might there be another explanation? No, a loop cannot even represent a repeating cycle of operations because completion of the last activity in one cycle prompts the first activity in the next cycle, not the first activity again in the same cycle.

Now before you say "Only a dummy would do this!", appreciate that such errors—when hidden in hundreds or thousands of other activities—are not as easily found in real-world networks as they were here. A good scheduling tool will find these errors and would be more polite in asking you to correct them than your boss would be.

Complete and accurate descriptions of all predecessor/successor relationships are mandatory. Effective scheduling and planning are impossible without them. We must ensure that:

- There is exactly one start and finish
- Activities are in proper order
- All relationships have been properly identified
- Correct logic is maintained throughout the entire network

Let us now work another example of twice as many activities. Suppose we wish to construct a new garage. How

Table 3-15   Schedule Setup

```
------------------------------------------------------------------------
SCHEDULE SETUP                                 DATE: _____

PROJECT NAME:   13-ACTIVITY GARAGE CONSTRUCTION_____
------------------------------------------------------------------------
```

ACTIVITY ID	DUR (DAYS)	PREDECESSOR/ RELATIONSHIP		SUCCESSOR/ RELATIONSHIP		ACTIVITY DESCRIPTION
1	1	None		2	F/S	Plan project
				3	F/S	
				4	F/S	
				5	F/S	
2	5	1	F/S	8	F/S	Construct door
3	20	1	F/S	7	F/S	Construct wall units
4	3	1	F/S	6	F/S	Level site
5	5	1	F/S	9	F/S	Construct roof units
6	7	4	F/S	7	F/S	Construct foundation
7	2	3	F/S	8	F/S	Install wall units
		6	F/S	9	F/S	
				11	F/S	
8	1	2	F/S	10	F/S	Install door
		7	F/S			
9	1	5	F/S	12	F/S	Erect roof
		7	F/S			
10	1	8	F/S	13	F/S	Paint door
11	2	7	F/S	13	F/S	Paint walls
12	2	9	F/S	13	F/S	Paint roof
13	1	10	F/S	None		Cleanup
		11	F/S			
		12	F/S			

```
------------------------------------------------------------------------
```

would we do this? Please now consider "13" to be your lucky number and carefully work the thirteen-activity example presented in Table 3-15. Assume a seven-day workweek and project start date to be October 1. Good luck!

Did you find:

- Project length to be twenty-seven days?
- The Critical Path to consist of activities 1, 3, 7, 9, 12, and 13?

Super! Your new garage will be ready by the end of October 27. But critical activities must not be delayed or this deadline will not be met. The start of other activities can be delayed, but by no more than their float value. Note the amount of scheduling freedom with activities 2, 4, 5, and 6. Also note the one-day values associated with activities 8, 10, and 11. If delayed by its float value, an activity will simply follow Late Start and still not affect project completion. If it is delayed by more, then project completion will also be delayed. This network may be summarized as shown in Table 3-16.

Other information provided by this (condensed) *Primavera* report is shown in Table 3-17.

This network may be diagrammed as shown in Figs. 3-17, 18, and 19.

Let us try another example. With only half the activities as the last network, the schedule from the Pac-10 will assuredly give you twice the fun (Table 3-18).

Did you find:

- Project length to be thirty-eight days?
- The Critical Path to split into two paths?

Super! The Critical Path splits at *A*. One portion goes through *B, D,* and *F;* the other through *C* before merging at *F*. This network may be summarized as shown in Table 3-19.

This network may be diagrammed as shown in Fig. 3-20A and 3-20B.

Now try this one from the Big Ten (Table 3-20).

Did you find:

- Project length to be twenty-nine days?
- Only *E* and *G* to be noncritical?

Super! This network may be summarized as shown in Table 3-21.

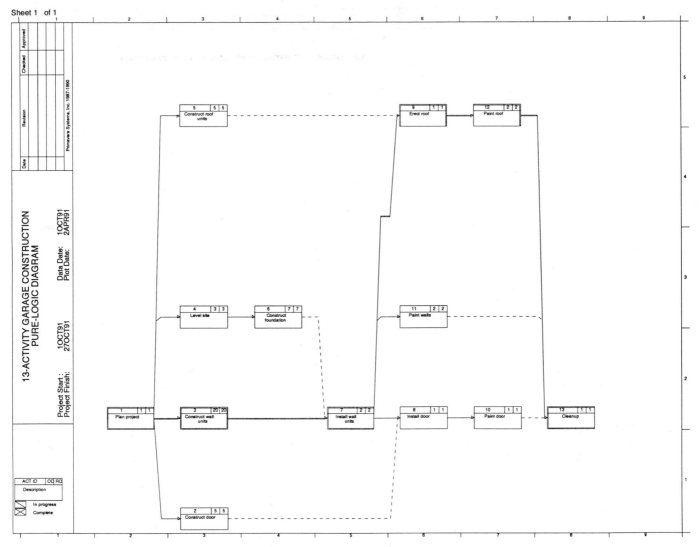

FIGURE 3-17. Pure-logic plot.

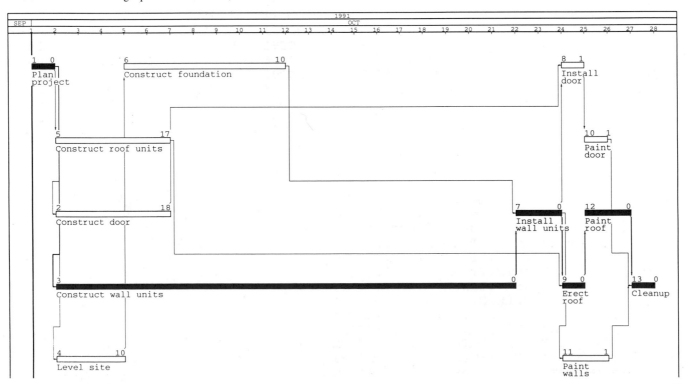

FIGURE 3-18. Time-logic plot.

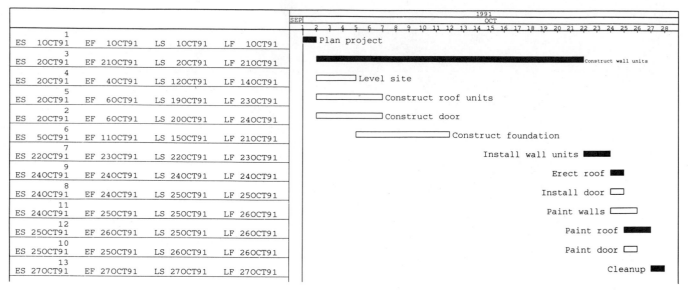

	1				
ES 1OCT91	EF 1OCT91	LS 1OCT91	LF 1OCT91		Plan project
	3				
ES 2OCT91	EF 21OCT91	LS 2OCT91	LF 21OCT91		Construct wall units
	4				
ES 2OCT91	EF 4OCT91	LS 12OCT91	LF 14OCT91		Level site
	5				
ES 2OCT91	EF 6OCT91	LS 19OCT91	LF 23OCT91		Construct roof units
	2				
ES 2OCT91	EF 6OCT91	LS 20OCT91	LF 24OCT91		Construct door
	6				
ES 5OCT91	EF 11OCT91	LS 15OCT91	LF 21OCT91		Construct foundation
	7				
ES 22OCT91	EF 23OCT91	LS 22OCT91	LF 23OCT91		Install wall units
	9				
ES 24OCT91	EF 24OCT91	LS 24OCT91	LF 24OCT91		Erect roof
	8				
ES 24OCT91	EF 24OCT91	LS 25OCT91	LF 25OCT91		Install door
	11				
ES 24OCT91	EF 25OCT91	LS 25OCT91	LF 26OCT91		Paint walls
	12				
ES 25OCT91	EF 26OCT91	LS 25OCT91	LF 26OCT91		Paint roof
	10				
ES 25OCT91	EF 25OCT91	LS 26OCT91	LF 26OCT91		Paint door
	13				
ES 27OCT91	EF 27OCT91	LS 27OCT91	LF 27OCT91		Cleanup

FIGURE 3-19. Gantt Chart.

Table 3-16 Schedule Summary

```
--------------------------------------------------------------------
SCHEDULE SUMMARY                            DATE: _____

PROJECT NAME:  13-ACTIVITY GARAGE CONSTRUCTION_____
--------------------------------------------------------------------
```

ACTIVITY ID		ORIG DUR	REM DUR	% DONE	EARLY START	EARLY FINISH	LATE START	LATE FINISH	TOTAL FLOAT	
1	*	1	1	0	1OCT91	1OCT91	1OCT91	1OCT91	0	*
2		5	5	0	2OCT91	6OCT91	20OCT91	24OCT91	18	
3	*	20	20	0	2OCT91	21OCT91	2OCT91	21OCT91	0	*
4		3	3	0	2OCT91	4OCT91	12OCT91	14OCT91	10	
5		5	5	0	2OCT91	6OCT91	19OCT91	23OCT91	17	
6		7	7	0	5OCT91	11OCT91	15OCT91	21OCT91	10	
7	*	2	2	0	22OCT91	23OCT91	22OCT91	23OCT91	0	*
8		1	1	0	24OCT91	24OCT91	25OCT91	25OCT91	1	
9	*	1	1	0	24OCT91	24OCT91	24OCT91	24OCT91	0	*
10		1	1	0	25OCT91	25OCT91	26OCT91	26OCT91	1	
11		2	2	0	24OCT91	25OCT91	25OCT91	26OCT91	1	
12	*	2	2	0	25OCT91	26OCT91	25OCT91	26OCT91	0	*
13	*	1	1	0	27OCT91	27OCT91	27OCT91	27OCT91	0	*

Table 3-17 Information Provided by a Condensed *Primavera* Report

```
====================================================
SCHEDULING STATISTICS FOR PROJECT GARAGE
        NUMBER OF ACTIVITIES........     13
        STARTED    ACTIVITIES........      0
        COMPLETED ACTIVITIES........      0
        NUMBER OF RELATIONSHIPS.....     17
        PERCENT COMPLETE............      0
        DATA DATE.................. 1OCT91
        START DATE................. 1OCT91
        IMPOSED FINISH DATE.......    NONE
        LATEST CALCULATED EF......27OCT91
====================================================
```

Table 3-18   Schedule Setup

```
------------------------------------------------------------------------
SCHEDULE SETUP                                    DATE: _____

PROJECT NAME:  7-ACTIVITY PROTOTYPE DEVELOPMENT_____
               CHASE (USC) AND AQUILANO (ARIZONA)
------------------------------------------------------------------------
```

ACTIVITY ID	DUR (DAYS)	PREDECESSOR/ RELATIONSHIP	SUCCESSOR/ RELATIONSHIP	ACTIVITY DESCRIPTION
A	21	None	B F/S C F/S	Design
B	5	A F/S	D F/S	Build prototype
C	7	A F/S	E F/S F F/S	Evaluate equipment
D	2	B F/S	E F/S F F/S	Test prototype
E	5	C F/S D F/S	G F/S	Write equipment report
F	8	C F/S D F/S	G F/S	Write methods report
G	2	E F/S F F/S	None	Write final report

Table 3-19   Schedule Summary

```
------------------------------------------------------------------------
SCHEDULE SUMMARY                                  DATE: _____

PROJECT NAME:  7-ACTIVITY PROTOTYPE DEVELOPMENT_____
------------------------------------------------------------------------
```

ACTIVITY ID		ORIG DUR	REM DUR	% DONE	EARLY START	EARLY FINISH	LATE START	LATE FINISH	TOTAL FLOAT	
A	*	21	21	0	1OCT91	21OCT91	1OCT91	21OCT91	0	*
B	*	5	5	0	22OCT91	26OCT91	22OCT91	26OCT91	0	*
C	*	7	7	0	22OCT91	28OCT91	22OCT91	28OCT91	0	*
D	*	2	2	0	27OCT91	28OCT91	27OCT91	28OCT91	0	*
F	*	8	8	0	29OCT91	5NOV91	29OCT91	5NOV91	0	*
E		5	5	0	29OCT91	2NOV91	1NOV91	5NOV91	3	
G	*	2	2	0	6NOV91	7NOV91	6NOV91	7NOV91	0	*

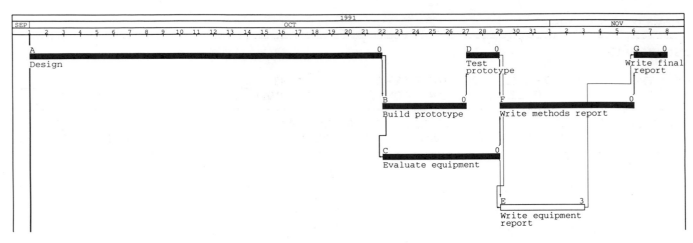

FIGURE 3-20A.   Time-logic plot.

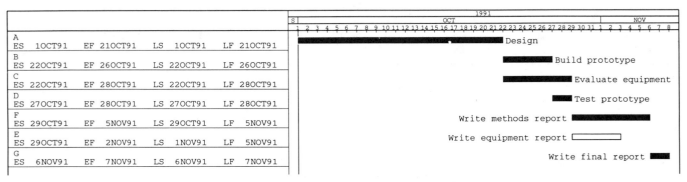

A							
ES	1OCT91	EF	21OCT91	LS	1OCT91	LF	21OCT91
B							
ES	22OCT91	EF	26OCT91	LS	22OCT91	LF	26OCT91
C							
ES	22OCT91	EF	28OCT91	LS	22OCT91	LF	28OCT91
D							
ES	27OCT91	EF	28OCT91	LS	27OCT91	LF	28OCT91
F							
ES	29OCT91	EF	5NOV91	LS	29OCT91	LF	5NOV91
E							
ES	29OCT91	EF	2NOV91	LS	1NOV91	LF	5NOV91
G							
ES	6NOV91	EF	7NOV91	LS	6NOV91	LF	7NOV91

FIGURE 3-20B.   Gantt Chart.

Table 3-20   Schedule Setup

```
---------------------------------------------------------------------
SCHEDULE SETUP                                    DATE: _____

PROJECT NAME:  WHITTEN-BENTLEY-HO EXAMPLE  (PURDUE)_____
---------------------------------------------------------------------
```

ACTIVITY ID	DUR (DAYS)	PREDECESSOR/ RELATIONSHIP		SUCCESSOR/ RELATIONSHIP		ACTIVITY DESCRIPTION
A	2	None		B	F/S	
B	3	A	F/S	C	F/S	
C	4	B	F/S	D	F/S	
				E	F/S	
D	5	C	F/S	F	F/S	
E	4	C	F/S	G	F/S	
				H	F/S	
F	3	D	F/S	G	F/S	
				H	F/S	
G	6	E	F/S	J	F/S	
		F	F/S			
H	5	E	F/S	I	F/S	
		F	F/S			
I	6	H	F/S	J	F/S	
J	1	G	F/S	None		
		I	F/S			

```
---------------------------------------------------------------------
```

Table 3-21   Schedule Summary

```
------------------------------------------------------------------------
SCHEDULE SUMMARY                                    DATE: _____

PROJECT NAME:   WHITTEN-BENTLEY-HO EXAMPLE (PURDUE)_____
------------------------------------------------------------------------
```

ACTIVITY ID		ORIG DUR	REM DUR	% DONE	EARLY START	EARLY FINISH	LATE START	LATE FINISH	TOTAL FLOAT	
A	*	2	2	0	1OCT91	2OCT91	1OCT91	2OCT91	0	*
B	*	3	3	0	3OCT91	5OCT91	3OCT91	5OCT91	0	*
C	*	4	4	0	6OCT91	9OCT91	6OCT91	9OCT91	0	*
D	*	5	5	0	10OCT91	14OCT91	10OCT91	14OCT91	0	*
E		4	4	0	10OCT91	13OCT91	14OCT91	17OCT91	4	
F	*	3	3	0	15OCT91	17OCT91	15OCT91	17OCT91	0	*
G		6	6	0	18OCT91	23OCT91	23OCT91	28OCT91	5	
H	*	5	5	0	18OCT91	22OCT91	18OCT91	22OCT91	0	*
I	*	6	6	0	23OCT91	28OCT91	23OCT91	28OCT91	0	*
J	*	1	1	0	29OCT91	29OCT91	29OCT91	29OCT91	0	*

```
------------------------------------------------------------------------
```

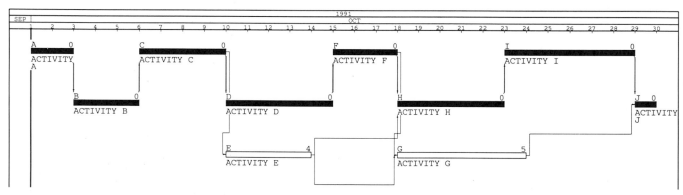

FIGURE 3-21A.   Time-logic plot.

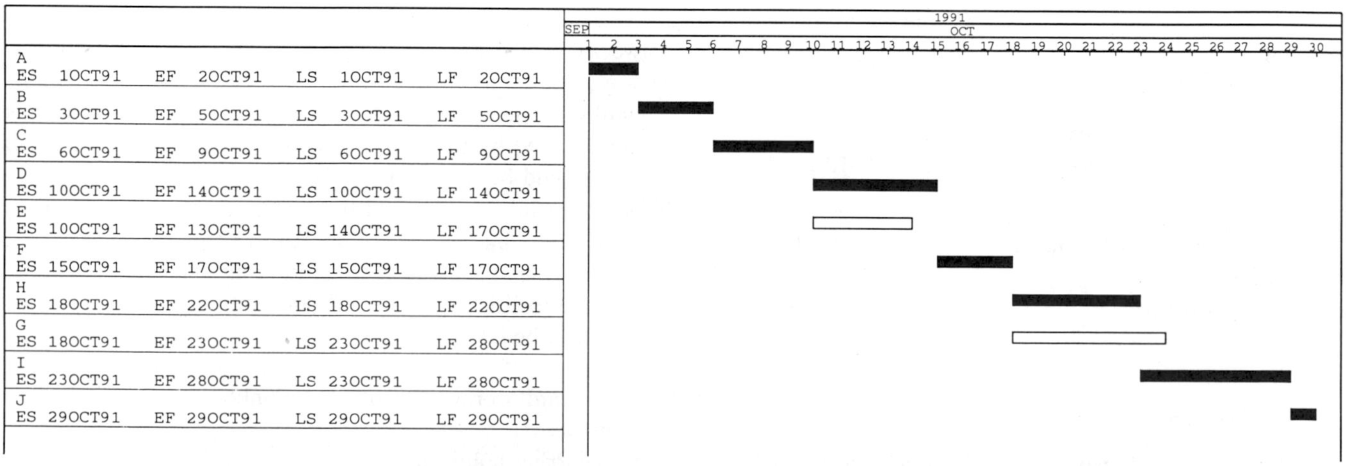

FIGURE 3-21B.   Gantt Chart.

Table 3-22   Schedule Setup

SCHEDULE SETUP   DATE: _____

PROJECT NAME: SOFTWARE DEVELOPMENT LIFE CYCLE_____
                 SHELLY (CONSULTANT) & CASHMAN (LONG BEACH CITY COLLEGE)

ACTIVITY ID	DUR (DAYS)	PREDECESSOR/ RELATIONSHIP		SUCCESSOR/ RELATIONSHIP		ACTIVITY DESCRIPTION
1	10	None		2	F/S	Prepare Requirements
				4	F/S	Definition Report
2	5	1	F/S	3	F/S	Organize project
3	3	2	F/S	5	F/S	Plan development phase
4	3	1	F/S	5	F/S	Plan design phase
5	20	3	F/S	6	F/S	Design system
		4	F/S	13	F/S	
6	2	5	F/S	7	F/S	Prepare system data
				17	F/S	
7	5	6	F/S	8	F/S	Write program pseudocode
8	17	7	F/S	9	F/S	Code program
9	5	8	F/S	10	F/S	Test and debug program
				19	F/S	
10	5	9	F/S	11	F/S	Prepare program documentation
11	3	10	F/S	12	F/S	Prepare system documentation
		16	F/S			
12	2	11	F/S	21	F/S	Arrange system support
13	2	5	F/S	14	F/S	Prepare system description
14	4	13	F/S	15	F/S	Prepare audits & controls
15	3	14	F/S	16	F/S	Prepare clerical procedures
16	3	15	F/S	11	F/S	Prepare training materials
17	4	6	F/S	18	F/S	Prepare System Resources Report
18	2	17	F/S	20	F/S	Plan installation phase
19	5	9	F/S	20	F/S	Test and debug system
20	3	18	F/S	21	F/S	Perform final system tests
		19	F/S			
21	1	12	F/S	None		Project finish
		20	F/S			

This network may be diagrammed as shown in Fig. 3-21A and 3-21B.

Finally, try to work the slightly longer, more complex example in Table 3-22.

Did you find:

- Project length to be seventy-eight days?
- The Critical Path to consist of activities 1–12 (except 4) and 21?

Super! This network may be summarized as shown in Table 3-23.

This network may be diagrammed as shown in Figs. 3-22 and 3-23.

CALENDARS

We all need time off from work in order to rest, catch up on things, and pursue our pleasures. When planning pro-

jects, therefore, it is necessary to take weekends, holidays, and other off days into account. A job that requires seven workdays to complete will require 1.4 (= 7/5) calendar weeks on the basis of a five-day workweek. Put another way, this same job would not be completed most months until (the end of) eight calendar days later. If two weekends are spanned by these seven workdays, the expected finish date would be ten calendar days away. If this job were to begin on July 8, it would be completed late on July 16 in most years, but as late as July 18 in some.

What this means is: The underlying calendar should reflect the realities of your work environment. You should be able to schedule:

- Standard workweeks of any number of workdays—not just five
- Recurring holidays
- One-time holidays

Table 3-23   Schedule Summary

```
------------------------------------------------------------------------
SCHEDULE SUMMARY                                    DATE: _____

PROJECT NAME:   SOFTWARE DEVELOPMENT LIFE CYCLE_____
------------------------------------------------------------------------
```

ACTIVITY ID		ORIG DUR	REM DUR	% DONE	EARLY START	EARLY FINISH	LATE START	LATE FINISH	TOTAL FLOAT	
1	*	10	10	0	1OCT91	10OCT91	1OCT91	10OCT91	0	*
2	*	5	5	0	11OCT91	15OCT91	11OCT91	15OCT91	0	*
3	*	3	3	0	16OCT91	18OCT91	16OCT91	18OCT91	0	*
4		3	3	0	11OCT91	13OCT91	16OCT91	18OCT91	5	
5	*	20	20	0	19OCT91	7NOV91	19OCT91	7NOV91	0	*
6	*	2	2	0	8NOV91	9NOV91	8NOV91	9NOV91	0	*
7	*	5	5	0	10NOV91	14NOV91	10NOV91	14NOV91	0	*
8	*	17	17	0	15NOV91	1DEC91	15NOV91	1DEC91	0	*
9	*	5	5	0	2DEC91	6DEC91	2DEC91	6DEC91	0	*
10	*	5	5	0	7DEC91	11DEC91	7DEC91	11DEC91	0	*
11	*	3	3	0	12DEC91	14DEC91	12DEC91	14DEC91	0	*
12	*	2	2	0	15DEC91	16DEC91	15DEC91	16DEC91	0	*
13		2	2	0	8NOV91	9NOV91	30NOV91	1DEC91	22	
14		4	4	0	10NOV91	13NOV91	2DEC91	5DEC91	22	
15		3	3	0	14NOV91	16NOV91	6DEC91	8DEC91	22	
16		3	3	0	17NOV91	19NOV91	9DEC91	11DEC91	22	
17		4	4	0	10NOV91	13NOV91	8DEC91	11DEC91	28	
18		2	2	0	14NOV91	15NOV91	12DEC91	13DEC91	28	
19		5	5	0	7DEC91	11DEC91	9DEC91	13DEC91	2	
20		3	3	0	12DEC91	14DEC91	14DEC91	16DEC91	2	
21	*	1	1	0	17DEC91	17DEC91	17DEC91	17DEC91	0	*

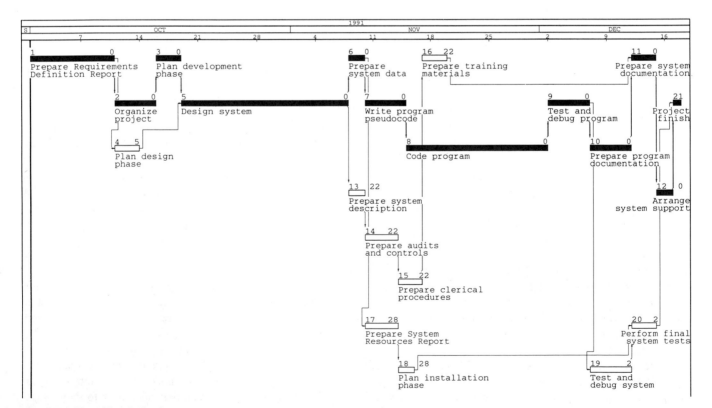

FIGURE 3-22.   Time-logic plot.

The following table shows the schedule data for the Gantt chart:

	1							
ES	1OCT91	EF	10OCT91	LS	1OCT91	LF	10OCT91	
	2							
ES	11OCT91	EF	15OCT91	LS	11OCT91	LF	15OCT91	
	4							
ES	11OCT91	EF	13OCT91	LS	16OCT91	LF	18OCT91	
	3							
ES	16OCT91	EF	18OCT91	LS	16OCT91	LF	18OCT91	
	5							
ES	19OCT91	EF	7NOV91	LS	19OCT91	LF	7NOV91	
	6							
ES	8NOV91	EF	9NOV91	LS	8NOV91	LF	9NOV91	
	13							
ES	8NOV91	EF	9NOV91	LS	30NOV91	LF	1DEC91	
	7							
ES	10NOV91	EF	14NOV91	LS	10NOV91	LF	14NOV91	
	14							
ES	10NOV91	EF	13NOV91	LS	2DEC91	LF	5DEC91	
	17							
ES	10NOV91	EF	13NOV91	LS	8DEC91	LF	11DEC91	
	15							
ES	14NOV91	EF	16NOV91	LS	6DEC91	LF	8DEC91	
	18							
ES	14NOV91	EF	15NOV91	LS	12DEC91	LF	13DEC91	
	8							
ES	15NOV91	EF	1DEC91	LS	15NOV91	LF	1DEC91	
	16							
ES	17NOV91	EF	19NOV91	LS	9DEC91	LF	11DEC91	
	9							
ES	2DEC91	EF	6DEC91	LS	2DEC91	LF	6DEC91	
	10							
ES	7DEC91	EF	11DEC91	LS	7DEC91	LF	11DEC91	
	19							
ES	7DEC91	EF	11DEC91	LS	9DEC91	LF	13DEC91	
	11							
ES	12DEC91	EF	14DEC91	LS	12DEC91	LF	14DEC91	
	20							
ES	12DEC91	EF	14DEC91	LS	14DEC91	LF	16DEC91	
	12							
ES	15DEC91	EF	16DEC91	LS	15DEC91	LF	16DEC91	
	21							
ES	17DEC91	EF	17DEC91	LS	17DEC91	LF	17DEC91	

FIGURE 3-23.   Gantt Chart.

- Same day off each year
- Range of days
- Suspend and resume dates
- Exceptions to any of the above

In this way, the resulting time schedule may be used directly without modification. Activities should not be scheduled on, nor resources applied to, any off day.

Recall the simple four-activity network that we studied first. The project used a seven-day calendar and ran nonstop from October 1 until completion ten days later on October 10. If a five-day calendar were used instead, when would it have finished? On October 14, as is shown in Table 3-24.

Although the project has been stretched out, activity relationships and the Critical Path remain the same in this example. The resulting time-logic plot and Gantt Chart are presented in Fig. 3-24A and 3-24B. Note how the time-logic activity bars narrow over nonworkdays (this could also have been done on the Gantt Chart). This isolates project inactive time from available time.

What about the garage? When will it be finished? Not until November 6, as is shown in Table 3-25.

Note how weekends off stretch the garage project well past the original October 27 finish date. In fact, activity 3

(construct wall units) alone extends two days beyond the original EF/LF date. What is your car worth?

The resulting time-logic plot and Gantt Chart are presented in Figs. 3-25 and 3-26.

Multiple Calendars

Now let us see how multiple calendars affect the scheduling process.

In all of the previous examples, everyone followed the same work schedule. But it does not always happen that way. Some persons may work five days a week, others six. Some may work seven days a week, others four. Where project team members work in different states, countries, or even for different companies, holidays often vary, and "one size does not fit all!"

It is necessary in such cases to establish a new *calendar,* or set of worktimes, for each major variance from the standard. This should be done before the schedule is created. For example, if most persons work five days a week but some work six, a separate calendar should be established for each workgroup. Calendar 1 represents standard worktimes—five days per week in this example—and Calendars 2, 3, and so on refer to the others according to their usage. Although a single calendar may suffice for most projects,

Table 3-24   Schedule Summary

```
------------------------------------------------------------------------
SCHEDULE SUMMARY                                    DATE: _____

PROJECT NAME:   4-ACTIVITY CRITICAL PATH METHOD (5-DAY WORKWEEK)_____
------------------------------------------------------------------------
```

ACTIVITY ID		ORIG DUR	REM DUR	% DONE	EARLY START	EARLY FINISH	LATE START	LATE FINISH	TOTAL FLOAT	
A	*	2	2	0	1OCT91	2OCT91	1OCT91	2OCT91	0	*
B	*	5	5	0	3OCT91	9OCT91	3OCT91	9OCT91	0	*
C		4	4	0	3OCT91	8OCT91	4OCT91	9OCT91	1	
D	*	3	3	0	10OCT91	14OCT91	10OCT91	14OCT91	0	*

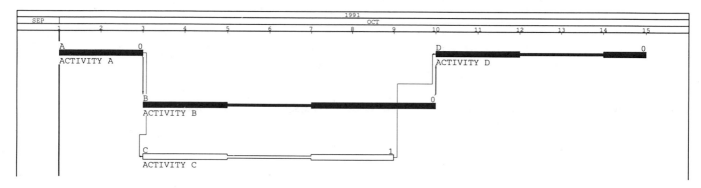

FIGURE 3-24A.   Time-logic plot.

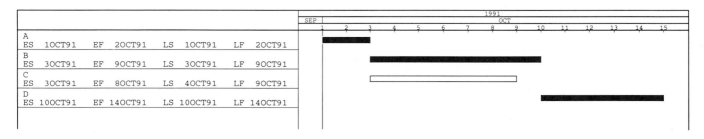

FIGURE 3-24B.   Gantt Chart.

Table 3-25   Schedule Summary

```
------------------------------------------------------------------------
SCHEDULE SUMMARY                                    DATE: _____

PROJECT NAME:   13-ACTIVITY GARAGE CONSTRUCTION (5-DAY WORKWEEK)_____
------------------------------------------------------------------------
```

ACTIVITY ID		ORIG DUR	REM DUR	% DONE	EARLY START	EARLY FINISH	LATE START	LATE FINISH	TOTAL FLOAT	
1	*	1	1	0	1OCT91	1OCT91	1OCT91	1OCT91	0	*
2		5	5	0	2OCT91	8OCT91	28OCT91	1NOV91	18	
3	*	20	20	0	2OCT91	29OCT91	2OCT91	29OCT91	0	*
4		3	3	0	2OCT91	4OCT91	16OCT91	18OCT91	10	
5		5	5	0	2OCT91	8OCT91	25OCT91	31OCT91	17	
6		7	7	0	7OCT91	15OCT91	21OCT91	29OCT91	10	
7	*	2	2	0	30OCT91	31OCT91	30OCT91	31OCT91	0	*
8		1	1	0	1NOV91	1NOV91	4NOV91	4NOV91	1	
9	*	1	1	0	1NOV91	1NOV91	1NOV91	1NOV91	0	*
10		1	1	0	4NOV91	4NOV91	5NOV91	5NOV91	1	
11		2	2	0	1NOV91	4NOV91	4NOV91	5NOV91	1	
12	*	2	2	0	4NOV91	5NOV91	4NOV91	5NOV91	0	*
13	*	1	1	0	6NOV91	6NOV91	6NOV91	6NOV91	0	*

```
------------------------------------------------------------------------
```

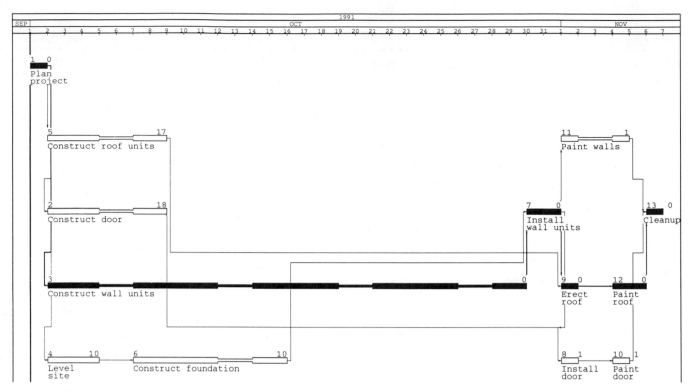

FIGURE 3-25.   Time-logic plot.

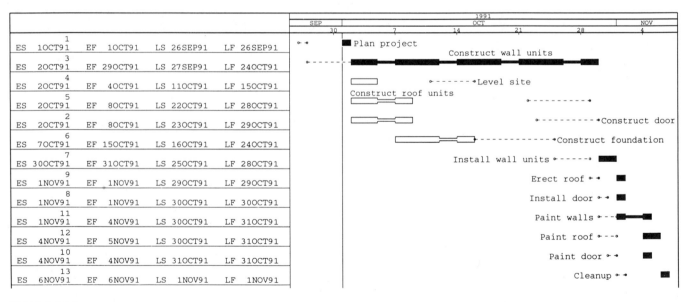

FIGURE 3-26.   Gantt Chart.

Primavera provides four user-defined calendars if needed. *Finest Hour,* which supports hourly or multiple-shift scheduling, supports thirty-one. Even if some nonwork periods are common to all calendars in the project, significant differences must be represented by their own calendars.

Multiple calendars based on different units of time must be redefined to the most precise. If one calendar must be a daily calendar, then the other calendar(s) must be daily

calendar(s), too, even if a weekly calendar might be adequate for the activities it schedules.

Each project activity will be scheduled—and required resources applied—only during the worktimes of its particular calendar. During non-worktimes:

- No activities will be scheduled
- No resources will be applied

Depending on the calendars and activity interdependencies, multiple-calendar scheduling calculations can become very complicated. Like so many other areas in effective project management, they are far better left to electronic computations than to manual.

Please study for a moment the effect on available workdays for each of the two calendars presented in Table 3-26.

Note the following from Table 3-26:

- Calendar 1 is a six-day workweek
- Calendar 2 is a five-day workweek
- Both calendars enjoy December 25 and January 1 off
- In addition, Calendar 2 enjoys December 24 off

Note in particular the two very different labor availability pools for each calendar: In this short time period of twenty-four days, Calendar 1 offers nineteen workdays, Calendar 2 only fifteen. Three Saturdays and the Calendar 2 December 24 holiday make the difference. Perhaps more important, it also means there are four days on which Calendar 1 activities may be scheduled but, ordinarily, not Calendar 2 counterparts. If resources from both calendars are needed on any of these four days, the project manager would either:

- Employ Calendar 2 resources at premium rates (i.e., overtime)
- Delay the activity until both calendars are again synchronized

The second approach, however, would:

- Risk project delay if the activity were critical
- Waste valuable float if it were not

If a ten-day activity starts December 18, it will complete December 30 under Calendar 1, but not until January 3 under Calendar 2. Do you think there will be much Calendar

---

Table 3-26   Multiple-Calendar Detail: 12/18/91–1/10/92

SUNDAY	MONDAY	TUESDAY	WEDNESDAY	THURSDAY	FRIDAY	SATURDAY
DATE.................................18DEC91				19DEC91	20DEC91	21DEC91
CALENDAR 1 WORKDAY.....................1				2	3	4
CALENDAR 2 WORKDAY.....................1				2	3	NO WORK
22DEC91	23DEC91	24DEC91	25DEC91	26DEC91	27DEC91	28DEC91
NO WORK	5	6	HOLIDAY	7	8	9
NO WORK	4	HOLIDAY	HOLIDAY	5	6	NO WORK
			----------------- 1992 -----------------			
29DEC91	30DEC91	31DEC91	1JAN92	2JAN92	3JAN92	4JAN92
NO WORK	10	11	HOLIDAY	12	13	14
NO WORK	7	8	HOLIDAY	9	10	NO WORK
5JAN92	6JAN92	7JAN92	8JAN92	9JAN92	10JAN92	
NO WORK	15	16	17	18	19	
NO WORK	11	12	13	14	15	

Table 3-27   Schedule Setup

SCHEDULE SETUP   DATE: _____

PROJECT NAME: FIVE-ACTIVITY TWO-CALENDAR NETWORK SETUP EXAMPLE_____

ACTIVITY ID	DUR (DAYS)	CAL	PREDECESSOR/ RELATIONSHIP	SUCCESSOR/ RELATIONSHIP	ACTIVITY DESCRIPTION
A	1	1	None	B F/S C F/S	
B	5	1	A F/S	D F/S	
C	5	2	A F/S	D F/S	
D	3	1	B F/S C F/S	E F/S	
E	5	1	D F/S	None	

----

2 production December 23? But if that were made a non-workday, the same activity would not finish until January 6. There would then be as many Calendar 2 days off as on. And it could have been completed under Calendar 1 one week (five workdays) earlier. What to do? What to do?

Now please study the two-calendar network in Table 3-27.

Make sure you are able to determine what is shown in Table 3-28.

The corresponding time-logic plot and Gantt Chart are shown in Fig. 3-27A and 3-27B.

The two paths through this network may be compared as shown in Table 3-29.

Do you see anything unusual? Remember two distinguishing features of the single-calendar Critical Path:

- It always made the longest path
- It alone determined project length

In Table 3-29, project length is fourteen workdays. Both the Critical Path and the non-Critical Path are that long. The Critical Path no longer exclusively determines project length. In this example, the non-Critical Path is just as long. It might even contain more workdays than the Critical Path!

Nor does the multiple-calendar Critical Path exclusively determine project end date. This is because project calendars:

- Do not match
- Often cause activities in other calendars to play "calendar catchup"

We saw this when D waited on C to finish. The Critical Path was affected by the calendar mix. Had C been assigned to Calendar 1, it, like B, could have finished on December 24. Activity D could then have started on December 26, and the project could have finished on January 4. On the other hand, had all activities proceeded under Calendar 2, the project would not have ended until January 9.

These findings are summarized in Tables 3-30 and 3-31 and Figs. 3-28 through 3-31.

Note for activity B the calendar-day differences between start dates and finish. For start dates, December 21–December 19 indicates two days, but for finish dates, December 27–December 24 indicates three. The reason is to allow activity B workers to enjoy Christmas if they did not begin progress on B on December 19 (ES). If they began on that day, they would already have completed B the day before Christmas under the ES schedule. If they began on December 20, they would enjoy Christmas off and finish on December 26. And if they began on December 21, they would:

- Follow Late Start schedule
- Enjoy Christmas off
- Finish on December 27 (LF)

It seems as if B contains float. It does: two days. As you would expect, float—like all other aspects of a multiple-calendar project—is measured by workday and mapped by activity calendar. That being done, it:

- Remains the difference between LF and EF (or LS and ES)
- Still represents how long the activity may be delayed without affecting the project finish date

For B, the float value remains two days even though:

- Two calendar dates (December 19 and 21) separate the start dates
- Three calendar dates (December 24 and 27) separate the finish dates

The project shown in Fig. 3-27A and 3-27B begins with activity A (one day under Calendar 1) on December 18. Since both B (Calendar 1) and C (Calendar 2) can start first thing the next day, Early Start for each is December 19. Each requires five days under its respective calendar. This

Table 3-28   Schedule Summary

```
------------------------------------------------------------------------------------
SCHEDULE SUMMARY                                     DATE: _____

PROJECT NAME:   TWO-CALENDAR 6/5 DAY WORKWEEK PROJECT_____
------------------------------------------------------------------------------------
```

ACTIVITY ID/CAL	ORIG DUR	REM DUR	% DONE	EARLY START	EARLY FINISH	LATE START	LATE FINISH	TOTAL FLOAT
A 1 *	1	1	0	18DEC91	18DEC91	18DEC91	18DEC91	0 *
B 1	5	5	0	19DEC91	24DEC91	21DEC91	27DEC91	2
C 2 *	5	5	0	19DEC91	27DEC91	19DEC91	27DEC91	0 *
D 1 *	3	3	0	28DEC91	31DEC91	28DEC91	31DEC91	0 *
E 1 *	5	5	0	2JAN92	7JAN92	2JAN92	7JAN92	0 *

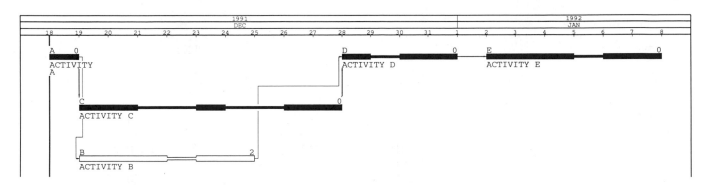

FIGURE 3-27A.   Time-logic plot.

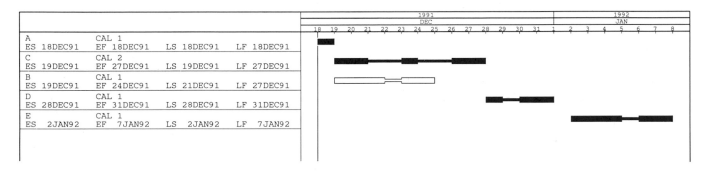

FIGURE 3-27B.   Gantt Chart.

Table 3-29   Paths Through the Network

	------------------- PATH -------------------	
	A-C-D-E	A-B-D-E
CRITICAL?	YES	NO
LENGTH	14 days	14 days
TOTAL FLOAT	0 days	2 days
CAN BE DELAYED?	NO	2 days (B only)

Table 3-30   Schedule Summary

```
-------------------------------------------------------------------------
SCHEDULE SUMMARY                                  DATE: _____

PROJECT NAME:   SAME AS 2-CALENDAR BUT CALENDAR 1 ONLY_____
-------------------------------------------------------------------------
```

ACTIVITY ID		ORIG DUR	REM DUR	% DONE	EARLY START	EARLY FINISH	LATE START	LATE FINISH	TOTAL FLOAT	
A	*	1	1	0	18DEC91	18DEC91	18DEC91	18DEC91	0	*
B	*	5	5	0	19DEC91	24DEC91	19DEC91	24DEC91	0	*
C	*	5	5	0	19DEC91	24DEC91	19DEC91	24DEC91	0	*
D	*	3	3	0	26DEC91	28DEC91	26DEC91	28DEC91	0	*
E	*	5	5	0	30DEC91	4JAN92	30DEC91	4JAN92	0	*

Table 3-31   Schedule Summary

```
------------------------------------------------------------------------------
SCHEDULE SUMMARY                                  DATE: _____

PROJECT NAME:   SAME AS 2-CALENDAR BUT CALENDAR 2 ONLY_____
------------------------------------------------------------------------------
ACTIVITY    ORIG    REM     %       EARLY      EARLY      LATE       LATE      TOTAL
   ID       DUR     DUR   DONE      START      FINISH     START      FINISH    FLOAT
--------    ----    ---   ----     -------    -------    -------    -------    -----
   A  *      1       1      0      18DEC91    18DEC91    18DEC91    18DEC91      0 *
   B  *      5       5      0      19DEC91    27DEC91    19DEC91    27DEC91      0 *
   C  *      5       5      0      19DEC91    27DEC91    19DEC91    27DEC91      0 *
   D  *      3       3      0      30DEC91     2JAN92    30DEC91     2JAN92      0 *
   E  *      5       5      0       3JAN92     9JAN92     3JAN92     9JAN92      0 *

------------------------------------------------------------------------------
```

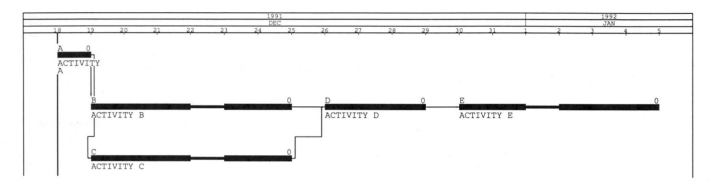

FIGURE 3-28.   Time-logic plot (Calendar 1 only).

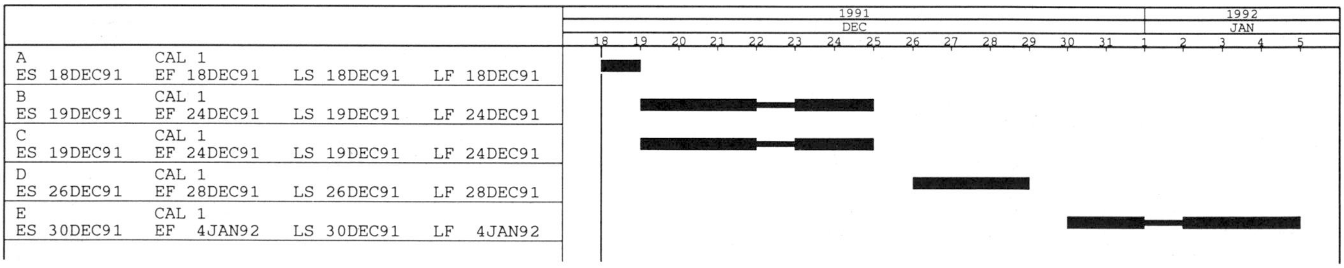

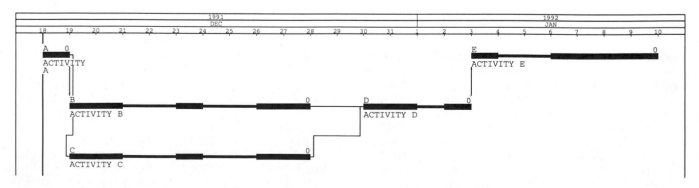

FIGURE 3-29.   Gantt Chart (Calendar 1 only).

FIGURE 3-30.   Time-logic plot (Calendar 2 only).

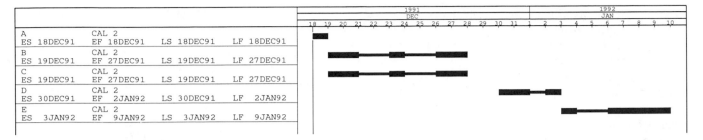

FIGURE 3-31.   Gantt Chart (Calendar 2 only).

means that *B* will be completed December 24, but *C* will not be completed until December 27. Even though the two activities started on the same date and the actual duration of each is the same (five days), their Early Finish dates differ because the calendars differ. The three-day variance is made up as follows:

- Two unmatched days off under Calendar 2: December 21 and 24
- December 25: also enjoyed as a day off by Calendar 1, but beyond EF for *B*

Two trails lead into *D*. The first, from *B*, can be completed by December 24 (*B*'s Early Finish), but the second, from *C*, is not scheduled to complete until December 27 (*C*'s Early Finish). Since *D* cannot start until the day after both *B* and *C* have completed, the earliest that *D* can occur is December 28. This date becomes Early Start for *D*.

If *C* were under Calendar 1 rather than 2, then it would—like *B*—finish December 24 and *D* could begin on the next workday, which would be December 26. But this is not the case. Even though *B* finishes December 24, *C* cannot finish until December 27, so *D* cannot start until December 28. Activity *D* takes three days to complete, so its Early Finish is December 31 (three workdays from its start on Calendar 1).

Because *E* is assigned to Calendar 1, it will begin on the next workday after its predecessor, *D* (also assigned to Calendar 1) completes. This day would be January 2. Activity *E* requires five days to complete. Its EF date, therefore, would be January 7.

Having calculated Early Start and Early Finish with a forward pass through the project, we must now calculate Late Start and Late Finish with a backward pass through the network—the same as is done for single-calendar projects.

Regardless of the number of project calendars, the earliest a project can be completed is its last-activity Early Finish date; that is, LF = EF unless an earlier deadline has been set. Therefore, Late Finish for *E* is set equal to Early Finish, or January 7. Late Start for *E* must equal Early Start, or January 2. Similarly, since *D* is critical (there are no other paths running in parallel), late dates must match the early, so are set to December 28 (LS) and 31 (LF).

Since we know that the Late Start for *D* is December 28, we also know that Late Finish for *D*'s predecessors must

be December 27. Late Start for *B* and *C* are found by subtracting their individual durations (five days) from Late Finish. This results in values of December 21 for *B* (Calendar 1) and December 19 for *C* (Calendar 2). Why the difference again? Activity *C* must begin no later than December 19—two days before *B*—because its calendar enjoys two days off (December 21 and 24) that *B*'s calendar does not.

It all balances out. Calendar 2 does not get a free ride. Although it enjoys more days off than Calendar 1, these same days off increase activity criticality when the workers do return. The backward pass through the network finishes by computing late dates for *A*. By inspection, these are both found to be December 18.

Even though the Critical Path still determines the project length and indicates the project end date, it does not exclusively do this. The calendar mix affects both. All this—and more—frequently happens in a multiple-calendar environment. By now something should be entirely obvious: You must take extreme care when dealing with multiple calendars. Accept all the help you can get!

Recall the last feature of the single-calendar Critical Path: It is the continuous chain(s) of zero-float activities. We have already seen how the multiple-calendar environment invalidates the other two characteristics. Will the third time be a charm? No. It even happens that the Critical Path may, and often does, contain activities with positive float!

Wow! Such activities, in the absence of date or time constraints (Chapters 5 and 6), can never be critical if only one calendar is used. But if the Critical Path contains activities from different calendars, some of the activities on this path may have positive float.

The result is that the activity:

- Has some starting time flexibility; or
- Is prevented from starting as early as otherwise could

Of course, delay beyond float values will delay successors and the project completion date.

This is not to say, however, that the Critical Path in a multiple-calendar project must always contain positive-float activities. A zero-float activity remains critical. In our earlier two-calendar, five-activity project, the Critical Path consisted of a continuous chain of activities, each with zero float (just as would occur in a single-calendar environment), even though activity *C* is scheduled under Calendar 2 and the others under Calendar 1.

Also in this sample network, Late Start equaled Early Start—as would occur in a single-calendar environment—for each critical activity. There is, therefore, no leeway in the starting times of any of these four activities. They can occur at one time only. If any of these four activities begins later, the project is delayed.

More often, however, the multiple-calendar Critical Path consists of some activities with zero float, as well as some with positive. Please study the five-activity project, based on the same two calendars as before, presented in Table 3-32.

A network sketch (Fig. 3-32) may help.

Observe in particular the float values for each activity in Table 3-33.

Note from Table 3-33:

• The Critical Path consists of activities *A, C, D,* and *E*
• Only *E* has a float value of zero
• Late Finish for *B* and *C* are the same, January 2, even though *C* is critical but *B* is not.

The two paths through the network may be compared as shown in Table 3-34.

Do you see anything unusual? Remember the last distinguishing feature of the single-calendar Critical Path: It consisted of only zero-float activities, none of which could be delayed. In the *A-C-D-E* Critical Path sequence described above, activities *A, C,* and *D*:

• Each contain some value of positive float
• May be delayed up to this float value and still not delay project finish

Only one of the four critical activities, *E*, follows the traditional critical-activity description. It contains no float and cannot be delayed.

Please study these results, which are plotted in Figs. 3-33, 3-34, and 3-35. Note the addition of the late-schedule activity bars to the Gantt Chart and how the Late Start time-logic network differs from the Early.

What determines the multiple-calendar Critical Path are the "driving predecessors," which were seen earlier in the single-calendar environment.

Table 3-32   Schedule Setup

```
---------------------------------------------------------------------------
SCHEDULE SETUP                                      DATE: _____

PROJECT NAME:   FIVE-ACTIVITY TWO-CALENDAR NETWORK SETUP EXAMPLE # 2_____
---------------------------------------------------------------------------
```

ACTIVITY ID	DUR (DAYS)	CAL	PREDECESSOR/ RELATIONSHIP	SUCCESSOR/ RELATIONSHIP	ACTIVITY DESCRIPTION
A	3	1	None	B F/S C F/S	
B	3	1	A F/S	D F/S	
C	5	2	A F/S	D F/S	
D	2	1	B F/S C F/S	E F/S	
E	2	2	D F/S	None	

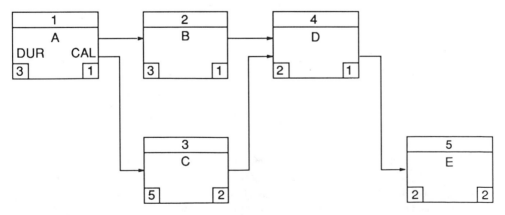

FIGURE 3-32.   Network setup diagram.

Table 3-33   Schedule Summary

```
----------------------------------------------------------------------
SCHEDULE SUMMARY                               DATE:  _____

PROJECT NAME:   TWO-CALENDAR PROJECT (#2) WITH POSITIVE-FLOAT CRITICAL PATH__
----------------------------------------------------------------------
```

ACTIVITY ID/CAL		ORIG DUR	REM DUR	% DONE	EARLY START	EARLY FINISH	LATE START	LATE FINISH	TOTAL FLOAT	
A	1 *	3	3	0	18DEC91	20DEC91	21DEC91	24DEC91	3	*
B	1	3	3	0	21DEC91	24DEC91	30DEC91	2JAN92	6	
C	2 *	5	5	0	23DEC91	31DEC91	26DEC91	2JAN92	1	*
D	1 *	2	2	0	2JAN92	3JAN92	3JAN92	4JAN92	1	*
E	2 *	2	2	0	6JAN92	7JAN92	6JAN92	7JAN92	0	*

Table 3-34   Paths Through the Network

	------------------ PATH ------------------	
	A-C-D-E	A-B-D-E
CRITICAL?	YES	NO
LENGTH	12 days	10 days
TOTAL FLOAT	5 days	10 days
CAN BE DELAYED?	YES (except E)	YES (except E)

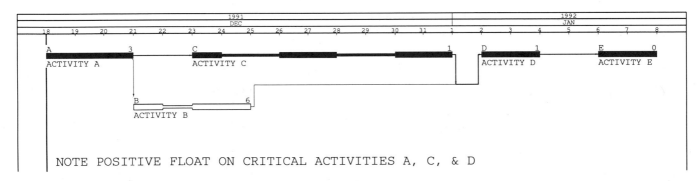

NOTE POSITIVE FLOAT ON CRITICAL ACTIVITIES A, C, & D

FIGURE 3-33.   Time-logic plot. The Critical Path can sometimes contain float.

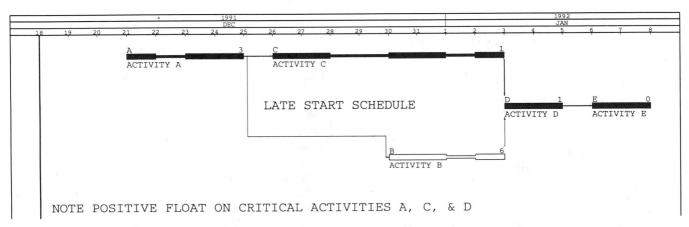

NOTE POSITIVE FLOAT ON CRITICAL ACTIVITIES A, C, & D

FIGURE 3-34.   Time-logic plot, Late Start schedule.

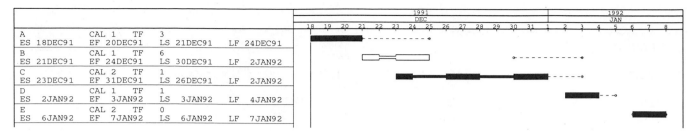

FIGURE 3-35.   Gantt Chart.

We must work from project finish to project start and identify these for each activity. A *driving predecessor*, you will recall, is an activity predecessor that determines when that particular activity can begin. There must always be a direct "cause and effect" relationship. Since the concept relates more to Early Start than to Late Start, only calculations made in the forward pass determine the driving relationships, even though the process is actually done as an additional step on the backward pass.

It is also possible that late-schedule driving relationships differ from the early. Since early-schedule values would have priority anyway, late-schedule calculations are unnecessary. *Primavera* denotes these driving predecessor relationships on each activity's detail screen.

Activity *E* is the last zero-float (LF = EF) activity in the network just presented. Since *E* has only one predecessor, *D* is undoubtedly its driver. Therefore, both *D* and *E* are on the Critical Path, even though only the latter has zero float. There is simply no other path.

But two trails lead into *D*—one from *B*, the other from *C*. We have already noted *B* and *C* Late Finish to be the same date: January 2. Is each a driving predecessor for *D*? Are both activities critical? No. Only *C* is.

We determine this as follows: Early Start for *D*, January 2, is conceptually moved up one workday to December 31 (January 1 is a holiday under Calendar 1). Now compare this with scheduled Early Finish dates for predecessors *B* and *C*. Clearly, the new *D* Early Start will violate the network logic at *C*. This is because *C*'s Early Finish is also December 31 and *D* cannot begin until *C* finishes. So *D* cannot begin December 31 because *C* will still be in progress. Such hypothetical violations of network logic always indicate a driving predecessor relationship. Therefore, *C* is both:

- A driving predecessor of *D*
- On the Critical Path (even with one day positive float)

Is it the only one? What about *B*? Since the network logic between *B* and *D* is not violated by the hypothetical December 31 Early Start (the conventional relationship with *B*'s Early Finish six days earlier would still be valid), *B* is not:

- A driving predecessor of *D*
- A driving predecessor of any other activity
- On the Critical Path

Its relatively high float gave us this clue, but it was only a clue and could not determine either way what *B*'s true status was.

Finally, since *A* is the only trail leading into *C*, *A* is clearly the driving predecessor for *C*. (It is also the driving predecessor for *B*.) Like activities *C* and *D*, *A* also has positive float, fully three days worth.

The Critical Path consists of activities *A*, *C*, *D*, and *E*. Of these, only *E* has zero float. The others required a method different from the single-calendar case to be identified and, therefore, managed.

The entire Critical Path is traced by performing this predecessor check, one relationship at a time. Some projects may have more than one Critical Path; each path is identified in precisely the same way. This method could also be used in a single-calendar environment, but there is no advantage in doing this.

FLOAT REVISITED

What if the project falls behind schedule—or never had sufficient time to begin with? Murphy had an interesting thought: "The sooner a project falls behind, the more time you have to catch up!"

Unfortunately, this is just not true. Somewhere these days must be made up. If they are not, the project will be delayed. By how much? The concept of "negative float" will tell us. Recall how float values are determined by differences in activity Early Start and Late Start:

- LS > ES: positive float (some scheduling leeway)
- LS = ES: zero float (critical and cannot be delayed)

By extension, we may define *negative float* as:

- LS < ES: negative float (super-critical; behind schedule)

Late Start earlier than Early Start?!! Sounds like something right out of Alice in Wonderland ("I'm late, I'm late, for an important date!" said the White Rabbit, not knowing himself to be in negative-float mode)! For here, late is early and early is late! What's going on here, anyway? Shouldn't early be early and late be late?

But the project management world is sometimes a topsyturvy world! Note how negative float is represented in the timeline-based Fig. 3-36.

It may all be explained as follows: The resulting value

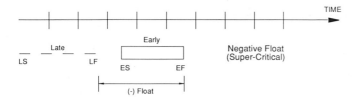

FIGURE 3-36. How float is represented in noncritical, critical, and super-critical activities.

clearly indicates the number of days we are behind schedule. The higher the (negative) number:

- The further behind we are
- The more the process (not necessarily the people) needs improvement
- The greater the importance of completing this activity over others

This number is still the difference between Late Start and Early Start (activity bars need not be, as pictured in Fig. 3-36, entirely disjoint). We would need to turn back the hands of time by this number of days in order to have all of our sins forgiven—for this activity's tardy condition, at least. "Rev mode" time!

Rev Mode: Break-neck work effort, with velocity approaching the speed of light and staff morale approaching zero, ordered by the boss to recover lost progress and counteract project *mis*management.

Single Calendar

Recall the simple four-activity network studied earlier. When mapped to a five-day workweek, the project was expected to finish on October 14. In 1991, this date is a Monday. No work is scheduled over the weekend. Now suppose the project must finish one (work)day earlier. The last workday prior to then is Friday, October 11. When must the project start? Would a weekend finishing deadline make any difference?

The concept of negative float provides the first answer: September 30. Project Late Finish is set to October 11, not

October 14 (EF) as would normally be done. Working back to the project's beginning, we find its Late Start now to be September 30, one workday prior to its Early Start on October 1. This one-workday-prior value is:

- The number of workdays project finish was moved up
- Represented by a -1 float value
- How far behind the project will be with a start on October 1
- The number of workdays prior to October 1 the project must start to meet the October 11 deadline

Since no work would be done Saturday or Sunday, a weekend deadline date would make no difference. We would still need to start on September 30. The schedule may be summarized as shown in Table 3-35.

Note that all activities are now critical or super-critical. Activity C has lost its scheduling flexibility. It must begin on October 3 and end on October 8, or else it will delay the project. The remaining activities must each begin one day earlier than originally scheduled or do the same. What is the new Critical Path? The more proper question would ask "paths." Although A-B-D is behind schedule with a start on October 1, A-C-D must still not be delayed by even one day and by definition qualifies as critical, too. We could call A-B-D the Super-Critical Path and A-C-D the Critical. In any case, the project must start on September 30 if it is to finish on October 11. Figures 3-37 and 3-38 present the associated time-logic plot and Gantt Chart. Time certainly flies, doesn't it? (Fig. 3-39).

Remember the garage project? When mapped to a five-day workweek, the project was expected to be finished on November 6. In 1991, this date is a Wednesday. Now suppose the garage needs to be ready first thing on Saturday, November 2. When must the project start? Thursday, September 26, as summarized below and shown in Table 3-36 and Figs. 3-40, 3-41, and 3-42.

To be ready on November 2, the project must finish by the end of November 1. This means we would lose three workdays—November 4, 5, and 6. The three days negative float is applied to each activity with the following results:

- Each activity's float value is reduced by three days
- Project length remains unchanged at twenty-seven days

Table 3-35 Schedule Summary

```
----------------------------------------------------------------------------------
SCHEDULE SUMMARY                                          DATE: _____

----------------------------------------------------------------------------------
PROJECT NAME:   4-ACTIVITY CPM (5-DAY WORKWEEK WITH 10/11/91 DEADLINE)_____
----------------------------------------------------------------------------------
```

ACTIVITY ID		ORIG DUR	REM DUR	% DONE	EARLY START	EARLY FINISH	LATE START	LATE FINISH	TOTAL FLOAT	
A	*	2	2	0	1OCT91	2OCT91	30SEP91	1OCT91	−1	*
B	*	5	5	0	3OCT91	9OCT91	2OCT91	8OCT91	−1	*
C	*	4	4	0	3OCT91	8OCT91	3OCT91	8OCT91	0	*
D	*	3	3	0	10OCT91	14OCT91	9OCT91	11OCT91	−1	*

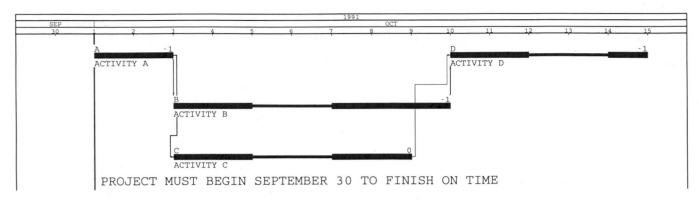

FIGURE 3-37.   Time-logic plot.

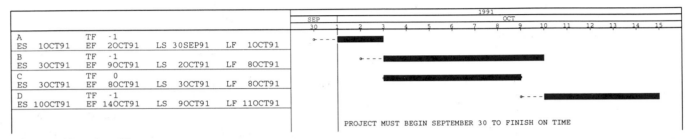

FIGURE 3-38.   Gantt Chart.

Table 3-36   Schedule Summary

SCHEDULE SUMMARY   DATE: _____

PROJECT NAME: 13-ACTIVITY GARAGE CONSTRUCTION_____

ACTIVITY ID		ORIG DUR	REM DUR	% DONE	EARLY START	EARLY FINISH	LATE START	LATE FINISH	TOTAL FLOAT	
1	*	1	1	0	1OCT91	1OCT91	26SEP91	26SEP91	-3	*
2		5	5	0	2OCT91	8OCT91	23OCT91	29OCT91	15	
3	*	20	20	0	2OCT91	29OCT91	27SEP91	24OCT91	-3	*
4		3	3	0	2OCT91	4OCT91	11OCT91	15OCT91	7	
5		5	5	0	2OCT91	8OCT91	22OCT91	28OCT91	14	
6		7	7	0	7OCT91	15OCT91	16OCT91	24OCT91	7	
7	*	2	2	0	30OCT91	31OCT91	25OCT91	28OCT91	-3	*
8	*	1	1	0	1NOV91	1NOV91	30OCT91	30OCT91	-2	*
9	*	1	1	0	1NOV91	1NOV91	29OCT91	29OCT91	-3	*
10	*	1	1	0	4NOV91	4NOV91	31OCT91	31OCT91	-2	*
11	*	2	2	0	1NOV91	4NOV91	30OCT91	31OCT91	-2	*
12	*	2	2	0	4NOV91	5NOV91	30OCT91	31OCT91	-3	*
13	*	1	1	0	6NOV91	6NOV91	1NOV91	1NOV91	-3	*

FIGURE 3-39.   "Time flies." *Source:* CSC Diagraph.

- The Critical Path has increased from six activities to nine; activities 8, 10, and 11 are now critical
- All work performed after October 15 could be (super) critical

  To finish on time we must do one of the following:

- Start three workdays earlier (September 26)
- Make up these three days along the way
- Follow a combination of both

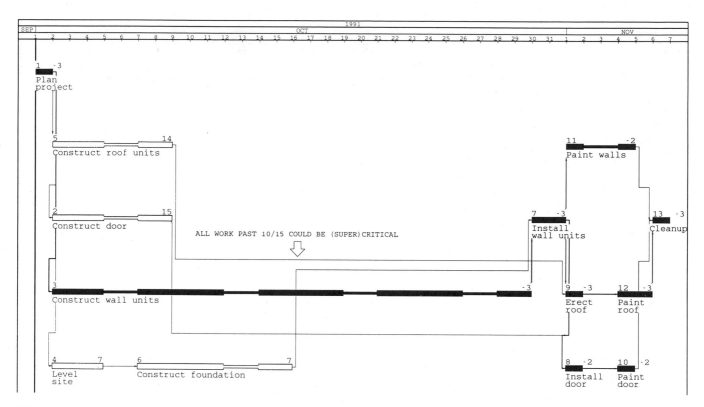

FIGURE 3-40.   Time-logic plot (Early Start schedule).

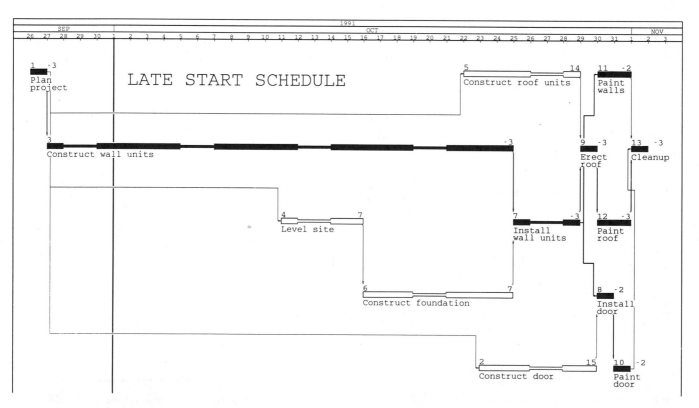

FIGURE 3-41.   Time-logic plot (Late Start schedule).

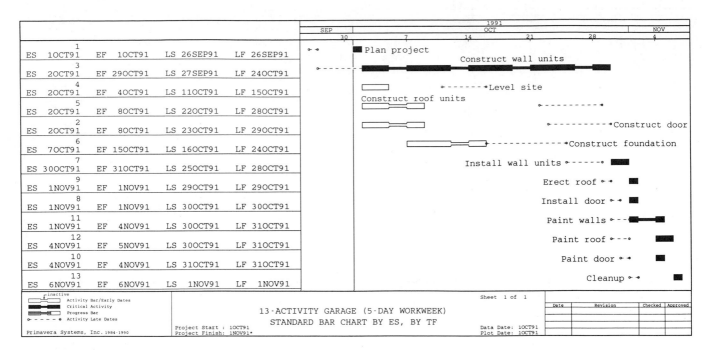

FIGURE 3-42.   Gantt Chart.

The Gantt Chart displays both the early and late schedules. If an activity (for example, "level site") has positive float, its late-schedule bar will be to the right of its early-schedule bar. The distance between EF and LF indicates your scheduling "bank account balance" (how much flexibility you have for that particular activity). But if an activity (for example, "plan project") has negative float, its late-schedule bar will be to the left of its early-schedule bar and indicate by how much your account is already "overdrawn." You have already spent more than all your float and must make it up before project finish. If you do not, your project will be late that many days—no exceptions!

Do not shoot the messenger if you do not like the message (Fig. 3-43)! If everything is coming up negatives instead of roses:

- Circle the wagons
- Batten down the hatches
- Hide from your boss (in a fortified stone bunker)
- Update your résumé

"I don't like your software," the boss once told me. "It shows I'm three months behind schedule!" Well, he was . . . on a six-month project (Fig. 3-44A and 3-44B)!

Most of the free world already knew that this project was very late! No production, no progress (Fig. 3-44C)! But without *P3,* or another such capable tool, how would he know:

- Exactly how far he was behind?
- How to catch up?
- Where best to invest time, resources, and effort?
- How not to make matters even worse?

FIGURE 3-43.   Your boss, if your project is late. *Source:* CSC Diagraph.

You should also do one thing more: If you elected to suppress late-schedule times (so that people would not wait until then to start), understand fully that super-critical Late Start always occurs *before* Early Start. Unless you somehow flag these activities as more urgent than indicated, you will make the problem even worse because only the (later) Early Start values would normally be displayed. Your project management software should let you display only the following if desired:

- Early Start and Early Finish for activities with positive float
- Early Start and Early Finish for activities with zero float
- Late Start and Late Finish for activities with negative float

It should also permit you to name any float value for activity selection purposes.

Noncritical Activities

What about noncritical activities? If negative-float activities demand the most attention and zero-float activities require almost as much, should we not be concerned at all with activities that (currently) contain some value of positive float? Should we just ignore Chase-and-Aquilano project activity *C*? After all, it does not affect the project's length. Can it ever? The answer is yes.

A noncritical activity always contains float. If properly controlled, this float is valuable in planning and controlling:

- Labor
- Materials
- Facilities
- Costs
- Time
- Other resources

Although noncritical activities do not directly affect the project completion date, they must of course still be accomplished. Moreover, in many projects, it is not the activities actually on the Critical Path that cause problems, but rather nearby noncritical activities, which for various reasons (including inattention) become critical.

It may happen that critical activities contain only small variances and can be treated as near certain in length. At the same time, activities not on the Critical Path may have larger variances that, if not closely monitored, could delay the project.

Thus, while it is important to control Critical Path activities, it may be just as useful to focus on those activities that:

- Are near, but not actually on, the Critical Path
- Contain a high degree of duration uncertainty

These activities can be subdivided as necessary to permit closer analysis. Some authors, myself included, have even suggested that the Critical Path approach be formally modified to simulate which activities are likely to cause project

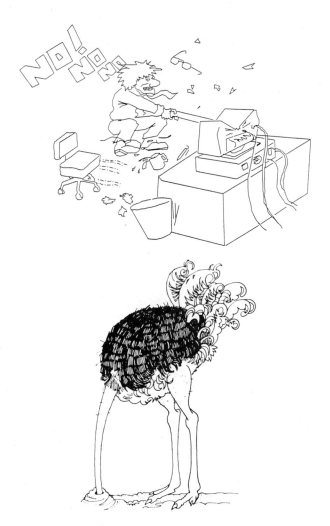

FIGURE 3-44 (A and B).   Your boss, if he or she is the reason why your project is late (initial reaction). *Source:* Unknown (A); Kerzner p. 761 (B).

FIGURE 3-44C.   Your boss, if he or she is the reason why your project is late (final reaction). *Source:* CSC Diagraph.

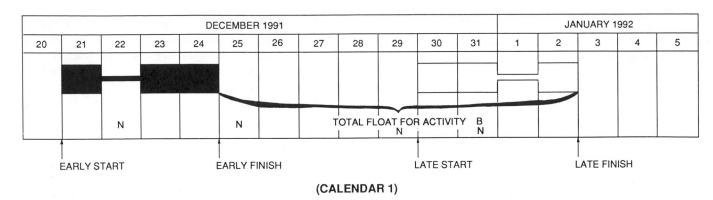

(CALENDAR 1)

FIGURE 3-45.   How to calculate float in a multiple-calendar environment.

delay. These activities—not just the Critical Path—would become the focus of managerial control. This idea certainly has merit. Why wait until these activities actually turn critical before they be controlled more closely?

Multiple Calendar

In a multiple-calendar project, float is measured according to the calendar to which an activity is assigned. Note in Fig. 3-45 how float may be represented for activity *B* (Calendar 1):

Activity *B* can finish as early as December 24 (EF) or as late as January 2 (LF). The workday difference between these two finish dates is six days, as measured by Calendar 1. There are also four nonworkdays in this span: December 22, Christmas Day, December 29, and New Year's Day. Expected duration is three days. The thirteen days between December 21 and January 2 may be classified as follows:

- Three days duration (variable and not necessarily contiguous)
- Four days off (as listed above and fixed)
- Six days float (none of the above seven days)

Activity *B* resources are best applied when this activity starts no earlier than December 21 and finishes no later than

January 2. Again, note well that the three days' duration need not be contiguous. Your software should allow you to stop and resume activities as required.

Had *B* scheduled under Calendar 2, a different date range would have resulted, as shown in Table 3-37 and Figure 3-46.

Note from Table 3-37 how the schedule for *B* has changed under Calendar 2. Early Start has moved right two days. This is because Calendar 2 does not work on December 21 (as does Calendar 1) or December 22 (both calendars are off). Early Finish has also slid (to December 27), but Late Finish remains January 2. If Late Finish were any later, *D*, *E*, and project finish would all be delayed. The workday difference between these two finish dates is only three days, as measured by Calendar 2. This is because there are now five nonworkdays in this eleven-day span: December 24, Christmas Day, December 28, December 29, and New Year's Day. Expected duration is still three days, again not necessarily contiguous. The eleven days between December 23 and January 2 may be classified as follows:

- Three days duration (variable and not necessarily contiguous)
- Five days off (as listed above and fixed; +1 from before)
- Three days float (none of the above eight days; −3 from before)

Table 3-37   Schedule Summary

```
-----------------------------------------------------------------------------
SCHEDULE SUMMARY                                     DATE: _____
-----------------------------------------------------------------------------
PROJECT NAME:   2-CALENDAR 6/5 DAY WORKWEEK PROJECT (#2); B UNDER CALENDAR 2_
-----------------------------------------------------------------------------
```

ACTIVITY ID/CAL		ORIG DUR	REM DUR	% DONE	EARLY START	EARLY FINISH	LATE START	LATE FINISH	TOTAL FLOAT	
A	1 *	3	3	0	18DEC91	20DEC91	21DEC91	24DEC91	3	*
B	2	3	3	0	23DEC91	27DEC91	30DEC91	2JAN92	3	
C	2 *	5	5	0	23DEC91	31DEC91	26DEC91	2JAN92	1	*
D	1 *	2	2	0	2JAN92	3JAN92	3JAN92	4JAN92	1	*
E	2 *	2	2	0	6JAN92	7JAN92	6JAN92	7JAN92	0	*

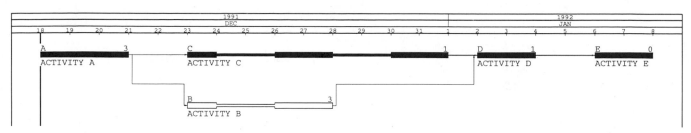

FIGURE 3-46A.   Time-logic plot.

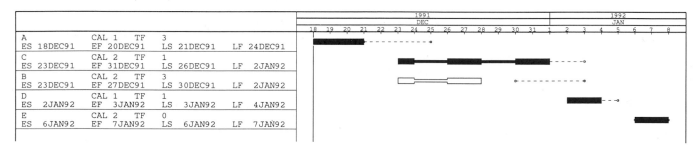

FIGURE 3-46B.   Gantt Chart.

Table 3-38   Schedule Summary

```
-----------------------------------------------------------------------------
SCHEDULE SUMMARY                                    DATE: _____

PROJECT NAME:  SAME AS BEFORE BUT WITH 1/6/92 FINISH_____
-----------------------------------------------------------------------------
```

ACTIVITY ID/CAL	ORIG DUR	REM DUR	% DONE	EARLY START	EARLY FINISH	LATE START	LATE FINISH	TOTAL FLOAT
A 1 *	3	3	0	18DEC91	20DEC91	17DEC91	19DEC91	-1 *
B 2	3	3	0	23DEC91	27DEC91	26DEC91	30DEC91	1
C 2 *	5	5	0	23DEC91	31DEC91	20DEC91	30DEC91	-1 *
D 1 *	2	2	0	2JAN92	3JAN92	31DEC91	2JAN92	-1 *
E 2 *	2	2	0	6JAN92	7JAN92	3JAN92	6JAN92	-1 *

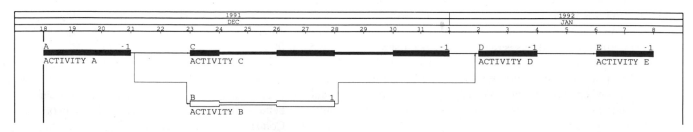

FIGURE 3-47A.   Time-logic plot.

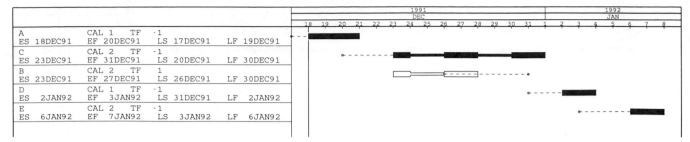

							1991 DEC														1992 JAN							
						18	19	20	21	22	23	24	25	26	27	28	29	30	31	1	2	3	4	5	6	7	8
A		CAL 1	TF	-1																							
ES 18DEC91	EF 20DEC91		LS 17DEC91		LF 19DEC91																						
C		CAL 2	TF	-1																							
ES 23DEC91	EF 31DEC91		LS 20DEC91		LF 30DEC91																						
B		CAL 2	TF	1																							
ES 23DEC91	EF 27DEC91		LS 26DEC91		LF 30DEC91																						
D		CAL 1	TF	-1																							
ES 2JAN92	EF 3JAN92		LS 31DEC91		LF 2JAN92																						
E		CAL 2	TF	-1																							
ES 6JAN92	EF 7JAN92		LS 3JAN92		LF 6JAN92																						

FIGURE 3-47B.   Gantt Chart.

The three days reduction in float was applied as follows:

• One day was changed into a holiday December 24
• The other two days pushed Early Start to December 23

Activity *B* resources are best applied when this activity starts no earlier than December 23 and finishes no later than January 2. Float, like other schedule details, must be measured according to its assigned calendar.

Now suppose the project must finish one day earlier—on January 6. What would be the effects? We might expect each activity would lose one day of float—the one day earlier that the project must finish. That would certainly produce an interesting Critical Path: One activity would have positive float, two would have zero, and one would have negative float.

Surprisingly, it does not turn out that way at all. Remember that the project must now start one day earlier if time cannot be made up along the way. Regardless of whatever float values each critical activity might have had before, each must now have the same value, −1, because each must start one day earlier (Table 3-38 and Fig. 3-47). Live and learn.

CONTIGUOUS AND INTERRUPTIBLE ACTIVITY DURATIONS

Because work cannot always progress contiguously (without interruption), your scheduling process should allow activities to be scheduled using either contiguous or interruptible activity durations. Duration type affects how the work progresses on an activity. *Contiguous duration* requires work to take place without interruption, based on the calendar to which the activity is assigned. *Interruptible duration,* by contrast, offers a more flexible scheduling method, in which work can be interrupted (as it often is). Of course, the duration itself remains the same. The work is just interrupted along the way.

Using interruptible durations is more flexible because you can make better use of float and available resources by working on an activity intermittently. Instead of working on an activity when time is critical or resources are short, work can start earlier and progress with interruptions—but without delaying project finish.

THE PROJECT STATUS MEETING

You have probably experienced "status" meetings in which the presenter:

• Discussed only the positive aspects of the project
• Beat his or her own drums and tooted his or her own horn
• Tried to oil the wheels of self-promotion
• Glossed over or totally ignored problems
• Had no guts but did have infinite (though unwarranted) pride

A better way exists and should be used. In addition to known problem areas, other topics likely to cause trouble should also be discussed. The typical "status" meeting or project review becomes a more progressive, more valuable risk-management session in which the top ten, say, items likely to jeopardize the entire project are investigated. Focus on things that:

• Really do, or can, make a difference
• The manager and team can do something about

Group identified risks go into appropriate categories, such as:

• Personnel shortfalls
• Unrealistic schedules and budgets
• Wrong requirements stated
• Continuous requirements changes
• Insufficient resources
• Inadequate training
• Error-prone processes

Calculate the accompanying risk exposure as the product of the probability of unsatisfactory outcome times the loss from this unsatisfactory outcome, or, in short, the "probability times the pain." For example, if failure probability equals 20 percent and the resulting loss would equal $1,000,000, the risk exposure would be (.20) × ($1,000,000), or $200,000.

There are several ways by which this may be done. *P3,* and perhaps your own software, provides several such tools, and most spreadsheets (including *20/20*) have this capability. The better statistical analysis and decision support tools (such as Comshare *IFPS/Plus* and *Executive Edge*) combine

Monte Carlo or other simulation models with AI-based* explanations of results.

Even if the loss cannot be expressed so precisely, you should at least score items on a 1-to-10 scale so that those with the highest risk exposure can receive the most attention. All possible one-on-one combinations should be systematically reviewed to determine proper ranking. If you have a PC, an outstanding tool to do this is *BestChoice3* by Sterling Castle.

Of course, you need not wait until there is a formal rules change to employ these analysis techniques. Your project may need them well before then. Use them!

Finally, if there exists a multiactivity path with float, an increase in duration of any one of the member activities will reduce the float available to the others. This process might also affect the float values in both the preceding and succeeding activities and may occur many times. The cumulative effect might be to alter, or at least split, the Critical Path, even though no single activity increased sufficiently in length to do this alone. It is crucial, therefore, that all aspects of your project's status be kept current, with daily updates reflecting this.

WHAT ELSE DO YOU DO WHEN YOUR PROJECT IS RUNNING LATE?

If your project seems to be running late, first make sure that it is indeed running late and does not just appear that way. The following symptoms are reliable trouble indicators:

- Project finish date gets later and later
- If project finish date is fixed:

    Negative-float magnitudes are increasing
    More activities have negative float
- Costs increase faster than planned for the work done
- Quality deteriorates
- Increased shortages of, and competition for, resources
- More problems with and arguments over time and other resources
- The boss:
    Gets chewed out again
    Takes it out again on his or her staff
    Orders the despicable, reprehensible Rev Mode

The following ten summary strategies and tactics might help bring your project back on track:

1. Check network logic for errors
2. Decrease activity durations where possible
3. Reduce noncritical-activity resources if possible to reduce resource contention
4. Place activities in parallel—use Start-to-Start or Finish-to-Finish relationships instead of Finish-to-Start
5. Remove unnecessary constraints
6. Apply more resources to reduce critical activity duration
7. Apply resources more effectively by improving processes and methods
8. Rearrange activities to avoid resource constraints
9. Use more capable resources—better-skilled people, better machines
10. Do "A −" work instead of "A +" work

---

*Artificial Intelligence. Computer-interpreted analysis that uses a set of rules provided by an expert or team of experts.

4

Precedence Diagram Method (PDM) Activity Relationships

We learned a great deal in the last chapter. But we made two major simplifications:

- Only conventional (F/S) relationships were used
- No progress had been made on any activity

NEEDED ENHANCEMENTS

This chapter will discuss all PDM relationships and the effect of progress on each.

In 1973, Professor Fondahl's activity-on-node (AON) format was expanded to include relationships other than the common Finish-to-Start. This enhanced methodology was named the *Precedence Diagram Method (PDM)*. In simplest terms, the problem with both activity-on-node and especially with activity-on-arrow methods may be seen in Fig. 4-1.

First, assume a conventional F/S relationship. Completion of A permits work on B and C to begin, but with no restriction on which activity:

- Starts first
- Starts last
- Finishes first
- Finishes last

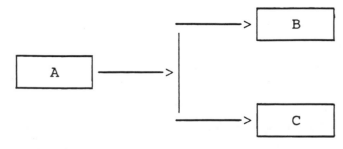

FIGURE 4-1.   Network setup diagram.

84

However, it might be possible that C can only start, or should start, sometime after B starts—not necessarily when A ends. Although completion of A is necessary, it is not sufficient. We saw this earlier in the Project HOME segment reproduced in Table 4-1.

We can begin to grout precast panels five days after they have been set. It is this five days, not the concrete slab curing time, that determines when activity 27 may begin. On the other hand, we do not need to wait until *all* concrete panels have been set to grout those that have been in place the required five days. Work on both activities may be done concurrently after this time. In this eleven-day segment, therefore, work may—and should—be done as follows:

- Days 1–5: Activity 26 only
- Days 6–10: Both activities 26 and 27
- Day 11: Activity 27 only

This could not be done in any format other than PDM. The consequences of both attempts would be unsatisfactory:

- Failed process if activity 27 began immediately upon completion of activity 24
- Unnecessary five-day delay if start of activity 27 waited until completion of activity 26

It might also happen that B cannot finish until C completes (or the other way around)—again, not necessarily related to when A completes. In Project HOME, for example, appliances must be set for hookup prior to the last five days electrical trimout and connection work (Table 4-2).

We must finish setting appliances (activity 117) five days before we finish electrical connections and trimout (activity 119), including appliance hookup. It is this five days that determines the latest date on which activity 117 can end

Table 4-1   Activity List, With Relationships and Durations

ACT ID	PRED/ REL		SUCC/ REL		ACTIVITY DESCRIPTION	DUR
22	11	F/S	24	F/S	Concrete slab on grade	5
	12	F/S				
	13	F/S				
24	22	F/S	26	F/S	Curing time	13
26	24	F/S	27	SS5	Set precast concrete panels	10
			30	F/S		
			50	F/S		
27	26	SS5	30	F/S	Grout precast panels	6
			50	F/S		

Table 4-2   Activity List, with Relationships and Durations

ACT ID	PRED/ REL		SUCC/ REL		ACTIVITY DESCRIPTION	DUR
115	109	F/S	117	F/S	Install cabinets	13
117	115	F/S	119	FF5	Set appliances	5
			128	F/S		
119	117	FF5	128	F/S	Electrical connections and trimout	12

(and from this the latest on which it can be started), not when activity 115 (install cabinets) has completed. On the other hand, we do not need to wait until *all* appliances have been set to begin final electrical connections; indeed these connections must begin two days before activity 117 in both the Early and the Late Start schedule. If the electrical outlet is ready, an appliance may be hooked up as soon as it is set. If not, the appliance—even if set—must wait for its hookup. Work on both activities may—and should—be done concurrently only until within five days of the finish of activity 119. No more work on activity 117 should be done during this time because it would interfere with progress on activity 119. In this twelve-day segment, therefore, work may—and should—be done as follows:

- Days 1–2: Activity 119 only
- Days 3–7: Both activities 117 and 119
- Days 8–12: Activity 119 only

This could not be done in any format other than PDM. Neither attempt would have a satisfactory consequence:

- Nothing to hook up if activity 117 did not make progress in time for activity 119
- Unnecessary seven-day delay if activity 119 waited until completion of activity 117

How do you represent these and similar situations in AOA format? You don't! You can't!

Because the activity-on-arrow format fails miserably just trying to represent these activities, it is used less and less

today. AON makes a better try, but still comes up short. The Precedence Diagram Method (PDM) is the format of overwhelming choice because it:

- Easily, but accurately, represents these more complex relationships
- Retains all the simplicity and clarity of the AON format

I strongly recommend that you learn and use PDM from the start or convert to it at the earliest possible time. There is no logical reason for you to put your project (and career) at undue risk by foolishly clinging to a methodology that does not, cannot, and will not accurately represent the realities of your project! Project management is often difficult enough; failure of the metrics themselves could make it impossible.

What cost PDM? A few extra minutes. What cost AOA or AON? Many extra:

- Hours
- Headaches
- Hurts
- Hassles

This is not the 4-H Club to which you might wish to belong!

The resulting time schedule is otherwise identical in both its computational procedures and presentation. Normally, these relationships are declared:

- After activities are identified
- Before duration estimates are applied

By using only the simple Finish-to-Start relationship in Chapter 3, we were able to proceed through the remaining steps without getting bogged down by the many advanced relationships that can, and often do, exist among activities. In actual practice, however, relationships are declared right after activities are listed, even before durations are applied.

Let us further distinguish between the conventional and the advanced relationships:

The F/S interpretation: When two or more activities must await the completion of an earlier activity, they are shown in diagrams as branching out in a "Y" to the right (Fig. 4-2). Each branch will retain its F/S relationship with the earlier activity because each activity depends only on predecessor completion. For example, it is certainly a good idea to land the airplane before unloading cargo or letting passengers off! But letting passengers off depends only upon whether or not the plane has landed, not on whether cargo is being unloaded. And cargo can be unloaded, also assuming the plane has landed, regardless of whether or not passengers are getting off. The F/S relationship correctly describes this situation.

The SS interpretation: The Start-to-Start relationship would be used if landing the plane is necessary, but not sufficient:

- Letting passengers off also depends on the start of cargo unloading, or
- Unloading cargo also depends on whether or not people have started to get off

On the other hand, it is also a good idea that all passengers and cargo be loaded before the plane takes off.

The F/S interpretation: When an activity cannot start until two or more activities have completed, it is represented by a "Y" branching to the left, with the earlier activities converging on the latter. Each branch will retain its F/S relationship with the earlier activities because each predecessor activity must complete before their common successor can start. The F/S relationship shown in Fig. 4-3 correctly describes this situation.

The FF interpretation: The Finish-to-Finish relationship would be used if taking off is necessary, but not sufficient:

- Completion of passenger loading also depends on cargo loading, or
- Completion of cargo loading also depends on passenger loading

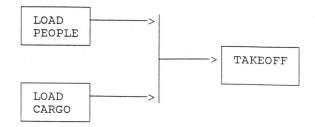

FIGURE 4-3.   Network setup diagram.

(Whatever you do, please continue to fly on Boeing airliners without concern about PDM relationships!)

In summary, the Precedence Diagram Method (PDM) is the better method because it:

- Supports all real-world relationships without restriction
- Complements the traditional Finish-to-Start relationship with the following additional representations:
    Start-to-Start
    Start-to-Finish
    Finish-to-Finish
- Permits the use of *lag* (the time duration of the relationship itself), which can show the offset between:
    Two starts
    Two finishes
    One start and one finish
- Never requires dummy activities
- Is more concise (two events and one activity are all contained in one box)
- Permits an easier numbering scheme better suited for grouping and sorting
- Is more flexible and easier to change

Primavera takes full advantage of PDM opportunities (impossible with activity-on-arrow format) by presenting useful information within node boundaries (Fig. 4-4).

Information provided for each activity includes:

- Activity identifier
- Activity description
- Relationships
- Original duration
- Remaining duration
- Percent complete

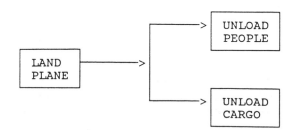

FIGURE 4-2.   Network setup diagram.

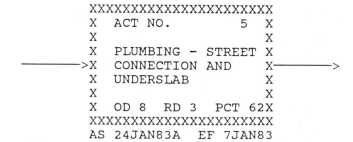

FIGURE 4-4.   Useful PDM activity information.

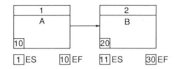

```
--------------------------------------------
CASE 1: No progress on A or B  |
--------------------------------------------
ACTIVITY DUR PROGRESS ES EF | ACTIVITY DUR PROGRESS ES EF GAIN
--------------------------------------------
   A    10  NONE    1  10 |   B    20  NONE   11  30 NONE
--------------------------------------------
```

FIGURE 4-5.   Network setup diagram.

* Early Start (or Actual Start)
* Early Finish (or Actual Finish)

Let us now study PDM relationships in greater depth and examine the effect of progress on each.

FINISH-TO-START RELATIONSHIPS

Single Calendar

In *Finish-to-Start (F/S)* relationships, predecessor progress improves successor Early Finish. It might also help to shorten the entire project. There are four cases to consider:

* No progress on A or B (Figs. 4-5, 4-6; Table 4-3)
* Progress on A, none on B (Figs. 4-7, 4-8; Table 4-4)
* Progress on B, none on A (Figs. 4-9, 4-10; Table 4-5)
* Progress on both A and B (Figs. 4-11, 4-12; Table 4-6)

Unless otherwise specified, assume a seven-day workweek and the *data date* (date as of which the measurement is set) to be 1 October 1991. Computation details for the four F/S cases are not given. You should be able to solve them readily by now. Computation details for the advanced relationships are more difficult and will be fully explained.

Multiple Calendars

We have already seen some of the effects that multiple calendars can have on the scheduling process. Please study Table 4-7, which reviews the two calendars presented in the last chapter.

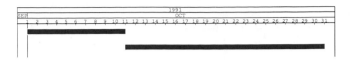

FIGURE 4-6.   Gantt Chart.

Recall the following from Table 4-7:

* Project start date is Wednesday, December 18
* Calendar 1 has a six-day workweek; Calendar 2 has a five-day workweek
* Both calendars enjoy December 25 and January 1 as off days
* In addition, Calendar 2 enjoys December 24 as an off day

In Fig. 4-13, the number in each activity's bottom right corner indicates its calendar assignment. All calculations in this example are based on the two calendars just presented and assume a December 18 data date unless otherwise specified.

Figure 4-14 is in bar chart format.

Note from Table 4-8 and Fig. 4-14 that activity *A:*

* Begins December 18
* Lasts five days
* Finishes December 23
* Contains one day of float

Assigned to Calendar 1, *A* enjoys only December 22 as a day off. Since *A* has completed on December 23, *B* could start on December 24. But this activity is assigned to Calendar 2, which enjoys both this day and Christmas as days off. These workers do not return until December 26; so although *B* could start December 24, it does not actually do so until after the two days off, or December 26. Work progresses on *B* for two days, until workers enjoy another two days off. They return December 30 and finish *B* later that day.

Consider this: What do activity *A* workers think about this situation? They work December 23 to finish *A* so that *B* can begin, but no one is "home" (or at work, as the case may be) to begin *B* until *A* workers have worked still another

Table 4-3   Schedule Summary

```
------------------------------------------------------------------
SCHEDULE SUMMARY                                DATE: _____

PROJECT NAME:  FINISH-TO-START RELATIONSHIP CASE 1_____
------------------------------------------------------------------
```

ACTIVITY ID		ORIG DUR	REM DUR	% DONE	EARLY START	EARLY FINISH	LATE START	LATE FINISH	TOTAL FLOAT	
A	*	10	10	0	1OCT91	10OCT91	1OCT91	10OCT91	0	*
B	*	20	20	0	11OCT91	30OCT91	11OCT91	30OCT91	0	*

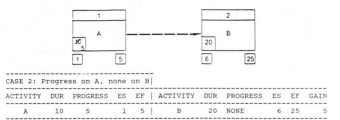

```
--------------------------------------------
CASE 2: Progress on A, none on B|
--------------------------------------------
ACTIVITY  DUR  PROGRESS  ES  EF | ACTIVITY  DUR  PROGRESS  ES  EF  GAIN
--------------------------------------------
   A      10     5        1   5 |    B      20   NONE       6  25   5
--------------------------------------------
```

FIGURE 4-7. Network setup diagram.

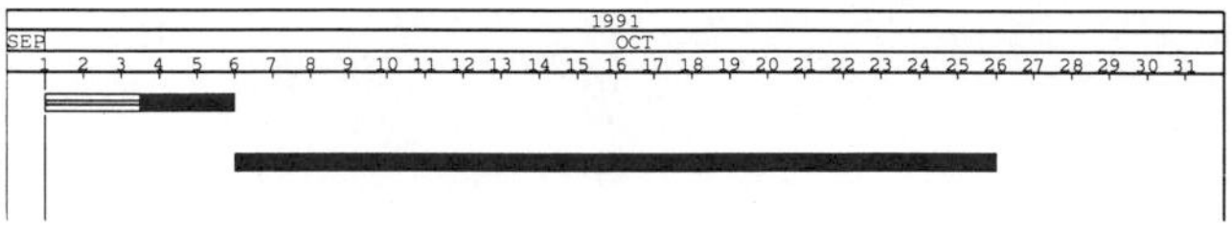

FIGURE 4-8. Gantt Chart.

Table 4-4 Schedule Summary

```
-------------------------------------------------------------------------
SCHEDULE SUMMARY                                     DATE: _____

PROJECT NAME:  FINISH-TO-START RELATIONSHIP CASE 2_____
-------------------------------------------------------------------------
```

ACTIVITY ID		ORIG DUR	REM DUR	% DONE	EARLY START	EARLY FINISH	LATE START	LATE FINISH	TOTAL FLOAT	
A	*	10	5	50	1OCT91	5OCT91	1OCT91	5OCT91	0	*
B	*	20	20	0	6OCT91	25OCT91	6OCT91	25OCT91	0	*

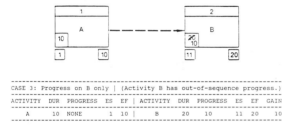

```
-----------------------------------------------------------
CASE 3: Progress on B only | (Activity B has out-of-sequence progress.)
-----------------------------------------------------------
ACTIVITY  DUR  PROGRESS  ES  EF | ACTIVITY  DUR  PROGRESS  ES  EF  GAIN
-----------------------------------------------------------
   A      10   NONE       1  10 |    B      20    10       11  20   10
-----------------------------------------------------------
```

FIGURE 4-9. Network setup diagram.

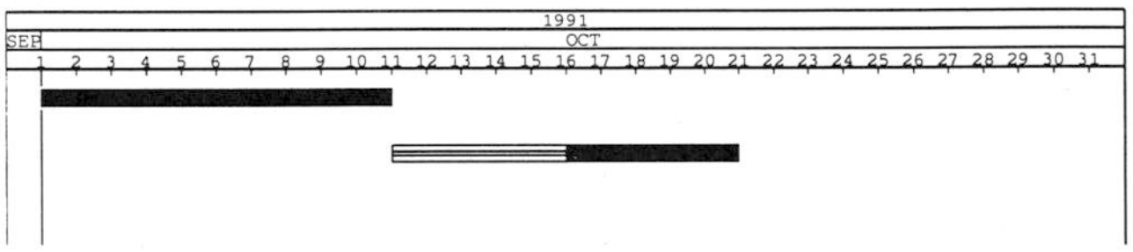

FIGURE 4-10. Gantt Chart.

Table 4-5 Schedule Summary

```
-------------------------------------------------------------------------
SCHEDULE SUMMARY                                     DATE: _____

PROJECT NAME:  FINISH-TO-START RELATIONSHIP CASE 3_____
-------------------------------------------------------------------------
```

ACTIVITY ID		ORIG DUR	REM DUR	% DONE	EARLY START	EARLY FINISH	LATE START	LATE FINISH	TOTAL FLOAT	
A	*	10	10	0	1OCT91	10OCT91	1OCT91	10OCT91	0	*
B	*	20	10	50	11OCT91	20OCT91	11OCT91	20OCT91	0	*

```
--------------------------------------------
CASE 4: Progress on both A and B|
--------------------------------------------
ACTIVITY  DUR  PROGRESS  ES  EF | ACTIVITY  DUR  PROGRESS  ES  EF  GAIN
--------------------------------------------
   A      10     5        1   5 |    B      20    10        6  15   15
--------------------------------------------
```

FIGURE 4-11. Network setup diagram.

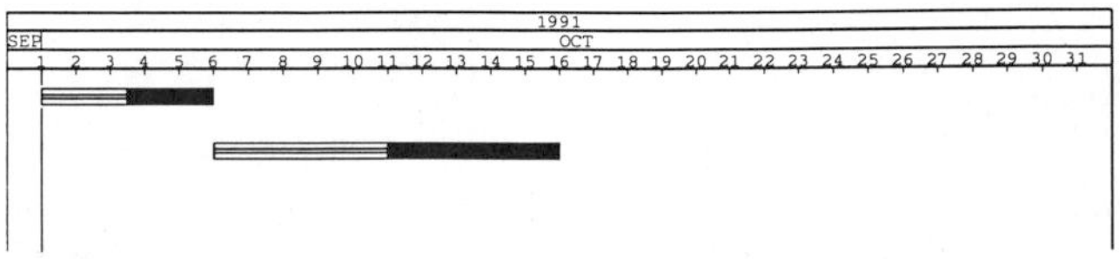

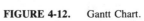

FIGURE 4-12. Gantt Chart.

Table 4-6 Schedule Summary

```
--------------------------------------------------------------------------------
SCHEDULE SUMMARY                                        DATE: _____

PROJECT NAME:  FINISH-TO-START RELATIONSHIP CASE 4_____
--------------------------------------------------------------------------------
ACTIVITY    ORIG   REM     %    EARLY     EARLY     LATE      LATE      TOTAL
   ID       DUR    DUR   DONE   START     FINISH    START     FINISH    FLOAT
--------    ----   ---   ----   -------   -------   -------   -------   -----
   A  *     10      5     50    1OCT91    5OCT91    1OCT91    5OCT91     0 *
   B  *     20     10     50    6OCT91    15OCT91   6OCT91    15OCT91    0 *
--------------------------------------------------------------------------------
```

Table 4-7 Multiple Calendar Detail

```
--------------------------------------------------------------------------------

 SUNDAY      MONDAY     TUESDAY    WEDNESDAY   THURSDAY    FRIDAY     SATURDAY
---------   ---------   ---------   ---------   ---------   ---------   ---------
DATE.................................18DEC91    19DEC91    20DEC91    21DEC91
CALENDAR 1 WORKDAY....................1          2          3          4
CALENDAR 2 WORKDAY....................1          2          3          NO WORK


22DEC91     23DEC91     24DEC91     25DEC91     26DEC91     27DEC91     28DEC91
NO WORK     5           6           HOLIDAY     7           8           9
NO WORK     4           HOLIDAY     HOLIDAY     5           6           NO WORK

                                 ------------------- 1992 -----------------
29DEC91     30DEC91     31DEC91    |1JAN92      2JAN92      3JAN92      4JAN92
NO WORK     10          11         |HOLIDAY     12          13          14
NO WORK     7           8          |HOLIDAY     9           10          NO WORK

5JAN92      6JAN92      7JAN92      8JAN92      9JAN92      10JAN92
NO WORK     15          16          17          18          19
NO WORK     11          12          13          14          15
--------------------------------------------------------------------------------
```

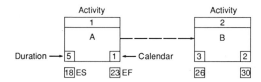

```
-------------------------------------------
BASELINE: No progress on A or B    |
-------------------------------------------
ACT  DUR  CAL  PROG   ES      EF | ACT  DUR  CAL  PROG   ES      EF
-------------------------------------------
A    5    1    NONE  12/18  12/23 | B    3    2    NONE  12/26  12/30
-------------------------------------------
```

FIGURE 4-13. Network setup diagram.

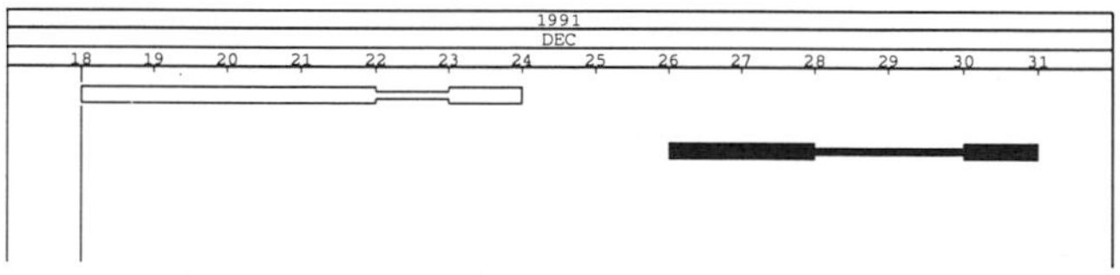

FIGURE 4-14. Gantt Chart.

Table 4-8 Schedule Summary

```
--------------------------------------------------------------------------------
SCHEDULE SUMMARY                                        DATE: _____

PROJECT NAME:  TWO-CALENDAR 6/5 DAY WORKWEEK PROJECT (CASE 1)_____
--------------------------------------------------------------------------------
ACTIVITY    ORIG   REM     %    EARLY     EARLY     LATE      LATE      TOTAL
 ID/CAL     DUR    DUR   DONE   START     FINISH    START     FINISH    FLOAT
--------    ----   ---   ----   -------   -------   -------   -------   -----
  A  1       5      5      0    18DEC91   23DEC91   19DEC91   24DEC91    1
  B  2  *    3      3      0    26DEC91   30DEC91   26DEC91   30DEC91    0 *
--------------------------------------------------------------------------------
```

Table 4-9   Schedule Summary

```
------------------------------------------------------------------------
SCHEDULE SUMMARY                                  DATE: _____

PROJECT NAME:  TWO-CALENDAR 6/5 DAY WORKWEEK PROJECT (CASE 2)_____
------------------------------------------------------------------------
```

ACTIVITY ID/CAL	ORIG DUR	REM DUR	% DONE	EARLY START	EARLY FINISH	LATE START	LATE FINISH	TOTAL FLOAT
A 1 *	5	5	0	18DEC91	23DEC91	13DEC91	23DEC91	0 *
B 1 *	3	3	0	24DEC91	27DEC91	24DEC91	27DEC91	0 *

Table 4-10   Schedule Summary

```
------------------------------------------------------------------------
SCHEDULE SUMMARY                                  DATE: _____

PROJECT NAME:  TWO-CALENDAR 6/5 DAY WORKWEEK PROJECT (CASE 3)_____
------------------------------------------------------------------------
```

ACTIVITY ID/CAL	ORIG DUR	REM DUR	% DONE	EARLY START	EARLY FINISH	LATE START	LATE FINISH	TOTAL FLOAT
A 2 *	5	5	0	18DEC91	26DEC91	18DEC91	26DEC91	0 *
B 2 *	3	3	0	27DEC91	31DEC91	27DEC91	31DEC91	0 *

Table 4-11   Schedule Summary

```
------------------------------------------------------------------------
SCHEDULE SUMMARY                                  DATE: _____

PROJECT NAME:  TWO-CALENDAR 6/5 DAY WORKWEEK PROJECT (CASE 4)_____
------------------------------------------------------------------------
```

ACTIVITY ID/CAL	ORIG DUR	REM DUR	% DONE	EARLY START	EARLY FINISH	LATE START	LATE FINISH	TOTAL FLOAT
A 2 *	5	5	0	18DEC91	26DEC91	18DEC91	26DEC91	0 *
B 1 *	3	3	0	27DEC91	30DEC91	27DEC91	30DEC91	0 *

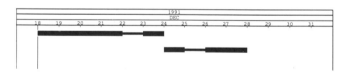

FIGURE 4-15.   Gantt Chart.

FIGURE 4-16.   Gantt Chart.

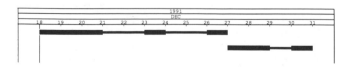

FIGURE 4-17.   Gantt Chart.

day, December 24! If I were the project manager, I would certainly make some changes to this schedule!

When would these two activities finish had they both been scheduled under Calendar 1? On December 27. This is because *B* would actually have started on December 24, not December 26 as under Calendar 2. Work would resume on December 26 after Christmas off and complete on December 27 (Table 4-9 and Figure 4-15).

Figure 4-15 is in bar chart format.

Now suppose that both activities had been scheduled under Calendar 2. When would they finish? Not until December 31 (Table 4-10).

Figure 4-16 is in bar chart format.

Finally, let *A* be scheduled under Calendar 2 and *B* under Calendar 1 (Table 4-11).

Figure 4-17 is in bar chart format.

Note that *B* would finish on December 30, the same date as in the first case, with the calendars reversed. But *A* in the first case had one day float; neither *A* nor *B* has any

Table 4-12 Schedule Summary: Cases 1, 2, 3, and 4

```
------------------------------------------------------------------------------
SCHEDULE SUMMARY                                    DATE: _____

PROJECT NAME:  TWO-CALENDAR 6/5 DAY WORKWEEK PROJECT_____
------------------------------------------------------------------------------
ACTIVITY   ORIG   REM     %    EARLY     EARLY     LATE      LATE      TOTAL
 ID/CAL    DUR    DUR   DONE    START     FINISH    START     FINISH    FLOAT

CASE 1
         ---------------------------------------------------------------------
  A  1       5     5     0    18DEC91   23DEC91   19DEC91   24DEC91     1
  B  2 *     3     3     0    26DEC91   30DEC91   26DEC91   30DEC91     0 *

CASE 2
         ---------------------------------------------------------------------
  A  1 *     5     5     0    18DEC91   23DEC91   18DEC91   23DEC91     0 *
  B  1 *     3     3     0    24DEC91   27DEC91   24DEC91   27DEC91     0 *
         ---------------------------------------------------------------------
CASE 3
         ---------------------------------------------------------------------
  A  2 *     5     5     0    18DEC91   26DEC91   18DEC91   26DEC91     0 *
  B  2 *     3     3     0    27DEC91   31DEC91   27DEC91   31DEC91     0 *
         ---------------------------------------------------------------------
CASE 4
         ---------------------------------------------------------------------
  A  2 *     5     5     0    18DEC91   26DEC91   18DEC91   26DEC91     0 *
  B  1 *     3     3     0    27DEC91   30DEC91   27DEC91   30DEC91     0 *
------------------------------------------------------------------------------
```

Table 4-13 Schedule Summary

	DECEMBER													
	18	19	20	21	22	23	24	25	26	27	28	29	30	31
CASE 1	A	A	A	A	–	A	?	–	B	B	–	–	B	
CASE 2	A	A	A	A	–	A	B	–	B	B				
CASE 3	A	A	A	–	–	A	–	–	A	B	–	–	B	B
CASE 4	A	A	A	–	–	A	–	–	A	B	B	–	B	

float in this case. And in more complex situations than this, the days would very likely be different. Once out of synchronization, the two schedules would probably continue to vary and to play "calendar catchup."

Combining all four cases, we would have what is illustrated in Table 4-12.

Table 4-13 illustrates the four cases in a different format (non-work days are denoted by a dash).

Table 4-13 shows how the four cases start out the same, but vary greatly after December 20. Several other observations may be made:

• Depending on which calendar combination is selected, these two activities may finish:
As early as December 27 (both activities assigned to Calendar 1)
As late as December 31 (both assigned to Calendar 2)

• Regardless of which calendar combination is selected:
Only *A* will be performed on 4 days
(December 18, 19, 20, and 23)
Only *B* will be performed December 27
No work will be performed December 22 or 25
Other days represent a mixture of:
A and *B*
A and holiday
B and holiday/??? (status unknown)
B and ???
Holiday and ???

START-TO-START RELATIONSHIPS

Single Calendar

None of the scheduling benefits described in the balance of this chapter is available to the less capable ADM and AON formats.

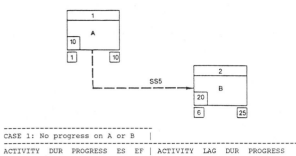

```
-----------------------------------------------
CASE 1: No progress on A or B   |
-----------------------------------------------
ACTIVITY DUR PROGRESS ES EF | ACTIVITY LAG DUR PROGRESS  ES EF
-----------------------------------------------
   A    10  NONE    1  10 |    B     SS5 20  NONE      6  25
-----------------------------------------------
```

FIGURE 4-18.   Network setup diagram.

In *Start-to-Start (SS)* relationships, the current activity and its successor activity must either start:

- At the same time, with one activity prompting the other
- At different times if successor start must lag behind the start of the current activity by a specified amount of time not to exceed 9,999 days in *Primavera*.

Start-to-Start relationships improve network efficiency by allowing related activities to operate mainly in parallel rather than sequentially. They are also a convenient way to mark important interface points among resources.

When assigning a Start-to-Start relationship to the current activity, do not forget to assign the proper relationship to its finish. A Start-to-Start relationship deals only with current activity start, never its end. Its finish must also be properly related to other successors. If it is not, it becomes an unintentional dangling activity.

There are, again, four general cases to consider. Assume a seven-day workweek for simplicity. Whenever two activities have a Start-to-Start relationship that includes lag, the start of a successor activity is based on the "effective duration" of the predecessor activity—that is, when the lag effects:

- Have been broken
- No longer constrain the successor

In a Start-to-Start relationship, a predecessor activity's "effective duration" is:

- Often simply the lag
- Assigned to workdays in its own calendar in a multiple-calendar project

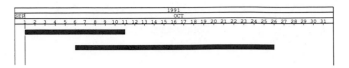

FIGURE 4-19.   Gantt Chart.

In the case presented in Fig. 4-18 and Table 4-14, *B* can (and should) start five days after *A* does; its Early Start is therefore October 6. It cannot start before then and should not start after.

An example: allowing concrete to dry for five days after pouring before placing a house frame over it. Have you ever noticed workers pouring concrete late on a Friday night? This is to take advantage of weekend drying. Pouring on Friday night allows framing to begin the following Thursday, whereas waiting until Monday would not allow framing to begin until at least the following Saturday, if not the following Monday. Heads-up scheduling in this case gained two to four days (assuming a five-day workweek).

For the next five days after that, work may be done on both *A* and *B* until *A* completes October 10. Another fifteen days of work are left on *B* at this point. The five days that both *A* and *B* worked concurrently reduces *B*'s Early Finish by the same amount—to October 25 (= 30 − 5).

This could not be properly handled by a conventional Finish-to-Start relationship. Although F/S lags are possible, they can only extend, but never compress, a schedule. If the five-day overlap could not be recognized, this situation would be handled like the F/S Case 1 just seen. It would indicate that thirty, not twenty-five, days were necessary. And if *A* and *B* were placed on two separate and unrelated paths, network logic would be violated. Both attempts to work around this problem are unacceptable. The second, "brute-force" logic change, is the more serious.

Figure 4-19 is in bar chart format.

Multiple Calendars

Shown in Fig. 4-20 are two activities, assigned to different calendars, with a Start-to-Start relationship and a lag of five days. The effective duration of *A* is five days, even though its actual duration is ten.

Figure 4-21 is in bar chart format.

If *A* starts December 18 under Calendar 1, it will lose its five-day lag effect late December 23, even though Early

Table 4-14   Schedule Summary

```
----------------------------------------------------------------------------
SCHEDULE SUMMARY                                    DATE: _____

PROJECT NAME:  START-TO-START RELATIONSHIP CASE 1_____
----------------------------------------------------------------------------
```

ACTIVITY ID		ORIG DUR	REM DUR	% DONE	EARLY START	EARLY FINISH	LATE START	LATE FINISH	TOTAL FLOAT	
A	*	10	10	0	1OCT91	10OCT91	1OCT91	10OCT91	0	*
B	*	20	20	0	6OCT91	25OCT91	6OCT91	25OCT91	0	*

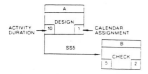

FIGURE 4-20.   Network setup diagram.

```
------------------------------------------------------------
CASE 1A: No progress on A or B; 1 trail between | LAG = SS5 ( Cal 1) |
------------------------------------------------------------
ACT  DUR  CAL  PROG   ES       EF | ACT  DUR  CAL  PROG   ES       EF
------------------------------------------------------------
A    10    1   NONE  12/18  12/30 | B    5     2   NONE  12/26   1/2
------------------------------------------------------------
```

FIGURE 4-21.   Gantt Chart.

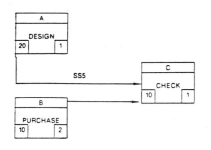

```
------------------------------------------------------------
CASE 1B: No progress on A or B; 2 trails to C | LAG = SS5 (Calendar 1)|
------------------------------------------------------------
ACT  DUR  CAL  PROG   ES       EF | ACT  DUR  CAL  PROG   ES       EF
------------------------------------------------------------
A    20    1   NONE  12/18   1/11 | B    10    2   NONE  12/18   1/3
C    10    1   NONE   1/4   1/15  |
------------------------------------------------------------
```

FIGURE 4-22.   Network setup diagram.

Finish is not until December 30. Note that lag in a Start-to-Start relationship always applies to the predecessor's calendar, as would be expected. In this case, the five days' lag is computed according to Calendar 1 workdays because *A* follows Calendar 1. Activity *B*, as a result, could begin December 24; but its calendar does not schedule work until December 26. This becomes *B*'s Early Start. Five (Calendar 2) workdays later, *B* completes on January 2. Because of the December 24 situation, *A* contains one day float and *B* contains none (Table 4-15).

Let us now look at a little more complex case, one in which a Calendar 1 activity with a Start-to-Start relationship is joined at its successor by a Calendar 2 activity with only a conventional Finish-to-Start relationships (Fig. 4-22 and Table 4-16). What would be the results?

Figure 4-23 is in bar chart format.

In the network segment in Fig. 4-22, both *A* and *B* precede *C*. Although *A* has a longer duration (twenty workdays), its effective duration on *C* is only five days. That is, the five-day SS5 constraint (measured under Calendar 1) no longer affects *C* after December 23. On the other hand, even though the duration of *B* (Calendar 2) is only ten days, all ten of these days continue to affect when *C* may begin. Since the net time trail through *B* is longer than it is through *A* (ten days compared with five), *C*'s Early Start is governed by *B*—not, as you might have guessed, by *A*. Activity *B* is a driving predecessor of *C*. If *A* follows the Early Start schedule:

- Both *A* and *B* can begin December 18
- Activity *B* is critical; *A* contains three days float
- The SS5 lag is broken December 23 and no longer constrains *C*

Table 4-15   Schedule Summary

```
------------------------------------------------------------------------------
SCHEDULE SUMMARY                                      DATE: _____
------------------------------------------------------------------------------
PROJECT NAME:  TWO-CALENDAR 6/5 DAY WORKWEEK PROJECT W/ SS5 RELATIONSHIP____
------------------------------------------------------------------------------
```

ACTIVITY ID/CAL		ORIG DUR	REM DUR	% DONE	EARLY START	EARLY FINISH	LATE START	LATE FINISH	TOTAL FLOAT	
A	1	10	10	0	18DEC91	30DEC91	19DEC91	31DEC91	1	
B	2 *	5	5	0	26DEC91	2JAN92	26DEC91	2JAN92	0	*

Table 4-16   Schedule Summary

```
------------------------------------------------------------------------------
SCHEDULE SUMMARY                                      DATE: _____
------------------------------------------------------------------------------
PROJECT NAME:  2-CALENDAR 6/5 DAY WORKWEEK PROJECT W/ FS & SS5 RELATIONSHIP_
------------------------------------------------------------------------------
```

ACTIVITY ID/CAL		ORIG DUR	REM DUR	% DONE	EARLY START	EARLY FINISH	LATE START	LATE FINISH	TOTAL FLOAT	
A	1	20	20	0	18DEC91	11JAN92	21DEC91	15JAN92	3	
B	2 *	10	10	0	18DEC91	3JAN92	18DEC91	3JAN92	0	*
C	1 *	10	10	0	4JAN92	15JAN92	4JAN92	15JAN92	0	*

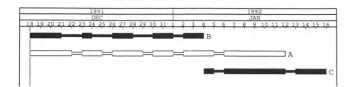

FIGURE 4-23.   Gantt Chart.

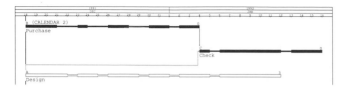

FIGURE 4-24.   Time-logic plot.

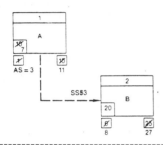

```
-----------------------------------------------------------------
CASE 2A: Progress on A, none on B.  Assume actual start date AS (for A)
         to be day 3 and reporting date to be day 5.  (DD - AS) < lag.
-----------------------------------------------------------------
ACTIVITY DUR PROGRESS ES EF | ACTIVITY LAG  DUR PROGRESS   ES EF
-----------------------------------------------------------------
   A     10     3      1 10 |    B      SS5  20  NONE        6 25
```

FIGURE 4-25.   Network setup diagram.

FIGURE 4-26.   Gantt Chart.

- Activity *B* is a driving predecessor of *C*
- Activity *B* finishes January 3 under Calendar 2
- Activity *C* begins the next day under Calendar 1 and finishes January 15
- Activity *A* finishes January 11, concurrently with progress on *C*

If *A* follows the Late Start schedule:

- The lag is not broken until December 27
- Both *A* and *C* finish January 15

The time-logic plot is presented in Fig. 4-24. Since schedule computations always invoke the longest time trail, they use the:

- Latest Early Start and Early Finish dates in the forward pass
- Earliest Late Start and Late Finish dates in the backward pass

Although the examples just discussed are activities in a daily multiple-calendar project, the methodology is equally valid for any type of multiple-calendar project. The time unit used for scheduling depends on the project requirements. It could be hourly, daily, weekly, monthly, or otherwise. But computations are greatly simplified if time units are the same. For most projects, daily is entirely sufficient.

Now suppose (Figure 4-25 and Table 4-17) that *A* has started, but *B* has not.

Figure 4-26 is in bar chart format.

In Start-to-Start relationships with lag, there are three values of interest:

- Original lag value (always measured by predecessor calendar)
- Data date (time as of which measurement is taken)
- Actual start (of predecessor)

Of these, only the data date will vary. The original lag value and actual start remain constant. These three values determine the remaining lag by the following equation:

Remaining lag =
$$\text{(Original lag} - \text{(Data date} - \text{Actual start date))}.$$

Table 4-17   Schedule Summary

```
-----------------------------------------------------------------------------
SCHEDULE SUMMARY                                    DATE: _____

PROJECT NAME:  START-TO-START RELATIONSHIP CASE 2A_____
-----------------------------------------------------------------------------
```

ACTIVITY ID		ORIG DUR	REM DUR	% DONE	EARLY START	EARLY FINISH	LATE START	LATE FINISH	TOTAL FLOAT	
A	*	10	7	30	3OCT91A	11OCT91		11OCT91	0	*
B	*	20	20	0	8OCT91	27OCT91	8OCT91	27OCT91	0	*

When (Data date − Actual start date) equals original lag, the lag effects are broken and no longer constrain the successor. This will happen on October 8 because 5 = (8 − 3).

In the above example:

- Original lag = 5
- Data date = 5
- Actual start = 3

Primavera first subtracts the Actual Start date from the data date. It then subtracts this value from the original lag to determine the remaining lag:

Remaining lag =
  (Original lag − (Data date − Actual start date))

  = (5 − (5 − 3))

  = 3 days

This remaining three-day lag is now measured from the data date—not Early or Actual Start—during schedule calculations. Therefore, the revised Early Start of *B* is calculated by adding the three remaining lag days to the data date:

Early Start of *B* = Remaining lag + Data date

  = 3 + 5

  = 8, as calculated above

As viewed on October 5, *B* will begin three days later, on October 8. Again, note well the following: You do *not* add the remaining lag value (3) directly to the original Early Start of *B* (6) for a value of 9. [Although *A* did not start until October 3, it recorded three days progress in the two days since and is one day ahead of expected pace, even though two days behind baseline target; if this (what you do *not* do) were done, this one day recovered progress would be lost on *B*.] The remaining lag value (3) is instead added only to the data date (5). The revised Early Start of *B* is, therefore, October 8. Regardless of how fast *A* progresses, five days must separate the start of *B* from the start of *A*. The duration of *B* remains 20 days, unaffected by progress

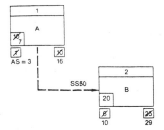

```
----------------------------------------------------------
CASE 2B: Progress on A, none on B.  Assume actual start date AS (for A)
         to be day 3 and reporting date to be day 10.  (DD - AS) > lag.
----------------------------------------------------------
ACTIVITY  DUR  PROGRESS  ES  EF | ACTIVITY  LAG  DUR  PROGRESS  ES  EF
----------------------------------------------------------
   A      10      3       1  10 |    B      SS5   20   NONE      6  25
----------------------------------------------------------
```

FIGURE 4-27.   Network setup diagram.

on *A* or the change in lag. *B* will finish the same two days (= 8 − 6) later as it started, or day 27 (= 25 + 2).

Now suppose *A* has started, *B* has not, and consider the additional details presented in Fig. 4-27 and Table 4-18.

Figure 4-28 is in bar chart format.

The remaining lag is again determined by the following equation:

Remaining lag =
  (Original lag − (Data date − Actual start date)).

When (Data date − Actual start date) equals original lag (in this case 5) the lag effects are broken and no longer constrain the successor. This will happen on October 8 because 5 = (8 − 3).

In the above example:

- Original lag = 5
- Data date = 10
- Actual start = 3

Primavera first subtracts the Actual Start date from the data date. It then subtracts this value from the original lag to determine the remaining lag:

Remaining lag =
  (Original lag − (Data date − Actual start date))

  = (5 − (10 − 3))

  = −2 days

Table 4-18 Schedule Summary

```
----------------------------------------------------------------------
SCHEDULE SUMMARY                              DATE: _____

PROJECT NAME:  START-TO-START RELATIONSHIP CASE 2B_____
----------------------------------------------------------------------
```

ACTIVITY ID	ORIG DUR	REM DUR	% DONE	EARLY START	EARLY FINISH	LATE START	LATE FINISH	TOTAL FLOAT
A *	10	7	30	3OCT91A	16OCT91		16OCT91	0 *
B *	20	20	0	10OCT91	29OCT91	10OCT91	29OCT91	0 *

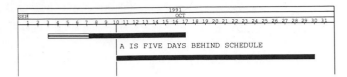

FIGURE 4-28.   Gantt Chart.

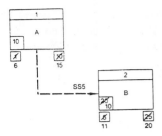

The negative value indicates that the lag expired two days before the data date, or October 8, as calculated earlier. But any lag value of zero or less is considered to be zero and have no further effect. When the lag expires:

• It loses all effect on *B*
• *A* and *B* may occur concurrently

This remaining lag value of 0 (*not* − 2) days is again measured from the data date—not the Early Start of *B* or the Actual Start of *A*—during schedule calculations. Therefore, the revised Early Start of *B* is calculated by adding the 0 remaining lag days to the data date:

Early Start of B = Remaining lag + Data date

$$= 0 + 10$$

$$= 10, \text{ as calculated above}$$

Beginning on October 8, when the lag effect disappears, the Early Start of *B* will be the data date. If the data date is October 10, *B* could also start then. In fact, *B* must start as soon as possible because it is already four days behind—two days because *A* started two days late (= 3 − 1) and two more days because *A* has made below-normal progress since.

As before, do *not* add the remaining lag value (0) directly to the original Early Start of *B* (6) for a value of 6. The remaining lag value (0) is instead added only to the data date (10) as we just did. The revised Early Start of *B* is, therefore, October 10. The duration of *B* remains twenty days, unaffected by progress on *A* or the elimination of lag. *B* will finish twenty days later, at the conclusion of October 29.

Now suppose (Fig. 4-29 and Table 4-19) that *B* has started, but *A* has not.

```
CASE 3:  Progress on B, none on A.   Assume reporting date to be day 6.
ACTIVITY  DUR  PROGRESS  ES  EF | ACTIVITY  LAG  DUR  PROGRESS     ES  EF
   A       10   NONE      1  10 |    B      SS5   20    10          6  25
```

FIGURE 4-29.   Network setup diagram.

FIGURE 4-30.   Gantt Chart.

Figure 4-30 is in bar chart format.

Activity *B* has made out-of-sequence progress. This topic will be discussed more fully at the end of this chapter. If *B* is really an SS successor to *A* and not a parallel activity, the five-day lag must continue to hold until *A* makes some progress. If further progress is made on *B* but not on *A*, there may come a point at which work on *B* must stop for as many as five days, until work finally begins on *A*. This, for example, includes allowing concrete to dry for five days before placing wall units on it. Even if all work on *B* were to finish before *A* is completed, it would not be considered complete without *A* finishing, too. More on this later.

It is now October 6 and not a lick o' work has been done on *A*. Under current conditions, the Early Start of *A* is now October 6. If work does not commence on *A*, it will continue to slide right—that is, be delayed. This means that the SS5 lag must now be measured from this (data) date, October 6, not from the originally-scheduled ES (October 1). Therefore, the Early Start of *B* is revised to October 11 by adding this lag (5) to the data date (6). Regardless of when *B*

Table 4-19   Schedule Summary

```
SCHEDULE SUMMARY                              DATE: _____

PROJECT NAME:  START-TO-START RELATIONSHIP CASE 3_____
```

ACTIVITY ID		ORIG DUR	REM DUR	% DONE	EARLY START	EARLY FINISH	LATE START	LATE FINISH	TOTAL FLOAT	
A	*	10	10	0	6OCT91	15OCT91	6OCT91	15OCT91	0	*
B	*	20	10	50	11OCT91	20OCT91	11OCT91	20OCT91	0	*

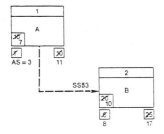

FIGURE 4-31.   Network setup diagram.

```
----------------------------------------------------------------
CASE 4:  Progress on both A and B.  Assume actual start date AS (for A)
         to be day 3 and reporting date to be day 5.  (DD - AS) < lag.
----------------------------------------------------------------
ACTIVITY DUR PROGRESS ES EF | ACTIVITY LAG DUR PROGRESS  ES EF
----------------------------------------------------------------
   A     10     3     1 10  |    B     SS5 20    10       6 25
----------------------------------------------------------------
```

FIGURE 4-32.   Gantt Chart.

actually started (not necessarily October 1), ten days progress have been made. In summary:

Early Start of B = Original lag + Data date

= 5 + 6

= 11, as calculated above

Again, note that you do *not* add the lag value (5) directly to the Early Start of B, even though in this situation lack of progress on A equated the data date to the original Early Start of B. The duration of B remains 20 days. Since ten days' progress has been recognized (after October 8), B will complete October 20, as we would expect. When will A complete? That, of course, depends on when it starts. If A begins on October 6, it will complete on October 15.

Finally, suppose (Fig. 4-31 and Table 4-20) that A and B have both started.

Figure 4-32 is in bar chart format.

This case is a combination of cases 2 and 3. When (Data date − Actual start date) equals the original lag, in this case 5, the lag effects are broken and no longer constrain the successor. This will happen on October 8 because 5 = (8 − 3).

In this example:

- Original lag = 5
- Data date = 5
- Actual start = 3

Primavera first subtracts the Actual Start date from the Data date. It then subtracts this value from the original lag to determine the remaining lag:

Remaining lag =

(Original lag − (Data date − Actual start date))

= (5 − (5 − 3))

= 3 days

This remaining three-day lag is now measured from the Data date—not from the Early or Actual Start—during schedule calculations. Therefore, the revised Early Start of B is calculated by adding the three remaining lag days to the data date:

Early Start of B = Remaining lag + Data date

= 3 + 5

= 8, as calculated above

As viewed on October 5, B will officially begin three days later, on October 8. Again, note the following: You do *not* add the remaining lag value (3) directly to the original Early Start of B (6) for a value of 9. (Although A did not start until October 3, it has recorded three days progress in the two days since and is one day ahead of expected pace, although it is two days behind baseline target; if this (what you do *not* do) were done, this one day recovered progress would be lost on B.) The remaining lag value (3) is instead added only to the data date (5); the revised Early Start of B is, therefore, October 8. Five days must separate the start of B from the start of A. The duration of B remains twenty days, unaffected by progress on A or the change in lag. Although the official Early Start of B was moved right two days by A, it will recognize its out-of-sequence progress

Table 4-20   Schedule Summary

```
------------------------------------------------------------------------------
SCHEDULE SUMMARY                                  DATE: _____

PROJECT NAME:  START-TO-START RELATIONSHIP CASE 4_____
------------------------------------------------------------------------------
```

ACTIVITY ID		ORIG DUR	REM DUR	% DONE	EARLY START	EARLY FINISH	LATE START	LATE FINISH	TOTAL FLOAT	
A	*	10	7	30	3OCT91A	11OCT91		11OCT91	0	*
B	*	20	10	50	8OCT91	17OCT91	8OCT91	17OCT91	0	*

```
-----------------------------------------------------------------
CASE 1A: No progress on A or B.  (Duration of A + lag) > duration of B.
-----------------------------------------------------------------
ACTIVITY  DUR  PROGRESS  ES  EF | ACTIVITY  LAG  DUR  PROGRESS  ES  EF
-----------------------------------------------------------------
    A      20   NONE     1   20 |    B      FF5   10   NONE     16  25
-----------------------------------------------------------------
```

FIGURE 4-33.   Network setup diagram.

after October 8, when the lag effect is broken, and finish ten days later, on October 17. Activity *A*, meanwhile, will continue to recognize the day it gained and will complete in nine days, on October 11.

FINISH-TO-FINISH RELATIONSHIPS

Single Calendar

In *Finish-to-Finish* (*FF*) relationships, the current activity and its successor activity must either finish:

- At the same time, with one activity prompting the other, or
- At different times if successor finish must lag behind the finish of the current activity by a specified amount of time not to exceed 9,999 days in *Primavera*.

Finish-to-Finish relationships are great for wrap-up activities. They tie related activities together by finish times and improve network efficiency for the same reason that Start-to-Start does—that is, enabling activities to work in parallel rather than in series.

There are once again four general cases to consider. Assume a seven-day workweek for simplicity. Whenever two activities have a Finish-to-Finish relationship that incudes lag, successor finish (and, therefore, start) is based on predecessor "effective duration"—that is, when the lag effects:

- Have been broken
- No longer constrain the successor

FIGURE 4-34.   Gantt Chart.

In a Finish-to-Finish relationship, predecessor "effective duration" is:

- Often simply the lag
- Assigned to workdays in the predecessor's calendar in a multiple-calendar project

But first we shall look at the single-calendar case (Fig. 4-33 and Table 4-21).

Figure 4-34 is in bar chart format.

With Start-to-Start relationships, we concerned ourselves with three values: original lag value, data date, and Actual Start. With Finish-to-Finish relationships, we concern ourselves with these:

- Original lag value (always measured by predecessor calendar)
- Data date (time at which measurement is taken)
- Predecessor Early Finish

The Finish-to-Finish lag value *applies* so long as:

(Early Finish of *A* − Data date + Original lag value)
$$> \text{Duration of } B$$

The Finish-to-Finish lag value *is disregarded* when:

(Early Finish of *A* − Data date + Original lag value)
$$< \text{Duration of } B$$

In the preceding example:

- Original lag = 5
- Data date = 1
- Early Finish = 20

Table 4-21   Schedule Summary

```
-----------------------------------------------------------------
SCHEDULE SUMMARY                                    DATE: _____

PROJECT NAME:  FINISH-TO-FINISH RELATIONSHIP CASE 1A_____
-----------------------------------------------------------------
```

ACTIVITY ID		ORIG DUR	REM DUR	% DONE	EARLY START	EARLY FINISH	LATE START	LATE FINISH	TOTAL FLOAT	
A	*	20	20	0	1OCT91	20OCT91	1OCT91	20OCT91	0	*
B	*	10	10	0	16OCT91	25OCT91	16OCT91	25OCT91	0	*

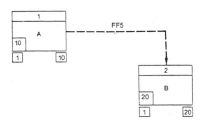

FIGURE 4-36.   Gantt Chart.

```
-----------------------------------------------------------------
CASE 1B: No progress on A or B; (Duration of A + lag) < duration of B.
-----------------------------------------------------------------
ACTIVITY  DUR  PROGRESS  ES  EF | ACTIVITY  LAG  DUR  PROGRESS  ES  EF
-----------------------------------------------------------------
   A      10    NONE      1  10 |    B      FF5   20   NONE       1  20
-----------------------------------------------------------------
```

FIGURE 4-35.   Network setup diagram.

Primavera first subtracts the data date from the Early Finish of A. It then adds this value to the original lag to compare with duration of B:

(Early Finish of A − Data date + Original lag value)

$$= (20 - 1 + 5)$$

$$= 24 \text{ days.}$$

Since this value (24) is greater than B duration (10), the FF5 lag holds.

The entire five days' lag is applied to the Early Finish of A (October 20) to determine the Early Finish of B (October 25). All ten days of B's duration is subtracted from then to find the Early Start of B (October 16).

This also could not be properly handled by a conventional Finish-to-Start relationship. As we saw earlier, F/S lags can only extend and not compress a schedule. If the five-day lag could not be recognized, this situation would be handled like the F/S Case 1 seen earlier (Fig. 4-5). It would indicate thirty, not twenty-five, days to be necessary. And if A and B were placed on two separate and unrelated paths, network logic would be violated. Both attempts to work around this problem are just as unacceptable here as they were in the Start-to-Start cases. As before, the second, "brute-force" logic change, is the more serious.

When will the FF5 lag lose its effect? October 15? If we solved the inequality for DD, we would certainly think so.

But a moving data date creates a moving target in A's Early Start. If the data date were October 15:

- Early Start of A would also be October 15
- Early Finish of A would be November 3
- The five-day lag would still apply in full
- Early Finish of B would be November 8 (five days after A)
- Early Start of B would be October 30

The FF5 lag will never lose its effect in this case. Now suppose the events in Fig. 4-35 and Table 4-22. Figure 4-36 is in bar chart format. Now assume:

- No progress has occurred on A or B
- The data date is October 1

The FF5 lag is not invoked because the trail through B indicates a later completion date, October 20, than would occur if these five days were added to the Early Finish of A, which would indicate an October 15 (= 10 + 5) finish for B. But B requires 20 days, until October 20, to complete. Lag or not, it cannot finish as early as October 15. Therefore, the lag value is ignored. This is true in all cases where the time difference between the Early Finish of A and the project data date, plus the original lag value, is less than the duration of B. At these times, the lag value has not taken effect and has no impact on B.

More formally, the Finish-to-Finish lag value is disregarded when:

(Early Finish of A − Data date + Original lag value)
< Duration of B.

In the example problem:

(Early Finish of A − Data date + Original lag value)

$$= (10 - 1 + 5)$$

$$= 14 \text{ days.}$$

Table 4-22   Schedule Summary

```
-----------------------------------------------------------------
SCHEDULE SUMMARY                                    DATE: _____
-----------------------------------------------------------------
PROJECT NAME:  FINISH-TO-FINISH RELATIONSHIP CASE 1B_____
-----------------------------------------------------------------
```

ACTIVITY ID		ORIG DUR	REM DUR	% DONE	EARLY START	EARLY FINISH	LATE START	LATE FINISH	TOTAL FLOAT
A		10	10	0	1OCT91	10OCT91	6OCT91	15OCT91	5
B	*	20	20	0	1OCT91	20OCT91	1OCT91	20OCT91	0 *

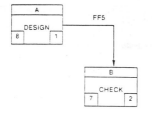

```
-----------------------------------------------------------------
CASE 1: No progress on A or B    | LAG = FF5 (Calendar 1) |
-----------------------------------------------------------------
ACT  DUR  CAL  PROG   ES      EF | ACT  DUR  CAL  PROG   ES     EF
-----------------------------------------------------------------
A     8    1   NONE  12/18  12/27 | B    7    2   NONE  12/23   1/3
-----------------------------------------------------------------
```

FIGURE 4-37.   Network setup diagram.

Since this is less than the duration of *B*, or twenty, the lag value does not apply. In fact, it cannot ever apply to these two activities because the equation above, when solved for the data date, has a meaningless solution of −5 days. Relative to the Early Finish of *A* and the lag value, *B*'s duration is simply too great.

If *A* followed the Late Start schedule, it would begin October 6 and finish October 15, five days before the Early (or Late) Finish of *B* on October 20. Strange coincidence? Not at all. In this case, *B* would drive *A*, not the other way around. The five days would be subtracted from the Early (or Late) Finish to find the Late Finish of *A* and, from this, its Late Start.

In summary, for these two activities:

• The lag value never affects *B*
• The lag value determines the Late Start schedule for *A*
• *A* and *B* may occur concurrently

Multiple Calendars

The multiple-calendar Finish-to-Finish situation is somewhat more difficult to understand than the corresponding Start-to-Start. Let us see why (Fig. 4-37 and Table 4-23).

Figure 4-38 is in bar chart format.

FIGURE 4-38.   Gantt Chart.

Table 4-23   Schedule Summary

```
-----------------------------------------------------------------
SCHEDULE SUMMARY                              DATE: _____
```

PROJECT NAME: TWO-CALENDAR 6/5 DAY WORKWEEK PROJECT W/ FF5 RELATIONSHIP____

ACTIVITY ID/CAL	ORIG DUR	REM DUR	% DONE	EARLY START	EARLY FINISH	LATE START	LATE FINISH	TOTAL FLOAT
A 1 *	8	8	0	18DEC91	27DEC91	18DEC91	27DEC91	0 *
B 2 *	7	7	0	23DEC91	3JAN92	23DEC91	3JAN92	0 *

If *A* begins on December 18, its effective duration is equal to:

Duration of *A* under Calendar 1 (8)	December 27 (*A* finish)
+ Finish-to-Finish lag under Calendar 1 (5)	January 3 (*B* finish)
− Duration of *B* under Calendar 2 (7)	December 23 (*B* start).

The effective Early Finish of *A* is therefore December 22.

In this relationship, unlike the others we have studied, predecessor effective duration can be negative. This will cause (or at least allow) a successor to start before its predecessor. Confused? The confusion goes away if we remember that FF activities are related by time of finish, not necessarily by time of start.

When two activities with this relationship are assigned to different calendars:

• Lag and predecessor duration are assigned to the predecessor's calendar
• Successor duration is always assigned to its own calendar

When the finish of a predecessor activity occurs just before a successor nonworkday, the successor activity's start is pushed one day at a time until the next available workday is found and the activity scheduled.

Now suppose the following (Fig. 4-39 and Table 4-24). Figure 4-40 is in bar chart format.

Cases 2A and 2B are similar to 1A and 1B except now the revised duration of *A* is used instead of its original. The remaining duration of *A* determines which of the two no-progress cases applies. In the situation described above, *A:*

• Began October 1
• Has recorded three days progress as of the October 3 data date
• Is one day ahead of schedule

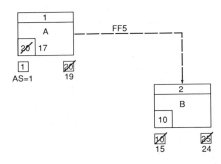

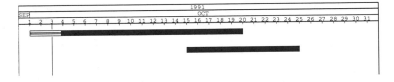

```
CASE 2A: Progress on A only.  Remaining DUR(A) + lag > duration of B.
--------------------------------------------------------------------
ACTIVITY  DUR  PROGRESS  ES  EF | ACTIVITY  LAG  DUR  PROGRESS  ES  EF
--------------------------------------------------------------------
   A      20      3      1   20 |    B      FF5   10   NONE      16  25
```

FIGURE 4-39. Network setup diagram.

FIGURE 4-40. Gantt Chart.

Table 4-24 Schedule Summary

```
---------------------------------------------------------------------------
SCHEDULE SUMMARY                                    DATE: _____

PROJECT NAME:  FINISH-TO-FINISH RELATIONSHIP CASE 2A_____
---------------------------------------------------------------------------
```

ACTIVITY ID	ORIG DUR	REM DUR	% DONE	EARLY START	EARLY FINISH	LATE START	LATE FINISH	TOTAL FLOAT
A *	20	17	15	1OCT91A	19OCT91		19OCT91	0 *
B *	10	10	0	15OCT91	24OCT91	15OCT91	24OCT91	0 *

The remaining duration of *A*, therefore, is:

Remaining duration = Original duration

− Progress to date

= 20 − 3

= 17 days.

To determine which Case 2 version applies, we need to add this value (17) and the original lag value (5), then compare this sum with the duration of *B*:

Compare: (Remaining DUR(*A*) + Original lag value) with DUR(*B*) = (17 + 5) = 22 days; DUR (*B*) = 10 days.

Case 2A properly handles this situation. The five-day lag still applies; *B* will finish on October 24, five days after *A*.

Now suppose the opposite (Fig. 4-41 and Table 4-25):

Figure 4-42 is in bar chart format.

The first order of business is to compare (Remaining DUR(*A*) + lag) with the duration of *B*. When we do, we find: (Remaining DUR(*A*) + Original lag value) = (7 + 5) = 12 days, and the duration of *B* to be more, or twenty days. Case 2*B* properly handles this situation. The five-day lag value never applies (except in reverse under the improbable Late Finish schedule). Activity *B* will finish at

least five days after *A*, very likely unaffected by the five-day lag. But it is already late and had better get started.

Now suppose (Fig. 4-43 and Table 4-26) that *B* has started, but *A* has not.

Figure 4-44 is in bar chart format.

As shown in Fig. 4-43 and Table 4-26), *B* has made out-of-sequence progress. The five-day lag always applies until *A* makes progress. This explains why the Early Finish of *B*

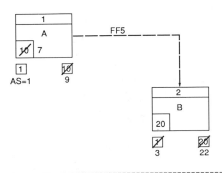

```
CASE 2B: Progress on A only.  Remaining DUR(A) + lag < duration of B.
--------------------------------------------------------------------
ACTIVITY  DUR  PROGRESS  ES  EF | ACTIVITY  LAG  DUR  PROGRESS  ES  EF
--------------------------------------------------------------------
   A      10      3      1   10 |    B      FF5   20   NONE      1   20
```

FIGURE 4-41. Network setup diagram.

Table 4-25   Schedule Summary

```
------------------------------------------------------------------------------
SCHEDULE SUMMARY                                        DATE: _____

PROJECT NAME:  FINISH-TO-FINISH RELATIONSHIP CASE 2B_____
------------------------------------------------------------------------------
ACTIVITY    ORIG   REM    %     EARLY     EARLY     LATE     LATE      TOTAL
   ID       DUR    DUR   DONE   START     FINISH    START    FINISH    FLOAT
--------    ----   ---   ----   -------   -------   -------  -------   -----
   A         10     7     30    1OCT91A   9OCT91             17OCT91     8
   B   *     20     20    0     3OCT91    22OCT91   3OCT91   22OCT91     0  *
------------------------------------------------------------------------------
```

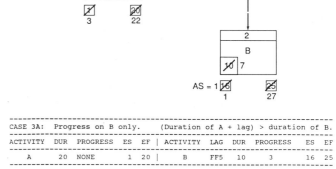

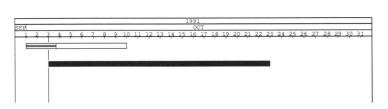

FIGURE 4-42.   Gantt Chart.

```
------------------------------------------------------------------------
CASE 3A:  Progress on B only.    (Duration of A + lag) > duration of B.
------------------------------------------------------------------------
ACTIVITY  DUR  PROGRESS  ES  EF | ACTIVITY  LAG  DUR  PROGRESS   ES  EF
   A       20    NONE     1  20 |    B       FF5   10     3       16  25
------------------------------------------------------------------------
```

FIGURE 4-43.   Network setup diagram.

Table 4-26   Schedule Summary

```
------------------------------------------------------------------------------
SCHEDULE SUMMARY                                        DATE: _____

PROJECT NAME:  FINISH-TO-FINISH RELATIONSHIP CASE 3A_____
------------------------------------------------------------------------------
ACTIVITY    ORIG   REM    %     EARLY     EARLY     LATE     LATE      TOTAL
   ID       DUR    DUR   DONE   START     FINISH    START    FINISH    FLOAT
--------    ----   ---   ----   -------   -------   -------  -------   -----
   A   *     20     20    0     3OCT91    22OCT91   3OCT91   22OCT91     0  *
   B   *     10     7     30    1OCT91A   27OCT91            27OCT91     0  *
------------------------------------------------------------------------------
```

FIGURE 4-44.   Gantt Chart.

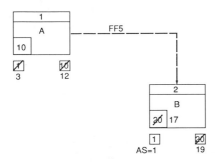

FIGURE 4-45.   Network setup diagram.

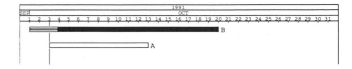

FIGURE 4-46.   Gantt Chart.

```
------------------------------------------------------------------------
CASE 3B:  Progress on B only.   (Duration of A + lag) < duration of B.
------------------------------------------------------------------------
ACTIVITY  DUR  PROGRESS  ES  EF | ACTIVITY  LAG  DUR  PROGRESS   ES  EF
------------------------------------------------------------------------
   A      10   NONE      1  10 |    B      FF5   20     3        1  20
------------------------------------------------------------------------
```

Table 4-27   Schedule Summary

```
---------------------------------------------------------------------------------
SCHEDULE SUMMARY                                    DATE: _____

PROJECT NAME:  FINISH-TO-FINISH RELATIONSHIP CASE 3B_____
---------------------------------------------------------------------------------
```

ACTIVITY ID	ORIG DUR	REM DUR	% DONE	EARLY START	EARLY FINISH	LATE START	LATE FINISH	TOTAL FLOAT
A	10	10	0	3OCT91	12OCT91	5OCT91	14OCT91	2
B *	20	17	15	1OCT91A	19OCT91		19OCT91	0 *

is so late: Although *B* has already started (October 1) and has only seven days duration remaining, it cannot officially (and perhaps technically) complete until five days after *A* finishes. Since *A* is not currently expected to finish until October 22 (assuming it begins on the October 3 data date), *B* cannot finish until October (22 + 5), or October 27. This is true with both the early and the late schedules.

Now suppose the opposite (Fig. 4-45 and Table 4-27).

Figure 4-46 is in bar chart format.

Activity *B* again has made out-of-sequence progress. The relationship between *A* and *B* is disregarded (except in reverse under the Late Finish schedule); both can occur independently of each other. This is because: (Remaining DUR(*A*) + Original lag value) = (10 + 5) = 15 days. The duration of *B* is more, or twenty days. But *A* is late and had better get started, especially since *B* is one day ahead of expected pace.

Finally, consider cases 4A and 4B, in which activity *A* is 100 percent complete. Please refer to Figures 4-47–4-50 and Tables 4-28–4-29.

The first order of business is to solve the inequality: [Original lag − (DD − Actual Finish of *A*)] ? DUR(*B*).

When we do, we find: [15 − (10 − 7)] > DUR(*B*) because 12 > 10.

These twelve days remaining lag:

- Still affect *B*
- Are measured, as usual, from the data date

Therefore, the Early Finish of *B* is found to be October 22: [Early Finish of *B* = Remaining lag + Data date] = 12 + 10 = 22, as calculated above.

Note as usual you do *not* add the remaining lag value (12) directly to the Actual Finish of *A* (7) to get October 19. It is only added to the data date as we just did. The duration of *B* remains ten days, unaffected by the completion of *A*. But *B* is now expected to finish three days earlier (since *A* did) and still meet the fifteen-day lag. This is because adding the original lag value (15) to the date *A* actually finished (7) gives October 22 as the revised Early Finish of *B*. The Early Start of *B* would, of course, be DUR(*B*) days earlier, or October 13. This is also three days earlier, and for the same reason.

The first order of business is once again to solve the inequality:

[Original lag − (DD − Actual Finish of *A*)] ? DUR(*B*).

When we do, we find: [5 − (10 − 7)] < DUR(*B*) because 2 < 10.

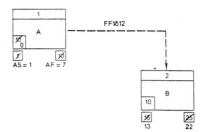

```
---------------------------------------------------------------------
CASE 4A:  A is 100% complete.  Assume A started October 1 and finished
          October 7.  Reporting date is October 10.  Furthermore:
          [Original lag - (DD - A Actual Finish)] > duration of B.
---------------------------------------------------------------------
ACTIVITY  DUR PROGRESS ES EF | ACTIVITY  LAG  DUR PROGRESS   ES  EF
---------------------------------------------------------------------
   A      10    10     1  10 |    B     FF15  10  NONE       16  25
---------------------------------------------------------------------
```

FIGURE 4-47.   Network setup diagram.

FIGURE 4-48.   Gantt Chart.

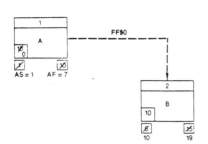

```
---------------------------------------------------------------------
CASE 4B:  A is 100% complete.  Assume A started October 1 and finished
          October 7.  Reporting date is October 10.  Furthermore:
          [Original lag - (DD - A Actual Finish)] < duration of B.
---------------------------------------------------------------------
ACTIVITY  DUR PROGRESS ES EF | ACTIVITY  LAG  DUR PROGRESS   ES  EF
---------------------------------------------------------------------
   A      10    10     1  10 |    B      FF5  10  NONE        6  15
---------------------------------------------------------------------
```

FIGURE 4-49.   Network setup diagram.

FIGURE 4-50.   Gantt Chart.

Table 4-28   Schedule Summary

```
-------------------------------------------------------------------------------
SCHEDULE SUMMARY                                          DATE: _____

PROJECT NAME:  FINISH-TO-FINISH RELATIONSHIP CASE 4A_____
-------------------------------------------------------------------------------
```

ACTIVITY ID	ORIG DUR	REM DUR	% DONE	EARLY START	EARLY FINISH	LATE START	LATE FINISH	TOTAL FLOAT
A	10	0	100	1OCT91A	7OCT91A			
B *	10	10	0	13OCT91	22OCT91	13OCT91	22OCT91	0 *

Table 4-29   Schedule Summary

```
-------------------------------------------------------------------------------
SCHEDULE SUMMARY                                          DATE: _____

PROJECT NAME:  FINISH-TO-FINISH RELATIONSHIP CASE 4B_____
-------------------------------------------------------------------------------
```

ACTIVITY ID	ORIG DUR	REM DUR	% DONE	EARLY START	EARLY FINISH	LATE START	LATE FINISH	TOTAL FLOAT
A	10	0	100	1OCT91A	7OCT91A			
B *	10	10	0	10OCT91	19OCT91	10OCT91	19OCT91	0 *

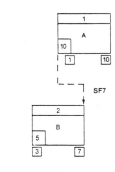

FIGURE 4-52.   Gantt Chart.

```
CASE 1: No progress on A or B  |
-------------------------------------------------------------------
ACTIVITY  DUR  PROGRESS  ES  EF  | ACTIVITY  LAG  DUR  PROGRESS  ES  EF
-------------------------------------------------------------------
   A      10    NONE     1   10  |    B      SF7   5    NONE      3   7
-------------------------------------------------------------------
```

FIGURE 4-51.   Network setup diagram.

The five-day lag will never apply, even in the late schedule. However, we cannot say that *A* and *B* can occur concurrently because *A* has already completed October 7 and *B* has not, as of October 10, even started.

START-TO-FINISH RELATIONSHIPS

Since the *Start-to-Finish* (*SF*) relationship can be better represented by the other three PDM relationships, it will not be as extensively discussed. In this type of relationship, a successor activity cannot complete until its predecessor starts. There may be a lag value (not to exceed 9,999 days in *Primavera*) associated with this relationship. A lag value means that the successor activity can finish *N* days after its predecessor starts. Sounds like a relay race in reverse! As a workaround (the actual result is to add complication to confusion!), negative lag values are often used. All this points out why:

- The SF relationship is the hardest to understand and explain
- It should be avoided unless absolutely necessary
- Other PDM relationships are preferable

There are once again four general cases to consider here. Assume a seven-day workweek for simplicity. Whenever two activities have a Start-to-Finish relationship that includes lag, a successor activity's finish is based on a predecessor activity's "effective duration"—that is, when the lag effects:

- Have been broken
- No longer constrain the successor

In a Start-to-Finish relationship, predecessor "effective duration" is:

- Often simply the lag
- Assigned to workdays in the predecessor's calendar in a multiple-calendar project

Case 1 (Fig. 4-51 and Table 4-30). Neither *A* nor *B* has started.

Figure 4-52 is in bar chart format.

Since *B* can finish seven days after *A* begins, it can complete on October 7 if *A* starts October 1. Activity *B* would then begin October 3. It may also complete as late as October 10 (Late Finish of *A*) without delaying the project or violating network logic. Late Start of Activity *B* is, therefore, October 6.

Case 2 consists of two parts. In each, *A* has started, *B* has not. (Figures 4-53–4-56 and Tables 4-31–4-32).

Assume that *A* began October 1 and the data date is October 4. The first order of business is once again to solve the inequality:

(Data date − Actual Start of *A*) ? Original lag

$$= (4 - 1) ? 7$$

$$= 3 < 7.$$

Therefore, the lag still applies. All of it? Not any more. The remaining lag, calculated as before, is equal to four (7 − (4 − 1)) days. This four-day value is measured as usual from the data date (October 4). Revised Early Finish of *B* is October (4 + 4), or October 8. Since the Late Finish of

Table 4-30   Schedule Summary

```
-------------------------------------------------------------------------------
SCHEDULE SUMMARY                                     DATE: _____

PROJECT NAME:   START-TO-FINISH RELATIONSHIP CASE 1_____
-------------------------------------------------------------------------------
```

ACTIVITY ID		ORIG DUR	REM DUR	% DONE	EARLY START	EARLY FINISH	LATE START	LATE FINISH	TOTAL FLOAT
A	*	10	10	0	1OCT91	10OCT91	1OCT91	10OCT91	0 *
B		5	5	0	3OCT91	7OCT91	6OCT91	10OCT91	3

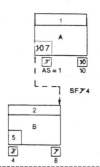

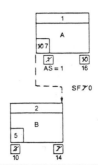

```
--------------------------------------------------------  --------------------------------------------------------
CASE 2A:  Progress on A only.  (Data date - A Actual Start) < orig lag.   CASE 2B:  Progress on A only.  (Data date - A Actual Start) > orig lag.
--------------------------------------------------------  --------------------------------------------------------
ACTIVITY  DUR  PROGRESS  ES  EF | ACTIVITY  LAG  DUR  PROGRESS   ES  EF    ACTIVITY  DUR  PROGRESS  ES  EF | ACTIVITY  LAG  DUR  PROGRESS   ES  EF
--------------------------------------------------------  --------------------------------------------------------
   A      10      3       1  10 |    B     SF7   5   NONE        3   7         A     10      3       1  10 |    B     SF7   5   NONE        3   7
--------------------------------------------------------  --------------------------------------------------------
```

FIGURE 4-53.   Network setup diagram.   **FIGURE 4-55.**   Network setup diagram.

FIGURE 4-54.   Gantt Chart.

Table 4-31   Schedule Summary

```
--------------------------------------------------------------------------------------------
```
SCHEDULE SUMMARY   DATE: _____

```
--------------------------------------------------------------------------------------------
```
PROJECT NAME: START-TO-FINISH RELATIONSHIP CASE 2A_____

```
--------------------------------------------------------------------------------------------
```

ACTIVITY ID	ORIG DUR	REM DUR	% DONE	EARLY START	EARLY FINISH	LATE START	LATE FINISH	TOTAL FLOAT
A *	10	7	30	1OCT91A	10OCT91		10OCT91	0 *
B	5	5	0	4OCT91	8OCT91	6OCT91	10OCT91	2

```
--------------------------------------------------------------------------------------------
```

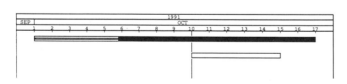

FIGURE 4-56.   Gantt Chart.

```
--------------------------------------------------------
CASE 3:  Progress on B, none on A.   Assume reporting date to be day 3.
--------------------------------------------------------
ACTIVITY  DUR  PROGRESS  ES  EF | ACTIVITY  LAG  DUR  PROGRESS   ES  EF
--------------------------------------------------------
   A      10    NONE      1  10 |    B     SF7   5     2         3   7
--------------------------------------------------------
```

FIGURE 4-57.   Network setup diagram.

Table 4-32   Schedule Summary

```
--------------------------------------------------------------------------------------------
```
SCHEDULE SUMMARY   DATE: _____

```
--------------------------------------------------------------------------------------------
```
PROJECT NAME: START-TO-FINISH RELATIONSHIP CASE 2B_____

```
--------------------------------------------------------------------------------------------
```

ACTIVITY ID	ORIG DUR	REM DUR	% DONE	EARLY START	EARLY FINISH	LATE START	LATE FINISH	TOTAL FLOAT
A *	10	7	30	1OCT91A	16OCT91		16OCT91	0 *
B	5	5	0	10OCT91	14OCT91	12OCT91	16OCT91	2

```
--------------------------------------------------------------------------------------------
```

Table 4-33   Schedule Summary

```
----------------------------------------------------------------------------
SCHEDULE SUMMARY                                    DATE: _____

PROJECT NAME:   START-TO-FINISH RELATIONSHIP CASE 3_____
----------------------------------------------------------------------------
```

ACTIVITY ID	ORIG DUR	REM DUR	% DONE	EARLY START	EARLY FINISH	LATE START	LATE FINISH	TOTAL FLOAT
A *	10	10	0	3OCT91	12OCT91	3OCT91	12OCT91	0 *
B	5	3	40	7OCT91	9OCT91	10OCT91	12OCT91	3

A and B is still two days later, the Late Start of B must again be October 6.

Now assume the data date to be October 10. The lag-effect inequality is solved as follows:

(Data date − Actual Start of A) ? Original lag

$$= (10 - 1) ? 7 =$$

$$9 > 7.$$

The lag no longer applies. It expired two days before, on October 8. When that happened, Early Start of B assumed data-date equality—October 10 under current conditions. Five days duration plus two days float means Late Finish of B is October 16. Since A cannot officially complete until B starts (even though the lag has expired, the SF relationship still holds), Late Finish of A is also October 16. This is true even if no more can be done on A itself. In the extreme case (again under current conditions), A could be done with all its work on October 10 and simply be waiting for B to begin until it, A, can report itself complete.

Case 3 considers progress on B, with none on A (Fig. 4-57 and Table 4-33.)

Figure 4-58 is in bar chart format.

Activity B has made out-of-sequence progress. The Start-to-Finish lag will continue to apply until A makes progress. If that occurs on October 3 (the current data date):

- Early Finish of B will be seven days later, or October 9
- Late Finish of A (and B) will be October 12

Case 4 (Fig. 4-59 and Table 4-34) considers progress on both A and B.

Figure 4-60 is in bar chart format.

The chart in Fig. 4-60 combines cases 2 and 3. *Primavera* subtracts from the lag value the elapsed time between Actual Start of A and the data date. The lag value expires when the difference between Actual Start of A and the data date is greater than this lag value. Then, the remaining duration of B is scheduled from the data date. Since A started October 21, Early Finish of B can be as soon as October 7. Late Finish for both activities is October 10 because A cannot complete any earlier.

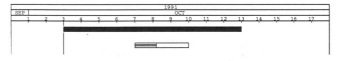

FIGURE 4-58.   Gantt Chart.

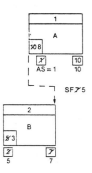

```
--------------------------------------------------------------------------
CASE 4:  Progress on both A and B.   Assume reporting date to be day 3.
--------------------------------------------------------------------------
ACTIVITY  DUR  PROGRESS  ES  EF | ACTIVITY  LAG  DUR  PROGRESS   ES  EF
--------------------------------------------------------------------------
   A      10      2      1  10 |    B      SF7   5      2         3   7
```

FIGURE 4-59.   Network setup diagram.

Table 4-34   Schedule Summary

```
----------------------------------------------------------------------------
SCHEDULE SUMMARY                                    DATE: _____

PROJECT NAME:   START-TO-FINISH RELATIONSHIP CASE 4_____
----------------------------------------------------------------------------
```

ACTIVITY ID	ORIG DUR	REM DUR	% DONE	EARLY START	EARLY FINISH	LATE START	LATE FINISH	TOTAL FLOAT
A *	10	8	20	1OCT91A	10OCT91		10OCT91	0 *
B	5	3	40	5OCT91	7OCT91	8OCT91	10OCT91	3

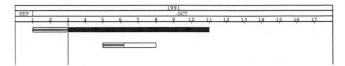

FIGURE 4-60.   Gantt Chart.

ADVANCED RELATIONSHIPS COMBINED

Let us now look at what happens when these advanced relationships are combined (assume a seven-day workweek) with others in a network. Please study the seven-activity network in Tables 4-35 and 4-36.

A diagram of this network is shown in Fig. 4-61.

The time-logic plot and Gantt Chart are presented in Figs. 4-62 and 4-63 respectively.

Note especially activity D. It seems to be, and is, at the center of everything—a real "spaghetti bowl" of relationships! It is also an excellent example of the effect of multiple lag values. You should be able to verify the following:

- Early Start of D is October 12 based on its F/S relationship with C
- It also has an overridden October 7 Early Start based on its SS relationship with B
- Late Finish of D is October 31, based on its trail through E and G
- It also has an overridden November 5 Late Finish based on its trail through F and G
- It must begin anytime between October 12 (ES) and October 17 (LS)
- It must finish anytime between October 26 (EF) through October 31 (LF)
- It contains five days float

Table 4-35   Schedule Setup

```
------------------------------------------------------------------------------
SCHEDULE SETUP                                        DATE:  _____

PROJECT NAME:  SEVEN-ACTIVITY COMPLEX NETWORK SETUP EXAMPLE_____
------------------------------------------------------------------------------
```

ACTIVITY ID	DUR (DAYS)	PREDECESSOR/ RELATIONSHIP	SUCCESSOR/ RELATIONSHIP	ACTIVITY DESCRIPTION
A	1	None	B F/S C F/S	
B	25	A F/S	D SS5 E F/S	
C	10	A F/S	D F/S	
D	15	B SS5 C F/S	E FF5 F SS5	
E	10	B F/S D FF5	G FF5	
F	20	D SS5	G SS5	
G	10	E FF5 F SS5	None	

Table 4-36   Schedule Summary

```
------------------------------------------------------------------------------
SCHEDULE SUMMARY                                      DATE:  _____

PROJECT NAME:  SEVEN-ACTIVITY COMPLEX-RELATIONSHIPS_____
------------------------------------------------------------------------------
```

ACTIVITY ID		ORIG DUR	REM DUR	% DONE	EARLY START	EARLY FINISH	LATE START	LATE FINISH	TOTAL FLOAT	
A	*	1	1	0	1OCT91	1OCT91	1OCT91	1OCT91	0	*
B	*	25	25	0	2OCT91	26OCT91	2OCT91	26OCT91	0	*
C		10	10	0	2OCT91	11OCT91	7OCT91	16OCT91	5	
D		15	15	0	12OCT91	26OCT91	17OCT91	31OCT91	5	
E	*	10	10	0	27OCT91	5NOV91	27OCT91	5NOV91	0	*
F		20	20	0	17OCT91	5NOV91	22OCT91	10NOV91	5	
G	*	10	10	0	1NOV91	10NOV91	1NOV91	10NOV91	0	*

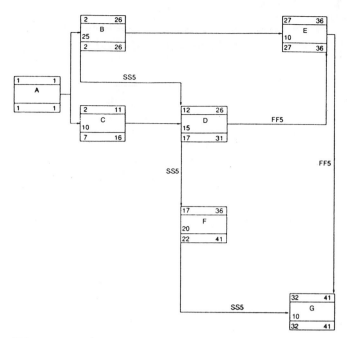

FIGURE 4-61.   Network setup diagram.

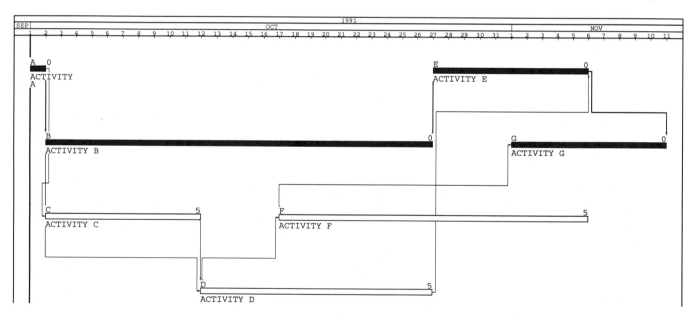

FIGURE 4-62.   Time-logic plot.

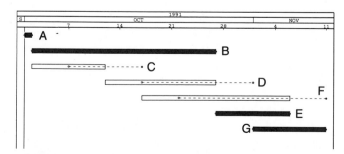

FIGURE 4-63.   Gantt Chart.

In the previous chapter we summarized the Finish-to-Start scheduling rules. Tables 4-37 (Early Schedule) and 4-38 (Late Schedule) summarize scheduling rules for the three major PDM relationships.

As with the forward pass, note that the times selected depend on the:

- Relationships between activities
- Any existing time delays (lags), leads, or other restraints

Remember Project HOME? That's good! Table 4-39 and Figs. 4-64, 4-65, and 4-66 revisit the logic. You should understand it much better now.

Table 4-37   Calculation of Early Start and Early Finish Times (Forward Pass)

ACTIVITY First	RELATIONSHIP Any	EARLY START (ES) Zero (always)	EARLY FINISH (EF) Activity duration
All sub- sequent: select latest of (1), (2), and (3)	(1) SS	ES of preceding activity	ES + activity duration
	(2) FS	EF of preceding activity	ES + activity duration
	(3) FF	EF of preceding activity, less own	EF of preceding activity

Table 4-38   Calculation of Late Start and Late Finish Times (Backward Pass)

ACTIVITY Last	RELATIONSHIP Any	LATE START (LS) LF - activity duration	LATE FINISH (LF) EF (always)
All prior: select earliest of (1), (2), and (3)	(1) SS	LS of following activity	LS of following activity, + own duration
	(2) FS	LF - activity duration	LS of following activity
	(3) FF	LF - activity duration	LF of following activity
First	Any	Zero (always)	

Table 4-39   Activity List, With Durations

```
----------------------------------------------------------------------
SCHEDULE SETUP                                    DATE: _____

PROJECT NAME:  58-ACTIVITY "HOME" HOUSING PROJECT (DALLAS, TEXAS)_____
               PRIMAVERA SYSTEMS, INC., BALA CYNWYD, PENNSYLVANIA 19004
----------------------------------------------------------------------
 ACT        PRED/          SUCC/
 ID          REL            REL    ACTIVITY DESCRIPTION              DUR
----------------------------------------------------------------------
  1     None           3  F/S    Layout                              5
  3      1  F/S        5  F/S    Soil stabilization                 15
  5      3  F/S        7  F/S    Plumbing - street connection and underslab 8
  7      5  F/S        9  F/S    Foundation excavation               5
  9      7  F/S       11  F/S    Granular fill                       7
                      12  F/S
                      13  F/S
 11      9  F/S       22  F/S    Underslab air conditioning freon line 5
 12      9  F/S       22  F/S    Underslab electrical line           7
 13      9  F/S       22  F/S    Termite protection                 13
 22     11  F/S       24  F/S    Concrete slab on grade              5
        12  F/S
        13  F/S
 24     22  F/S       26  F/S    Curing time                        13
 26     24  F/S       27  SS5    Set precast concrete panels        10
                      30  F/S
                      50  F/S
 27     26  SS5       30  F/S    Grout precast panels                6
                      50  F/S
 30     26  F/S       32  F/S    Install metal stairs               50
        27  F/S
 32     30  F/S       34  F/S    Plates, lintels, and roof trusses  23
 34     32  F/S       41  F/S    Redwood fascia, soffit, & plywood decking 20
 41     34  F/S       43  F/S    Dry sheeting                        5
                      58  F/S
 43     41  F/S       45  F/S    Stock bulk material inside building  4
 45     43  F/S       47  F/S    Set infill panel framing            3
 47     45  F/S       49  F/S    Windows                             5
 49     47  F/S       66  F/S    Wood siding                         8
 50     26  F/S       52  F/S    Frame interior walls               20
        27  F/S       53  F/S
                      54  F/S
 52     50  F/S       58  F/S    Install tub, stack out plumbing     4
 53     50  F/S       66  F/S    Pull wire; rough in electric & telephone 15
 54     50  F/S       66  F/S    TV wire pulling                     8
 58     41  F/S       66  F/S    Roof shingles                      15
        52  F/S
 66     49  F/S       67  SS2    Wall insulation                     5
        53  F/S       68  SS3
        54  F/S       70  F/S
        58  F/S
 67     66  SS2      128  F/S    Concrete stairs                     5
 68     66  SS3      128  F/S    Exterior railings                   6
 70     66  F/S       72  F/S    Sheetrock walls                    25
 72     70  F/S       74  F/S    Tape and bed                       20
                      76  FF5
 74     72  F/S      128  F/S    Blow on ceiling insulation         10
```

Table 4-39   Continued

```
------------------------------------------------------------------------
SCHEDULE SETUP                                        DATE: _____

PROJECT NAME:   58-ACTIVITY "HOME" HOUSING PROJECT (DALLAS, TEXAS)_____
                PRIMAVERA SYSTEMS, INC., BALA CYNWYD, PENNSYLVANIA 19004
------------------------------------------------------------------------
```

ACT ID	PRED/ REL		SUCC/ REL		ACTIVITY DESCRIPTION	DUR
76	72	FF5	78	F/S	Fur down for ceiling air conditioner	5
78	76	F/S	80	F/S	Air conditioning rough in	10
80	78	F/S	87	F/S	Sheetrock fur downs	4
87	80	F/S	89	F/S	Tape and bed fur downs	15
89	87	F/S	91	F/S	Texture walls and ceilings	13
			93	F/S		
91	89	F/S	95	F/S	Bathroom tile	5
93	89	F/S	95	F/S	Doors and trim	10
95	91	F/S	99	F/S	Painting	20
	93	F/S	100	F/S		
99	95	F/S	128	F/S	Hardware	5
100	95	F/S	107	F/S	Vinyl wall covering	8
107	100	F/S	109	F/S	Cleanup	5
109	107	F/S	112	F/S	Resilient flooring and bases	10
			113	F/S		
			114	F/S		
			115	F/S		
112	109	F/S	128	F/S	Paneling, finish carpentry, and millwork	14
113	109	F/S	128	F/S	Install condensers and A/C trimout	10
114	109	F/S	128	F/S	TV trimout	5
115	109	F/S	117	F/S	Install cabinets	13
			118	F/S		
117	115	F/S	119	FF5	Set appliances	5
			128	F/S		
118	115	F/S	123	F/S	Plumbing connections and trimout	13
119	117	FF5	128	F/S	Electrical connections and trimout	12
123	118	F/S	128	F/S	Bathroom accessories	5
128	67	F/S	136	F/S	Cleanup	10
	68	F/S				
	74	F/S				
	99	F/S				
	112	F/S				
	113	F/S				
	114	F/S				
	117	F/S				
	119	F/S				
	123	F/S				
136	128	F/S	138	F/S	Paint touchup	5
138	136	F/S	140	F/S	Install carpeting	15
140	138	F/S	142	F/S	Install drapes	5
142	140	F/S	144	F/S	Cleanup	10
144	142	F/S	146	F/S	Punch list	10
146	144	F/S	None		Building complete	5

```
------------------------------------------------------------------------
                              *** TOTAL WORKDAYS ***                 597
------------------------------------------------------------------------
```

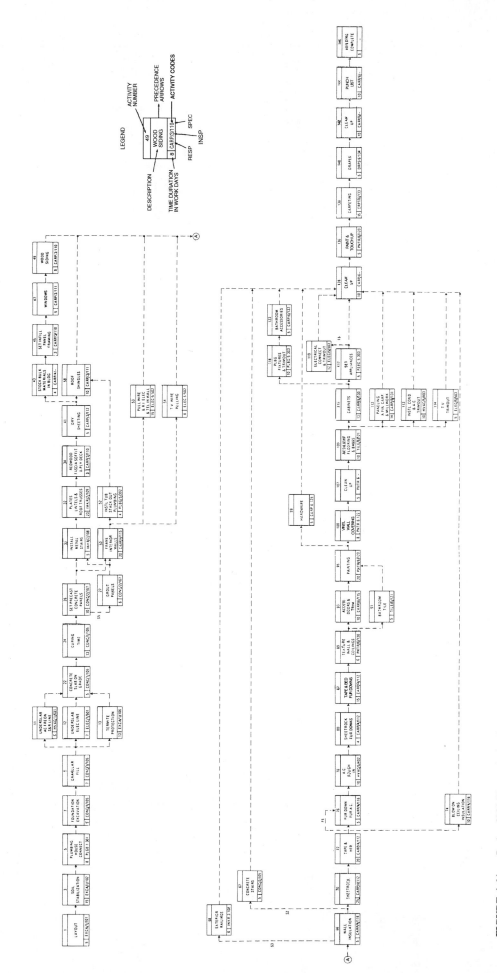

FIGURE 4-64. Project HOME pure-logic plot.

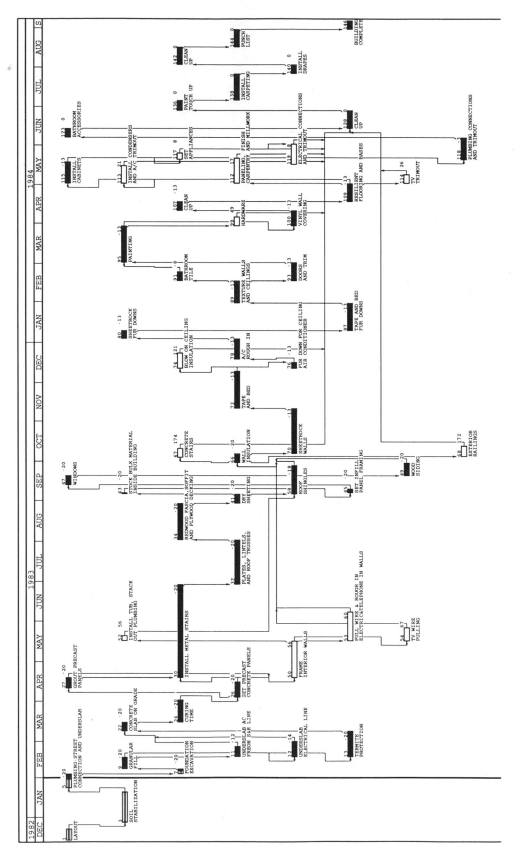

FIGURE 4-65. Project HOME time-logic plot.

114

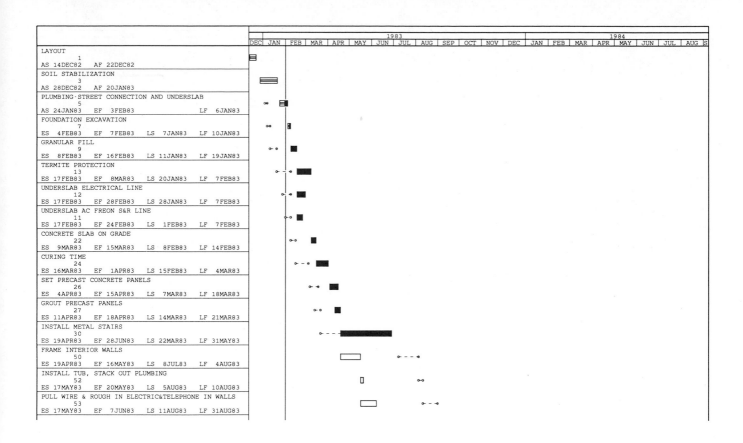

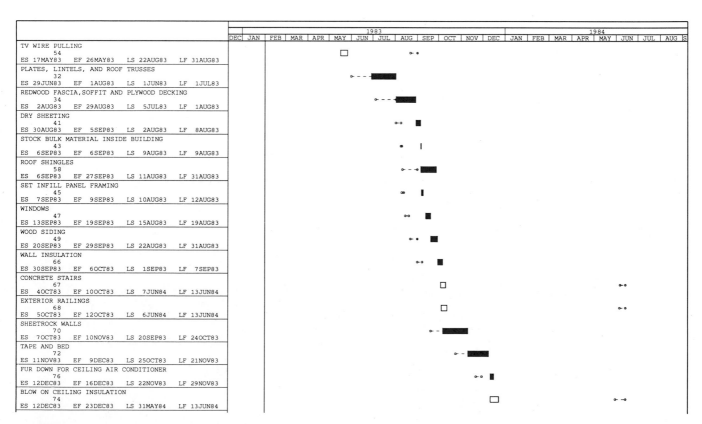

FIGURE 4-66. Project HOME Gantt Chart.

		1983													1984								
	DEC	JAN	FEB	MAR	APR	MAY	JUN	JUL	AUG	SEP	OCT	NOV	DEC	JAN	FEB	MAR	APR	MAY	JUN	JUL	AUG	S

A/C ROUGH IN
78
ES 19DEC83   EF 3JAN84   LS 30NOV83   LF 13DEC83

SHEETROCK FUR DOWNS
80
ES 4JAN84   EF 9JAN84   LS 14DEC83   LF 19DEC83

TAPE AND BED FUR DOWNS
87
ES 10JAN84   EF 30JAN84   LS 20DEC83   LF 11JAN84

TEXTURE WALLS AND CEILINGS
89
ES 31JAN84   EF 16FEB84   LS 12JAN84   LF 30JAN84

DOORS AND TRIM
93
ES 17FEB84   EF 1MAR84   LS 31JAN84   LF 13FEB84

BATHROOM TILE
91
ES 17FEB84   EF 23FEB84   LS 7FEB84   LF 13FEB84

PAINTING
95
ES 2MAR84   EF 29MAR84   LS 14FEB84   LF 12MAR84

VINYL WALL COVERING
100
ES 30MAR84   EF 10APR84   LS 13MAR84   LF 22MAR84

HARDWARE
99
ES 30MAR84   EF 5APR84   LS 7JUN84   LF 13JUN84

CLEAN UP
107
ES 11APR84   EF 17APR84   LS 23MAR84   LF 29MAR84

RESILIENT FLOORING AND BASES
109
ES 18APR84   EF 1MAY84   LS 30MAR84   LF 12APR84

INSTALL CABINETS
115
ES 2MAY84   EF 18MAY84   LS 13APR84   LF 1MAY84

PANELING, FINISH CARPENTRY AND MILLWORK
112
ES 2MAY84   EF 21MAY84   LS 25MAY84   LF 13JUN84

INSTALL CONDENSERS AND A/C TRIMOUT
113
ES 2MAY84   EF 15MAY84   LS 31MAY84   LF 13JUN84

TV TRIMOUT
114
ES 2MAY84   EF 8MAY84   LS 7JUN84   LF 13JUN84

ELECTRICAL CONNECTIONS AND TRIMOUT
119
ES 17MAY84   EF 1JUN84   LS 29MAY84   LF 13JUN84

		1983													1984								
	DEC	JAN	FEB	MAR	APR	MAY	JUN	JUL	AUG	SEP	OCT	NOV	DEC	JAN	FEB	MAR	APR	MAY	JUN	JUL	AUG	S

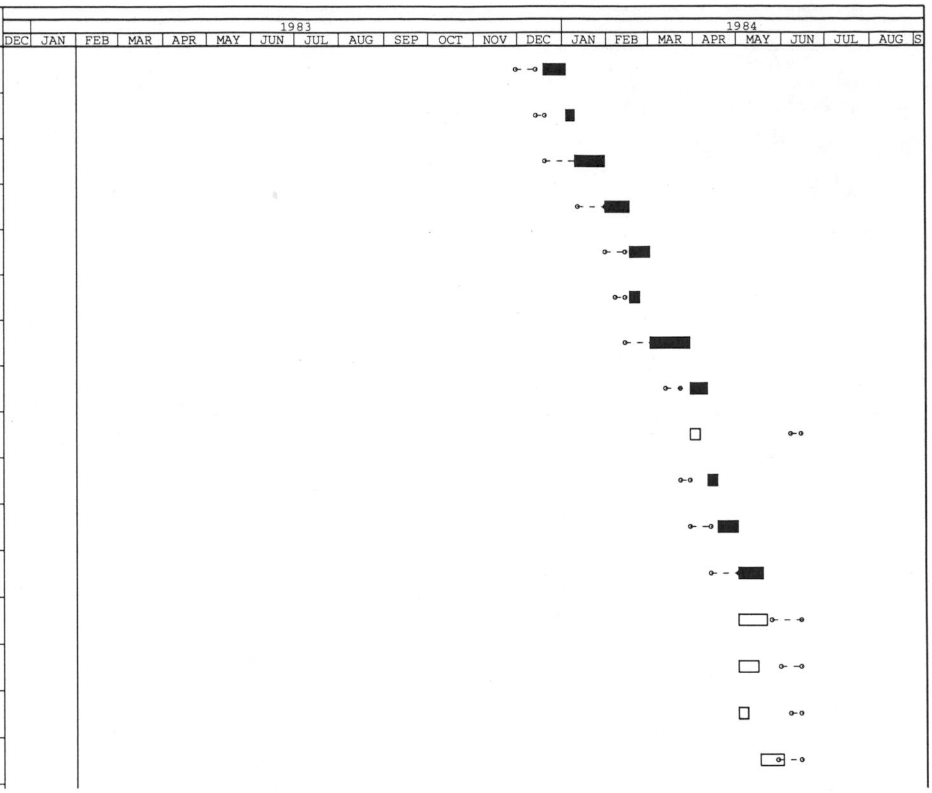

PLUMBING CONNECTIONS AND TRIMOUT
118
ES 21MAY84   EF 6JUN84   LS 16MAY84   LF 1JUN84

SET APPLIANCES
117
ES 21MAY84   EF 25MAY84   LS 31MAY84   LF 6JUN84

BATHROOM ACCESSORIES
123
ES 7JUN84   EF 13JUN84   LS 7JUN84   LF 13JUN84

CLEAN UP
128
ES 14JUN84   EF 27JUN84   LS 14JUN84   LF 27JUN84

PAINT TOUCH UP
136
ES 28JUN84   EF 5JUL84   LS 28JUN84   LF 5JUL84

INSTALL CARPETING
138
ES 6JUL84   EF 26JUL84   LS 6JUL84   LF 26JUL84

INSTALL DRAPES
140
ES 27JUL84   EF 2AUG84   LS 27JUL84   LF 2AUG84

CLEAN UP
142
ES 3AUG84   EF 16AUG84   LS 3AUG84   LF 16AUG84

PUNCH LIST
144
ES 17AUG84   EF 30AUG84   LS 17AUG84   LF 30AUG84

BUILDING COMPLETE
146
ES 31AUG84   EF 6SEP84   LS 31AUG84   LF 6SEP84

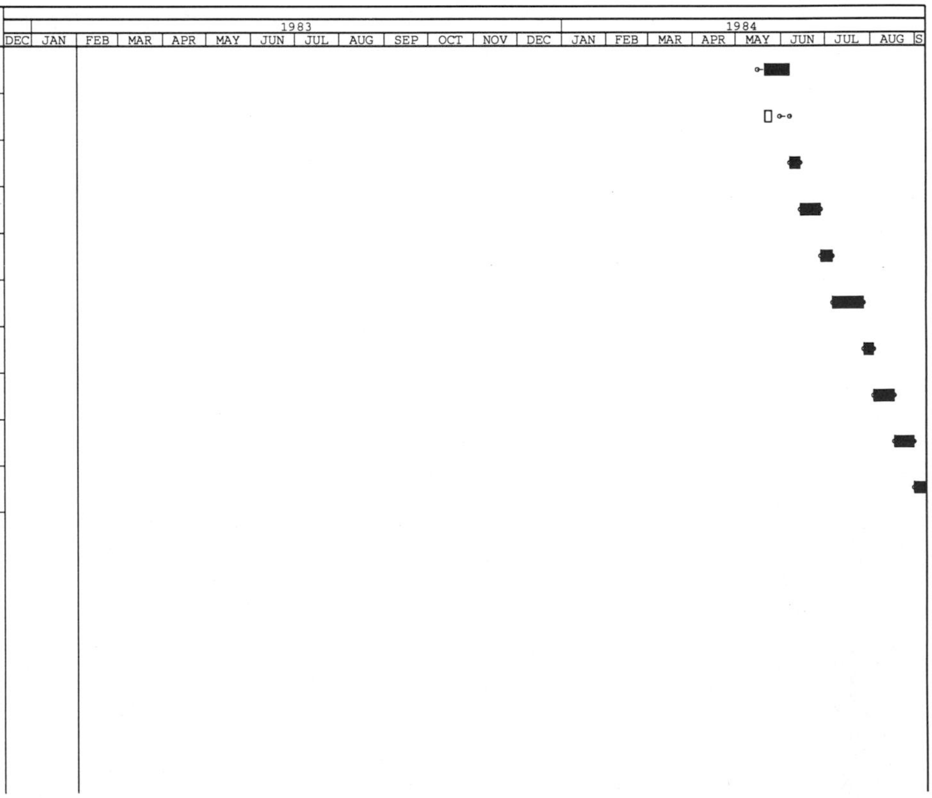

FIGURE 4-66.   Continued.

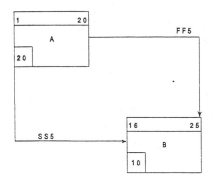

FIGURE 4-67.   Network setup diagram.

FIGURE 4-68.   Gantt Chart.

Table 4-40   Schedule Summary

```
------------------------------------------------------------------------
SCHEDULE SUMMARY                                    DATE: _____

PROJECT NAME:  2-ACTIVITY CONTIGUOUS DURATION EXAMPLE_____
------------------------------------------------------------------------
ACTIVITY    ORIG    REM     %     EARLY      EARLY     LATE      LATE      TOTAL
   ID       DUR     DUR   DONE    START      FINISH    START     FINISH    FLOAT
--------    ----    ---   ----   -------    -------   -------   -------    -----
     A  *    20      20     0    1OCT91     20OCT91   1OCT91    20OCT91      0 *
     B  *    10      10     0    16OCT91    25OCT91   16OCT91   25OCT91      0 *
------------------------------------------------------------------------
```

CONTIGUOUS ACTIVITIES REVISITED

We introduced this topic in the previous chapter. Now we shall investigate the scheduling effects of each method. They extend to relationships as well as duration. Study the small contiguous-duration network presented in Fig. 4-67.

The summary report is shown in Table 4-40.

Figure 4-68 is in bar chart format.

In the network above, B can begin five days after A; however, B cannot finish until five days after A completes. Using contiguous duration (that is, uninterrupted progress), the Finish-to-Finish relationship governs the Early Start of B. Since all work on B must take place without interruption:

- Finish of B is pushed five days after A completes, or October 25
- Start of B is pulled to within ten days (duration of B) of finish, or October 16

INTERRUPTIBLE ACTIVITIES REVISITED

If interruptible duration is used instead, the "PUSH-ME-PULL-YOU" network changes as shown in Fig. 4-69.

The summary report would look like Table 4-41.

Figure 4-70 is in bar chart format.

By specifying interruptible duration, finish of B is still five days after A completes, yet B can now begin five days (not fifteen) after A starts, in accordance with the SS5 relationship. Activity B duration remains 10 days, but the work can be done intermittently between October 6 and October 25; it is not forced to occur only during the last ten

days. No float is introduced even though ten days exist between Early Start and Late Start; the finish date, October 25, is the same under both schedules.

In networks where float does occur, you must choose which type to use:

- *Start float*—workperiod difference between Early Start and Late Start
- *Finish float*—workperiod difference between Early Finish and Late Finish

Primavera can, if desired, automatically select the *most critical float,* which is the lower value of the start and finish float. These values sometimes differ in an interruptible-

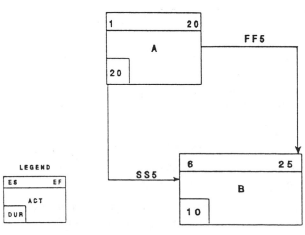

FIGURE 4-69.   Network setup diagram.

Table 4-41   Schedule Summary

```
------------------------------------------------------------------------
SCHEDULE SUMMARY                              DATE: _____

PROJECT NAME:   2-ACTIVITY INTERRUPTIBLE DURATION EXAMPLE_____
------------------------------------------------------------------------
```

ACTIVITY ID	ORIG DUR	REM DUR	% DONE	EARLY START	EARLY FINISH	LATE START	LATE FINISH	TOTAL FLOAT
A *	20	20	0	1OCT91	20OCT91	1OCT91	20OCT91	0 *
B *	10	10	0	6OCT91	25OCT91	16OCT91	25OCT91	0 *

```
------------------------------------------------------------------------
```

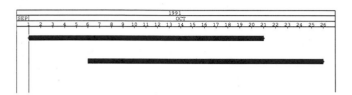

FIGURE 4-70.   Gantt Chart.

duration environment because an activity's start and finish times are calculated independently of, and are unaffected by, one another for scheduling purposes—almost as two separate pseudo-activities. Contiguous activity duration calculations, on the other hand, always schedule start and finish dates together; a relationship such as FF governs the activity start date, as seen earlier.

OUT-OF-SEQUENCE PROGRESS REVISITED

Out-of-sequence progress is work completed for an activity before it is logically scheduled to occur. We have already seen several such instances. Let us now explore the topic further. First, is it desirable? That depends. Although it is best to follow the planned schedule, this is not always possible. Delays can and frequently do occur. Instead of crying "Woe is me!" and doing nothing on later activities, do what you can, where you can, to contribute something to overall progress during this time. Too much out-of-sequence progress, however, should be avoided—especially when it disrupts orderly work flow or demands excessive storage space for incomplete assemblies.

Activities can (and, if appropriate, should) progress out of turn or even complete before all of their predecessors finish. At least one predecessor, however, must finish by then, otherwise the "successor":

- Is really a parallel activity
- Should have been scheduled as such

The real issue is when out-of-sequence progress should be recognized. There are two options:

- Wait until all predecessors have finished (*retained logic*)
- Immediately recognize this progress in full (*progress override*)

For simplicity, only retained logic has been used so far. Each method has its own advantages and disadvantages. If you find out-of-sequence progress, determine which method better represents your project reporting needs. The key question is this: Can progress continue on out-of-sequence activities, or must they wait until predecessor relationships are satisfied as planned?

Please study Figure 4-71. Regardless of how it is reported, work has been accomplished on *B*. In fact, no more can be done on *B* because it has been finished.

Retained Logic

In the retained logic method, an activity such as *B* with out-of-sequence progress:

- Is scheduled according to network logic
- Cannot officially complete until *all* of its predecessor activities—all the way back to network beginning—have also finished.

Its prime benefit is additional protection against an incomplete activity falling through the cracks. Its disadvantage is an overly pessimistic view of project progress. In the short example above, *C* will not complete until October 20.

The summary report would look like Table 4-42.

Figure 4-72 is in bar chart format.

Progress Override

On the other hand, you may instead claim all progress made on any activity—regardless of predecessor completion status. If this progress override method is used, an activity with progress would be unaffected by incomplete prede-

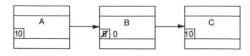

FIGURE 4-71.   Network setup diagram.

Table 4-42   Schedule Summary

```
------------------------------------------------------------------------------
SCHEDULE SUMMARY                                       DATE: _____

PROJECT NAME:  ABC RETAINED LOGIC EXAMPLE_____
------------------------------------------------------------------------------
ACTIVITY     ORIG   REM    %     EARLY     EARLY     LATE      LATE     TOTAL
   ID        DUR    DUR   DONE   START     FINISH    START     FINISH   FLOAT
--------     ----   ---   ----   -------   -------   -------   -------  -----
   A  *      10     10     0    1OCT91    10OCT91   1OCT91    10OCT91    0 *
   B          5      0    100
   C  *      10     10     0    11OCT91   20OCT91   11OCT91   20OCT91    0 *
------------------------------------------------------------------------------
```

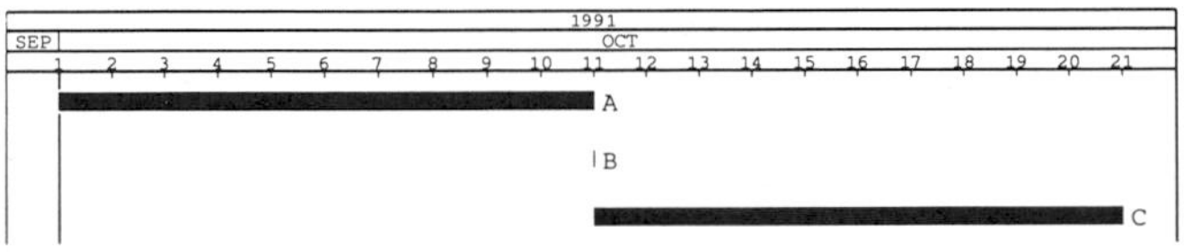

FIGURE 4-72.   Gantt Chart.

cessor activities. The out-of-sequence progress activity (*B*) is treated, for reporting purposes only, as if it had no predecessors (*A*). It can progress without delay due to network logic. In the short example above, *C* will now complete on October 10. This is because:

- *A* is no longer treated as a predecessor
- *B* is finished
- *C* may progress independently of and in parallel with *A*; in fact, *C* may start even if *A* cannot.

Of course, *B* is finished regardless of which reporting method is used.

The summary report would look like Table 4-43.
Figure 4-73 is in bar chart format.
The progress override method:
- More accurately measures current project status
- Allows a better look ahead into what, if any, makeup activities may be worked on

Please now study the five-activity network setup in Table 4-44.

Figure 4-74 is in network diagram format.
The resulting summary (retained-logic) report is shown in Table 4-45.
Figure 4-75 is in bar chart format.
Note that *D* has recorded two days' out-of-sequence progress before *A* and *C* have ended—or even begun. The nine-day (= 10 − 1) progress bar is proportionally divided into two parts—progress made and remaining duration. Using this method, the remaining four days work for *D* (a critical activity) are not scheduled until both its predecessors, *A* and *C,* complete. Of course, *C* cannot complete, either, until *A* does. The five-day lag holds until progress is made on *A,* or until the data date exceeds its value. The project expects to finish on October 11.

By contrast, the progress override method would see things as shown in Fig. 4-76.

The resulting summary (progress override) report is shown in Table 4-46.
Figure 4-77 is in bar chart format.
When progress override is used, the predecessor relationship between *C* and *D* is disregarded to the point that *C*:

- Is now an open end
- Introduces float on the path into *D,* which is no longer critical

The project expects to finish October 8, three days earlier than under the retained logic method. Note how the bar representing *D* has been scaled back, to four days, and

Table 4-43   Schedule Summary

```
------------------------------------------------------------------------------
SCHEDULE SUMMARY                                       DATE: _____

PROJECT NAME:  ABC PROGRESS OVERRIDE EXAMPLE_____
------------------------------------------------------------------------------
ACTIVITY     ORIG   REM    %     EARLY     EARLY     LATE      LATE     TOTAL
   ID        DUR    DUR   DONE   START     FINISH    START     FINISH   FLOAT
--------     ----   ---   ----   -------   -------   -------   -------  -----
   A  *      10     10     0    1OCT91    10OCT91   1OCT91    10OCT91    0 *
   B          5      0    100
   C  *      10     10     0    1OCT91    10OCT91   1OCT91    10OCT91    0 *
------------------------------------------------------------------------------
```

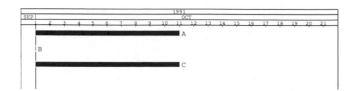

FIGURE 4-73.   Gantt Chart.

Table 4-44   Schedule Setup

```
------------------------------------------------------------------------------
SCHEDULE SETUP                                         DATE: _____

PROJECT NAME:   5-ACTIVITY NETWORK RETAINED LOGIC/PROGRESS OVERRIDE EXAMPLE__
                PRIMAVERA SYSTEMS, INC., BALA CYNWYD, PENNSYLVANIA 19004
------------------------------------------------------------------------------
```

ACTIVITY ID	DUR (DAYS)	PREDECESSOR/ RELATIONSHIP	SUCCESSOR/ RELATIONSHIP	PROGRESS TO DATE (DAYS)
A	2	None	B F/S	
			C F/S	
B	4	A F/S	E F/S	
C	3	A F/S	D F/S	
D	6	C F/S	E F/S	2
E	2	D F/S	None	

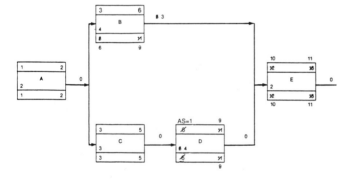

LEGEND

FIGURE 4-74.   Network setup diagram.

Table 4-45   Schedule Summary

```
------------------------------------------------------------------------------
SCHEDULE SUMMARY                                      DATE: _____

PROJECT NAME:   5-ACTIVITY NETWORK RL/PO EXAMPLE:   RETAINED LOGIC_____
------------------------------------------------------------------------------
```

ACTIVITY ID		ORIG DUR	REM DUR	% DONE	EARLY START	EARLY FINISH	LATE START	LATE FINISH	TOTAL FLOAT	
A	*	2	2	0	1OCT91	2OCT91	1OCT91	2OCT91	0	*
B		4	4	0	3OCT91	6OCT91	6OCT91	9OCT91	3	
C	*	3	3	0	3OCT91	5OCT91	3OCT91	5OCT91	0	*
D	*	6	4	33	1OCT91A	9OCT91		9OCT91	0	*
E	*	2	2	0	10OCT91	11OCT91	10OCT91	11OCT91	0	*

120

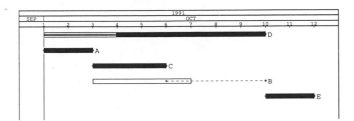

FIGURE 4-75.   Gantt Chart.

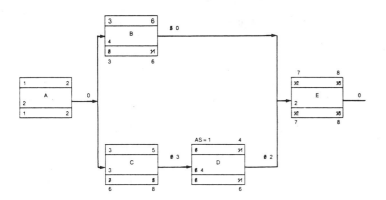

FIGURE 4-76.   Network setup diagram.

Table 4-46   Schedule Summary

```
------------------------------------------------------------------------
SCHEDULE SUMMARY                              DATE: _____

PROJECT NAME:  5-ACTIVITY NETWORK RL/PO EXAMPLE:  PROGRESS OVERRIDE_____
------------------------------------------------------------------------
```

ACTIVITY ID		ORIG DUR	REM DUR	% DONE	EARLY START	EARLY FINISH	LATE START	LATE FINISH	TOTAL FLOAT	
A	*	2	2	0	1OCT91	2OCT91	1OCT91	2OCT91	0	*
B	*	4	4	0	3OCT91	6OCT91	3OCT91	6OCT91	0	*
C		3	3	0	3OCT91	5OCT91	6OCT91	8OCT91	3	
D		6	4	33	1OCT91A	4OCT91		6OCT91	2	
E	*	2	2	0	7OCT91	8OCT91	7OCT91	8OCT91	0	*

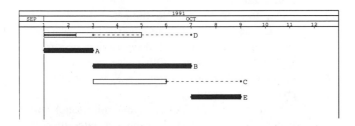

FIGURE 4-77.   Gantt Chart.

proportionately divided according to progress made and remaining duration.

PROJECT REVIEW, UPDATE AND CONTROL

Update and review your project frequently—weekly if not daily. Also do this when unexpected or significant changes occur in:

- Network logic
- Activity time estimates
- Resource availability
- Constraints and delivery times

Report all progress to date (the data date) and make any necessary changes to network logic. Once these changes have been made, recalculate the schedule to determine necessary revisions for the remaining activities.

Measure progress by recording the actual time taken by each activity, both completed and in progress. Completed activities no longer constrain the future schedule, but may have materially altered it. Actual dates should be recorded to serve as historical data for planning another project.

For incomplete activities, also re-evaluate their likely duration in light of progress already made and the time (including delays) expended so far. This idea is the basis of the earned-value measurement technique, which will be discussed in Chapter 12. The revised duration should measure the entire time between the activity's start and its finish. Include an explanation of why delays occurred and how much time was lost. In *Primavera*, this could be done in the nine-line scratchpad log associated with each activity.

The progress measurement procedure must, of course:

- Commence with the start of the project
- Continue in time through the entire network to produce valid activity dates; as the project proceeds, the data date moves left to right toward completion of the project

Besides revising the schedule with the actual duration of completed activities and re-evaluating activities in progress, change the durations of unstarted activities in light of more up-to-date information. At the same time, alter activity relationships, constraints, and resource requirements if necessary. Once all appropriate changes have been made, recompute the schedule and generate new reports.

Compare actual performance with planned (that is, the baseline or target). Clearly, the most important information will be the effect on:

- Project completion date
- Intermediate activities, deadlines, and constraints
- Float values, especially on critical or near-critical activities
- Resource requirements (to be discussed later)

Without consistent and objective performance measurement (you cannot manage what you cannot measure), it is

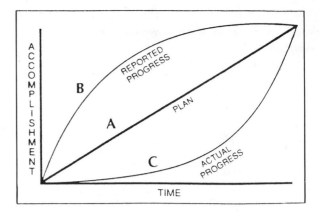

FIGURE 4-78.   Reality compared with perception.

nearly impossible to make necessary critical judgments. Fig. 4-78 illustrates the point.

In the absence of objective, precise measures, human nature will describe project status as following Line B: "I'm doing just super. Really great shape! Ahead of schedule and below budget. I really must have my act together! Mostly wrap-up stuff at this point!" But Line C shows reality:

- Slow start
- Minimal progress until panic sets in
- Frenzied rev-mode accomplishment to finish

Objective, precise, and reliable metrics are needed for effective project management and control. Track how long it really takes to do the identifiable work, and why. Record actual hours for each resource by activity and compare the figures with reported progress values. If a team member, for example, works only forty hours on an activity, but claims eight days progress—or if (s)he says that (s)he is "90 percent complete" in six days on a ten-day activity—then:

- Something is seriously wrong
- (S)he is severely afflicted with the "90 percent complete pseudo-hero" syndrome
- An investigation should be made

Earned value analysis, the most capable metric available today to measure actual progress, will be discussed at length in Chapter 12.

Costs, although not yet discussed, will obviously be of great interest, too. If the update indicates that both the objective project completion date and intermediate deadlines will likely be met, little need be done except perhaps to ensure the plan is still on budget. Otherwise, congratulations on a fine job so far. "Steady as she goes!" is, for now, the ordered project course and speed.

But if the forecasted project (or other milestone) completion date cannot be met (Late Finish is later than the desired deadline), then immediate planning must be done.

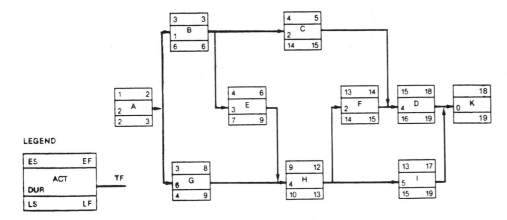

FIGURE 4-79.   Network setup diagram.

Although it will vary in detail from project to project, it must effectively reduce project time as a whole or reduce the time of that network portion leading to an intermediate deadline. We shall learn how to do this in Chapter 9.

Consider the ten-activity, no-deadline network shown in Fig. 4-79.

The resulting summary schedule is shown in Table 4-47.

Figure 4-80 is in bar chart format.

If the project must finish October 18, the Critical Path would run through activities *A, G, H, F, D,* and *K*—each having zero days float. The project deadline looks attainable. The constrained network is shown in Fig. 4-81.

The resulting summary report is shown in Table 4-48.

Figure 4-82 is in bar chart format.

Now suppose it is October 10. The project deadline is still October 18, and the network looks like Fig. 4-83.

Note the following changes since the baseline:

- *A, B,* and *G* have completed (remaining duration equals zero)
- *E* has one day remaining
- *C* has made two days progress, but original duration has been revised to four
- *J,* a new (and currently non-critical) activity, has been added
- We have fallen one day behind schedule; unless performance is improved (along the *E-H-F-D* trail), the project will finish two days late, October 20.

The resulting summary report is shown in Table 4-49.

The resulting Gantt Chart comparison is shown in Fig. 4-84. Presented in Table 4-50 is a sample *P3*-generated turnaround document to facilitate the reporting and updating

Table 4-47   Schedule Summary

```
------------------------------------------------------------------------------
SCHEDULE SUMMARY                                 DATE: _____

PROJECT NAME:  10-ACTIVITY PROGRESS REPORTING EXAMPLE  (BASELINE)_____
------------------------------------------------------------------------------
```

ACTIVITY ID	ORIG DUR	REM DUR	% DONE	EARLY START	EARLY FINISH	LATE START	LATE FINISH	TOTAL FLOAT
A	2	2	0	1OCT91	2OCT91	2OCT91	3OCT91	1
B	1	1	0	3OCT91	3OCT91	6OCT91	6OCT91	3
C	2	2	0	4OCT91	5OCT91	14OCT91	15OCT91	10
D	4	4	0	15OCT91	18OCT91	16OCT91	19OCT91	1
E	3	3	0	4OCT91	6OCT91	7OCT91	9OCT91	3
F	2	2	0	13OCT91	14OCT91	14OCT91	15OCT91	1
G	6	6	0	3OCT91	8OCT91	4OCT91	9OCT91	1
H	4	4	0	9OCT91	12OCT91	10OCT91	13OCT91	1
I	5	5	0	13OCT91	17OCT91	15OCT91	19OCT91	2
K	0	0	0		18OCT91		19OCT91	1

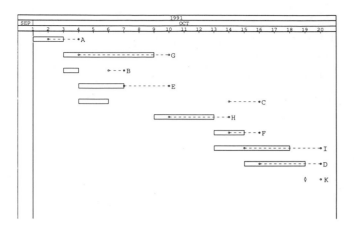

FIGURE 4-80.   Gantt Chart.

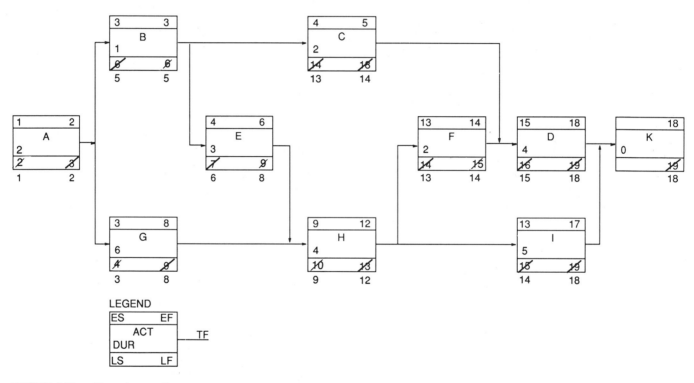

FIGURE 4-81.   Network setup diagram.

of progress. The three completed activities were not selected because they no longer require status reports. Milestone *K*, project finish, was not selected because it is not directly updated. The remaining seven (incomplete) activities were selected from within the range Data Date and (Data Date + 10 days), that is, October 10–20.

Only the very basic scheduling information is presented in Table 4-50. *Primavera* actually provides several dozen format and content options from which to build a customized report. These report options will be discussed more extensively in Chapter 7.

Table 4-48   Schedule Summary

```
------------------------------------------------------------------------------------
SCHEDULE SUMMARY                                          DATE:  _____

PROJECT NAME:  10-ACTIVITY PROGRESS REPORTING EXAMPLE (BASELINE)_____
------------------------------------------------------------------------------------
```

ACTIVITY ID		ORIG DUR	REM DUR	% DONE	EARLY START	EARLY FINISH	LATE START	LATE FINISH	TOTAL FLOAT	
A	*	2	2	0	1OCT91	2OCT91	1OCT91	2OCT91	0	*
B		1	1	0	3OCT91	3OCT91	5OCT91	5OCT91	2	
C		2	2	0	4OCT91	5OCT91	13OCT91	14OCT91	9	
D	*	4	4	0	15OCT91	18OCT91	15OCT91	18OCT91	0	*
E		3	3	0	4OCT91	6OCT91	6OCT91	8OCT91	2	
F	*	2	2	0	13OCT91	14OCT91	13OCT91	14OCT91	0	*
G	*	6	6	0	3OCT91	8OCT91	3OCT91	8OCT91	0	*
H	*	4	4	0	9OCT91	12OCT91	9OCT91	12OCT91	0	*
I		5	5	0	13OCT91	17OCT91	14OCT91	18OCT91	1	
K	*	0	0	0		18OCT91		18OCT91	0	*

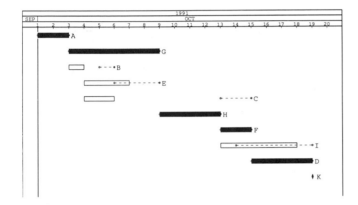

FIGURE 4-82.   Gantt Chart.

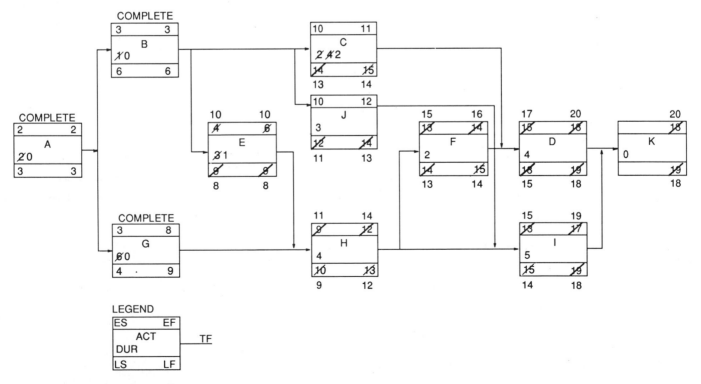

FIGURE 4-83.   Network setup diagram.

Table 4-49   Schedule Summary

```
------------------------------------------------------------------------
SCHEDULE SUMMARY                                      DATE: _____

PROJECT NAME:  10-ACTIVITY PROGRESS REPORTING EXAMPLE (10/10 STATUS SUMMARY)
------------------------------------------------------------------------
```

ACTIVITY ID		ORIG DUR	REM DUR	% DONE	EARLY START	EARLY FINISH	LATE START	LATE FINISH	TOTAL FLOAT	
A		0	0	100	2OCT91A	3OCT91A				
B		0	0	100	4OCT91A	4OCT91A				
C		4	2	50	10OCT91	11OCT91	13OCT91	14OCT91	3	
D	*	4	4	0	17OCT91	20OCT91	15OCT91	18OCT91	-2	*
E	*	3	1	67	10OCT91	10OCT91	8OCT91	8OCT91	-2	*
F	*	2	2	0	15OCT91	16OCT91	13OCT91	14OCT91	-2	*
G		0	0	100	4OCT91A	9OCT91A				
H	*	4	4	0	11OCT91	14OCT91	9OCT91	12OCT91	-2	*
I	*	5	5	0	15OCT91	19OCT91	14OCT91	18OCT91	-1	*
J		3	3	0	10OCT91	12OCT91	11OCT91	13OCT91	1	
K	*	0	0	0		20OCT91		18OCT91	-2	*

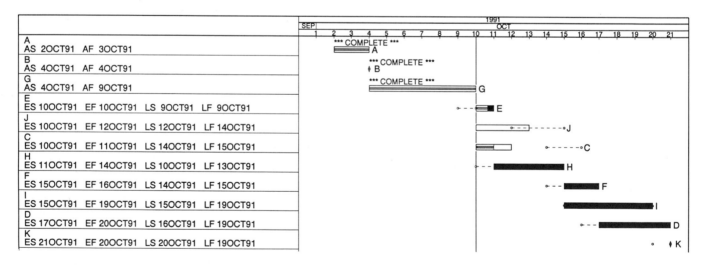

FIGURE 4-84.   Target-comparison Gantt Chart.

Table 4-50   Turnaround Document

```
-----------------------------------------------------------------------------
TURNAROUND DOCUMENT                                    DATE: _____

PROJECT NAME:   10-ACTIVITY PROGRESS REPORTING EXAMPLE (10/10 STATUS SUMMARY)
-----------------------------------------------------------------------------
```

ACTIVITY ID	ORIG DUR	REM DUR	%	CODES	ACTIVITY DESCRIPTION	SCHEDULED START	FINISH
E	3	1	67		Activity E	10OCT91	10OCT91
J	3	3	0		Activity J	10OCT91	12OCT91
C	4	2	50		Activity C	10OCT91	11OCT91
H	4	4	0		Activity H	11OCT91	14OCT91
F	2	2	0		Activity F	15OCT91	16OCT91
I	5	5	0		Activity I	15OCT91	19OCT91
D	4	4	0		Activity D	17OCT91	20OCT91

5
PDM Date Constraints

We shall study two things in this chapter:

- Time estimates
- Date constraints

TIME ESTIMATES

The usefulness and benefits of a schedule depend heavily on good time estimates. Your objective should always be maximum cost-effective accuracy. It is crucial that you use the best staff and tools available for this process.

The estimating process should:

- Be as realistic as possible
- Be based on history, if available (some activities have been done many times in the past)
- Take into account all likely conditions and circumstances

Time estimates should be based on normal:

- Staff or work team expected to do the work
- Working conditions

It may be advisable to break some activities into smaller parts. By doing this, it will be possible to identify component tasks for which estimates:

- Exist (from a previous project with similar activities/tasks), or
- May at least now be more easily determined from scratch

If standards (or records with integrity) are available, you should make full use of this experience. Estimates should be based on the time required for similar activities or tasks, varied to meet any special conditions expected, or on the basis of other differences between the present situation and the one from which the data come. With regression or cross-tabulation analyses of historical data, one can relate the estimate to one or more independent variables that will accurately predict most, if not nearly all, of the new-activity duration. Then, using rational analytical methods, provide best-guess estimates ("guesstimates") on the remaining portion not covered by standards or experience. In this way, a much smaller percentage of the activity must be estimated from scratch. This results in a process that is:

- Easier to do
- More accurate to use
- Less risky

Consult and listen to the "worker bees" who have performed similar processes in the past. Their insight and experience may prove invaluable in helping to set realistic time-and-cost expectations. Their added support, from feeling that they are involved, will certainly help, too.

As a general rule, the estimated time should represent a 50 percent probability of success; that is, there should be a 50 percent chance that the activity will be completed within the stated time. Although often not an easy process, it is always an important process. Remember that you will be measured on the extent to which your project is satisfactorily completed—both on time and on budget. Your time objective is declared here and nowhere else. There is no substitute for honesty and accuracy—and historical records, if done the same way. In scheduling, the past can be very helpful in forecasting the future.

If your project is to design, code, modify, cost, or evaluate software, the de-facto estimating metric is *Function Point Analysis (FPA)*. Its accuracy—and, therefore, usefulness—is literally orders of magnitude greater than the more conventional (but never accurate) source lines of code—which, of course, requires the code be written first (super forecasting value!). FPA, on the other hand, accurately and effectively measures or estimates the following software-project values:

- System business value, as seen by the user
- Project size, cost, and development time
- Information systems staff productivity and quality
- Attribute analysis: process and project characteristics (education, tools, experience, work environment, and so on)
- Maintenance, modification, and customization efforts
- Make-vs.-buy decision support
- Benefits of *I-CASE* (Integrated Computer-Aided Software Engineering) and other tools.
- Trends and variances
- Results of process-improvement efforts

These activity duration estimates *must* be realistic. Even if difficult (especially when no prior history exists), this is not "SWAG time" or time to fire up your computer's random number generator (Fig. 5-1)!

There is sometimes a tendency to be overly optimistic and to underestimate times. Usually this is done to "look good" and "be a hero." Be (instead) very careful, though! This attitude does not serve you well because it may:

- Simply be impossible to meet these objectives even with otherwise satisfactory performance
- Unnecessarily cause you to expedite your schedule at premium rates
- Create a false impression that you really can finish within this desired time, which in turn will lead to strained staff relations

If your project misses the due date only because you declared insufficient times, you will not:

- Look good

- Be called "Hero"
- Be called anything I may put in print! (Fig. 5-2).

With more realistic time estimates, you may actually have:

- Finished on time, or even early
- Not needed to expedite your schedule at premium rates
- Been perceived to be more competent

But now is not the time to convince anyone of that. Fur will be flying and heads will be rolling. One of them will probably be yours! Even before project finish, it is unlikely that revised, more realistic times will be approved. Fitz-Gerald says schedule first, advertise later:

> "Promise no more than what you can deliver—
> but deliver what you promise!"

The more common tendency is to overestimate activity completion times. This does not serve you well, either, because:

- Project length expands to meet the time thought to be available
- Supporting resources should be made available to other activities

Overestimating activity durations may prevent your company from bidding on a project—or winning a bid already submitted. The results may be:

- Lost contracts
- Idle equipment
- Revenue opportunity costs
- Personnel layoffs

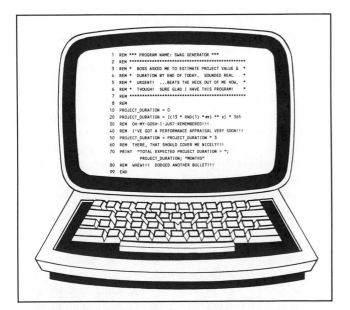

```
1   REM *** PROGRAM NAME: SWAG GENERATOR ***
2   REM ****************************************
3   REM *  BOSS ASKED ME TO ESTIMATE PROJECT VALUE &  *
4   REM *  DURATION BY END OF TODAY.  SOUNDED REAL    *
5   REM *  URGENT!  ...BEATS THE HECK OUT OF ME HOW,  *
6   REM *  THOUGH!  SURE GLAD I HAVE THIS PROGRAM!    *
7   REM ****************************************
8   REM
10  PROJECT_DURATION = 0
20  PROJECT_DURATION = [(13 * RND(1) * √т) ** e] * 365
30  REM  OH-MY-GOSH-I-JUST-REMEMBERED!!!
40  REM  I'VE GOT A PERFORMANCE APPRAISAL VERY SOON!!!
50  PROJECT_DURATION = PROJECT_DURATION * 3
60  REM  THERE, THAT SHOULD COVER ME NICELY!!!!
70  PRINT  "TOTAL EXPECTED PROJECT DURATION = ";
              PROJECT_DURATION; "MONTHS"
80  REM  WHEW!!!  DODGED ANOTHER BULLET!!!
99  END
```

FIGURE 5-1.   A BASIC "SWAG generator" that really works!

FIGURE 5-2.   "Did the boss have much to say?"

People will remember who padded the time estimates and caused these problems.

And if you develop a reputation for crying "Wolf!" too often and inflating your time estimates, later project requests will automatically be cut back—even if they are reasonable.

What?!! No "fudge factor"?!! Sorry! But please read on.

Few things will accelerate progress. Many will impede it. Both experience and Murphy's Law find this to be commonly true: Progress is more easily delayed than made. Even the best plans may be disrupted by such unforeseen things as:

* Bad weather
* Faulty materials
* Sickness
* Work stoppages
* Murphy's Law

There is, unfortunately, usually a much greater chance that an activity will be late than be early. A workable solution might be the following: Similar to "Management Reserve" funds set aside to cover unexpected cash outlays, insert near the end of the network (and important milestones along the way) certain contingency activities. The purpose is to absorb possible delays without degrading the accuracy of time estimates for individual activities. This will provide the following benefits:

* Activity durations will be more accurate, yet still feasible
* Project finish estimates will not be incorrectly lengthened
* Float provided only for the possibility of such delays will not be wasted
* Vendor delays and similar contingencies may be tracked directly
* Resulting estimates will establish and maintain a better, more accurate historical base from which to estimate future activity times; if contingency time were loaded into these estimates, it may be impossible—or simply forgotten—to remove them later when no longer needed

The last point merits further discussion. Past project experience—time requirements, resource consumption, process sequences, costs, and the like can be invaluable when predicting future needs, including pricing bids and proposals. The greater the similarity between past and current or future activities, the more useful this historical information will be. If current or future activities will take place in an environment materially different from the past—more education and training, better equipment, and so on—then appropriate adjustments should be made to duration estimates. Still, it is easier (and much more accurate) to make these adjustments than to start from scratch each time. It also allows more effective contingency analysis.

But be very careful! Watch out for padded times to handle any contingencies. Suppose a vendor is frequently three days late delivering needed supplies. (I would say: Time to select a new vendor.) Should these three days be loaded into activities requiring these supplies? No! Although late-delivery activities would ("everything else being equal") still finish on time and no-delay activities would (under the same assumption) finish three days early, it is absolutely inappropriate to pad activity durations with these contingencies. For one thing, it covers up the vendor's sloppy performance and demonstrates no pain to your organization. For another, it artificially inflates future cost and time estimates—especially if the vendor's performance improves or another, more reliable vendor is chosen instead. What's wrong with that? It appears that you are busier than you actually are, and need more resources than you really do. It also invokes Murphy's Law: The project that pays the most will be offered when there is *seemingly* no time to deliver the services. Unless "provision for late-vendor deliveries" is removed from the historical base, the resulting damage to the estimating process will never completely go away.

Effective estimating requires the following three-step process:

* Perform a complete and careful analysis of all relevant factors
* Include like-activity experience from a similar environment
* Modify both the above as necessary to reflect current requirements

Remember that the law of large numbers will work in your favor. Both underestimates and overestimates will even out over the project as a whole.

A mistake as serious as it is common is to force a desired completion time on the schedule or on the activities themselves. You should take extreme care that deadlines or desired completion times *not* influence estimated activity durations in any way. Otherwise, "desirable" durations will be used to meet the "desirable" finish date instead of realistic durations accurately—if not desirably—indicating the finish date.

The *only* variable for determining durations is product quality specification. If you are willing to accept a product of lower quality, you can finish earlier. If, however, you want a more capable, higher-quality, more reliable product, it takes longer. Period. No "Bibbidi bobbidi boo!" magic for you! Do it right the *first* time.

You cannot always have something just because you want it—no matter how badly or for how noble a cause.

The same applies here. Your estimates will not be realistic if you allow project deadlines to influence individual activity estimates. You will not want to commit to these times, either. Let the system "do its thing." It works, and works well. (But the "GIGO Effect" also applies!) If an activity requires N days, schedule it for N days.

Note that although CPM does not require the three time estimates (optimistic time, most likely time, and "Murphy's Law time") required for each PERT activity, you may still estimate CPM times in precisely the same manner as is required by PERT. This may in fact be more appropriate in highly uncertain fields and will be discussed further when we research PERT in Chapter 8.

DATE CONSTRAINTS

Accurate project modeling requires PDM relationships. Sometimes, however,

- No logical relationship exists between activities
- Existing relationships are inadequate

In these cases, we can apply certain schedule restrictions to reflect project requirements. Known as *constraints,* these restrictions are applied to activity start or finish times (sometimes both) and can be specified as one or more of the following:

- Imposed schedule dates *(date constraints)*
- Limits on duration
- Limits on float

If you do not take these constraints into account, your network logic will be invalid. But excessive use of constraints will do the same thing. I once observed a network of one thousand activities, in which *every* activity was assigned at least one constraint! Needless to say, correct scheduling was impossible on this project.

Judicious use of constraints can provide the following benefits:

- Restrict or distribute float to critical network segments
- Control standalone activities within a network
- Smooth the use of resources
- Eliminate resource conflicts
- Control subproject network logic
- Meet external requirements under which the project must operate

Examples of such external requirements include:

- Contractual requirement
- Management decree
- Needed personnel, equipment, and the like will not arrive before a certain date
- Project deliverable is seasonal or pertains to a certain holiday
- Contract milestone dates are mandatory
- Needed funds will not be available before a certain date
- A key person is available only on specified days
- All outdoor activities must be completed before the beginning of winter
- Wheat crop must be harvested by June 25

We shall discuss date constraints in this chapter and duration/float constraints in the next.

Despite proper activity relationships and durations, an earlier completion date is often more desirable or even essential. In these cases, the calculated activity dates:

- Do not reflect true project realities
- Must be changed accordingly

If these date constraints are applied before network logic is calculated, much reshuffling will be saved, particularly in a manual environment. Although reasons differ from instance to instance, there will be times when an activity or the entire project is absolutely required to take place:

- Before a fixed date
- On a fixed date
- After a fixed date

A date constraint is any imposed schedule date (treated as fixed) applied to the date:

- Before which an activity cannot start or finish
- On which it must start or finish
- After which it cannot start or finish.

Indirectly, it can also refer to a duration restriction. This is because duration implies the dates on which an activity can, should, or must proceed—and must finish. In general, you can use date constraints when a particular date must be the controlling factor of an activity or network. However, they must not be:

- Applied arbitrarily
- Allowed to override required network logic (especially activity relationships and start or finish dates) without valid justification

Date constraints are usually applied before the "Big Four" dates are calculated, but are sometimes applied after then to fine-tune the network. Also note well: Date constraints are applied *only* when they create a tighter schedule, not when they indicate an "easier" one. The test is the resulting effect on float: Less float indicates a "harder" schedule (constraint applied), more float an "easier" (constraint not applied).

Therefore, an imposed December 1 Early Start would not (unless mandatory) affect a computed December 15 Early Start because the two weeks earlier start represents more time in which to do the project. But it is a good idea anyway to note these constraints because they may affect future schedules—even if not the current. If, however, the same (December 15) activity were required to start no earlier than December 30, it would be rescheduled to that date because the start fifteen days later represents less time.

On the other hand, if the project is required to finish before the calculated Early Finish date, it will be necessary to:

- Reduce project length by shortening one or more critical activities
- Examine the new network to ensure another, longer path did not arise
- Repeat this process as necessary

The total reduction necessary is the difference between calculated Early Finish and the imposed (finish-no-later-than) end date.

If the required project finish date is after the calculated Early Finish (or Late Finish) date, it is *not* advisable to delay the project accordingly. Although this extra time might look like a free ride, it would foolishly increase costs.

The effects on intermediate activities are much the same,

but usually harder to determine—especially if the activity occurs in a sequence of noncritical activities. But the same rule holds: Date constraints apply only when they result in a tighter, not easier, schedule—that is, a schedule with less float.

The seven date constraints are:

- Start no earlier than (SNET)
- Finish no earlier than (FNET)
- Start no later than (SNLT)
- Finish no later than (FNLT)
- Start on (ON)
- Mandatory start (MS)
- Mandatory finish (MF)

The first four allow activities to fall into place wherever appropriate and still meet the general time requirement that they not start before, nor end after, a given time. The last three narrow to only a single day the time window during which an activity can start or must complete. Because of this greater scheduling flexibility, it is recommended that the first four constraints be used when necessary in favor of the others.

Sometimes the distinction is not clearly made, the results not really intended. Often, people will informally state that something must be done "on" a specified date, when in actuality it only need be done *by* this date. You are not being picky to ask for a clarification. The benefit to both of you is a more realistic, more flexible schedule.

Let us look at each of these date constraints in greater detail. To do this, we shall employ a six-activity network with an October 17 fixed ending date (Tables 5-1 and 5-2).

Figure 5-3 is shown in network diagram format, and 5-4 in bar chart format.

Table 5-1   Activity List, With Relationships and Durations

```
-------------------------------------------------------------------------------
SCHEDULE SETUP                                      DATE: _____

PROJECT NAME:  SIX-ACTIVITY NETWORK DATE CONSTRAINTS EXAMPLE_____
               PRIMAVERA SYSTEMS, INC., BALA CYNWYD, PENNSYLVANIA 19004
-------------------------------------------------------------------------------
ACTIVITY    DUR      PREDECESSOR/      SUCCESSOR/
   ID      (DAYS)    RELATIONSHIP      RELATIONSHIP    ACTIVITY DESCRIPTION
--------   ------   -------------     -----------    --------------------
   A         3      None              B   F/S
                                      D   F/S
   B         7      A   F/S           C   F/S
   C         5      B   F/S           F   F/S
   D         2      A   F/S           E   F/S
   E         4      D   F/S           F   F/S
   F         2      C   F/S           None; 10/17 deadline
                    E   F/S
-------------------------------------------------------------------------------
```

Table 5-2   Schedule Summary

```
-------------------------------------------------------------------------------
SCHEDULE SUMMARY                                    DATE: _____

PROJECT NAME:  SIX-ACTIVITY NETWORK DATE CONSTRAINTS EXAMPLE (BASELINE)_____
-------------------------------------------------------------------------------
```

ACTIVITY ID		ORIG DUR	REM DUR	% DONE	EARLY START	EARLY FINISH	LATE START	LATE FINISH	TOTAL FLOAT	
A	*	3	3	0	1OCT91	3OCT91	1OCT91	3OCT91	0	*
B	*	7	7	0	4OCT91	10OCT91	4OCT91	10OCT91	0	*
C	*	5	5	0	11OCT91	15OCT91	11OCT91	15OCT91	0	*
D		2	2	0	4OCT91	5OCT91	10OCT91	11OCT91	6	
E		4	4	0	6OCT91	9OCT91	12OCT91	15OCT91	6	
F	*	2	2	0	16OCT91	17OCT91	16OCT91	17OCT91	0	*

```
-------------------------------------------------------------------------------
```

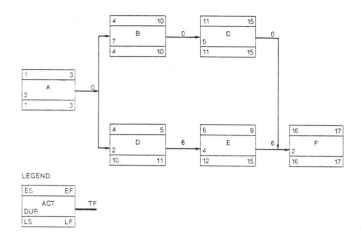

FIGURE 5-3.   Network setup diagram.

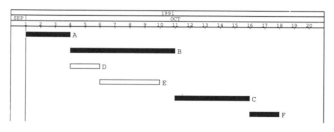

FIGURE 5-4.   Gantt Chart.

Multiple Calendars

The multiple-calendar effect on each constraint will be examined immediately after the single-calendar case. Activities *D* and *E* are assigned to Calendar 2. All activities must complete by January 8. The project employs the same calendar (Table 5-3) as already seen.

Table 5-4 summarizes the schedule in tabular format. Figure 5-5 is shown in network diagram format, and 5-6 in bar chart format.

START NO EARLIER THAN (SNET)

When an *SNET* constraint is applied, the activity (or entire project):

- Must not start before this date
- May begin after then if not critical

This affects Early Start. Calculated Early Start is compared with the assigned SNET constraint; the later of the two times is selected. This constraint is often used in cases where equipment delivery is necessary for the start of an activity.

Single Calendar

In Fig. 5-7, an October 11 SNET constraint is imposed on *D*. Because this date is later than the calculated Early Start of October 4, the constraint applies and affects:

Table 5-3   Multiple Calendar Detail, December 18, 1991–January 10, 1992

SUNDAY	MONDAY	TUESDAY	WEDNESDAY	THURSDAY	FRIDAY	SATURDAY
DATE...................................18DEC91				19DEC91	20DEC91	21DEC91
CALENDAR 1 WORKDAY.....................1				2	3	4
CALENDAR 2 WORKDAY.....................1				2	3	NO WORK
22DEC91	23DEC91	24DEC91	25DEC91	26DEC91	27DEC91	28DEC91
NO WORK	5	6	HOLIDAY	7	8	9
NO WORK	4	HOLIDAY	HOLIDAY	5	6	NO WORK
			------------------ 1992 ------------------			
29DEC91	30DEC91	31DEC91	1JAN92	2JAN92	3JAN92	4JAN92
NO WORK	10	11	HOLIDAY	12	13	14
NO WORK	7	8	HOLIDAY	9	10	NO WORK
5JAN92	6JAN92	7JAN92	8JAN92	9JAN92	10JAN92	
NO WORK	15	16	17	18	19	
NO WORK	11	12	13	14	15	

Table 5-4   Schedule Summary

```
-----------------------------------------------------------------------------
SCHEDULE SUMMARY                                    DATE: _____
-----------------------------------------------------------------------------
PROJECT NAME:   TWO-CALENDAR DATE CONSTRAINTS EXAMPLE (BASELINE)_____
-----------------------------------------------------------------------------
```

ACTIVITY ID/CAL	ORIG DUR	REM DUR	% DONE	EARLY START	EARLY FINISH	LATE START	LATE FINISH	TOTAL FLOAT
A 1 *	3	3	0	18DEC91	20DEC91	18DEC91	20DEC91	0 *
B 1 *	7	7	0	21DEC91	30DEC91	21DEC91	30DEC91	0 *
C 1 *	5	5	0	31DEC91	6JAN92	31DEC91	6JAN92	0 *
D 2	2	2	0	23DEC91	26DEC91	27DEC91	30DEC91	2
E 2	4	4	0	27DEC91	2JAN92	31DEC91	6JAN92	2
F 1 *	2	2	0	7JAN92	8JAN92	7JAN92	8JAN92	0 *

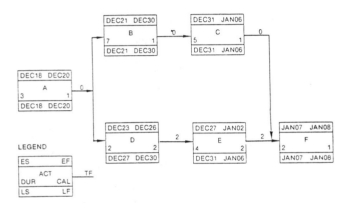

FIGURE 5-5.   Network setup diagram.

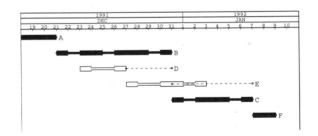

FIGURE 5-6.   Gantt Chart.

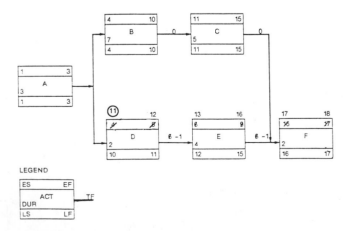

FIGURE 5-7.   Network setup diagram.

- Early Start of *D*
- Early Finish of *D*
- All activities leading from *D*

It does not, however, affect Late Start or Late Finish.

The resulting summary report is shown in Table 5-5, and in bar chart format (Fig. 5-8).

Did you remember to restrict project finish to October 17? If not, your late dates will probably be off by one day (Table 5-6).

Note what happened to these values in Table 5-6:

- Available float for *D*
- Available float for successor activities of *D*
- The Critical Path
- Project finish date

The seven days by which Early Start of *D* was delayed:

- Used up all six days (and more) available float for *D*
- Decreased float for successor activities of *D*
- Turned both *D* and its successors super-critical
- Split the Critical Path
- Delayed normal project finish by the one day resulting negative float to October 18

If, instead, an October 8 SNET constraint were imposed on *C*, the schedule dates in this network would not change. This is because the calculated Early Start of October 11 is later than the constraint. The SNET constraint would be disregarded and have no effect on *C* or any other activity under current conditions.

Multiple Calendars

Multiple-calendar constraints are calculated like their single-calendar counterparts. However, schedule dates may vary because of differences in available worktime across calendars. Suppose a December 30 SNET constraint is placed on *D*. Because this date is later than the calculated Early Start of December 23 and results in a tighter schedule, the con-

Table 5-5   Schedule Summary

```
------------------------------------------------------------------------------------
SCHEDULE SUMMARY                                    DATE: _____

PROJECT NAME:   START NO EARLIER THAN (SNET) EXAMPLE_____
------------------------------------------------------------------------------------
```

ACTIVITY ID		ORIG DUR	REM DUR	% DONE	EARLY START	EARLY FINISH	LATE START	LATE FINISH	TOTAL FLOAT	
A	*	3	3	0	1OCT91	3OCT91	1OCT91	3OCT91	0	*
B	*	7	7	0	4OCT91	10OCT91	4OCT91	10OCT91	0	*
C	*	5	5	0	11OCT91	15OCT91	11OCT91	15OCT91	0	*
D	*	2	2	0	11OCT91*	12OCT91	10OCT91	11OCT91	-1	*
E	*	4	4	0	13OCT91	16OCT91	12OCT91	15OCT91	-1	*
F	*	2	2	0	17OCT91	18OCT91	16OCT91	17OCT91	-1	*

Table 5-6   Schedule Summary

```
------------------------------------------------------------------------------------
SCHEDULE SUMMARY                                    DATE: _____

PROJECT NAME:   START NO EARLIER THAN EXAMPLE WITHOUT OCTOBER 17 DEADLINE_____
------------------------------------------------------------------------------------
```

ACTIVITY ID		ORIG DUR	REM DUR	% DONE	EARLY START	EARLY FINISH	LATE START	LATE FINISH	TOTAL FLOAT	
A		3	3	0	1OCT91	3OCT91	2OCT91	4OCT91	1	
B		7	7	0	4OCT91	10OCT91	5OCT91	11OCT91	1	
C		5	5	0	11OCT91	15OCT91	12OCT91	16OCT91	1	
D	*	2	2	0	11OCT91*	12OCT91	11OCT91	12OCT91	0	*
E	*	4	4	0	13OCT91	16OCT91	13OCT91	16OCT91	0	*
F	*	2	2	0	17OCT91	18OCT91	17OCT91	18OCT91	0	*

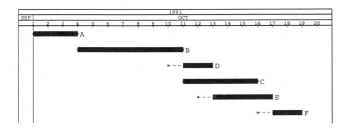

FIGURE 5-8.   Gantt Chart.

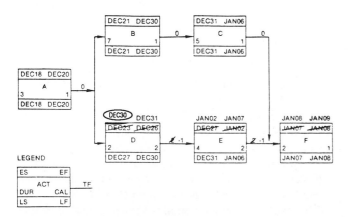

FIGURE 5-9.   Network setup diagram.

straint affects both *D* and the early dates of all activities leading from it. If, on the other hand, the imposed SNET constraint were earlier than December 23, the original schedule calculations would still hold (Fig. 5-9).

The resulting summary report is shown in Table 5-7, and in bar chart format (Fig. 5-10).

FINISH NO EARLIER THAN (FNET)

When an *FNET* constraint is applied, the activity (or entire project):

- Must not finish before this date
- May end after then if not critical

This affects Early Finish. It functions exactly like the SNET constraint except it applies to Early Finish rather than Early Start. It changes the schedule only if the FNET constraint is later than calculated Early Finish. This constraint is usually applied only to activities with few (if any) predecessors and ones that must be accomplished just in time for another task, or the next project phase. This constraint can be used to remove some, but not all, of an activity's float.

Table 5-7   Schedule Summary

```
------------------------------------------------------------------------------------
SCHEDULE SUMMARY                                               DATE:  _____

PROJECT NAME:   TWO-CALENDAR START NO EARLIER THAN (SNET) EXAMPLE_____
------------------------------------------------------------------------------------
ACTIVITY    ORIG   REM    %    EARLY     EARLY      LATE      LATE      TOTAL
ID/CAL      DUR    DUR   DONE   START    FINISH     START    FINISH     FLOAT
--------    ----   ---   ----  -------   -------   -------   -------    -----
  A  1 *     3      3     0    18DEC91   20DEC91   18DEC91   20DEC91      0 *
  B  1 *     7      7     0    21DEC91   30DEC91   21DEC91   30DEC91      0 *
  C  1 *     5      5     0    31DEC91    6JAN92   31DEC91    6JAN92      0 *
  D  2 *     2      2     0    30DEC91*  31DEC91   27DEC91   30DEC91     -1 *
  E  2 *     4      4     0     2JAN92    7JAN92   31DEC91    6JAN92     -1 *
  F  1 *     2      2     0     8JAN92    9JAN92    7JAN92    8JAN92     -1 *
------------------------------------------------------------------------------------
```

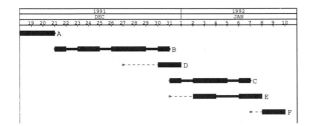

FIGURE 5-10.   Gantt Chart.

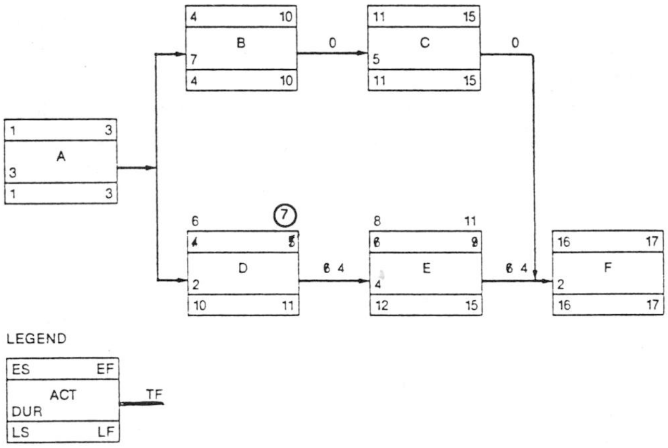

FIGURE 5-11.   Network setup diagram.

Single Calendar

In the diagram in Fig. 5-11, an October 7 FNET constraint is imposed on *D*. Because this date is later than the calculated Early Finish of October 5, the constraint applies and affects:

- Early Finish of *D*
- Early Start of *D*
- All activities leading from *D*.

It does not, however, affect Late Start or Late Finish.

The resulting summary report is shown in Table 5-8, and in bar chart format (Fig. 5-12).

Note what has happened to the following values:

- Available float for *D*
- Available float for successor activities of *D*

The two days by which Early Start of *D* was delayed:

- Used up two days available float for *D*, leaving four
- Decreased float for successor activities of *D* by the same amount until this chain joined the Critical Path coming down from *C*

If, on the other hand, the FNET constraint were earlier than October 5, the schedule dates in this network would not change. This is because the calculated Early Finish of October 5 is later than the constraint. The FNET constraint would be disregarded and have no effect on *D* or any other activity under current conditions.

Multiple Calendars

Suppose a December 30 FNET constraint is placed on *D*. Because this date is later than the calculated Early Finish of December 26 and results in a tighter schedule, the constraint affects both *D* and the early dates of all activities leading from it (all are made critical) until the original Critical Path is rejoined at *F*. If, on the other hand, the imposed FNET constraint were earlier than December 26, the original schedule calculations would still hold (Fig. 5-13).

The resulting summary report is shown in Table 5-9, and in bar chart format (Fig. 5-14).

Table 5-8   Schedule Summary

```
------------------------------------------------------------------------
SCHEDULE SUMMARY                                    DATE: _____

PROJECT NAME:   FINISH NO EARLIER THAN (FNET) EXAMPLE_____
------------------------------------------------------------------------
```

ACTIVITY ID		ORIG DUR	REM DUR	% DONE	EARLY START	EARLY FINISH	LATE START	LATE FINISH	TOTAL FLOAT	
A	*	3	3	0	1OCT91	3OCT91	1OCT91	3OCT91	0	*
B	*	7	7	0	4OCT91	10OCT91	4OCT91	10OCT91	0	*
C	*	5	5	0	11OCT91	15OCT91	11OCT91	15OCT91	0	*
D		2	2	0	6OCT91	7OCT91*	10OCT91	11OCT91	4	
E		4	4	0	8OCT91	11OCT91	12OCT91	15OCT91	4	
F	*	2	2	0	16OCT91	17OCT91	16OCT91	17OCT91	0	*

Table 5-9   Schedule Summary

```
------------------------------------------------------------------------
SCHEDULE SUMMARY                                    DATE: _____

PROJECT NAME:   TWO-CALENDAR FINISH NO EARLIER THAN (FNET) EXAMPLE_____
------------------------------------------------------------------------
```

ACTIVITY ID/CAL			ORIG DUR	REM DUR	% DONE	EARLY START	EARLY FINISH	LATE START	LATE FINISH	TOTAL FLOAT	
A	1	*	3	3	0	18DEC91	20DEC91	18DEC91	20DEC91	0	*
B	1	*	7	7	0	21DEC91	30DEC91	21DEC91	30DEC91	0	*
C	1	*	5	5	0	31DEC91	6JAN92	31DEC91	6JAN92	0	*
D	2	*	2	2	0	27DEC91	30DEC91*	27DEC91	30DEC91	0	*
E	2	*	4	4	0	31DEC91	6JAN92	31DEC91	6JAN92	0	*
F	1	*	2	2	0	7JAN92	8JAN92	7JAN92	8JAN92	0	*

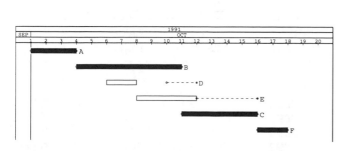

FIGURE 5-12.   Gantt Chart.

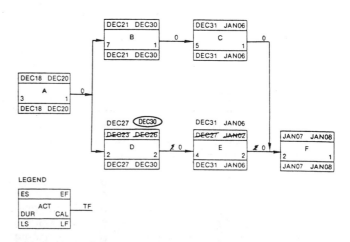

FIGURE 5-13.   Network setup diagram.

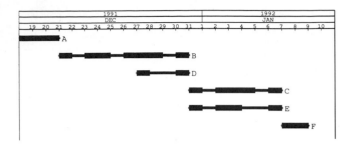

FIGURE 5-14.   Gantt Chart.

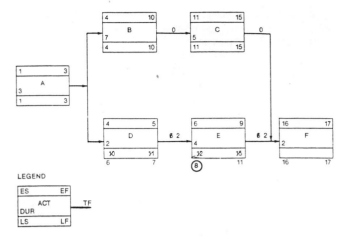

FIGURE 5-15.   Network setup diagram.

START NO LATER THAN (SNLT)

When an *SNLT* constraint is applied, the activity (or entire project):

- Must start before this date

This affects Late Start. It changes the schedule only if the SNLT constraint is earlier than calculated Late Start. This constraint is usually the result of an agreement that an activity will begin on or before a particular date already advertised. It sometimes relates to weather and other conditions. Although it is really on-time activity/project completion that is desired, an SNLT constraint is often applied "activity-duration" days prior to this desired finish. This action:

- Provides both greater and earlier visibility of effort
- Locks in a deadline start date not subject to schedule changes
- May also help reduce float in successive activities

Single Calendar

In the diagram in Fig. 5-15, an October 8 SNLT constraint is imposed on *E*. Because this date is earlier than the calculated Late Start of October 12, the constraint applies and affects:

- Late Start of *E*
- Late Finish of *E*
- All non-critical activities leading into *E*

It does not, however, affect Early Start or Early Finish.

The resulting summary report is shown in Table 5-10, and in bar chart format (Fig. 5-16).

Note what has happened to the following values:

- Available float for *E*
- Available float for predecessor activities of *E*

The four days by which Late Start of *E* was moved up:

- Used up four days available float for *E*, leaving two
- Decreased float for non-critical predecessors of *E*

If, on the other hand, you impose an SNLT constraint later than October 12 on *E*, the schedule dates in this network will not change. This is because the calculated Late Start of October 12 is earlier than the constraint. The SNLT constraint would be disregarded and have no effect on *E* or any other activity under current conditions.

Table 5-10   Schedule Summary

```
---------------------------------------------------------------------------
SCHEDULE SUMMARY                                       DATE: _____

PROJECT NAME:   START NO LATER THAN (SNLT) EXAMPLE_____
---------------------------------------------------------------------------
```

ACTIVITY ID		ORIG DUR	REM DUR	% DONE	EARLY START	EARLY FINISH	LATE START	LATE FINISH	TOTAL FLOAT	
A	*	3	3	0	1OCT91	3OCT91	1OCT91	3OCT91	0	*
B	*	7	7	0	4OCT91	10OCT91	4OCT91	10OCT91	0	*
C	*	5	5	0	11OCT91	15OCT91	11OCT91	15OCT91	0	*
D		2	2	0	4OCT91	5OCT91	6OCT91	7OCT91	2	
E		4	4	0	6OCT91	9OCT91	8OCT91*	11OCT91	2	
F	*	2	2	0	16OCT91	17OCT91	16OCT91	17OCT91	0	*

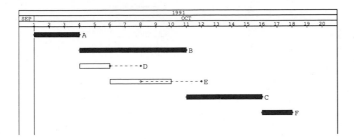

FIGURE 5-16.   Gantt Chart.

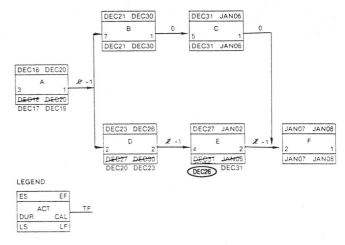

FIGURE 5-17.   Network setup diagram.

Multiple Calendars

Suppose a December 26 SNLT constraint is placed on *E*. Because this date is earlier than the calculated Late Start of December 31 and results in a tighter schedule, the constraint affects both *E* and the late dates of all activities preceding it. If, on the other hand, the imposed SNLT constraint were later than December 31, the original schedule calculations would still hold (Fig. 5-17).

The resulting summary report is shown in Table 5-11, and in bar chart format (Fig. 5-18).

FINISH NO LATER THAN (FNLT)

When an *FNLT* constraint is applied, the activity (or entire project):

- Must finish by this date

This affects Late Finish and is the most common date constraint. Cinderella's date to the ball had an FNLT midnight constraint. Calculated Late Finish is compared with the assigned FNLT constraint, and the earlier of the two times is selected. This will reduce the float of the constrained

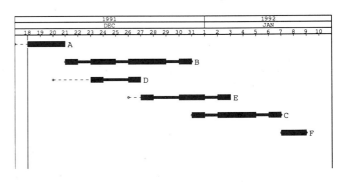

FIGURE 5-18.   Gantt Chart.

Table 5-11   Schedule Summary

```
------------------------------------------------------------------------------
SCHEDULE SUMMARY                                    DATE: _____

PROJECT NAME:  TWO-CALENDAR START NO LATER THAN (SNLT) EXAMPLE_____
------------------------------------------------------------------------------
```

ACTIVITY ID/CAL	ORIG DUR	REM DUR	% DONE	EARLY START	EARLY FINISH	LATE START	LATE FINISH	TOTAL FLOAT
A 1 *	3	3	0	18DEC91	20DEC91	17DEC91	19DEC91	−1 *
B 1 *	7	7	0	21DEC91	30DEC91	21DEC91	30DEC91	0 *
C 1 *	5	5	0	31DEC91	6JAN92	31DEC91	6JAN92	0 *
D 2 *	2	2	0	23DEC91	26DEC91	20DEC91	23DEC91	−1 *
E 2 *	4	4	0	27DEC91	2JAN92	26DEC91*	31DEC91	−1 *
F 1 *	2	2	0	7JAN92	8JAN92	7JAN92	8JAN92	0 *

activity (and its predecessors) by the amount of the difference. Critical activities will now turn super-critical and non-critical activities may, if they lose all their float, turn critical. If this happens, we shall need to recalculate the entire work to see if the Critical Path has:

• Remained the same
• Shifted to include the constrained activities
• Split into two or more paths

The FNLT constraint is often used to set intermediate completion dates or milestones. It is very similar to the SNLT constraint described earlier. When applying these (and other) constraints, make sure that they give the desired effects. Avoid placing both an SNET and an FNLT constraint on the same path, if possible. If that must be done, be sure to declare which has precedence over the other if a tiebreaker is necessary. Even so, the results produced may be misleading or unintended—and require extra special care in interpretation.

The decision to give precedence to one or the other constraint will both simplify calculations and clarify results. This is because the calculations need take into account only the primary constraint. The secondary constraint can then be compared with the appropriate calculated event time to determine the probable effect.

In the diagram in Fig. 5-19, an October 9 FNLT constraint is imposed on *E*. Because this date is earlier than the calculated Late Finish of October 15, the constraint applies and affects:

• Late Finish of *E*
• Late Start of *E*
• All non-critical activities leading into *E*

It does not, however, affect Early Start or Early Finish.
The resulting summary report is shown in Table 5-12, and in bar chart format (Fig. 5-20).
Note what has happened to the following values:

• Available float for *E*
• Available float for predecessor activities of *E*

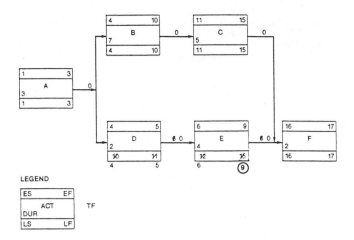

FIGURE 5-19.   Network setup diagram.

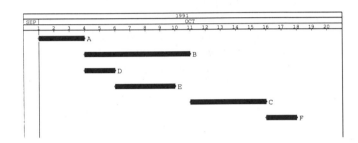

FIGURE 5-20.   Gantt Chart.

The six days by which Late Finish of *E* was moved up:

• Used up all six days available float for *E*, leaving none
• Decreased float for *E*'s non-critical predecessor activities
• Turned *D* and *E* critical
• Split the Critical Path into two: *A-B-C-F* and *A-D-E-F*

If, on the other hand, you impose an FNLT constraint later than October 15 on *E*, the schedule dates in this network will not change. This is because the calculated Late Finish of October 15 is earlier than the constraint. The constraint would be disregarded and have no effect on *E* or any other activity under current conditions.

Table 5-12   Schedule Summary

```
---------------------------------------------------------------------------------
SCHEDULE SUMMARY                                    DATE: _____

PROJECT NAME:   FINISH NO LATER THAN (FNLT) EXAMPLE_____
---------------------------------------------------------------------------------
```

ACTIVITY ID		ORIG DUR	REM DUR	% DONE	EARLY START	EARLY FINISH	LATE START	LATE FINISH	TOTAL FLOAT	
A	*	3	3	0	1OCT91	3OCT91	1OCT91	3OCT91	0	*
B	*	7	7	0	4OCT91	10OCT91	4OCT91	10OCT91	0	*
C	*	5	5	0	11OCT91	15OCT91	11OCT91	15OCT91	0	*
D	*	2	2	0	4OCT91	5OCT91	4OCT91	5OCT91	0	*
E	*	4	4	0	6OCT91	9OCT91	6OCT91	9OCT91*	0	*
F	*	2	2	0	16OCT91	17OCT91	16OCT91	17OCT91	0	*

Multiple Calendars

Suppose (Figure 5-21) a December 31 FNLT constraint is placed on *E*. Because this date is earlier than the calculated Late Finish of January 6 and results in a tighter schedule, the constraint affects both *E* and the late dates of all activities preceding it. If, on the other hand, the imposed FNLT constraint were later than January 6, the original schedule calculations would still hold (Fig. 5-5).

The resulting summary report is shown in Table 5-13, and in bar chart format (Fig. 5-22).

In summary, the four major constraints affect the schedule as shown in Fig. 5-23.

START ON (ON)

This constraint operates as if both an SNET and an SNLT restriction imposed on the same activity. By setting both Early Start and Late Start to the imposed date, the Start On constraint revises:

- ES and EF only if the constraint is later than calculated Early Start
- LS and LF only if the constraint is earlier than calculated Late Start

This constraint, therefore, can:

- Delay Early Start to satisfy the imposed date
- Accelerate Late Start to do the same thing
- Protect network logic more faithfully than Mandatory Start

Use this constraint with caution.

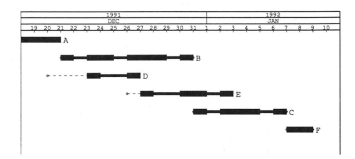

FIGURE 5-22. Gantt Chart.

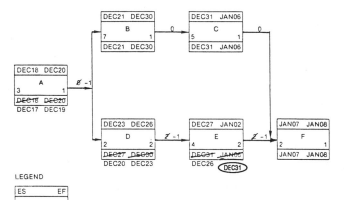

FIGURE 5-21. Network setup diagram.

```
            SNET    FNET
          ┌─────────────┐
          │  ES     EF  │
          │             │
          │             │
          │  LS     LF  │
          └─────────────┘
            SNLT    FNLT
```

```
-----------------------------------------------------------------------
CONSTRAINT                      AFFECTS   CALENDAR CHANGED IF CONSTRAINT:
-----------------------------------------------------------------------
Start no earlier than   (SNET)    ES      later than computed Early Start
Finish no earlier than  (FNET)    EF        "      "      "      "   Finish
Start no later than     (SNLT)    LS      earlier  "      "    Late Start
Finish no later than    (FNLT)    LF        "      "      "      "   Finish
-----------------------------------------------------------------------
```

FIGURE 5-23. How date constraints affect the "Big Four" dates.

Table 5-13 Schedule Summary

```
-----------------------------------------------------------------------
SCHEDULE SUMMARY                              DATE: _____


PROJECT NAME:  TWO-CALENDAR FINISH NO LATER THAN (FNLT) EXAMPLE_____
-----------------------------------------------------------------------
ACTIVITY    ORIG   REM    %    EARLY     EARLY     LATE      LATE    TOTAL
 ID/CAL     DUR    DUR   DONE  START     FINISH    START     FINISH  FLOAT
--------   ----   ---   ----  -------   -------   -------   -------  -----
  A  1  *    3      3     0   18DEC91   20DEC91   17DEC91   19DEC91   -1 *
  B  1  *    7      7     0   21DEC91   30DEC91   21DEC91   30DEC91    0 *
  C  1  *    5      5     0   31DEC91    6JAN92   31DEC91    6JAN92    0 *
  D  2  *    2      2     0   23DEC91   26DEC91   20DEC91   23DEC91   -1 *
  E  2  *    4      4     0   27DEC91    2JAN92   26DEC91   31DEC91*  -1 *
  F  1  *    2      2     0    7JAN92    8JAN92    7JAN92    8JAN92    0 *
-----------------------------------------------------------------------
```

Single Calendar

In Fig. 5-24, an October 13 Start On constraint is imposed on *C*. Because this date is later than the calculated Early Start of October 11, the constraint applies and affects:

- Early Start of *C*
- Early Finish of *C*
- All activities leading from *C*

It does not, however, affect Late Start or Late Finish in this particular case (but could in others) because the scheduled October 11 Late Start is earlier than the October 13 constraint.

The resulting summary report is shown in Table 5-14, and in bar chart format (Fig. 5-25).

Note what has happened to the following values:

- Available float for *C*
- Available float for successor activities of *C*

The two days by which *C* early dates were delayed:

- Turned both *C* and *F* super-critical by the same two days
- Extended the project by the same two days to October 19

Multiple Calendars

Suppose a December 30 Start On constraint is imposed on *E* (Fig. 5-26). Because this date is later than the calculated Early Start of December 27 and results in a tighter early schedule, the restriction applies. Since the constraint is also earlier than the scheduled December 31 Late Start, it applies in the late schedule as well. Both Early Start and Late Start are set to December 30. The overall result is a decrease in float for both *E* (2 days) and its predecessor, *D* (1 day). Hope December 30 turned out to be a very special day!

The resulting summary report is shown in Table 5-15, and in bar chart format (Fig. 5-27).

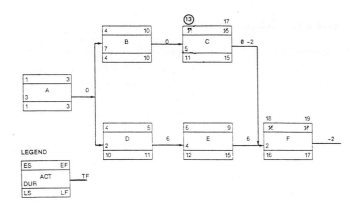

FIGURE 5-24.   Network setup diagram.

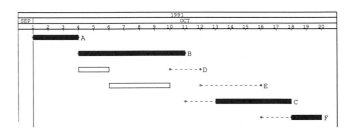

FIGURE 5-25.   Gantt Chart.

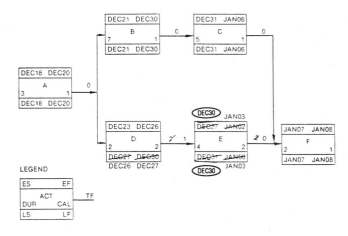

FIGURE 5-26.   Network setup diagram.

Table 5-14   Schedule Summary

```
--------------------------------------------------------------------------------
SCHEDULE SUMMARY                                      DATE: _____

PROJECT NAME:  START ON (ON) EXAMPLE_____
--------------------------------------------------------------------------------
```

ACTIVITY ID		ORIG DUR	REM DUR	% DONE	EARLY START	EARLY FINISH	LATE START	LATE FINISH	TOTAL FLOAT	
A	*	3	3	0	1OCT91	3OCT91	1OCT91	3OCT91	0	*
B	*	7	7	0	4OCT91	10OCT91	4OCT91	10OCT91	0	*
C	*	5	5	0	13OCT91*	17OCT91	11OCT91*	15OCT91	-2	*
D		2	2	0	4OCT91	5OCT91	10OCT91	11OCT91	6	
E		4	4	0	6OCT91	9OCT91	12OCT91	15OCT91	6	
F	*	2	2	0	18OCT91	19OCT91	16OCT91	17OCT91	-2	*

Table 5-15   Schedule Summary

```
------------------------------------------------------------------------
SCHEDULE SUMMARY                                   DATE: _____

PROJECT NAME:  TWO-CALENDAR START ON (ON) EXAMPLE_____
------------------------------------------------------------------------
ACTIVITY   ORIG   REM    %     EARLY     EARLY     LATE      LATE    TOTAL
 ID/CAL    DUR    DUR   DONE   START     FINISH    START     FINISH  FLOAT
--------   ----   ---   ----   -------   -------   -------   ------- -----
  A  1 *    3      3     0     18DEC91   20DEC91   18DEC91   20DEC91   0 *
  B  1 *    7      7     0     21DEC91   30DEC91   21DEC91   30DEC91   0 *
  C  1 *    5      5     0     31DEC91    6JAN92   31DEC91    6JAN92   0 *
  D  2      2      2     0     23DEC91   26DEC91   26DEC91   27DEC91   1
  E  2 *    4      4     0     30DEC91*   3JAN92   30DEC91*   3JAN92   0 *
  F  1 *    2      2     0      7JAN92    8JAN92    7JAN92    8JAN92   0 *
------------------------------------------------------------------------
```

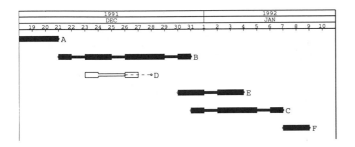

FIGURE 5-27.   Gantt Chart.

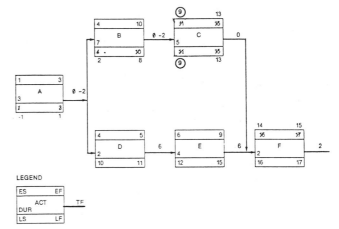

FIGURE 5-28.   Network setup diagram.

MANDATORY START (MS)

The Mandatory Start constraint is similar to the Start On constraint because, like ON, it sets both Early Start and Late Start equal to the imposed date. The activity (or project) must start only on this specified date and neither before nor after. Use this constraint when the kick-off party date cannot be changed.

The Mandatory Start constraint differs from the Start On restriction because:

- It is never overridden by schedule calculations
- It may violate network logic by forcing an activity to have dates earlier than its predecessors
- It affects late dates of all predecessors
- It affects early dates of all successors

Use only with extreme caution! Also, avoid imposing a mandatory-start date that occurs on a nonworkday, for obvious reasons!

Single Calendar

In Fig. 5-28, an October 9 Mandatory Start constraint is imposed on C. This moves both Early Start and Late Start up two days, from October 11 to October 9. It also moves up Early Finish and Late Finish by the same two days, from October 15 to October 13.

But wait! In so doing, we have forced a "squeeze play" and scheduled C to start ("or else!") on October 9, even though its predecessor, B, cannot finish until the next day, October 10. Activity B is suddenly two days behind, even before project start. This shows how the Mandatory Start constraint can sometimes violate network logic.

What we need to do is to rob Peter to pay Paul: The two days' earlier (mandatory) start on C:

- Moves F early dates up two days
- Creates two days float in F
- Must be plowed back to reduce A and B Late Start and Late Finish

In other words:

- Predecessor activities of C revise late dates and decrease float
- Successor activities of C revise early dates and increase float
- Predecessor activities of C apply this float to counteract constraint effects

Table 5-16   Schedule Summary

```
------------------------------------------------------------------------
SCHEDULE SUMMARY                                DATE: _____

PROJECT NAME:  MANDATORY START (MS) EXAMPLE_____
------------------------------------------------------------------------
```

ACTIVITY ID		ORIG DUR	REM DUR	% DONE	EARLY START	EARLY FINISH	LATE START	LATE FINISH	TOTAL FLOAT	
A	*	3	3	0	1OCT91	3OCT91	29SEP91	1OCT91	-2	*
B	*	7	7	0	4OCT91	10OCT91	2OCT91	8OCT91	-2	*
C	*	5	5	0	9OCT91*	13OCT91	9OCT91*	13OCT91	0	*
D		2	2	0	4OCT91	5OCT91	10OCT91	11OCT91	6	
E		4	4	0	6OCT91	9OCT91	12OCT91	15OCT91	6	
F	*	2	2	0	14OCT91	15OCT91	16OCT91	17OCT91	2	*

The resulting summary report is shown in Table 5-16, and in bar chart format (Fig. 5-29).

Note what has happened to the following values:

- Available float for predecessors of *C*
- Available float for successors of *C*

The two days by which both *C* start dates were moved up:

- Turned both *A* and *B* super-critical by the same two days
- Introduced two days' float of doubtful value in *F*
- Reduced project duration by the same two days to fifteen (if early schedule is followed)

Multiple Calendars

Suppose a December 30 Mandatory Start constraint is imposed on *E* (Fig. 5-30). This forces its start dates, even though *D* is scheduled to finish on December 26 (EF). Activities following *E* might revise their early dates (this does not quite happen here, though); those preceding it will revise their late dates, as does happen here. The overall result is a decrease in float along the path. Unlike the single-calendar example, this MS constraint does not violate network logic, but does not allow activities to flow as efficiently as they could. Hope December 30 turned out to be a very special day!

The resulting summary report is shown in Table 5-17, and in bar chart format (Fig. 5-31).

MANDATORY FINISH (MF)

The activity (or project) must finish only on this specified date and neither before nor after. Use this constraint when the completion ceremony date cannot be changed. Both Early Finish and Late Finish are set to this imposed completion date. As was the case with Mandatory Start:

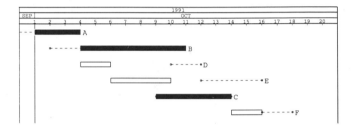

FIGURE 5-29.   Gantt Chart.

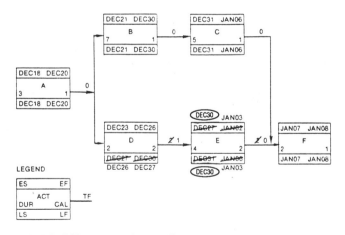

FIGURE 5-30.   Network setup diagram.

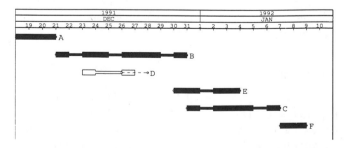

FIGURE 5-31.   Gantt Chart.

Table 5-17   Schedule Summary

```
------------------------------------------------------------------------------
SCHEDULE SUMMARY                                      DATE: _____

PROJECT NAME:  TWO-CALENDAR MANDATORY START (MS) EXAMPLE_____
------------------------------------------------------------------------------
```

ACTIVITY ID/CAL			ORIG DUR	REM DUR	% DONE	EARLY START	EARLY FINISH	LATE START	LATE FINISH	TOTAL FLOAT	
A	1	*	3	3	0	18DEC91	20DEC91	18DEC91	20DEC91	0	*
B	1	*	7	7	0	21DEC91	30DEC91	21DEC91	30DEC91	0	*
C	1	*	5	5	0	31DEC91	6JAN92	31DEC91	6JAN92	0	*
D	2		2	2	0	23DEC91	26DEC91	26DEC91	27DEC91	1	
E	2	*	4	4	0	30DEC91*	3JAN92	30DEC91*	3JAN92	0	*
F	1	*	2	2	0	7JAN92	8JAN92	7JAN92	8JAN92	0	*

- It is never overridden by schedule calculations
- It may violate network logic by forcing an activity to have dates earlier than its predecessors
- It affects late dates of all predecessor activities
- It affects early dates of all successor activities

Be very careful with this constraint, too. Avoid imposing a mandatory-finish date:

- As a project completion date (use an imposed *project,* rather than activity, finish date instead)
- That occurs on a nonworkday (again for obvious reasons)

Single Calendar

In Fig. 5-32, an October 8 Mandatory Finish constraint is imposed on *B.* This moves both Early Finish and Late Finish up two days, from October 10 to October 8. It also moves up Early Start and Late Start by the same two days, from October 4 to October 2.

But wait! In so doing, we have again forced a "squeeze play" and scheduled *B* to start ("or else!") on October 2, even though its predecessor, *A,* cannot finish until the next day, October 3. Activity *A* is suddenly two days behind, even before project start. This again shows how the Mandatory Finish constraint can sometimes violate network logic.

We again need to rob Peter to pay Paul: The two days earlier (mandatory) start on *B:*

- Moves *C* and *F* early dates up two days
- Creates two days float in *C* and *F*
- Must be plowed back to reduce Late Start and Late Finish of *A*

In other words:

- Predecessors of *B* revise late dates and decrease float
- Successors of *B* revise early dates and increase float
- Predecessors of *B* apply this float to counteract constraint effects

The resulting summary report is shown in Table 5-18, and in bar chart format (Fig. 5-33).

Note what has happened to the following values:

- Available float for predecessors of *B*
- Available float for successors of *B*

The two days by which both finish dates of *B* were moved up:

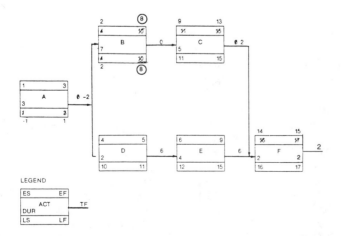

FIGURE 5-32.   Network setup diagram.

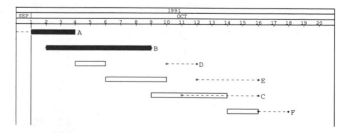

FIGURE 5-33.   Gantt Chart.

Table 5-18   Schedule Summary

```
------------------------------------------------------------------------
SCHEDULE SUMMARY                                    DATE: _____

PROJECT NAME:  MANDATORY FINISH (MF) EXAMPLE_____
------------------------------------------------------------------------
```

ACTIVITY ID		ORIG DUR	REM DUR	% DONE	EARLY START	EARLY FINISH	LATE START	LATE FINISH	TOTAL FLOAT	
A	*	3	3	0	1OCT91	3OCT91	29SEP91	1OCT91	-2	*
B	*	7	7	0	2OCT91	8OCT91*	2OCT91	8OCT91*	0	*
C		5	5	0	9OCT91	13OCT91	11OCT91	15OCT91	2	
D		2	2	0	4OCT91	5OCT91	10OCT91	11OCT91	6	
E		4	4	0	6OCT91	9OCT91	12OCT91	15OCT91	6	
F		2	2	0	14OCT91	15OCT91	16OCT91	17OCT91	2	

- Turned *A* super-critical by the same two days
- Introduced two days float of doubtful value in *C* and *F*
- Reduced project duration by the same two days to fifteen (if early schedule is followed)

Multiple Calendars

Suppose a January 3 Mandatory Finish constraint is imposed on *C* (Fig. 5-34). This causes *C* to start December 28, violating its (early-schedule) relationship with *B*. Activity *F*, which succeeds *C*, revises its early dates. *A* and *B*, which precede *C*, revise their late dates. The overall result is a general disruption of the network:

- *A* and *B* turn super-critical
- *C* remains critical (but with different dates)
- *F* gains two days of useless float

If this were a required milestone, one does what is necessary. Still, if there were any other way to do it "naturally" . . .

The resulting summary report is shown in Table 5-19, and in bar chart format (Fig. 5-35).

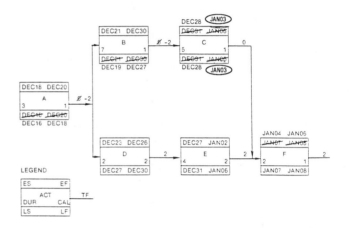

FIGURE 5-34.   Network setup diagram.

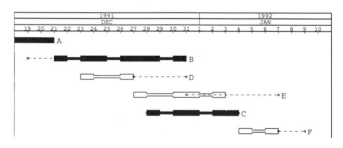

FIGURE 5-35.   Gantt Chart.

Table 5-19   Schedule Summary

```
------------------------------------------------------------------------
SCHEDULE SUMMARY                                    DATE: _____

PROJECT NAME:  TWO-CALENDAR MANDATORY FINISH (MF) EXAMPLE_____
------------------------------------------------------------------------
```

ACTIVITY ID/CAL			ORIG DUR	REM DUR	% DONE	EARLY START	EARLY FINISH	LATE START	LATE FINISH	TOTAL FLOAT	
A	1	*	3	3	0	18DEC91	20DEC91	16DEC91	18DEC91	-2	*
B	1	*	7	7	0	21DEC91	30DEC91	19DEC91	27DEC91	-2	*
C	1	*	5	5	0	28DEC91	3JAN92*	28DEC91	3JAN92*	0	*
D	2		2	2	0	23DEC91	26DEC91	27DEC91	30DEC91	2	
E	2		4	4	0	27DEC91	2JAN92	31DEC91	6JAN92	2	
F	1		2	2	0	4JAN92	6JAN92	7JAN92	8JAN92	2	

6
PDM Duration Constraints

In this chapter we shall study *duration constraints*. A duration constraint is any limit applied to how long an activity may take. They can be used when both the following apply:

- Actual duration is unknown
- Relationships, or a date, govern duration calculations

They also include constraints that control activity or path float. We have already seen one example in the hammock activity mentioned earlier.

Listed below are the four duration constraints:

- Expected finish (XF)
- Hammock activity (HA)
- Zero free float (ZFF)
- Zero total float (ZTF)

These four constraints are mutually exclusive. Only one may be applied to a particular activity at any given time.

EXPECTED FINISH (XF)

An *expected finish* constraint is a user-specified date which:

- Updates the schedule
- Redefines affected activity duration
- Serves as a forced end point in a "what if" analysis

The remaining duration of XF activities is the workday difference between:

- Calculated Early Start
- Assigned expected finish

Be sure that the expected finish date is not earlier than scheduled Early Start. Otherwise, the activity's remaining duration becomes zero. This condition, of course, should exist only for completed activities.

Single Calendar

In Fig. 6-1, an October 11 Expected Finish constraint is imposed on *D*, notwithstanding an October 4 Early Start and an original duration of only two days. This constraint replaces the calculated October 5 Early Finish. At the same time, the revised Early Finish date increases *D*'s duration to eight days, computed as the difference between the:

- Calculated October 4 Early Start
- Assigned October 11 XF constraint

The original Late Start of October 10 was moved up to October 4, which is only by coincidence the activity's Early Start. In this example, the net effect is to begin *D* at Early Start but not finish until Late Finish, thereby applying all available float to duration. As a result, both *D* and *E* are now critical, as are the other four activities.

The resulting summary report is shown in Table 6-1, and in bar chart format (Fig. 6-2).

Note what has happened to the following values:

- Duration of *D*
- Available float for *D*
- Available float for *E*

The six days by which Early Finish of *D* was delayed:

- Used up all available float for *D* and *E*
- Delayed Early Start of *E* until October 12, as though an FNET constraint had been applied to *D*
- Turned both *D* and *E* critical
- Introduced a second Critical Path through *D* and *E*

This example emphasizes an earlier point: Durations should reflect project realities and not be unjustifiably influenced by actual dates chosen more to make someone a "hero" than to meet project needs.

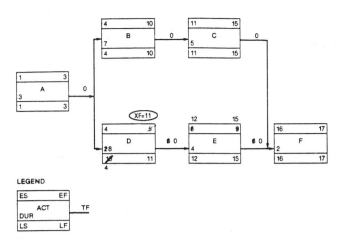

FIGURE 6-1.   Network setup diagram.

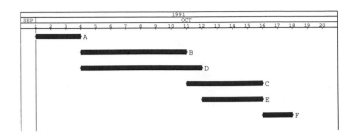

FIGURE 6-2.   Gantt Chart.

Table 6-1   Schedule Summary

```
-------------------------------------------------------------------
SCHEDULE SUMMARY                              DATE: _____

PROJECT NAME:   EXPECTED FINISH (XF) EXAMPLE_____
-------------------------------------------------------------------
ACTIVITY    ORIG    REM     %     EARLY     EARLY    LATE     LATE     TOTAL
  ID        DUR     DUR    DONE   START    FINISH   START   FINISH    FLOAT
--------    ----    ---    ----   -------  -------  -------  -------   -----
   A  *      3       3      0     1OCT91   3OCT91   1OCT91   3OCT91     0  *
   B  *      7       7      0     4OCT91  10OCT91   4OCT91  10OCT91     0  *
   C  *      5       5      0    11OCT91  15OCT91  11OCT91  15OCT91     0  *
   D  *      8       8*     0     4OCT91  11OCT91*  4OCT91  11OCT91     0  *
   E  *      4       4      0    12OCT91  15OCT91  12OCT91  15OCT91     0  *
   F  *      2       2      0    16OCT91  17OCT91  16OCT91  17OCT91     0  *
-------------------------------------------------------------------
```

Multiple Calendars

Suppose a December 30 Expected Finish constraint is imposed on *D* (Fig. 6-3). Because this date is later than the calculated Early Finish of December 28:

- Duration increases from two days to four
- Float is reduced from two days to zero
- *D* and *E* turn critical
- The Critical Path splits to include this trail

The resulting summary report is shown in Table 6-2, and in bar chart format (Fig. 6-4).

HAMMOCK ACTIVITIES (HA)

You are probably already familiar with one type of hammock activity (Fig. 6-5).

In project management, a *hammock activity* refers to a summary activity whose duration is calculated after the rest

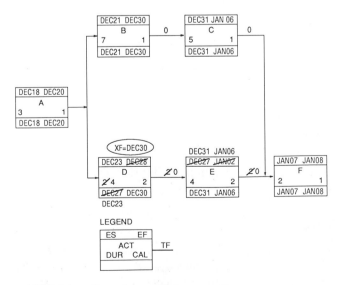

FIGURE 6-3.   Network setup diagram.

Table 6-2   Schedule Summary

```
-----------------------------------------------------------------------------
SCHEDULE SUMMARY                                      DATE: _____

PROJECT NAME:   TWO-CALENDAR EXPECTED FINISH (XF) EXAMPLE_____
-----------------------------------------------------------------------------
```

ACTIVITY ID/CAL		ORIG DUR	REM DUR	% DONE	EARLY START	EARLY FINISH	LATE START	LATE FINISH	TOTAL FLOAT	
A	1 *	3	3	0	18DEC91	20DEC91	18DEC91	20DEC91	0	*
B	1 *	7	7	0	21DEC91	30DEC91	21DEC91	30DEC91	0	*
C	1 *	5	5	0	31DEC91	6JAN92	31DEC91	6JAN92	0	*
D	2 *	4	4*	0	23DEC91	30DEC91*	23DEC91	30DEC91	0	*
E	2 *	4	4	0	31DEC91	6JAN92	31DEC91	6JAN92	0	*
F	1 *	2	2	0	7JAN92	8JAN92	7JAN92	8JAN92	0	*

of the network is scheduled. The primary purpose of a hammock activity is to summarize for a user-specified set of project activities the:

- Early and late dates
- Duration

Hammock dates are based only on the calculated dates of an activity's predecessor and successor activities. A hammock activity has a unique activity number and description, but no fixed duration; this depends on the lengths of the underlying activities it summarizes. The hammock activity duration, computed (and therefore known) only after the rest of the network, is calculated from the:

- Earliest Early Start date (of its SSO predecessor)
- Latest Early Finish date (of its FFO successor)

These relationships always hold true. A hammock activity cannot start until the first contained activity begins, instantaneously before. For this reason, the first contained activity is considered a predecessor to the hammock; the hammock cannot begin or exist without it. The hammock activity, conversely, is considered a successor to the anchor. In either case, the lag is zero because the two activities commence almost simultaneously.

Similarly, the hammock and the last contained activity

finish almost simultaneously. Although it might seem, therefore, that the hammock should be considered the successor, keep in mind that the FFO relationship makes this matter moot. For simplicity and balance, the hammock is considered the anchor activity predecessor.

As these contained times change, so does the hammock. Inserting a hammock between two otherwise unrelated activities creates a *reporting* relationship, the hammock, even if none existed prior to this action. It does *not*, however, create a *logical* relationship.

A hammock activity should have at least one predecessor activity and one successor activity, but may have more. The predecessor activity with the earliest Early Start is assigned an SSO relationship to define hammock start; the successor activity with the latest Early Finish is assigned an FFO relationship to define hammock end.

A hammock with no predecessor activities is assumed to start on the data date, and a hammock without successor activities to end on the project completion date. A hammock activity with no predecessors or successors spans all activ-

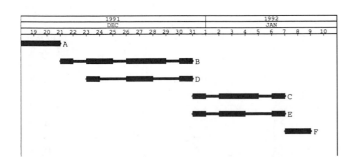

FIGURE 6-4.   Gantt Chart.

FIGURE 6-5.   Hammock activity. *Source:* CSC Diagraph.

ities between the data date and the project finish date (imposed if it exists, otherwise Early Finish), thereby providing a quick summary of project duration remaining.

Hammock duration is first calculated after the forward (early-dates) pass. It is recalculated after the reverse (late-dates) pass through the network. Note well that the forward-pass duration will equal the reverse-pass duration only under certain ideal conditions. If any underlying activities make progress out of sequence or have imposed constraints, the two values will be different. As long as the reason for this is understood, there is no cause for alarm.

Single Calendar

Note in Fig. 6-6 hammock activity H, which has:

- A zero-lag Start-to-Start relationship with D
- A zero-lag Finish-to-Finish relationship with E
- October 4 Early Start (from D)
- October 10 Late Start (from D)
- October 9 Early Finish (from E)
- October 15 Late Finish (from E)
- Six days duration (computed as usual but only after all other activities)
- Six days float

The resulting summary report is shown in Table 6-3, and in bar chart format (Fig. 6-7).

To establish a hammock activity:

1. Add the hammock activity to the project
2. Define the activity as a hammock
3. Define all predecessors; declare an SSO relationship with the activity whose Early Start is earliest
4. Define all successors; declare an FFO relationship with the activity whose Early Finish is latest
5. Compute the network schedule to determine hammock duration and dates

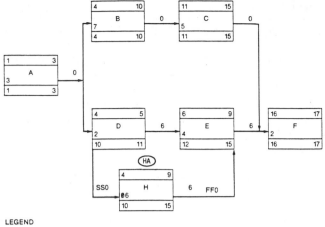

FIGURE 6-6.   Network setup diagram.

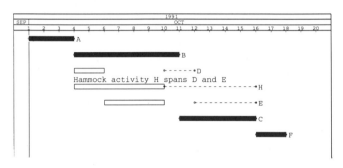

FIGURE 6-7.   Gantt Chart.

Table 6-3   Schedule Summary

```
-------------------------------------------------------------------
SCHEDULE SUMMARY                              DATE: _____

PROJECT NAME:   HAMMOCK ACTIVITY (HA) EXAMPLE_____
-------------------------------------------------------------------
```

ACTIVITY ID		ORIG DUR	REM DUR	% DONE	EARLY START	EARLY FINISH	LATE START	LATE FINISH	TOTAL FLOAT	
A	*	3	3	0	1OCT91	3OCT91	1OCT91	3OCT91	0	*
B	*	7	7	0	4OCT91	10OCT91	4OCT91	10OCT91	0	*
C	*	5	5	.0	11OCT91	15OCT91	11OCT91	15OCT91	0	*
D		2	2	0	4OCT91	5OCT91	10OCT91	11OCT91	6	
E		4	4	0	6OCT91	9OCT91	12OCT91	15OCT91	6	
F	*	2	2	0	16OCT91	17OCT91	16OCT91	17OCT91	0	*
H		6	6*	0	4OCT91	9OCT91	10OCT91	15OCT91	6	

Multiple Calendars

A hammock activity can summarize more than just two activities as in the above case. Suppose *H* summarizes activities *A*, *D*, and *E* as shown in Fig. 6-8.

The resulting summary report is shown in Table 6-4, and in bar chart format (Fig. 6-9).

ZERO FREE FLOAT (ZFF)

Free float is float owned by an activity that, if used, will *not* change the float in later activities. The name *zero free float* follows from the fact that a ZFF activity is entirely free to use this float without affecting any other activity times or float values.

The zero free float (also known as the as-late-as-possible) constraint maximizes the use of available float by turning an activity critical on the late schedule. It also delays resource consumption. This is to allow a positive-float activity to start as late as possible without delaying its successors, and is done by setting activity Early Finish equal to the earliest Early Start of all successors. Early Start is reset to Late Start. If activity float is already zero or negative, a zero free float constraint cannot be applied. ZFF activities may only progress contiguously; they cannot be interrupted without delaying project finish.

Single Calendar

Note in Fig. 6-10 how a zero free float constraint affects *E*.

The resulting summary report is shown in Table 6-5, and in bar chart format (Fig. 6-11).

This means that *E* could start as late as October 12 without delaying its successor, *F*. It also means that *E* is critical, since available free float is now zero and the early dates have been reset to the late.

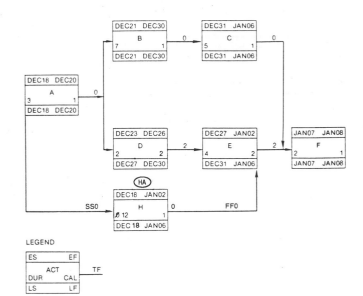

FIGURE 6-8. Network setup diagram.

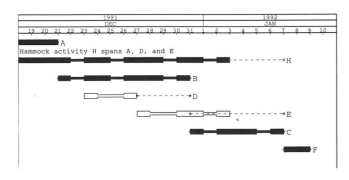

FIGURE 6-9. Gantt Chart.

Table 6-4   Schedule Summary

```
--------------------------------------------------------------------
SCHEDULE SUMMARY                               DATE: _____

PROJECT NAME:  TWO-CALENDAR HAMMOCK ACTIVITY (HA) EXAMPLE_____
--------------------------------------------------------------------
```

ACTIVITY ID/CAL	ORIG DUR	REM DUR	% DONE	EARLY START	EARLY FINISH	LATE START	LATE FINISH	TOTAL FLOAT
A 1 *	3	3	0	18DEC91	20DEC91	18DEC91	20DEC91	0 *
B 1 *	7	7	0	21DEC91	30DEC91	21DEC91	30DEC91	0 *
C 1 *	5	5	0	31DEC91	6JAN92	31DEC91	6JAN92	0 *
D 2	2	2	0	23DEC91	26DEC91	27DEC91	30DEC91	2
E 2	4	4	0	27DEC91	2JAN92	31DEC91	6JAN92	2
F 1 *	2	2	0	7JAN92	8JAN92	7JAN92	8JAN92	0 *
H 1 *	12	12*	0	18DEC91	2JAN92	18DEC91	6JAN92	0 *

Table 6-5   Schedule Summary

```
--------------------------------------------------------------------------------
SCHEDULE SUMMARY                                      DATE: _____

PROJECT NAME:  ZERO FREE FLOAT (ZFF) EXAMPLE_____
--------------------------------------------------------------------------------
ACTIVITY    ORIG    REM     %      EARLY     EARLY      LATE      LATE    TOTAL
   ID       DUR     DUR   DONE     START    FINISH     START    FINISH    FLOAT
--------    ----    ---   ----    -------   -------    ------    ------    -----
   A  *      3       3     0      1OCT91    3OCT91     1OCT91   3OCT91     0  *
   B  *      7       7     0      4OCT91   10OCT91     4OCT91  10OCT91     0  *
   C  *      5       5     0     11OCT91   15OCT91    11OCT91  15OCT91     0  *
   D         2       2     0      4OCT91    5OCT91    10OCT91  11OCT91     6
   E  *      4       4     0     12OCT91*  15OCT91*   12OCT91  15OCT91     0  *
   F  *      2       2     0     16OCT91   17OCT91    16OCT91  17OCT91     0  *
--------------------------------------------------------------------------------
```

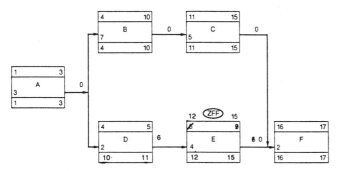

FIGURE 6-10.   Network setup diagram.

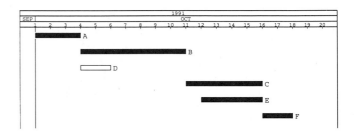

FIGURE 6-11.   Gantt Chart.

The schedule dates for *F* have not been changed in any way, but both paths leading into *F* are now critical, not just the *A-B-C-F* path.

Multiple Calendars

If a ZFF constraint were applied to *E,* the results would be as illustrated in Fig. 6-12.

The resulting summary report is shown in Table 6-6, and in bar chart format (Fig. 6-13).

ZERO TOTAL FLOAT (ZTF)

Total float represents the amount of excess time that can be made available for the completion of an activity if the:

• Preceding activity completes at its earliest date and
• Succeeding activity starts at its latest date

Total float differs from free float, which is owned by an individual activity. Total float, by comparison:

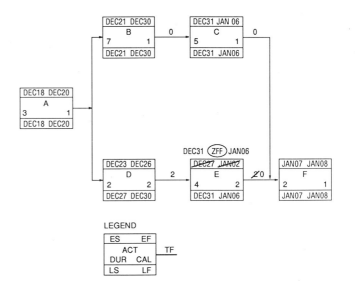

FIGURE 6-12.   Network setup diagram.

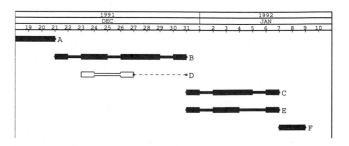

FIGURE 6-13.   Gantt Chart.

Table 6-6 Schedule Summary

```
------------------------------------------------------------------------------
SCHEDULE SUMMARY                                   DATE:  _____

PROJECT NAME:   TWO-CALENDAR ZERO FREE FLOAT (ZFF) EXAMPLE_____
------------------------------------------------------------------------------
ACTIVITY    ORIG    REM     %     EARLY     EARLY     LATE      LATE    TOTAL
 ID/CAL     DUR     DUR   DONE    START     FINISH    START     FINISH  FLOAT
--------    ----    ---   ----   -------   -------   -------   ------- -----
   A  1  *    3      3     0    18DEC91   20DEC91   18DEC91   20DEC91   0  *
   B  1  *    7      7     0    21DEC91   30DEC91   21DEC91   30DEC91   0  *
   C  1  *    5      5     0    31DEC91    6JAN92   31DEC91    6JAN92   0  *
   D  2       2      2     0    23DEC91   26DEC91   27DEC91   30DEC91   2
   E  2  *    4      4     0    31DEC91*   6JAN92*  31DEC91    6JAN92   0  *
   F  1  *    2      2     0     7JAN92    8JAN92    7JAN92    8JAN92   0  *
------------------------------------------------------------------------------
```

- Must be shared by all activities along a float (non-critical) path
- Affects successor activity and float times when used

A *zero total float* constraint makes any noncritical activity turn critical on the early schedule. This is done by:

- Setting the late dates equal to the early
- Reducing activity float to zero

The name *zero total float* follows from the fact this constraint dries up the total amount of float from the entire (noncritical) path on which it was applied. A series of ZTF activities is like consecutive green lights: no waiting. The constraint is sometimes called as-soon-as-possible, since even float activities must now follow the early schedule. Late dates of predecessor activities are also affected. If activity float is already zero or negative, a zero total float constraint cannot be applied.

This technique is effective in accomplishing the following:

- Increase resource allocation priorities
- Meet milestones off the Critical Path
- Effect a tighter, more ambitious schedule in general

Single Calendar

Note in Fig. 6-14 how a zero total float constraint affects *E*.

The resulting summary report is shown in Table 6-7, and in bar chart format (Fig. 6-15).

Activity *E* is now scheduled to start October 6 under both the early and the late schedule. Late dates, once October 12 and October 15, are now reset to early, or October 6 and October 9. This means *E* is now critical, since available float equals zero.

The schedule dates for *F* have not been changed in any way. But both paths leading into *F* are now critical, not just *A-B-C-F*.

What about *D*? We just learned that the late dates of predecessor activities would also be moved up when a zero total float constraint is applied to an activity. Therefore, *D* must move Late Start and Late Finish up by the same six days, to October 4 and October 5. *D* has no more float and has also turned critical. The zero total float constraint was applied to *E*, but affected *D* just the same, as would be expected by the name: The total amount of available float in the float path is zero.

Table 6-7 Schedule Summary

```
------------------------------------------------------------------------------
SCHEDULE SUMMARY                                   DATE:  _____

PROJECT NAME:   ZERO TOTAL FLOAT (ZTF) EXAMPLE_____
------------------------------------------------------------------------------
ACTIVITY    ORIG    REM     %     EARLY     EARLY     LATE      LATE    TOTAL
   ID       DUR     DUR   DONE    START     FINISH    START     FINISH  FLOAT
--------    ----    ---   ----   -------   -------   -------   ------- -----
   A     *    3      3     0     1OCT91    3OCT91    1OCT91    3OCT91   0  *
   B     *    7      7     0     4OCT91   10OCT91    4OCT91   10OCT91   0  *
   C     *    5      5     0    11OCT91   15OCT91   11OCT91   15OCT91   0  *
   D     *    2      2     0     4OCT91    5OCT91    4OCT91    5OCT91   0  *
   E     *    4      4     0     6OCT91    9OCT91    6OCT91*   9OCT91*  0  *
   F     *    2      2     0    16OCT91   17OCT91   16OCT91   17OCT91   0  *
------------------------------------------------------------------------------
```

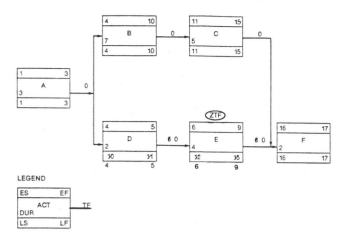

LEGEND

FIGURE 6-14.   Network setup diagram.

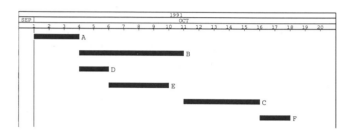

FIGURE 6-15.   Gantt Chart.

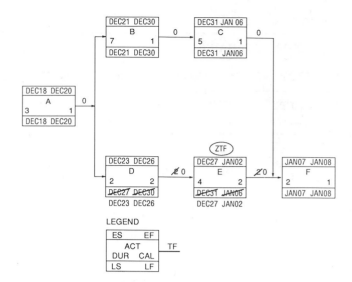

LEGEND

FIGURE 6-16.   Network setup diagram.

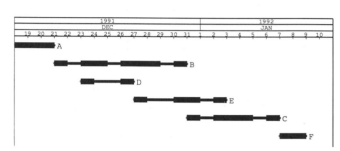

FIGURE 6-17.   Gantt Chart.

Another Critical Path is created through activities A, D, E, and F. What used to be six days of float between E and F is no longer. E cannot under the new schedule finish any later than October 9, and F still cannot start any earlier than October 16 because of its driving predecessor, C. The indicated six-day float between E and F:

- Has technically disappeared and can no longer be used
- Is nevertheless still actually available if needed

The result in this example is like synchronizing all traffic lights to green—only to wait for a train at the final intersection!

Multiple Calendars

If a ZTF constraint were applied to E, the results would be as illustrated in Fig. 6-16.

The resulting summary report is shown in Table 6-8, and in bar chart format (Fig. 6-17).

CONSTRAINTS REVISITED

As another example of how constraints affect network schedule dates, we shall examine the ten-activity project shown in Fig. 6-18 one constraint at a time.

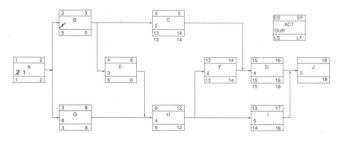

FIGURE 6-18.   Network setup diagram.

The resulting summary report is shown in Table 6-9.

The time-logic plot is shown in Fig. 6-19, and in bar chart format (Fig. 6-20).

An October 10 Start No Earlier Than constraint on H is illustrated in Fig. 6-21.

The resulting summary report is shown in Table 6-10, and in bar chart format (Fig. 6-22).

Table 6-8 Schedule Summary

```
--------------------------------------------------------------------------------
SCHEDULE SUMMARY                                         DATE: _____

PROJECT NAME:  TWO-CALENDAR ZERO TOTAL FLOAT (ZTF) EXAMPLE_____
--------------------------------------------------------------------------------
ACTIVITY    ORIG   REM    %     EARLY     EARLY      LATE      LATE     TOTAL
 ID/CAL     DUR    DUR   DONE   START     FINISH     START     FINISH   FLOAT
--------   ----   ---   ----   -------   -------    -------   -------   -----
   A  1 *    3      3     0    18DEC91   20DEC91    18DEC91   20DEC91     0 *
   B  1 *    7      7     0    21DEC91   30DEC91    21DEC91   30DEC91     0 *
   C  1 *    5      5     0    31DEC91    6JAN92    31DEC91    6JAN92     0 *
   D  2 *    2      2     0    23DEC91   26DEC91    23DEC91   26DEC91     0 *
   E  2 *    4      4     0    27DEC91    2JAN92    27DEC91*   2JAN92*    0 *
   F  1 *    2      2     0     7JAN92    8JAN92     7JAN92    8JAN92     0 *
--------------------------------------------------------------------------------
```

Table 6-9 Schedule Summary

```
--------------------------------------------------------------------------------
SCHEDULE SUMMARY                                         DATE: _____

PROJECT NAME:  10-ACTIVITY ADVANCED RELATIONSHIPS EXAMPLE (BASELINE)_____
--------------------------------------------------------------------------------
ACTIVITY    ORIG   REM    %     EARLY     EARLY      LATE      LATE     TOTAL
   ID       DUR    DUR   DONE   START     FINISH     START     FINISH   FLOAT
--------   ----   ---   ----   -------   -------    -------   -------   -----
   A  *      2      2     0     1OCT91    2OCT91     1OCT91    2OCT91     0 *
   B         1      1     0     3OCT91    3OCT91     5OCT91    5OCT91     2
   C         2      2     0     4OCT91    5OCT91    13OCT91   14OCT91     9
   D  *      4      4     0    15OCT91   18OCT91    15OCT91   18OCT91     0 *
   E         3      3     0     4OCT91    6OCT91     6OCT91    8OCT91     2
   F  *      2      2     0    13OCT91   14OCT91    13OCT91   14OCT91     0 *
   G  *      6      6     0     3OCT91    8OCT91     3OCT91    8OCT91     0 *
   H  *      4      4     0     9OCT91   12OCT91     9OCT91   12OCT91     0 *
   I         5      5     0    13OCT91   17OCT91    14OCT91   18OCT91     1
   J  *      0      0     0              18OCT91              18OCT91     0 *
--------------------------------------------------------------------------------
```

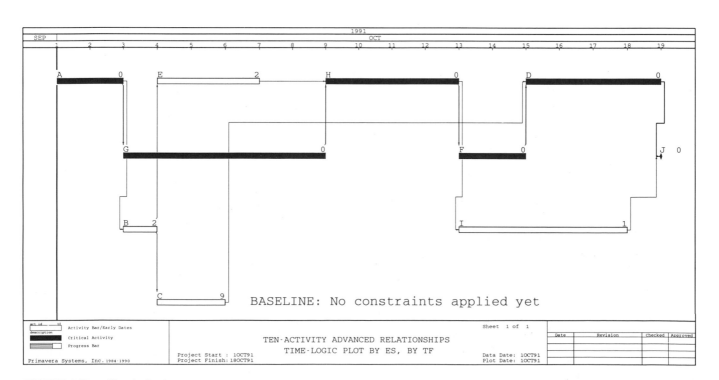

FIGURE 6-19. Time-logic plot.

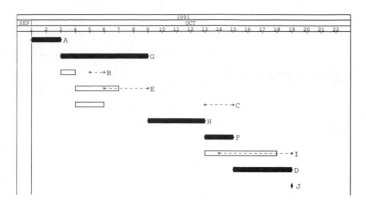

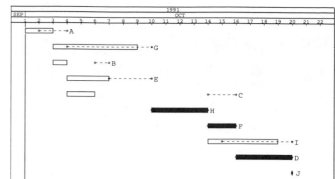

FIGURE 6-20. Gantt Chart.

FIGURE 6-22. Gantt Chart.

Table 6-10 Schedule Summary

```
------------------------------------------------------------------------------
SCHEDULE SUMMARY                                    DATE: _____

PROJECT NAME:  10-ACTIVITY START NO EARLIER THAN (SNET) EXAMPLE_____
------------------------------------------------------------------------------
```

ACTIVITY ID		ORIG DUR	REM DUR	% DONE	EARLY START	EARLY FINISH	LATE START	LATE FINISH	TOTAL FLOAT	
A		2	2	0	1OCT91	2OCT91	2OCT91	3OCT91	1	
B		1	1	0	3OCT91	3OCT91	6OCT91	6OCT91	3	
C		2	2	0	4OCT91	5OCT91	14OCT91	15OCT91	10	
D	*	4	4	0	16OCT91	19OCT91	16OCT91	19OCT91	0	*
E		3	3	0	4OCT91	6OCT91	7OCT91	9OCT91	3	
F	*	2	2	0	14OCT91	15OCT91	14OCT91	15OCT91	0	*
G		6	6	0	3OCT91	8OCT91	4OCT91	9OCT91	1	
H	*	4	4	0	10OCT91*	13OCT91	10OCT91	13OCT91	0	*
I		5	5	0	14OCT91	18OCT91	15OCT91	19OCT91	1	
J	*	0	0	0		19OCT91		19OCT91	0	*

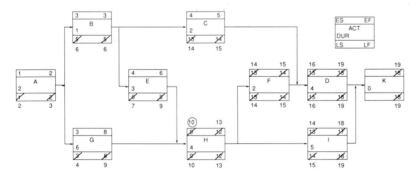

FIGURE 6-21. Network setup diagram.

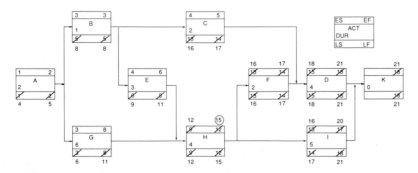

FIGURE 6-23. Network setup diagram.

156

An October 15 Finish No Earlier Than constraint on *H* is illustrated in Fig. 6-23.

The resulting summary report is shown in Table 6-11, and in bar chart format (Fig. 6-24).

An October 7 Start No Later Than constraint on *H* is illustrated in Fig. 6-25.

The resulting summary report is shown in Table 6-12, and in bar chart format (Fig. 6-26).

An October 10 Finish No Later Than constraint on *H* is illustrated in Fig. 6-27.

The resulting summary report is shown in Table 6-13, and in bar chart format (Fig. 6-28).

An October 10 Start On constraint on *H* is illustrated in Fig. 6-29.

The resulting summary report is shown in Table 6-14, and in bar chart format (Fig. 6-30).

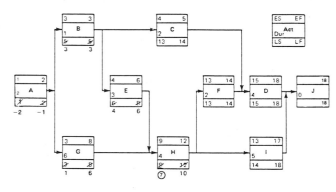

FIGURE 6-24.   Gantt Chart.

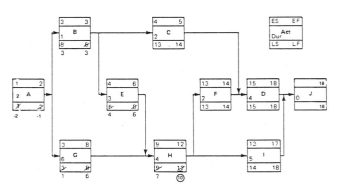

FIGURE 6-26.   Gantt Chart.

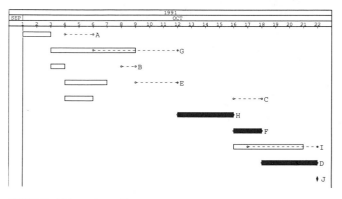

FIGURE 6-25.   Network setup diagram.

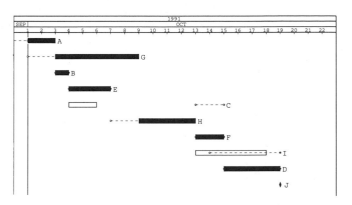

FIGURE 6-27.   Network setup diagram.

Table 6-11   Schedule Summary

SCHEDULE SUMMARY   DATE: _____

PROJECT NAME: 10-ACTIVITY FINISH NO EARLIER THAN (FNET) EXAMPLE_____

ACTIVITY ID	ORIG DUR	REM DUR	% DONE	EARLY START	EARLY FINISH	LATE START	LATE FINISH	TOTAL FLOAT
A	2	2	0	1OCT91	2OCT91	4OCT91	5OCT91	3
B	1	1	0	3OCT91	3OCT91	8OCT91	8OCT91	5
C	2	2	0	4OCT91	5OCT91	16OCT91	17OCT91	12
D *	4	4	0	18OCT91	21OCT91	18OCT91	21OCT91	0 *
E	3	3	0	4OCT91	6OCT91	9OCT91	11OCT91	5
F *	2	2	0	16OCT91	17OCT91	16OCT91	17OCT91	0 *
G	6	6	0	3OCT91	8OCT91	6OCT91	11OCT91	3
H *	4	4	0	12OCT91	15OCT91*	12OCT91	15OCT91	0 *
I	5	5	0	16OCT91	20OCT91	17OCT91	21OCT91	1
J *	0	0	0		21OCT91		21OCT91	0 *

Table 6-12   Schedule Summary

```
-----------------------------------------------------------------------
SCHEDULE SUMMARY                                   DATE: _____

PROJECT NAME:  10-ACTIVITY START NO LATER THAN (SNLT) EXAMPLE_____
-----------------------------------------------------------------------
```

ACTIVITY ID		ORIG DUR	REM DUR	% DONE	EARLY START	EARLY FINISH	LATE START	LATE FINISH	TOTAL FLOAT	
A	*	2	2	0	1OCT91	2OCT91	29SEP91	30SEP91	-2	*
B	*	1	1	0	3OCT91	3OCT91	3OCT91	3OCT91	0	*
C		2	2	0	4OCT91	5OCT91	13OCT91	14OCT91	9	
D	*	4	4	0	15OCT91	18OCT91	15OCT91	18OCT91	0	*
E	*	3	3	0	4OCT91	6OCT91	4OCT91	6OCT91	0	*
F	*	2	2	0	13OCT91	14OCT91	13OCT91	14OCT91	0	*
G	*	6	6	0	3OCT91	8OCT91	1OCT91	6OCT91	-2	*
H	*	4	4	0	9OCT91	12OCT91	7OCT91*	10OCT91	-2	*
I		5	5	0	13OCT91	17OCT91	14OCT91	18OCT91	1	
J	*	0	0	0		18OCT91		18OCT91	0	*

Table 6-13   Schedule Summary

```
-----------------------------------------------------------------------
SCHEDULE SUMMARY                                   DATE: _____

PROJECT NAME:  10-ACTIVITY FINISH NO LATER THAN (FNLT) EXAMPLE_____
-----------------------------------------------------------------------
```

ACTIVITY ID		ORIG DUR	REM DUR	% DONE	EARLY START	EARLY FINISH	LATE START	LATE FINISH	TOTAL FLOAT	
A	*	2	2	0	1OCT91	2OCT91	29SEP91	30SEP91	-2	*
B	*	1	1	0	3OCT91	3OCT91	3OCT91	3OCT91	0	*
C		2	2	0	4OCT91	5OCT91	13OCT91	14OCT91	9	
D	*	4	4	0	15OCT91	18OCT91	15OCT91	18OCT91	0	*
E	*	3	3	0	4OCT91	6OCT91	4OCT91	6OCT91	0	*
F	*	2	2	0	13OCT91	14OCT91	13OCT91	14OCT91	0	*
G	*	6	6	0	3OCT91	8OCT91	1OCT91	6OCT91	-2	*
H	*	4	4	0	9OCT91	12OCT91	7OCT91	10OCT91*	-2	*
I		5	5	0	13OCT91	17OCT91	14OCT91	18OCT91	1	
J	*	0	0	0		18OCT91		18OCT91	0	*

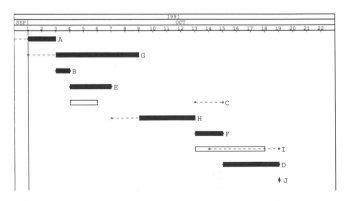

FIGURE 6-28.   Gantt Chart.

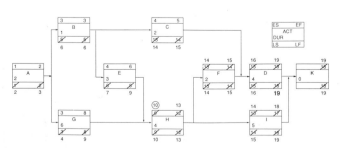

FIGURE 6-29.   Network setup diagram.

Table 6-14   Schedule Summary

```
SCHEDULE SUMMARY                                    DATE: _____
```

PROJECT NAME: 10-ACTIVITY START ON (SO) EXAMPLE_____

ACTIVITY ID		ORIG DUR	REM DUR	% DONE	EARLY START	EARLY FINISH	LATE START	LATE FINISH	TOTAL FLOAT	
A		2	2	0	1OCT91	2OCT91	2OCT91	3OCT91	1	
B		1	1	0	3OCT91	3OCT91	6OCT91	6OCT91	3	
C		2	2	0	4OCT91	5OCT91	14OCT91	15OCT91	10	
D	*	4	4	0	16OCT91	19OCT91	16OCT91	19OCT91	0	*
E		3	3	0	4OCT91	6OCT91	7OCT91	9OCT91	3	
F	*	2	2	0	14OCT91	15OCT91	14OCT91	15OCT91	0	*
G		6	6	0	3OCT91	8OCT91	4OCT91	9OCT91	1	
H	*	4	4	0	10OCT91*	13OCT91	10OCT91*	13OCT91	0	*
I		5	5	0	14OCT91	18OCT91	15OCT91	19OCT91	1	
J	*	0	0	0		19OCT91		19OCT91	0	*

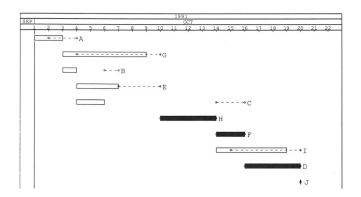

FIGURE 6-30.   Gantt Chart.

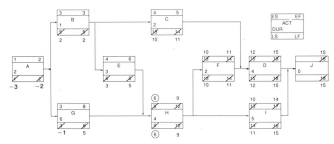

FIGURE 6-31.   Network setup diagram.

Table 6-15   Schedule Summary

```
SCHEDULE SUMMARY                                    DATE: _____
```

PROJECT NAME: 10-ACTIVITY MANDATORY START (MS) EXAMPLE_____

ACTIVITY ID		ORIG DUR	REM DUR	% DONE	EARLY START	EARLY FINISH	LATE START	LATE FINISH	TOTAL FLOAT	
A	*	2	2	0	1OCT91	2OCT91	28SEP91	29SEP91	-3	*
B	*	1	1	0	3OCT91	3OCT91	2OCT91	2OCT91	-1	*
C		2	2	0	4OCT91	5OCT91	10OCT91	11OCT91	6	
D	*	4	4	0	12OCT91	15OCT91	12OCT91	15OCT91	0	*
E	*	3	3	0	4OCT91	6OCT91	3OCT91	5OCT91	-1	*
F	*	2	2	0	10OCT91	11OCT91	10OCT91	11OCT91	0	*
G	*	6	6	0	3OCT91	8OCT91	30SEP91	5OCT91	-3	*
H	*	4	4	0	6OCT91*	9OCT91	6OCT91*	9OCT91	0	*
I		5	5	0	10OCT91	14OCT91	11OCT91	15OCT91	1	
J	*	0	0	0		15OCT91		15OCT91	0	*

An October 6 Mandatory Start constraint on *H* is illustrated in Fig. 6-31.

The resulting summary report is shown in Table 6-15, and in bar chart format (Fig. 6-32).

An October 14 Mandatory Finish constraint on *H* is illustrated in Fig. 6-33.

The resulting summary report is shown in Table 6-16, and in bar chart format (Fig. 6-34).

An October 15 Expected Finish constraint on *H* is illustrated in Fig. 6-35.

The resulting summary report is shown in Table 6-17, and in bar chart format (Fig. 6-36).

A Zero Free Float constraint on *C* is illustrated in Fig. 6-37.

The resulting summary report is shown in Table 6-18, and in bar chart format (Fig. 6-38).

A Zero Total Float constraint on *C* is illustrated in Fig. 6-39.

The resulting summary report is shown in Table 6-19, and in bar chart format (Fig. 6-40).

A Hammock Activity summarizing *G* and *H* is illustrated in Fig. 6-41.

The resulting summary report is shown in Table 6-20, and in bar chart format (Fig. 6-42).

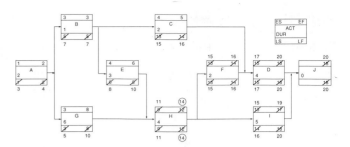

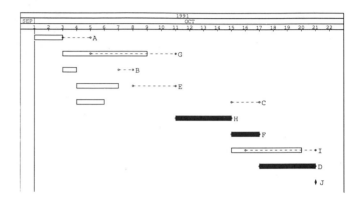

FIGURE 6-33.   Network setup diagram.

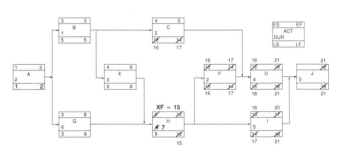

FIGURE 6-34.   Gantt Chart.

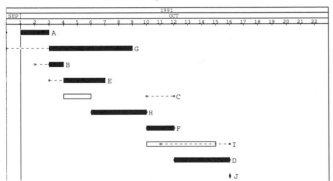

FIGURE 6-32.   Gantt Chart.

FIGURE 6-35.   Network setup diagram.

Table 6-16   Schedule Summary

```
------------------------------------------------------------------------------------
SCHEDULE SUMMARY                                          DATE:  _____

PROJECT NAME:  10-ACTIVITY MANDATORY FINISH (MF) EXAMPLE_____
------------------------------------------------------------------------------------
```

ACTIVITY ID		ORIG DUR	REM DUR	% DONE	EARLY START	EARLY FINISH	LATE START	LATE FINISH	TOTAL FLOAT	
A		2	2	0	1OCT91	2OCT91	3OCT91	4OCT91	2	
B		1	1	0	3OCT91	3OCT91	7OCT91	7OCT91	4	
C		2	2	0	4OCT91	5OCT91	15OCT91	16OCT91	11	
D	*	4	4	0	17OCT91	20OCT91	17OCT91	20OCT91	0	*
E		3	3	0	4OCT91	6OCT91	8OCT91	10OCT91	4	
F	*	2	2	0	15OCT91	16OCT91	15OCT91	16OCT91	0	*
G		6	6	0	3OCT91	8OCT91	5OCT91	10OCT91	2	
H	*	4	4	0	11OCT91	14OCT91*	11OCT91	14OCT91*	0	*
I		5	5	0	15OCT91	19OCT91	16OCT91	20OCT91	1	
J	*	0	0	0	20OCT91			20OCT91	0	*

```
------------------------------------------------------------------------------------
```

Table 6-17   Schedule Summary

```
------------------------------------------------------------------------
SCHEDULE SUMMARY                                    DATE: _____

PROJECT NAME:  10-ACTIVITY EXPECTED FINISH (XF) EXAMPLE_____
------------------------------------------------------------------------
```

ACTIVITY ID		ORIG DUR	REM DUR	% DONE	EARLY START	EARLY FINISH	LATE START	LATE FINISH	TOTAL FLOAT	
A	*	2	2	0	1OCT91	2OCT91	1OCT91	2OCT91	0	*
B		1	1	0	3OCT91	3OCT91	5OCT91	5OCT91	2	
C		2	2	0	4OCT91	5OCT91	16OCT91	17OCT91	12	
D	*	4	4	0	18OCT91	21OCT91	18OCT91	21OCT91	0	*
E		3	3	0	4OCT91	6OCT91	6OCT91	8OCT91	2	
F	*	2	2	0	16OCT91	17OCT91	16OCT91	17OCT91	0	*
G	*	6	6	0	3OCT91	8OCT91	3OCT91	8OCT91	0	*
H	*	4	7*	0	9OCT91	15OCT91	9OCT91	15OCT91	0	*
I		5	5	0	16OCT91	20OCT91	17OCT91	21OCT91	1	
J	*	0	0	0		21OCT91		21OCT91	0	*

```
------------------------------------------------------------------------
```

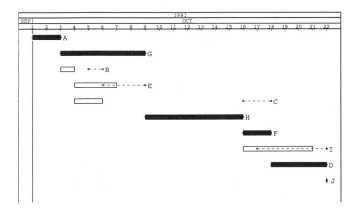

FIGURE 6-36.   Gantt Chart.

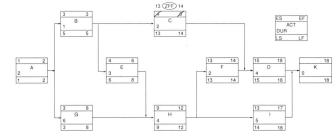

FIGURE 6-37.   Network setup diagram.

Table 6-18   Schedule Summary

```
------------------------------------------------------------------------
SCHEDULE SUMMARY                                    DATE: _____

PROJECT NAME:  10-ACTIVITY ZERO FREE FLOAT (ZFF) EXAMPLE_____
------------------------------------------------------------------------
```

ACTIVITY ID		ORIG DUR	REM DUR	% DONE	EARLY START	EARLY FINISH	LATE START	LATE FINISH	TOTAL FLOAT	
A	*	2	2	0	1OCT91	2OCT91	1OCT91	2OCT91	0	*
B		1	1	0	3OCT91	3OCT91	5OCT91	5OCT91	2	
C	*	2	2	0	13OCT91*	14OCT91*	13OCT91	14OCT91	0	*
D	*	4	4	0	15OCT91	18OCT91	15OCT91	18OCT91	0	*
E		3	3	0	4OCT91	6OCT91	6OCT91	8OCT91	2	
F	*	2	2	0	13OCT91	14OCT91	13OCT91	14OCT91	0	*
G	*	6	6	0	3OCT91	8OCT91	3OCT91	8OCT91	0	*
H	*	4	4	0	9OCT91	12OCT91	9OCT91	12OCT91	0	*
I		5	5	0	13OCT91	17OCT91	14OCT91	18OCT91	1	
J	*	0	0	0		18OCT91		18OCT91	0	*

```
------------------------------------------------------------------------
```

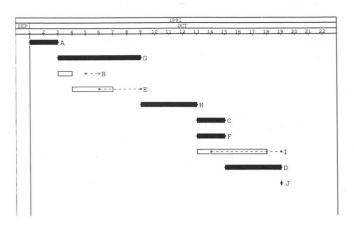

FIGURE 6-38.   Gantt Chart.

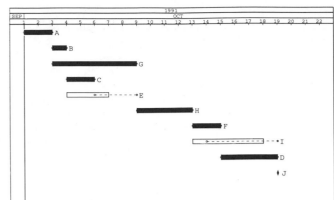

FIGURE 6-40.   Gantt Chart.

Table 6-19   Schedule Summary

```
----------------------------------------------------------------------
SCHEDULE SUMMARY                                 DATE: _____

PROJECT NAME:  10-ACTIVITY ZERO TOTAL FLOAT (ZTF) EXAMPLE_____
----------------------------------------------------------------------
```

ACTIVITY ID		ORIG DUR	REM DUR	% DONE	EARLY START	EARLY FINISH	LATE START	LATE FINISH	TOTAL FLOAT	
A	*	2	2	0	1OCT91	2OCT91	1OCT91	2OCT91	0	*
B	*	1	1	0	3OCT91	3OCT91	3OCT91	3OCT91	0	*
C	*	2	2	0	4OCT91	5OCT91	4OCT91*	5OCT91*	0	*
D	*	4	4	0	15OCT91	18OCT91	15OCT91	18OCT91	0	*
E		3	3	0	4OCT91	6OCT91	6OCT91	8OCT91	2	
F	*	2	2	0	13OCT91	14OCT91	13OCT91	14OCT91	0	*
G	*	6	6	0	3OCT91	8OCT91	3OCT91	8OCT91	0	*
H	*	4	4	0	9OCT91	12OCT91	9OCT91	12OCT91	0	*
I		5	5	0	13OCT91	17OCT91	14OCT91	18OCT91	1	
J	*	0	0	0		18OCT91		18OCT91	0	*

```
----------------------------------------------------------------------
```

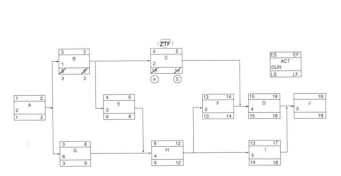

FIGURE 6-39.   Network setup diagram.

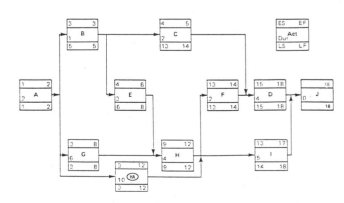

FIGURE 6-41.   Network setup diagram.

Table 6-20   Schedule Summary

```
------------------------------------------------------------------------
SCHEDULE  SUMMARY                                    DATE: _____

PROJECT NAME:   10-ACTIVITY HAMMOCK ACTIVITY (HA) EXAMPLE_____
------------------------------------------------------------------------
```

ACTIVITY ID		ORIG DUR	REM DUR	% DONE	EARLY START	EARLY FINISH	LATE START	LATE FINISH	TOTAL FLOAT	
A	*	2	2	0	1OCT91	2OCT91	1OCT91	2OCT91	0	*
B		1	1	0	3OCT91	3OCT91	5OCT91	5OCT91	2	
C		2	2	0	4OCT91	5OCT91	13OCT91	14OCT91	9	
D	*	4	4	0	15OCT91	18OCT91	15OCT91	18OCT91	0	*
E		3	3	0	4OCT91	6OCT91	6OCT91	8OCT91	2	
F	*	2	2	0	13OCT91	14OCT91	13OCT91	14OCT91	0	*
G	*	6	6	0	3OCT91	8OCT91	3OCT91	8OCT91	0	*
H	*	4	4	0	9OCT91	12OCT91	9OCT91	12OCT91	0	*
HAMMOCK	*	10*	10*	0	3OCT91	12OCT91	3OCT91	12OCT91	0	*
I		5	5	0	13OCT91	17OCT91	14OCT91	18OCT91	1	
J	*	0	0	0		18OCT91		18OCT91	0	*

```
------------------------------------------------------------------------
```

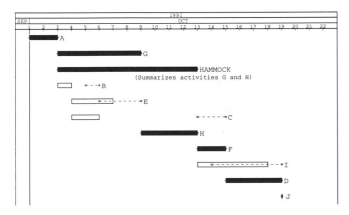

FIGURE 6-42.   Gantt Chart.

7
How to Produce Good Status Reports

THE NEED FOR GOOD STATUS REPORTS

All the planning and scheduling work that we have done will be of little value to your project team unless you clearly organize your material and present it in a useful and understandable manner. This is especially true in a manual (non computerized) environment. If insufficient care is taken in laying out and presenting the network, the result may be so complicated and cluttered with mumbo-jumbo that only a rocket scientist would be able to understand it. Reports must be clear, complete, and accurate. They must effectively communicate important project information—especially if the audience is from a nontechnical background. Otherwise, the network—no matter how well designed or carefully thought out—will soon:

- Be ignored from the start by all but the very enthusiastic (who may soon lose much of this enthusiasm!)
- Fall into disuse

Successful people make the effort required to plan their life and organize their time and activities. Applying this criteria to your project will provide the seven benefits listed by Randolph and Posner (page 51):

1. You will have a more realistic plan—one that gives a more accurate picture of what will happen as your project progresses.
2. You will be better able to anticipate what the next step should be.
3. You will know where to concentrate your attention to be sure the project stays on schedule and within the budget.
4. You will be able to anticipate bottlenecks and other coordination problems before they occur, so that you

can take action to correct a delay before it becomes severe.
5. You will have a valuable tool to enhance coordination and communication among project team members.
6. You will have a tool that helps build commitment because it publicly identifies responsibilities and deadlines, and creates an awareness of interdependencies.
7. You will have a tool that leads to completion of projects on time, within budget, and according to quality standards.

In a manual environment, there will always be much trial and error—and schedule rearrangement—before a final "clean copy" is produced. Each network change subsequent to that—be it an addition, a deletion, or even the most simple of changes—will send your draftspersons "back to the drawing board!" In all cases, you must give careful attention to the orderly arrangement of activities. Standard conventions must be followed, common sense used. The flow of time is always represented from left to right. Even in a pure-logic diagram, earlier activities should be presented, as much as possible, to the left of later activities. Ensuring that everything fits in its proper place requires careful planning and attention to detail.

It may be useful, therefore, to design multiple report formats to provide each recipient only that information he or she needs to do the job: "no need, no read!" Your software should provide complete control over what information is selected, what is presented, what is masked from view, and how it is all organized—by total project, by manager, by resource, sort order, and so on. It should also remember who gets what by maintaining a file of report templates which may be used as the basis of future reports.

A good E-mail (electronic mail) system, such as Digital

Equipment Corporation's *ALL-IN-1*, simplifies report distribution. Reports may, for example, easily be:

- Imported into *ALL-IN-1* or another E-mail system
- Combined with letters, other reports, spreadsheets, graphics, and so on
- Transmitted electronically throughout the entire computer network to eliminate time and space barriers.

USEFUL PRESENTATION GUIDELINES

In both the pure-logic and the time-logic plots, the following rules must also be observed:

- Activities in a pure-logic plot should be placed in neat boxes or circles that are properly spaced, of uniform size, and include additional necessary detail
- Activities in a time-logic plot should be placed in neat boxes or rectangles that are properly spaced by start and finish times in direct proportion to duration and scaled to a timeline presented on chart top or bottom
- Connecting arrows representing conventional relationships and the flow of time should be drawn straight and horizontally with only the ends turned to connect into later activities
- Connecting arrows representing other component activities in a complex relationship (Start-to-Start or Finish-to-Finish) should be drawn straight and vertically with only the ends turned
- Arrow heads should always point to the later activity
- When absolutely necessary for (unrelated) arrows to cross, one arrow should bridge the other or include a slight break at the meeting point
- Activity descriptions should be clear, concise, fit within

their bounds, and not contain abbreviations or codes not readily understood
- Divide the network into clear areas of responsibility so that it is unnecessary to scan the whole network to locate activities at a single location, or for which one individual or work group is responsible; this is done by dividing the network into horizontal zones, each of which represents a different work group or physical location

Your software should provide extensive selection, sorting, and formatting capabilities in addition to its standard reports portfolio. These reports, both standard and custom, should allow you to:

- Select any valid project portion
- View it from any perspective, at any level, in any format

Primavera, for example, provides:

- A four-level gated Boolean selection process
- Up to twenty sort keys
- Control-break summarizing—all on any data field

Primavera provides sixty-six standard reports distributed among the sixteen categories shown in Table 7-1.

Primavera also provides a cafeteria-style report generator in which desired information is selected and arranged from a generous list of available items. Extensive content and format options enable fast and easy customized report production from literally hundreds of possibilities.

<<Bon appetit!>>

Finally, *Primavera* provides presentation-quality graphics such as the time-logic plots and Gantt Charts already seen. We shall see the resource, cost, and loading charts in later chapters.

Table 7-1   Major *Primavera* Report Categories

```
    I.   Tabular schedules
   II.   Bar charts
  III.   Network logic diagrams
   IV.   Resource usage
         A. Resource usage
         B. Cumulative resource usage
         C. Resource control
         D. Productivity
         E. Earned value (units)
         F. Tabular resource usage
    V.   Costs
         A. Resource cost
         B. Cumulative cost profile
         C. Cost control
         D. Cost, price, and rates control
         E. Earned value (costs)
         F. Tabular costs
   VI.   Resource loading
```

PROJECT HOME SCHEDULE REPORTS

The Project HOME reports detailed in the following tables are only a few of the many possible. They display some of the ways in which schedules may be presented and customized to reflect individual information needs and preferences.

Project Schedule Sorted by Early Start, by Total Float

Probably the most useful, the report illustrated in Table 7-2 presents all or selected activities by Early Start and within these, by increasing float. For each activity listed, it provides the activity identifier, original and remaining durations, per-

Table 7-2   Project Schedule Sorted by Early Start and Total Float

```
-----------------------------------------------------------------------------------------------------------------
AMERICAN COMMUNITY DEVELOPERS, INC.          PRIMAVERA PROJECT PLANNER          BRIAN'S DUPLICATE OF PROJECT "HOME"

REPORT DATE  12FEB83  RUN NO.   1            PROJECT SCHEDULE                   START DATE 13DEC82  FIN DATE  6SEP84

PROJECT SCHEDULE SORTED BY EARLY START AND TOTAL FLOAT                          DATA DATE   1FEB83  PAGE NO.    1
```

ACTIVITY ID	ORIG DUR	REM DUR	%	ACTIVITY DESCRIPTION	EARLY START	EARLY FINISH	LATE START	LATE FINISH	TOTAL FLOAT
1	5	0	100	LAYOUT	14DEC82A	22DEC82A			
3	15	0	100	SOIL STABILIZATION	28DEC82A	20JAN83A			
5	8	3	62	PLUMBING-STREET CONNECTION AND UNDERSLAB	24JAN83A	3FEB83		6JAN83	-20
7	5	2	60	FOUNDATION EXCAVATION	4FEB83	7FEB83	7JAN83	10JAN83	-20
9	7	7	0	GRANULAR FILL	8FEB83	16FEB83	11JAN83	19JAN83	-20
13	13	13	0	TERMITE PROTECTION	17FEB83	8MAR83	20JAN83	7FEB83	-20
12	7	7	0	UNDERSLAB ELECTRICAL LINE	17FEB83	28FEB83	28JAN83	7FEB83	-14
11	5	5	0	UNDERSLAB AC FREON S&R LINE	17FEB83	24FEB83	1FEB83	7FEB83	-12
22	5	5	0	CONCRETE SLAB ON GRADE	9MAR83	15MAR83	8FEB83	14FEB83	-20
24	13	13	0	CURING TIME	16MAR83	1APR83	15FEB83	4MAR83	-20
26	10	10	0	SET PRECAST CONCRETE PANELS	4APR83	15APR83	7MAR83	18MAR83	-20
27	6	6	0	GROUT PRECAST PANELS	11APR83	18APR83	14MAR83	21MAR83	-20
30	50	50	0	INSTALL METAL STAIRS	19APR83	28JUN83	22MAR83	31MAY83	-20
50	20	20	0	FRAME INTERIOR WALLS	19APR83	16MAY83	8JUL83	4AUG83	56
52	4	4	0	INSTALL TUB, STACK OUT PLUMBING	17MAY83	20MAY83	5AUG83	10AUG83	56
53	15	15	0	PULL WIRE & ROUGH IN ELECTRIC&TELEPHONE IN WALLS	17MAY83	7JUN83	11AUG83	31AUG83	60
54	8	8	0	TV WIRE PULLING	17MAY83	26MAY83	22AUG83	31AUG83	67
32	23	23	0	PLATES, LINTELS, AND ROOF TRUSSES	29JUN83	1AUG83	1JUN83	1JUL83	-20
34	20	20	0	REDWOOD FASCIA,SOFFIT AND PLYWOOD DECKING	2AUG83	29AUG83	5JUL83	1AUG83	-20
41	5	5	0	DRY SHEETING	30AUG83	5SEP83	2AUG83	8AUG83	-20
43	4	1	62	STOCK BULK MATERIAL INSIDE BUILDING	6SEP83	6SEP83	9AUG83	9AUG83	-20
58	15	15	0	ROOF SHINGLES	6SEP83	27SEP83	11AUG83	31AUG83*	-18
45	3	3	0	SET INFILL PANEL FRAMING	7SEP83	9SEP83	10AUG83	12AUG83	-20
47	5	5	0	WINDOWS	13SEP83	19SEP83	15AUG83	19AUG83	-20
49	8	8	0	WOOD SIDING	20SEP83	29SEP83	22AUG83	31AUG83	-20
66	5	5	0	WALL INSULATION	30SEP83*	6OCT83	1SEP83*	7SEP83	-20
67	5	5	0	CONCRETE STAIRS	4OCT83	10OCT83	7JUN84	13JUN84	174
68	6	6	0	EXTERIOR RAILINGS	5OCT83	12OCT83	6JUN84	13JUN84	172
70	25	25	0	SHEETROCK WALLS	7OCT83	10NOV83	20SEP83	24OCT83	-13
72	20	20	0	TAPE AND BED	11NOV83	9DEC83	25OCT83	21NOV83	-13
76	5	5	0	FUR DOWN FOR CEILING AIR CONDITIONER	12DEC83	16DEC83	22NOV83	29NOV83	-13
74	10	10	0	BLOW ON CEILING INSULATION	12DEC83	23DEC83	31MAY84	13JUN84	121
78	10	10	0	A/C ROUGH IN	19DEC83	3JAN84	30NOV83	13DEC83	-13
80	4	4	0	SHEETROCK FUR DOWNS	4JAN84	9JAN84	14DEC83	19DEC83	-13
87	15	15	0	TAPE AND BED FUR DOWNS	10JAN84	30JAN84	20DEC83	11JAN84	-13
89	13	13	0	TEXTURE WALLS AND CEILINGS	31JAN84	16FEB84	12JAN84	30JAN84	-13
93	10	10	0	DOORS AND TRIM	17FEB84	1MAR84	31JAN84	13FEB84	-13
91	5	5	0	BATHROOM TILE	17FEB84	23FEB84	7FEB84	13FEB84	-8
95	20	20	0	PAINTING	2MAR84	29MAR84	14FEB84	12MAR84	-13
100	8	8	0	VINYL WALL COVERING	30MAR84	10APR84	13MAR84	22MAR84	-13
99	5	5	0	HARDWARE	30MAR84	5APR84	7JUN84	13JUN84	49
107	5	5	0	CLEAN UP	11APR84	17APR84	23MAR84	29MAR84	-13
109	10	10	0	RESILIENT FLOORING AND BASES	18APR84	1MAY84	30MAR84	12APR84	-13
115	13	13	0	INSTALL CABINETS	2MAY84	18MAY84	13APR84*	1MAY84	-13

Table 7-2   Continued

```
AMERICAN COMMUNITY DEVELOPERS, INC.        PRIMAVERA PROJECT PLANNER          BRIAN'S DUPLICATE OF PROJECT "HOME"

REPORT DATE  12FEB83  RUN NO.    1          PROJECT SCHEDULE                   START DATE 13DEC82  FIN DATE  6SEP84

PROJECT SCHEDULE SORTED BY EARLY START AND TOTAL FLOAT                          DATA DATE   1FEB83  PAGE NO.    2
```

ACTIVITY ID	ORIG DUR	REM DUR	%	ACTIVITY DESCRIPTION	EARLY START	EARLY FINISH	LATE START	LATE FINISH	TOTAL FLOAT
112	14	14	0	PANELING, FINISH CARPENTRY AND MILLWORK	2MAY84	21MAY84	25MAY84	13JUN84	17
113	10	10	0	INSTALL CONDENSERS AND A/C TRIMOUT	2MAY84	15MAY84	31MAY84	13JUN84	21
114	5	5	0	TV TRIMOUT	2MAY84	8MAY84	7JUN84	13JUN84	26
119	12	12	0	ELECTRICAL CONNECTIONS AND TRIMOUT	17MAY84	1JUN84	29MAY84	13JUN84	8
118	13	13	0	PLUMBING CONNECTIONS AND TRIMOUT	21MAY84	6JUN84	16MAY84	1JUN84*	-3
117	5	5	0	SET APPLIANCES	21MAY84	25MAY84	31MAY84	6JUN84	8
123	5	5	0	BATHROOM ACCESSORIES	7JUN84	13JUN84	7JUN84	13JUN84	0
128	10	10	0	CLEAN UP	14JUN84	27JUN84	14JUN84	27JUN84	0
136	5	5	0	PAINT TOUCH UP	28JUN84	5JUL84	28JUN84	5JUL84	0
138	15	15	0	INSTALL CARPETING	6JUL84	26JUL84	6JUL84	26JUL84	0
140	5	5	0	INSTALL DRAPES	27JUL84	2AUG84	27JUL84	2AUG84	0
142	10	10	0	CLEAN UP	3AUG84	16AUG84	3AUG84	16AUG84	0
144	10	10	0	PUNCH LIST	17AUG84	30AUG84	17AUG84	30AUG84	0
146	5	5	0	BUILDING COMPLETE	31AUG84	6SEP84	31AUG84	6SEP84	0

cent complete, special codes if applicable, activity description, Early Start and Early Finish dates, Late Start and Late Finish dates, and total float. All project activities may be selected for inclusion, or only those meeting user-specified criteria.

Project Schedule Sorted by Total Float, by Early Start

The report illustrated in Table 7-3 provides the same information as the report shown in Table 7-2, but in reverse order. The Critical Path consists of all activities with zero or negative float.

Project Schedule (with Log) Sorted by Early Start, by Total Float

The report illustrated in Table 7-4 adds additional information to selected project activities. This nine-line log (only five are used in the sample report) may be used as shown here to refer to specific drawings, to provide additional detail, to explain important changes or decisions, or for any other note-taking purpose.

Project Schedule Sorted by Resource, by Early Start

The report illustrated in Table 7-5 provides the same information as the reports shown in Tables 7-2 through 7-4, but divides the project into a collection of smaller segments by a given criteria—resources, for example. It provides a project subschedule that includes only those activities of interest to a given resource. Each worker category is provided its own schedule details uncluttered by those of other worker groups.

Project Schedule with Analysis and Successors Sorted by Activity

The report shown in Table 7-6 provides additional information on the status or particular details of a project, and also lists activity predecessors and successors.

Project Schedule with Predecessor/Successor Analysis Sorted by Activity

The report illustrated in Table 7-7 is similar to that shown in Table 7-6. It is also organized by activity identifier and indicates both activity predecessor(s) and successor(s)—in the same format as reports shown in Tables 7-2 through 7-5.

Critical Path

The report shown in Table 7-8 graphs the Critical Path and for each activity shows:

- Predecessor(s) and successor(s)
- Special logic relationships
- Activity identifier
- Activity description
- Total float
- Original duration (OD)
- Remaining duration (RD)
- Percent complete (PCT)
- Early Start (ES)
- Early Finish (EF)
- Actual start (AS) or finish (AF)

Table 7-3   Project Schedule Sorted by Total Float and Early Start

ACTIVITY ID	ORIG DUR	REM DUR	%	ACTIVITY DESCRIPTION	EARLY START	EARLY FINISH	LATE START	LATE FINISH	TOTAL FLOAT
1	5	0	100	LAYOUT	14DEC82A	22DEC82A			
3	15	0	100	SOIL STABILIZATION	28DEC82A	20JAN83A			
5	8	3	62	PLUMBING-STREET CONNECTION AND UNDERSLAB	24JAN83A	3FEB83		6JAN83	-20
7	5	2	60	FOUNDATION EXCAVATION	4FEB83	7FEB83	7JAN83	10JAN83	-20
9	7	7	0	GRANULAR FILL	8FEB83	16FEB83	11JAN83	19JAN83	-20
13	13	13	0	TERMITE PROTECTION	17FEB83	8MAR83	20JAN83	7FEB83	-20
22	5	5	0	CONCRETE SLAB ON GRADE	9MAR83	15MAR83	8FEB83	14FEB83	-20
24	13	13	0	CURING TIME	16MAR83	1APR83	15FEB83	4MAR83	-20
26	10	10	0	SET PRECAST CONCRETE PANELS	4APR83	15APR83	7MAR83	18MAR83	-20
27	6	6	0	GROUT PRECAST PANELS	11APR83	18APR83	14MAR83	21MAR83	-20
30	50	50	0	INSTALL METAL STAIRS	19APR83	28JUN83	22MAR83	31MAY83	-20
32	23	23	0	PLATES, LINTELS, AND ROOF TRUSSES	29JUN83	1AUG83	1JUN83	1JUL83	-20
34	20	20	0	REDWOOD FASCIA,SOFFIT AND PLYWOOD DECKING	2AUG83	29AUG83	5JUL83	1AUG83	-20
41	5	5	0	DRY SHEETING	30AUG83	5SEP83	2AUG83	8AUG83	-20
43	4	1	62	STOCK BULK MATERIAL INSIDE BUILDING	6SEP83	6SEP83	9AUG83	9AUG83	-20
45	3	3	0	SET INFILL PANEL FRAMING	7SEP83	9SEP83	10AUG83	12AUG83	-20
47	5	5	0	WINDOWS	13SEP83	19SEP83	15AUG83	19AUG83	-20
49	8	8	0	WOOD SIDING	20SEP83	29SEP83	22AUG83	31AUG83	-20
66	5	5	0	WALL INSULATION	30SEP83*	6OCT83	1SEP83*	7SEP83	-20
58	15	15	0	ROOF SHINGLES	6SEP83	27SEP83	11AUG83	31AUG83*	-18
12	7	7	0	UNDERSLAB ELECTRICAL LINE	17FEB83	28FEB83	28JAN83	7FEB83	-14
70	25	25	0	SHEETROCK WALLS	7OCT83	10NOV83	20SEP83	24OCT83	-13
72	20	20	0	TAPE AND BED	11NOV83	9DEC83	25OCT83	21NOV83	-13
76	5	5	0	FUR DOWN FOR CEILING AIR CONDITIONER	12DEC83	16DEC83	22NOV83	29NOV83	-13
78	10	10	0	A/C ROUGH IN	19DEC83	3JAN84	30NOV83	13DEC83	-13
80	4	4	0	SHEETROCK FUR DOWNS	4JAN84	9JAN84	14DEC83	19DEC83	-13
87	15	15	0	TAPE AND BED FUR DOWNS	10JAN84	30JAN84	20DEC83	11JAN84	-13
89	13	13	0	TEXTURE WALLS AND CEILINGS	31JAN84	16FEB84	12JAN84	30JAN84	-13
93	10	10	0	DOORS AND TRIM	17FEB84	1MAR84	31JAN84	13FEB84	-13
95	20	20	0	PAINTING	2MAR84	29MAR84	14FEB84	12MAR84	-13
100	8	8	0	VINYL WALL COVERING	30MAR84	10APR84	13MAR84	22MAR84	-13
107	5	5	0	CLEAN UP	11APR84	17APR84	23MAR84	29MAR84	-13
109	10	10	0	RESILIENT FLOORING AND BASES	18APR84	1MAY84	30MAR84	12APR84	-13
115	13	13	0	INSTALL CABINETS	2MAY84	18MAY84	13APR84*	1MAY84	-13
11	5	5	0	UNDERSLAB AC FREON S&R LINE	17FEB83	24FEB83	1FEB83	7FEB83	-12
91	5	5	0	BATHROOM TILE	17FEB84	23FEB84	7FEB84	13FEB84	-8
118	13	13	0	PLUMBING CONNECTIONS AND TRIMOUT	21MAY84	6JUN84	16MAY84	1JUN84*	-3
123	5	5	0	BATHROOM ACCESSORIES	7JUN84	13JUN84	7JUN84	13JUN84	0
128	10	10	0	CLEAN UP	14JUN84	27JUN84	14JUN84	27JUN84	0
136	5	5	0	PAINT TOUCH UP	28JUN84	5JUL84	28JUN84	5JUL84	0
138	15	15	0	INSTALL CARPETING	6JUL84	26JUL84	6JUL84	26JUL84	0
140	5	5	0	INSTALL DRAPES	27JUL84	2AUG84	27JUL84	2AUG84	0
142	10	10	0	CLEAN UP	3AUG84	16AUG84	3AUG84	16AUG84	0
144	10	10	0	PUNCH LIST	17AUG84	30AUG84	17AUG84	30AUG84	0
146	5	5	0	BUILDING COMPLETE	31AUG84	6SEP84	31AUG84	6SEP84	0
119	12	12	0	ELECTRICAL CONNECTIONS AND TRIMOUT	17MAY84	1JUN84	29MAY84	13JUN84	8
117	5	5	0	SET APPLIANCES	21MAY84	25MAY84	31MAY84	6JUN84	8
112	14	14	0	PANELING, FINISH CARPENTRY AND MILLWORK	2MAY84	21MAY84	25MAY84	13JUN84	17
113	10	10	0	INSTALL CONDENSERS AND A/C TRIMOUT	2MAY84	15MAY84	31MAY84	13JUN84	21
114	5	5	0	TV TRIMOUT	2MAY84	8MAY84	7JUN84	13JUN84	26
99	5	5	0	HARDWARE	30MAR84	5APR84	7JUN84	13JUN84	49
50	20	20	0	FRAME INTERIOR WALLS	19APR83	16MAY83	8JUL83	4AUG83	56
52	4	4	0	INSTALL TUB, STACK OUT PLUMBING	17MAY83	20MAY83	5AUG83	10AUG83	56
53	15	15	0	PULL WIRE & ROUGH IN ELECTRIC&TELEPHONE IN WALLS	17MAY83	7JUN83	11AUG83	31AUG83	60
54	8	8	0	TV WIRE PULLING	17MAY83	26MAY83	22AUG83	31AUG83	67
74	10	10	0	BLOW ON CEILING INSULATION	12DEC83	23DEC83	31MAY84	13JUN84	121
68	6	6	0	EXTERIOR RAILINGS	5OCT83	12OCT83	6JUN84	13JUN84	172

Table 7-4   Project Schedule (With Log) Sorted by Early Start and Total Float

```
-----------------------------------------------------------------------------------------------------------
AMERICAN COMMUNITY DEVELOPERS, INC.          PRIMAVERA PROJECT PLANNER          BRIAN'S DUPLICATE OF PROJECT "HOME"

REPORT DATE  12FEB83  RUN NO.    3              PROJECT SCHEDULE                 START DATE 13DEC82  FIN DATE  6SEP84

PROJECT SCHEDULE (WITH LOG) SORTED BY EARLY START AND TOTAL FLOAT                DATA DATE   1FEB83  PAGE NO.   2
```

ACTIVITY ID	ORIG DUR	REM DUR	%		ACTIVITY DESCRIPTION	EARLY START	EARLY FINISH	LATE START	LATE FINISH	TOTAL FLOAT
66	5	5	0		WALL INSULATION	30SEP83*	6OCT83	1SEP83*	7SEP83	-20
				1	Drawing # 12345A					
				2	Subcontractor: Jones Corp.					
				3	Contact Amy, 316-555-1212					
				4	Material + "load factor"					
				5	*** ORDER ASAP ***					
67	5	5	0		CONCRETE STAIRS	4OCT83	10OCT83	7JUN84	13JUN84	174
68	6	6	0		EXTERIOR RAILINGS	5OCT83	12OCT83	6JUN84	13JUN84	172
70	25	25	0		SHEETROCK WALLS	7OCT83	10NOV83	20SEP83	24OCT83	-13
72	20	20	0		TAPE AND BED	11NOV83	9DEC83	25OCT83	21NOV83	-13
76	5	5	0		FUR DOWN FOR CEILING AIR CONDITIONER	12DEC83	16DEC83	22NOV83	29NOV83	-13
74	10	10	0		BLOW ON CEILING INSULATION	12DEC83	23DEC83	31MAY84	13JUN84	121
78	10	10	0		A/C ROUGH IN	19DEC83	3JAN84	30NOV83	13DEC83	-13
80	4	4	0		SHEETROCK FUR DOWNS	4JAN84	9JAN84	14DEC83	19DEC83	-13
87	15	15	0		TAPE AND BED FUR DOWNS	10JAN84	30JAN84	20DEC83	11JAN84	-13
89	13	13	0		TEXTURE WALLS AND CEILINGS	31JAN84	16FEB84	12JAN84	30JAN84	-13
93	10	10	0		DOORS AND TRIM	17FEB84	1MAR84	31JAN84	13FEB84	-13
146	5	5	0		BUILDING COMPLETE	31AUG84	6SEP84	31AUG84	6SEP84	0

Table 7-5   Project Schedule Sorted by Worker Category and Early Start

```
-----------------------------------------------------------------------------------------------------------
AMERICAN COMMUNITY DEVELOPERS, INC.          PRIMAVERA PROJECT PLANNER          BRIAN'S DUPLICATE OF PROJECT "HOME"

REPORT DATE  12FEB83  RUN NO.    4              PROJECT SCHEDULE                 START DATE 13DEC82  FIN DATE  6SEP84

PROJECT SCHEDULE SORTED BY WORKER CATEGORY AND EARLY START                       DATA DATE   1FEB83  PAGE NO.   2
```

CARPENTER

ACTIVITY ID	ORIG DUR	REM DUR	%		ACTIVITY DESCRIPTION	EARLY START	EARLY FINISH	LATE START	LATE FINISH	TOTAL FLOAT
50	20	20	0		FRAME INTERIOR WALLS	19APR83	16MAY83	8JUL83	4AUG83	56
34	20	20	0		REDWOOD FASCIA,SOFFIT AND PLYWOOD DECKING	2AUG83	29AUG83	5JUL83	1AUG83	-20
41	5	5	0		DRY SHEETING	30AUG83	5SEP83	2AUG83	8AUG83	-20
43	4	1	62		STOCK BULK MATERIAL INSIDE BUILDING	6SEP83	6SEP83	9AUG83	9AUG83	-20
58	15	15	0		ROOF SHINGLES	6SEP83	27SEP83	11AUG83	31AUG83*	-18
45	3	3	0		SET INFILL PANEL FRAMING	7SEP83	9SEP83	10AUG83	12AUG83	-20
47	5	5	0		WINDOWS	13SEP83	19SEP83	15AUG83	19AUG83	-20

Table 7-5   Continued

```
-----------------------------------------------------------------------------------------------------
AMERICAN COMMUNITY DEVELOPERS, INC.         PRIMAVERA PROJECT PLANNER         BRIAN'S DUPLICATE OF PROJECT "HOME"

REPORT DATE  12FEB83  RUN NO.    4           PROJECT SCHEDULE                 START DATE 13DEC82  FIN DATE  6SEP84

PROJECT SCHEDULE SORTED BY WORKER CATEGORY AND EARLY START                    DATA DATE   1FEB83  PAGE NO.    2
```

ACTIVITY ID	ORIG DUR	REM DUR	%	ACTIVITY DESCRIPTION	EARLY START	EARLY FINISH	LATE START	LATE FINISH	TOTAL FLOAT
49	8	8	0	WOOD SIDING	20SEP83	29SEP83	22AUG83	31AUG83	-20
66	5	5	0	WALL INSULATION	30SEP83*	6OCT83	1SEP83*	7SEP83	-20
70	25	25	0	SHEETROCK WALLS	7OCT83	10NOV83	20SEP83	24OCT83	-13
72	20	20	0	TAPE AND BED	11NOV83	9DEC83	25OCT83	21NOV83	-13
76	5	5	0	FUR DOWN FOR CEILING AIR CONDITIONER	12DEC83	16DEC83	22NOV83	29NOV83	-13
74	10	10	0	BLOW ON CEILING INSULATION	12DEC83	23DEC83	31MAY84	13JUN84	121
80	4	4	0	SHEETROCK FUR DOWNS	4JAN84	9JAN84	14DEC83	19DEC83	-13
87	15	15	0	TAPE AND BED FUR DOWNS	10JAN84	30JAN84	20DEC83	11JAN84	-13
93	10	10	0	DOORS AND TRIM	17FEB84	1MAR84	31JAN84	13FEB84	-13
99	5	5	0	HARDWARE	30MAR84	5APR84	7JUN84	13JUN84	49
115	13	13	0	INSTALL CABINETS	2MAY84	18MAY84	13APR84*	1MAY84	-13
112	14	14	0	PANELING, FINISH CARPENTRY AND MILLWORK	2MAY84	21MAY84	25MAY84	13JUN84	17
123	5	5	0	BATHROOM ACCESSORIES	7JUN84	13JUN84	7JUN84	13JUN84	0
128	10	10	0	CLEAN UP	14JUN84	27JUN84	14JUN84	27JUN84	0
142	10	10	0	CLEAN UP	3AUG84	16AUG84	3AUG84	16AUG84	0
144	10	10	0	PUNCH LIST	17AUG84	30AUG84	17AUG84	30AUG84	0

```
-----------------------------------------------------------------------------------------------------
AMERICAN COMMUNITY DEVELOPERS, INC.         PRIMAVERA PROJECT PLANNER         BRIAN'S DUPLICATE OF PROJECT "HOME"

REPORT DATE  12FEB83  RUN NO.    4           PROJECT SCHEDULE                 START DATE 13DEC82  FIN DATE  6SEP84

PROJECT SCHEDULE SORTED BY WORKER CATEGORY AND EARLY START                    DATA DATE   1FEB83  PAGE NO.    3

CONCRETE WORKER
```

ACTIVITY ID	ORIG DUR	REM DUR	%	ACTIVITY DESCRIPTION	EARLY START	EARLY FINISH	LATE START	LATE FINISH	TOTAL FLOAT
7	5	2	60	FOUNDATION EXCAVATION	4FEB83	7FEB83	7JAN83	10JAN83	-20
9	7	7	0	GRANULAR FILL	8FEB83	16FEB83	11JAN83	19JAN83	-20
22	5	5	0	CONCRETE SLAB ON GRADE	9MAR83	15MAR83	8FEB83	14FEB83	-20
24	13	13	0	CURING TIME	16MAR83	1APR83	15FEB83	4MAR83	-20
26	10	10	0	SET PRECAST CONCRETE PANELS	4APR83	15APR83	7MAR83	18MAR83	-20
27	6	6	0	GROUT PRECAST PANELS	11APR83	18APR83	14MAR83	21MAR83	-20
67	5	5	0	CONCRETE STAIRS	4OCT83	10OCT83	7JUN84	13JUN84	174

```
-----------------------------------------------------------------------------------------------------
AMERICAN COMMUNITY DEVELOPERS, INC.         PRIMAVERA PROJECT PLANNER         BRIAN'S DUPLICATE OF PROJECT "HOME"

REPORT DATE  12FEB83  RUN NO.    4           PROJECT SCHEDULE                 START DATE 13DEC82  FIN DATE  6SEP84

PROJECT SCHEDULE SORTED BY WORKER CATEGORY AND EARLY START                    DATA DATE   1FEB83  PAGE NO.    4

CARPET LAYER
```

ACTIVITY ID	ORIG DUR	REM DUR	%	ACTIVITY DESCRIPTION	EARLY START	EARLY FINISH	LATE START	LATE FINISH	TOTAL FLOAT
138	15	15	0	INSTALL CARPETING	6JUL84	26JUL84	6JUL84	26JUL84	0

Table 7-5   Continued

```
--------------------------------------------------------------------------------------------
AMERICAN COMMUNITY DEVELOPERS, INC.        PRIMAVERA PROJECT PLANNER        BRIAN'S DUPLICATE OF PROJECT "HOME"

REPORT DATE  12FEB83  RUN NO.   4          PROJECT SCHEDULE                 START DATE 13DEC82 FIN DATE  6SEP84

PROJECT SCHEDULE SORTED BY WORKER CATEGORY AND EARLY START                  DATA DATE   1FEB83  PAGE NO.   5
```

DRAPE HANGER

ACTIVITY ID	ORIG DUR	REM DUR	%	ACTIVITY DESCRIPTION	EARLY START	EARLY FINISH	LATE START	LATE FINISH	TOTAL FLOAT
140	5	5	0	INSTALL DRAPES	27JUL84	2AUG84	27JUL84	2AUG84	0

```
--------------------------------------------------------------------------------------------
AMERICAN COMMUNITY DEVELOPERS, INC.        PRIMAVERA PROJECT PLANNER        BRIAN'S DUPLICATE OF PROJECT "HOME"

REPORT DATE  12FEB83  RUN NO.   4          PROJECT SCHEDULE                 START DATE 13DEC82 FIN DATE  6SEP84

PROJECT SCHEDULE SORTED BY WORKER CATEGORY AND EARLY START                  DATA DATE   1FEB83  PAGE NO.   6
```

ELECTRICIAN

ACTIVITY ID	ORIG DUR	REM DUR	%	ACTIVITY DESCRIPTION	EARLY START	EARLY FINISH	LATE START	LATE FINISH	TOTAL FLOAT
12	7	7	0	UNDERSLAB ELECTRICAL LINE	17FEB83	28FEB83	28JAN83	7FEB83	-14
53	15	15	0	PULL WIRE & ROUGH IN ELECTRIC&TELEPHONE IN WALLS	17MAY83	7JUN83	11AUG83	31AUG83	60
54	8	8	0	TV WIRE PULLING	17MAY83	26MAY83	22AUG83	31AUG83	67
114	5	5	0	TV TRIMOUT	2MAY84	8MAY84	7JUN84	13JUN84	26
119	12	12	0	ELECTRICAL CONNECTIONS AND TRIMOUT	17MAY84	1JUN84	29MAY84	13JUN84	8

```
--------------------------------------------------------------------------------------------
AMERICAN COMMUNITY DEVELOPERS, INC.        PRIMAVERA PROJECT PLANNER        BRIAN'S DUPLICATE OF PROJECT "HOME"

REPORT DATE  12FEB83  RUN NO.   4          PROJECT SCHEDULE                 START DATE 13DEC82 FIN DATE  6SEP84

PROJECT SCHEDULE SORTED BY WORKER CATEGORY AND EARLY START                  DATA DATE   1FEB83  PAGE NO.   7
```

EXCAVATOR

ACTIVITY ID	ORIG DUR	REM DUR	%	ACTIVITY DESCRIPTION	EARLY START	EARLY FINISH	LATE START	LATE FINISH	TOTAL FLOAT
1	5	0	100	LAYOUT	14DEC82A	22DEC82A			
3	15	0	100	SOIL STABILIZATION	28DEC82A	20JAN83A			
13	13	13	0	TERMITE PROTECTION	17FEB83	8MAR83	20JAN83	7FEB83	-20

```
--------------------------------------------------------------------------------------------
AMERICAN COMMUNITY DEVELOPERS, INC.        PRIMAVERA PROJECT PLANNER        BRIAN'S DUPLICATE OF PROJECT "HOME"

REPORT DATE  12FEB83  RUN NO.   4          PROJECT SCHEDULE                 START DATE 13DEC82 FIN DATE  6SEP84

PROJECT SCHEDULE SORTED BY WORKER CATEGORY AND EARLY START                  DATA DATE   1FEB83  PAGE NO.   8
```

HEATING VENTILATING AND AIR CONDITIONING

ACTIVITY ID	ORIG DUR	REM DUR	%	ACTIVITY DESCRIPTION	EARLY START	EARLY FINISH	LATE START	LATE FINISH	TOTAL FLOAT
11	5	5	0	UNDERSLAB AC FREON S&R LINE	17FEB83	24FEB83	1FEB83	7FEB83	-12
78	10	10	0	A/C ROUGH IN	19DEC83	3JAN84	30NOV83	13DEC83	-13
113	10	10	0	INSTALL CONDENSERS AND A/C TRIMOUT	2MAY84	15MAY84	31MAY84	13JUN84	21

Table 7-5 Continued

AMERICAN COMMUNITY DEVELOPERS, INC.   PRIMAVERA PROJECT PLANNER   BRIAN'S DUPLICATE OF PROJECT "HOME"

REPORT DATE 12FEB83 RUN NO.   4   PROJECT SCHEDULE   START DATE 13DEC82 FIN DATE 6SEP84

PROJECT SCHEDULE SORTED BY WORKER CATEGORY AND EARLY START   DATA DATE   1FEB83 PAGE NO.   9

IRON WORKER

ACTIVITY ID	ORIG DUR	REM DUR	%	ACTIVITY DESCRIPTION	EARLY START	EARLY FINISH	LATE START	LATE FINISH	TOTAL FLOAT
30	50	50	0	INSTALL METAL STAIRS	19APR83	28JUN83	22MAR83	31MAY83	-20
32	23	23	0	PLATES, LINTELS, AND ROOF TRUSSES	29JUN83	1AUG83	1JUN83	1JUL83	-20
68	6	6	0	EXTERIOR RAILINGS	5OCT83	12OCT83	6JUN84	13JUN84	172

AMERICAN COMMUNITY DEVELOPERS, INC.   PRIMAVERA PROJECT PLANNER   BRIAN'S DUPLICATE OF PROJECT "HOME"

REPORT DATE 12FEB83 RUN NO.   4   PROJECT SCHEDULE   START DATE 13DEC82 FIN DATE 6SEP84

PROJECT SCHEDULE SORTED BY WORKER CATEGORY AND EARLY START   DATA DATE   1FEB83 PAGE NO.   10

PLUMBER

ACTIVITY ID	ORIG DUR	REM DUR	%	ACTIVITY DESCRIPTION	EARLY START	EARLY FINISH	LATE START	LATE FINISH	TOTAL FLOAT
5	8	3	62	PLUMBING-STREET CONNECTION AND UNDERSLAB	24JAN83A	3FEB83		6JAN83	-20
52	4	4	0	INSTALL TUB, STACK OUT PLUMBING	17MAY83	20MAY83	5AUG83	10AUG83	56
118	13	13	0	PLUMBING CONNECTIONS AND TRIMOUT	21MAY84	6JUN84	16MAY84	1JUN84*	-3
117	5	5	0	SET APPLIANCES	21MAY84	25MAY84	31MAY84	6JUN84	8

AMERICAN COMMUNITY DEVELOPERS, INC.   PRIMAVERA PROJECT PLANNER   BRIAN'S DUPLICATE OF PROJECT "HOME"

REPORT DATE 12FEB83 RUN NO.   4   PROJECT SCHEDULE   START DATE 13DEC82 FIN DATE 6SEP84

PROJECT SCHEDULE SORTED BY WORKER CATEGORY AND EARLY START   DATA DATE   1FEB83 PAGE NO.   11

PAINTER

ACTIVITY ID	ORIG DUR	REM DUR	%	ACTIVITY DESCRIPTION	EARLY START	EARLY FINISH	LATE START	LATE FINISH	TOTAL FLOAT
89	13	13	0	TEXTURE WALLS AND CEILINGS	31JAN84	16FEB84	12JAN84	30JAN84	-13
95	20	20	0	PAINTING	2MAR84	29MAR84	14FEB84	12MAR84	-13
100	8	8	0	VINYL WALL COVERING	30MAR84	10APR84	13MAR84	22MAR84	-13
107	5	5	0	CLEAN UP	11APR84	17APR84	23MAR84	29MAR84	-13
136	5	5	0	PAINT TOUCH UP	28JUN84	5JUL84	28JUN84	5JUL84	0

AMERICAN COMMUNITY DEVELOPERS, INC.   PRIMAVERA PROJECT PLANNER   BRIAN'S DUPLICATE OF PROJECT "HOME"

REPORT DATE 12FEB83 RUN NO.   4   PROJECT SCHEDULE   START DATE 13DEC82 FIN DATE 6SEP84

PROJECT SCHEDULE SORTED BY WORKER CATEGORY AND EARLY START   DATA DATE   1FEB83 PAGE NO.   12

TILE SETTER

ACTIVITY ID	ORIG DUR	REM DUR	%	ACTIVITY DESCRIPTION	EARLY START	EARLY FINISH	LATE START	LATE FINISH	TOTAL FLOAT
91	5	5	0	BATHROOM TILE	17FEB84	23FEB84	7FEB84	13FEB84	-8
109	10	10	0	RESILIENT FLOORING AND BASES	18APR84	1MAY84	30MAR84	12APR84	-13

Table 7-6 Project Schedule (With Analysis and Successors) Sorted by Activity Number
----

AMERICAN COMMUNITY DEVELOPERS, INC.   PRIMAVERA PROJECT PLANNER   BRIAN'S DUPLICATE OF PROJECT "HOME"

REPORT DATE 12FEB83 RUN NO.   5   PROJECT SCHEDULE   START DATE 13DEC82 FIN DATE 6SEP84

PROJECT SCHEDULE (WITH ANALYSIS AND SUCCESSORS) SORTED BY ACTIVITY NUMBER   DATA DATE   1FEB83 PAGE NO.   1

ACTIVITY ID	ORIG DUR	REM DUR	%	ACTIVITY DESCRIPTION	EARLY START	EARLY FINISH	LATE START	LATE FINISH	TOTAL FLOAT
1	5	0	100	LAYOUT	14DEC82A	22DEC82A			
				WORKPERIOD	2	8			
				CODE EXCA=1=101=					
				S.L.D.F., 3.FS 0. 0. ,					
3	15	0	100	SOIL STABILIZATION	28DEC82A	20JAN83A			
				WORKPERIOD	11	27			
				CODE EXCA=1=102=					
				S.L.D.F., 5.FS 0. 3. -20,					
5	8	3	62	PLUMBING-STREET CONNECTION AND UNDERSLAB	24JAN83A	3FEB83		6JAN83	-20
				WORKPERIOD	29	37		17	
				CODE PLBG=1=301=					
				S.L.D.F., 7.FS 0. 2. -20,					
7	5	2	60	FOUNDATION EXCAVATION	4FEB83	7FEB83	7JAN83	10JAN83	-20
				WORKPERIOD	38	39	18	19	
				CODE CONC=1=105=					
				S.L.D.F., 9.FS 0. 7. -20,					
9	7	7	0	GRANULAR FILL	8FEB83	16FEB83	11JAN83	19JAN83	-20
				WORKPERIOD	40	46	20	26	
				CODE CONC=1=105=					
				S.L.D.F., 11.FS 0. 5. -12, 12.FS 0. 7. -14					
				S.L.D.F., 13.FS 0. 13. -20,					

Turnaround Document

The turnaround document option is shown in Table 7-9. It adds an update line (or lines) to any *Primavera* report format, including those that will be seen in later chapters of this book. The option allows easy progress reporting by filling in current values when different from shown. A good E-mail system simplifies responses and provides the same benefits that have been noted for report distribution.

Primavera supports character-based printers, as well as graphics. Sample Gantt Charts are shown in Tables 7-10, 7-11, and 7-12.

For each activity listed (Table 7-10; sorted by Early Start and total float), note that we are provided its description, identifier, original duration, remaining duration, percent complete, special codes if applicable, float, and schedule dates. These schedule dates, in turn, provide additional information in their (user-specified) coding scheme, defined similarly to the following:

E = early schedule
L = late schedule
H = holiday
⊙ = other nonworkday
A = actual start/finish date
* = data date
V = leveled activity (to be defined in Chapter 10)

Note the visual effect of float. If activity float is positive, the early-schedule "E" character string will be above and

Table 7-7   Project Schedule (With Predecessors and Successors) Sorted by Activity Number

```
------------------------------------------------------------------------------------------------------------
AMERICAN COMMUNITY DEVELOPERS, INC.          PRIMAVERA PROJECT PLANNER          BRIAN'S DUPLICATE OF PROJECT "HOME"

REPORT DATE  12FEB83  RUN NO.   6            PROJECT SCHEDULE                   START DATE 13DEC82  FIN DATE  6SEP84

PROJECT SCHEDULE (WITH PREDECESSORS AND SUCCESSORS) SORTED BY ACTIVITY NUMBER        DATA DATE   1FEB83  PAGE NO.   1
```

ACTIVITY ID	ORIG DUR	REM DUR	%		ACTIVITY DESCRIPTION	EARLY START	EARLY FINISH	LATE START	LATE FINISH	TOTAL FLOAT
1	5	0	100		LAYOUT	14DEC82A	22DEC82A			
.. 3	15	0	100 S FS	0	SOIL STABILIZATION	28DEC82A	20JAN83A			
3	15	0	100		SOIL STABILIZATION	28DEC82A	20JAN83A			
.. 1	5	0	100 P FS	0	LAYOUT	14DEC82A	22DEC82A			
.. 5	8	3	62 S FS	0	PLUMBING-STREET CONNECTION AND UNDERSLAB	24JAN83A	3FEB83		6JAN83	-20
5	8	3	62		PLUMBING-STREET CONNECTION AND UNDERSLAB	24JAN83A	3FEB83		6JAN83	-20
.. 3	15	0	100 P FS	0	SOIL STABILIZATION	28DEC82A	20JAN83A			
.. 7	5	2	60 S FS	0	FOUNDATION EXCAVATION	4FEB83	7FEB83	7JAN83	10JAN83	-20
7	5	2	60		FOUNDATION EXCAVATION	4FEB83	7FEB83	7JAN83	10JAN83	-20
.. 5	8	3	62 P FS	0	PLUMBING-STREET CONNECTION AND UNDERSLAB	24JAN83A	3FEB83		6JAN83	-20
.. 9	7	7	0 S FS	0	GRANULAR FILL	8FEB83	16FEB83	11JAN83	19JAN83	-20
9	7	7	0		GRANULAR FILL	8FEB83	16FEB83	11JAN83	19JAN83	-20
.. 7	5	2	60 P FS	0	FOUNDATION EXCAVATION	4FEB83	7FEB83	7JAN83	10JAN83	-20
.. 11	5	5	0 S FS	0	UNDERSLAB AC FREON S&R LINE	17FEB83	24FEB83	1FEB83	7FEB83	-12
.. 12	7	7	0 S FS	0	UNDERSLAB ELECTRICAL LINE	17FEB83	28FEB83	28JAN83	7FEB83	-14
.. 13	13	13	0 S FS	0	TERMITE PROTECTION	17FEB83	8MAR83	20JAN83	7FEB83	-20
11	5	5	0		UNDERSLAB AC FREON S&R LINE	17FEB83	24FEB83	1FEB83	7FEB83	-12
.. 9	7	7	0 P FS	0	GRANULAR FILL	8FEB83	16FEB83	11JAN83	19JAN83	-20
.. 22	5	5	0 S FS	0	CONCRETE SLAB ON GRADE	9MAR83	15MAR83	8FEB83	14FEB83	-20
12	7	7	0		UNDERSLAB ELECTRICAL LINE	17FEB83	28FEB83	28JAN83	7FEB83	-14
.. 9	7	7	0 P FS	0	GRANULAR FILL	8FEB83	16FEB83	11JAN83	19JAN83	-20
.. 22	5	5	0 S FS	0	CONCRETE SLAB ON GRADE	9MAR83	15MAR83	8FEB83	14FEB83	-20
13	13	13	0		TERMITE PROTECTION	17FEB83	8MAR83	20JAN83	7FEB83	-20
.. 9	7	7	0 P FS	0	GRANULAR FILL	8FEB83	16FEB83	11JAN83	19JAN83	-20
.. 22	5	5	0 S FS	0	CONCRETE SLAB ON GRADE	9MAR83	15MAR83	8FEB83	14FEB83	-20
22	5	5	0		CONCRETE SLAB ON GRADE	9MAR83	15MAR83	8FEB83	14FEB83	-20
.. 11	5	5	0 P FS	0	UNDERSLAB AC FREON S&R LINE	17FEB83	24FEB83	1FEB83	7FEB83	-12
.. 12	7	7	0 P FS	0	UNDERSLAB ELECTRICAL LINE	17FEB83	28FEB83	28JAN83	7FEB83	-14
.. 13	13	13	0 P FS	0	TERMITE PROTECTION	17FEB83	8MAR83	20JAN83	7FEB83	-20
.. 24	13	13	0 S FS	0	CURING TIME	16MAR83	1APR83	15FEB83	4MAR83	-20
24	13	13	0		CURING TIME	16MAR83	1APR83	15FEB83	4MAR83	-20
.. 22	5	5	0 P FS	0	CONCRETE SLAB ON GRADE	9MAR83	15MAR83	8FEB83	14FEB83	-20
.. 26	10	10	0 S FS	0	SET PRECAST CONCRETE PANELS	4APR83	15APR83	7MAR83	18MAR83	-20

Table 7-8 Critical Path Summary

```
------------------------------------------------------------------------------------------------
AMERICAN COMMUNITY DEVELOPERS, INC.          PRIMAVERA PROJECT PLANNER          BRIAN'S DUPLICATE OF PROJECT "HOME"

REPORT DATE  12FEB83  RUN NO.   7            NETWORK PATH ANALYSIS             START DATE 13DEC82 FIN DATE  6SEP84

CRITICAL PATH SUMMARY                                                          DATA DATE   1FEB83  PAGE NO.   1
------------------------------------------------------------------------------------------------
        XXXXXXXXXXXXXXXXXXXXXX
        X                    X
        X                    X
        X                    X
        X   NO PREDECESSORS  X--------->
        X                    X          |
        X                    X          |
        X                    X          |
        XXXXXXXXXXXXXXXXXXXXXX          |
                                        |
                 -------------          |
                 |
                 V
        XXXXXXXXXXXXXXXXXXXXXX    XXXXXXXXXXXXXXXXXXXXXX    XXXXXXXXXXXXXXXXXXXXXX    XXXXXXXXXXXXXXXXXXXXXX
        X ACT NO.         1 X    X ACT NO.         3 X    X ACT NO.         5 X    X ACT NO.         7 X
        X                   X    X                   X    X                   X    X                   X
 TOTAL  X  LAYOUT          X FS 0 X  SOIL            X FS 0 X  PLUMBING-STREET X FS 0 X  FOUNDATION     X FS 0
 FLOAT  X                  X----->X  STABILIZATION   X----->X  CONNECTION AND  X----->X  EXCAVATION     X----->
  -20   X                   X    X                   X    X  UNDERSLAB         X    X                   X     |
        X                   X    X                   X    X                   X    X                   X     |
        XOD   5 RD   0 PCT100X    XOD  15 RD   0 PCT100X    XOD   8 RD   3 PCT 62X    XOD   5 RD   2 PCT 60X   |
        XXXXXXXXXXXXXXXXXXXXXX    XXXXXXXXXXXXXXXXXXXXXX    XXXXXXXXXXXXXXXXXXXXXX    XXXXXXXXXXXXXXXXXXXXXX   |
        ES 14DEC82A EF 22DEC82A   ES 28DEC82A EF 20JAN83A   ES 24JAN83A EF  3FEB83    ES  4FEB83  EF  7FEB83  |
                                                                                                             |
             ----------------------------------------------------------------------------------------------
             |
             V
        XXXXXXXXXXXXXXXXXXXXXX    XXXXXXXXXXXXXXXXXXXXXX    XXXXXXXXXXXXXXXXXXXXXX    XXXXXXXXXXXXXXXXXXXXXX
        X ACT NO.         9 X    X ACT NO.        13 X    X ACT NO.        22 X    X ACT NO.        24 X
        X                   X    X                   X    X                   X    X                   X
 TOTAL  X  GRANULAR FILL   X FS 0 X  TERMITE         X FS 0 X  CONCRETE SLAB ON X FS 0 X  CURING TIME    X FS 0
 FLOAT  X                  X----->X  PROTECTION      X----->X  GRADE           X----->X               X----->
  -20   X                   X    X                   X    X                   X    X                   X     |
        X                   X    X                   X    X                   X    X                   X     |
        XOD   7 RD   7 PCT  0X    XOD  13 RD  13 PCT  0X    XOD   5 RD   5 PCT  0X    XOD  13 RD  13 PCT  0X   |
        XXXXXXXXXXXXXXXXXXXXXX    XXXXXXXXXXXXXXXXXXXXXX    XXXXXXXXXXXXXXXXXXXXXX    XXXXXXXXXXXXXXXXXXXXXX   |
        ES  8FEB83 EF 16FEB83     ES 17FEB83 EF  8MAR83     ES  9MAR83 EF 15MAR83     ES 16MAR83 EF  1APR83   |
                                                                                                             |
             ----------------------------------------------------------------------------------------------
             |
             V
        XXXXXXXXXXXXXXXXXXXXXX    XXXXXXXXXXXXXXXXXXXXXX    XXXXXXXXXXXXXXXXXXXXXX    XXXXXXXXXXXXXXXXXXXXXX
        X ACT NO.        26 X    X ACT NO.        27 X    X ACT NO.        30 X    X ACT NO.        32 X
        X                   X    X                   X    X                   X    X                   X
 TOTAL  X  SET PRECAST     X SS 5 X  GROUT PRECAST   X FS 0 X  INSTALL METAL   X FS 0 X  PLATES, LINTELS, X FS 0
 FLOAT  X  CONCRETE PANELS X----->X  PANELS          X----->X  STAIRS          X----->X  AND ROOF TRUSSES X----->
  -20   X                   X    X                   X    X                   X    X                   X     |
        X                   X    X                   X    X                   X    X                   X     |
        XOD  10 RD  10 PCT  0X    XOD   6 RD   6 PCT  0X    XOD  50 RD  50 PCT  0X    XOD  23 RD  23 PCT  0X   |
        XXXXXXXXXXXXXXXXXXXXXX    XXXXXXXXXXXXXXXXXXXXXX    XXXXXXXXXXXXXXXXXXXXXX    XXXXXXXXXXXXXXXXXXXXXX   |
        ES  4APR83 EF 15APR83     ES 11APR83 EF 18APR83     ES 19APR83 EF 28JUN83     ES 29JUN83 EF  1AUG83   |
                                                                                                             |
             ----------------------------------------------------------------------------------------------
             |
             V
        TO ACTIVITY # 34 (REDWOOD FASCIA, SOFFIT, AND PLYWOOD DECKING)
```

Table 7-9   Turnaround Document

```
----------------------------------------------------------------------------------------------
AMERICAN COMMUNITY DEVELOPERS, INC.        PRIMAVERA PROJECT PLANNER      BRIAN'S DUPLICATE OF PROJECT "HOME"

REPORT DATE  12FEB83  RUN NO.   8          PROJECT SCHEDULE              START DATE 13DEC82  FIN DATE  6SEP84

TURNAROUND DOCUMENT                                                      DATA DATE   1FEB83  PAGE NO.   1

CARPENTER
```

ACTIVITY ID	ORIG DUR	REM DUR	%	CODE	ACTIVITY DESCRIPTION	EARLY START	EARLY FINISH	LATE START	LATE FINISH	TOTAL FLOAT
50	20	20	0	115	FRAME INTERIOR WALLS	19APR83	16MAY83	8JUL83	4AUG83	56
34	20	20	0	110	REDWOOD FASCIA, SOFFIT AND PLYWOOD DECKING	2AUG83	29AUG83	5JUL83	1AUG83	-20
41	5	5	0	112	DRY SHEETING	30AUG83	5SEP83	2AUG83	8AUG83	-20
43	4	1	62		STOCK BULK MATERIAL INSIDE BUILDING	6SEP83	6SEP83	9AUG83	9AUG83	-20
58	15	15	0	111	ROOF SHINGLES	6SEP83	27SEP83	11AUG83	31AUG83*	-18
45	3	3	0	110	SET INFILL PANEL FRAMING	7SEP83	9SEP83	10AUG83	12AUG83	-20
47	5	5	0	111	WINDOWS	13SEP83	19SEP83	15AUG83	19AUG83	-20
49	8	8	0	110	WOOD SIDING	20SEP83	29SEP83	22AUG83	31AUG83	-20
66	5	5	0	116	WALL INSULATION	30SEP83*	6OCT83	1SEP83*	7SEP83	-20
70	25	25	0	112	SHEETROCK WALLS	7OCT83	10NOV83	20SEP83	24OCT83	-13
72	20	20	0	112	TAPE AND BED	11NOV83	9DEC83	25OCT83	21NOV83	-13

NOTES:

Table 7-10   Double-Bar Weekly Gantt Chart Sorted by Early Start and Total Float

```
-------------------------------------------------------------------------------------------------------------
AMERICAN COMMUNITY DEVELOPERS, INC.           PRIMAVERA PROJECT PLANNER              BRIAN'S DUPLICATE OF PROJECT "HOME"

REPORT DATE  12FEB83  RUN NO.   9             PROJECT SCHEDULE                       START DATE 13DEC82  FIN DATE  6SEP84

PROJECT SCHEDULE: DOUBLE-BAR WEEKLY GANTT CHART SORTED BY EARLY START AND TOTAL FLOAT          DATA DATE   1FEB83  PAGE NO.    2

                                                                                              WEEKLY-TIME PER.   1
-------------------------------------------------------------------------------------------------------------
                                                          03  07  07  04  02  06  04  01  05  03  07  05  02  06  05  02
................ACTIVITY DESCRIPTION...................   JAN FEB MAR APR MAY JUN JUL AUG SEP OCT NOV DEC JAN FEB MAR APR
ACTIVITY ID  OD   RD  PCT    CODES    FLOAT    SCHEDULE    83  83  83  83  83  83  83  83  83  83  83  83  84  84  84  84
-----------  ---- --- --- ------------ -----   --------   ---------------------------------------------------------------
GROUT PRECAST PANELS                           EARLY       .  *.  .   .EE .   .   .   .   .   .   .   .   .   .   .   .
         27   6    6   0             -20  LATE       .  *.  .LL .   .   .   .   .   .   .   .   .   .   .   .   .
ES = 11APR83       EF = 18APR83    LS = 14MAR83     LF = 21MAR83

INSTALL METAL STAIRS                           EARLY       .  *.  .   . EEEEEEEEEEE.  .   .   .   .   .   .   .   .   .
         30  50   50   0             -20  LATE       .  *.  . LLLLLLLLLLL.  .   .   .   .   .   .   .   .   .   .
ES = 19APR83       EF = 28JUN83    LS = 22MAR83     LF = 31MAY83

FRAME INTERIOR WALLS                           EARLY       .  *.  .   . EEEEE .   .   .   .   .   .   .   .   .   .   .
         50  20   20   0              56  LATE       .  *.  .   .   .   .   LLLLL .   .   .   .   .   .   .   .
ES = 19APR83       EF = 16MAY83    LS = 8JUL83      LF = 4AUG83

INSTALL TUB, STACK OUT PLUMBING                EARLY       .  *.  .   .   . E  .   .   .   .   .   .   .   .   .   .
         52   4    4   0              56  LATE       .  *.  .   .   .   .   LL  .   .   .   .   .   .   .   .
ES = 17MAY83       EF = 20MAY83    LS = 5AUG83      LF = 10AUG83

PULL WIRE & ROUGH IN ELECTRIC&TELEPHONE IN WALLSEARLY       .  *.  .   .   . EEEE .   .   .   .   .   .   .   .   .
         53  15   15   0              60  LATE       .  *.  .   .   .   .   .LLLL. .   .   .   .   .   .   .
ES = 17MAY83       EF = 7JUN83     LS = 11AUG83     LF = 31AUG83

TV WIRE PULLING                                EARLY       .  *.  .   .   . EE .   .   .   .   .   .   .   .   .   .
         54   8    8   0              67  LATE       .  *.  .   .   .   .   .   LL. .   .   .   .   .   .   .
ES = 17MAY83       EF = 26MAY83    LS = 22AUG83     LF = 31AUG83

PLATES, LINTELS, AND ROOF TRUSSES              EARLY       .  *.  .   .   .   . EEEEE .   .   .   .   .   .   .   .
         32  23   23   0             -20  LATE       .  *.  .   .   .   LLLLL. .   .   .   .   .   .   .   .
ES = 29JUN83       EF = 1AUG83     LS = 1JUN83      LF = 1JUL83

REDWOOD FASCIA,SOFFIT AND PLYWOOD DECKING       EARLY       .  *.  .   .   .   . EEEEE. .   .   .   .   .   .   .
         34  20   20   0             -20  LATE       .  *.  .   .   .   LLLLL .   .   .   .   .   .   .   .
ES = 2AUG83        EF = 29AUG83    LS = 5JUL83      LF = 1AUG83

DRY SHEETING                                   EARLY       .  *.  .   .   .   .   . EE .   .   .   .   .   .   .
         41   5    5   0             -20  LATE       .  *.  .   .   .   .   LL .   .   .   .   .   .   .   .
ES = 30AUG83       EF = 5SEP83     LS = 2AUG83      LF = 8AUG83

STOCK BULK MATERIAL INSIDE BUILDING            EARLY       .  *.  .   .   .   .   .   E  .   .   .   .   .   .   .
         43   4    1  62             -20  LATE       .  *.  .   .   .   .   .L  .   .   .   .   .   .   .
ES = 6SEP83        EF = 6SEP83     LS = 9AUG83      LF = 9AUG83

ROOF SHINGLES                                  EARLY       .  *.  .   .   .   .   . EEEE. .   .   .   .   .   .
         58  15   15   0             -18  LATE       .  *.  .   .   .   .   .LLLL. .   .   .   .   .   .   .
ES = 6SEP83        EF = 27SEP83    LS = 11AUG83     LF = 31AUG83
```

Table 7-11   Single-Bar Weekly Gantt Chart Sorted by Early Start and Total Float

```
----------------------------------------------------------------------------------------
AMERICAN COMMUNITY DEVELOPERS, INC.        PRIMAVERA PROJECT PLANNER        BRIAN'S DUPLICATE OF PROJECT "HOME"

REPORT DATE 12FEB83 RUN NO.   10           PROJECT SCHEDULE                 START DATE 13DEC82  FIN DATE  6SEP84

PROJECT SCHEDULE: SINGLE-BAR WEEKLY GANTT CHART SORTED BY EARLY START AND TOTAL FLOAT      DATA DATE   1FEB83  PAGE NO.   2


                                                                                          WEEKLY-TIME PER.   1

----------------------------------------------------------------------------------------
                                                 03   07  07  04  02  06  04  01  05  03  07  05  02  06  05  02
..............ACTIVITY DESCRIPTION..............  JAN  FEB MAR APR MAY JUN JUL AUG SEP OCT NOV DEC JAN FEB MAR APR
ACTIVITY ID OD  RD PCT    CODES   FLOAT  SCHEDULE  83   83  83  83  83  83  83  83  83  83  83  83  84  84  84  84
----------- ---- ---- --- ------------- -----  --------  ------------------------------------------------------------
GROUT PRECAST PANELS                        CURRENT   .  *.  .LL--EE .   .   .    .    .    .    .    .    .    .    .
      27   6    6   0                  -20            .  *.          .   .   .    .    .    .    .    .    .    .    .
ES = 11APR83       EF = 18APR83     LS = 14MAR83   LF = 21MAR83

INSTALL METAL STAIRS                        CURRENT   .  *.  . LLLLEEEEEE/EEEE.   .    .    .    .    .    .    .    .
      30   50   50  0                  -20            .  *.          .   .   .    .    .    .    .    .    .    .    .
ES = 19APR83       EF = 28JUN83     LS = 22MAR83   LF = 31MAY83

FRAME INTERIOR WALLS                        CURRENT   .  *.  .   . EEEEE++++++LLLLL   .    .    .    .    .    .    .
      50   20   20  0                   56            .  *.  .   .   .   .    .    .    .    .    .    .    .    .
ES = 19APR83       EF = 16MAY83     LS =  8JUL83   LF =  4AUG83

INSTALL TUB, STACK OUT PLUMBING             CURRENT   .  *.  .   .   . E++++++++++LL   .    .    .    .    .    .    .
      52   4    4   0                   56            .  *.  .   .   .   .    .    .    .    .    .    .    .    .
ES = 17MAY83       EF = 20MAY83     LS =  5AUG83   LF = 10AUG83

PULL WIRE & ROUGH IN ELECTRIC&TELEPHONE IN WALLSCURRENT  .  *.  .   .   . EEEE+++++++LLLL.   .    .    .    .    .    .
      53   15   15  0                   60            .  *.  .   .   .   .    .    .    .    .    .    .    .    .
ES = 17MAY83       EF =  7JUN83     LS = 11AUG83   LF = 31AUG83

TV WIRE PULLING                             CURRENT   .  *.  .   .   . EE+++++++++++LL.   .    .    .    .    .    .
      54   8    8   0                   67            .  *.  .   .   .   .    .    .    .    .    .    .    .    .
ES = 17MAY83       EF = 26MAY83     LS = 22AUG83   LF = 31AUG83

PLATES, LINTELS, AND ROOF TRUSSES           CURRENT   .  *.  .   .   .   LLLL/EEEEE   .    .    .    .    .    .    .
      32   23   23  0                  -20            .  *.  .   .   .   .    .    .    .    .    .    .    .    .
ES = 29JUN83       EF =  1AUG83     LS =  1JUN83   LF =  1JUL83

REDWOOD FASCIA,SOFFIT AND PLYWOOD DECKING    CURRENT  .  *.  .   .   .   . LLLL/EEEE.   .    .    .    .    .    .
      34   20   20  0                  -20            .  *.  .   .   .   .    .    .    .    .    .    .    .    .
ES =  2AUG83       EF = 29AUG83     LS =  5JUL83   LF =  1AUG83

DRY SHEETING                                CURRENT   .  *.  .   .   .   .   LL--EE   .    .    .    .    .    .    .
      41   5    5   0                  -20            .  *.  .   .   .   .    .    .    .    .    .    .    .    .
ES = 30AUG83       EF =  5SEP83     LS =  2AUG83   LF =  8AUG83

STOCK BULK MATERIAL INSIDE BUILDING         CURRENT   .  *.  .   .   .   .   .L---E   .    .    .    .    .    .    .
      43   4    1  62                  -20            .  *.  .   .   .   .    .    .    .    .    .    .    .    .
ES =  6SEP83       EF =  6SEP83     LS =  9AUG83   LF =  9AUG83

ROOF SHINGLES                               CURRENT   .  *.  .   .   .   .   .LLLLEEEE.   .    .    .    .    .    .
      58   15   15  0                  -18            .  *.  .   .   .   .    .    .    .    .    .    .    .    .
ES =  6SEP83       EF = 27SEP83     LS = 11AUG83   LF = 31AUG83
```

Table 7-12   Single-Bar Weekly Gantt Chart Sorted by Worker Category and Early Start

```
-----------------------------------------------------------------------------------------------------
AMERICAN COMMUNITY DEVELOPERS, INC.        PRIMAVERA PROJECT PLANNER          BRIAN'S DUPLICATE OF PROJECT "HOME"

REPORT DATE  12FEB83  RUN NO.   11         PROJECT SCHEDULE                   START DATE 13DEC82  FIN DATE  6SEP84

PROJECT SCHEDULE: SINGLE-BAR WEEKLY GANTT CHART SORTED BY WORKER CATEGORY AND EARLY START    DATA DATE   1FEB83  PAGE NO.    1

CARPENTER                                                                                   WEEKLY-TIME PER.   1
-----------------------------------------------------------------------------------------------------
                                                        03  07  07  04  02  06  04  01  05  03  07  05  02  06  05  02
.................ACTIVITY DESCRIPTION...................  JAN FEB MAR APR MAY JUN JUL AUG SEP OCT NOV DEC JAN FEB MAR APR
ACTIVITY ID OD  RD  PCT    CODES     FLOAT     SCHEDULE   83  83  83  83  83  83  83  83  83  83  83  83  84  84  84  84
----------- ---- ---- --- -- ------------ -----  --------  -----------------------------------------------------------
FRAME INTERIOR WALLS                          CURRENT    . *.   .   . EEEEE++++++LLLLL   .   .   .   .   .   .   .   .
      50  20  20   0            56                       . *.   .   .   .   .   .   .   .   .   .   .   .   .   .   .
ES = 19APR83       EF = 16MAY83    LS =  8JUL83   LF =  4AUG83

REDWOOD FASCIA,SOFFIT AND PLYWOOD DECKING     CURRENT    . *.   .   .   .   .   . LLLL/EEEE.  .   .   .   .   .   .   .
      34  20  20   0           -20                       . *.   .   .   .   .   .   .   .   .   .   .   .   .   .   .
ES =  2AUG83       EF = 29AUG83    LS =  5JUL83   LF =  1AUG83

DRY SHEETING                                  CURRENT    . *.   .   .   .   .   .   . LL--EE  .   .   .   .   .   .   .
      41   5   5   0           -20                       . *.   .   .   .   .   .   .   .   .   .   .   .   .   .   .
ES = 30AUG83       EF =  5SEP83    LS =  2AUG83   LF =  8AUG83

STOCK BULK MATERIAL INSIDE BUILDING           CURRENT    . *.   .   .   .   .   .   .  .L---E  .   .   .   .   .   .   .
      43   4   1  62           -20                       . *.   .   .   .   .   .   .   .   .   .   .   .   .   .   .
ES =  6SEP83       EF =  6SEP83    LS =  9AUG83   LF =  9AUG83

ROOF SHINGLES                                 CURRENT    . *.   .   .   .   .   .   . .LLLLEEEE.  .   .   .   .   .   .
      58  15  15   0           -18                       . *.   .   .   .   .   .   .   .   .   .   .   .   .   .   .
ES =  6SEP83       EF = 27SEP83    LS = 11AUG83   LF = 31AUG83

SET INFILL PANEL FRAMING                      CURRENT    . *.   .   .   .   .   .   .  .L---E  .   .   .   .   .   .   .
      45   3   3   0           -20                       . *.   .   .   .   .   .   .   .   .   .   .   .   .   .   .
ES =  7SEP83       EF =  9SEP83    LS = 10AUG83   LF = 12AUG83

WINDOWS                                       CURRENT    . *.   .   .   .   .   .   . L---EE  .   .   .   .   .   .   .
      47   5   5   0           -20                       . *.   .   .   .   .   .   .   .   .   .   .   .   .   .   .
ES = 13SEP83       EF = 19SEP83    LS = 15AUG83   LF = 19AUG83

WOOD SIDING                                   CURRENT    . *.   .   .   .   .   .   .  LL--EE.   .   .   .   .   .   .
      49   8   8   0           -20                       . *.   .   .   .   .   .   .   .   .   .   .   .   .   .   .
ES = 20SEP83       EF = 29SEP83    LS = 22AUG83   LF = 31AUG83

WALL INSULATION                               CURRENT    . *.   .   .   .   .   .   .  LL--EE   .   .   .   .   .   .
      66   5   5   0           -20                       . *.   .   .   .   .   .   .   .   .   .   .   .   .   .   .
ES = 30SEP83       EF =  6OCT83    LS =  1SEP83   LF =  7SEP83

SHEETROCK WALLS                               CURRENT    . *.   .   .   .   .   .   .   . LLEEE/EE  .   .   .   .   .   .
      70  25  25   0           -13                       . *.   .   .   .   .   .   .   .   .   .   .   .   .   .   .
ES =  7OCT83       EF = 10NOV83    LS = 20SEP83   LF = 24OCT83

TAPE AND BED                                  CURRENT    . *.   .   .   .   .   .   .   .  LLEE/EE  .   .   .   .   .
      72  20  20   0           -13                       . *.   .   .   .   .   .   .   .   .   .   .   .   .   .   .
ES = 11NOV83       EF =  9DEC83    LS = 25OCT83   LF = 21NOV83

FUR DOWN FOR CEILING AIR CONDITIONER          CURRENT    . *.   .   .   .   .   .   .   .  . LL-E  .   .   .   .   .
      76   5   5   0           -13                       . *.   .   .   .   .   .   .   .   .   .   .   .   .   .   .
ES = 12DEC83       EF = 16DEC83    LS = 22NOV83   LF = 29NOV83
```

to the left of the late-schedule "L" string. The offset represents the amount of float. Positive-float activities include activities 50 and 52 (fifty-six days), activity 53 (sixty days), and activity 54 (sixty-seven days).

If activity float equals zero, the early-schedule "E" character string will line up precisely over the late-schedule "L" string immediately below. These activities (none are shown in the sample report) are, of course, critical activities; they cannot be delayed.

And if activity float is negative, the early-schedule character string will be above and to the right of the late-schedule string, the offset again representing magnitude (and in this case, situation severity). These activities are super-critical. The indicated amount of time must be made up, or else the project will be delayed accordingly. Activities 27, 30, 32, 34, 41, 43, and 58 are all super-critical.

If the two schedule lines are combined into one (see Tables 7-11 and 7-12), the following additional float symbols may also be used:

+ = positive float
− = negative float
/ = overlap between early and late schedule ranges

Table 7-11 presents all Table 7-10 activities in the same ES, TF order. Table 7-12 presents only those project activities of interest to the carpenter. Other worker categories could also have their own subproject reports.

Regardless of format details, these Gantt Charts are Gantt Charts done *right*—they summarize, but do not replace, the crucial logic "under the covers."

Now that we have completed this trip through the network and presented our findings, what do we do next?

8
Introduction to PERT

HOW PERT DIFFERS FROM CPM

In our discussion of CPM activity duration, we learned that PERT does not differ greatly from AOA CPM except that it requires three time estimates for each activity:

- Optimistic time
- Most likely time
- "Murphy's Law time"

The "three time estimate" requirement allows the use of statistics to estimate the probability the project will complete before a given time.

ACTIVITY TIME ESTIMATES

Estimated activity time combines the three time estimates as follows:

$$= \frac{[\text{optimistic time} + (4 * \text{most likely time}) + \text{pessimistic time}]}{6}$$

$$= \frac{[a + 4m + b]}{6}$$

We may define *optimistic time* as the minimum reasonable time in which an activity can be completed if everything goes exceptionally well: the best time possible given one hundred actual or imaginary performances. Optimistic time should occur about 1 percent of the time; faster times than this should occur less than 1 percent of the time.

Pessimistic time is the maximum reasonable time in which an activity would be completed if everything goes exceptionally poorly: the worst time possible given one hundred actual or imaginary performances—if Murphy's Law is the Law of the Land (or, at least of your project). Although you might think it occurs all the time, at least to you, pessimistic time should occur about 1 percent of the time;

slower times than this should occur less than 1 percent of the time.

Most likely time is, not surprisingly, always somewhere between these two outlying values. It is the most realistic amount of time an activity might consume: the mean time of one hundred actual or imaginary performances and the value whose probability of completion is 50 percent. Note that this time is weighted quadruple either the optimistic or pessimistic time. This:

- Supports the underlying PERT assumption of a beta distribution
- Makes further sense, in that the outlying values should each occur no more often than 1 percent of the time

Of course, if the difference between the optimistic time and the most likely time equals the difference between the pessimistic time and the most likely time, the estimated time is reduced simply to the most likely time. That is, if $(m - a) = (b - m)$, then the estimated time becomes simply m. But this happens only infrequently and by coincidence.

It is *not* appropriate to force symmetry around m if the values selected do not represent reality. The underlying PERT statistical theory says only that optimistic and pessimistic times on average each occur only 1 percent of the time. It does not say or imply that the absolute differences from the most likely time will necessarily be equal. This error:

- Would always affect probability calculations for on-time completion
- May also affect project duration calculations

People sometimes have difficulty estimating even the most likely time. Determining a and b becomes a "Federal

181

project." This totally disrupts accuracy and has caused most project managers to abandon the three-value PERT method in favor of the single-value CPM. Moreover, although a PERT network could be represented in PDM format, most PERT literature and project management software uses the more cumbersome, less capable activity-on-arrow (I-J) format.

When (rarely) necessary to do this, my approach is to export schedules directly into good spreadsheet software (like *20/20*) and then to conduct simulations accordingly. If desired, the newly calculated estimated times may then be re-introduced back into the network and the resulting PDM schedule calculated. If just the probability of on-time completion is sought, only super-critical, critical, and near-critical activities need be considered.

PROBABILITY OF ON-TIME COMPLETION

The probability that this project will complete by the time indicated depends on the amount of uncertainty in estimated activity times. By definition, each activity's estimated time measures this uncertainty as a variance equal to the square of one-sixth the difference between the two extremes *a* and *b*:

$$\sigma^2 = \frac{(b - a)^2}{6^2}$$

The greater the difference between *a* and *b*:

- The larger the variance
- The smaller the probability this activity will complete by the indicated time

For example, if we have an activity for which $a = 10$, $m = 22$, and $b = 28$, then the estimated time will be:

$$\frac{(10 + 4 * 22 + 28)}{6}, \text{ or 21 days}$$

By definition, there is a 50 percent chance that the actual duration will equal this twenty-one-day value. The remaining 50 percent of the time, activity duration will be different. Of this, half will be longer than twenty-one days, half will be shorter.

If, and only if, $|a - m| = |b - m|$ will this remaining percentage be distributed evenly left and right of twenty-one days. At the same time, the variance for this activity would be:

$$\frac{(28 - 10)^2}{6^2}, \text{ or 9 days}$$

This means the estimated time for this activity is equal to twenty-one days, but the variance, nine days, is rather high and indicates much uncertainty as to just how long it really will take.

But suppose we were even more uncertain about these times. Let us now assume optimistic time is equal to five days and pessimistic time is equal to thirty. The estimated time for this activity would now be:

$$\frac{(5 + 4 * 22 + 30)}{6}$$

or 20.5 days, which we could round to 21. The variance for these new times, however, would almost double to:

$$\frac{(30 - 5)^2}{6^2}$$

17.4 days, even though the spread $(b - a)$ increased only by 7 days $(= [30 - 28] + [10 - 5])$. This means the estimated time for this activity, still 21 days (actually, 20.5), is even less certain than before.

When (and only when) *a, b,* and *m* all equal each other:

- Variance is equal to zero
- It is a virtual certainty the activity will complete in *m* time units
- There is almost no chance it will complete either sooner or later

In the sample case, estimated time would obviously be:

$$\frac{(22 + 4 * 22 + 22)}{6}$$

or 22 days and the variance would, as advertised, be equal to 0:

$$\frac{(22 - 22)^2}{6^2}$$

or 0 days. There is negligible chance this activity will take any shorter or longer than twenty-two days.

Continue this process for each project activity. Calculate the Critical Path exactly as before, except use the weighted time estimates for duration.

Having calculated activity variance and the Critical Path, we may now determine the probability of completing the project by a given date.

The first step is to total the variances for each activity on the Critical Path. Although some activities may be close to the Critical Path, they are not considered unless they actually turn critical, which could happen for the same reasons as with CPM activities. (Of course, here as there, it would be wise to simulate and ask "what if" questions.)

Next, take the square root of this value.

Now subtract the earliest expected completion time (TE) for the last project activity—like CPM Early Finish—from the project due date (D) and divide this difference by the square-root value determined above. This gives the number of standard deviations the project due date varies from the earliest expected completion time (TE):

$$Z = \frac{D - T_E}{\sqrt{\sum \sigma_{cp}^2}}$$

Where Z = number of standard deviations the project due date is from the expected completion date

D = project due date

T_E = earliest expected completion time for last project activity

$\sum \sigma_{cp}^2$ = sum of the variances along the Critical Path

This Z-value represents the number of standard deviations the project due date is from the expected completion time. If the magnitude of Z is large:

- The two dates are not close in time, and/or
- Critical Path variance is small

If Z equals zero:

- The two dates are precisely the same, regardless of Critical Path variance
- The project has a 50 percent chance of on-time completion

The sign of Z is very important. If the project due date is after the earliest expected completion date, then "WHOOPIE!!!"—a high Z-value is desirable because it represents a high probability the project will complete on or before the due date. But if the Z-value is negative (because the earliest expected completion date is after the project due date), the higher its value, the more miserable things will be for you because this represents a high probability the project will complete late. As before, this could occur if the two dates are not close in time ("Mission Impossible"?), or if the Critical Path variance is small. The latter case tells us Critical Path activity times are reasonably certain but too long. They must be shortened, or the project deadline extended, in order to improve the probability of on-time completion.

An abbreviated Z-table is presented in Table 8-1. Probability values are rounded.

WORKED EXAMPLE

Let us look with a PERT perspective at the thirty-eight-day network from Chapter 3 and see if we can determine the probability this project will complete on time (Table 8-2).

First, draw a network diagram, such as Fig. 8-1.

Next, calculate the appropriate expected-time and variance values for each activity and determine the Critical Path. Add the critical expected times and variances as shown in Table 8-3.

Note how the Critical Path splits at event 1 (the completion of activity 0–1). Even though by definition the expected times (ET) associated with each path must be equal (seven days along activity 1–3 does indeed equal the sum of five days and two days for activities 1–2 and 2–3), we see the variances for each path are quite different. The one-activity path has $2\frac{7}{9}$ days, the two-activity path only $1\frac{1}{9}$ (these variances are determined by activity a, m, and b values, not the number of path activities themselves).

So we must decide which value to use in arriving at the probability of on-time completion. Prudence tells us always to select the path with the largest total variance. This is because:

- Less controllable things demand closer management attention and effort
- It represents a greater likelihood of exclusive criticality

On this basis, then, we select and add the variances associated with activities 0–1, 1–3, 3–5, and 5–6, or 11.89. Note that most of this variance came from activity 0–1; this is not unusual in research, design, or other new-activity projects for which adequate time histories do not exist.

Will we complete the project on time? This depends on the project due date. The earliest expected completion time is thirty-eight days. If the due date is also thirty-eight days, we have only a 50 percent chance of finishing our project on time.

For due dates other than those in which $D = TE$ (and for which, therefore, $Z = 0$), the moderate 11.89-day vari-

Table 8-1   PERT Z-Probabilities

Z value (+)	Probability %	Z value (−)	Probability %
+0.00	50	−0.00	50
+0.25	60	−0.25	40
+0.50	69	−0.50	31
+0.75	77	−0.75	23
+1.00	84	−1.00	16
+1.25	89	−1.25	11
+1.50	93	−1.50	7
+1.75	96	−1.75	4
+2.00	98	−2.00	2
+2.25	99	−2.25	1
+2.50	99.4	−2.50	0.6
+2.75	99.7	−2.75	0.3
+3.00	99.9	−3.00	0.1

184   Chapter 8: Introduction to PERT

Table 8-2   Activity List With Relationships and Durations
```
------------------------------------------------------------------------
SCHEDULE SETUP                                      DATE: _____

PROJECT NAME:    EIGHT-ACTIVITY PERT NETWORK EXAMPLE_____
                 CHASE (USC) AND AQUILANO (ARIZONA)
------------------------------------------------------------------------
   ACTIVITY                                                      ACTIVITY
     ID       PREDECESSOR     a     m     b    EXPECTED TIME (ET) VARIANCE
   --------   -----------    ---   ---   ---   ------------------ --------
     0-1      None           10    22    28
     1-2      0-1             4     4    10
     2-3      1-2             1     2     3
     1-3      0-1             4     6    14
 D   3-4      1-3, 2-3        -     -     -
     4-5      3-4             1     5     9
     3-5      1-3, 2-3        7     8     9
     5-6      3-5, 4-5        2     2     2
------------------------------------------------------------------------
```

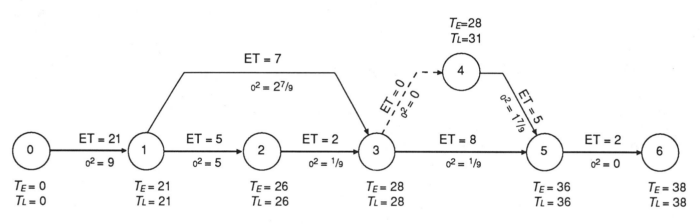

FIGURE 8-1.   Network setup diagram.

Table 8-3   Schedule Setup
```
------------------------------------------------------------------------
SCHEDULE SETUP                                      DATE: _____

PROJECT NAME:    EIGHT-ACTIVITY PERT NETWORK EXAMPLE_____
                 CHASE (USC) AND AQUILANO (ARIZONA)
------------------------------------------------------------------------
   ACTIVITY                                                      ACTIVITY
     ID        PREDECESSOR      a    m    b   EXPECTED TIME (ET) VARIANCE
   --------    -----------     ---  ---  ---  ------------------ --------
     0-1 *     None            10   22   28          21          * 9
     1-2 *     0-1              4    4   10           5            1
     2-3 *     1-2              1    2    3           2              1/9
     1-3 *     0-1              4    6   14           7          * 2-7/9
 D   3-4       1-3, 2-3         -    -    -           -          -----
     4-5    1-3, 2-3, 3-4       1    5    9           5            1-7/9
     3-5 *     1-3, 2-3         7    8    9           8          *   1/9
     5-6 *     3-5, 4-5         2    2    2           2          * 0
   ---------                                         ---         ------
     SUM:                                             38         *11-8/9
------------------------------------------------------------------------
```

ance will have more effect. If the due date were given as thirty-five days, we are in a world of hurt. Solving the Z-transform equation studied earlier would give:

$$Z = \frac{D - T_E}{\sqrt{\sum \sigma_{cp}^2}}$$

$$= \frac{(35 - 38)}{\sqrt{(11.89)}}$$

$$= -0.87$$

We see from a statistics "Areas of the Cumulative Standard Normal Distribution Table" that a Z-value of −0.87 means we have only little more than 19 percent chance of finishing this project in thirty-five days. Recall our earlier mention of negative Z's with high variances. Suppose we were to reduce activity 0–1 variance by half, to 4.5 days. Would this help or hurt? Clue: "Ouch!" Our chances would drop to only 13.57 percent because we:

- Could no longer hope as much to reduce activity 0–1 expected time
- Would be more certain we actually need twenty-one days (not fewer) to finish it

- Would also be more certain we really do need thirty-eight days (not fewer) to complete the entire project

What if the due date is three days after the earliest expected completion time? Would we be 81 percent (= 100 − 19) certain of completing our project on time? Yes! This situation would give a Z-value of +0.87, which translates to an 80.79 percent probability.

If, as above, we halved activity 0–1 variance, our chances of on-time completion would increase to 86.43 percent because it:

- Not surprisingly equals 100 percent less the 13.57 percent other-side-of-the-coin value just calculated
- Would be more certain we need only twenty-one days (not more) to finish it
- Would also be more certain we need only thirty-eight days (not more) to complete the entire project

But human nature being human nature, and bosses being bosses, you would probably be given only eight weeks, or forty days, to complete your project because this would look better on a wall calendar, or in a report to their management. So your respective probabilities would drop somewhat to 71.90 percent and 76.73 percent. Sorry!

This concludes our introduction to PERT.

9
Time-Cost Trade-Off Methodologies

WHY TIME-COST TRADE-OFFS ARE NECESSARY

Project managers are often given the option (and usually the mad-panic emergency requirement) of applying additional funds and resources to:

- Reduce activity duration
- Recover lost progress
- Meet deadlines

We have already discussed why time estimates should be both accurate and realistic. Assuming they are, note well the following: Any arbitrary and capricious cutting of durations without valid justification—although perhaps indicating on paper (or on the screen) that the project will complete earlier—will almost certainly result in an invalid, unworkable schedule. Just because something is wanted—no matter how badly or for how noble a cause—does not mean it can be realistically achieved! When the project manager in days of old was faced with a schedule overrun, he or she would merely:

- Snip a little here
- Snip a little there
- Snip a little everywhere from the Gantt Chart

to reduce project length. Managers with more modern tools (but with not-so-modern methodologies) may go berserk with a Gantt-Chart screen painter.

Another way is to apply an across-the-board percentage reduction of random magnitude ("Your budget has been cut 7.61 percent") with no thought whatsoever as to effectiveness or even the feasibility of such actions. Effective reduction in project length can only be achieved by acceptable:

- Rearrangement of activities
- Redefinition of relationships (including use of PDM methodologies)
- Reductions in critical activity durations

Often the most time-saving discovery is also the easiest: Some activities can, and should, be performed concurrently.

Careful examination of each of the following is mandatory:

- The network as a whole
- Each individual activity
- Resource requirements

Project length is always determined by the length of the current Critical Path. If this path changes, project length may also. If critical activities cannot be rearranged, project length may be shortened only by reductions in their durations.

HOW TIME AND MONEY RELATE TO EACH OTHER

But no amount of effort, time, money, people, resources, and so on to reduce noncritical activity durations will have the slightest effect on project length. Only critical and supercritical activities determine project length. Only they can reduce it.

Ways by which this may be done include:

1. Increase personnel. Up to a point, most operations can be speeded up by:

- Adding more people (both permanent new hires and loaned-in temporaries)
- Introducing shift work
- Assigning overtime
- Subcontracting work

Use of additional personnel is probably the simplest and the most common. There is, of course, a limit to the additional human resources that can be applied. To exceed this limit:

- Is always wasteful
- Can even impede instead of improve things

    Murphy sees it this way: "Adding people to a late project only makes it later!"
    Finally, there are some activities for which there can be no time reduction at all. Can nine women each contribute one month concurrent pregnancy to bring forth birth in thirty days? If so, contact Frederick ("The Mythical Man–Month") Brooks ASAP!

2. Allocate more plant, equipment, or other resources. This added plant and equipment may be either bought or leased. As with human resources, however, there is usually a practical limit to the amount that can be applied on any particular operation. Beyond this limit, things only interfere with each other. Some resources not currently used (such as excess space) or wasted (such as time) may never be used. A common method of reducing project length is to redeploy resources from noncritical to critical activities. The converse never reduces project length and may, in fact, lengthen it because the resource pool available to critical activities is smaller.

3. Use special or alternate materials. Using special, often more expensive, materials can help reduce activity durations. Or, the same materials may be used, but delivery expedited by utilizing, for example, same-day or overnight delivery services. It is *not* acceptable, however, to use materials that are of inferior quality or impose a greater risk on workers' safety. Even the world's biggest project is not as valuable as one human life.

4. Implement improved methods and processes. Most competitive enterprises are aware of and try to achieve savings through:

    - Total Quality Management (TQM)
    - Better work methods
    - Continuous process improvements
    - "Working smarter, not harder"
    - Automation, but only after improvements to the work process

These improved work methods are, of course, both applicable and valuable to *all* project activities, but will reduce project length only to the extent that they reduce critical and super-critical activity durations.
    Complicating these calculations is the fact that project managers are (and should be) as concerned with the cost of completing a project as they are with the time. Their conflicting objectives are to:

- Ensure customer satisfaction
- Make the boss happy (Mission Impossible?)
- Achieve deliverable quality goals
- Meet the deadline
- Control expenditures
- Develop a minimum-cost schedule consistent with customer requirements and project commitments

    This minimum-cost project scheduling routine is formally known as the *Least Cost Method* and correctly assumes a relationship between activity completion time and project cost.
    On one hand, it costs money to expedite an activity using the methods listed above. These costs:

- Are called *activity direct costs*
- Increase as project length is reduced

    They typically include a combination of personnel, materials, facilities, plant, and equipment costs.
    On the other hand, it also costs money to sustain (or lengthen) the project because of overhead costs, administrative costs, penalty costs, opportunity costs, and perhaps also lost incentive payments. These costs:

- Are called *project indirect costs*
- Decrease as project length is reduced

    Since activity direct costs and project indirect costs are opposing costs that are both dependent upon time, the scheduling problem is, therefore, to find the project length that minimizes the sum of these two sets of costs—or, in other words, finds the optimum point in a time–cost tradeoff.
    Another way of putting this is to say that we need to:

- Compare direct and indirect costs over a range of project lengths
- Select that project length at which their sum is at a minimum

    This is also the project time objective for which a "Do it ASAP" order was given in the absence of clearer, more precise criteria. If the indicated expenses extend well into the future, say beyond one year, you should strongly consider discounting these values by the cost of capital or other acceptable discount factors. These calculations are best performed using a spreadsheet. More on this in Chapter 11.
    It is therefore necessary to introduce cost into PDM time computations. For each activity, both critical and noncritical, there exists a range of costs, over a range of durations, which may be represented by a simple time-cost curve. The Least Cost Method evaluates the time–cost tradeoff within the range of two curve points of special importance:

- Normal cost/time
- Crash cost/time

Working day by day, the Least Cost Method selects that project length for which the sum of the direct costs and indirect costs is least.

The number of times this process must be repeated to find this point will vary by project. Appreciate that there are no acceptable shortcuts that give valid results.

Having made the necessary critical-activity time reductions, the schedule should be recomputed and examined to ensure that the deadline can now be met. It is possible that the reduction of the original Critical Path has:

- Created another path
- Simply caused it to shift somewhere else

If the deadline still cannot be met, the new Critical Path must be examined and the process repeated until one of two things is decided:

- The project deadline will be met, at a cost of $\$_____.\_\_\_\_\_$.
- The project deadline will not be met, regardless of cost

There are often many ways to reduce project length. The effect of each alternative may be measured by simulation, in which the project is rescheduled many times for contingencies, each time incorporating one of the alternatives. The results are compared to determine which alternative would be most beneficial. The more capable decision support tools (such as Comshare *IFPS/Plus,* which was mentioned earlier) even provide AI-based explanations of optimized results.

Note well that simulation should not be reserved for unsatisfactory projects only. It should also be used to:

- Understand your project better
- Improve projects generally
- Compare alternative plans
- Make good schedules even better

It is clearly advantageous to do this by computer. Doing so provides the following benefits:

- Reduces required effort
- Permits ready analysis of a very large number of alternatives
- Greatly reduces time required
- Eliminates all of the risk of experimentation including adverse effects on staff morale

The ultimate benefit of this "better information faster" result is that you can apply keen and timely managerial judgment as to what you must do and what you should not do. It points out where extra effort is needed to meet time limits and where such effort would be wasted. Another benefit is that you can:

- Simulate reality
- Evaluate results
- Select alternatives with good results
- Reject those with unsatisfactory results

all without time or financial risk, or negative impact on the morale of the project team—as would happen if you had actually implemented one of the unsatisfactory options.

How fast is fast? A matter of minutes. The "value of perfect information" is high. Its cost is cheap. The time is negligible.

WORKED EXAMPLES

Consider a fun problem provided by Armstrong-Wright "across the sea":

The Case of the Optimum-Cost Window Washer

Assume a window washer:

- Cleans an average of ten windows an hour
- Works an eight-hour day
- Earns $4 an hour

We need to know:

- How long should it take to wash all 2,400 windows in a building?
- How much should it cost?

Time and cost factors may be summarized as follows.
Time: 10 windows/hour, 6 minutes/window.
Cost: $4.00/hour, $0.40/window.
The cost of cleaning all 2,400 windows is, therefore,

$$\frac{2400 * 32}{10 * 8} = \$960,$$

and the time required is equal to thirty days.

A small car, used to transport equipment, costs $16 a day, so the total cost is equal to:

$960 for the window washer (from above)
$480 for the car ($16/day * 30 days)
$1440 total cost for one person and one car for thirty days.

If two window washers (assume equal pay rates) can be employed without getting in each other's way, the work can be completed in only half the time, or fifteen days, at a cost of $960:

$$\frac{2 * 2,400 * 32}{2 * 10 * 8},$$

so the total cost is equal to:

$960 for the two window washers (from above)
$240 for the car ($16/day * 15 days)
$1200 total cost for two persons and one car for fifteen days.

If each works two hours a day overtime at double-time pay, the time is reduced to:

$$\frac{2400}{10 * 10 * 2} = 12 \text{ days, but the cost has risen to } \$1344:$$

$768 for the two persons' regular pay 2 * $32/day * 12 days

$384 overtime pay [2 * (2 * $4/hour) * 2 hours/day * 12 days]

$192 for the car ($16/day * 12 days)

$1344 total cost for two persons and one car for twelve days.

Now assume that use of special lighting equipment, also costing $16 a day, enables them to work two additional hours overtime at night. They will now be able to complete the job in ten days:

$$\frac{2400}{10 * 12 * 2} = 10 \text{ days, and at a cost of } \$1600:$$

$640 for the two persons' regular pay (2 * $32/day * 10 days)

$640 overtime pay [2 * (2 * $4/hour) * 4 hours/day * 10 days]

$160 for the car ($16/day * 10 days)

$160 for the lighting equipment ($16/day * 10 days)

$1600 total cost for two persons, lights, and one car for ten days.

To reduce the time even further, and because safety regulations prohibit more than twelve hours work per day or more than two hours work at night, we employ a third window washer at the same rate of pay. But now they are all in each others' way and, worse, must share the only available special hoist fitted to the building. And it still takes ten days to do the work—no sooner. Since three persons are now employed (underemployed?), the cost has increased to $2240:

$960 for the three persons' regular pay (3 * $32/day * 10 days)

$960 overtime pay [3 * (2 * $4/hour) * 4 hours/day * 10 days]

$160 for the car ($16/day * 10 days)

$160 for the lighting equipment ($16/day * 10 days)

$2240 total cost for three persons, lights, and one car for ten days

Note well:

- No amount of extra expense will reduce project length below the ten days (cost = $1600) crash time
- No amount of extra time will reduce project cost below the $1200 (length = 15 days) normal cost

In fact, allowing too much or too little time can:

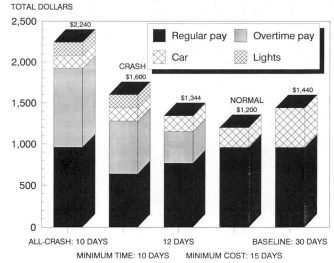

THE CASE OF THE OPTIMUM-COST WINDOW WASHER

FIGURE 9-1. Window washer time-cost tradeoff options. The case of the optimum-cost window washer.

- Produce an inefficient situation
- Drive up costs

In this example, we considered the entire window-washing operation as a single, independent project. For this reason, we were interested in all five cost/time points and how well we were able to complete our project relative to the chosen objective:

- Minimize total cost; do the job in fifteen days for $1200, or
- Minimize total time; do the job in ten days for $1600

On the other hand, if this entire operation were only a single activity, only the *crash* and *normal* points would be calculated:

- Crash: 10 days, $1600
- Normal: 15 days, $1200

We shall soon define these points more formally. The activity would be priced as shown in Fig. 9-1.

Four-Activity Branched Network

Let us now more formally determine the least-cost project schedule using the simple four-activity network that we employed previously (Fig. 9-2, Table 9-1), and in bar chart format (Fig. 9-3).

We need to know the project's daily indirect costs (assume these to be $10/day for each of eight days, then to increase $5 per day each day thereafter) and the following four items for each activity:

1. *Normal time (NT):* typical activity duration; the minimum time to achieve the normal cost

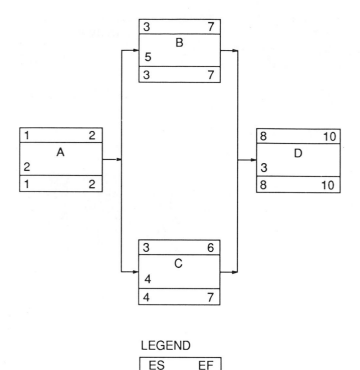

LEGEND

ES	EF
ACT	
DUR	
LS	LF

FIGURE 9-2.   Network setup diagram.

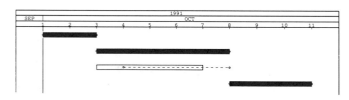

FIGURE 9-3.   Gantt Chart.

2. *Normal cost (NC):* the cost associated with normal time; the lowest expected activity cost (and the lower of the two cost figures under each node in Fig. 9-4) using normal means and avoiding overtime, use of extra or special staff, resources, or materials

3. *Crash time (CT):* the shortest possible activity duration; the absolute minimum time necessary to complete an activity

4. *Crash cost (CC):* the cost associated with crash time; the minimum cost of using whatever means possible to achieve the crash time; the greater of the two cost figures under each node in Fig. 9-4

We are now ready to work the five-step example.

Step 1

Prepare a Complete Cost/Time Network in PDM Format

Begin by adding the four time and cost values to each activity. Be sure not to get these values confused. Within the activity box (Fig. 9-4), duration is presented in (NT,CT) order. Below the box, cost is presented in (CC,NC) order.

Step 2

Determine the Cost Per Day to Expedite Each Activity

Relationships between activity time and activity cost may be shown graphically by:

- Plotting the coordinates (NT,NC) and (CT,CC) for each activity and day between crash time and normal time
- Connecting this series of points by the appropriate form

If the relationship between activity time and activity cost is linear (or reasonably close to it), only the end points need be plotted. The slope of the connecting line represents the cost per day to expedite this activity. This value is calculated as follows:

$$Slope = [(CC - NC)/(NT - CT)]$$

Table 9-1   Schedule Setup

```
--------------------------------------------------------------------------------
SCHEDULE SETUP                                      DATE: _____

PROJECT NAME:   FOUR-ACTIVITY LEAST COST METHOD EXAMPLE_____
                CHASE (USC) AND AQUILANO (ARIZONA)
--------------------------------------------------------------------------------
```

ACTIVITY ID	DUR (DAYS)	PREDECESSOR/ RELATIONSHIP	SUCCESSOR/ RELATIONSHIP	ACTIVITY DESCRIPTION
A	2	None	B F/S C F/S	
B	5	A F/S	D F/S	
C	4	A F/S	D F/S	
D	3	B F/S C F/S	None	

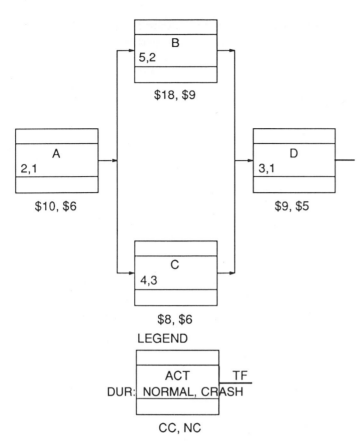

LEGEND

	ACT	TF
DUR:	NORMAL, CRASH	
	CC, NC	

FIGURE 9-4.   Network setup diagram, with costs.

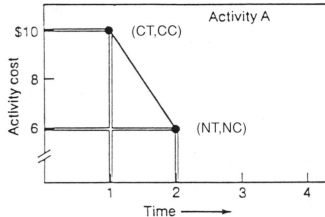

FIGURE 9-5.   Activity A normal/crash times and costs.

For example, in the graph presented in Fig. 9-5 for *A,* duration is plotted on the X-axis and cost is plotted on the Y-axis. The two coordinates would be:

- (NT,NC), or (2, $6)
- (CT,CC), or (1, $10)

The slope would be equal to [(CC − NC)/(NT − CT)]
= [($10 − $6)/(2 − 1)]
= $4/day to expedite *A.*

Activities *B, C,* and *D* would be calculated precisely the same way. Daily expediting costs would be $3, $2, and $2, respectively. These values and supporting calculations are summarized in Table 9-2.

Note in particular the last two columns entitled "Cost per day to expedite" and "Number of days activity may be shortened." These values are graphed in Fig. 9-6 and will be needed in Step 4.

If, however, the relationship between activity time and activity cost is nonlinear, separate expediting costs must be calculated for each day. The average linear slope cannot be used. Functions to be used in these cases include:

- The first derivative of the curve at that day's point
- An appropriate step function

More on these later, and how to use them in these rare situations. Usually, the linear slope approximation is entirely satisfactory—especially when considering:

- That most activities will be scheduled at either normal or crash values

Table 9-2   Normal and Crash Times and Costs, by Activity

Activity	(CC − NC)	(NT − CT)	$\dfrac{(CC - NC)}{(NT - CT)}$	Cost/day to Expedite	# Days Activity May Be Shortened
A	$10 − $6	(2 − 1)	$\dfrac{\$10 - \$6}{(2 - 1)}$	$4	1
B	$18 − $9	(5 − 2)	$\dfrac{\$18 - \$9}{(5 - 2)}$	$3	3
C	$ 8 − $6	(4 − 3)	$\dfrac{\$ 8 - \$6}{(4 - 3)}$	$2	1
D	$ 9 − $5	(3 − 1)	$\dfrac{\$ 9 - \$5}{(3 - 1)}$	$2	2

NORMAL/CRASH TIMES/COSTS BY ACTIVITY

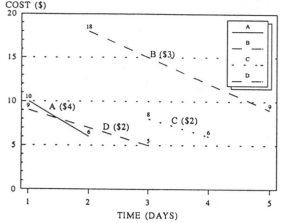

FIGURE 9-6.   Normal and crash times and costs, by activity.

- The project as a whole
- Underlying precision levels of other measurements, especially time

The linear slope approximation will provide a uniform rate of cost increase as a function of time decrease. For activities not scheduled at normal or crash values, it will introduce only a small inaccuracy (slightly higher than actual) at intermediate points.

The linear slope approximation has two other advantages:

- It is much easier and less costly to produce and use
- It is more likely to be used; people would probably resent producing and using a highly-detailed cost schedule, but in most cases have no problem with straight-line approximations

Even with this approximation, though, the Least Cost Method will still entail a considerable amount of work. To calculate and use the actual cost/time value for each activity:

- Greatly complicates calculations
- Exponentially increases the number of required computations

This is not a job for the:

- Rushed
- Bored
- Faint of heart
- Unfortunate individuals without project management tools!

Even with electronic scheduling, absolute accuracy is probably not worth the very great extra effort required. In light of the project as a whole and its underlying precision, the linear approximation is usually satisfactory.

Nevertheless, there are special cases, easy to recognize, in which the linear approximation would introduce an error too large to ignore. This usually occurs when duration re-

duction beyond a certain limit results in a quantum jump in cost. This may result from the need to employ a completely different:

- Method or process
- Equipment type
- Material

Examples include:

- Next-day delivery by air, instead of normal surface transportation
- Using a new (instead of repaired) replacement part

In these and other similar circumstances, straight-line accuracy may be inadequate for times between normal and crash.

Look, for example, at Fig. 9-7, which illustrates the time–cost tradeoff for next-day air freight delivery in comparison with normal ground means.

The square corner at the top left of the figure represents next-day delivery, when materials cannot wait for later delivery.

Two other sources of error may be:

- Large activities that are really small subprojects needing more detail
- Hammock activities

These can be rectified by dividing these large activities into an appropriate number of smaller ones.

The best way to deal with potential errors is the following:

- Compute costs using the straight-line method for all activities
- Re-examine those activities with durations between normal and crash

If the indicated error is too large, say more than 10 percent, provide these activities with more accurate costs for their respective durations. It would also be a good idea to specially mark these activities in case durations must change.

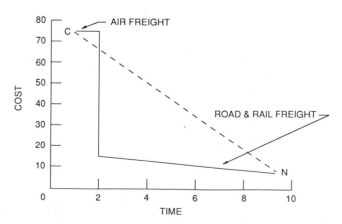

FIGURE 9-7.   Step-function time–cost tradeoff options.

It is also necessary to consider how shortening one activity would affect others. If a certain method or equipment type is used on several activities, and reducing one of these activities requires an alternative method or equipment type, the effects on the other activities must be analyzed. To use both methods or equipment types is probably uneconomical. In some cases, they may be incompatible, their concurrent use impossible. This often happens in organizations with multiple computer hardware environments.

On the other hand, if the alternative method or equipment can be used on other activities, their costs and durations must also be re-examined. Choose whichever option is best for the project as a whole. Successful project management requires "systems orientation" problem-solving skills.

In summary, the error must be viewed in light of:

- The degree of underlying precision in time and cost estimates. It makes no sense to estimate costs at a precision of 99 percent or higher if times have been estimated at only 90 percent precision. But if the error is too large to ignore, recalculate the point(s) more accurately.
- The cost of greater precision. This cost should not, of course, exceed its value. Calculating only a few points on either side of the initial least-cost point should be all that is necessary to achieve acceptable accuracy. As a general guideline:

  A positive error indicates a shorter activity duration for least cost

  A negative error indicates a longer activity duration for least cost

Step 3

Compute the Critical Path

We have already done this in Chapter 3. The Critical Path consists of activities *A, B,* and *D;* its expected duration is ten days. Project normal direct cost is the total direct cost of all activities performed at normal cost, or $26. Remember to include all activities, not just critical activities. Project normal time is ten days, as was already found, and is the duration of all critical activities performed at normal time (Fig. 9-8).

Figure 9-9 is in bar chart format.

Step 4

Shorten the Critical Path at Least Cost

The object of this step is to determine the project's *crash point,* or combination of crash time and crash cost. The project crash point represents the minimum cost for the minimum amount of time. The process involves systematically shortening the Critical Path (or paths), which in turn reduces total project length. The project crash point is found when project length has been so reduced that:

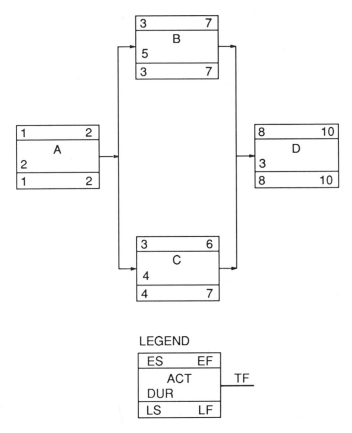

FIGURE 9-8.   Network setup diagram.

- All critical activities are at crash times
- Further reduction in time is not possible

Noncritical activity durations can be expanded even beyond their normal times by absorbing any available float. If, however, they are reduced to their crash times (or anything less than normal), regardless of whether or not they become critical, project length will still be determined by the fully-crashed Critical Paths. The only difference will be an unnecessary increase in cost. This cost is:

- Called the project *all-crash cost*
- Always higher than the project crash cost

All-crash situations frequently arise when senior management is faced with very difficult deadlines and:

- Does not, as they should, understand formal scheduling methodologies
- Panics and comes unglued

FIGURE 9-9.   Gantt Chart.

- Orders *all* work to be done at fastest speed possible, regardless of:

  Effect on the schedule

  Cost

  Effect on quality

Instead, emphasize only critical activities. Begin with the normal cost/normal time schedule. Then reduce the Critical Path one day by shortening that activity whose daily expediting cost is least. Expedite only critical activities! Crashing noncritical activities will only:

- Waste money and effort
- Not reduce project duration
- Create worthless extra float
- Waste time better invested on other, critical activities
- Make a joke of the expediting process (if all activities are urgent, how are the *more* urgent activities identified now?)

Next, recompute the network, find the new Critical Path(s), and reduce it one day, too, exactly as we did earlier. Repeat this procedure until:

- Completion time is satisfactory, or
- No further reductions in project completion time are possible

Note well: When multiple Critical Paths exist, *each* path must be concurrently compressed. Expediting only one Critical Path will merely:

- Shift one Critical Path exclusively to the other
- Not reduce project duration
- Waste the money spent on the effort

Let us now return to our four-activity Chase and Aquilano network. In the original (normal cost/time) state (Table 9-3), we know:

- The Critical Path consists of activities *A, B,* and *D*
- Expected project duration is ten days
- Total direct cost of all network activities is $26 (= $6 + $9 + $6 + $5)

We need to select that *critical* activity—*A, B,* or *D*—whose daily expediting cost is least. From the cost/time slope values calculated in Table 9-2 and entitled "Cost per day to expedite," we see that:

- Reducing *A* one day would cost $4
- Reducing *B* one day would cost $3
- Reducing *D* one day would cost $2

We are not concerned with reduction costs of *C* because it is noncritical.

Because *D*'s $2 cost is less than either *A*'s ($4) or *B*'s ($3), we select *D* as the activity to expedite. Activity *D* will cost $2 more to complete, or $7, but require one less day, or two days. Similarly, the total network direct costs will increase by the same $2, to $28; and project completion time will be shortened one day, to nine (Table 9-4). The Critical Path remains constant along *A-B-D*.

At this point, we now know:

- The Critical Path is still activities *A-B-D*
- Expected project duration is nine days
- Total direct cost of all network activities is $28 (= $6 + $9 + $6 + $7)

Are we done yet? Not at all. We need to repeat the process over and over until one of the following conditions occurs:

- The project deadline will be met, at a cost of $____.____
- The project deadline will not be met, regardless of cost

We again select the least costly activity to expedite; it is again *D*. This assumes the expediting cost remained constant at $2 and did not, as it sometimes does, increase. Activity *D* will now cost $2 more to complete, or $9, but require one less day, or one day total duration.

As it is now at crash time (and cost), no further time improvements can come from *D*. Any more money would only be wasted. Activity *D* is "crashed out" and no longer need be considered.

Total network direct costs will increase by the same $2,

Table 9-3   Schedule Summary

```
----------------------------------------------------------------------------------------
SCHEDULE SUMMARY                                          DATE:  _____

PROJECT NAME:  FOUR-ACTIVITY LEAST COST METHOD EXAMPLE (NORMAL COST/TIME)___
----------------------------------------------------------------------------------------
ACTIVITY     ORIG    REM     %     EARLY     EARLY     LATE      LATE      CURR
   ID        DUR     DUR    DONE    START    FINISH    START    FINISH     COST
--------     ----    ---    ----   -------   -------   -------   -------    ----
      A  *    2       2      0     1OCT91    2OCT91    1OCT91    2OCT91    $ 6
      B  *    5       5      0     3OCT91    7OCT91    3OCT91    7OCT91    $ 9
      C       4       4      0     3OCT91    6OCT91    4OCT91    7OCT91    $ 6
      D  *    3       3      0     8OCT91   10OCT91    8OCT91   10OCT91    $ 5
----------------------------------------------------------------------------------------
* TOTALS *   10  (CRITICAL PATH ONLY)       10OCT91            10OCT91     $26
----------------------------------------------------------------------------------------
```

Table 9-4   Schedule Summary

```
--------------------------------------------------------------------------------
SCHEDULE SUMMARY                                    DATE: _____

PROJECT NAME:  FOUR-ACTIVITY LEAST COST METHOD EXAMPLE (CHANGE 1)_____
--------------------------------------------------------------------------------
ACTIVITY    ORIG    REM     %     EARLY      EARLY     LATE      LATE      CURR
   ID       DUR     DUR    DONE   START      FINISH    START     FINISH    COST
--------    ----    ---    ----   -------    -------   -------   -------   ----
   A  *      2       2      0     1OCT91     2OCT91    1OCT91    2OCT91    $ 6
   B  *      5       5      0     3OCT91     7OCT91    3OCT91    7OCT91    $ 9
   C         4       4      0     3OCT91     6OCT91    4OCT91    7OCT91    $ 6
   D  *      2       2      0     8OCT91     9OCT91    8OCT91    9OCT91    $ 7
--------------------------------------------------------------------------------
* TOTALS *   9 (CRITICAL PATH ONLY)          9OCT91             9OCT91    $28
--------------------------------------------------------------------------------
```

to $30; and project completion time will be shortened one day, to eight (Table 9-5). We are now done with activity D, but not with the network. At this point we now know:

- The Critical Path is still activities A-B-D
- Expected project duration is eight days
- Total direct cost of all network activities is $30 (= $6 + $9 + $6 + $9)

The Critical Path remains at A-B-D, but further time improvements can still be made in A (one day) and B (three days). Because it costs only $3 to expedite B and $4 to expedite A, we decide to spend $3 and shorten B by one day, to four, increasing completion cost $3, to $12. This, in turn, reduces project length to seven days and increases its cost to $33 (Table 9-6). At this point, we now know:

- The Critical Path includes activities A-B-D (but read on!)
- Expected project duration is seven days
- Total direct cost of all network activities is $33 (= $6 + $12 + $6 + $9)

Now, at this point you might be tempted to throw $6 more at B, expecting project length to drop the remaining two days left until B crash time.

Gotcha!—lead yourself not into this temptation! Remember that after each recalculation we also need to recompute the Critical Path. And when we do this, we discover that the Critical Path has now split in two. The first path still consists of activities A-B-D and requires seven days, as just calculated. But the other path, A-C-D, which had been separated from the Critical Path only by:

- The single day of float in C, or,
- The one day by which B was just expedited

also requires seven days to complete (= 2 + 4 + 1).

This means that *both* paths must be considered. As always, we select the least-cost solution, and, surprise, it turns out that A, not B or C, is cheapest.

Why? We can reduce project length one day, to six, by crashing A alone at a cost of $4. But crashing B, at a cost of $3:

Table 9-5   Schedule Summary

```
--------------------------------------------------------------------------------
SCHEDULE SUMMARY                                    DATE: _____

PROJECT NAME:  FOUR-ACTIVITY LEAST COST METHOD EXAMPLE (CHANGE 2)_____
--------------------------------------------------------------------------------
ACTIVITY    ORIG    REM     %     EARLY      EARLY     LATE      LATE      CURR
   ID       DUR     DUR    DONE   START      FINISH    START     FINISH    COST
--------    ----    ---    ----   -------    -------   -------   -------   ----
   A  *      2       2      0     1OCT91     2OCT91    1OCT91    2OCT91    $ 6
   B  *      5       5      0     3OCT91     7OCT91    3OCT91    7OCT91    $ 9
   C         4       4      0     3OCT91     6OCT91    4OCT91    7OCT91    $ 6
   D  *      1       1      0     8OCT91     8OCT91    8OCT91    8OCT91    $ 9
--------------------------------------------------------------------------------
* TOTALS *   8 (CRITICAL PATH ONLY)          8OCT91             8OCT91    $30
--------------------------------------------------------------------------------
```

Table 9-6   Schedule Summary

```
--------------------------------------------------------------------------
SCHEDULE SUMMARY                                          DATE: _____

PROJECT NAME:   FOUR-ACTIVITY LEAST COST METHOD EXAMPLE (CHANGE 3)_____
--------------------------------------------------------------------------
ACTIVITY    ORIG    REM     %     EARLY     EARLY     LATE     LATE    CURR
   ID       DUR     DUR   DONE    START     FINISH    START    FINISH  COST
--------    ----    ---   ----   -------   -------   -------  -------  ----
    A  *     2       2     0     1OCT91    2OCT91    1OCT91   2OCT91   $ 6
    B  *     4       4     0     3OCT91    6OCT91    3OCT91   6OCT91   $12
    C  *     4       4     0     3OCT91    6OCT91    3OCT91   6OCT91   $ 6
    D  *     1       1     0     7OCT91    7OCT91    7OCT91   7OCT91   $ 9
--------------------------------------------------------------------------
* TOTALS *   7 (CRITICAL PATH ONLY)        7OCT91             7OCT91   $33
--------------------------------------------------------------------------
```

- Only shifts the Critical Path to *A-C-D* alone
- Leaves project completion time unchanged at seven days

    Similarly, crashing only *C,* at a cost of $2:

- Only shifts the Critical Path to *A-B-D* alone
- Also leaves project completion time unchanged at seven days

When multiple Critical Paths exist, we need to crash the least-cost activity on *each* contributing path. This rule requires that we crash both *B* ($3) and *C* ($2) for a total cost of $5—and it explains why it was less expensive to crash *A* ($4) than *B* and *C* together ($5). Project completion time is now six days (Table 9-7), its total direct costs have now increased $4, to $37, and the pickin's are getting slimmer! At this point we now know:

- The Critical Path has split in two: *A-B-D* and *A-C-D*
- Expected project duration is six days
- Total direct cost of all network activities is $37 (= $10 + $12 + $6 + $9)

But now *A* is at crash time (and cost). Only *B* and *C* crashed together (for $5 a day) can shorten the project any more. Activities *A* and *D,* both "crashed out," can have no further effect.

We now apply the $5 determined above and reduce both *B* and *C* by one day, lowering project length to five days, but increasing total direct costs to $42 (Table 9-8). Now *C* joins *A* and *D* in being "crashed out." *B* still has one day left until it is, too. In summary:

- The Critical Path is still split in two: *A-B-D* and *A-C-D*
- Expected project duration is five days
- Total direct cost of all network activities is $42 (= $10 + $15 + $8 + $9)

    Figure 9-10 is shown in bar chart format.

    Would it be worth the cost to expedite *B* by one more day? No. Here is why:

- Project completion time would remain at five days
- The $3 spent expediting *B* would be wasted

Table 9-7   Schedule Summary

```
--------------------------------------------------------------------------
SCHEDULE SUMMARY                                          DATE: _____

PROJECT NAME:   FOUR-ACTIVITY LEAST COST METHOD EXAMPLE (CHANGE 4)_____
--------------------------------------------------------------------------
ACTIVITY    ORIG    REM     %     EARLY     EARLY     LATE     LATE    CURR
   ID       DUR     DUR   DONE    START     FINISH    START    FINISH  COST
--------    ----    ---   ----   -------   -------   -------  -------  ----
    A  *     1       1     0     1OCT91    1OCT91    1OCT91   1OCT91   $10
    B  *     4       4     0     2OCT91    5OCT91    2OCT91   5OCT91   $12
    C  *     4       4     0     2OCT91    5OCT91    2OCT91   5OCT91   $ 6
    D  *     1       1     0     6OCT91    6OCT91    6OCT91   6OCT91   $ 9
--------------------------------------------------------------------------
* TOTALS *   6 (CRITICAL PATH ONLY)        6OCT91             6OCT91   $37
--------------------------------------------------------------------------
```

Table 9-8   Schedule Summary

```
------------------------------------------------------------------------
SCHEDULE SUMMARY                                    DATE: _____

PROJECT NAME:  FOUR–ACTIVITY LEAST COST METHOD EXAMPLE (CHANGE 5)_____
------------------------------------------------------------------------
ACTIVITY     ORIG    REM     %     EARLY    EARLY    LATE    LATE    CURR
   ID        DUR     DUR   DONE    START   FINISH   START  FINISH   COST
--------     ----    ---   ----   -------  -------  ------- ------- ----
    A  *      1       1      0    1OCT91   1OCT91   1OCT91  1OCT91   $10
    B  *      3       3      0    2OCT91   4OCT91   2OCT91  4OCT91   $15
    C  *      3       3      0    2OCT91   4OCT91   2OCT91  4OCT91   $ 8
    D  *      1       1      0    5OCT91   5OCT91   5OCT91  5OCT91   $ 9
------------------------------------------------------------------------
* TOTALS *    5 (CRITICAL PATH ONLY)             5OCT91          5OCT91   $42
------------------------------------------------------------------------
```

This is because the Critical Path would now shift to *A-C-D* alone, but would still require—because *A*, *C*, and *D* are all "crashed out"—five days to complete (Table 9-9).

Figure 9-11 is shown in bar chart format.

It makes no sense to raise total direct costs to $45 when project length would not be shortened. The one remaining day until *B* reaches crash time:

- Has no relationship with *C*
- Cannot be used to reduce *C* or the Critical Path any further

The earliest this project can ever complete is five days, and it would cost $42 to do it. We may, therefore, say this four-activity project has:

- A crash point of five days and $42
- An all-crash point of five days and $45

Let us take a moment to review what we have done. Starting with the lowest cost/time activities, we reduced critical activities one by one to their respective crash points. We continued this procedure until:

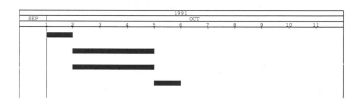

FIGURE 9-10.   Gantt Chart.

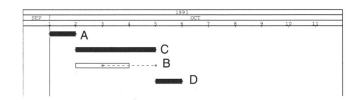

FIGURE 9-11.   Gantt Chart.

Table 9-9   Schedule Summary

```
------------------------------------------------------------------------
SCHEDULE SUMMARY                                    DATE: _____

PROJECT NAME:  FOUR–ACTIVITY LEAST COST METHOD EXAMPLE (CHANGE 6)_____
------------------------------------------------------------------------
ACTIVITY     ORIG    REM     %     EARLY    EARLY    LATE    LATE    CURR
   ID        DUR     DUR   DONE    START   FINISH   START  FINISH   COST
--------     ----    ---   ----   -------  -------  ------- ------- ----
    A  *      1       1      0    1OCT91   1OCT91   1OCT91  1OCT91   $10
    B         2       2      0    2OCT91   3OCT91   3OCT91  4OCT91   $18
    C  *      3       3      0    2OCT91   4OCT91   2OCT91  4OCT91   $ 8
    D  *      1       1      0    5OCT91   5OCT91   5OCT91  5OCT91   $ 9
------------------------------------------------------------------------
* TOTALS *    5 (CRITICAL PATH ONLY)             5OCT91          5OCT91   $45
------------------------------------------------------------------------
```

- All critical activities are reduced to crash, or
- Another Critical Path is created

When multiple Critical Paths exist, it is necessary to reduce each path concurrently. This is done by selecting one activity from each Critical Path with a combined cost/time rate lower than the corresponding rate of any other critical-activity combination.

When one activity (such as A and D) is common to both Critical Paths, reducing that activity will shorten both paths by the same amount. Naturally, a common activity should be shortened when its cost/time rate is lower than the corresponding rate for a combination of noncommon activities.

As project length reduction approaches the crash point:

- More and more Critical Paths will be created
- Many more comparisons will be necessary to determine the best choice to crash

Even closer to the crash point, there will usually be just as many Critical Paths—or more—but fewer comparisons are necessary because fewer are now possible; most activities have been crashed out and need not be considered for further reduction.

Even for a simple project, does this process appear:

- Time-consuming?
- Tedious?
- Boring?
- Subject to errors?
- Like something you would rather have a computer do?

For each activity, all that is needed to process this all-important step electronically is:

- Two durations—normal and crash
- Two costs—normal and crash
- Rate of cost increase (cost/time rate)
- A few nanoseconds of time

With this information, any number of scenarios—both real and simulated—between normal and crash points can quickly be analyzed. The minimum-cost project length can readily be obtained.

For each activity, all that is needed to process this all-important step by hand is:

- Two durations—normal and crash
- Two costs—normal and crash
- Rate of cost increase (cost/time rate)
- Lots of patience
- A millennium of time

Table 9-10 summarizes these calculations. Is this a good deal? We have:

- Reduced project length 50 percent (= 5 days/10 days)
- Simultaneously increased total direct costs more than 61 percent (= $42/$26)

We still need to answer the following questions:

- How long should the project be?
- Should we expedite any activities?
- If so, which ones?
- Can we plot project cost/time curves?
- What about the straight-line approximation method—is it valid?
- Are we having fun yet?

Similarly to individual activities, project scenarios may be represented by a cost function of time between normal and crash points. Somewhere between these two limits, project length relates to a minimum project cost, which consists of both direct and indirect costs. The three points of greatest interest are:

- Project normal cost/time
- Project crash cost/time
- Project minimum cost

Unlike individual activities, project cost/time curves cannot be straight-line approximated without unacceptable loss of accuracy. Recall that most activities fell on one or the other limit, normal or crash. Only a few did not. The total variance of these activities was negligible in relation to all other project activities.

For most projects, however, the situation is exactly the

Table 9-10   Crash-the-Path Summary Calculations

Current Critical Path	Remaining # Days May Be Shortened	Cost/day to Expedite Options	Least-cost Activity to Expedite	Total Direct Costs	Project Completion Time
ABD	All times and costs are normal			$26	10
ABD	A-1, B-3, D-2	A-4, B-3, D-2	D	28	9
ABD	A-1, B-3, D-1	A-4, B-3, D-2	D	30	8
ABD	A-1, B-3	A-4, B-3	B	33	7
ABCD	A-1, B-2, C-1	A-4, B-3, C-2	A	37	6
ABCD	B-2, C-1	B-3, C-2	B & C*	42	5
ABCD	B-1	B-3	B	45	5

* Must be crashed together

opposite. An intermediate point between the normal and crash points will often provide the least cost. And, of course, there is no law of large numbers to help out: We are talking of a single point, and it *must* be accurate! Your entire project schedule is represented by it! So, too, are the chances that you will finish your project:

- On time
- On cost
- On specification
- Still on the payroll!

For projects as a whole, the straight-line "approximation" is no approximation at all, but instead introduces an error of unacceptable magnitude.

Step 5

Plot Project Direct, Indirect, and Total-Cost Curves Against Time, Then Find the Minimum-Cost Schedule
We have already determined both contributing cost sets:

- Direct (in the previous step)
- Indirect (given earlier as a constant $10 per day until they increased by an additional $5 per day after the eighth day)

We now need to:

- Plot this range of values
- Select project length whose *total* (not just direct!) costs are lowest

To do this, we need "*20/20* foresight," so to speak. Note the following concerning Fig. 9-12:

- Possible project completion times in days are plotted on the X-axis
- Costs (direct, indirect, and total) in monetary units are plotted on the Y-axis

Total project costs are the sum of daily direct and indirect costs. It is essential to use *total* costs, not just direct costs, even though the indirect component is usually:

- Harder to conceptualize
- More difficult to measure

But if not included, the indicated answer will almost always be very wrong.

This cost-curve series ranges from project crash to project normal. The project length represented by the lowest total cost may be readily identified. From this length may be

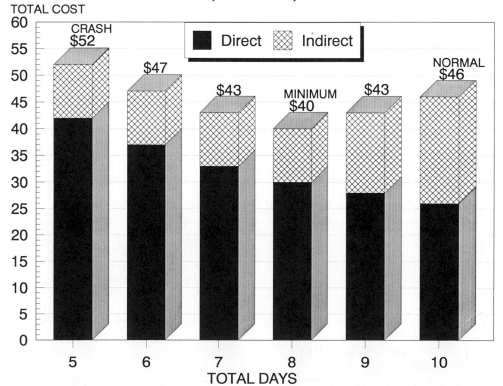

FIGURE 9-12.   Project direct, indirect, and total costs by duration.

determined necessary cost and duration details for each activity.

For example, the total cost for a project of:

- Five days duration is $42 (direct) + $10 (indirect), or $52
- Six days duration is $37 (direct) + $10 (indirect), or $47
- Nine days duration is $28 (direct) + $15 (indirect), or $43
- Ten days duration is $26 (direct) + $20 (indirect), or $46

The total-cost curve is clearly lowest for an eight-day schedule, which costs $40 (Fig. 9-12). Therefore, we should choose to complete this project in eight days, not ten as originally planned (Table 9-11).

Figure 9-13 is shown in bar chart.

Any other completion time—whether earlier or later—would unnecessarily cost you more money. It really does not matter whether these costs are direct or indirect. In either case, you would have:

- Chosen a nonoptimal solution
- Cost your organization unnecessarily

Unfortunately, many people will select the ten-day schedule because:

- Total direct costs for it are least
- Indirect costs are often:
    Misunderstood
    Harder to measure than direct costs
    Thought to represent voodoo accounting

But they must be considered nevertheless. If you did not consider them and selected the ten-day schedule instead, you would have unnecessarily:

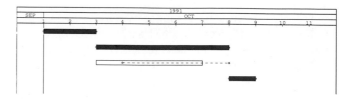

FIGURE 9-13.   Gantt Chart.

- Wasted $6 (= $46 − $40)
- Incurred a useless 15 percent cost overrun
- Wasted two days' production opportunities

On the other hand, some people will unfortunately select the five-day, $52 schedule because it is the shortest. Since, they reason, the project is out of the way, indirect costs will be minimized and facilities may be used for another project. Once again, we need to consider where *all* costs, including direct costs, are least. The direct costs are simply too high near the crash point. In fact, they are higher than the total eight-day schedule in costs, both direct and indirect.

If you selected the five-day schedule, you would have unnecessarily:

- Wasted $12 (= $52 − $40)
- Incurred a useless 30 percent cost overrun

When should the project begin? Still October 1, to end October 8 in a seven-day work week environment. It would be unwise to wait until October 3, to finish on October 10—even though this date was acceptable originally. The current expectation is an October 8 finish. Anything later would be considered late, fairly or otherwise.

What happens if the project starts late? That depends upon how late it starts (Table 9-12).

Table 9-11   Least-Cost Summary Schedule, with Costs

```
------------------------------------------------------------------------------------
SCHEDULE SUMMARY                                      DATE: _____

PROJECT NAME:  FOUR-ACTIVITY LCM EXAMPLE: MINIMUM-COST SOLUTION (8 DAYS)____
------------------------------------------------------------------------------------
```

ACTIVITY ID		ORIG DUR	REM DUR	% DONE	EARLY START	EARLY FINISH	LATE START	LATE FINISH	CURR COST
A	*	2	2	0	1OCT91	2OCT91	1OCT91	2OCT91	$ 6
B	*	5	5	0	3OCT91	7OCT91	3OCT91	7OCT91	$ 9
C		4	4	0	3OCT91	6OCT91	4OCT91	7OCT91	$ 6
D	*	1	1	0	8OCT91	8OCT91	8OCT91	8OCT91	$ 9

```
------------------------------------------------------------------------------------
* TOTALS *     8  (CRITICAL PATH ONLY)       8OCT91               8OCT91      $30
INDIRECT COSTS (8 DAYS)                                                       $10
------------------------------------------------------------------------------------
TOTAL COSTS (DIRECT + INDIRECT)                                               $40
------------------------------------------------------------------------------------
```

Table 9-12   Delayed Start Summary Calculations

Start date	Days Available	Activities Yet to Crash	Total Project Cost
October 1	8	None	$40
October 2	7	B	$43
October 3	6	A, B	$47
October 4	5 (All-crash)	A, B, (B & C)	$52
October 5	4	*** MISSION IMPOSSIBLE ***	

If the project starts October 5 or later, there is nothing further money can do to advance the completion date. If it starts October 2–4, follow the same process as earlier beginning with:

- *D* at crash point
- Total costs at $40

to meet the October 8 deadline and go as far as necessary to recover lost progress. Again, no amount of money will reduce project length below five days.

Remember that a completed activity can no longer be expedited. If the least-expedition-cost bounces between a later activity and an earlier, the earlier should be expedited first, while still possible. Although this solution might cost a little more by expediting activities out of strict least-cost sequence, it will recover lost progress while still possible and avoid crunches further along in the project.

Also remember that crash times limit our options here, too, just as they did when we looked to minimize total project costs. The project has already been shortened by two days and may be shortened by three more, but cannot under any circumstances be compressed more than that. Time now rules supreme—even over money.

Even with an October 4 start, you are held to full-game responsibility but are forced to:

- Sit out one and one-half quarters
- Pay $12 more to do so

Unless John Elway is your quarterback, I would not place any bets! Thus, you should practice the following:

- To stay on budget, start on time.
- To stay on time, start on budget

Why did the project start late, anyway? This question must be researched fairly, taking into account all relevant facts and circumstances. If, for instance, one discovers that the previous project ran overtime or that resources needed for the current project were unavailable, it would not be appropriate to hammer the current project manager (even if convenient and handy) for starting late!

He or she would love to begin on time and get off to a good start; most people would. But this would depend on the availability of needed resources. What if a project using these same resources is running late? Who would ever shut that project down for eight days in order to begin another? So the project manager starting late really is:

- Not the creator of bad news
- Only the bearer of bad news!

Moral: Don't shoot the messenger if you don't like the message! (It seems as if we have said this before!)

10
Resource Allocation and Control

The time–cost tradeoff examples discussed in Chapter 9 are not at all unusual. However, they assumed that unlimited resources, money, materials, equipment, and people were available and could be applied to:

- An on-schedule project to:
    Expedite completion
    Minimize cost
- A late project to restore lost progress

RESOURCE LIMITATIONS

In these examples, only time was limited. Resources were not. The objective was to minimize total costs while maintaining the target completion date. The project could easily and readily obtain all resources needed to execute every activity according to schedule. Very often we find that this assumption—and the resulting schedule—does not represent project realities. Other, more typical situations include:

- Time-limited resources
- Quantity-limited resources
- (Usually and unfortunately) both time- and quantity-limited resources

These situations are either actual conditions or simulations produced to develop contingency plans.

In a *time-limited* resource condition, restrictions are placed on when certain resources are available. During these periods, sufficient resource quantities are available to satisfy each activity. Outside of these periods, the resource is either available in insufficient quantities or not available at all. The resource allocation procedure for this situation should:

- Establish resource quantities required to comply with time restrictions
- Level (even out) resource usage during crash periods

On the other hand, a *quantity-limited* resource condition occurs when there are insufficient resources to satisfy scheduled activity demands. Resource *leveling* and *smoothing*—to be discussed in greater detail later—revises the plan so that:

- Quantities in excess of available are not required
- Available quantities are usable at all times

The real world is usually a complicated combination of these two situations: Insufficient resources are available for inadequate lengths of time. This chapter expands the scheduling methodology to consider the effects of limited, overworked, and/or constrained resources.

There is often competition for resources—especially personnel—between projects and among concurrent activities. For most activities, resource availability affects activity duration as follows:

- Up to a certain point, adding more resources will reduce duration (this will generally not be a linear relationship due to increased coordination, politics, turf battles, and so on)
- Beyond this point, adding extra resources will only make matters worse because everyone will be in each other's way, in addition to the other problems already listed.

But duration clearly affects resource availability. *Catch-22?* No doubt about it! See Figure 10-1.

Tradeoffs among the following must be evaluated by the project manager:

- Resource availability
- Duration
- Costs
- Performance

FIGURE 10-1. "Decisions, decisions!" *Source:* Kerzner, p. 761.

Tradeoffs are always based on project constraints. Kerzner (p. 762; some examples mine) summarizes commonly-imposed constraints as shown in Table 10-1.

Many factors contribute to the decision to sacrifice time, cost, performance, or combinations of these. Note well that it is not always possible to sacrifice one of these items without affecting the others. Reducing time could have a serious impact on both performance and cost, especially if overtime is required. But never let *your* project get caught in the no-man's land between cheap enough and good enough.

Some go so far as to contend that all three elements can never simultaneously be held constant. They argue performance, time, and cost represent the three points of a triangle (illustrated in Fig. 10-2) and that emphasizing any two by definition precludes the third. But I, by contrast, argue that your objective should be to do it on schedule, do it on budget, and do it right the *first* time. Satisfy your customer *completely*.

The literature provides little guidance on the subject. But a recent report by management consultants McKinsey & Company, quoted in *Fortune* magazine, estimates that certain projects finishing on time but reasonably over budget are 140 percent more profitable than if they had finished on budget but six months late. This is probably due to the:

- Leverage of project benefits
- Time value of money (discussed in the next chapter)

Unfortunately, many project managers and their bosses regard this trilogy as a circus juggling act in which the true cause of problems is never found; instead, apparent symptoms are brought under temporary control by tossing the other two elements into the air (Fig. 10-3). Then, when one of these falls out of tolerance (and causes another flap), it is grabbed and the element just held is launched—and so on. Nothing is ever brought under permanent control, but

Table 10-1   Time–Cost Tradeoffs, Holding Some Parameter(s) Fixed

ONE ELEMENT FIXED AT A TIME			
TYPICAL EXAMPLE	TIME	COST	PERFORMANCE
Capital equipment	Fixed	Variable	Variable
Moonlighter	Variable	Fixed	Variable
Research and Development	Variable	Variable	Fixed
TWO ELEMENTS FIXED AT A TIME			
TYPICAL EXAMPLE	TIME	COST	PERFORMANCE
Consultant	Fixed	Fixed	Variable
Capital equipment	Fixed	Variable	Fixed
Non-process equipment	Variable	Fixed	Fixed
THREE ELEMENTS FIXED OR VARIABLE AT A TIME			
TYPICAL EXAMPLE	TIME	COST	PERFORMANCE
What your boss demands	Fixed	Fixed	Fixed
No constraints/tradeoff	Variable	Variable	Variable

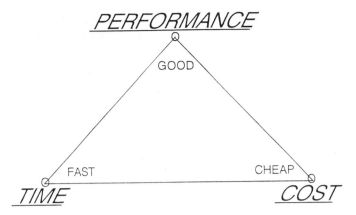

FIGURE 10-2.   Time-cost-performance tradeoff triangle.

the activity level is so high that people seem pleased, nonetheless, with the hurry-scurry rev-mode effort and circus atmosphere, if not the positive results.

RESOURCE ALLOCATION

Resource allocation, assigning necessary resources to individual activities, often receives more attention today than any other aspect of project management. Reasons for this emphasis include:

- Extremely complex mathematics that until just a few moons ago was computed only by "big iron" machines too expensive to make it worthwhile for most projects
- The worldwide inflation spiral since the 1973 oil crisis that has relentlessly pushed resource costs higher and higher, making it more important to manage them well

FIGURE 10-3.   Project management seen as a three-ball juggling act.

- The high cost of capital. This affects many large plant construction, capital investment, and research and development projects—none of which can typically be financed internally through retained earnings.

The biggest irony is that people have become much more expensive, despite flat or even declining real wages.

Ideally, project managers would like to use some precise and logical way to ensure that scarce project resources:

- Are and will continue to be optimally (most cost-effectively) used
- Have an availability level that is never exceeded

Unfortunately, these goals are very difficult to achieve. This is especially true when other objectives (such as minimizing project length or cost), at cross purposes with this goal, are also sought.

The mathematical complexity of the problem is due to the following: For every possible activity starting time, there are generally multiple (*P3* allows unlimited) resources required. Within these different starting times, there are many, many possible combinations of resources. Therefore, for a project of even moderate size, there is usually a vast number of combinations to evaluate. In fact, total resource optimization with respect to time, cost, and other project objectives still requires much more iron and horsepower than most companies have or could ever afford.

The saving factors are these:

- Allocation efficiencies well in excess of 90 percent are possible (*P3*: 98 + percent)
- Many other uncertainties in the underlying schedule would make even a "perfectly optimized" allocation plan less than perfect anyway.

The second point merits further discussion. Recall your algebra and other math classes. You will remember that an answer's precision is only as good as the least-precise contributing number. Considering that durations are rarely more than 90–95 percent accurate, it is not worth going crazy over resource allocation precisions.

Even though perfection is virtually impossible, the project manager must still manage his or her resources effectively. This requires:

- Careful, skillful judgment of the situation in general
- Strong consideration of the software-recommended solution in particular.

The resource allocation procedure uses your skill and judgment as a project planner, and supplements—not replaces—these with a set of decision rules carried out and reported by the computer system. Careful review and evaluation of the computer-generated resource plan assists you in smoothing out irregularities and resolving resource conflicts. Although no consistent set of decision rules can be developed that optimally solves all network situations, they nevertheless:

- Are useful
- Produce enlightening information
- Provide conclusions approximating full-scale optimization

While powerful analytical tools, leveling and smoothing do not produce optimal solutions; they evaluate options. There is virtually an unlimited number of ways to assign resources in a network so that the ultimate choice can be made by a knowledgeable, skillful project manager. Rather than accept the results of any leveling run at face value, take time to consider alternatives.

On the other hand, leveling takes away much scheduling flexibility. Indicated activity dates should be followed quite closely because the late schedule, not resource-leveled, may still assume resource availability in excess of actual amounts. Since the resource shortages have not been solved, there would be no choice but to delay the project beyond Late Finish.

Resource constraints, while increasingly important, not only complicate, but even alter, some of the basic game rules. Often resource availability:

- Influences scheduling
- Changes an already acceptable plan

As another example, the longest activity sequence under constrained-resource conditions may well represent a Critical Path different from that under unlimited resource conditions.

Still another difference is that, under constrained-resource conditions, there may exist many Early Start schedules, not just one! This is because float is not as useful a planning tool when resources are inadequate. Float, as we learned earlier, guarantees only the availability of time, not the availability of resources. Careful review, analysis, and evaluation of this resource plan will assist you in smoothing out irregularities and resolving resource conflicts. Nothing less is acceptable. Without adequate resources, your project will not get done the way you want it done.

Fortunately, one of the main advantages of the network model for project planning and control is the ease by which resource information can be generated and analyzed. There are only two requirements:

- Each activity's resource requirements must be identified separately
- Activities with variable resource requirements must represent each situation as a separate subactivity if they cannot be represented by lags

Remember, though, no consistent set of decision rules can be developed that will solve all network situations. Later we shall look at eight such methods and their relative effectiveness. None produces an optimal schedule. To develop an optimal allocation process for a complex network with multiple resources requires time and expense well beyond its value in most cases.

But the project manager who fails to do his or her best is the project manager who is throwing money to the winds! If you insist on doing this, please do so only when the winds are blowing in my direction!

Resource allocation, including leveling and smoothing, is a technique that allows:

- Normal buildup at project start
- Relatively constant usage during the major time period of the work
- Normal tapering off and winding down at project conclusion, bringing it to a smooth, orderly close

Resource allocation, then, is performed for much the same reason that cost analysis is, to measure and ensure the most economic use of resources. There is, however, a significant difference. Whereas only two general cost types are considered (direct and indirect), resources are of many categories with widely differing characteristics.

The main steps in resource allocation are:

- Estimate and schedule required resources
- Determine resource availability
- Allocate resources
- Replan as necessary

Clearly, a manual operation of infinite plug-and-chug calculations is no way to earn manager-of-the-year honors!

Your people will have neither time nor energy left to carry out the plan they manually calculated. (Oh, well, it was probably wrong anyway!)

This point also merits further discussion. Whether in a manual environment or a computerized one, any error or inefficiency in activity relationships or durations:

- Must be corrected—no exceptions
- Requires the entire network (beyond completed activities) to be recalculated.

Included in this recalculation, of course, must be a new resource allocation plan. The same is also true for evaluating the impact of schedule changes. *Time is critical and speed is urgent!*

It is simply impossible to perform your job duties satisfactorily unless you can produce and evaluate this information in a timely manner. Networks in excess of fifty activities do not, and cannot, meet this requirement unless done by computer. Processing by computer:

- Saves both time and costs
- Is inexpensive, reliable, and flexible
- Provides capabilities that are impossible in a manual environment

It does not require that you do anything extra—that is, anything you should not already be doing. You may not do these things in a manual environment because:

- You do not have time
- It is easier to cheat and get away with things

Both the following are needed and provided:

• A high degree of accuracy
• A low degree of cost

For all but the smallest projects (twenty-five to thirty activities), the software investment represents a negligible percentage (as low as 0.0005 percent of total project revenue) of total project cost and is a big money-maker if the following other benefits are considered:

• Better information faster
• Reduced labor expenses
• Reduced material expenses
• Reduced indirect costs
• Less overhead costs
• More effective resource utilization
• More or earlier revenue
• A better deliverable
• Enhanced professionalism
• A more satisfied customer.

But remember: Although a computer can detect some errors in logic, it absolutely depends on the planner for proper activity sequences. It can construct the network very quickly, but its accuracy depends heavily on that of underlying activity relationships and durations. No amount of programming brilliance can correct faulty planning. It will instead only mess things up at electronic speed, with only human speed available to correct the problems. *GIGO!*

Before proceeding with resource allocation, leveling, and smoothing, we need to:

• Recognize the main resource categories
• Understand their different characteristics

Capital

Capital is a resource provided either as:

• A lump sum at project beginning or end
• By receipts at regular or required intervals throughout—perhaps at successful milestone completion or production of an acceptable deliverable.

In either case, what is not used in one time period is usually carried forward to the next and is not lost. But idle capital, although not expended, is a waste of earning power; it would be better used to pay current expenses or earn interest. Like other resources, the objective is to complete the project with the most effective use of capital.

Personnel

Unlike capital, idle labor and personnel cannot be carried forward. For example, suppose five persons are hired for two days. On the first day, there is only enough work for two persons. This does not mean that eight persons will be available the next day. If eight persons are actually needed on the second day, then three more must be hired. What was lost on the first day can never be carried over to the second.

We must also consider the flexibility by which persons may be assigned jobs, too. Understand well that labor in general, and people in particular, vigorously guard their right to carry out only the tasks for which they have been employed. Even if lower on the learning curve, an army of jacks-of-all-trades would greatly simplify resource allocation, but the reality of things says this is impossible. Therefore, arbitrary allocation of personnel to activities without careful examination of required skills can, and usually will, be disastrous.

Human resources are flexible only to the extent that they can be moved from one location to another, provided the work is of the same category. But unused resources can never be carried over or applied elsewhere.

An elite, highly trained resource pool should be established to support:

• New projects
• Projects undergoing major schedule or requirements revisions
• Projects in trouble and in desperate need of correcting counsel

When this "tiger team" is no longer needed on one project, it can be assigned, collectively or individually, to other projects needing its services. This arrangement would require the support of senior management; high quality is always in high demand and jealously guarded. Understandably, if you are fortunate enough to have an Andrea, a Lynn, a Mary, or a Phil (any of whom I would select over *two* future draft choices!) on *your* team, you want to keep them there!

Plant and Equipment

Plant and equipment is either owned, leased, or rented by the enterprise carrying out the project. Unused plant and equipment represents a direct loss, either in terms of rental charges, depreciation, or loss of monetary earning power. As with personnel, most plant and equipment must be used when available, or heavy losses will result. Unused plant capacity or equipment hours cannot be carried over to a future date: "Use it or lose it!" Depending on both size and function, some plant and equipment may be moved from one location to another on appropriate work.

Materials and Supplies

Materials and supplies are usually purchased when required. If purchased too early:

• Capital is unnecessarily tied up
• Interest on this capital is wasted
• Some will spoil or decline in quality.

This explains the great interest in *just-in-time (JIT)* processes: to reduce the amount of capital tied up in inventory carrying costs. Materials and supplies allocated for, but unused in, one period may be carried forward to the next.

But purchasing materials too few or too late may embarrassingly delay your project. I have seen several instances in which a new Information System (none of them mine!) was delayed because nobody remembered to purchase the checks or other special forms. "For the want of a nail . . ."

Space

A frequently overlooked but nonetheless vital resource for most projects is the space required to conduct the project. Examples include the following:

- Office area
- Meeting rooms
- Shop floor work area
- Factory accommodation
- Warehouse

Some, even all, of this space may be unneeded after project completion. Space requires careful planning. Generally, once purchased, leased, or rented, space cannot readily be expanded or reduced. But space availability is so important it often is a controlling factor in maintaining planned progress and expenditures. In the extreme case, it may even determine whether or not the project may be done at all.

Space unused in one time period cannot be added to space available in the next. For example, if a warehouse has ten thousand square feet of floor space but only five thousand square feet are used, there will still be only ten thousand square feet available for use in the next period, and certainly not fifteen thousand! At the same time, it is both unlikely and undesirable that the excess five thousand square feet could be rented out to someone else. Space is quite inflexible as far as movement is concerned.

THE BASIC RESOURCE-ALLOCATION PROCESS

Resources needed for each activity are estimated and then aggregated, or combined, for each resource type, using the same method as is used to calculate expenditures. Manual resource-allocation computation is:

- Another job of extreme boredom
- A challenge to human sanity

Often a project includes many resource categories having but one thing in common: There is usually not enough of any particular resource. This brings us to the next step, which is to schedule the resource amounts available throughout the project. Resources are usually specified at two availability levels:

- *Normal:* the level already or easily made available

- *Maximum:* the highest level of resource availability; the level reserved to expedite delayed activities, for emergencies, or for other extreme circumstances. It usually involves higher amounts or expenditure rates

It would be desirable to establish different resource availability limits over the project time frame. *Primavera* allows you to specify up to six time intervals for each availability level; the maximum-level intervals need not equal the normal-level intervals. This ensures that variances in resource availability that may affect your project's completion date are taken into account. At the same time, although an activity may be on the Critical Path, it often happens (if activity resource levels vary) that certain portions have float, excess resources assigned, or both.

For even greater accuracy, then, establish a separate activity for each subactivity whose increased resource requirements are likely to turn it critical (by extending duration). At a minimum, keep in mind that not all portions of an activity may be maxed-out, even though the entire activity is critical.

Inevitably, this process will show that required levels are sometimes:

- Greater than maximum (beyond availability)
- Equal to available (between normal and obtainable)
- Less than available (less than normal)

To maximize efficiency and economy, these peaks and valleys must somehow be leveled off, yet not delay the project schedule or negatively affect the quality of your end product or service.

DETERMINING PROJECT COMPLETION DATE WITH A FIXED RESOURCE LIMIT

Let us first consider a common situation: determining project length given a fixed resource limit. Project managers frequently work with limited resources—especially personnel. We must determine how to handle those activities whose durations assume resource availability in excess of actual. We set up the baseline with a diagram and a table, both shown in Fig. 10-4.

The resulting summary report is shown in Table 10-2, and in bar chart format (Fig. 10-5).

A profile for each needed resource [such as the "Persons" table (Table 10-3) and the *Primavera* chart (Fig. 10-6)] must clearly show the following:

- Required resource totals for each time period
- Normal and maximum limits (not done yet)
- When required resources exceed these levels so appropriate action may be taken well in advance of a last-minute panic-emergency crisis

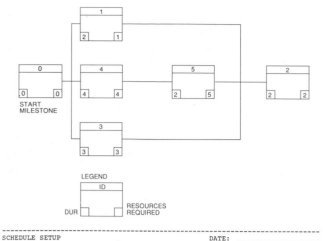

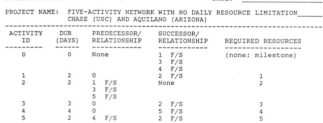

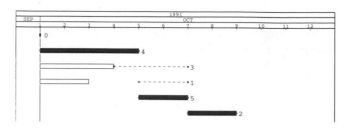

FIGURE 10-5.   Gantt Chart.

```
-------------------------------------------------------------
SCHEDULE SETUP                              DATE: _____
-------------------------------------------------------------
PROJECT NAME:  FIVE-ACTIVITY NETWORK WITH NO DAILY RESOURCE LIMITATION_____
               CHASE (USC) AND AQUILANO (ARIZONA)
-------------------------------------------------------------
ACTIVITY   DUR     PREDECESSOR/      SUCCESSOR/
   ID     (DAYS)   RELATIONSHIP      RELATIONSHIP    REQUIRED RESOURCES
-------   ------   ------------      ------------    ------------------
   0        0      None              1  F/S          (none; milestone)
                                     3  F/S
                                     4  F/S
   1        2      0                 2  F/S               1
   2        2      1  F/S            None                 2
                   3  F/S
                   5  F/S
   3        3      0                 2  F/S               3
   4        4      0                 5  F/S               4
   5        2      4  F/S            2  F/S               5
-------------------------------------------------------------
```

FIGURE 10-4.   Activity list, with relationships, durations, and resources.

The declared resource limits must be allowed to change over time, as is allowed by *Primavera*. The baseline (un-limited-resource) load is shown in Table 10-3.

Important schedule facts include the following:

- The Critical Path is activities 4, 5, and 2
- Project length is eight days, October 1 to October 8
- Two activities contain float: activities 1 (four days) and 3 (three days)
- Daily resource requirements vary from two to eight persons under the early schedule, and from two to nine persons under the late. These values are graphed in Fig. 10-6

Table 10-2   Schedule Summary

```
-------------------------------------------------------------------------------
SCHEDULE SUMMARY                                    DATE: _____
```

PROJECT NAME: FIVE-ACTIVITY NETWORK WITH NO DAILY RESOURCE LIMITATION_____

ACTIVITY ID		ORIG DUR	REM DUR	% DONE	EARLY START	EARLY FINISH	LATE START	LATE FINISH	TOTAL FLOAT	
1		2	2	0	1OCT91	2OCT91	5OCT91	6OCT91	4	
2	*	2	2	0	7OCT91	8OCT91	7OCT91	8OCT91	0	*
3		3	3	0	1OCT91	3OCT91	4OCT91	6OCT91	3	
4	*	4	4	0	1OCT91	4OCT91	1OCT91	4OCT91	0	*
5	*	2	2	0	5OCT91	6OCT91	5OCT91	6OCT91	0	*

Table 10-3   Resource Loading Table

```
-------------------------------------------------------------------------------
RESOURCE LOADING TABLE:   PERSONS                   DATE: _____
```

PROJECT NAME: FIVE-ACTIVITY NETWORK WITH NO DAILY RESOURCE LIMITATION_____

					DAY			
ACTIVITY	1	2	3	4	5	6	7	8
1	1	1						
2							2	2
3	3	3	3					
4	4	4	4	4				
5					5	5		
TOTALS	8	8	7	4	5	5	2	2

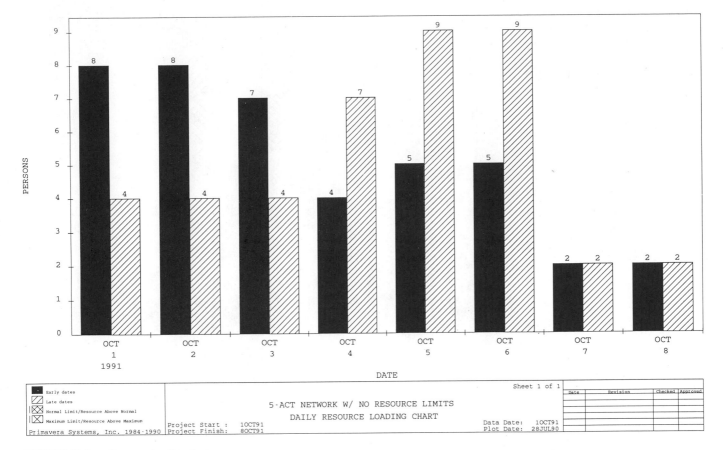

FIGURE 10-6.   Resource loading chart.

A sample *P3* screen is provided, again FYI only, in Fig. 10-7. As with relationships and durations, these values could have been graphically assigned instead. Do note, however, that *Primavera* measures resources ("Units per Day") to the nearest hundredth-unit. This greatly helps in the leveling and smoothing processes discussed shortly.

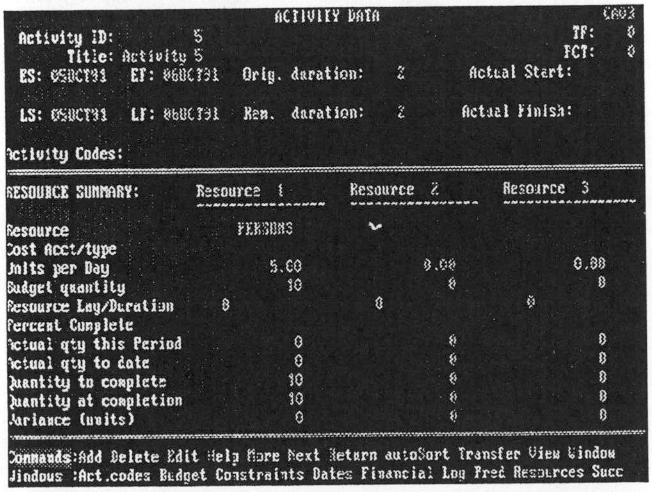

FIGURE 10-7.   *Primavera* resource input screen (Primavera Systems, Inc.).

In order to complete in eight days, the project assumed that:

• Unlimited resources were available each day
• All persons reported for work with the correct skills

If both of these assumptions are not met, the project has no choice but to slide. How much it will be delayed depends on the individual facts and circumstances.

RESOURCE LEVELING

We approach this topic first by example, then by formal discussion. Assume that an absolute limit of five workers per day has been imposed. What effect will this have on our schedule? Recall the eight-day schedule assumed unlimited resource availability and took full advantage of this in the first three days of the early schedule:

• October 1: eight workers
• October 2: eight workers
• October 3: seven workers

The rest of the early schedule, October 4 through October 8, would be unaffected by the resource limit. But the late schedule, ten person-days over limit, faces an even harder objective. The impact on both early and late schedules is presented in Fig. 10-8.

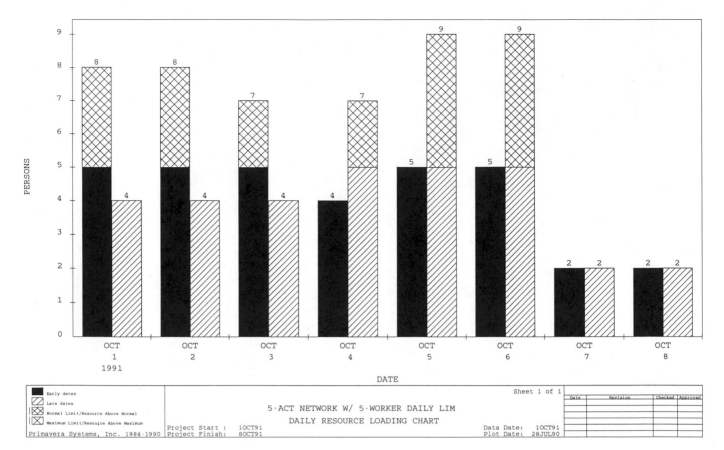

FIGURE 10-8.   Resource loading chart.

But limiting the first three days to only five workers, instead of seven or eight, as used previously, clearly requires that the project schedule be extended. The scheduling objective is to:

- Minimize excess duration (alternate objective: minimize total cost)
- Comply with the five-person limit on all days
- Avoid breaking up worker teams that must remain intact to do their work (ever try to hang ceiling sheetrock alone?)
- Maintain proper logic

Not easy. But remember this: Your computer wants to be your friend. And "a friend in need is a friend indeed." Use all of its power to determine the very best possible solution.

Although critical-activity resource allocation is strictly bound (limiting resources will increase activity duration and lengthen the project), there is some flexibility with non-critical activities: Resources may be allocated at any time between Early Start and Late Finish. Working day by day between these two times, the objective is to:

- Identify the period that minimizes total resource requirements
- Reschedule the activity to that time

As was true for float, these times need not be contiguous. Your software should allow you to stop and resume activities as required—especially when more effective resource allocations result.

As policy, it is wise to select the earliest possible time at which an activity can be scheduled with sufficient resources. This is to allow time to overcome possible delays in the future.

Another way might be to reduce an activity's resources and to allow its duration to rise by an amount not to exceed the available float. This, however, may not be possible in all situations. Some worker teams simply cannot be broken up, as we have already seen with sheetrockers. The same holds true for other resources. Not all things can come in smaller packages.

Required resource quantities might still be greater than available resource quantities. In these circumstances, there is no option but to increase either or both of the following:

- Project length
- Availability of those particular resources

No exceptions!

It is to your great advantage to know how to calculate constrained schedules, and to evaluate the resulting impact on enterprise business objectives. A common lament (quoted from *InformationWeek,* 25 June 1990, p. 15) says: "Finance would approve a business unit plan that depended on a major IS (Information Systems) project and then deny IS the people it needed to carry out the project. After a while, rational people just say to hell with it!"

This frustration is not limited to information systems. Accept all the help and ammo you can get!

First, look at the resource-loading chart in Fig. 10-9 to verify that no day exceeds the five-person limit. Does your answer match the *Primavera* solution shown in Table 10-4?

The leveled loading table is shown in Table 10-5, and is in bar chart format (Fig. 10-10).

Note that the project has now been extended three additional days to a total of eleven. It will now finish on October 11. This is not just because the eight-day schedule incorporated three days on which the number of workers exceeded the five-person limit. We cannot get off that easily! We must, as always, take into account both precedence relationships and team loading constraints. On any given day, we can either load the entire activity team or none of it. We cannot on any day, for any reason:

- Break up an activity work team
- Exceed the five-worker limitation

If we have not already done so, we should at this point question the very wisdom of such a limit on the number of workers. Sometimes no feasible alternatives are possible. More commonly, though, such limits are:

- Arbitrarily applied
- Politically motivated
- Knee-jerk reactions
- Foolish and unwise

They also occur because of the mystic nature of indirect costs, which, as seen earlier, are:

- Misunderstood
- Harder to measure
- Thought to represent voodoo accounting

Whatever their reason, such limits often unnecessarily cost your company:

- Money
- Time
- Professional respect

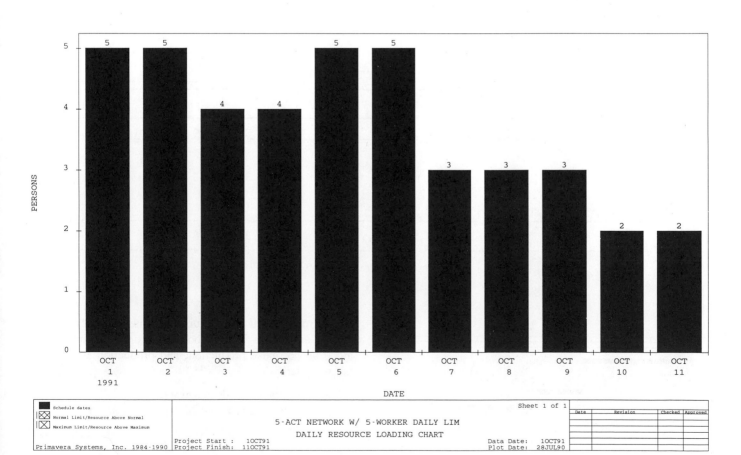

FIGURE 10-9.   Resource loading chart.

Table 10-4   Resource Leveling Analysis Report

```
-------------------------------------------------------------------------
RESOURCE LEVELING ANALYSIS REPORT                    DATE: _____

PROJECT NAME:   LEVELED FIVE-ACTIVITY, FIVE-WORKER NETWORK_____
-------------------------------------------------------------------------
```

ACT/CAL RESOURCE	DAILY USAGE	TF	EARLY START NORM	EARLY START MAX	DELAYED BY PRED OR RES DATE	TF	NORM	MAX	LEVELED START	FINISH
4 1 Activity 4		0							1OCT91	4OCT91
PERSONS	4.00	0	5.00	5.00					1OCT91	4OCT91
5 1 Activity 5		0							5OCT91	6OCT91
PERSONS	5.00	0	5.00	5.00					5OCT91	6OCT91
3 1 Activity 3		3			7OCT91	-3			7OCT91	9OCT91
PERSONS	3.00	3	1.00	1.00	7OCT91	-3	5.00	5.00	7OCT91	9OCT91
1 1 Activity 1		4							1OCT91	2OCT91
PERSONS	1.00	4	1.00	1.00					1OCT91	2OCT91
2 1 Activity 2		0			1OOCT91	-3			1OOCT91	11OCT91
PERSONS	2.00	0	2.00	2.00	1OOCT91	-3	5.00	5.00	1OOCT91	11OCT91

Table 10-5   Resource Loading Table

```
-------------------------------------------------------------------------
RESOURCE LOADING TABLE                               DATE: _____

PROJECT NAME:   LEVELED FIVE-ACTIVITY, FIVE-WORKER NETWORK_____
-------------------------------------------------------------------------
```

						DAY					
ACT	1	2	3	4	5	6	7	8	9	10	11
1	1	1									
2										2	2
3							3	3	3		
4	4	4	4	4							
5					5	5					
TOTALS	5	5	4	4	5	5	3	3	3	2	2

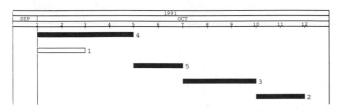

FIGURE 10-10.   Gantt Chart.

The road to Hell (and the unemployment office!) is often paved, as they say, with good intentions. But intentions alone do not make production, and production alone does not necessarily:

- Satisfy customer needs and wants
- Accumulate long-term wealth for your company

These, I would think, would also be your needs and wants!

But let us assume the project manager has:

- Performed a complete evaluation
- Found the five-worker constraint to be acceptable

How do we schedule this project under the five-worker limit? The first three days did not comply with the limit. We need to look at each day in turn to determine how best to load the work.

October 1

October 1 is currently loaded with activities 1, 3, and 4. Since only activity 4 is critical, it is loaded first. It requires four persons. Activity 3 contains one less day float than activity 1 but must be slid because it requires three persons, which would exceed the daily limit. The only choice left is to load activity 1, bringing the total load to five.

What do we do with the three persons displaced by the limit? Some possibilities include:

- Training
- Loaning them out to other projects
- Having them take compensatory time in a flex-time arrangement

Otherwise, "Congratulations!", you have just trashed twenty-four person-hours of production in one day! Maybe these workers will have something to do October 2.

October 2

But this day looks just like the previous day. No work for Team 3 on October 2, either! Activity 4, still critical, is loaded first. This repeats the prior day's situation. Activity 1 is again scheduled to round out the limit. Since it is not a critical activity, its work-in-process status is a consideration, but not a determining factor. If appropriate, the balance could be done later. It is still too early for activities 5 and 2. They, like activity 3, also require too many resources.

Hopefully, teams are scheduled in advance and not at the last minute. Counting noses and then loading the work force "herky-jerky" does not:

- Permit effective scheduling of alternate time uses
- Afford workers the respect and dignity they deserve

October 3

Activity 4 is still critical and underway. It is again scheduled first, leaving as before one worker in balance. But activity 1 was completed on October 2. It can no longer use this odd-lot remainder. Neither can any other activity. It is still too early for activities 5 and 2 anyway. Team 3 cannot be broken and is again slid. No other activities beside activity 4 can be scheduled; we must simply go at 80 percent—more opportunity costs!

October 4

Same as October 3. Don't give up, Team 3!

October 5–6

When will Team 3 get to work—on October 5? No, sorry! On this day, both activities 1 and 4 have completed, so there are no activities underway. Activity 2 requires that all other activities be completed first, so it will not contend for resources. It is face-off time at center ice for resources! Activity 5 requires the entire five-person restriction, so it meets the limit alone until it is completed—which takes care of October 6 as well as pushes activity 3 all the way to October 7. Hope Team 3 has not been forgotten all this time!

Remember the four days float contained in activity 1? Had it been delayed for any reason, it could work any two days but these until October 9.

October 7–9

Now the situation is this:

- Activities 1, 4, and 5 have completed
- Activity 2 must await completion of activity 3 before it can begin

Work can proceed (finally!) only on activity 3 for the next three days. Even though it requires only three workers, the two activity-2 persons cannot work until activity 3 completes—unless somehow the two activities could be carried out concurrently. But this would violate network logic and is rejected. We must operate at only 60 percent of potential (more opportunity costs!) for the next three days. This brings us to the end of October 9—one day after we would have finished under the old schedule—and we still need to do activity 2.

October 10–11

We "do 2 in two" and finish our worker-constrained schedule in eleven days, on October 11, as advertised earlier.

Could we have done any better? No. This is the best we can do—even if it will not win a blue ribbon from the Project Management Institute!

Maybe if we looked at the resulting network (Fig. 10-11) for float, we would see something! Well, we won't. Only activity 1 has usable float because the three days listed for activities 4 and 5 arise strictly from the three-day delay in project completion. In constrained-resource environments, float no longer guarantees resource—or even time—flexibility. Only activity 1 can be delayed without extending the project beyond eleven days. But even it cannot work October 5 or 6 because activity 5 will on both days totally consume all available resources under the limit.

Activity 1, therefore, really contains only five days float ($= 4 + 3 - 2$) because no work may be done on October 5–6. Usable float occurs only October 3–4 and October 7–9. Float must take into account resource availability as well as time.

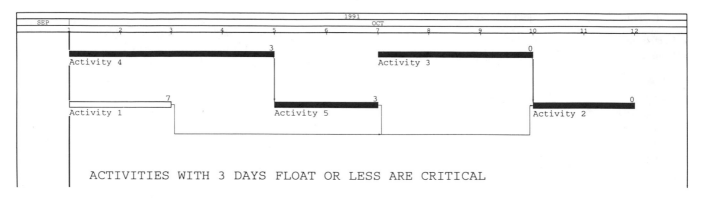

ACTIVITIES WITH 3 DAYS FLOAT OR LESS ARE CRITICAL

FIGURE 10-11. Time-logic plot.

How about the other activities? Activity 2 could not be started until all others had been completed; it could not even be combined in parallel with activity 3 because activity 3 had to be done first. Activity 3 has no float and could not be moved ahead or back. It lost its place in line under the old schedule but could not be moved up under the new because:

• Other activities had already consumed the full five-person limit
• Partial team loading was not allowed

It could not be delayed without also delaying both activity 2 and the entire project even more. Team 3 probably even took some heat for "delaying" activity 2! Glad I didn't work on Team 3.

Have you ever noticed how the supply of office "boo-birds" greatly exceeds the demand for them? Think about this bit of wisdom from Notre Dame football coach Lou Holtz: "Most people in this world just observe. They don't ever make anything or build anything; they just observe and are critics."

Activities 4 (sometimes with 1) and 5:

• Met the daily worker limit
• Suffered no delay
• Have no usable float

Activities 4 and 5 lead off the lengthened Critical Path, which also includes postponed activities 3 and 2. Activity slippage:

• Comes with the resource-constrained territory
• Increases idle time
• Makes effective scheduling more difficult
• May be counterproductive

It may, in fact, be more difficult to load idle teams with work in so piecemeal an environment than to justify the cost of removing the worker limit.

These are not easy things to manage, but must be managed nonetheless. Who told you that project management would be easy, anyway? If she did (Fig. 10-12) you should

have taken her crystal ball, magic wand, enchanted slippers, or something!

You should now see how these methodologies (not my-thologies!) relate and why you should also use *all* the tools in your toolbox, not just the one you happen to grab first. Now you can be a project manager, not just an adding machine!

Before solving more examples, we need to identify some formal resource allocation processes. Because of the complex mathematics involved, the literature has little to say on the subject. Two sources, however, provide the following excellent summaries.

Chase and Aquilano (pp. 322–3) provide the simplest, least quantitative heuristic approach:

1. Schedule the network assuming unlimited resources. For each day, examine all activities, across all projects, to

FIGURE 10-12. "I see for you . . . excellent health, lots of riches, and optimized project schedules!" *Source:* Unknown.

determine cumulative requirements. Next, allocate resources serially in time; start on the first day and schedule all jobs possible. Consistent with network logic, begin with the activity with the highest requirements (for example, activity 4)—then look to other candidates in decreasing requirements order (activities 3 and 1) until you find that activity (1) whose requirements, when added to the highest-consuming activity, do not exceed the limit. Continue as long as the limit is not exceeded. Repeat the entire process beginning with the second-highest consuming activity, and so on. An activity already underway gets first use of the resource; its successors cannot be started until this activity is completed.

2. When several activities compete for the same resource, give preference to jobs with the least float, but only if their predecessors have been completed. If several activities have identical float, apply all needed resources in Early Start order.

3. Reschedule noncritical activities to free resources for super-critical or critical activities. Remember, critical activities—those with zero float (there are other cases, too)—must start and finish exactly as scheduled. And super-critical activities need all the help they can get!

4. Level resource usage to minimize overtime, unproductive time, and spot shortages in skills and equipment. In a manual environment, only one resource—the current most critical—should be leveled at a time. Evaluate its results before leveling the next most critical resource, and so on. In a computerized environment, level as many as appropriate on each run. *Primavera* levels up to forty resources (in user-specified priority) per run.

5. Recompute float for each incomplete (both underway and unstarted) activity to reflect its delay

Other possible schedule priorities include:

- Shortest duration
- Longest duration
- Least uncertainty
- Most concurrent activities
- By organization

Want to race the computer? You would be more likely to win Lotto America than that contest! Sorting out this mess by hand would assuredly finish off the balance of your annual budget. Do not allow your project team to go to the top of tall buildings or high bridges during this time!

Is this the best we can do? Yes. But in a more complex situation, we could only say, "Probably." No one heuristic—or combination—can always produce the best results. What works well in one case may not work in another. The opposite also holds true. As an added complication, each heuristic is likely to produce a different schedule. It is impossible to guarantee that a particular heuristic, or combination thereof, will produce the best results. The problem must be solved numerous times, each time employing a different method, then the best solution chosen—as if you did not already have plenty to do!

Nevertheless, such procedures are widely used in practice. Although not the best possible, they are usually "good enough" for planning purposes. The better performers make error margins of less than 10 percent possible and less than 20 percent probable. This is usually acceptable—especially in light of duration uncertainties and underlying estimates of resource requirements. Because these procedures are relatively easy to use, it is more likely that they will be.

Moder, Phillips, and Davis (Chapter 7) discuss a more formal methodology and also summarize others by relative effectiveness.

Burgess Resource Leveling Algorithm

For each day, calculate the sum of the resource-requirements square. This squares-sum decreases as:

- Peaks are leveled
- Valleys are raised

It reaches a minimum for a schedule that is level, or as close to level as possible. The objective is to follow a series of decreasing daily squares-sums until this best-fit schedule can be determined. Presented in detail:

1. List project activities in ascending order by number and include for each activity:
   Early Start
   Duration
   Float
2. Starting with the last activity, schedule it period by period to give it the lowest possible sum of squares of resource requirements for each time unit. If more than one schedule gives the same total sum of squares, then schedule the activity as late as possible in order to provide all preceding activities as much float as possible.
3. Holding the last activity fixed, repeat Step 2 on the next to last network activity, taking advantage of any float that may have been available as result of Step 2.
4. Continue Step 3 until the first activity in the list has been considered; this completes the first rescheduling cycle.
5. Repeat Steps 2 through 4 until no further reduction in the total squares-sum is possible, noting that an activity may only move right under this scheme.
6. If the resource is particularly critical, repeat Steps 1 through 5 with a different ordering still by precedence.
7. Choose the best schedule of those obtained in Steps 5 and 6.
8. Make final adjustments to the schedule chosen in Step 7, taking into account factors not considered in the basic scheduling procedure.
9. Punt! (Quick kick?)—and let the computer do all this stuff for you.

Other heuristic models can also be used. Again, the results vary by project detail. But several studies have found the minimum-float MINSLACK heuristic most often produces the best stand-alone results (Table 10-6).

But the research has also concluded the following:

• Resource allocation procedures all follow one basic rule: Activity priorities are set according to some specified re-source-availability criterion. The corresponding activities are then scheduled accordingly if:

Their predecessors have been completed
Adequate resources are available

• There are two general methods by which resource-allocation heuristics may be applied. According to Moder, Phillips, and Davis (p. 203):

Table 10-6   Effectiveness of Various Resource Allocation Methodologies

RULE	(a)	(b)	DESCRIPTION
1. Minimum Activity Slack (MINSLK)	29	5.6	Schedules first those activities with lowest total float (slack)
2. Minimum Late Finish Time (LFT)	20	6.7	Schedules first those activities with earliest Late Finish
3. Resource Scheduling Method (RSM)	14	6.8	Priority index calculated on the basis of pairwise comparison of activity Early Finish and Late Start times, giving preference roughly in order of increasing LF times
4. Random Activity Selection (RAN)	5	11.4	Priority given to jobs selected at random, subject to resource availability limits
5. Greatest Resource Demand (GRD)	13	13.1	Schedules first those activities with greatest resource demand in order to complete potential bottleneck activities
6. Greatest Resource Utilization (GRU)	2	13.1	Gives priority to that group of activities which results in the minimum amount of idle resources in each scheduling interval; involves an integer linear programming algorithm
7. Shortest Imminent Operations (SIO)	1	15.3	Schedules first those activities with shortest durations in an attempt to complete the greatest number of activities within a given timespan
8. Most Jobs Possible (MJP)	2	16.0	Gives priority to the largest possible group of jobs which can be scheduled in a time interval; involves an integer linear programming

KEY
(a) = percentage of problems in which found best duration (higher values desirable)
(b) = percent increase above optimal duration (lower values desirable)

- A *serial* scheduling procedure "is one in which all activities of the project are ranked in order of priority as a single group, using some heuristic, and then scheduled one at a time (i.e., serially). Activities that cannot be started at their early start time are progressively delayed until sufficient resources are available." The process allows partial loading.
- A *parallel* scheduling procedure is one in which "all activities starting in a given time period are ranked as a group in order of priority and resources allocated according to this priority as long as available. When an activity cannot be scheduled in a given time period for lack of resources, it is delayed until the next time period. At each successive time period a new rank-ordering of all eligible activities is made and the process continued until all activities have been scheduled." The process does not allow partial loading.

- The choice of allocation procedure (serial or parallel) is sometimes more significant than the choice of scheduling heuristic
- The parallel method is more difficult because partial loading is not permitted
- The serial method can sometimes produce shorter schedules—but often violates network logic in the process. (*Primavera* does not use this method)

We have already seen this. Recall the sheetrockers. If an activity requires two people working together as a team and not separately (putting up ceiling sheetrock certainly qualifies!), having only one person available will:

- Not satisfy the resource requirement
- Delay the activity under the parallel method until two persons are available

The serial method, though, would allow this activity to start. I pity the poor sheetrocker who must now work alone! The serial method cannot combine resource requirements unless told to do so. The parallel method always does.

At the same time, the parallel method can emulate the serial method. Suppose an activity can be performed by one or two persons not working as a team. To accommodate

progress by only one, split the activity into two parallel activities (similarly designated, such as 73A and 73B), each requiring one worker. Progress on each may then be reported independently.

Because it is more flexible and does not violate network logic, the parallel allocation method is superior and should be used.

You must determine which rule set is best for your particular problem. It is not necessarily the method with the highest current individual batting average. But the extraordinary cost of the "perfect" solution must be weighed against its value, again remembering that underlying duration imprecisions will indicate a solution different from optimal anyway. Consider, for example, the following two arithmetic problems:

$$(0.123456789) \qquad (0.123456789)$$
$$\times\ 0.99 \qquad\qquad \times\ 0.990000000.$$

The first may be confidently expressed to only two decimal places, the second to nine. If durations are estimated only to the nearest day, there is no point going hog wild on allocation processes. And, avoiding a loser may be more important than picking the very best.

Primavera combines the two best stand-alone decision rules as follows:

- Earliest Late Start
- Least total float

Activities are sorted in increasing Late Start order and, within these dates, in increasing total-float sequence.

You can redefine or fine-tune these criteria by specifying up to ten schedule parameter or activity codes. Because of this "have-it-your-way" approach, efficiencies above 98 percent are both possible and common.

Encouraged, let us now solve the second resource-allocation problem as shown in Table 10-7.

Table 10-7   Schedule Setup

```
-----------------------------------------------------------------------------
SCHEDULE SETUP                               DATE: _____
```

PROJECT NAME: FIVE-ACTIVITY NETWORK WITH NO DAILY RESOURCE LIMITATION_____
               PRIMAVERA SYSTEMS, INC., BALA CYNWYD, PENNSYLVANIA 19004

ACTIVITY ID	DUR (DAYS)	PREDECESSOR/ RELATIONSHIP	SUCCESSOR/ RELATIONSHIP	REQUIRED RESOURCES
A	4	None	B SS0 C F/S D F/S	2
B	6	A SS0	E F/S	1
C	3	A F/S	E F/S	2
D	3	A F/S	E FF0	1
E	2	B F/S C F/S	None	2

The resulting summary report is shown in Table 10-8, and in bar chart format (Fig. 10-13).

The Critical Path consists of activities *A, C,* and *E,* each of which requires two persons per day. Noncritical activities *B* and *D* each require one person. Project length is nine days, from October 1 through October 9.

This results in the loading chart shown in Table 10-9.

Now assume that only two workers are available each day. The current (early) schedule requires three workers on most days and four workers on two. Only on the last two days are just two workers needed. The impact on both early and late schedules is presented in Tables 10-10 and 10-11 and Fig. 10-14.

Note how the two-worker limitation extends the project

Table 10-8   Schedule Summary

```
-----------------------------------------------------------------------------------
SCHEDULE SUMMARY                                          DATE: _____

PROJECT NAME:  FIVE-ACTIVITY NETWORK WITH NO DAILY RESOURCE LIMITATION_____
-----------------------------------------------------------------------------------
```

ACTIVITY ID		ORIG DUR	REM DUR	% DONE	EARLY START	EARLY FINISH	LATE START	LATE FINISH	TOTAL FLOAT	
A	*	4	4	0	1OCT91	4OCT91	1OCT91	4OCT91	0	*
B		6	6	0	1OCT91	6OCT91	2OCT91	7OCT91	1	
C	*	3	3	0	5OCT91	7OCT91	5OCT91	7OCT91	0	*
D		3	3	0	5OCT91	7OCT91	7OCT91	9OCT91	2	
E	*	2	2	0	8OCT91	9OCT91	8OCT91	9OCT91	0	*

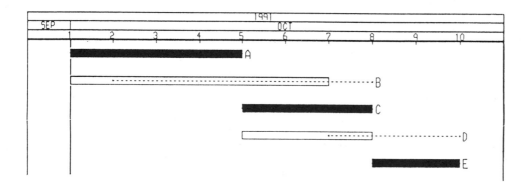

FIGURE 10-13.   Gantt Chart.

Table 10-9   Resource Loading Table

```
-----------------------------------------------------------------------------------
RESOURCE LOADING TABLE                                   DATE: _____

PROJECT NAME:  FIVE-ACTIVITY NETWORK WITH NO DAILY RESOURCE LIMITATION_____
-----------------------------------------------------------------------------------
```

				DAY				
ACT	1	2	3	4	5	6	7	8	9
A	2	2	2	2					
B	1	1	1	1	1	1			
C					2	2	2		
D					1	1	1		
E								2	2
TOTALS	3	3	3	3	4	4	3	2	2

Table 10-10   Resource Leveling Analysis Report

```
--------------------------------------------------------------------------------
RESOURCE LEVELING ANALYSIS REPORT                    ⸱      DATE: _____

PROJECT NAME:  LEVELED FIVE-ACTIVITY, FIVE-WORKER NETWORK_____
--------------------------------------------------------------------------------
ACT/CAL   DAILY ----EARLY START--- --DELAYED BY PRED OR RES--     LEVELED
RESOURCE  USAGE  TF  NORM    MAX    DATE    TF  NORM    MAX    START    FINISH
--------- ----- ---- ------ ------ ------- ---- ------ ------ -------  -------

A  1 Activity A    4                                          |1OCT91   4OCT91
   PERSONS 2.00    4  2.00   2.00                             |1OCT91   4OCT91

B  1 Activity B    6                 5OCT91   -3              |5OCT91  10OCT91
   PERSONS 1.00    6   .00    .00     5OCT91   -3  2.00   2.00|5OCT91  10OCT91

C  1 Activity C    3                11OCT91   -6              |11OCT91 13OCT91
   PERSONS 2.00    3  1.00   1.00   11OCT91   -6  2.00   2.00|11OCT91 13OCT91

D  1 Activity D    3                                          |5OCT91   7OCT91
   PERSONS 1.00    3  1.00   1.00                             |5OCT91   7OCT91

E  1 Activity E    2                14OCT91   -6              |14OCT91 15OCT91
   PERSONS 2.00    2  1.00   1.00   14OCT91   -6  2.00   2.00|14OCT91 15OCT91
--------------------------------------------------------------------------------
```

Table 10-11   Resource Loading Table

```
--------------------------------------------------------------------------------
RESOURCE LOADING TABLE                               DATE: _____

PROJECT NAME:  FIVE-ACTIVITY NETWORK WITH 2-WORKER RESOURCE LIMITATION_____
--------------------------------------------------------------------------------
                                   DAY
```

ACT	1	2	3	4	5	6	7	8	9	10	11	12	13	14	15
A	2	2	2	2											
B					1	1	1	1	1	1					
C											2	2	2		
D					1	1	1								
E														2	2
TOTALS	2	2	2	2	2	2	2	1	1	1	2	2	2	2	2

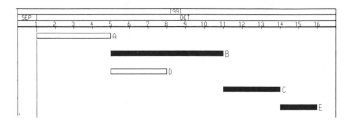

FIGURE 10-14.   Gantt Chart.

from its original nine-day duration to fifteen. Leadoff activity *A* starts and finishes under the original schedule. But the resource limitation delays *B* until October 5—three days later than original Late Start. It also delays *C* until October 11—six days later than original Late Start. If *C* could be loaded serially, it could begin three days earlier. Since it cannot, these three days can only be loaded at 50 percent. Activity *D* avoids slippage because it needs only one worker, who complements the person working on *B* October 5 through

October 7 (and three days beyond). Activity *E* cannot start until *C* completes—also six days later than original Late Start. The Critical Path has changed from *A-C-E* to *B-C-E* even though this solution still depends on *A* to start on time.

Figure 10-15 reviews how many person-days were rearranged by the two-worker daily limit.

Now suppose you must do the following:

- Use multiple resources
- Observe maximum daily limits
- Maintain resource team assignments

The parallel allocation method must be used; the serial method is unacceptable.

Study the network in Table 10-12 and note the following daily resource limits:

- *A*: 5
- *B*: 3
- *C*: 4

For example, activity 2 can begin only if both the following are concurrently available:

- Four workers of resource *A*
- Two workers of resource *C*

Activity 1 requires two of each. The remaining activities require the specified quantities of each resource.

Where do we begin? What do we do? First, let us determine (Table 10-13) our unlimited-resource schedule dates.

Figure 10-16 is in bar chart format.

The impact on both early and late schedules is presented in Fig. 10-17. Note the following early-schedule resource bottlenecks:

- Resource *A*: 5 days (October 3 through October 7) @ 1 worker over the limit
- Resource *B*: 2 days (October 6 through October 7) @ 2 workers over the limit

These bottlenecks may also be presented by day:

October 3 through October 5: Resource *A* is overworked by one worker

October 6 through October 7: Resource *A* is overworked by one worker; Resource *B* is overworked by two workers

The loading table is shown in Table 10-14.

What to do? What to do? Working day by day, assign resources by Late Start, by total float as summarized by *P3* in Table 10-15.

The leveled loading table is shown in Table 10-16 and graphically in Fig. 10-18.

Figure 10-19 is in bar chart format.

The revised schedule:

- Drops activities 1 and 2 from the Critical Path

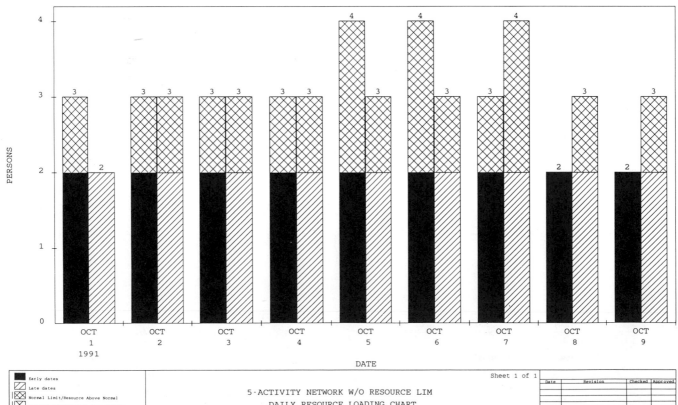

FIGURE 10-15. Resource loading chart.

Table 10-12   Schedule Setup

```
------------------------------------------------------------------------
SCHEDULE SETUP                                    DATE: _____

PROJECT NAME:  SEVEN-ACTIVITY NETWORK WITH THREE-RESOURCE LIMITATION_____
               PRIMAVERA SYSTEMS, INC., BALA CYNWYD, PENNSYLVANIA 19004
------------------------------------------------------------------------
```

ACTIVITY ID	DUR (DAYS)	PREDECESSOR/ RELATIONSHIP	SUCCESSOR/ RELATIONSHIP	REQUIRED RESOURCES A	B	C
1	2	None	2 F/S	2	0	2
			3 F/S			
2	3	1 F/S	4 F/S	4	0	2
			5 F/S			
3	5	1 F/S	6 F/S	2	1	2
4	3	2 F/S	6 F/S	2	3	1
			7 F/S			
5	2	2 F/S	6 F/S	2	1	1
6	2	3 F/S	7 F/S	4	2	2
		4 F/S				
		5 F/S				
7	3	4 F/S	None	3	1	3
		6 F/S				

Table 10-13   Schedule Summary

```
----------------------------------------------------------------------
SCHEDULE SUMMARY                                  DATE: _____

PROJECT NAME:  SEVEN-ACTIVITY NETWORK WITH THREE-RESOURCE LIMITATION_____
----------------------------------------------------------------------
```

ACTIVITY ID		ORIG DUR	REM DUR	% DONE	EARLY START	EARLY FINISH	LATE START	LATE FINISH	TOTAL FLOAT	
1	*	2	2	0	1OCT91	2OCT91	1OCT91	2OCT91	0	*
2	*	3	3	0	3OCT91	5OCT91	3OCT91	5OCT91	0	*
3		5	5	0	3OCT91	7OCT91	4OCT91	8OCT91	1	
4	*	3	3	0	6OCT91	8OCT91	6OCT91	8OCT91	0	*
5		2	2	0	6OCT91	7OCT91	7OCT91	8OCT91	1	
6	*	2	2	0	9OCT91	10OCT91	9OCT91	10OCT91	0	*
7	*	3	3	0	11OCT91	13OCT91	11OCT91	13OCT91	0	*

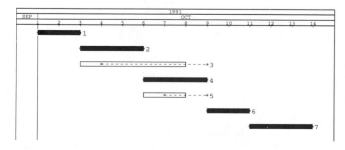

FIGURE 10-16.   Gantt Chart.

• Still assumes them to start on time
• Contains no days in which resource demand exceeds availability
• Requires an additional five days to achieve this condition

This was also the number of days in which demand for the most overworked resource, *A*, exceeded its availability. But *B*, short two persons for as many days, played a more crucial part. Let us look at the schedule more closely.

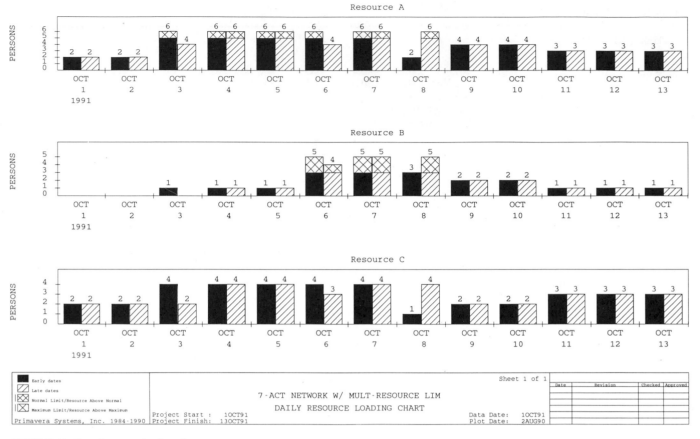

FIGURE 10-17. Resource loading chart.

Table 10-14   Resource Loading Table

```
------------------------------------------------------------------------
RESOURCE LOADING TABLE                      DATE: _____

PROJECT NAME:  SEVEN-ACTIVITY NETWORK WITH THREE-RESOURCE LIMITATION_____
------------------------------------------------------------------------
                                DAY
------------------------------------------------------------------------
```

ACT	1	2	3	4	5	6	7	8	9	10	11	12	13
	ABC	ABC	ABC	ABC	ABC	ABC	ABC	ABC	ABC	ABC	ABC	ABC	ABC
1	202	202											
2			402	402	402								
3			212	212	212	212	212						
4						231	231	231					
5						211	211						
6									422	422			
7											313	313	313

```
------------------------------------------------------------------------
TOTALS:
------------------------------------------------------------------------
A:    2    2    6*   6*   6*   6*   6*   2    4    4    3    3    3
B:    0    0    1    1    1    5*   5*   3    2    2    1    1    1
C:    2    2    4    4    4    4    4    1    2    2    3    3    3
------------------------------------------------------------------------
PROBLEM DAYS:    A    A    A    AB   AB
------------------------------------------------------------------------
```

Table 10-15   Resource Leveling Analysis Report

```
------------------------------------------------------------------------------
RESOURCE LEVELING ANALYSIS REPORT                      DATE: _____

PROJECT NAME:  LEVELED SEVEN-ACTIVITY, THREE-RESOURCE NETWORK_____
------------------------------------------------------------------------------
```

ACT/CAL RESOURCE	DAILY USAGE	----EARLY START--- TF	NORM	MAX	--DELAYED BY PRED OR RES-- DATE	TF	NORM	MAX	LEVELED START	FINISH
1 1 Activity 1		2							1OCT91	2OCT91
A	2.00	2	5.00	5.00					1OCT91	2OCT91
C	2.00	2	4.00	4.00					1OCT91	2OCT91
2 1 Activity 2		3							3OCT91	5OCT91
A	4.00	3	5.00	5.00					3OCT91	5OCT91
C	2.00	3	4.00	4.00					3OCT91	5OCT91
3 1 Activity 3		5			6OCT91	-2			6OCT91	10OCT91
A	2.00	5	1.00	1.00	6OCT91	-2	5.00	5.00	6OCT91	10OCT91
B	1.00	5	3.00	3.00	6OCT91	-2	3.00	3.00	6OCT91	10OCT91
C	2.00	5	2.00	2.00	6OCT91	-2	4.00	4.00	6OCT91	10OCT91
4 1 Activity 4		3			11OCT91	-5			11OCT91	13OCT91
A	2.00	3	3.00	3.00	11OCT91	-5	5.00	5.00	11OCT91	13OCT91
B	3.00	3	2.00	2.00	11OCT91	-5	3.00	3.00	11OCT91	13OCT91
C	1.00	3	2.00	2.00	11OCT91	-5	4.00	4.00	11OCT91	13OCT91
5 1 Activity 5		2							6OCT91	7OCT91
A	2.00	2	3.00	3.00					6OCT91	7OCT91
B	1.00	2	2.00	2.00					6OCT91	7OCT91
C	1.00	2	2.00	2.00					6OCT91	7OCT91
6 1 Activity 6		2			14OCT91	-5			14OCT91	15OCT91
A	4.00	2	3.00	3.00	14OCT91	-5	5.00	5.00	14OCT91	15OCT91
B	2.00	2	2.00	2.00	14OCT91	-5	3.00	3.00	14OCT91	15OCT91
C	2.00	2	2.00	2.00	14OCT91	-5	4.00	4.00	14OCT91	15OCT91
7 1 Activity 7		3			16OCT91	-5			16OCT91	18OCT91
A	3.00	3	3.00	3.00	16OCT91	-5	5.00	5.00	16OCT91	18OCT91
B	1.00	3	.00	.00	16OCT91	-5	3.00	3.00	16OCT91	18OCT91
C	3.00	3	3.00	3.00	16OCT91	-5	4.00	4.00	16OCT91	18OCT91

October 1–2

The first two days are straightforward. Although technically no longer critical, activity 1 must still start October 1 or else delay the project. It uses only two units of A (40 percent) and two of C (50 percent). No other activity can start because 1 must finish first. Activity 1 proceeds with no resource contention until completion the next day.

October 3–5

Activity 2 starts because its predecessor finished. Although both it and activity 3 have the same Early Start, activity 2 is critical, so must start. It uses four units of A (80 percent) and two of C (50 percent). Now only one unit of A is available for activity 3, which requires two. Activity 3 must

therefore wait until 2 is finished with A on October 5. This is true even though resources B and C are available; unless all three are available in sufficient quantities, the activity cannot be scheduled and none can be used.

October 6–7

Once activity 2 completes on October 5, the correct resource combination (2 of A, 1 of B, and 2 of C) is finally available; activity 3 may start on October 6. Now only two units of B are available for activity 4, which requires all three. Activity 4 must wait until 3 is finished with B on October 10. This is true even though:

- Activity 4 is critical and should start October 6
- Resources A and C are available

Table 10-16   Resource Loading Table

```
--------------------------------------------------------------------------
RESOURCE LOADING TABLE                                    DATE: _____

PROJECT NAME:  LEVELED SEVEN-ACTIVITY, THREE-RESOURCE NETWORK_____
--------------------------------------------------------------------------
                                DAY
_____
ACT  1   2   3   4   5   6   7   8   9   10  11  12  13  14  15  16  17  18
     ABC ABC ABC ABC ABC ABC ABC ABC ABC ABC ABC ABC ABC ABC ABC ABC ABC ABC
  1  202 202
  2          402 402 402
  3          DELAY——————>212 212 212 212 212
  4                  DELAY————————————>231 231 231
  5                  211 211
  6                          DELAY————————————>422 422
  7                              DELAY————————————>313 313 313
--------------------------------------------------------------------------
TOTALS:
--------------------------------------------------------------------------
A:   2   2   4   4   4   4   4   2   2   2   2   2   2   4   4   3   3   3
B:   0   0   0   0   0   2   2   1   1   1   3   3   3   2   2   1   1   1
C:   2   2   2   2   2   3   3   2   2   2   1   1   1   2   2   3   3   3
--------------------------------------------------------------------------
PROBLEM DAYS:    NONE
--------------------------------------------------------------------------
```

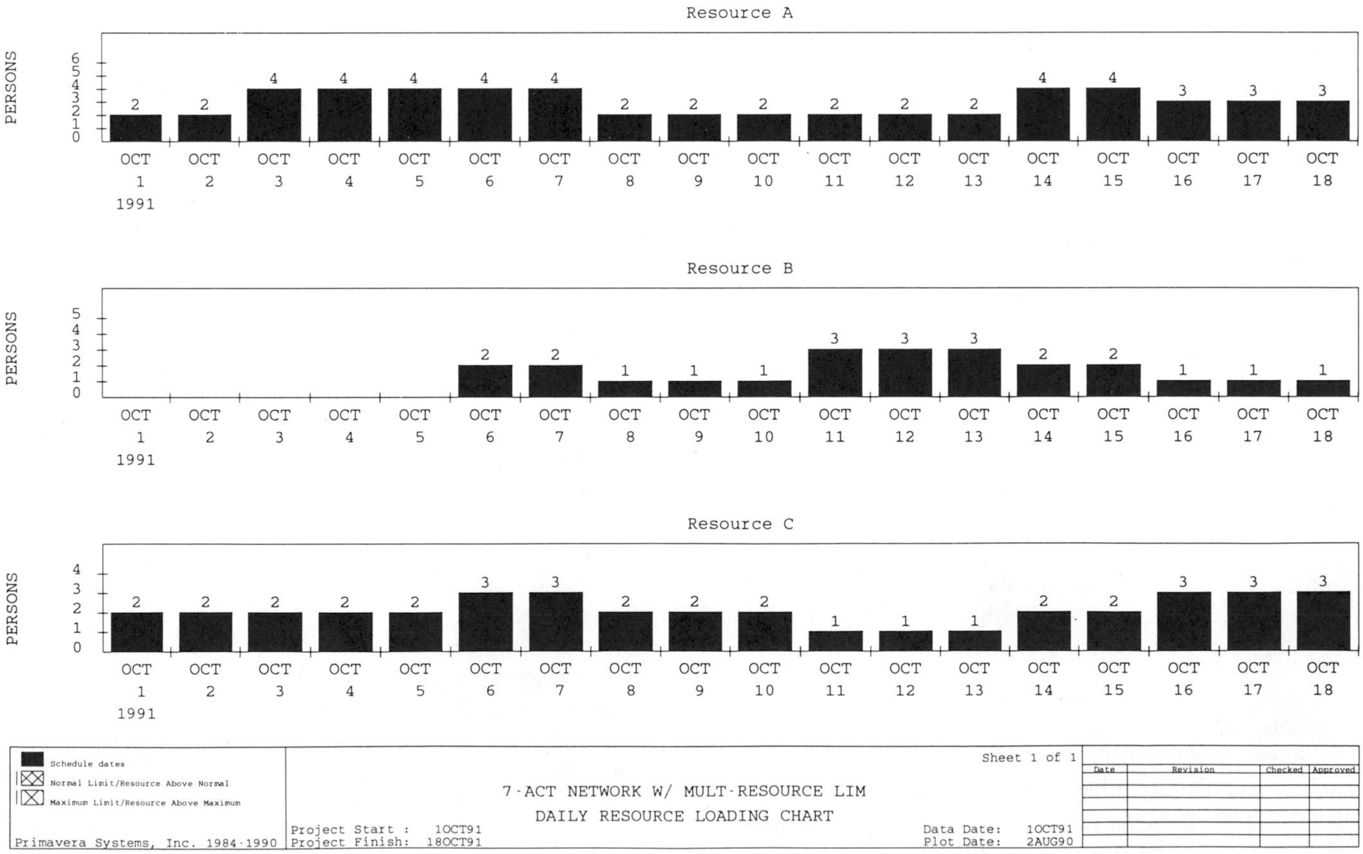

FIGURE 10-18.   Resource loading chart.

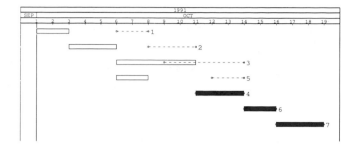

FIGURE 10-19.   Gantt Chart.

But activity 3 is already two days behind under the late schedule. Unless all three resources are available, the activity cannot be scheduled and none can be used. The unavailability of resource *B* proves costly to activity 4 and the entire project; it forces a five-day delay in each.

What about activity 5? It also wants to begin October 6 and use two units of *A* and one each of the others. Normally, activity 4 would have priority over activity 5 because of its earlier Late Start. But now activity 5 can:

- Take a very big advantage of the delay in activity 4
- Start without delay since all needed resources are available
- Finish on October 7 as originally scheduled

October 8–10
Activities 1, 2, and 5 have completed. Activity 3 is still underway and as before requires one unit of *B*. Since activity 4 requires the entire three-unit limit of *B*, it still cannot start until activity 3 is finished—even though activity 5 released its one unit of *B* to add to the other not utilized.

October 11–13
With activity 3 now finished, activity 4 can finally start, five days late, on October 11 and proceed until completion three days later. Activity 6 cannot start because:

- All predecessors (activities 3, 4, and 5) have not completed
- *A* and *B* resource requirements for activity 4 are too high

October 14–15
Activity 6 can finally start on October 14, also five days late, because activity 4 finishes the previous evening. But now activity 6 is only starting when the original schedule would have already ended. It proceeds until completion the next day.

October 16–18
Activity 7 finally begins on October 16, also five days late, with no resource contention (all other activities have completed) and finishes three days later.

Project Post-Audit

Recall project objectives:

- Comply with stated resource limits
- Minimize project length

The leveled schedule sometimes reaches, but never exceeds, these resource limits. It requires five extra days—no less. This represents a 38 percent time overrun and probably a similar cost overrun, too, when indirect costs are included. The big play of the game seems to be the five-day delay in activity 4, all for the want of just one more unit of *B* when needed. After October 5, there were only three days (activity 4) on which *B* demand equalled its availability. Somewhere, somehow, if we had only tried a little harder on October 6 . . .

Too many people would rather stage their own version of Custer's Last Stand than to admit they should have:

- Tried a little harder
- Never set or accepted an arbitrary resource limit
- Changed this limit when prudent

The solution is simply to apply resource limits that:

- Vary by need over time
- Use available resources more effectively

A contradiction? Not at all. Often additional resources may be borrowed from other projects or resource pools. Temporary help may also be available. At the same time, extra workers may be loaned out, when they are no longer needed by your project, to one that does, and so on. This maintains a high level of flexibility in the personnel pool, but requires three things to do this:

- Openmindedness by all concerned
- A commitment to use this arrangement both fairly and wisely
- The ability to establish and track variable resource levels

The normal resource limit is used during resource-constrained leveling to take advantage of network float. During leveling, activities may be delayed (to the leveled date) if they contain any (positive) float. If an activity cannot be scheduled without exceeding the normal resource limit, and without exhausting all of the float, the resource availability limit is then immediately moved to the maximum level previously defined for this resource and time frame. In effect, the normal limit is used on a "take-it-or-leave-it" basis.

Using the maximum resource limit, the activity may be leveled (scheduled to start) to any date between Early Start and Late Start if this (maximum) resource level is sufficient. If the activity still cannot be scheduled without inducing negative float:

- The activity will be considered leveled on its early dates (even though the schedule did not change)
- The overload condition will be indicated in the leveling analysis report

There is, however, no way the project end date can be maintained in this case unless additional resources are applied when and where needed; it will always slip. In the extreme case, the project might never be finished. Later, we shall determine how many resources must be applied, and when and where, to meet a given project deadline.

In resource-constrained environments, the normal and maximum resource limits are sometimes the same; this happens when the resource limitations are more important than the project end date. These limits (normal and maximum) should be set exactly at the level of resource availability. Then, anytime the limit is exceeded, the activities will be delayed until sufficient resources become available. *Primavera* will identify these activities as well as those that can never be scheduled under current resource limitations.

Note well: If there is no difficulty meeting given resource requirements, no matter how high, you:

- Do not have a leveling problem
- Should not try to create one!

RESOURCE SMOOTHING

You may, however, wish to smooth resource usage in order to reduce overall resource costs. In this case, set:

- The maximum resource limit a little higher than required to meet peaks
- The normal resource limit a little lower than actual

Smoothing gradually increases resource availability from normal level to maximum level in a series of smaller steps, rather than in one large jump (as is done with simple leveling). It nudges the availability ceiling upward a little at a time to see if "just a little more" would make it possible to schedule the activity. Smoothing is superior to simple leveling because it fine-tunes resource requirements. Straight leveling has no choice but to assign the maximum resource quantity if the normal quantity is insufficient; smoothing assigns only what is needed somewhere between these two values and is therefore less wasteful.

The difference between these two resource limits (normal and maximum) is divided by *Primavera* into ten equal increments. If the difference is too much, the resulting:

- Increments will be large
- Resource allocation profile will look choppy

If the difference is too little, the smoothing routine will:

- Have little flexibility
- Level the resource profile as though normal and maximum limits were the same, or very close to it

Primavera can level up to forty resources at a time in user-specified priority, with or without smoothing. Do not, however, level additional resources in subsequent leveling runs without first recalculating the schedule. In a manual

environment, recalculate the schedule after *each* resource is leveled or smoothed.

The previous example, of course, cannot be smoothed because there is no difference between the normal and the maximum resource limits. But the leveled schedule may still be shortened by judicious application of extra resources.

Recall from the leveling analysis report (Table 10-15) the five-day delay in activity 4. A one-unit shortage in resource *B* delayed the start of activity 4 from October 6 to October 11.

Providing one more unit of resource *B* from October 6 through October 8 (while activity 3 is underway) would allow activity 4 to start and would also shorten project length three days (Fig. 10-20).

Now activity 3 wants to return to its original Early Start on October 3. When given the one unit of resource *A* needed, the project ends October 14 (Fig. 10-21).

Next, activity 5 wants one more unit each of resources *A* and *B* to return to its October 6 Early Start. Without significant changes elsewhere, this premium application would (much like all-crash) be wasted. The project end date remains October 14. This (Figs. 10-22, 10-23, and 10-24) is the best we can do in the absence of cost information. If, however, strict resource-limit compliance was required, we would leave our original eighteen-day schedule intact.

Finally, recall that some project management tools (including *P3*) allow interruptible activity durations and resource lags. This offers a more flexible scheduling method because work can be, as it often is, interrupted. It can also provide, in networks more complex than the example just

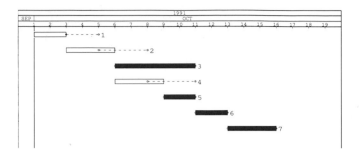

FIGURE 10-20.   Gantt Chart.

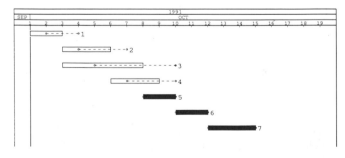

FIGURE 10-21.   Gantt Chart.

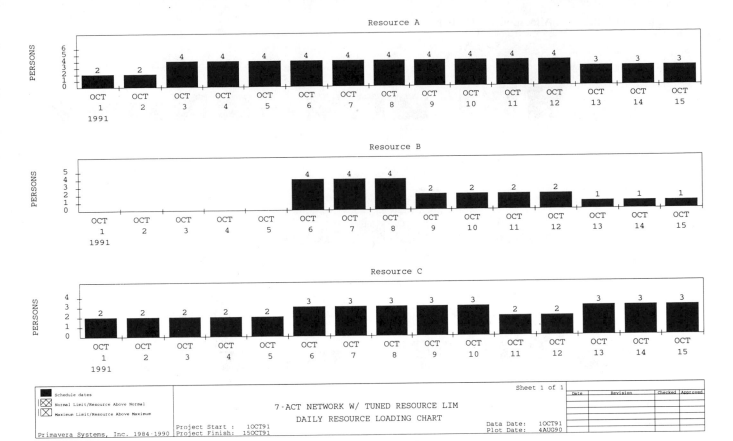

FIGURE 10-22. Resource loading chart (fix 1).

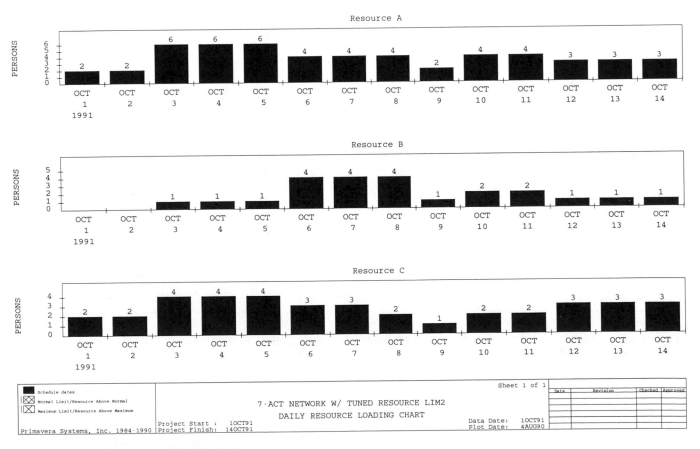

FIGURE 10-23. Resource loading chart (fix 2).

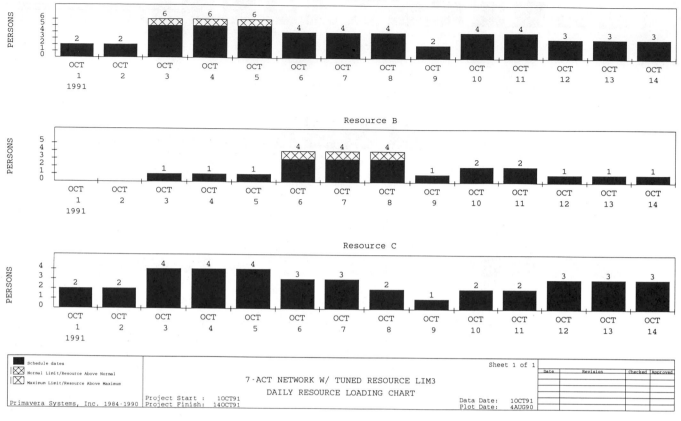

FIGURE 10-24.   Resource loading chart (fix 3).

worked, a more compact schedule. Using the same rules as before, the eighteen-day leveled schedule is reduced, first, to fifteen days, then to fourteen days. Unlike the previous (contiguous) schedule, however, the next iteration returns the network to the unleveled thirteen-day baseline. The real benefits of interruptible scheduling become apparent only in longer, more complex networks.

Judicious application of extra resources reduced project duration four days, from eighteen to fourteen days. The key is to apply extra resources only where they are really needed.

Multiple Calendars

The preceding rules also apply to multiple-calendar projects. Suppose the same seven-activity, three-resource project were performed instead in the familiar two-calendar environment. Let activities 1, 2, and 5 be performed under Calendar 1 and the others be performed under Calendar 2. If no resource limits are applied, the baseline schedule would be as shown in Table 10-17.

Figure 10-25 is in bar chart format.

Table 10-17   Schedule Summary

```
----------------------------------------------------------------------------------
SCHEDULE SUMMARY                                      DATE: _____

PROJECT NAME:   2-CALENDAR, 7-ACTIVITY, 3-RESOURCE NETWORK (BASELINE)_____
----------------------------------------------------------------------------------
```

ACTIVITY ID/CAL		ORIG DUR	REM DUR	% DONE	EARLY START	EARLY FINISH	LATE START	LATE FINISH	TOTAL FLOAT
1	1	2	2	0	18DEC91	19DEC91	26DEC91	27DEC91	6
2	1	3	3	0	20DEC91	23DEC91	28DEC91	31DEC91	6
3	2	5	5	0	20DEC91	30DEC91	30DEC91	6JAN92	4
4	2	3	3	0	26DEC91	30DEC91	2JAN92	6JAN92	4
5	1	2	2	0	24DEC91	26DEC91	4JAN92	6JAN92	8
6	2	2	2	0	31DEC91	2JAN92	7JAN92	8JAN92	4
7	2	3	3	0	3JAN92	7JAN92	9JAN92	13JAN92	4

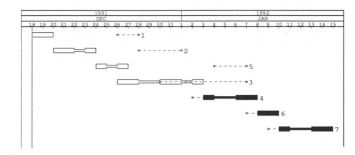

FIGURE 10-25.   Gantt Chart.

FIGURE 10-26.   Gantt Chart.

Table 10-18   Resource Leveling Analysis Report

```
---------------------------------------------------------------------------
RESOURCE LEVELING ANALYSIS REPORT                    DATE: _____

PROJECT NAME:  LEVELED 2-CALENDAR, 7-ACTIVITY, 3-RESOURCE NETWORK_____
---------------------------------------------------------------------------
```

ACT/CAL RESOURCE	DAILY USAGE	TF	EARLY START NORM	MAX	DELAYED BY DATE	TF	PRED OR RES NORM	MAX	LEVELED START	FINISH
1 1 Activity 1		6							18DEC91	19DEC91
A	2.00	6	5.00	5.00					18DEC91	19DEC91
C	2.00	6	4.00	4.00					18DEC91	19DEC91
2 1 Activity 2		6							20DEC91	23DEC91
A	4.00	6	5.00	5.00					20DEC91	23DEC91
C	2.00	6	4.00	4.00					20DEC91	23DEC91
3 2 Activity 3		4			26DEC91	2			26DEC91	2JAN92
A	2.00	4	1.00	1.00	26DEC91	2	5.00	5.00	26DEC91	2JAN92
B	1.00	4	3.00	3.00	26DEC91	2	3.00	3.00	26DEC91	2JAN92
C	2.00	4	2.00	2.00	26DEC91	2	4.00	4.00	26DEC91	2JAN92
4 2 Activity 4		4			3JAN92	-1			3JAN92	7JAN92
A	2.00	4	3.00	3.00	3JAN92	-1	5.00	5.00	3JAN92	7JAN92
B	3.00	4	2.00	2.00	3JAN92	-1	3.00	3.00	3JAN92	7JAN92
C	1.00	4	2.00	2.00	3JAN92	-1	4.00	4.00	3JAN92	7JAN92
5 1 Activity 5		8							24DEC91	26DEC91
A	2.00	8	5.00	5.00					24DEC91	26DEC91
B	1.00	8	3.00	3.00					24DEC91	26DEC91
C	1.00	8	4.00	4.00					24DEC91	26DEC91
6 2 Activity 6		4			8JAN92	-1			8JAN92	9JAN92
A	4.00	4	3.00	3.00	8JAN92	-1	5.00	5.00	8JAN92	9JAN92
B	2.00	4	2.00	2.00	8JAN92	-1	3.00	3.00	8JAN92	9JAN92
C	2.00	4	2.00	2.00	8JAN92	-1	4.00	4.00	8JAN92	9JAN92
7 2 Activity 7		4			10JAN92	-1			10JAN92	14JAN92
A	3.00	4	3.00	3.00	10JAN92	-1	5.00	5.00	10JAN92	14JAN92
B	1.00	4	.00	.00	10JAN92	-1	3.00	3.00	10JAN92	14JAN92
C	3.00	4	3.00	3.00	10JAN92	-1	4.00	4.00	10JAN92	14JAN92

```
---------------------------------------------------------------------------
```

Because of extensive "calendar catch-up," no activity under either calendar is without float. The Critical Path is but a wandering trail. If the project begins December 18, it should finish sometime between January 7 and January 13. It could start as late as December 26 and still finish by then.

Now suppose the same resource limits as before (5-3-4) are applied to resources *A, B,* and *C.* In both the early and the late schedules, there are three days on which *A* exceeds its limit by one unit, two days on which *B* exceeds its limit by one unit, and one day on which *B* exceeds its limit by two units. Resource *C* is within limits on all days, as before. When leveled using interruptible activities and the parallel allocation method, only one day is added to the original unconstrained (late) schedule (Table 10-18).

Figure 10-26 is in bar chart format.

The baseline and leveled daily resource loading charts are presented in Figs. 10-27 and 10-28.

A sample Project HOME resource profile is provided in Tables 10-19 and 10-20 (cumulative values are presented in Table 10-21). Appreciate the great value of such reports! They warn—up to *eighty-eight years* in advance—of impending resource shortages that could delay your project. This warning allows you plenty of time to take appropriate action:

- Hire or borrow extra personnel
- Schedule overtime
- Raise the approved resource limits
- Delay project completion by accepting given resource limits

Table 10-19, for example, clearly warns in early February 1983 of impending plumber shortages in May and June 1984. Not all activities requiring plumbers will get done. The project manager must decide what to do about this but fortunately has:

- Fifteen months
- A whole portfolio of other analytical reports

This indicated analysis should include all resources, across all activities, not just plumbers in the spring of 1984. Suppose for simplicity, though, that we leveled only plumbers. The resulting reports (Tables 10-22 through 10-24) show that we can comply with the seven-plumber limit *only* if the project is delayed five workdays (note the five days negative float), to finish September 13 instead of September 6.

The resulting resource loading and (leveled) Gantt Charts are presented in Figures 10-29 through 10-31.

No further reductions are possible without extending the

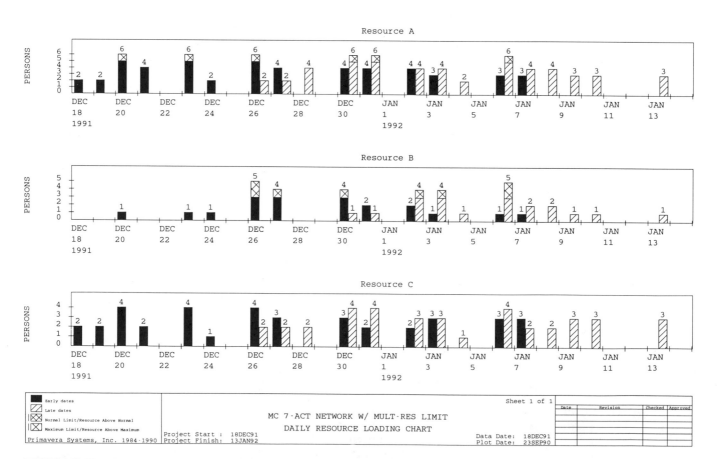

FIGURE 10-27.   Resource loading chart (baseline).

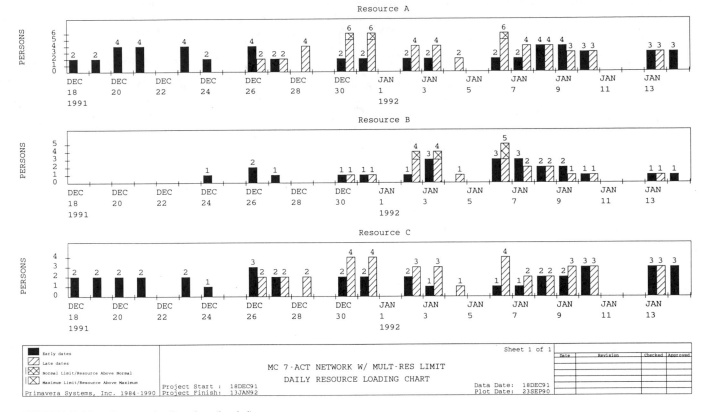

FIGURE 10-28.   Resource loading chart (leveled).

project beyond September 6. Unless we raise the maximum availability level these three weeks and find more plumbers:

- Not all plumbing work will get done
- The project will be delayed accordingly
- You will get chewed out by the boss, and by your customer

No, NO, **NO**!!! You should know by now:

- Things don't always go according to desired plan
- A winner never quits—and a quitter never wins (Fig. 10-32)

When you're ahead, don't let up—and when you're behind, don't give up. Instead, we need to determine the cost of acquiring additional temporary resources during these three weeks and compare this cost with the financial benefits of earlier project completion. When we do, we must also evaluate the impact that other "super-short" resources will have on project schedule and cost. Under the circumstances, the prudent course of action would be to hire extra plumbers for those thirteen days.

TWO USEFUL INDICES

Let us now set up another, slightly longer, example, as shown in Table 10-25, and in bar chart format (Fig. 10-33).

Daily and cumulative requirements for resources X and

Y are shown in Figs. 10-34 through 10-37. These (right-axis) cumulative requirements curves may be used to:

- Schedule activities
- Plan, track, and control resources

This may be done before and during project implementation. After the project has started, actual cumulative resource usage and forecasted requirements should always lie within the closed area bounded by the:

- Early-schedule curve (always on top)
- Late-schedule curve (always on bottom)

If actual cumulative resource usage falls below the LS curve, then:

- The project is behind schedule
- Resource requirements were overestimated
- Both

Conversely, if it exceeds the ES curve, then:

- The project is ahead of schedule
- Resource requirements were underestimated
- Both

Use these curves to plan resource quantities and timing. Resource critically is indicated by the total magnitude and by the average-usage slope.

The cumulative eighteen-day total for resource X is 111 units. This is true regardless of whether the early, the late,

Table 10-19 Daily Resource Usage (Actual and Forecast) and Availability by Resource

```
-------------------------------------------------------------------------------------------------------
AMERICAN COMMUNITY DEVELOPERS, INC.          PRIMAVERA PROJECT PLANNER          BRIAN'S DUPLICATE OF PROJECT "HOME"

REPORT DATE  12FEB83  RUN NO.   12           RESOURCE PROFILE                  START DATE 13DEC82  FIN DATE  6SEP84

DAILY RESOURCE USAGE (ACTUAL AND FORECAST) AND AVAILABILITY BY RESOURCE        DATA DATE   1FEB83  PAGE NO.    1
-------------------------------------------------------------------------------------------------------
RESOURCE: PLUMBERS
         16.........
            ..       .      .      .      .      .      .      .      .     .|----------------------------------------
            ..       .      .      .      .      .      .      .      .     .|       PRIMAVERA PROJECT PLANNER
            ..       .      .   .----21 May 1984    .      .      .      .  .|
            ..       .      .      |      .      .      .      .      .     .| RESOURCE/COST PROFILE AND CUMULATIVE CURVE
  P      14.........................|...................................... .|
  E         ..       .      .      |      .      .      .      .      .     .|              LEGEND
  R         ..       .      .      |      .      .      .      .      .     .|
  S         ..       .      .  EEEEE  .    .----6 June 1984   .      .      .|------------------------------------------
  O         ..       .      .  EEEEE  .      .|     .      .      .      .   .|
  N      12.................EEEEE...........|.....................................| E - BASED ON EARLY SCHEDULE
  |         ..       .      .  EEEEE  .      .|     .      .      .      .   .|
  D         ..       .      .  EEEEE  .      .|     .      .      .      .   .| L - BASED ON LATE SCHEDULE
  A         ..       .      .  EEEEE  .      .|     .      .      .      .   .|
  Y         ..       .      .  EEEEE  .      .|     .      .      .      .   .| A - ACTUAL DATES
  S      10.................EEEEE..EEEEE..EEE..........................| 
            ..       .      .  EEEEE  EEEEE  EEE    .      .      .      .   .| - - NORMAL AVAILABILITY
            ..       .      .  EEEEE  EEEEE  EEE    .      .      .      .   .|
            ..       .      .  EEEEE  EEEEE  EEE    .      .      .      .   .| = - MAXIMUM AVAILABILITY
            ..       .      .  EEEEE  EEEEE  EEE    .      .      .      .   .|
          8.................EEEEE..EEEEE..EEE...........................| / - WHERE TWO OR MORE CURVES INTERSECT
            ..       .      .  EEEEE  EEEEE  EEE    .      .      .      .   .|
            ..       .      .  EEEEE  EEEEE  EEE    .      .      .      .   .| T - BASED ON TARGET 1 SCHEDULE
          7 ====================EEEEE==EEEEE==EEE=================================|
            ..       .      .  EEEEE  EEEEE  EEE    .      .      .      .   .| * - DATA DATE
          6.................EEEEE..EEEEE..EEE...........................|
            ..       .      .  EEEEE  EEEEE  EEE    .      .      .      .   .| V - BASED ON RESOURCE-LEVELED SCHEDULE
            ..       .      .  EEEEE  EEEEE  EEE    .      .      .      .   .|
          5 ----------------EEEEE--EEEEE--EEE----------------------------|
            ..       .      .  EEEEE  EEEEE  EEE    .      .      .      .   .
          4.................EEEEE..EEEEE..EEE...........................
            ..       .      .  EEEEE  EEEEE  EEE    .      .      .      .   .      .      .      .      .
            ..       .      .  EEEEE  EEEEE  EEE    .      .      .      .   .      .      .      .      .
            ..       .      .  EEEEE  EEEEE  EEE    .      .      .      .   .      .      .      .      .
            ..       .      .  EEEEE  EEEEE  EEE    .      .      .      .   .      .      .      .      .
          2.................EEEEE..EEEEE..EEE...........................
            ..       .      .  EEEEE  EEEEE  EEE    .      .      .      .   .      .      .      .      . E  EEEEE
            ..       .      .  EEEEE  EEEEE  EEE    .      .      .      .   .      .      .      .      . E  EEEEE
            ..       .      .  EEEEE  EEEEE  EEE    .      .      .      .   .      .      .      .      . E  EEEEE
            ..       .      .  EEEEE  EEEEE  EEE    .      .      .      .   .      .      .      .      . E  EEEEE
          0.................EEEEE..EEEEE..EEE...............................................E..EEEEE.
            30     07     14     21     28     04     11     18     25     02     09     16     23     30     06     13     20
            APR    MAY    MAY    MAY    MAY    JUN    JUN    JUN    JUN    JUL    JUL    JUL    JUL    JUL    AUG    AUG    AUG
            84     84     84     84     84     84     84     84     84     84     84     84     84     84     84     84     84
```

Table 10-20   Resource Loading Report by Week, by Activity

```
-------------------------------------------------------------------------------------------------------------------
AMERICAN COMMUNITY DEVELOPERS, INC.        PRIMAVERA PROJECT PLANNER         BRIAN'S DUPLICATE OF PROJECT "HOME"


REPORT DATE 12FEB83  RUN NO.   13          RESOURCE LOADING REPORT           START DATE 13DEC82 FIN DATE  6SEP84


RESOURCE LOADING REPORT BY WEEK, BY ACTIVITY   TOTAL USAGE FOR WEEK BEGINNING      DATA DATE   1FEB83  PAGE NO.   1
-------------------------------------------------------------------------------------------------------------------

ACTIVITY   ACTIVITY DESCRIPTION                                             20MAY 21MAY 22MAY 23MAY 24MAY 25MAY 26MAY
   ID                                                                       1984  1984  1984  1984  1984  1984  1984
----- -----  ------------------------------------------------------------   ----- ----- ----- ----- ----- ----- -----

PLUMBERS                                           UNITS = PERSON-DAY


     5  PLUMBING-STREET CONNECTION AND UNDERSLAB
    52  INSTALL TUB, STACK OUT PLUMBING
   117  SET APPLIANCES                                                        3     3     3     3     3
   118  PLUMBING CONNECTIONS AND TRIMOUT                                     10    10    10    10    10
   144  PUNCH LIST
----- -----                                                                 ----- ----- ----- ----- ----- ----- -----

*** TOTAL PLUMBERS ***                                                       13    13    13    13    13
===================================================================================================================
```

Table 10-21   Cumulative Weekly Resource Usage (Actual and Forecast) by Resource

```
-------------------------------------------------------------------------------------------------------------------
AMERICAN COMMUNITY DEVELOPERS, INC.        PRIMAVERA PROJECT PLANNER         BRIAN'S DUPLICATE OF PROJECT "HOME"


REPORT DATE  12FEB83  RUN NO.   14         RESOURCE CUMULATIVE CURVE         START DATE 13DEC82 FIN DATE  6SEP84


CUMULATIVE WEEKLY RESOURCE USAGE (ACTUAL AND FORECAST) BY RESOURCE           DATA DATE   1FEB83  PAGE NO.   1
-------------------------------------------------------------------------------------------------------------------

RESOURCE: PLUMBERS
C     250..........*.....................................................................................................
U      ..  .  *.  .  .  .  .  .  .  .  .  .  .  .  .  .  .  .  .  .  .  .  .  .  .  *  .  .  .  .  .  .  .  .  .  .  .
M      ..  .  *.  .  .  .  .  .  .  .  .  .  .  .  .  .  .  .  .  .  .  .  .  .  .  *  .  .  .  .  .  .  .  .  .  .  .
U      ..  .  *.  .  .  .  .  .  .  .  .  .  .  .  .  .  .  .  .  .  .  .  .  .  .  *  .  .  .  . ./////////////////////
L      ..  .  *.  .  .  .  .  .  .  .  .  .  .  .  .  .  .  .  .  .  .  .  .  .  .  *  .  .  .  ./ .  .  .  .  .  .  .
A     200..........*.......................................................................////////////TTTTTTTTTTTTTTTTTTTTTTTTTTTTTTTTTTT
T      ..  .  *.  .  .  .  .  .  .  .  .  .  .  .  .  .  .  .  .  .  .  .  .  .  .  L.  .  T  .  .  .  .  .  .  .  .
I      ..  .  *.  .  .  .  .  .  .  .  .  .  .  .  .  .  .  .  .  .  .  .  .  .  .  TTTTTTTTTTT.  .  .  .  .  .  .  .
V      ..  .  *.  .  .  .  .  .  .  .  .  .  .  .  .  .  .  .  .  .  .  .  .  .  .  E.  .  .  .  .  .  .  .  .  .  .
E      ..  .  *.  .  .  .  .  .  .  .  .  .  .  .  .  .  .  .  .  .  .  .  .  .  .  T  .  .  .  .  .  .  .  .  .  .
      150..........*.......................................................................................................
P      ..  .  *.  .  .  .  .  .  .  .  .  .  .  .  .  .  .  .  .  .  .  .  .  .  .  .  .  .  .  .  .  .  .  .  .  .
E      ..  .  *.  .  .  .  .  .  .  .  .  .  .  .  .  .  .  .  .  .  .  .  .  .  .  L.  .  .  .  .  .  .  .  .  .
R      ..  .  *.  .  .  .  .  .  .  .  .  .  .  .  .  .  .  .  .  .  .  .  .  .  .  .  .  .  .  .  .  .  .  .  .
S      ..  .  *.  .  .  .  .  .  .  .  .  .  .  .  .  .  .  .  .  .  .  .  .  .  .  .TE  .  .  .  .  .  .  .  .  .
O     100..........*.......................................................................................................
N      ..  .  *.  .  .  .  .  .  .  .  .  .  .  .  .  .  .  .  .  .  .  .  .  .  .  .  .  .  .  .  .  .  .  .  .  .
|      ..  .  *.  .  .  .  .  .  .  .  .  .  .  .  .  .  .  .  .  .  .  .  .  .  .  .L  .  .  .  .  .  .  .  .  .  .
D      ..  .  *.  .  .  .  .  .  .  .  .  .  .  .  .  .  .  .  .  .  .  .  .  .  .  .  .  .  .  .  .  .  .  .  .  .
A      ..  .  *.  .  .  .  .  .  .  .  .  .  .  .  .  .  .  .  .  .  .  .  .  .  .  T  .  .  .  .  .  .  .  .  .  .
Y      50..........*..........T7//////////////////////////////////////////////////E....................................
S      ..  .  *.  .  .  .  .  .  .  .  .  .  .  .  .  .  .  .  .  .  .  .  .  .  .  .  .  .  .  .  .  .  .  .  .  .
      ..  .  TT///////////////LLLLLLLLLLLLL  .  .  .  .  .  .  .  .  .  .  .  .  .  .  .  .  .  .  .  .  .  .  .  .
      ..  .  *.  .  .  .  .  .  .  .  .  .  .  .  .  .  .  .  .  .  .  .  .  .  .  .  .  .  .  .  .  .  .  .  .  .
      ..  .T *.  .  .  .  .  .  .  .  .  .  .  .  .  .  .  .  .  .  .  .  .  .  .  .  .  .  .  .  .  .  .  .  .  .
       0..........*.......................................................................................................

        06  03  07  07  04  02  06  04  01  05  03  07  05  02  06  05  02  07  04  02  06  03  01  05  03  07  04
       DEC JAN FEB MAR APR MAY JUN JUL AUG SEP OCT NOV DEC JAN FEB MAR APR MAY JUN JUL AUG SEP OCT NOV DEC JAN FEB
       82  83  83  83  83  83  83  83  83  83  83  83  83  84  84  84  84  84  84  84  84  84  84  84  84  85  85
```

Table 10-22   Results of Leveling Resource "Plumbers" by Late Start, by Total Float

```
-----------------------------------------------------------------------------------------------------------------
AMERICAN COMMUNITY DEVELOPERS, INC.            PRIMAVERA PROJECT PLANNER              BRIAN'S DUPLICATE OF PROJECT "HOME"

REPORT DATE 12FEB83  RUN NO.  13L          RESOURCE LEVELING ANALYSIS REPORT          START DATE 13DEC82 FIN DATE  6SEP84

RESULTS OF LEVELING RESOURCE "PLUMBERS" BY LATE START, BY TOTAL FLOAT          DATA DATE  1FEB83  PAGE NO.   1
    USING PROGRESS OVERRIDE AND INTERRUPTIBLE ACTIVITIES
-----------------------------------------------------------------------------------------------------------------
            CAL     DAILY RES REM --------EARLY START------- ------DELAYED BY PRED----- ------DELAYED BY RES.-----    LEVELED
ACTIVITY ID RESOURCE USAGE LAG DUR  DATE   TF  NORM   MAX    DATE   TF  NORM   MAX    DATE   TF  NORM   MAX   START   FINISH
---------- -------- ----- --- --- ------ ---- ------ ------ ------ ---- ------ ------ ------ ---- ------ ------ ------- -------
***** WARNING:  THE FOLLOWING ACTIVITY COULD NOT BE SCHEDULED WITHIN RESOURCE LIMITS
      5  1 PLUMBING-STREET   3 1FEB83  -20                                                                 1FEB83  3FEB83
         PLUMBERS 11.67      3 1FEB83  -20  5.00   7.00                                                    1FEB83  3FEB83

     52  1 INSTALL TUB, STA  4 17MAY83  56                                                                 17MAY83 20MAY83
         PLUMBERS  5.00      4 17MAY83  56  5.00   7.00                                                    17MAY83 20MAY83

***** WARNING:  THE FOLLOWING ACTIVITY COULD NOT BE SCHEDULED WITHIN RESOURCE LIMITS
    118  1 PLUMBING CONNECT 13 21MAY84  -3                                                                 21MAY84  6JUN84
         PLUMBERS 10.23     13 21MAY84  -3  5.00   7.00                                                    21MAY84  6JUN84

    117  1 SET APPLIANCES    5 21MAY84   8                              7JUN84  -5                          7JUN84 13JUN84
         PLUMBERS  2.60      5 21MAY84   8   .00    .00                 7JUN84  -5  5.00   7.00  7JUN84 13JUN84

    144  1 PUNCH LIST       10 17AUG84   0           24AUG84  -5                                            24AUG84  6SEP84
         PLUMBERS  2.00     10 17AUG84   0  5.00   7.00 24AUG84  -5  5.00   7.00                            24AUG84  6SEP84

         **************************** LATEST CALCULATED EF AFTER LEVELING WITH SMOOTHING........13SEP84 ****************************
=================================================================================================================
```

Table 10-23   Leveled Project Schedule Sorted by Early Start and Total Float

```
-----------------------------------------------------------------------------------------------------------------
AMERICAN COMMUNITY DEVELOPERS, INC.            PRIMAVERA PROJECT PLANNER              BRIAN'S DUPLICATE OF PROJECT "HOME"

REPORT DATE 12FEB83  RUN NO.   1L              PROJECT SCHEDULE                       START DATE 13DEC82 FIN DATE  6SEP84

LEVELED PROJECT SCHEDULE SORTED BY EARLY START AND TOTAL FLOAT                  DATA DATE  1FEB83  PAGE NO.   1
----- -----  ---- ---- - ---  ----------------------------------------  -------- -------- -------- -------- -----
ACTIVITY   ORIG REM                        ACTIVITY DESCRIPTION           LEVELED  LEVELED   LATE     LATE   TOTAL
   ID      DUR  DUR   %                                                    START   FINISH    START   FINISH  FLOAT
----- -----  ---- ---- - ---  ----------------------------------------  -------- -------- -------- -------- -----
      118    13   13  0       PLUMBING CONNECTIONS AND TRIMOUT           21MAY84   6JUN84  16MAY84  1JUN84*    -3
      119    12   12  0       ELECTRICAL CONNECTIONS AND TRIMOUT          5JUN84  20JUN84  29MAY84 13JUN84     -5
      117     5    5  0       SET APPLIANCES                              7JUN84  13JUN84  31MAY84  6JUN84     -5
      123     5    5  0       BATHROOM ACCESSORIES                        7JUN84  13JUN84   7JUN84 13JUN84      0
      128    10   10  0       CLEAN UP                                   21JUN84   5JUL84  14JUN84 27JUN84     -5
      136     5    5  0       PAINT TOUCH UP                              6JUL84  12JUL84  28JUN84  5JUL84     -5
      138    15   15  0       INSTALL CARPETING                          13JUL84   2AUG84   6JUL84 26JUL84     -5
      140     5    5  0       INSTALL DRAPES                              3AUG84   9AUG84  27JUL84  2AUG84     -5
      142    10   10  0       CLEAN UP                                   10AUG84  23AUG84   3AUG84 16AUG84     -5
      144    10   10  0       PUNCH LIST                                 24AUG84   6SEP84  17AUG84 30AUG84     -5
      146     5    5  0       BUILDING COMPLETE                           7SEP84  13SEP84  31AUG84  6SEP84     -5
```

Table 10-24   Turnaround Document

```
------------------------------------------------------------------------------------------------------------------------
AMERICAN COMMUNITY DEVELOPERS, INC.        PRIMAVERA PROJECT PLANNER         BRIAN'S DUPLICATE OF PROJECT "HOME"

REPORT DATE  12FEB83  RUN NO.    8L        PROJECT SCHEDULE                  START DATE 13DEC82  FIN DATE  6SEP84

TURNAROUND DOCUMENT                                                         DATA DATE   1FEB83  PAGE NO.    1
```

PLUMBER

ACTIVITY ID	ORIG DUR	REM DUR	%	CODE	ACTIVITY DESCRIPTION	LEVELED START	LEVELED FINISH	LATE START	LATE FINISH	TOTAL FLOAT
5	8	3	62	301	PLUMBING-STREET CONNECTION AND UNDERSLAB	24JAN83A	3FEB83		6JAN83	-20
52	4	4	0	302	INSTALL TUB, STACK OUT PLUMBING	17MAY83	20MAY83	5AUG83	10AUG83	56
118	13	13	0	303	PLUMBING CONNECTIONS AND TRIMOUT	21MAY84	6JUN84	16MAY84	1JUN84*	-3
117	5	5	0	303	SET APPLIANCES	7JUN84	13JUN84	31MAY84	6JUN84	-5

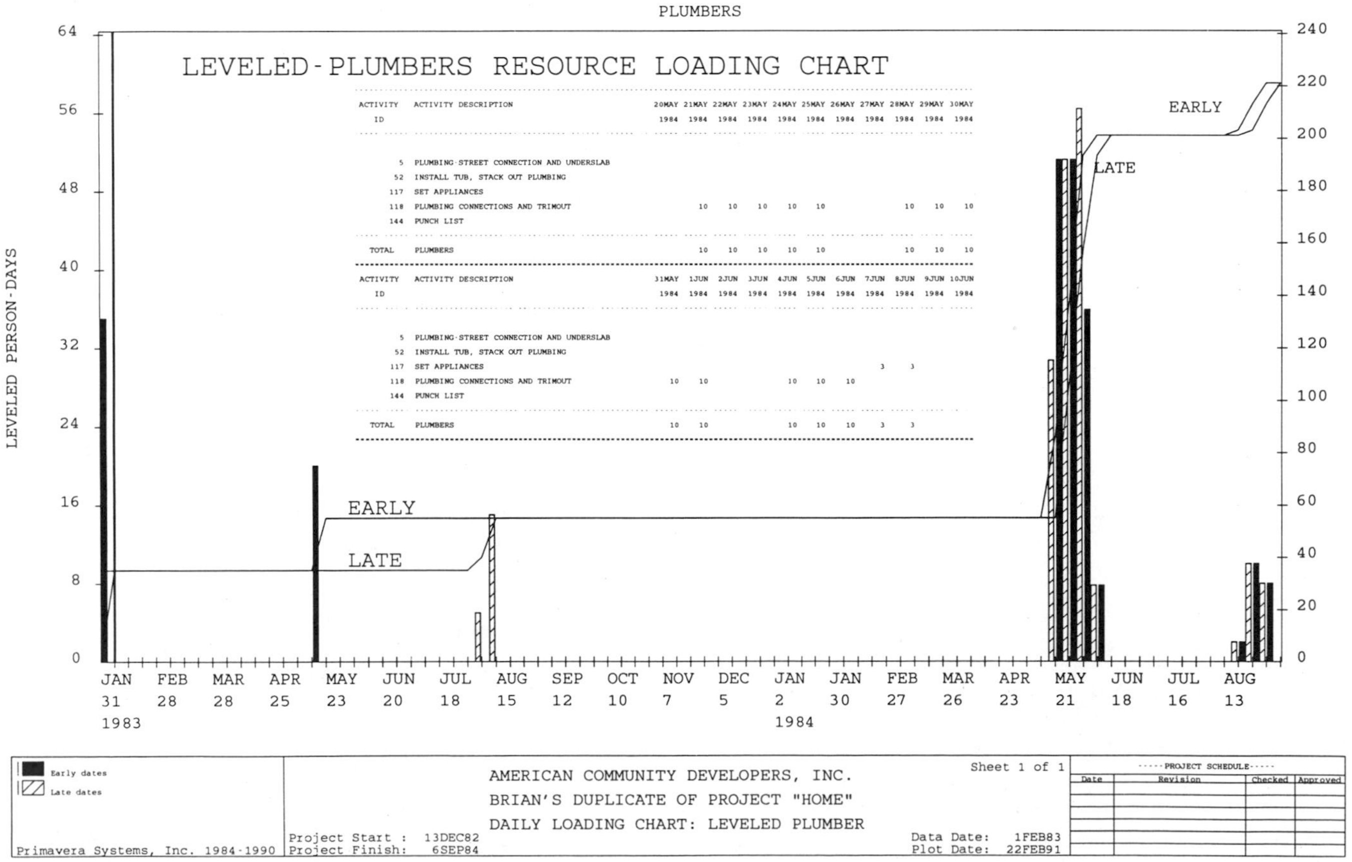

FIGURE 10-29.   Leveled HOME resource loading chart (plumbers).

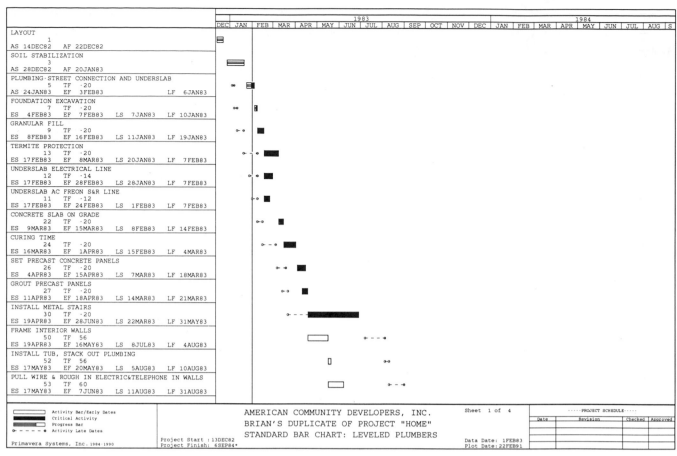

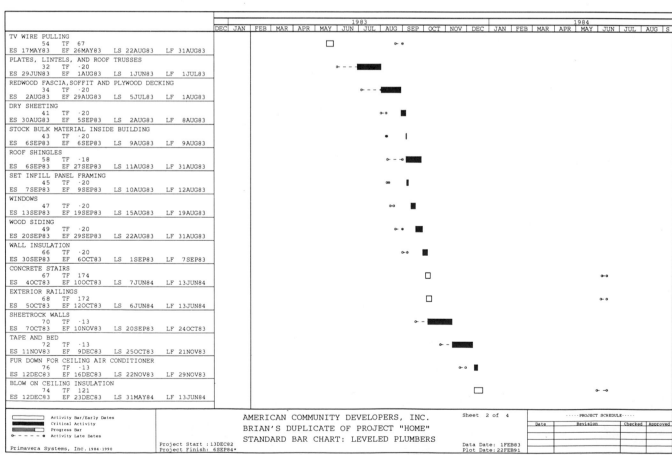

FIGURE 10-30. Leveled HOME Gantt Chart with detail for activity 117 on.

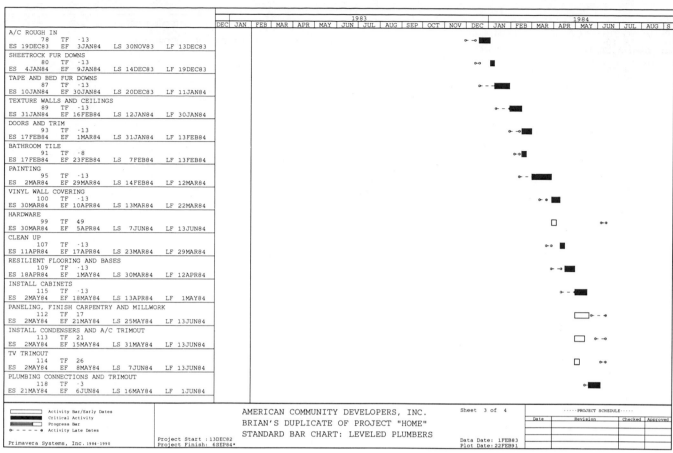

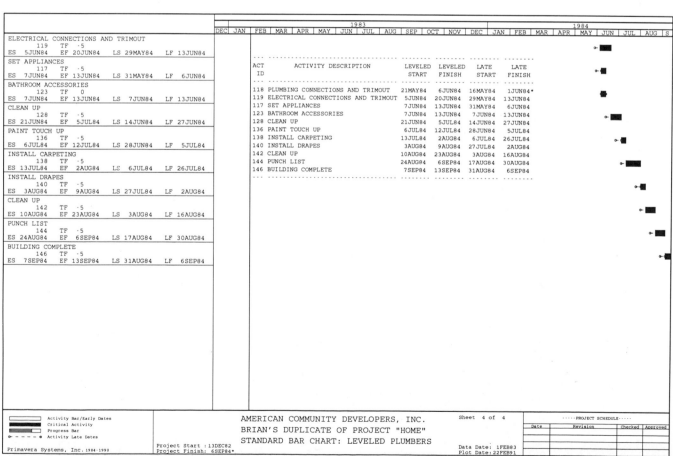

FIGURE 10-30. Continued

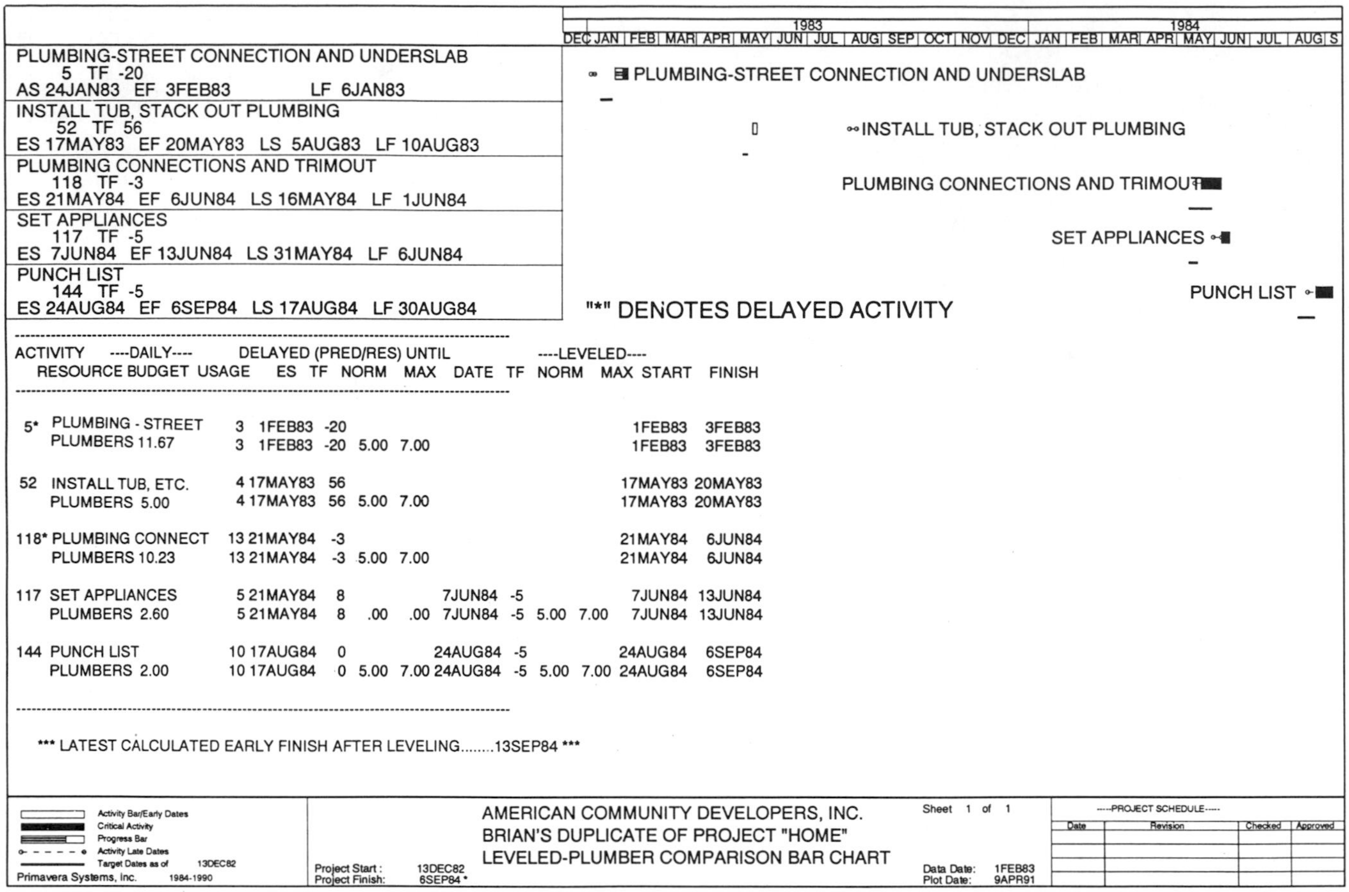

FIGURE 10-31. Leveled HOME Gantt target-comparison chart.

Table 10-25 Schedule Setup

```
------------------------------------------------------------------------
SCHEDULE SETUP                              DATE: _____

PROJECT NAME:  ELEVEN-ACTIVITY NETWORK WITH DUAL-RESOURCE CONSTRAINTS_____
               MODER, PHILLIPS, AND DAVIS (AUTHORS)
------------------------------------------------------------------------
```

ACTIVITY ID	DUR (DAYS)	PREDECESSOR/ RELATIONSHIP		SUCCESSOR/ RELATIONSHIP		REQUIRED RESOURCES X	Y
0	0	None		A	F/S	Milestone; none	
				B	F/S		
A	3	0	F/S	C	F/S	3	2
				D	F/S		
B	5	0	F/S	G	F/S	2	4
C	6	A	F/S	I	F/S	3	1
D	2	A	F/S	E	F/S	4	3
				F	F/S		
E	3	D	F/S	J	F/S	2	0
F	3	D	F/S	H	F/S	1	1
G	4	B	F/S	H	F/S	3	1
H	5	F	F/S	T	F/S	2	2
		G	F/S				
I	4	C	F/S	J	F/S	3	2
J	2	E	F/S	K	F/S	4	1
		I	F/S				
K	3	J	F/S	T	F/S	5	4
T	0	H	F/S	None		Milestone; none	
		K	F/S				

FIGURE 10-32. "I don't wanna play anymore!" *Source:* Fujikawa, Gyo, *Let's Play,* Zokeisha Publications, Ltd., Japan, 1975.

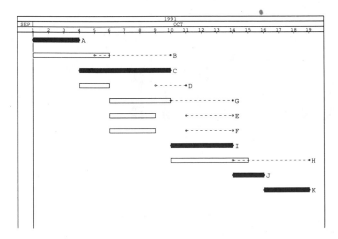

FIGURE 10-33. Gantt Chart.

or an intermediate schedule is used—although each schedule would have different values along the way. This total may be divided by project length to compute the average daily requirement:

$$\text{Average daily requirement} = \frac{\text{Total quantity needed}}{\text{Project length}}$$

$$= \frac{111 \text{ total units}}{18 \text{ days}}$$

$$= 6.17 \text{ units/day}$$

Now suppose resource X is available at a maximum level of seven units per day. In this case, a total of 126 units ($= 18 * 7$) could be expended, if necessary, over the 18 project days. Since only 111 are actually required, it seems unlikely that shortages of X would delay the project. The *Criticality Index,* the ratio of required to available resources, also supports this conclusion:

$$\text{Criticality index} = \frac{\text{Average daily units required}}{\text{Maximum daily amount available}}$$

$$= \frac{6.17}{7.00}$$

$$= 0.8814$$

Using total values will provide a little greater precision:

$$\text{Criticality index} = \frac{\text{Total units required}}{\text{Total amount available}}$$

$$= \frac{111}{126}$$

$$= 0.8810$$

Now suppose only six units are available each day. What is the new criticality index? Can we still expect to finish our project in eighteen days?

$$\text{Criticality index} = \frac{\text{Average daily units required}}{\text{Maximum daily amount available}}$$

$$= \frac{6.17}{6.00}$$

$$= 1.0283$$

Using total values will provide a little greater precision:

$$\text{Criticality index} = \frac{\text{Total units required}}{\text{Total amount available}}$$

$$= \frac{111}{108}$$

$$= 1.0278$$

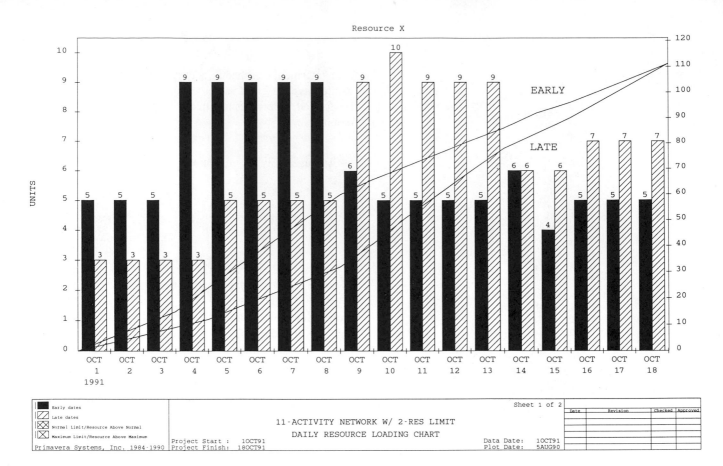

FIGURE 10-34. X resource loading chart.

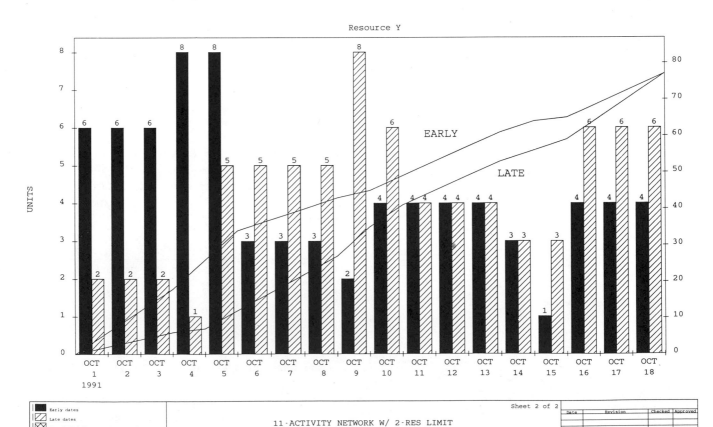

FIGURE 10-35. Y resource loading chart.

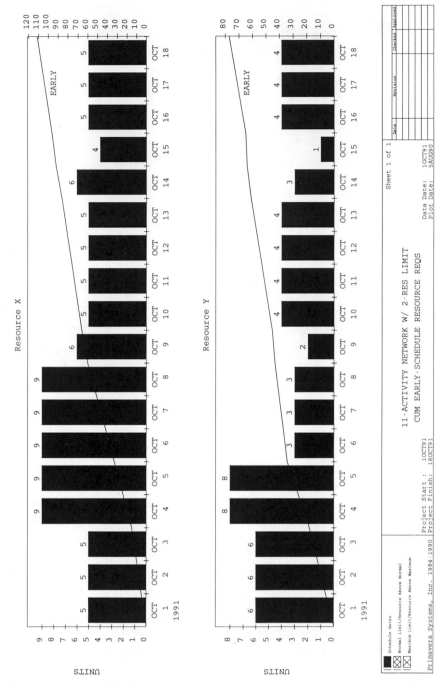

FIGURE 10-36. Resource loading chart (early schedule).

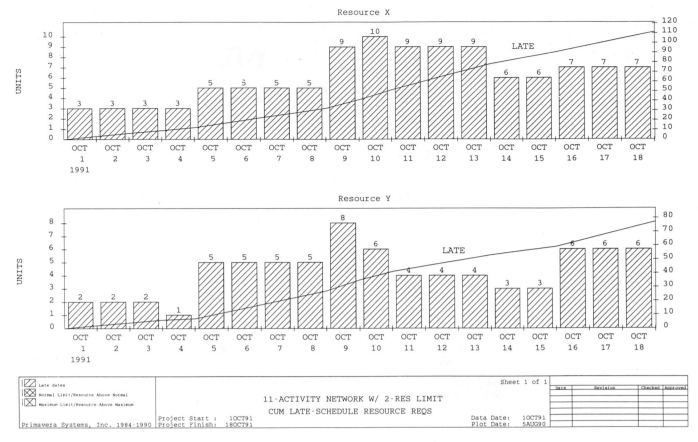

FIGURE 10-37.   Resource loading chart (late schedule).

Because the availability of *X* falls short by three units, the project will be extended beyond eighteen days, since no more than 97 percent (= 108/111) of the *X* work will be completed by October 18. The project manager must determine if this delay is acceptable. If it is not, he or she must somehow acquire—probably at premium rates—three additional units of *X* over the eighteen-day period. Otherwise, the project will take longer to complete. The higher the criticality index, the more tightly constrained the resource and the more likely its shortages will cause project delay. But how much delay? When, where, and why?

Is the criticality index too simple to be of use? No. But never use it alone! Its greatest weakness is the underlying serial-method assumption (a no-no in the real world!), which provides a more optimistic view of the situation than is justified. For example, it indicates that a seven-limit schedule should easily finish by October 18. But it does not tell you the following:

- Activities *E, F, G,* and *H* found no *X* units when needed
- Activities *D* and *K* found too few *X* units when needed
- The project cannot actually finish until October 19

It also indicates that a six-limit schedule should finish around noon on October 19. But it does not tell you the following:

- Activities *E, F, J,* and *K* found no *X* units when needed
- Activities *D* and *I* found too few *X* units when needed
- The project cannot actually finish until October 22

The *X*-constrained schedule is presented in Fig. 10-38.

The preceding examples assumed that the need for resource *X*:

- Began at project start
- Continued without interruption through project finish

If, however, a resource:

- Cannot be used until sometime into the project (contains *resource lag*)
- Is not needed continuously until the end

the timespan over which the criticality index is calculated must be reduced from total project length to actual-use duration. Otherwise, the actual average daily requirements will be higher than computed, and the criticality index will be too low.

Moder, Phillips, and Davis (pp. 199–200) provide a good example of this problem. Assume in a project of two hundred days that:

- Concrete is needed only between days 65 and 184
- A total of one million cubic yards is required

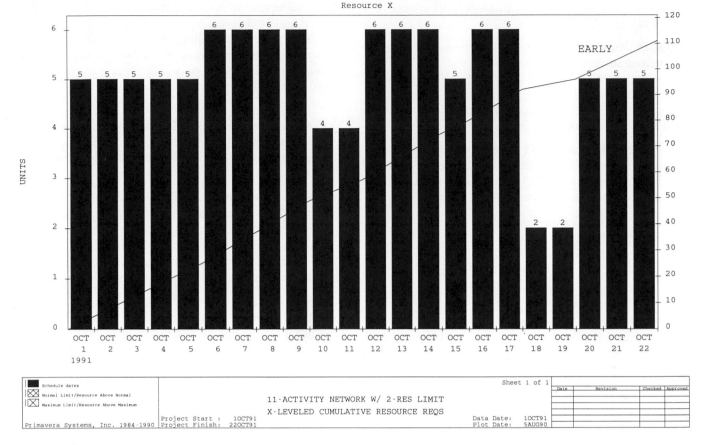

FIGURE 10-38.   Resource loading chart.

• A maximum of six thousand cubic yards per day is available

Will concrete delay the project beyond day 200? It depends on the time frame used.

If we compute the criticality index as before, using total project length, we find the average daily requirement to be five thousand cubic yards and the criticality index to be 0.8333. According to these figures, concrete would not be a constraining resource and would not delay the project beyond two hundred days. But this is misleading. Recall that concrete is actually needed for only 60 percent of project duration—from days 65 through 184—not for 100 percent.

Therefore, a better measure of constraint would begin with day 65 and end with day 184:

$$\text{Average daily requirement} = \frac{\text{Total quantity needed}}{\text{Time actually required}}$$

$$= \frac{1{,}000{,}000 \text{ cu. yds.}}{(184 - 65) \text{ days}}$$

$$= 8333 \text{ cu. yds./day}$$

The criticality index is likewise much higher:

$$\text{Criticality index} = \frac{\text{Total units required}}{\text{Total amount available}}$$

$$= \frac{1{,}000{,}000}{720{,}000}$$

$$= 1.3889$$

Because concrete is needed only 60 percent of the time, the actual average daily requirement and the criticality index exceed earlier calculations by the same 67 percent ($= (200/(184 - 65))$) amount.

This leads to a totally different conclusion from before: Only 720,000 cubic yards ($= 120$ days $* 6000$ cu. yds./day) can be poured over the indicated 120-day period, and project delays beyond day 184 (and 200) will occur. Because of the nature of concrete, the total delay is likely to exceed just the 46.7 days ($= (1{,}000{,}000 - 720{,}000)/6000$) indicated by the shortage alone. That is, concrete must be poured in complete job lots and not simply added to already-dried areas. It will be extremely difficult to recover these forty-seven days; although some out-of-sequence work may be possible, most areas will be unable to support it:

• Some areas will simply not be ready
• Other areas will be ready but do not want to work around wet concrete

- Still others will be ready but cannot work around dry assemblies

Other situations similar to this include cases of irregular or intermittent resource requirements.

In cases such as this, and in general, a minimum daily estimate may be obtained by drawing a line at time points T1 and T2 within (or on) the ES-LS cumulative requirements envelope such that the:

- Lower data point at time T1 represents the L1 cumulative resource requirements under the early schedule
- Upper data point at time T2 represents the L2 cumulative resource requirements under the late schedule

The slope of this line represents the average daily requirements and may be calculated as:

$$\frac{(L2 - L1)}{(T2 - T1)}$$

The criticality index may be computed from this value, as demonstrated earlier. Like the average, this value is likely to vary from day to day and should be evaluated accordingly.

Write Moder, Phillips, and Davis (p. 201),

"The use of the cumulative resource requirements curves provides an approach for estimating the impact of resource constraints, either in advance of or in the absence of more sophisticated procedures. The procedure could also be used, if desired, as a basis for setting activity priorities in project scheduling. To do this, all resources required by the project could first be ranked by criticality; this listing could then be used to rank the activities, putting those that require the most critical resource(s) at the top of the list. Then the activities could be scheduled in the order listed."

DETERMINING PROJECT STAFFING LEVEL WITH A FIXED DEADLINE

The previous examples focused on the earliest time a resource-constrained project could complete. We learned that activities could be delayed by any of the following conditions:

- Insufficient resource quantity at activity start time
- Required resources not available for the entire duration
- Activity predecessors delayed by one or both the above.

We now need to look at the other side of the same coin—that is, how to staff a project, knowing the date by which it must be completed.

Additional resources must be acquired and utilized to meet overload conditions. This includes the area above the maximum availability line—an area generally considered "beyond availability" when the completion date could slip. Not so here: *The deadline must be met!*

Since the project end date is inflexible, an activity must *never* be delayed beyond Late Start—regardless of indicated resource usage. If it were delayed, the project end date would also be delayed. We must not allow this!

Time-constrained leveling (including smoothing) is used when the project end date is firm and must be met. To take advantage of smoothing in time-constrained problems, the normal and maximum resource limits should be set so that the:

- Normal limit is the desired staffing level (not just a little below as in the previous resource-constrained situation)
- Maximum limit is a tolerable peak condition (it may need to change)

If the activity contains float, but the normal resource limit is insufficient to schedule the activity, the smoothing routine raises the availability limit by one-tenth the difference between the normal and maximum limits, and tries again. If this is still inadequate, *Primavera* raises the availability another one-tenth the difference, and so on, until the activity:

- Can be scheduled without delay
- Cannot be scheduled without a higher maximum resource limit

Primavera will tell you what activities need more resources than are currently available. It will also tell you when these resources are needed and exactly how many more must be applied to meet the fixed schedule dates.

Smoothing, like leveling in general, will conserve project schedule dates. Unlike straight leveling, it does this with a minimum of resources.

Do not, however, assume that resource leveling or smoothing will solve all of your staffing problems at all times. In many instances, resource smoothing cannot occur because there is no positive float over which to smooth the particular activities. If the project end date is fixed, activities (with zero float) on the Critical Path will not be smoothed.

During leveling with smoothing, only activities that would be delayed, due to insufficient resources, beyond Early Start are considered eligible. Those activities that have sufficient resources are not delayed just to smooth the resource profile; delaying these activities for this reason alone would be risky and inadvisable. At the same time, activities are never delayed beyond Late Start in order to accomplish smoothing; this would delay the project and is also not advised.

In a sense, this problem is much like the crash-the-path examples studied earlier. In those examples, extra money was applied to buy time, sometimes through additional resource acquisition. In this problem, we seek sufficient resource levels to:

- Meet an imposed deadline
- Minimize resource costs (including acquisition and release)

These two objectives are, of course, at cross purposes and must be resolved as a balanced compromise. Let us revisit the earlier Chase and Aquilano five-activity network but for simplicity:

- Remove activity 4
- Shorten activity 1 to one day
- Remove all sequence restrictions

Our objective is to determine the daily number of workers needed to complete the project in four days. Severe penalties will be applied if the project finishes late. The primary consideration is to meet this deadline. Within this objective, however, we seek to:

- Allow normal buildup at project beginning
- Establish relatively constant usage during most of the project
- Provide normal winding down at project conclusion for a smooth close

We want to do this in as cost-effective a manner as possible. Resource acquisition and release costs are omitted here for simplification, but they should be included in your project.

Table 10-26 and Fig. 10-39 summarize our first try, loading by early schedule. This arrangement is also called a left-justified schedule. The work load could be better balanced; even though the average loading level is six, daily loads vary: from eight and ten workers on the first two days, to three workers on both of the last two days.

The left-justified schedule disappointed us. So, back to the drawing board we go. What about loading everyone as late as possible—a right-justified schedule? The Late Start results are presented in Table 10-27 and Fig. 10-40.

This looks even more ridiculous and provides no benefit other than to defer peak loading requirements until the end of the project. Although this is sometimes desirable (the concept of the *time value of money* encourages delaying costs as long as possible), the risks here are:

- Unavailability of workers should initial project activities complete early
- An excess of workers, unable to recover lost progress if these initial activities complete late

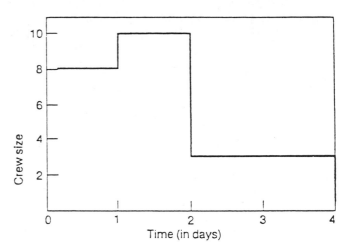

FIGURE 10-39.   Resource loading chart (left justified).

- Severe penalties if the project finishes late (regardless of reason)

So the third time, shown in Table 10-28 and Fig. 10-41, does indeed turn out to be the charm.

Note that the:

- Project is still completed in four days, as required
- Workload is better balanced (varying only from five to eight workers—a range of just three throughout the project instead of an average of eight

$$[= ((10 - 3) + (10 - 1))/2]$$

as in the previous two schedules
- Labor loading curve has a lower peak than the previous two

This is the best we can do without additional cost and payoff information.

Table 10-26   Resource Loading Table

RESOURCE LOADING TABLE			DATE: _____
PROJECT NAME: LEFT-JUSTIFIED SCHEDULE TO MEET FIXED-SCHEDULE DATE_____			

	DAY			
ACT	1	2	3	4
1	1			
2	2	2		
3		3	3	3
4 (OMITTED)				
5	5	5		
TOTALS	8	10	3	3

Table 10-27   Resource Loading Table

```
------------------------------------------------------------------------
RESOURCE LOADING TABLE                         DATE:  _____

PROJECT NAME:   RIGHT-JUSTIFIED SCHEDULE TO MEET FIXED-SCHEDULE DATE_____
------------------------------------------------------------------------
```

	DAY			
ACT	1	2	3	4
1	1			
2			2	2
3		3	3	3
4 (OMITTED)				
5			5	5
TOTALS	1	3	10	10

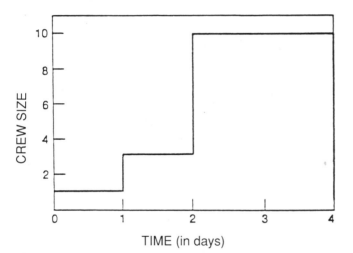

FIGURE 10-40.   Resource loading chart (right justified).

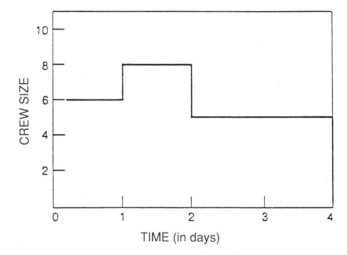

FIGURE 10-41.   Resource loading chart (best).

Table 10-28   Resource Loading Table

```
------------------------------------------------------------------------
RESOURCE LOADING TABLE                         DATE:  _____

PROJECT NAME:   CENTER-BALANCED SCHEDULE TO MEET FIXED-SCHEDULE DATE_____
------------------------------------------------------------------------
```

	DAY			
ACT	1	2	3	4
1	1			
2			2	2
3		3	3	3
4 (OMITTED)				
5	5	5		
TOTALS	6	8	5	5

Some authors contend that an ideal solution produces a perfect rectangle. But it is not that easy or simple! In fact, more persons are often needed in the middle of a project than at its beginning or end. This is because more activities are likely to be in progress then. Under ideal circumstances, personnel not needed until (or past) the middle of a project may be:

- Effectively employed on other projects—perhaps during their peak periods
- Provided needed training to enhance their skills and value to your organization and project

So whether a particular loading curve is optimal depends on:

- Project requirements
- All costs involved, both direct and indirect

This is exactly how we solved our minimum-cost scheduling problems. Since project length and staffing levels are related to each other and are both driven by monetary considerations, it makes perfect sense to use the same basic methodology for each problem, changing processes only as necessary.

Now suppose we have another project, set up as shown in Table 10-29, with a mandatory October 22 finish.

Assume that seven workers are normally available. When leveled, the resulting summary report would look as is shown in Table 10-30.

This schedule, although efficient and compact, finishes three days late and is, therefore, unacceptable. The deadline cannot be met simply by a better schedule. More workers must be added—but when? To what activities?

For an initial solution, keep the normal staff value but remove the seven-person maximum. This does reduce pro-

Table 10-29 Schedule Setup

```
------------------------------------------------------------------------------
SCHEDULE SETUP                                  DATE: _____

PROJECT NAME:   EIGHT-ACTIVITY FIXED-SCHEDULE STAFFING EXAMPLE_____
                ARMSTRONG-WRIGHT (AUTHOR)
------------------------------------------------------------------------------
```

ACTIVITY ID	DUR (DAYS)	PREDECESSOR/ RELATIONSHIP		SUCCESSOR/ RELATIONSHIP		REQUIRED RESOURCES
A	6	None		B	F/S	8
				E	F/S	
B	4	A	F/S	C	F/S	4
C	3	B	F/S	D	F/S	6
D	4	C	F/S	H	F/S	4
		G	F/S			
E	1	A	F/S	F	F/S	2
F	3	E	F/S	G	F/S	3
G	3	F	F/S	H	F/S	4
H	5	D	F/S	None		4
		G	F/S			

Table 10-30 Schedule Summary

```
------------------------------------------------------------------------------
SCHEDULE SUMMARY                                DATE: _____

PROJECT NAME:   8-ACTIVITY FIXED-SCHEDULE STAFFING EXAMPLE: INITIAL ATTEMPT__
------------------------------------------------------------------------------
```

ACTIVITY ID		ORIG DUR	REM DUR	% DONE	EARLY START	EARLY FINISH	LATE START	LATE FINISH	TOTAL FLOAT	
A		6	6	0	1OCT91	6OCT91	4OCT91	9OCT91	3	
B		4	4	0	7OCT91	10OCT91	10OCT91	13OCT91	3	
C		3	3	0	11OCT91	13OCT91	14OCT91	16OCT91	3	
D		4	4	0	14OCT91	17OCT91	17OCT91	20OCT91	3	
E		1	1	0	7OCT91	7OCT91	14OCT91	14OCT91	7	
F		3	3	0	8OCT91	10OCT91	15OCT91	17OCT91	7	
G	*	3	3	0	18OCT91	20OCT91	18OCT91	20OCT91	0	*
H	*	5	5	0	21OCT91	25OCT91	21OCT91	25OCT91	0	*

ject length to the required twenty-two days and results in the loading chart seen in Fig. 10-42. But is this the best we can do? No, improvements in efficiency are still possible, even though a shorter project length is not.

To find these improvements, recompute the network with the following options:

1. Maximum = eight workers
2. Smoothing
3. Progress override
4. Interruptible activities

This results in a more efficient loading table (Fig. 10-43) that requires only eight workers, not ten as before.

The resulting schedule is shown in Table 10-31.

The resulting Gantt Chart is shown in Fig. 10-44.

A partial loading chart is shown in Table 10-32.

Note how the required staffing level varies from a low of four to a high of eight over the twenty-two day project span. Consider the following if you tried to do this manually: If you have children who play with blocks, or if you can remember when you did (do you still?), you know that children will generally knock down the tallest block first. This is essentially what you must do in a manual environment to reduce required resource pool variation and size:

- Assign critical-activity resources to the lowest blocks (bounded by ES, EF, and the required resource level)
- Assign noncritical resources to similarly-bounded blocks atop the critical—as in the stacked bar chart shown in Fig. 10-45
- Rearrange (Fig. 10-46) non-critical activities, without increasing project length, by pushing the highest block(s) down to an appropriate level (it, or they, must fit without moving any others) and repeating the process as often as necessary until no further leveling can be done

Only noncritical activities can participate in push-the-highest-block processes. If you reduce critical-activity resources, you will always:

- Delay the activity or increase its duration
- Unnecessarily delay your project

Never take resources from a critical activity! Never apply premium cost resources to a noncritical activity!

To finish on time, start on time. Never let an activity slide past Late Start. Be careful—apply resources wisely and do not waste your float!

Figure 10-46 represents only two-thirds the variance $(= [(8 - 4)/(10 - 4)])$ of the first twenty-two day, unlimited-resource schedule evaluated. It also means easier load-

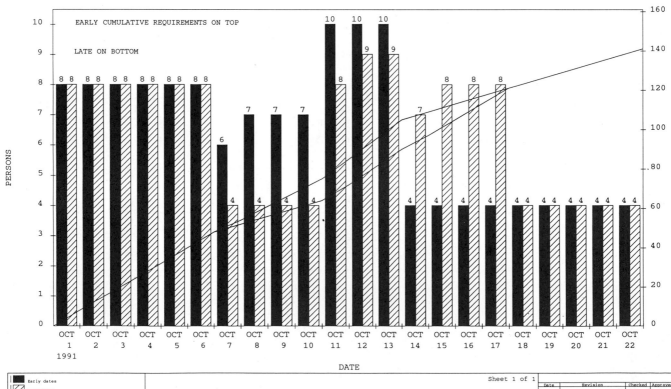

FIGURE 10-42. Resource loading chart (preliminary).

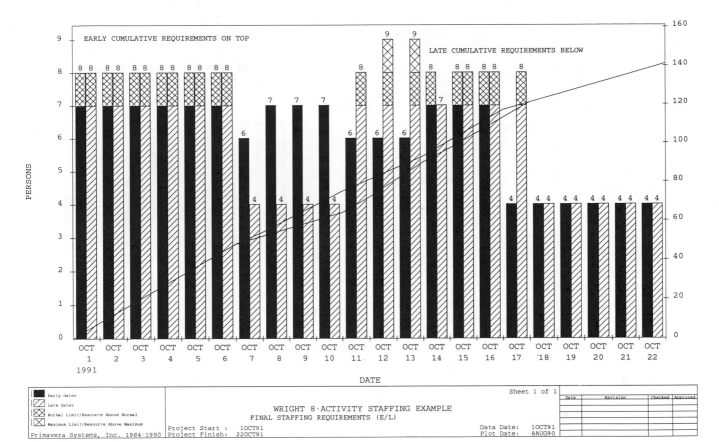

FIGURE 10-43. Resource loading chart (final).

Table 10-31 Schedule Summary

```
-------------------------------------------------------------------------
SCHEDULE SUMMARY                               DATE: _____

PROJECT NAME:  8-ACTIVITY FIXED-SCHEDULE STAFFING EXAMPLE: FINAL SOLUTION___
-------------------------------------------------------------------------
```

ACTIVITY ID		ORIG DUR	REM DUR	% DONE	EARLY START	EARLY FINISH	LATE START	LATE FINISH	TOTAL FLOAT	
A	*	6	6	0	1OCT91	6OCT91	1OCT91	6OCT91	0	*
B	*	4	4	0	7OCT91	10OCT91	7OCT91	10OCT91	0	*
C	*	3	3	0	11OCT91	13OCT91	11OCT91	13OCT91	0	*
D	*	4	4	0	14OCT91	17OCT91	14OCT91	17OCT91	0	*
E		1	1	0	7OCT91	7OCT91	11OCT91	11OCT91	4	
F		3	3	0	8OCT91	10OCT91	12OCT91	14OCT91	4	
G		3	3	0	14OCT91	16OCT91	15OCT91	17OCT91	1	
H	*	5	5	0	18OCT91	22OCT91	18OCT91	22OCT91	0	*

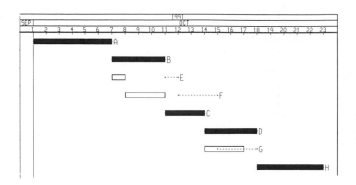

FIGURE 10-44.   Gantt Chart.

ing, as evidenced by the big jump in loading efficiency from the earlier 76.6 percent all the way up to 92.8 percent. In each case, assume that all workers selected must remain on the project payroll until October 17. On that date, all but four workers may be reassigned to other projects. These values are computed as follows:

Schedule of twenty-two days, ten workers:

$$\frac{[(6 * 8) + (1 * 6) + (3 * 7) + (3 * 10) + (9 * 4)]}{16 \text{ days @ 10 workers/day} + 6 \text{ days @ 4 workers/day}}$$

$$= \frac{141 \text{ actual person-days}}{184 \text{ possible person-days}}$$

$$= \underline{76.6\%}$$

Schedule of twenty-two days, eight workers:

$$\frac{[(6 * 8) + (1 * 6) + (3 * 7) + (3 * 6) + (3 * 8) + (6 * 4)]}{16 \text{ days @ 8 workers/day} + 6 \text{ days @ 4 workers/day}}$$

$$= \frac{141 \text{ actual person-days}}{152 \text{ possible person-days}}$$

$$= \underline{92.8\%}$$

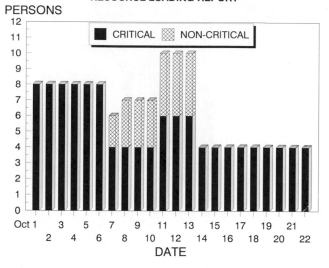

FIGURE 10-45.   Resource loading chart (baseline).

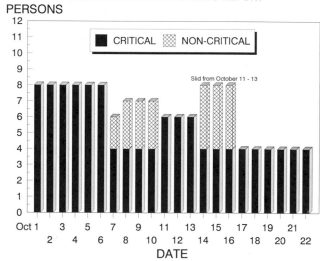

FIGURE 10-46.   Resource loading chart (leveled).

Table 10-32   Resource Loading Table

```
------------------------------------------------------------------------------------
RESOURCE LOADING TABLE (PARTIAL)                         DATE: _____

PROJECT NAME:   8-ACTIVITY FIXED-SCHEDULE STAFFING EXAMPLE: FINAL SOLUTION____
------------------------------------------------------------------------------------
```

ACTIVITY ID	6OCT 1991	7OCT 1991	8OCT 1991	9OCT 1991	10OCT 1991	11OCT 1991	12OCT 1991	13OCT 1991	14OCT 1991	15OCT 1991	16OCT 1991
A	8										
B		4	4	4	4						
C						6	6	6			
D									4	4	4
E		2									
F			3	3	3						
G									4	4	4
H											
TOTALS:	8	6	7	7	7	6	6	6	8	8	8

which is delightfully high for any project. Note that 141 person-days were required in each case, but one solution required 25 percent more people for the same 16 days than the other with no schedule reduction or other benefit provided.

The remaining 7.2 percent (eleven person-days) should be used wisely—training, miscellaneous administrative duties, and so on. For so small a time period, it probably would not be worthwhile to loan these workers out.

Our objective in this example was to balance project requirements (twenty-two-day deadline) against minimum staff availability. We have succeeded.

Table 10-33   Schedule Setup

```
---------------------------------------------------------------------------------
SCHEDULE SETUP                                    DATE: _____

PROJECT NAME:   73-ACTIVITY "BIG ONE" NETWORK WITH DUAL-RESOURCE REQUIREMENTS
                MODER, PHILLIPS, AND DAVIS (AUTHORS)
---------------------------------------------------------------------------------
```

ACTIVITY ID	DUR (DAYS)	PREDECESSOR/ RELATIONSHIP		SUCCESSOR/ RELATIONSHIP		REQUIRED RESOURCES	
						X	Y
1	0	None		2	F/S	Milestone; none	
				28	F/S		
2	2	1	F/S	3	F/S	1	0
				4	F/S		
				5	F/S		
				12	F/S		
				29	F/S		
				47	F/S		
3	3	2	F/S	6	F/S	1	0
				9	F/S		
				11	F/S		
4	6	2	F/S	8	F/S	0	1
5	5	2	F/S	10	F/S	1	0
				13	F/S		
6	4	3	F/S	7	F/S	1	0
		29	F/S	8	F/S		
7	4	6	F/S	14	F/S	1	0
8	4	4	F/S	14	F/S	0	1
		6	F/S				
9	7	3	F/S	15	F/S	0	1
10	8	5	F/S	15	F/S	1	0
				16	F/S		
11	6	3	F/S	17	F/S	1	0
				18	F/S		
12	7	2	F/S	18	F/S	0	1
13	3	5	F/S	19	F/S	1	0
14	2	7	F/S	20	F/S	0	1
		8	F/S				
15	4	9	F/S	20	F/S	0	1
		10	F/S				
16	12	10	F/S	20	F/S	1	0
				21	F/S		
17	5	11	F/S	22	F/S	1	0
18	9	11	F/S	25	F/S	0	2
		12	F/S	40	F/S		
		30	F/S				
19	8	13	F/S	55	F/S	0	1

(continued)

Table 10-33   Continued

SCHEDULE SETUP   DATE: _____

PROJECT NAME: 73-ACTIVITY "BIG ONE" NETWORK WITH DUAL-RESOURCE REQUIREMENTS
                 MODER, PHILLIPS, AND DAVIS (AUTHORS)

ACTIVITY ID	DUR (DAYS)	PREDECESSOR/ RELATIONSHIP		SUCCESSOR/ RELATIONSHIP		REQUIRED RESOURCES	
						$\underline{X}$	$\underline{Y}$
20	8	14	F/S	23	F/S	0	2
		15	F/S				
		16	F/S				
21	4	16	F/S	23	F/S	1	0
				24	F/S		
22	13	17	F/S	25	F/S	1	0
23	10	20	F/S	26	F/S	0	1
		21	F/S	43	F/S		
24	3	21	F/S	26	F/S	1	0
				43	F/S		
25	13	18	F/S	27	F/S	0	1
		22	F/S				
26	7	23	F/S	71	F/S	0	1
		24	F/S	72	F/S		
27	8	25	F/S	71	F/S	0	1
				72	F/S		
28	1	1	F/S	29	F/S	1	0
				30	F/S		
				32	F/S		
				33	F/S		
				47	F/S		
29	3	2	F/S	6	F/S	1	0
		28	F/S	31	F/S		
				47	F/S		
30	9	28	F/S	18	F/S	0	1
31	6	29	F/S	36	F/S	0	1
32	9	28	F/S	36	F/S	1	0
				37	F/S		
33	2	28	F/S	34	F/S	1	0
				35	F/S		
34	8	33	F/S	38	F/S	1	0
35	9	33	F/S	38	F/S	0	1
36	6	31	F/S	58	F/S	0	1
		32	F/S				
37	12	32	F/S	39	F/S	1	0
				40	F/S		
38	8	34	F/S	58	F/S	0	1
		35	F/S				
39	4	37	F/S	41	F/S	1	0
				42	F/S		

Table 10-33   Continued

SCHEDULE SETUP   DATE: _____

PROJECT NAME: 73-ACTIVITY "BIG ONE" NETWORK WITH DUAL-RESOURCE REQUIREMENTS
               MODER, PHILLIPS, AND DAVIS (AUTHORS)

ACTIVITY ID	DUR (DAYS)	PREDECESSOR/ RELATIONSHIP		SUCCESSOR/ RELATIONSHIP		REQUIRED RESOURCES	
						X	Y
40	5	18	F/S	42	F/S	0	1
		37	F/S				
41	8	39	F/S	43	F/S	0	1
				44	F/S		
42	11	39	F/S	45	F/S	0	1
		40	F/S				
43	6	23	F/S	46	F/S	0	3
		24	F/S				
		41	F/S				
44	6	41	F/S	46	F/S	1	0
45	7	42	F/S	71	F/S	0	1
				72	F/S		
46	3	43	F/S	70	F/S	0	3
		44	F/S				
47	3	2	F/S	48	F/S	1	0
		28	F/S	49	F/S		
		29	F/S				
48	1	47	F/S	50	F/S	1	0
				51	F/S		
49	14	47	F/S	67	F/S	0	1
				68	F/S		
50	3	48	F/S	52	F/S	1	0
51	7	48	F/S	55	F/S	0	1
52	10	50	F/S	53	F/S	2	0
				54	F/S		
				55	F/S		
				56	F/S		
53	9	52	F/S	57	F/S	2	0
				58	F/S		
54	6	52	F/S	59	F/S	1	0
55	10	19	F/S	59	F/S	0	2
		51	F/S				
		52	F/S				
56	3	52	F/S	60	F/S	2	0
57	6	53	F/S	61	F/S	2	0
				62	F/S		
58	13	36	F/S	66	F/S	0	2
		38	F/S				
		53	F/S				
59	6	54	F/S	67	F/S	0	2
		55	F/S	68	F/S		

Table 10-33   Continued

SCHEDULE SETUP   DATE: _____

PROJECT NAME: 73-ACTIVITY "BIG ONE" NETWORK WITH DUAL-RESOURCE REQUIREMENTS
                MODER, PHILLIPS, AND DAVIS (AUTHORS)

ACTIVITY ID	DUR (DAYS)	PREDECESSOR/ RELATIONSHIP		SUCCESSOR/ RELATIONSHIP		REQUIRED RESOURCES	
						X	Y
60	10	56	F/S	67	F/S	0	1
				68	F/S		
61	4	57	F/S	63	F/S	1	0
				64	F/S		
				67	F/S		
				68	F/S		
62	3	57	F/S	65	F/S	1	0
				66	F/S		
63	3	61	F/S	70	F/S	1	0
64	8	61	F/S	70	F/S	1	0
65	8	62	F/S	71	F/S	1	0
				72	F/S		
66	12	58	F/S	69	F/S	0	3
		62	F/S				
67	7	49	F/S	70	F/S	0	1
		59	F/S				
		60	F/S				
		61	F/S				
68	6	49	F/S	70	F/S	0	1
		59	F/S				
		60	F/S				
		61	F/S				
69	7	66	F/S	71	F/S	0	3
				72	F/S		
70	13	46	F/S	73	F/S	2	3
		63	F/S				
		64	F/S				
		67	F/S				
		68	F/S				
71	5	26	F/S	73	F/S	2	3
		27	F/S				
		45	F/S				
		65	F/S				
		69	F/S				
72	5	26	F/S	73	F/S	2	3
		27	F/S				
		45	F/S				
		65	F/S				
		69	F/S				
73	0	70	F/S	None		Milestone; none	
		71	F/S				
		72	F/S				

Table 10-34 Project BIG ONE Schedule Setup

```
--------------------------------------------------------------------------------
SCHEDULE SUMMARY                                    DATE: _____

PROJECT NAME:  73-ACTIVITY "BIG ONE" NETWORK BY EARLY START AND TOTAL FLOAT_
--------------------------------------------------------------------------------
```

ACTIVITY ID		ORIG DUR	REM DUR	% DONE	EARLY START	EARLY FINISH	LATE START	LATE FINISH	TOTAL FLOAT	
1	*	0	0	0	1OCT91		1OCT91		0	*
2	*	2	2	0	1OCT91	2OCT91	1OCT91	2OCT91	0	*
28		1	1	0	1OCT91	1OCT91	2OCT91	2OCT91	1	
33		2	2	0	2OCT91	3OCT91	17OCT91	18OCT91	11	
32		9	9	0	2OCT91	14OCT91	18OCT91	30OCT91	12	
30		9	9	0	2OCT91	14OCT91	31OCT91	12NOV91	21	
29	*	3	3	0	3OCT91	7OCT91	3OCT91	7OCT91	0	*
5		5	5	0	3OCT91	9OCT91	4OCT91	10OCT91	1	
3		3	3	0	3OCT91	7OCT91	21OCT91	23OCT91	12	
4		6	6	0	3OCT91	10OCT91	23OCT91	30OCT91	14	
12		7	7	0	3OCT91	11OCT91	4NOV91	12NOV91	22	
35		9	9	0	4OCT91	16OCT91	21OCT91	31OCT91	11	
34		8	8	0	4OCT91	15OCT91	22OCT91	31OCT91	12	
47	*	3	3	0	8OCT91	10OCT91	8OCT91	10OCT91	0	*
9		7	7	0	8OCT91	16OCT91	24OCT91	1NOV91	12	
6		4	4	0	8OCT91	11OCT91	25OCT91	30OCT91	13	
11		6	6	0	8OCT91	15OCT91	25OCT91	1NOV91	13	
31		6	6	0	8OCT91	15OCT91	28OCT91	4NOV91	14	
10		8	8	0	10OCT91	21OCT91	11OCT91	22OCT91	1	
13		3	3	0	10OCT91	14OCT91	30OCT91	1NOV91	14	
48	*	1	1	0	11OCT91	11OCT91	11OCT91	11OCT91	0	*
49		14	14	0	11OCT91	30OCT91	18NOV91	5DEC91	26	
50	*	3	3	0	14OCT91	16OCT91	14OCT91	16OCT91	0	*
7		4	4	0	14OCT91	17OCT91	31OCT91	5NOV91	13	
8		4	4	0	14OCT91	17OCT91	31OCT91	5NOV91	13	
51		7	7	0	14OCT91	22OCT91	5NOV91	13NOV91	16	
37		12	12	0	15OCT91	30OCT91	31OCT91	15NOV91	12	
19		8	8	0	15OCT91	24OCT91	4NOV91	13NOV91	14	
17		5	5	0	16OCT91	22OCT91	4NOV91	8NOV91	13	
36		6	6	0	16OCT91	23OCT91	5NOV91	12NOV91	14	
18		9	9	0	16OCT91	28OCT91	13NOV91	25NOV91	20	
52	*	10	10	0	17OCT91	30OCT91	17OCT91	30OCT91	0	*
38		8	8	0	17OCT91	28OCT91	1NOV91	12NOV91	11	
14		2	2	0	18OCT91	21OCT91	6NOV91	7NOV91	13	
16		12	12	0	22OCT91	6NOV91	23OCT91	7NOV91	1	
15		4	4	0	22OCT91	25OCT91	4NOV91	7NOV91	9	
22		13	13	0	23OCT91	8NOV91	11NOV91	27NOV91	13	
53	*	9	9	0	31OCT91	12NOV91	31OCT91	12NOV91	0	*
55		10	10	0	31OCT91	13NOV91	14NOV91	27NOV91	10	
39		4	4	0	31OCT91	5NOV91	18NOV91	21NOV91	12	
56		3	3	0	31OCT91	4NOV91	19NOV91	21NOV91	13	
54		6	6	0	31OCT91	7NOV91	20NOV91	27NOV91	14	
40		5	5	0	31OCT91	6NOV91	26NOV91	2DEC91	18	
60		10	10	0	5NOV91	18NOV91	22NOV91	5DEC91	13	
41		8	8	0	6NOV91	15NOV91	22NOV91	3DEC91	12	
20		8	8	0	7NOV91	18NOV91	8NOV91	19NOV91	1	
21		4	4	0	7NOV91	12NOV91	14NOV91	19NOV91	5	
42		11	11	0	7NOV91	21NOV91	3DEC91	17DEC91	18	
25		13	13	0	11NOV91	27NOV91	28NOV91	16DEC91	13	
58	*	13	13	0	13NOV91	29NOV91	13NOV91	29NOV91	0	*
57		6	6	0	13NOV91	20NOV91	19NOV91	26NOV91	4	
24		3	3	0	13NOV91	15NOV91	29NOV91	3DEC91	12	
59		6	6	0	14NOV91	21NOV91	28NOV91	5DEC91	10	
44		6	6	0	18NOV91	25NOV91	4DEC91	11DEC91	12	
23		10	10	0	19NOV91	2DEC91	20NOV91	3DEC91	1	

(continued)

255

Table 10-34   Continued

```
------------------------------------------------------------------------
SCHEDULE SUMMARY                                     DATE:  _____

PROJECT NAME:  73-ACTIVITY "BIG ONE" NETWORK BY EARLY START AND TOTAL FLOAT_
------------------------------------------------------------------------
```

ACTIVITY ID		ORIG DUR	REM DUR	% DONE	EARLY START	EARLY FINISH	LATE START	LATE FINISH	TOTAL FLOAT	
62		3	3	0	21NOV91	25NOV91	27NOV91	29NOV91	4	
61		4	4	0	21NOV91	26NOV91	29NOV91	4DEC91	6	
45		7	7	0	22NOV91	2DEC91	18DEC91	26DEC91	18	
65		8	8	0	26NOV91	5DEC91	17DEC91	26DEC91	15	
64		8	8	0	27NOV91	6DEC91	5DEC91	16DEC91	6	
67		7	7	0	27NOV91	5DEC91	6DEC91	16DEC91	7	
68		6	6	0	27NOV91	4DEC91	9DEC91	16DEC91	8	
63		3	3	0	27NOV91	29NOV91	12DEC91	16DEC91	11	
27		8	8	0	28NOV91	9DEC91	17DEC91	26DEC91	13	
66	*	12	12	0	2DEC91	17DEC91	2DEC91	17DEC91	0	*
43		6	6	0	3DEC91	10DEC91	4DEC91	11DEC91	1	
26		7	7	0	3DEC91	11DEC91	18DEC91	26DEC91	11	
46		3	3	0	11DEC91	13DEC91	12DEC91	16DEC91	1	
70		13	13	0	16DEC91	1JAN92	17DEC91	2JAN92	1	
69	*	7	7	0	18DEC91	26DEC91	18DEC91	26DEC91	0	*
71	*	5	5	0	27DEC91	2JAN92	27DEC91	2JAN92	0	*
72	*	5	5	0	27DEC91	2JAN92	27DEC91	2JAN92	0	*
73	*	0	0	0		2JAN92		2JAN92	0	*

Now let us solve another, somewhat bigger problem. Although weighing in at seventy-three activities, the largest network in the book, project BIG ONE is still:

- 9,927 activities shorter than
- Only 0.73 percent the capacity of

MS-DOS *Primavera* limits (31,927 activities and 0.23 percent for VAX/VMS hardware). First, schedule the network (Moder, Phillips, and Davis, pp. 222–3) suggested by the setup shown in Table 10-33 and solved in Table 10-34. Allocate resources as indicated. Display the results in a time-logic plot and Gantt Chart, noting critical activities, busy times, and float values. Produce a resource loading chart for resources *X* and *Y*.

Now assume the boss tries to be a hero, goes on another cost-cutting rampage, and issues the following memo: "Since no single activity needs more than 2 *X* and 3 *Y*, only these amounts will be funded until after January 1." Assuming the project (and its staff) are still around, when will it now end? What is the new Critical Path, and when are project busy times? How do float patterns before January 1 change after then? Compare your answers with the *Primavera* solutions given in Figs. 10-47 through 10-53.

More Project HOME Resource Reports

Two more (many more are possible!) Project HOME resource reports are presented on the following pages:

- Resource Control Activity Report (Table 10-35)
- Resource Monthly Usage Report (Table 10-36)

The first report is organized by activity, by resource, by cost account, and by account category. Within each of these categories, the following information is presented:

- Unit of measure
- Budgeted unit amount
- Percent complete
- Actual usage to date
- Actual usage this period
- Estimated usage to complete
- Forecasted usage to complete
- Variance

The second report provides monthly information on normal and maximum availability limits by resource; and, for both early and late schedules, presents:

- Actual resource usage this time period (month in this example)
- Cumulative usage to date
- Average between the two schedules

Corresponding cost information is provided on other reports to be seen later. Many other reports are possible. Together, they constitute a set of information as concise as it is complete and necessary.

Do not even attempt to manage your project without these, and other, reports! Resources constitute one of the three necessary components of effective project management (along with time and performance) and must be managed every bit as carefully as the other two.

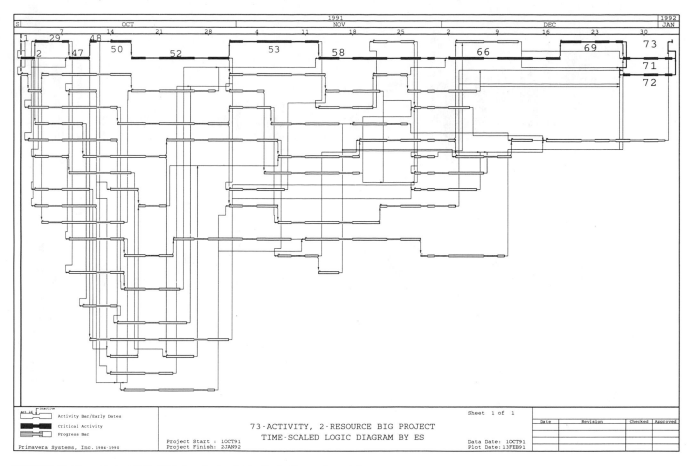

FIGURE 10-47. Project BIG ONE time-logic plot by Early Start and total float.

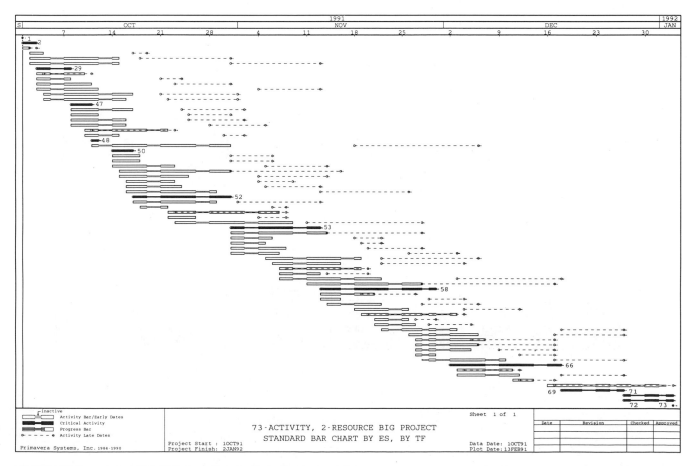

FIGURE 10-48. Project BIG ONE Gantt Chart by Early Start and total float.

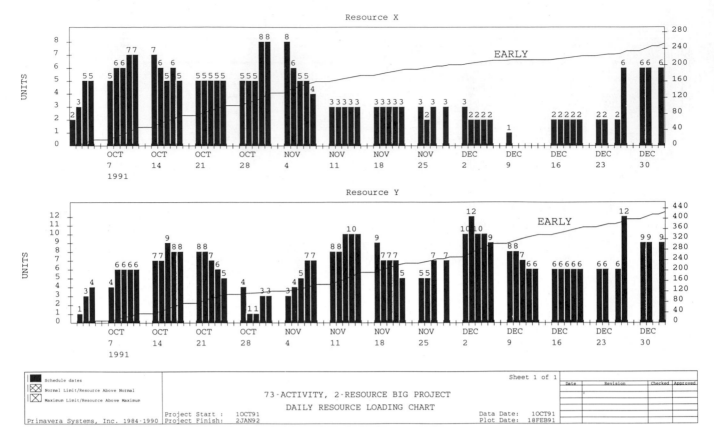

FIGURE 10-49. Project BIG ONE baseline resource loading chart.

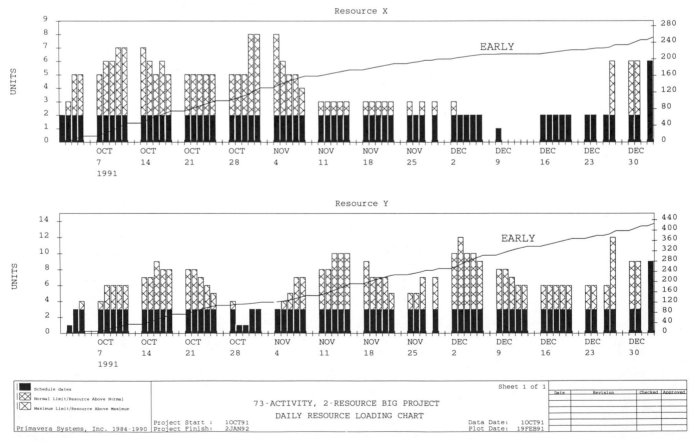

FIGURE 10-50. Project BIG ONE excess-amounts resource loading chart.

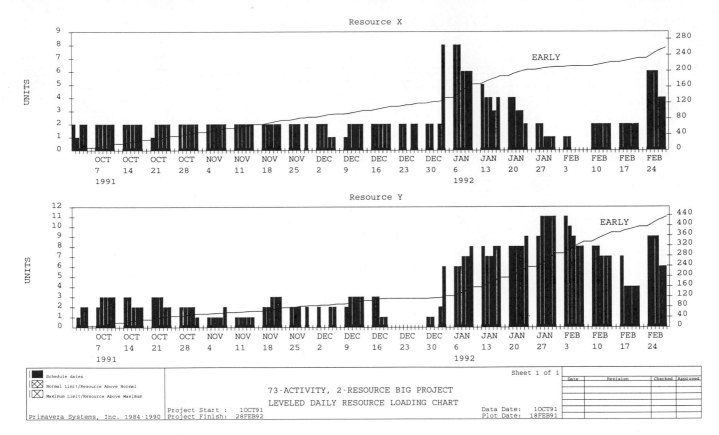

FIGURE 10-51. Project BIG ONE leveled-resource loading chart.

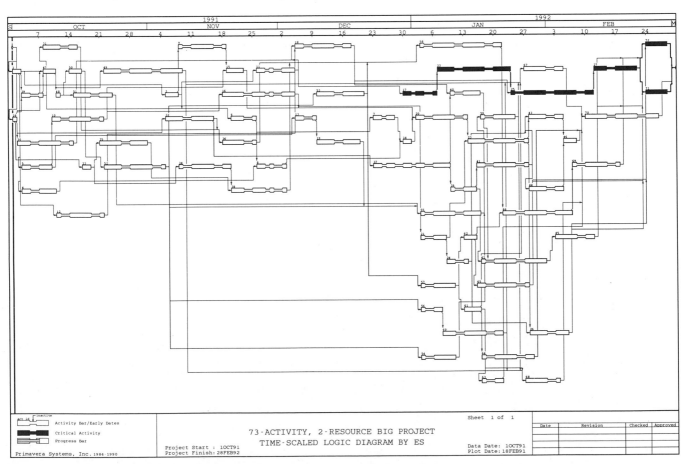

FIGURE 10-52. Project BIG ONE leveled time-logic plot sorted by Early Start and total float. Project busy time has now moved to January; the new Critical Path, which does not even get organized until then, shares only wrap-up activities 71–73 with the old Critical Path.

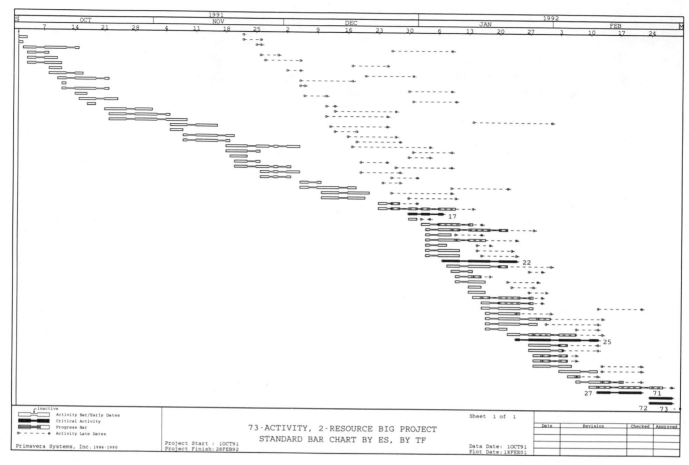

FIGURE 10-53.   Project BIG ONE leveled Gantt Chart sorted by Early Start and total float. Huge, but largely unusable, float values before January 1 collapse after then as resource constraints are removed.

Table 10-35   Resource Control Activity Report

```
----------------------------------------------------------------------------------------------------
AMERICAN COMMUNITY DEVELOPERS, INC.        PRIMAVERA PROJECT PLANNER        BRIAN'S DUPLICATE OF PROJECT "HOME"

REPORT DATE 12FEB83  RUN NO.  15         RESOURCE CONTROL ACTIVITY REPORT        START DATE 13DEC82  FIN DATE  6SEP84

RESOURCE USAGE AND CONTROL REPORT SORTED BY ACTIVITY NUMBER                    DATA DATE   1FEB83  PAGE NO.   1
----------------------------------------------------------------------------------------------------
```

ACTIVITY ID	RESOURCE	COST ACCOUNT	ACCOUNT CATEGORY	UNIT MEAS	BUDGET	PCT CMP	ACTUAL TO DATE	ACTUAL THIS PERIOD	ESTIMATE TO COMPLETE	FORECAST	VARIANCE

```
    1  LAYOUT
       RD    0 AS 14DEC82  AF 22DEC82

       LABORERS        101L LABOR   PDAY     15 100        0            0            15           15            0
                                         ------------ --- ------------ ------------ ------------ ------------ ------------
       TOTAL :                            15   0        0            0            15           15            0
    3  SOIL STABILIZATION
       RD    0 AS 28DEC82  AF 20JAN83

       LABORERS        102L LABOR   PDAY     20 100        0            0            20           20            0
                                         ------------ --- ------------ ------------ ------------ ------------ ------------
       TOTAL :                            20   0        0            0            20           20            0
    5  PLUMBING-STREET CONNECTION AND UNDERSLAB
       RD    3 AS 24JAN83  EF  3FEB83        LF  6JAN83  TF  -20

       LABORERS        301L LABOR   PDAY     32  62        0            0            32           32            0
                                         ------------ --- ------------ ------------ ------------ ------------ ------------
       TOTAL :                            32   0        0            0            32           32            0
    7  FOUNDATION EXCAVATION
       RD    2 ES  4FEB83  EF  7FEB83  LS  7JAN83  LF 10JAN83  TF  -20

       LABORERS        105L LABOR   PDAY     20  60        0            0            20           20            0
                                         ------------ --- ------------ ------------ ------------ ------------ ------------
       TOTAL :                            20   0        0            0            20           20            0
    9  GRANULAR FILL
       RD    7 ES  8FEB83  EF 16FEB83  LS 11JAN83  LF 19JAN83  TF  -20

       LABORERS        105L LABOR   PDAY     35   0        0            0            35           35            0
                                         ------------ --- ------------ ------------ ------------ ------------ ------------
       TOTAL :                            35   0        0            0            35           35            0
   13  TERMITE PROTECTION
       RD   13 ES 17FEB83  EF  8MAR83  LS 20JAN83  LF  7FEB83  TF  -20

       TOTAL :                             0   0        0            0             0            0            0
   22  CONCRETE SLAB ON GRADE
       RD    5 ES  9MAR83  EF 15MAR83  LS  8FEB83  LF 14FEB83  TF  -20

       LABORERS        105L LABOR   PDAY     25   0        0            0            25           25            0
                                         ------------ --- ------------ ------------ ------------ ------------ ------------
       TOTAL :                            25   0        0            0            25           25            0
   24  CURING TIME
       RD   13 ES 16MAR83  EF  1APR83  LS 15FEB83  LF  4MAR83  TF  -20

       TOTAL :                             0   0        0            0             0            0            0


                                         ------------ --- ------------ ------------ ------------ ------------ ------------
*** REPORT TOTAL ***                      451   0        0            0           451          451            0
====================================================================================================
```

Table 10-36   Resource Usage Report

```
-------------------------------------------------------------------------------------------------------------
AMERICAN COMMUNITY DEVELOPERS, INC.          PRIMAVERA PROJECT PLANNER          BRIAN'S DUPLICATE OF PROJECT "HOME"

REPORT DATE  12FEB83  RUN NO.    16          RESOURCE USAGE REPORT - MONTHLY          START DATE 13DEC82  FIN DATE  6SEP84

RESOURCE USAGE REPORT BY RESOURCE, BY MONTH, AND BY SCHEDULE                       DATA DATE   1FEB83  PAGE NO.    1
-------------------------------------------------------------------------------------------------------------
```

PERIOD BEGINNING	AVAILABLE NORMAL	AVAILABLE MAXIMUM	EARLY SCHEDULE USAGE	EARLY SCHEDULE CUMULATIVE	LATE SCHEDULE USAGE	LATE SCHEDULE CUMULATIVE	EARLY/LATE AVG. USAGE	EARLY/LATE AVG. CUMULATIVE
CARPENTERS					UNIT OF MEASURE = PERSON-DAYS			
1DEC82	8	12	0	0	0	0	0	0
1JAN83	13	20	0	0	0	0	0	0
DATA DATE								
1FEB83	13	20	0	0	0	0	0	0
1MAR83	13	20	0	0	0	0	0	0
1APR83	13	20	36	36	0	0	18	18
1MAY83	13	20	44	80	0	0	22	40
1JUN83	13	20	0	80	0	0	0	40
1JUL83	10	15	0	80	88	88	44	84
1AUG83	10	15	41	121	112	200	77	161
1SEP83	10	15	83	204	74	274	79	239
1OCT83	10	15	118	322	181	455	150	389
1NOV83	10	15	269	591	297	752	283	672
1DEC83	10	15	161	752	54	806	108	779
1JAN84	15	25	88	840	36	842	62	841
1FEB84	15	25	18	858	18	860	18	859
1MAR84	15	25	8	866	10	870	9	868
1APR84	15	25	36	902	142	1012	89	957
1MAY84	15	25	174	1076	16	1028	95	1052
1JUN84	15	25	50	1126	98	1126	74	1126
1JUL84	15	25	0	1126	0	1126	0	1126
1AUG84	15	25	40	1166	40	1166	40	1166
1SEP84	0	0	0	1166	0	1166	0	1166

```
+------------------------------------------------+
|    Resource: CARPENTR                          |
| Description: CARPENTERS                         |
|       Units: PERSON-DAYS                        |
+------------------------------------------------+
| Normal limit    Max limit       Through         |
| ~~~~~~~~~~~~    ~~~~~~~~~       ~~~~~~~          |
|                                                 |
|        8            12         01JAN83          |
|       13            20         01JUL83          |
|       10            15         01JAN84          |
|       15            25         01SEP84          |
|        0             0                          |
+------------------------------------------------+
```

11
Accounting and Cost-Benefit Analysis

PROJECT MANAGEMENT BY COMPREHENSIVE RESOURCE ALLOCATION AND CONTROL

In the previous chapter, we studied how resource constraints affected a single project. We learned that one of two things must be done after float, leveling, and perhaps smoothing had been used to fullest advantage but still are inadequate to meet project objectives:

- Add sufficient resources to finish the project on time
- Hold resources steady and let the project finish date slide

There are no other choices. We have effectively dealt with both challenges.

But this simplified case—in which a single project employs a single resource pool—is rare: if only life would be so simple! Usually many projects, although nominally independent of each other, simultaneously compete for a common, limited resource pool. This often comes as a big surprise to the uninitiated. Why? The competition for resources usually begins in the requirements definition and funding stages.

Resource commitments are often made at the micro level without regard to demands or overall macro availabilities. So, when Project 1 wants three programmers, Project 2 wants five programmers, and Project 3 wants two programmers, the resource providers say, "Sure!" to each project manager. Although everything is very fluid and poorly-defined at this stage, resources are always thought to be available at the micro level.

The problem occurs when the pseudo-commitments to all three projects are totalled. For the first time, the resource provider realizes (s)he promised three project managers a total of ten programmers when only seven are actually avail-

able. The sum of the promised micro-level resource requirements is always greater than the actual macro-level availability.

Thus, there is resource contention even before the project starts. When this happens, activity sequencing and resource allocation decisions must take into account the effect on all projects needing a given resource, not just the project under review.

How do you prioritize the resources needed to support critical activities across multiple projects? What should you do when one project manager correctly says "*My* Critical Path is more critical than *your* Critical Path"?

The problem is expanded because projects often depend on regular lines of authority—in political competition among themselves for senior management's recognition—for resources. Essentially, we need to treat each individual project as a master resource allocation plan subproject, still recognizing, of course, that each project is related to the others only by this dependence on a common resource pool and not by network logic.

Clearly, the following capabilities are crucial for effective and comprehensive multiple-project resource allocation and control:

- Combine projects for resource allocation purposes
- Prioritize resource assignments within this larger context

Moder, Phillips, and Davis (pp. 194–195) explain how such complexities can, without proper tools, rapidly explode to unmanageable levels. Please study Fig. 11-1, which depicts a three-project scheduling situation involving the same number of resource categories. For simplicity, assume an activity uses only one unit of one resource type. This one unit, however, is the only one available and must therefore be shared among the three projects.

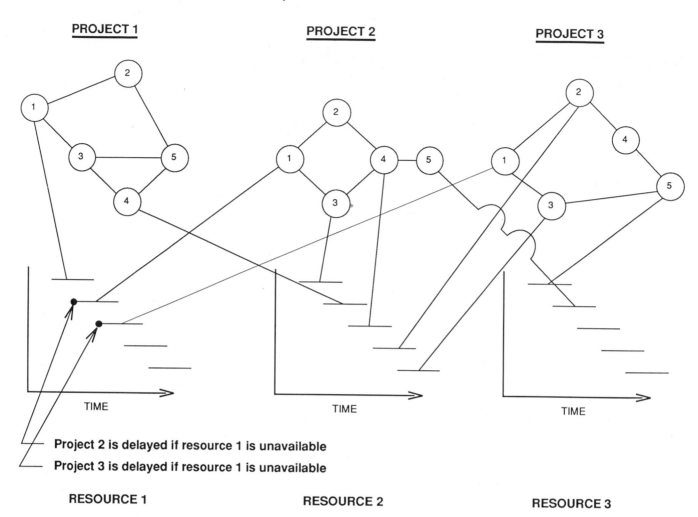

FIGURE 11-1.   Why resource conflicts spread across projects.

It is easy to imagine the domino effect that resource conflicts could cause. The consequences affect not only the activity and project under review, but possibly all other projects supported by the resource pool. Depending on activity float, network logic, and project finish times, the impact could be severe. For example, delaying activity 3 of project 1 (to resolve the conflict with activity 1 of project 2) might cause the following:

- Delays in project 1 successor activities 4 and 5
- As a result of the above, creation of additional resource conflicts (which must be resolved) among all activities (including 4 and 5 in project 1) requiring resource types 2 and 3
- As a result of this, creation of additional delays in projects 2 and 3—and possibly even in project 1 once more

So here we go again! From even this simple model, we can see that Murphy's Law again holds true: Any time we wish to isolate an item for study, we find it is interconnected to every other item in the universe! In practice, such multiproject scheduling problems involve:

- Dozens of projects
- Thousands of activities
- Unlimited resources

They may only be solved by high-octane software installed on iron of similarly high horsepower.

We have already indicated that prioritizing is often used to level resources within subprojects or across multiple projects. This allows you, the project manager, to control your resources even more closely and to apply them wisely—to the "most critical of the critical" activities.

Before leveling can begin, all candidate activities are rounded up to form a sequence that represents the natural logic of the combined network. Referred to as a "topological sequence," this collection represents the order in which activities must take place, maintaining as closely as possible the given defined logic of the contributing project.

In some topological-sequence networks, two or more adjacent activities in the global order could be resequenced with no effect on overall integrity. This permits fine-tuning and enables the assignment of priorities among activities.

The "topological sequence" ensures that an activity becomes eligible for leveling if, and only if:

- All its predecessors have been leveled
- It has sufficient resources

Within this sequence, you should be able to assign user-specified priority values to eligible parallel (both single and multiple project) activities in resource contention. *Primavera,* for example, allows ten different sort fields based on activity codes, schedule parameter codes, user-defined priority codes, or any other valid basis consistent with network logic and acceptable scheduling rules. User-specified examples include:

- Customer importance
- Project priority
- Cost/schedule consequence
- Management preferences

By introducing additional codes for ordering activities, and by providing control over how these codes are selected and sorted, it is possible to accommodate actual needs and preferences—not "take a chance with chance."

You still, of course, have the Late-Start-Total-Float prioritizing method—and many others—which works exceptionally well for most networks. This rule set attempts to ensure that activities most crucial to the project completion date are served first.

But some merged networks require a better way to reflect and manage the more subtle choices among competing activities. This "better way" does exist in the form of user-specified priorities.

If several projects are to be merged into one larger network, multiple code fields should be used to establish priorities. Activities within each contributing project should be assigned a distinct priority value for use in leveling. The project name should also be preserved in a code field (or encoded within the activity identifier itself). When that is done, assign a second code field to indicate the relative leveling priority. Be certain when leveling to select this field as the primary sort field. In *Primavera,* up to ten such priority-code fields may be used for resource allocation, leveling, and smoothing.

Predecesors will, as they should, always be leveled before their successors—regardless of codes assigned to the successor. You must not (nor would you want to!) alter network logic; out-of-sequence progress notwithstanding, the first activity in a chain is always leveled first, regardless of the priority codes assigned to those that occur later.

Multiple-project resource assignment is accomplished using a parallel-allocation algorithm similar to the single-project case. Activities are ordered first by internal network logic, then by user-specified priorities. For any given time, each activity's resource requirements are compared with current resource availability. If all required resources are available for the entire activity duration (not necessarily contiguous), the activity is scheduled without delay. If all requested resources are not available for the entire time

needed, but the maximum level would allow activity scheduling, this resource quantity is assigned to the requesting activity, which is then scheduled on its early dates.

If, however, any required resource is unavailable in sufficient quantity for the entire duration, the activity is delayed until all needed resources become available. This ensures proper loading and also avoids excessive resource swapping in and out of activities, which in the extreme can result in the playing out of another corollary of Murphy's Law: The rate of change will at such point exceed the rate of progress. Of course, successors will be delayed, too.

If multiple activities are topologically eligible for consideration, the higher-priority activity is served before the lower-priority activity, as would be expected. This is why good user-specified priorities are as crucial as they are beneficial. The process repeats and compares the unserved activity with others to determine relative service priority, and so on.

Since hammock activities only summarize their various contributing activities, they are not subject to leveling or smoothing regardless of whether or not resources have been assigned to the hammock.

In one extreme—that in which a project contains no relationships among the contributing activities—the priority codes alone would dictate leveled activity dates (provided, of course, sufficient resources are available). The reason priority codes control in this situation is that every activity is eligible based on the topological sort order.

In the opposite extreme—in which only a single activity chain is tightly integrated into one super-project—priority codes would have no effect on leveled dates. This is because the topological sequence alone would provide a unique sequence of eligible activities.

Most cases lie somewhere between these two extremes. Two otherwise unconnected parallel chains may be prioritized relative to each other by assigning a priority code to each that can later be invoked at sort time. The chain whose activities are at the top of the sorted priority-code list is considered first since the topological sequence is indifferent to which chain is leveled first. Since *you* probably care which is leveled first, be sure to assign priority codes wisely and consider all other activities, across all other projects, that may compete for the same resources at the same time.

The resource-allocation process then proceeds as in the single-project case because the resource requirements have now been combined into one project for assignment purposes. Always review report recommendations to determine:

- If the suggested solutions are workable
- Whether or not usage exceeds maximum resource availability

At the same time, you should also review a complete schedule report to determine the effect on activities excluded from the analysis report because they did not require leveled resources.

Review the resource leveling analysis reports carefully. You may even wish to "monkey around" a little with activity sequences that cause resource overloads or create sharp spikes in resource usage. Ways by which this may be done include:

- Modify network logic
- Reschedule and relevel activities
- Perform various other "what if" contingency analyses with the project management software
- Export information to your spreadsheet and do the analyses there

Target–comparison schedule reports compare current project status with planned progress and are extremely useful to evaluate alternatives. If leveling (and smoothing) results are acceptable, you must reincorporate these dates into the network and apply constraints to leveling-delayed activities.

Do not, however, apply the resource constraints if any of the following applies:

- You leveled resources only to understand your network better
- You only did contingency analyses to see the effects resource limitations might have
- You have not decided that the project plan is workable

If, though, you find the leveling (and smoothing) results acceptable, you should apply necessary constraints to activities delayed during leveling. This shows that you accept why the activity must be delayed—resource limitations more restrictive than when the initial schedule was computed under unlimited-resource conditions. As you apply network resource constraints, it is a good practice to code the reason for doing so. Then, at some later date, you may:

- Remember why they were placed
- Determine if they are still needed
- Remove the resource constraints if no longer needed

These codes also enable you to select only resource-constrained activities and:

- Generate special constrained-activity reports
- Produce batch update records
- Export selected records to your spreadsheet for further analysis and batch-update rewrite from there. Either way is both easy and effective

Early-Start constraints represent the best way to incorporate these resource-driven constraints into the network. By doing this, the schedule may be recalculated as progress is recorded. You are automatically assured that the new schedule dates will be no earlier than permitted if this schedule were again leveled. This is important in the single-project environment but mandatory in the multiproject environment.

This protection in place, you should level again as often as necessary to determine whether or not any:

- Old resource bottlenecks have been cleared
- New bottlenecks impede your ability to meet the current project schedule

Resource leveling and smoothing are very powerful analytical tools that provide near-optimal solutions, effectively and quickly. Given the low cost to produce and the other underlying network uncertainties, they can evaluate multiple options with entirely sufficient accuracy. But since there is an almost unlimited number of ways to assign network resources, it is still highly worthwhile:

- To consider alternatives
- To accept the recommendations of a knowledgeable project manager

A fire needs three elements to ignite and burn—fuel, heat, and oxygen; the absence of any one element will extinguish the fire. A project also requires three elements:

- Planning
- Organization
- Control

These are required by all management processes, not just projects. Like the fire that goes out, if all three project management requirements are not present, what "goes out" will be you, the project manager—out the door!

We have already discussed various aspects of all three of the necessary elements. Let us now look at *control* in greater depth. Project management can never be truly successful unless it is controlled, as well as planned and organized.

And project control can never be truly successful unless there is some means to measure actual work performance in terms of:

- Cost
- Progress value
- Schedules

A project rarely goes entirely according to plan: "No major project is ever completed on time, within budget, with the same staff that started it, nor does the project do what it is supposed to do. Yours will not be the first!"—Murphy.

The earlier problems are recognized, the earlier corrective action can be initiated to eliminate—or at least to minimize—the impact on planned costs and schedules. Problems at any project stage must be handled promptly and effectively. Mistakes made and problems left unsolved early in the game rapidly increase the "FUBAR-Factor" (*F*ouled *U*p *B*eyond *A*ll *R*epair) under which the remainder of the project must operate. The cost to fix errors and solve problems increases exponentially with time. Sometimes not even the best of teams can recover from mistakes early in the game. Both information and time are of the most critical essence.

A comprehensive resource allocation and control system is needed and must provide performance measurement capabilities. Proper measurement is absolutely critical to project success. You cannot manage what you cannot measure. Jones, quoted in *Function Point Analysis*, p. 3, further noted:

1. Debits never equal credits.
2. Expenses always exceed revenues.
3. Trial balances don't.
4. Balance sheet doesn't.
5. Liquidity tends to run out.
6. Fixed assets get loose.
7. Net income is not income.
8. Pro forma is without form.
9. Retained earnings aren't.
10. Working capital doesn't.
11. Return on investment won't.
12. Payback period doesn't pay back, period.
13. GAAP is a four-letter word (meaning SWAG).

FIGURE 11-2.   Murphy's 13 special laws of accountancy.

"Scientific progress in every field has been heavily dependent upon the ability to take accurate measurements. Progress in all of the sciences has been significantly obliged to progress in measurement for progress to occur in the science itself."

Reports must be complete, accurate, reliable, meaningful, and, above all, timely indications of when and where management must take corrective action. Performance problems must be easily visible at multiple detail levels or vantage points of company work centers, trade skills, and the project Work Breakdown Structure (WBS). They must also easily summarize details and "drill down" to provide more. AI-based decision support systems (such as Comshare *IFPS/Plus* and *Executive Edge*) residing atop the resource pool for more extensive quantitative analysis have recently grown in popularity.

Of course, these reports should also "catch people doing something right" so that management can, and hopefully will, offer commendations where warranted. Remember: A pat on the back is only a few inches away from a kick in the pants—but is miles ahead in results!

If you have not already made friends with accounting, you must immediately do this. The balance of this chapter (including the applications of Murphy's Law noted in Fig. 11-2) is required reading for all but the CPA's who might be tuned in. While by no means a complete treatment, this accounting and cost-benefit analysis summary will:

* Give you a solid foundation on which to build further knowledge
* Provide a quick but effective review of important principles if you have forgotten your debits and credits

A BRIEF SUMMARY OF ACCOUNTING PRINCIPLES

In *Accounting: Text and Cases,* Anthony and Reece effectively discuss the managerial accounting concepts and rules that are very briefly summarized below.

Generally Accepted Accounting Principles (GAAP) requires the use of a double-entry bookkeeping system in which each accounting transaction is expressed by a debit amount and an equal and offsetting credit amount. This makes possible the rule, to which there is absolutely no exception, that for each transaction the debit amount (or the sum of all the debit amounts, if there are more than one) must equal the credit amount (or the sum of all the credit amounts). It is also why we refer to accounting and bookkeeping as double-entry. It follows that the recording of a transaction in which debits do not equal credits is incorrect. It also follows that, for all the accounts combined, the sum of the debit balances must equal the sum of all the corresponding credit balances; otherwise, something has been done incorrectly. Thus, the debit and credit arrangement provides a useful means of checking the accuracy by which the transactions have been recorded.

The equality of debits and credits is maintained simply by specifying that asset accounts, which are recorded on the Balance Sheet, are increased on the debit side, while liabilities and owners' equity accounts, which also are recorded on the Balance Sheet, are increased on the credit side. The account balances, when totaled, will then conform to the two equations:

* Assets = Liabilities + Owners' Equity
* Debits = Credits

This arrangement, in turn, gives rise to three rules:

* Increases in asset accounts are debits; decreases are credits
* Increases in liability accounts are credits; decreases are debits
* Increases in owners' equity accounts are credits; decreases are debits

We can derive the rules for expense and revenue accounts, which are recorded on the Income/Profit and Loss Statement, if we recall that:

* Expenses are decreases in owners' equity
* Revenues are increases in owners' equity

Since owners' equity accounts decrease on the debit side, expenses increase on the debit side; and since owners' equity accounts increase on the credit side, revenues increase on the credit side. In summary:

* Increases in expense accounts are debits
* Increases in revenue accounts are credits

Each of these five rules is illustrated in the examples shown in Table 11-1. Note that assets—"good" things—and expenses—"bad" things—both increase on the debit side. Also note that liability and revenue accounts both increase on the credit side. This illustrates the fact that "debit" and "credit" are neutral terms; they do not connote value judgments. Instead, they indicate only the side of the paper, left or right, on which to post an entry. Other meanings have been added later.

These five account categories may be combined into the summary "Where-Got/Where-Gone" diagram shown in Table 11-2. GAAP requires that *costs* be matched to *revenues,* not the other way around. (Note: GAAP says, "Match costs

Table 11-1   Examples of Debits and Credits

ASSETS		=	LIABILITIES		+	OWNERS' EQUITY	
Cash on Hand			Accounts Payable			Retained Earnings	
DR	CR		DR	CR		DR	CR
+	–		–	+		–	+
Expenses						Revenues	
Wages and Salaries						Sales	
DR	CR					DR	CR
+							+

to revenues." Murphy says, "Increase costs to exceed revenues.")

Employing the use of these examples, we may determine the Balance Sheet/Income Statement results (Table 11-3) of the following twelve transactions:

1. You sell $95,000 worth of goods. These products cost $57,000 to produce.
2. You borrow $50,000 from the bank.
3. You repay this loan, plus $5,000 interest.
4. You issue $75,000 worth of common stock.
5. You invest $2,000 to acquire software. (You will be surprised how many people miss this one! Hint: stay out of the Expense column!)
6. You purchase $2,000 worth of office supplies and consume half.
7. You write off a $32,000 bad debt against the Accounts Receivable Bad Debt Reserve.
8. You purchase a new car for $12,000 entirely on credit. No payments have yet been made.
9. You pay $25,000 in wages and salaries.
10. You recognize one month's insurance expenses of $1,000, premiums for which have already been paid.
11. You pay three months' rent in advance, totaling $3,000.
12. You receive a $7,000 remittance from an Accounts Receivable customer.

Although Assets increased $82,000, Liabilities increased $12,000 and Owners' Equity increased $75,000; this $5,000 difference between the two sides

$$(= \$82,000 - (\$12,000 + \$75,000))$$

is because expenses exceeded revenues for the period by $5,000.

Debits and credits to certain special accounts are not directly covered by these rules, but can be deduced from them. For example, consider the account Returned Goods, which is a deduction from Sales. We know that Sales is a revenue account and that increases to it are, therefore, recorded on the credit side. Since Returned Goods is a deduction from Sales, it must be treated in the opposite way from Sales. Returned Goods, therefore, increase on the debit side.

Two other important terms must now be defined. First, a *ledger* is simply a group of related accounts to which financial journal transactions are recorded. Second, prior to setting up an accounting system, a list is usually prepared showing each item for which a ledger account is to be maintained. This list is called the *chart of accounts*. Each account on the list is numbered in such a way as to facilitate arrangement, grouping, and sorting. For example, all asset accounts may be numbered 100–199, all liability accounts 200–299, all owners' equity accounts 300–399, expense accounts 400–499, and all revenue accounts 500–599, then each subdivided by successive layers according to both division and topic ("bean jar").

Table 11-2   Accounting in a Nutshell

DEBITS (Uses)				(Sources) CREDITS
+			Assets	–
–		=	Liabilities	+
–		+	Owners' Equity	+
+	Expenses		Revenues	+

Table 11-3   Results, in Thousands of Dollars or Other Monetary Units

#	ASSETS DR	ASSETS CR	LIABILITIES DR	LIABILITIES CR	EQUITY DR	EQUITY CR	EXPENSES DR	EXPENSES CR	REVENUE DR	REVENUE CR
(1)	95									95
		57					57			
(2)	50			50						
(3)		50	50							
		5					5			
(4)	75					75				
(5)	2	2								
(6)	2	2								
		1					1			
(7)		10					10			
(8)	12			12						
(9)		25					25			
(10)		1					1			
(11)	2	3					1			
(12)	7	7								
DR	<u>245</u>		<u>50</u>		<u>0</u>		<u>100</u>		<u>0</u>	
CR		<u>163</u>		<u>62</u>		<u>75</u>		<u>0</u>		<u>95</u>

TOTAL DEBITS = $<u>395,000</u>

TOTAL CREDITS = $<u>395,000</u>

Finally, it is important to know the relationship between the Balance Sheet and the Income/Profit and Loss Statement.

We have already seen the Balance Sheet in operation when balancing the equation:

Total Assets = Total Liabilities + Owners' Equity

To understand this equation better, we need at this point to define several more important terms:

1. *Total assets:* Total monetary value of all economic resources controlled by an organization whose cost at the time of acquisition could be objectively measured. By definition, must always equal the sum of Total Liabilities and Owners' Equity.

   Current assets: Cash, inventory, accounts receivable, and other assets that are reasonably expected to be converted into cash, or sold, or consumed during the normal operating cycle of the organization (usually one year).

   Fixed assets: Real property (land), plant, and equipment. The current net value of plant and equipment is its original cost less all accumulated *depreciation* (which is that fraction of an asset's cost converted during the current accounting period into an expense to reflect asset consumption through both deterioration and obsolescence), which may in turn be computed by a variety of ways—of which the straight-line, the double-declining balance, and the sum-of-years-digits methods are the most common. Land is never depreciated.

   Other assets: Intangible assets and assets not easily categorized as either current or fixed.

2. *Total liabilities:* Total monetary value of all claims against the organization's assets.

   Current liabilities: Accounts payable, notes payable, estimated taxes, accrued expenses payable, and other liabilities that are expected to be satisfied either by the use of current assets or by the creation of other current liabilities during the normal operating cycle of the organization (usually one year).

   Noncurrent liabilities: Long-term debt and other liabilities due beyond the end of the normal operating cycle of the organization (usually one year).

3. *Owners' equity:* Excess (deficit) of Total Assets over Total Liabilities.

   Paid-in capital: Capital stock and other paid-in capital invested by the owners in the organization.

   Retained earnings: Difference between the organization's total earnings to date and the total amount of dividends paid to date to the shareholders. Retained earnings represent that part of the total earnings that have been retained by the organization for its own use.

The Income/Profit and Loss Statement, seen earlier, summarizes the organization's financial performance for a given time period, usually month, quarter, or year. In its most basic form:

Net Income = Total Revenues − Total Expenses

To this must now be added Retained Earnings:

Ending Retained Earnings =

Net Income
+ Beginning Retained Earnings
− Dividends

We have already seen Retained Earnings and Dividends in the Balance Sheet. We now need to define the two remaining terms—Revenues and Expenses—and to distinguish the latter from Costs in general.

Revenues: Increases in Owners' Equity resulting from operation of the entity (including, especially, providing goods and services to customers), recognized in the period in which these goods are shipped or services are rendered, and against which accompanying costs are matched.

Expenses: Cost items (see below) that are subtracted from revenue in that accounting period in which the corresponding revenue is realized (or, if a cost item cannot be associated with the revenue of some future accounting period), resulting in a decrease to Owners' Equity. Expenses are *not* to be confused with asset acquisition (such as the investment in software), which is a cost, and perhaps also an expenditure—but is *not* an expense unless the asset is entirely consumed during the same year (highly unlikely with software!). Expenses also include:

- *Inventories:* assets that become expenses when products are sold
- *Prepaid expenses:* assets purchased, but not yet consumed, prior to this year (or other accounting period)
- *Depreciation:* defined above under Fixed Assets

Note well the distinction between costs and expenses. Costs refer to the amount of resources used for any purpose, the monetary value of which may be objectively measured. Expenses are one type of cost. Asset acquisition is another. The accounting treatment for each cost type is, however, very different from the other! This is summarized in Table 11-4.

Final discussion point: In a 7 May 1990 letter to *InformationWeek,* James Kinder quoted former Citicorp chairperson Walter Wriston as follows:

"Today the biggest asset in business is intellectual capital, the software that actually runs the business, controls the operation, and makes it productive. But how do we treat software? Because software came after the Industrial Revolution, because it isn't tangible, we expense most of it."

Managers face a major challenge to fit the tools of the Industrial Age into the workings of the Information Age. Most people know a good pump will deliver flow well in excess of required priming quantity and would never expect a pump to work properly without it. They also understand that a financial institution will not pay them interest unless they invest some funds there. Yet, how many of the same people think investment in critically-important software is like throwing water and money to the winds?

Kinder concludes: "It's interesting that most don't believe software is an asset, probably because they can't see it or touch it."

Barker would call this "paradigm paralysis." This author would call it reckless, irresponsible management.

Retained Earnings is the only direct connection between the Balance Sheet and the Income/Profit and Loss Statement. Because it shows why changes occurred between two years in the Retained Earnings account, the Income/Profit and Loss Statement may be considered a special (and very important) case of the Statement of Changes in Financial Position; and thus it is considered by GAAP to be a better test of financial performance over time than is the Balance Sheet, which is merely a financial snapshot of a single day and is therefore subject to extensive "window dressing."

A complete Balance Sheet and Income Statement is provided in Table 11-5 to show how these concepts all tie together into an accurate working financial model of a typical business. Following this is a summary discussion of cost-benefit analysis methodologies.

As a project manager, you will probably be most concerned with expenses: wages, salaries, materials, overtime, and so on. However, you should still be familiar with all

Table 11-4   Differences Between Asset Acquisition and Expense

```
ASSET ACQUISITION                    EXPENSE

* Is NOT subtracted from revenue     * Is ALWAYS subtracted from revenue
* Does NOT affect Net Income         * Reduces Net Income
* Does NOT affect Owners' Equity     * Reduces Owners' Equity
* Exchanges one asset for another    * Usually reduces Current Assets
* Example:  software acquisition     * Example:  pay power & light bill
   dr.  Software Inventory...1,000       dr.  Accounts Payable...500
      cr.  Cash............  1,000          cr.  Cash...........  500
   (Revenue unaffected)                 (Charged against revenue)
```

Table 11-5 Integrated Year-1 Balance Sheet, Year-2 Income Statement, and Year-2 Balance Sheet

INTEGRATED YEAR 1 BALANCE SHEET, YEAR 2 INCOME STATEMENT, AND YEAR 2 BALANCE SHEET

------BALANCE SHEET (YEAR 1) IN THOUSANDS OF DOLLARS------

```
*** ASSETS ***
=============
Current assets
  Cash                                     546
  Inventory                             12,194
  Accounts receivable                   10,103
  Prepaid expenses; other                  997
Total current assets                            23,840
Fixed assets                            26,666
  Less: accumulated depreciation        12,410
Net fixed assets                                14,256
Other assets                                       181
TOTAL ASSETS                                    38,277
=============                                    ======

*** LIABILITIES ***
==================
Current liabilities
  Accounts payable                       5,088
  Notes payable and current debt         2,398
  Other                                  5,406
Total current liabilities                       12,892
Long-term debt; other                            3,000
TOTAL LIABILITIES                               15,892
=================                                ======

*** OWNERS' EQUITY ***
=====================
Capital stock                                    5,000
Retained earnings (from current-year P&L)       17,385
TOTAL OWNERS' EQUITY                            22,385
====================                            ======

*** TOTAL LIABILITIES AND OWNERS' EQUITY ***    38,277
===========================================     ======

*** CHECK: ***
DO TOTAL ASSETS = (TL + OE)?     * YES! *
===========================      =======
```

------INCOME STATEMENT (YEAR 2) x $1,000------

```
Gross sales                                   $79,614
  Less: returns and allowances                 (1,326)
  Less: sales discounts                        (2,810)
Net sales                                     $75,478
  Less: cost of sales                         (52,227)
Gross margin                                  $23,251
  Less: expenses                              (10,785)

Income before taxes                           $12,466
  Less: provision for income taxes             (4,986)
*** NET INCOME ***                             $7,480
==================                             ======

Plus: beginning retained earnings             $17,385
Less: dividends                                (5,748)
*** ENDING RETAINED EARNINGS ***              $19,117
================================               ======
```

------BALANCE SHEET (YEAR 2) IN THOUSANDS OF DOLLARS------

```
*** ASSETS ***
=============
Current assets
  Cash                                     515
  Inventory                             10,883
  Accounts receivable                   10,191
  Prepaid expenses; other                1,062
Total current assets                            22,651
Fixed assets                            26,190
  Less: accumulated depreciation        12,778
Net fixed assets                                13,412
Other assets                                       173
TOTAL ASSETS                                    36,236
=============                                    ======

*** LIABILITIES ***
==================
Current liabilities
  Accounts payable                       3,849
  Notes payable and current debt           887
  Other                                  4,383
Total current liabilities                        9,119
Long-term debt; other                            3,000
TOTAL LIABILITIES                               12,119
=================                                ======

*** OWNERS' EQUITY ***
=====================
Capital stock                                    5,000
Retained earnings (from year-2 P&L)             19,117
TOTAL OWNERS' EQUITY                            24,117
====================                            ======

*** TOTAL LIABILITIES AND OWNERS' EQUITY ***    36,236
===========================================     ======

*** CHECK: ***
DO TOTAL ASSETS = (TL + OE)?     * YES! *
===========================      =======
```

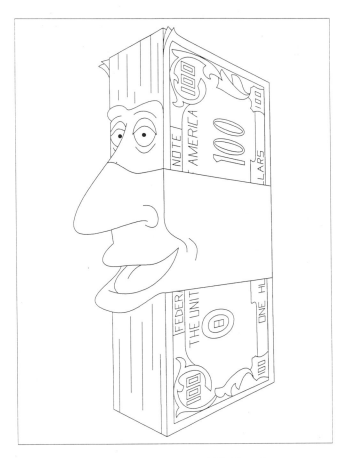

FIGURE 11-3.   "Money talks!" *Source:* CSC Diagraph.

these other terms, and their relationships among each other. Looking at your project in the context of the overall accounting picture will enable you to make better decisions faster, be more effective, and be regarded as more professional. The cost-benefit analysis material will help you sell your project to the corporate purse-keepers. *Good luck and good accounting* (Fig. 11-3)!

COST-BENEFIT ANALYSIS

In *Computer Information Systems Development: Analysis and Design,* Powers, Adams, and Mills present a short but effective cost-benefit analysis discussion summarized below.

Costs and benefits are tradeoffs used to decide:

- Whether or not to proceed or continue with a particular project
- Which of two or more projects to fund if moneys for all are not available

Cost-benefit analyses might also demonstrate why a project should be approved even if cash is not available today but will be made available tomorrow as a direct result of the project.

Tangible costs and benefits can be readily measured in monetary terms. Intangible costs and benefits are just as real, and just as important, but are harder to measure in monetary units. All four categories—both one-time and ongoing—must be included, however, in any analysis to ensure validity.

Projects should be considered capital investments that provide a stream of benefits over a number of future years and, accordingly, consider the time value of money. The value of money today is not the same as its future value. If you deposit $1 today at 7 percent interest, it would in one year increase to $1.07. On this same basis, the dollar would have a value of $1.07 if it were invested in a one-year project.

Suppose instead, that you put your dollar away in a drawer, rather than depositing it in a financial institution. When you remove the bill after a year, it is worth less than when you put it away. Inflation has deprived your dollar of some of its purchasing power. At the very least, you have missed an opportunity for a 7 percent growth. You also missed the opportunity to pay current expenses. Either way, you have experienced the cost of a missed opportunity—an *opportunity cost.*

No matter how you apply available funds, the value of money changes over time. Money has a time value that must be considered in guiding investment decisions. A dollar today is not worth the same as a dollar tomorrow—or yesterday. In general, it is advisable to:

- Enjoy revenues as soon as possible
- Delay paying expenses for as long as possible (without penalty), unless they are substantially discounted for early payment

As a capital investment, a project competes with other financial alternatives and investment opportunities. When resources are limited, not all opportunities can be funded. Those that do not support the goals and objectives of an enterprise will probably be, as they should, rejected outright. Those that do must compete for limited amounts of funding and show why they are financially preferable to other uses of needed funds.

For example, assume that a new system will cost $60,000 and is expected to save $20,000 annually for a three-year anticipated life. Is this a good investment? Or would it be better to deposit this amount in a financial institution?

At first glance, the system investment appears sound. However, $60,000 invested for three years at 8 percent would grow to $75,583. On this basis, the system investment is not cost-effective—unless there are other valid reasons for its development.

Because the value of money changes over time, it is desirable to establish some common denominator for comparison—a factor that makes it possible to state values in constant monetary units. The most common such reference point for comparing values over time is the present year—the value of money right now.

Future economic values are discounted backward in time at given rates (the *discount factor*) to arrive at their *present values*. The discounted rates represent projected interest earnings, inflation losses, the cost of capital, *IRR (Internal Rate of Return)*, or other meaningful changes in the value of money over time. Senior management must either set, or at least agree to, these rates.

Any future monetary value can be discounted to its present value through multiplication by a *present value factor (PVF)*, which is equal to:

$$\frac{1}{(1 + i)^n}$$

where i = interest rate and n = number of years. If i = 7 percent and n = one year, the PVF equals 0.935. If i increases to 8 percent, PVF decreases to 0.926. If i increases to 10 percent, the PVF decreases further to 0.909; if i increases to 12 percent, the PVF drops to 0.893. At i = 15 percent, PVF = 0.870.

In general, the PVF decreases with:

• Higher discount rates (i)
• Longer times (n)

It increases with:

• Lower discount rates (i)
• Shorter times (n)

Values may be computed directly, perhaps in a spreadsheet, or extracted from a present value table, a portion of which is presented in Table 11-6.

The present value goes down fast, doesn't it! If you could earn 10 percent on your investment, but only put your dollar away in a drawer, that same dollar is really worth only 90.9 cents a year from now. If you could earn 15 percent but did the same thing, the dollar, in five years, would be worth less than half its current value.

As an example of how a discount table is used, assume that a new system costs $19,000 and is expected to produce a savings of $20,000 at the end of one year. Also assume that the money could be invested risk-free at 10 percent over the same period. If the discounted value of $20,000 savings is less than the required $19,000 investment, the project will not produce comparable returns. In financial terms alone, the discounted value of $20,000 at 10 percent over one year represents the maximum amount that should be spent on the project.

Note the use of the word "returns" instead of "savings." Preferred by this author, too, *returns* correctly implies that money and other resources are:

• Made available for other, better uses
• Not necessarily "saved," which generally means:
   Improved Net Income
   Reduced expenses
   Firing "surplus" or "excess" people (brutal, ruthless terms!)

The present value calculation is straightforward. The present value factor (.909) is either computed or is found in the table at the intersection of the 10 percent column and the one-year row. It is then multiplied by the principal amount, or: $20,000 * .909 = $18,180.

On financial grounds, the project should be rejected because the required $19,000 investment exceeds the $18,180 present value. The company would do better to invest its $19,000 at 10 percent for the same year.

The use of present values of future amounts:

• Recognizes the time value of money
• Equates different investment opportunities with differing costs, benefits, discount rates, and lengths of investment periods to a common measurement standard

One important application of this concept is known as *net present value (NPV)*.

An investment net present value is measured in monetary units and equals:

• The sum of the present values of the benefits (returns) less:
• The sum of the present values of the investments (costs)

The resulting value can be positive, zero, or negative. The algebraic sign of the value reflects the investment's rate of return with respect to a given discount rate.

For example, consider the costs and benefits given for the following opportunity:

Development costs = $153,500 (current year)
                              + $32,600 (one year later)
Projected savings by year = $19,800; $46,725; $62,650;
                              $68,220; and $75,200

Table 11-6   Partial Discount Table

YEAR	8%	10%	12%	15%
1	.926	.909	.893	.870
2	.857	.826	.797	.756
3	.794	.751	.712	.658
4	.735	.683	.636	.572
5	.681	.621	.567	.497

The net present value method:

- Discounts both costs and benefits to the current year
- Compares the resulting (discounted) values, altered for risk as appropriate

Table 11-7 assumes that an acceptable alternative investment opportunity at 10 percent is available.

The positive NPV ($13,838) indicates that the projected rate of return exceeds the 10 percent comparison value. Therefore, investing in the system will produce greater monetary returns than the alternative investment—by a total value (measured in current-year monetary units) of $13,838. Note that the NPV does not indicate the exact investment rate of return, only the dollar amount by which it exceeds the benchmark base of 10 percent. A positive NPV indicates that the projected return on investment is greater than the alternative considered. Therefore, we do know that investment in the system would produce a rate of return greater than 10 percent, even though we do not know just what the exact value is. The exact value, if desired, may be computed by means of a goal-seeking operation in your spreadsheet or decision support system.

A zero NPV:

- Indicates financial equality between the two investment opportunities
- Means that the system rate of return precisely equals the alternative (10 percent)
- Produces a tie that must be resolved by other means if both opportunities cannot be funded

A negative NPV indicates that the projected return for the investment is less than the comparative value. Note well that a negative NPV does not necessarily mean a project is unprofitable; it only means its rate of return is less than the comparison amount. Again, the precise value may, if desired, be calculated with goal-seeking.

NPV can also be used to compare two or more alternative proposed projects. For example, assume Project A costs $10,000 and will produce $4,000 savings a year for five years. Project B costs $100,000 and returns savings of $30,000 a year for five years. The length of expected benefits need not be the same but, as seen here, may be. Assuming that only one project can be funded and that the minimum acceptable rate of return is 12 percent, which project should be approved?

Shame on anyone who says Project A because it is "cheaper"! From the NPV calculations shown in Table 11-8, B should be funded before A.

Both project NPVs are positive, so both qualify; each return rate exceeds the 12 percent minimum. Which project, then, is the better investment?

On an NPV basis alone, Project B is. Its NPV ($8,143) is almost double that of A's ($4,419). But the returns on each project must be related to the required dollar investments. This is done by comparing the net present value coefficient (NPV coefficient) for each project.

The *NPV coefficient* is the ratio between the net present value and the investment amount. The coefficient is a percentage value that can be used to compare projects. The two projects are compared in Table 11-9.

Table 11-7   Net Present Value Calculations, $i = 10\%$

YEAR	INVESTMENT COST	10% PRESENT VALUE FACTOR	INVESTMENT PV	RETURNS	10% PVF	RETURNS PV
0	$153,500	1.0000	$153,500		1.0000	$0
1	$32,600	0.9091	$29,636	$19,800	0.9091	$18,000
2		0.8264		$46,725	0.8264	$38,616
3		0.7513		$62,650	0.7513	$47,070
4		0.6830		$68,220	0.6830	$46,595
5		0.6209		$75,200	0.6209	$46,693
TOTALS	$186,100		$183,136			$196,974

```
            $196,974  PV(RETURNS)
            $183,136  PV(INVESTMENT)
NPV =       $13,838
```

Table 11-8   Project-Comparison NPV Calculations, $i = 12\%$

				PROJECT A			

YEAR	INVESTMENT COST	12% PRESENT VALUE FACTOR	INVESTMENT PV	RETURNS	12% PVF	RETURNS PV
0	$10,000	1.0000	$10,000		1.0000	$0
1		0.8929		$4,000	0.8929	$3,571
2		0.7972		$4,000	0.7972	$3,189
3		0.7118		$4,000	0.7118	$2,847
4		0.6355		$4,000	0.6355	$2,542
5		0.5674		$4,000	0.5674	$2,270
	$10,000		$10,000			$14,419

```
          $14,419  PV(RETURNS)
          $10,000  PV(INVESTMENT)
NPV =      $4,419
```

				PROJECT B			

YEAR	INVESTMENT COST	12% PRESENT VALUE FACTOR	INVESTMENT PV	RETURNS	12% PVF	RETURNS PV
0	$100,000	1.0000	$100,000		1.0000	$0
1		0.8929		$30,000	0.8929	$26,786
2		0.7972		$30,000	0.7972	$23,916
3		0.7118		$30,000	0.7118	$21,353
4		0.6355		$30,000	0.6355	$19,066
5		0.5674		$30,000	0.5674	$17,023
	$100,000		$100,000			$108,143

```
          $108,143  PV(RETURNS)
          $100,000  PV(INVESTMENT)
NPV =       $8,143
```

These results indicate that Project A has a much higher *return on investment (ROI)* than Project B does. Although these values do not represent the actual rates of return, they do provide a basis for comparison that recognizes the costs of investment, as well as the returns.

If funds are limited (let me know immediately if they are not!), the better investment might be Project A because it produces more than half the net savings as does B—but on only 10 percent of the investment. Now, that's leverage! If the remaining $90,000 can be invested to net at least

Table 11-9   NPV Coefficient Calculations, $i = 12\%$

PROJECT A	PROJECT B
NPV Coefficient = NPV/Investment $$= \$ \frac{4,419}{\$10,000}$$ $$= \underline{0.44}$$	NPV Coefficient = NPV/Investment $$= \$ \frac{8,143}{\$100,000}$$ $$= \underline{0.08}$$

$3,724 (the difference between $8,143 and $4,419), both Project *A* and this third option (perhaps a slightly smaller Project *B*) should be selected. It should not be too hard to net this amount from a $90,000 investment because it represents an ROI on the margin of only 4.14 percent.

The deciding factor (tiebreaker), if needed, should be when projects are expected to break even. The earlier a

project breaks even (cumulative net costs equal cumulative net returns), the sooner it will begin to provide lasting financial benefit.

Regardless of ROI values, payback periods, and other financial indicators, no project should be funded unless it materially and substantially supports the business goals of an enterprise. It is even sometimes strategic to approve

Table 11-10   Typical Business Objectives

CATEGORY	OBJECTIVE	EXPLANATION: BY IMPLEMENTING PRODUCTS OR PROCESSES THAT:
1. **FINANCES**	A. Increase revenues	* Contribute to increasing sales and profits
	B. Reduce expenses	* Cost less to buy, use, maintain, or replace; or that permit cost savings in related areas
	C. Increase productivity	* Enable more or better work output as a function of required input (time, money, facilities, people) through process improvement
	D. Improve cash flow	* Better manage revenue income and expense outflow
2. **GROWTH AND CHANGE**	A. Ensure capacity	* Handle current peak loads, avoid slippages and opportunity costs, and provide for future expansion
	B. Increase flexibility	* Can perform multiple functions
	C. Provide for future needs	* Support long-term stability and viability; meet future business goals, objectives, and opportunities; counter competitive challenges

3. **OPERATIONS**   A. Simplify operations   * Are easier to learn and use

              B. Increase efficiency   * Increase or improve work output, through process improvement, of people using them

              C. Increase flexibility   * Can accommodate even unexpected changes and short-notice needs

              D. Improve reliability   * Fail less often and/or can be repaired/restored more quickly if they do

              E. Acquire capabilities   * Perform new or additional functions

4. **MANAGEMENT**   A. Simplify management   * Streamline the management process by underlying-process improvement

              B. Increase control   * Permit more effective management

              C. Improve planning   * Provide tools to capture and process information to be used in forecasting and planning operations

5. **SERVICE TO OTHERS**   A. Improve service   * Increase quantity, quality, type, or speed of service provided

              B. Achieve recognition   * Demonstrate the effectiveness and professionalism of your operation

6. **HUMAN RESOURCES**   A. Develop personnel   * Help personnel learn new skills or acquire additional capabilities

              B. Reduce turnover   * Promote job satisfaction and improve morale

---

projects unlikely to return a profit if other unmeasurable benefits will also accrue. Who but Boeing could—and did—build *Air Force One?*

Consider the business objectives (presented in Table 11-10) that Tratec suggests *your* project funding request should satisfy.

If none of the objectives in Table 11-10 seem to work, Murphy's Law (and human nature) suggests that the prioritized budgeting criteria presented in Table 11-11 be used instead.

Table 11-11   How Projects Are Really Funded

```
1. EGO
2. POWER
3. MONEY
4. COMPANY BENEFIT
```

12
Project Cost Accounting and Forecasting

THE NEED FOR COST CONTROL

We studied basic accounting principles in the last chapter in order to understand cost control in this. Cost control evaluates:

- Actual costs relative to budget
- Progress relative to baseline
- Progress relative to budget
- Schedule performance and efficiency
- Earned value measurements

The essential ingredients of cost control include:

- Activity networks with identifiable work quantities (in units and costs, and in both actual and budgeted amounts)
- Cost accounts that relate each activity to its contributing resources and that lend themselves to effective detail, grouping, summarizing, and sorting
- Budget estimates (not SWAGs!) for each cost account
- Charge codes to which personnel can readily and accurately bill time
- Personnel capable of allocating costs from vendor invoice and various other sources to cost account
- Accurate, timely progress reporting with quantity details; percentage complete; materials; labor, money, and other resources employed by activity
- Good communication and working relationships between project staff and accounting department personnel

Despite wide variances, most cost control systems follow an operational cycle that is founded in the Work Breakdown Structure (WBS) and is similar to progress control:

- Estimate costs
- Plan the work
- Work the plan

- Forecast expenditures
- Measure progress and costs
- Re-estimate costs
- Replan, reforecast, and so on

The specific form and content depend on:

- Project type
- Management needs
- Capital sources
- Several other factors

Each activity must be assigned a cost estimate when duration is estimated. Unfortunately, cost history is usually by work or labor category, not by individual activities—which often involve:

- Multiple work categories
- Partial work categories

Your accounting system *must* provide sufficient detail to accommodate both situations. If it does not, it should be enhanced so that it can. Otherwise, cost estimating will:

- Essentially start from scratch each time
- Be unable to take advantage of past history
- Produce values of doubtful accuracy, benefit, and reliability
- Be a real hassle
- Not be performed, except under duress

These problems will only be compounded with time. A current, reliable, and useful cost base must be maintained. New activities can look to it for initial values—which can then be modified (often by skilled judgment) to reflect unique considerations. When completed, these activities can report experience—both good and bad—for use in future cost estimates.

278

Note well that costs depend primarily on the process performed (and include needed people and resources), not on the end deliverable. In this way, appropriate cost modules that duplicate the process under review may be selected and used with only minor fine-tuning. Completely new estimates are unnecessary and probably unreliable. Use past history where possible to forecast future needs.

This procedure will require more initial effort but less sustaining. You say that you don't have time to perform it? Will you have time later to clean up a total disaster? Perhaps—if you seriously overbid your project (you lost the deal) or underbid it (you lost your job!).

There is a better way: Do it right the FIRST time!

As a moderating solution, it is acceptable to distribute costs across multiple activities by relative proportion. Provided that the total amount apportioned is correct, the actual amounts distributed need only be moderately accurate. As several work category costs may be assigned to a single activity, a table or report should be prepared to avoid confusion.

Cost coding, like its resource counterpart, provides the following benefits:

- Increased simplicity and accuracy through standardization
- Allocation prioritization
- Greater information reporting flexibility and value

Indirect costs can be similarly apportioned and coded. Finally, a hammock activity can be used to allocate costs to a group of activities where even the apportionment method is too difficult, much the same as with activities too complex to break down into their time components. The hammock activity is assigned the (work category) total cost for member activities. If greater precision is needed, assign costs to the individual activities. The hammock activity should be used only as a last resort.

The cost-estimating and update process should be done the same time as the following:

- Work Breakdown Structure (WBS) definition
- Activity duration estimating
- Critical Path scheduling
- Least cost scheduling
- Overall network planning
- Major milestones
- Post-project review

Once each activity has been assigned an estimated cost, and start and finish dates, it is possible to forecast expenditure for:

- Any project date
- Any project component (resource, activity, key person, and so on)
- The entire project

If your project does not exceed eighty-eight years (I hope it does not!), *Primavera* will:

- Forecast future cost and schedule status

- Determine current cost and schedule status
- Review past cost and schedule status

To evaluate schedule performance, both time and cost:

- Examine project milestones
- Compare actual cumulative time and cost experience with planned target values and the work performed
- Analyze slippages and recovery

Cost data are accumulated by individual work packages, then summarized ("rolled up") into higher WBS levels. Summary cost information may also be presented in greater detail by a drill-down process. Both uses show why proper work package design was stressed so heavily in the discussion of WBS.

Baseline, or target, schedules can be established to measure cost and performance as the project progresses. The project manager can measure actual work performed according to a defined schedule and evaluate alternative courses of action to meet objectives if actual progress fails to meet expected progress. Project control requires the project manager to:

- Completely and objectively monitor activities in process
- Note, thank, and encourage persons found "doing something right"
- Identify and fairly evaluate corrective actions to restore progress
- Select, implement, and monitor the most effective actions

Schedule control methodologies evaluate actual progress relative to time. Cost control methodologies evaluate actual progress relative to budgeted costs. Together, these two techniques—if implemented properly—provide the project manager with an objective evaluation of the health of his or her project.

Proper WBS setup and good cost/schedule reporting become especially important when we remember that the hardest part of maintaining cost control is establishing an effective correspondence between activity codes used for scheduling and the codes used for cost accumulation. This procedure:

- Is crucial to project success
- Must be done carefully
- Should be included in the Work Breakdown Structure (WBS)
- Must relate each work package (including resources applied and milestones accomplished) to its corresponding cost account(s)
- Is a necessary management responsibility and not a software-induced difficulty

Software only helps (in some cases, requires) you to do what you should do anyway, but maybe have not done because it was:

- Impossible to do right with limited time, people, money, or other resources

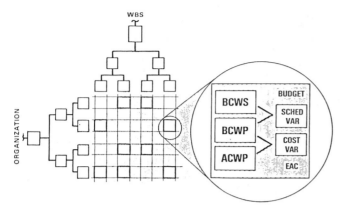

FIGURE 12-1.   How the work package assigns WBS financial performance responsibility to the organization chart. *Source:* Kerzner.

Table 12-1   Key Financial Indicators

	ACTUAL	BUDGETED
PERFORMED	ACWP	BCWP
SCHEDULED	N/A	BCWS

- Too easy to cheat and *think* you could get away with it
- Both

But remember: What goes around, comes around.

Selection of appropriate work packages depends on the project. To provide effective control, you should ensure that each work package corresponds to responsibility assignments as well as project elements. Then, you can track the performance of each responsible manager (Kerzner p. 748) (Fig. 12-1).

THREE LEVELS OF ANALYTICAL SOPHISTICATION

Cost control methodologies can be applied at one of three general levels of sophistication:

Level 1: Compare actual costs with budgeted costs. Compute variances to identify potential problem areas.

Level 2: Combine cost estimates to complete each activity with actual cost data. Analyze variances between estimated costs at completion and budgeted costs at completion.

Level 3: Compare Actual Cost for Work Performed (ACWP)—and Budgeted Cost for Work Scheduled (BCWS)—with Budgeted Cost for Work Performed (BCWP) to determine variances from baseline. Obtain additional, more useful, information by:

- Evaluating the rate at which costs are expended to accomplish activities
- Determining reasons for activity performance variances, including:
  Spending rate differs because insufficient work was accomplished
  Cost/work unit differs, even though scheduled quantity was achieved

Each of these three methodologies will now be discussed in more detail. Keep Table 12-1 in mind.

Level 1

Study Fig. 12-2.

Level 1: Compare actual costs with budgeted costs, or (BCWS − ACWP). Compute variances to identify potential problem areas. In Fig. 12-2, cumulative ACWP costs have exceeded budgeted BCWS amounts. The spending rate is higher than planned. Whether or not the project will finish on time and on budget cannot be determined from this diagram. We do not know whether the apparent cost overruns will continue, get worse, or correct themselves by the target date. Expenditure rates may be either:

- Estimated averages over the time period under review
- Actual amounts, including all rate changes, over the same time

Although any date may be selected as the reporting date, chosen times usually correspond to intervals at which progress must be reported: weekly, monthly, quarterly, or upon reaching a major milestone.

A good start, but we cannot be finished yet—too many unanswered questions.

Level 2

Study Fig. 12-3.

Level 2: The project manager can:

- Provide cost estimates to complete each activity
- Combine these with actual cost data

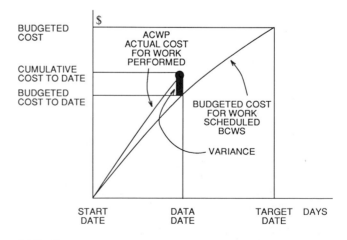

FIGURE 12-2.   Level-1 analysis.

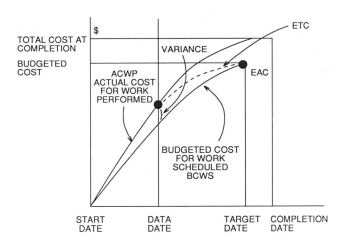

FIGURE 12-3.   Level-2 analysis.

FIGURE 12-4.   *"Keep searching!" Source:* CSC Diagraph.

- Compare this sum with budgeted costs, or

$$[BCWS - (ACWP + ETC)]$$

Although actual ACWP costs currently exceed budgeted BCWS amounts, this situation is expected to correct itself by the original target finish date. This is because we now look into the future, as well as into the past. The Estimate to Complete (ETC) is:

- Added to the cumulative actual cost to date (ACWP) to provide the Estimate at Completion (EAC)
- Represented by the line segment between these points:
   (Data date, ACWP)
   (Target date, EAC)

The EAC is compared with the budgeted value (BCWS) for that date in order to compute the variance. For this project, remaining costs are expected to occur:

- More slowly than planned for the rest of the project
- Much more slowly than they already have

The convergence of the ETC line with the BCWS line shows that the project manager believes he or she can "pull this one out." The project is expected to finish on time and on budget, despite current cost status. Since *Level 2* does not really deal with time, however, but only with cost, we must go to *Level 3* to evaluate both items together (Fig. 12-4).

Level 3

Study Fig. 12-5.

Level 3: Compare Actual Cost for Work Performed (ACWP)—and Budgeted Cost for Work Scheduled (BCWS)—with Budgeted Cost for Work Performed (BCWP) to determine variances from baseline. Obtain additional, more useful, information by:

- Evaluating the rate at which costs are expended to accomplish activities
- Determining reasons for activity performance variances, including:
   Spending rate differs because insufficient work was accomplished
   Cost/work unit differs, even though scheduled quantity was achieved

In 1964, the U.S. Air Force proved why cost and schedule variances must be analyzed together:

- Cost variance (levels 1 and 2) only compares deviations from the BCWS budget and does not meaningfully relate work accomplished to work scheduled
- Schedule variance compares actual progress with planned progress, but does not include costs

Each variance contained what the other lacked. But how could they be related for better understanding?

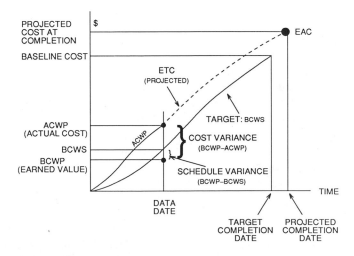

FIGURE 12-5.   Level-3 analysis.

Table 12-2 Key Financial Indicators, With Variances

<------- COST ------->

	ACTUAL	BUDGETED	
PERFORMED	ACWP	BCWP	S K E D
SCHEDULED	N/A	BCWS	

The Department of Defense understood the problem and provided a solution: DOD Instruction 7000.2, *Cost/Schedule Control Systems Criteria (C/SCSC),* which it continues to improve and requires its contractors to follow.

This methodology establishes a baseline against which both cost and schedule performance may be uniformly and objectively measured. Known in short as *earned value analysis,* it calculates the fair monetary value of work satisfactorily completed to date. It also effectively relates ACWP values to BCWS estimates through the common BCWP standard. Earned value reports can summarize cost and schedule performance for each WBS or organization level.

Even if not mandatory in your environment, it makes sense to implement the methodology anyway. Its principal advantage: It supplies the missing link between actual and budget—and between production and plan—correlating in the process the:

- Work package
- Organizational responsibility
- Work Breakdown Structure (WBS)
- Budget
- Schedule

Recall Table 12-1 and study Table 12-2, which includes these two important variances.

EARNED VALUE ANALYSIS

Formal definitions for each key indicator follow:

Budgeted Cost for Work Scheduled (BCWS): This is a time-phased cost plan to accomplish the project. It is a baseline, "let's-try-for-this" objective that shows how much work should take place if everything is performed exactly in accordance with the plan. In *P3,* an entire project schedule (with costs and resources) may be set aside as this baseline against which progress and cost experience may be measured. It equals the product, of (total cost) budget and percentage complete, on which the target activity should be as of the data date. Other terms for BCWS are Scheduled Budget and Planned Earned Value. It answers the question, "What did you want to spend?"

Actual Cost for Work Performed (ACWP): This represents the costs actually incurred for the work accomplished during a specific time period, or accumulated through a certain point in time. The cost of the work is *independent*

of both its value and its planned (expected) amount. It answers the question, "What did you actually spend?"

Budgeted Cost for Work Performed (BCWP): This measures the *actual value,* not cost, of work accomplished to date. This value (sometimes called Actual Earned Value) is central to C/SCSC earned value analysis. It is based on:

- Expected cost (or resource requirement) to achieve the work element
- Degree to which it has been accomplished

The BCWP excludes both schedule and unit price variances. It measures what has been done, and what it is worth, not what it took to do it. It equals the product of resource percentage complete and resource budget; or, if resource percentage complete is unknown, the product of schedule percentage complete and resource budget. It answers the question, "What is it really worth?"

Again note well: The BCWP is *independent* of the actual work effort time or cost. It anchors the variance chart in Table 12-2. It serves as a standard, reliable baseline *from* which monetary variances are measured, and *over* which percentage variances are computed. Without it, effective project reporting and analysis is impossible.

A variance occurs when BCWP is compared with BCWS or ACWP and found to be different. Cost and schedule variances may be formally defined as follows:

- The *schedule,* or *performance, variance* is the difference (measured in monetary units) between the work accomplished and the work planned, or:

Schedule variance =
Budgeted Cost for Work Performed (BCWP)
− Budgeted Cost for Work Scheduled (BCWS).

A positive (favorable) schedule variance occurs if the work accomplished (BCWP) exceeds the planned effort (BCWS). This means that the project is ahead of schedule as measured in cost—rather than time—performance units. If the resulting value were negative, the project would be behind schedule, again measured in units of cost, not units of time. A negative schedule variance indicates that you did not accomplish as much work as you had planned for the money. Note that schedule variance considers only the amount of work and the accomplished effort. It does not rank activities by importance. Do not use schedule variance alone to monitor progress. Schedule variance may be:

- Calculated by time period or cumulative to date
- Rolled up (summarized) to the next higher WBS/OBS/CA level
- Reported only if outside certain acceptable ranges

It may also be expressed as a percentage:

$$\text{Schedule variance (\%)} = \frac{(\text{BCWP} - \text{BCWS})}{(\text{BCWP})}.$$

- The *cost variance* is the difference (measured in monetary units) between the work accomplished and its actual cost, or:

Cost variance =
  Budgeted Cost for Work Performed (BCWP)
  − Actual Cost for Work Performed (ACWP).

A positive (favorable) cost variance occurs if the value of the work accomplished (BCWP) exceeds its actual cost (ACWP). This means that the project is ahead of cost schedule. It also means the work effort has cost less than its resulting (BCWP) value. If this variance were negative, the project would be behind cost schedule, which indicates that more money was spent than was budgeted for the amount of work done. Do not use cost variance alone to monitor progress or expenditure rate. Cost variance may be:

- Calculated by time period or cumulative to date
- Rolled up (summarized) to the next higher WBS/OBS/CA level
- Reported only if outside certain acceptable ranges

It may also be expressed as a percentage:

$$Cost\ variance\ (\%) = \frac{(\text{BCWP} - \text{ACWP})}{(\text{BCWP})}.$$

- The *total variance* is the difference between ACWP and BCWS. Even if interesting, it is not, as indicated earlier (level-1 discussion), really useful. It mixes two useful variances linked only by their common earned-value base into a total that:

- Cannot be properly interpreted or evaluated
- Does not shed light on the nature of the differences between planned effort and accomplished effort
- Has little or no analytical value

You may also wish to employ two performance indices. Based on (and not to be confused with) the preceding variances, these indices compute the percentage variance and not just the magnitude:

1. *Schedule performance index (SPI):* This indicator measures project (or a given item) schedule efficiency as a percentage of the planned earned value (BCWS). Also called the *production rate,* it is calculated as follows:

% Schedule performance index (SPI) =
  (BCWP/BCWS) * 100.

An SPI above 100 percent:

- Corresponds to a positive variance
- Indicates that an item (or the project) is ahead of schedule
- Is favorable and desirable

An SPI below 100 percent corresponds to a negative variance and indicates an item (or the project) is behind schedule. Be aware of low-SPI activities. Locate and correct problem areas, especially if they cause, or might soon cause, the entire project to fall behind schedule. Do not use the schedule performance index alone to monitor progress and performance. The schedule performance index may be:

- Calculated by time period or cumulative to date
- Rolled up (summarized) to the next higher WBS/OBS/CA level
- Reported only if outside certain acceptable ranges

2. *Cost performance index (CPI):* This indicator measures project (or a given item) cost efficiency as a percentage of actual costs (ACWP). It is calculated as follows:

% Cost performance index (CPI) =
  (BCWP/ACWP) * 100.

A CPI above 100 percent:

- Corresponds to a positive variance
- Indicates that an item (or the project) cost is doing better than planned
- Is favorable and desirable

A CPI below 100 percent corresponds to a negative variance and indicates the cost performance for an item (or the project) to be less than planned. Be aware of low-CPI activities. Locate and correct problem areas, especially if they are causing—or might soon cause—the entire project to overrun costs. Do not use the cost performance index alone to monitor cost performance. The cost performance index may be:

- Calculated by time period or cumulative to date
- Rolled up (summarized) to the next higher WBS/OBS/CA level
- Reported only if outside certain acceptable ranges

The project manager must identify these variances, determine their true causes, and take appropriate followup action:

- Corrective action for those below objectives
- Complimentary action for those above

WORKED EXAMPLES

Let us now work some examples. When performing variance analysis, Kerzner (p. 735) suggests we ask the following five questions:

- What caused the variance?
- What is the impact on time, cost, and performance?
- What is the impact on other efforts, if any?
- What corrective action is planned or underway?
- What are the expected results of the corrective action?

Assume that an activity involves the construction of fifty widgets in as many days at an estimated cost of $300 each.

The total fifty-day production cost is $15,000. If only thirty articles have been completed (at an actual cost of $12,000) when all were supposed to have been:

- Actual Cost for Work Performed (ACWP) = $12,000 (given)
- Budgeted Cost for Work Performed (BCWP) = $9,000 (= 30 * $300)
- Budgeted Cost for Work Scheduled (BCWS) = $15,000 (@ 50 days)
- Estimate to completion (ETC) = $8,000
- Estimate at completion (EAC) = $20,000

How are we doing with this activity? Not very well. We have used all of our time, but produced only 60 percent (= 30/50) what we should have. And we used 80 percent (= $12,000/$15,000) of our allocated budget to produce this 60 percent. Clearly, we are behind schedule and over budget. (No, you are not 20 percent under budget—you have not done all of your work!) If this continues, this activity will complete with results that you do not wish to include in your next letter home:

- Duration will jump from 50 days to 83.3 days (67 percent too slow)
- Total cost will jump from $15,000 to $20,000 (33 percent too costly)

More formally presented:

- *Cost variance =*
  (BCWP − ACWP) = ($9,000 − $12,000) = −$3,000
  or, expressed as a percentage,
  −$3,000/$9,000 = −33%, as noted above.
- *Schedule variance =*
  (BCWP − BCWS) = ($9,000 − $15,000) = −$6,000
  or, expressed as a percentage,
  −$6,000/$9,000 = −67%, as noted above.
- *FUBAR Factor:* Very high

No awards for you! Better luck next time, if there is one (Fig. 12-6).

The project manager should have seen these warning flags long before this and taken more effective action. Levine (p. 243) provides the following discussion:

"When the earned value approach is combined with forecasting you have the best of both worlds. . . . It is essential to project control that performance be measured while there is still time to

FIGURE 12-6.   The boss, if your project is over budget. *Source:* CSC Diagraph.

take corrective action and also that the effect of the periodic review and corrective actions is revealed by the trend data extrapolated from these periodic measurements and reviews."

Assume (Levine, pp. 243–8) that an activity entails one hundred cable connections, each of which requires 0.8 hour (48 minutes) and $20. Budget values for this activity are:

- Time: 80 hours
  (= 0.8 hour/connection * 100 connections)
- Cost: $2,000
  (= $20/connection * 100 connections).

The project is divided into four equal periods. No cables are to be connected in the first period, thirty in the second, forty in the third, and the rest in the fourth. This produces the quarterly BCWS values shown in Table 12-3.

Your second-period report card is shown in Table 12-4. How are you doing? First, compute applicable values:

- ACWP = $500 (= $25/hour * 20 hours)
- BCWP = $400 (= $20/connection * 20 connections)
- BCWS = $600 (given)
- Cost variance = (BCWP − ACWP)
  = $400 − $500 = ($100)
- Schedule variance = (BCWP − BCWS)
  = $400 − $600 = ($200)

Table 12-3   BCWS Values by Quarter

MEASURED ITEM	2 BASE	2 ACTUAL	3 BASE	3 ACTUAL	4 BASE	4 ACTUAL
# CONNECTIONS	30		40		30	
TOTAL HOURS	24		32		24	
TOTAL COST	$600		$800		$600	

Table 12-4   Second-Quarter Results

MEASURED ITEM	2 BASE	2 ACTUAL	3 BASE	3 ACTUAL	4 BASE	4 ACTUAL
# CONNECTIONS	30	20	40		30	
TOTAL HOURS	24	20	32		24	
TOTAL COST	$600	$500	$800		$600	

So far, not very well on this activity, either. What does the future look like? Any of several formulas may be used to calculate final values. The answers:

- Are based on the same data
- Make different assumptions about future performance
- May vary widely
- Are equally legitimate

If the future is assumed to be directly proportional to past experience, the EAC would equal $2,500 (= ACWP/BCWP * total BCWS) = ($500/$400 * $2,000). If, on the other hand, all sins are assumed forgiven (for this activity, at least), the EAC would equal $2,100 (= $500 + (100% − 20%) * $2,000).

Your third-period report card is shown in Table 12-5.

How are you doing now? First, compute applicable (cumulative) values:

- ACWP = $1300 (= $25/hour * 52 hours)
- BCWP = $1200 (= $20/connection * 60 connections)
- BCWS = $1400 (given)
- Cost variance = (BCWP − ACWP)
  = $1,200 − $1,300 = ($100)
- Schedule variance = (BCWP − BCWS)
  = $1,200 − $1,400 = ($200)

Although third-quarter results are commendable, they recovered no second-quarter cost overruns or lost progress. For this reason, cost and schedule variances remain unchanged. But the EAC has improved:

- Pessimistic view: $2,167 (= $1,300/$1,200 * $2,000)
- Optimistic view: $2,100
  (= $1,300 + (100% − 60%) * $2,000)

Project objectives are within reach. GO FOR IT!!!

Your fourth-period report card, shown in Table 12-6, shows that you did it!

How are you doing now? Again, compute applicable (cumulative) values:

- ACWP = $2,000 (= $25/hour * 80 hours)
- BCWP = $2,000 (= $20/connection * 100 connections)
- BCWS = $2,000 (given)
- Cost variance = (BCWP − ACWP)
  = $2,000 − $2,000 = $0
- Schedule variance = (BCWP − BCWS)
  = $2,000 − $2,000 = $0

Congratulations! On time and on budget (Fig. 12-7)!

Project variance analysis (Table 12-7) is the weighted sum of its component activities. Kerzner again (p. 746):

ESTIMATE AT COMPLETION (EAC)
  = (360/340) * $579,000 = $613,059
OVERRUN = ($613,059 − $579,000) = $34,059
COST SUMMARY: Approximately 5.9 percent over budget
SCHEDULE SUMMARY: Approximately 32.4 percent behind schedule, primarily due to no progress on activities 4 and 6.

These three examples represent several of thirteen possible cases spelled out well by Kerzner (pp. 742–743) (Table 12-8).

In each of these thirteen cases, variances are computed as before (Fig. 12-8):

- *Cost variance*
  = Actual Earned Value (BCWP) − Actual Costs (ACWP)
- *Schedule/Performance variance*
  = Actual Earned Value (BCWP) − Planned Earned Value (BCWS)

CASE 1: This is the baseline situation. The project is precisely on schedule and on budget. Both cost and schedule variances equal zero, and both performance indices equal 100 percent.

CASE 2: Costs are 50 percent too high (= $600/$400) and the project is way behind schedule: Only half (= $400/$800) of the work is being accomplished. Both

Table 12-5   Third-Quarter Results

MEASURED ITEM	2 BASE	2 ACTUAL	3 BASE	3 ACTUAL	4 BASE	4 ACTUAL
# CONNECTIONS	30	20	40	40	30	
TOTAL HOURS	24	20	32	32	24	
TOTAL COST	$600	$500	$800	$800	$600	

Table 12-6   Fourth-Quarter Results

MEASURED ITEM	2 BASE	ACTUAL	3 BASE	ACTUAL	4 BASE	ACTUAL
# CONNECTIONS	30	20	40	40	30	40
TOTAL HOURS	24	20	32	32	24	28
TOTAL COST	$600	$500	$800	$800	$600	$700

FIGURE 12-7.   "You done good!"

COST AND SCHEDULE VARIANCES   ## PERFORMANCE INDICES

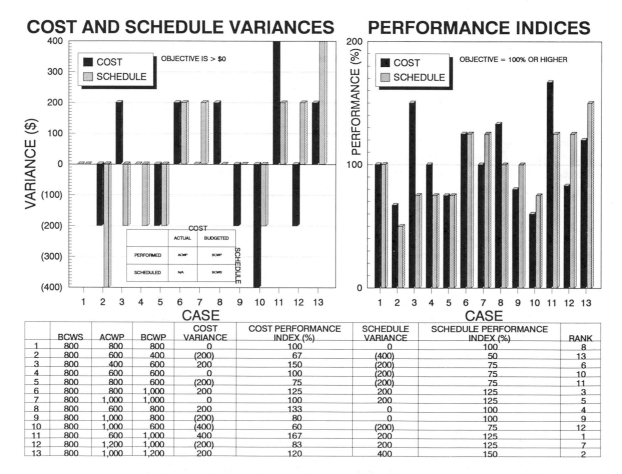

	BCWS	ACWP	BCWP	COST VARIANCE	COST PERFORMANCE INDEX (%)	SCHEDULE VARIANCE	SCHEDULE PERFORMANCE INDEX (%)	RANK
1	800	800	800	0	100	0	100	8
2	800	600	400	(200)	67	(400)	50	13
3	800	400	600	200	150	(200)	75	6
4	800	600	600	0	100	(200)	75	10
5	800	800	600	(200)	75	(200)	75	11
6	800	800	1,000	200	125	200	125	3
7	800	1,000	1,000	0	100	200	125	5
8	800	600	800	200	133	0	100	4
9	800	1,000	800	(200)	80	0	100	9
10	800	1,000	600	(400)	60	(200)	75	12
11	800	600	1,000	400	167	200	125	1
12	800	1,200	1,000	(200)	83	200	125	7
13	800	1,000	1,200	200	120	400	150	2

FIGURE 12-8.   Cost variances, schedule variances, and performance indices.

Table 12-7   Project Variance = Weighted Sum of Its Component Tasks

ACTIVITY	STATUS	BCWS	ACWP	BCWP	VARIANCES(%) SCHEDULE	COST
1	Complete	100	100	100	0	0
2	Complete	50	55	50	0	-10
3	Complete	50	40	50	0	20
4	Not started	70	0	0	-100	N/A
5	Complete	90	140	90	0	-55.5
6	Not started	40	0	0	-100	N/A
7	Started	50	25	50	0	50
					-32.4	-5.9
(ASSUME TOTAL PROJECT BUDGET = $579,000)						
TOTALS						

performance indices are much less than 100 percent. This is the worst of the thirteen sample cases presented here. Time for a new project manager if things do not turn around fast.

CASE 3: In this case there is good news and bad news. The good news: We are performing work efficiently (cost performance index is well over 100 percent). The bad: We are behind schedule.

CASE 4: Work is not being accomplished according to schedule (we are behind schedule), but costs are being maintained for what has been done.

CASE 5: Costs are on target with schedule, but work is 25 percent behind schedule because it is performed at only 75 percent (= $600/$800) efficiency.

CASE 6: Because we are operating at 125 percent efficiency (that is, higher on the learning curve), work is ahead of schedule by 25 percent but still within scheduled costs.

CASE 7: We are operating at 100 percent efficiency and work is being accomplished ahead of schedule. Costs are being maintained according to budget.

CASE 8: Work is on schedule and costs are under budget.

CASE 9: Work is on schedule, but costs are over budget.

CASE 10: Like case 2, this situation might indicate time for a new project manager. Work is 25 percent behind schedule and costs are nearly double what they should be. This situation, very bad, indicates that work is being accomplished inefficiently.

CASE 11: The opposite of cases 2 and 10, this situation indicates that the project manager will enjoy a big Christmas bonus. Performance is 25 percent ahead of schedule and costs are 40 percent lower than planned. World-class numbers!

CASE 12: Work is being done inefficiently, which would indicate a possible cost overrun. But since performance is ahead of schedule, the final outcome is unclear: It may be a cost overrun or a schedule underrun. Cost overruns do not necessarily mean that there will be a final overrun because work may, as here, be getting done faster than planned. Of course, the percentage of cost overrun should not vary greatly from the percentage of schedule advantage.

CASE 13: This is the second best of the thirteen cases presented. Although actual costs are greater than budgeted,

Table 12-8   Thirteen Possible BCWS/ACWP/BCWP Variance Costs

CASE	PLANNED EARNED VALUE (BCWS)	ACTUALS (ACWP)	ACTUAL EARNED VALUE (BCWP)
1	800	800	800
2	800	600	400
3	800	400	600
4	800	600	600
5	800	800	600
6	800	800	1000
7	800	1000	1000
8	800	600	800
9	800	1000	800
10	800	1000	600
11	800	600	1000
12	800	1200	1000
13	800	1000	1200

performance is ahead of schedule and work is being accomplished very efficiently. Performance is 50 percent ahead of schedule and costs are 17 percent lower than planned.

What happens if the cost basis or expenditure rates change? Easy. Use the new values! Activity cost estimates should be revised as often as necessary so that actual and estimated expenditures converge, not diverge, as the project progresses. Accuracy should improve with progress.

At the same time, it will also be necessary, if changes are material, to recompute the following:

- Schedule
- Resource allocations
- Least-cost calculations
- Liabilities and expenditure forecasts
- Cash flow analysis (keep your cash flow flowing!)

A heads-up "look-ahead" attitude will provide the following benefits:

- Greater time in which to act (not react)
- More options
- Increased decision effectiveness

Measuring Earned Value

The key to measuring earned value is accurate performance assessment. The earned value methodology recognizes that cost measurement is:

- Relatively easy for completed work packages
- Difficult and subject to error for underway activities with open work packages. How complete are, and what is the value of, the following?
    Work in process?
    A half-built building?
    Only the foundation?
    Only the blueprints?
    Only the idea?
    Seventy-three lines of COBOL source code?

Of the two estimating methods commonly used, the preferred method requires the project manager to determine the actual percentage of each work package completed. Use valid measures to determine these values. If, for example, your project is software development or maintenance, use Function Points—not lines of code—to measure earned value. (*Function Points* are the state-of-the-art metric for measuring project size, duration, required resources, quality base, earned value, and many other useful criteria.)

This, in general, will provide:

- A more accurate and extremely useful progress estimate
- Better knowledge of current project status
- Progressive, methodical "divide and conquer" time and cost estimates (not even John Elway should be expected to complete a one-hundred-yard "Hail, Mary!" pass)
- Guidance for needed corrective action
- Help in building a better base from which future proposals may be written or contract prices established

The other technique (the "fifty-fifty" rule) is less preferable but is suitable for large projects with many open work packages. It simply assumes that:

- A completed package has earned its full BCWP value
- An unopened package has a value of zero
- An open but incomplete package is valued at one-half its BCWS

Although this method may appear arbitrary at first glance, it eliminates the risk of unbounded optimism in the early stages of a project. The law of large numbers helps, too: When a large number of packages are open and individual packages do not span more than one reporting period, the fifty-fifty rule is, on balance, satisfactory.

Of course, the assumed 50 percent BCWS value could, where possible, be altered to allow more accurate work-in-process measurement. Further refinements will then approach first-method accuracy.

Earned Value Resource Analysis

The project manager should know both the "what" and the "why" of things. Like cost variance analysis, earned value resource analysis is done at one of three levels of sophistication. In its simplest form, the percentage of activity complete may be multiplied by current budget as a (very) rough earned value estimate. This should be updated with each schedule change. Not bad, but only as a start.

A better approach estimates the percentage complete for each of an activity's resources at each update. These percentages often:

- Vary among themselves
- Differ from duration percent complete

You may find this method especially useful for resources:

- With "long-lead" procurement times
- Whose usage rate materially varies from the other resources in the activity under review

Update each resource individually and periodically, or as needed.

The best and most advanced method requires a set of cost accounts, as well as resources. The cost account structure can correspond to:

- A job cost accounting system
- Work Breakdown Structure (WBS)

Assign a cost account to each resource. When updating, declare a percentage complete for each resource, as was done above. To review earned value status, produce an Earned Value Report prepared in either units or cost.

This advanced level permits earned value review at intermediate (and final) summary levels. For example, suppose your cost account scheme contains a division "7080" which consists of departments "7081" through "7089." A summary earned value analysis report, by cost or by unit, may be generated for each department (or other cost account). These reports, in turn, may be summarized for division "7080," or the total report may be produced directly with no departmental reports created.

On the other hand, you might want a detailed earned value analysis report only for certain cost types—such as all programming labor in cost account "7861" expended on new systems. In this case, request the Earned Value Report (by cost or by unit) for cost account "7861PNS," if this is how it was defined in the cost accounts dictionary.

Reports may also be produced at any desired WBS level. For example, to evaluate performance for major WBS area #2 (at the first level of the WBS), produce an Earned Value Report (by cost or by unit), requesting all account codes between 200000000000 and 299999999999. You could just as easily request only a desired portion of these accounts, such as 212560000000 through 212561000099, or any other range.

Finally, you may want to examine current-schedule progress relative to baseline. This comparison is made in the Earned Value Report, which presents ACWP, BCWP, BCWS, and percentage complete for each activity and cost account. It also provides both cost and schedule variances, and the budgeted/estimated completion estimates. Combine this information with the various rate analysis reports to understand the underlying variances.

Many projects must control performance within subcontractual or other vendor relationships. The project cost accounting system must be able to select and compute costs by vendor (or by resource) to track:

- Costs
- Trends
- Vendor performance
- Variances
- Other important items

This approach might require that the cost account number (or, preferably, an activity code) encode the subcontractor performing the work. A simple report could show which activities this subcontractor is doing. Many other reports could also be produced.

The ability to review earned value at multiple levels, from multiple perspectives, is crucial. Reports to serve any intended purpose must be immediately available to provide:

- Summary briefing to senior management and the customer
- Detailed precision for in-depth analysis, evaluation, and management response

The Master Toolbox

Use whatever tool is appropriate for the job. Examples from my world include:

- Decision support: Comshare *IFPS/Plus, Executive Edge*
- Office automation (including E-mail): DEC *ALL-IN-1*
- Project management: *Primavera Project Planner*
- Spreadsheet: Access Technology *20/20* (with *Database Connection* and *ALL-IN-1* interface)
- Statistical analysis: BBN *RS/1, Explore*
- Word processor: Microsoft *Word*, DEC *WPS+*

Project HOME workers brought (and used) more than one tool. You should, too. Use your other tools as needed!

Sample Project HOME cost and performance reports are presented in Tables 12-9 through 12-19. These reports may be summarized as follows:

Cost Profile

This report (Table 12-9) summarizes daily, weekly, or monthly project costs by account number (or all-cost totals). It shows both actual and forecasted expenditures. (It looks as though someone ought to be on friendly terms with a loan officer to get through the September 1983 cash crunch!)

Cumulative Cost Profile

This report (Table 12-10) accumulates costs by day, week, or month for a given account number, or for cost totals—for both early and late project schedule forecasts. It shows both actual and forecasted expenditures. Note the big jump in September 1983; Table 12-9 showed why this is expected to happen.

Cost Control Activity Report

This report (Table 12-11) details costs to date by activity, by resource, by cost account, and by account category. The following information is also provided:

- Unit of measure
- Budgeted amount
- Percent complete
- Actual costs to date
- Actual costs this period
- Estimated costs to complete
- Forecasted costs to complete
- Variance

Summary Cost Report

This report (Table 12-12) summarizes costs to date by resource. For each of these, the following information is provided:

- Unit of measure
- Budgeted amount
- Percent complete
- Actual costs to date
- Actual costs this period
- Estimated costs to complete
- Forecasted costs to complete
- Variance

Monthly Tabular Cost Report

This report (Table 12-13) provides a cash flow analysis and forecast. Expenditures by period and over time are presented for both the early and the late schedules. This report quantifies actual expenditures and forecasts future outlays. It can also calculate average values between the two schedules or compare current-schedule expense status with the baseline plan (not shown).

Table 12-9   Cost Profile

```
- - - - - - - - - - - - - - - - - - - - - - - - - - - - - - - - - - - - - - - - - - - - - - - - - - - - - - - - - - - - -
AMERICAN COMMUNITY DEVELOPERS, INC.          PRIMAVERA PROJECT PLANNER              BRIAN'S DUPLICATE OF PROJECT "HOME"

REPORT DATE  12FEB83  RUN NO.   17           COST PROFILE                           START DATE 13DEC82  FIN DATE  6SEP84

WEEKLY COST (ACTUAL AND FORECAST) BY ACCOUNT NUMBER                                 DATA DATE   1FEB83  PAGE NO.    1
- - - - - - - - - - - - - - - - - - - - - - - - - - - - - - - - - - - - - - - - - - - - - - - - - - - - - - - - - - - - -
COST ACCOUNT: *** ALL ***
      200000.......*..........................................................................................................
            .. .  *. .   .    .    .   .  . . .   . E .  .   .   .    .   .   .    .   .  .   .  .   .  .   .   .   .   .   .
            .. .  *. .   .    .    .   .  . . .   . E .  .   .   .    .   .   .    .   .  .   .  .   .  .   .   .   .   .   .
            .. .  *. .   .    .    .   .  . . .   . E .  .   .   .    .   .   .    .   .  .   .  .   .  .   .   .   .   .   .
            .. .  *. .   .    .    .   .  . . .   . E .  .   .   .    .   .   .    .   .  .   .  .   .  .   .   .   .   .   .
      180000.......*............................E....................................................................
            .. .  *. .   .    .    .   .  . . .   . E .  .   .   .    .   .   .    .   .  .   .  .   .  .   .   .   .   .   .
            .. .  *. .   .    .    .   .  . . .   . E .  .   .   .    .   .   .    .   .  .   .  .   .  .   .   .   .   .   .
            .. .  *. .   .    .    .   .  . . .   . E .  .   .   .    .   .   .    .   .  .   .  .   .  .   .   .   .   .   .
            .. .  *. .   .    .    .   .  . . .   E E .  .   .   .    .   .   .    .   .  .   .  .   .  .   .   .   .   .   .
      160000.......*........................EEE..................................................................
            .. .  *. .   .    .    .   .  . . .   EEE .  .   .   .    .   .   .    .   .  .   .  .   .  .   .   .   .   .   .
            .. .  *. .   .    .    .   .  . . .   EEE .  .   .   .    .   .   .    .   .  .   .  .   .  .   .   .   .   .   .
            .. .  *. .   .    .    .   .  . . .   EEE .  .   .   .    .   .   .    .   .  .   .  .   .  .   .   .   .   .   .
  C         .. .  *. .   .    .    .   .  . . .   EEE .  .   .   .    .   .   .    .   .  .   .  .   .  .   .   .   .   .   .
  O   140000.......*........................EEE..................................................................
  S         .. .  *. .   .    .    .   .  . . .   EEE .  .   .   .    .   .   .    .   .  .   .  .   .  .   .   .   .   .   .
  T         .. .  *. .   .    .    .   .  . . .   EEE .  .   .   .    .   .   .    .   .  .   .  .   .  .   .   .   .   .   .
            .. .  *. .   .    .    .   .  . . .   EEE .  .   .   .    .   .   .    .   .  .   .  .   .  .   .   .   .   .   .
            .. .  *. .   .    .    .   .  . . .   EEE .  .   .   .    .   .   .    .   .  .   .  .   .  .   .   .   .   .   .
  P   120000.......*........................EEE..................................................................
  E         .. .  *. .   .    .    .   .  . . .   EEE .  .   .   .    .   .   .    .   .  .   .  .   .  .   .   .   .   .   .
  R         .. .  *. .   .    .    .   .  . . .   EEE .  .   .   .    .   .   .    .   .  .   .  .   .  .   .   .   .   .   .
            .. .  *. .   .    .    .   .  . . .   EEE .  .   .   .    .   .   .    .   .  .   .  .   .  .   .   .   .   .   .
  W         .. .  *. .   .    .    .   .  . . .   EEE .  .   .   .    .   .   .    .   .  .   .  .   .  .   .   .   .   .   .
  E   100000.......*........................EEE..................................................................
  E         .. .  *. .   .    .    .   .  . . .   EEE .  .   .   .    .   .   .    .   .  .   .  .   .  .   .   .   .   .   .
  K         .. .  *. .   .    .    .   .  . . .   EEE .  .   .   .    .   .   .  E .  .   .  .   .  .   .  .   .   .   .   .
            .. .  *. .   .    .    .   .  . . .   EEE .  .   .   .    .   .   .  E .  .   .  .   .  .   .  .   .   .   .   .
            .. .  *. .   .    .    .   .  . . .   EEE .  .   .   .    .   .   .  E .  .   .  .   .  .   .  .   .   .   .   .
       80000.......*........................EEEE.............................E................................
            .. .  *. .   .    .    .   .  . . .   EEEE.  .   .   .    .   .   .  E .  .   .  .   .  .   .  .   .   .   .   .
            .. .  *. .   .    .    .   .  . . .   EEEE.  .   .   .    .   .   .  E .  .   .  .   .  .   .  .   .   .   .   .
            .. .  *. .   .    .    .   .  . . .   EEEE.  .   .   .    .   .   .  E .  .   .  .   .  .   .  .   .   .   .   .
            .. .  *. .   .    .    .   .  . . .   EEEE.  .   .   .    .   .   .  E .  .   .  .   .  .   .  .   .   .   .   .
       60000.......*........................EEEE.............................E................................
            .. .  *. .   .    .    .   .  . . .   EEEE.  .   .   .    .   .   .  E .  .   .  .   .  .   .  .   .   .   .   .
            .. .  *. .   .    .    .   .  . . .   EEEE.  .   .   .    .   .   .  E .  .   .  .   .  .   .  .   .   .   .   .
            .. .  *. .   .    .    .   .  . . .   EEEE.  .   .   .    .   .   .  E .  .   .  .   .  .   .  .   .   .   .   .
       40000.......*........................EEEE.............................E................................
            .. .  *. .   .    .    .   .  . . .   EEEE.  .   .   .    .   .   .  E .  .   .  .   .  .   .  .   .   .   .   .
            .. .  *. .   .    .    .   .  . . .   EEEE.  .   .   .    .   .   .  E .  .   .  .   .  .   .  .   .   .   .   .
            .. .  *. .   .  EE .    .   .  . . .   EEEE.  .   .   .    .   .   E E .  .   .  .   .  .   .  .   .   .   .   .
       20000.......*........EE..............EEEE...........................E.E..............................
            .. .  E. .   .  EE . E .   .  . . .   EEEE.  .   .   .    .   . EEEE .  .   .  .   .  .   .  .   .   .   .   .
            .. .  E. .   .  EE . E .   .  . . .   EEEE.  .   .   .    .   . EEEEE .  .   .  .   .  .   .  .   .   .   .   .
            .. .  EE  .   .  EE . E .   .  . . .   EEEE.   .E EEEE .   .   . EEEEE .  .   .  .   .  .   .  .   .   .   .   .
            .. .  EE  E   EE . EE .  EEEE.  EEEEEEE  EEEEEEE  .   .  EE  EEEEEE .EE .EEE.  .   .  .   .  .   .   .   .   .
          0.......EEE..EE..EEEEEEEEEEEEEEEEEEEEEEEEEEEEEEEEEEEEEEEEEEEEEEEEEEEEE.EEEEEEEEEEEEEEEEE...........................
                 03   07  07  04  02   06  04  01   05  03   07  05  02   06  05  02   07  04  02   06  03  01   05  03   07  04  04
                 JAN  FEB MAR APR MAY  JUN JUL AUG  SEP OCT  NOV DEC JAN  FEB MAR APR  MAY JUN JUL  AUG SEP OCT  NOV DEC  JAN FEB MAR
                 83   83  83  83  83   83  83  83   83  83   83  83  84   84  84  84   84  84  84   84  84  84   84  84   85  85  85
```

Table 12-10   Cumulative Cost Profile

```
------------------------------------------------------------------------------------------------------------
AMERICAN COMMUNITY DEVELOPERS, INC.          PRIMAVERA PROJECT PLANNER          BRIAN'S DUPLICATE OF PROJECT "HOME"

REPORT DATE  12FEB83  RUN NO.   18           COST CUMULATIVE CURVE             START DATE 13DEC82  FIN DATE  6SEP84

CUMULATIVE WEEKLY COST (ACTUAL AND FORECAST) BY ACCOUNT NUMBER                 DATA DATE   1FEB83  PAGE NO.    1
------------------------------------------------------------------------------------------------------------
COST ACCOUNT: *** ALL ***
      2000000.......*...............................................................................................
           .. .    *.   .     .     .     .     .     .     .     .     .     .     .     .     .     .     .     .
           .. .    *.   .     .     .     .     .     .     .     .     .     .     .     .     .     .     .     .
           .. .    *.   .     .     .     .     .     .     .     .     .     .     .     .     .     .     .     .
           .. .    *.   .     .     .     .     .     .     .     .     .     .     .     .     .     .     .     .
      1800000.......*.............................................................................................
           .. .    *.   .     .     .     .     .     .     .     .     .     .     .     .     .     .     .     .
           .. .    *.   .     .     .     .     .     .     .     .     .     .     .     .     .     .     .     .
           .. .    *.   .     .     .     .     .     .     .     .     .     .     .     .     .     .     .     .
           .. .    *.   .     .     .     .     .     .     .     .     .     .     .     .     .     .     .     .
      1600000.......*.............................................................................................
           .. .    *.   .     .     .     .     .     .     .     .     .     .     .     .     .     .     .     .
           .. .    *.   .     .     .     .     .     .     .     .     .     .     .     .     .     .     .     .
           .. .    *.   .     .     .     .     .     .     .     .     .     .     .     .     .     .     .     .
 C         .. .    *.   .     .     .     .     .     .     .     .     .     .     .     .     .     .     .     .
 U    1400000.......*.............................................................................................
 M         .. .    *.   .     .     .     .     .     .     .     .     .     .     .     .     .     .     .     .
 U         .. .    *.   .     .     .     .     .     .     .     .     .     .     .     .     .     .     .     .
 L         .. .    *.   .     .     .     .     .     .     .     .     .     .     .     .     .     .     .     .
 A         .. .    *.   .     .     .     .     .     .     .     .     .     .     .     .     .     .     .     .
 T    1200000.......*.............................................................................................
 I         .. .    *.   .     .     .     .     .     .     .     .     .     .     .     .     .     .     .     .
 V         .. .    *.   .     .     .     .     .     .     .     .     .     .     .   . ///////////////////////////
 E         .. .    *.   .     .     .     .     .     .     .     .     .     .   E////////// .     .     .     .
           .. .    *.   .     .     .     .     .     .     .     .     .     . EEL   .     .     .     .     .
 C    1000000.......*.............................................................................................
 O         .. .    *.   .     .     .     .     .     .     .     .     .   .E L.   .     .     .     .     .
 S         .. .    *.   .     .     .     .     .     .     .     .   . EELL   .     .     .     .     .
 T         .. .    *.   .     .     .     .     .     .     .   . EE////////LL   .     .     .     .
           .. .    *.   .     .     .     .     .     .   . L//////////LL.   .     .     .     .     .
       800000.......*................................L////E...........................................
           .. .    *.   .     .     .     .     . LLLL/////E.   .     .     .     .     .     .
           .. .    *.   .     .     .     .     .   .   . E .   .     .     .     .     .     .
           .. .    *.   .     .     .     .   . L   .     .     .     .     .     .     .     .
       600000.......*.............................................................................................
           .. .    *.   .     .     .     .     .     .     .     .     .     .     .     .     .
           .. .    *.   .     .     .     .     .     .     .     .     .     .     .     .     .
           .. .    *.   .     .     .   .E   .     .     .     .     .     .     .     .     .
           .. .    *.   .     .     . L   .     .     .     .     .     .     .     .     .
       400000.......*.............................................................................................
           .. .    *.   .     .     .     .     .     .     .     .     .     .     .     .
           .. .    *.   .     .     . E   .     .     .     .     .     .     .     .     .
           .. .    *.   .     .     .     .     .     .     .     .     .     .     .     .
           .. .    *.   .     .     .     .     .     .     .     .     .     .     .     .
       200000.......*.......................L.....................................................
           .. .    *.   .     .   . E.   .     .     .     .     .     .     .     .     .
           .. .    *.   .   . EEEEEE/////EEE .   .     .     .     .     .     .     .
           .. .    *..LLLL//////LLLLLL.   .     .     .     .     .     .     .     .
           .. .    *. L  E   .     .     .     .     .     .     .     .     .     .
            0.......//////EEEE..............................................................
             03  07  07  04  02   06  04  01   05  03   07  05  02   06  05  02   07  04  02   06  03  01   05  03   07  04  04
             JAN FEB MAR APR MAY  JUN JUL AUG  SEP OCT  NOV DEC JAN  FEB MAR APR  MAY JUN JUL  AUG SEP OCT  NOV DEC  JAN FEB MAR
             83  83  83  83  83   83  83  83   83  83   83  83  84   84  84  84   84  84  84   84  84  84   84  84   85  85  85
```

Table 12-11 Cost Control Activity Report

```
--------------------------------------------------------------------------------------------------------
AMERICAN COMMUNITY DEVELOPERS, INC.        PRIMAVERA PROJECT PLANNER           BRIAN'S DUPLICATE OF PROJECT "HOME"

REPORT DATE  12FEB83  RUN NO.   19         COST CONTROL ACTIVITY REPORT        START DATE 13DEC82  FIN DATE  6SEP84

COST CONTROL REPORT SORTED BY ACTIVITY NUMBER, RESOURCE, AND COST ACCOUNT      DATA DATE  1FEB83  PAGE NO.   1
--------------------------------------------------------------------------------------------------------
```

ACTIVITY ID	RESOURCE	COST ACCOUNT	ACCOUNT CATEGORY	UNIT MEAS	BUDGET	PCT CMP	ACTUAL TO DATE	ACTUAL THIS PERIOD	ESTIMATE TO COMPLETE	FORECAST	VARIANCE
1 LAYOUT											
RD 0 AS 14DEC82 AF 22DEC82											
	SURVEYOR	101L	LABOR	PDAY	852.00	100	.00	.00	852.00	852.00	.00
	LABORERS	101L	LABOR	PDAY	1224.00	100	.00	.00	1224.00	1224.00	.00
	TOTAL :				2076.00	0	.00	.00	2076.00	2076.00	.00
3 SOIL STABILIZATION											
RD 0 AS 28DEC82 AF 20JAN83											
	LABORERS	102L	LABOR	PDAY	1632.00	100	.00	.00	1632.00	1632.00	.00
	TOTAL :				1632.00	0	.00	.00	1632.00	1632.00	.00
5 PLUMBING-STREET CONNECTION AND UNDERSLAB											
RD 3 AS 24JAN83 EF 3FEB83 LF 6JAN83 TF -20											
	LABORERS	301L	LABOR	PDAY	3360.00	62	.00	.00	3360.00	3360.00	.00
	PLUMBERS	301L	LABOR	PDAY	3990.00	62	.00	.00	3990.00	3990.00	.00
	PIPING	301M	MATERIAL	LF	700.00	62	.00	.00	700.00	700.00	.00
	TOTAL :				8050.00	0	.00	.00	8050.00	8050.00	.00
7 FOUNDATION EXCAVATION											
RD 2 ES 4FEB83 EF 7FEB83 LS 7JAN83 LF 10JAN83 TF -20											
	LABORERS	105L	LABOR	PDAY	1632.00	60	.00	.00	1632.00	1632.00	.00
	OP ENG	105L	LABOR	PDAY	1200.00	60	.00	.00	1200.00	1200.00	.00
	DOZER	105E	EQUIP.	EA	9710.00	60	.00	.00	9710.00	9710.00	.00
	TOTAL :				12542.00	0	.00	.00	12542.00	12542.00	.00
9 GRANULAR FILL											
RD 7 ES 8FEB83 EF 16FEB83 LS 11JAN83 LF 19JAN83 TF -20											
	LABORERS	105L	LABOR	PDAY	2856.00	0	.00	.00	2856.00	2856.00	.00
	STONE	105M	MATERIAL	CY	390.00	0	.00	.00	390.00	390.00	.00
	TOTAL :				3246.00	0	.00	.00	3246.00	3246.00	.00
11 UNDERSLAB AC FREON S&R LINE											
RD 5 ES 17FEB83 EF 24FEB83 LS 1FEB83 LF 7FEB83 TF -12											
	TOTAL :				.00	0	.00	.00	.00	.00	.00
12 UNDERSLAB ELECTRICAL LINE											
RD 7 ES 17FEB83 EF 28FEB83 LS 28JAN83 LF 7FEB83 TF -14											
	TOTAL :				.00	0	.00	.00	.00	.00	.00
*** REPORT TOTAL ***				1130858.93	0	.00	.00	1130858.93	1130858.93	.00

Table 12-12   Summary Cost Report

```
------------------------------------------------------------------------------------------------------------
AMERICAN COMMUNITY DEVELOPERS, INC.          PRIMAVERA PROJECT PLANNER           BRIAN'S DUPLICATE OF PROJECT "HOME"

REPORT DATE  12FEB83  RUN NO.   20           SUMMARY COST REPORT                 START DATE 13DEC82  FIN DATE  6SEP84

SUMMARY COST/VARIANCE REPORT BY RESOURCE                                         DATA DATE  1FEB83  PAGE NO.   1
------------------------------------------------------------------------------------------------------------
```

RESOURCE	UNIT MEAS	BUDGET	PCT CMP	ACTUAL TO DATE	ACTUAL THIS PERIOD	ESTIMATE TO COMPLETE	FORECAST	VARIANCE
AIRCOND - AIR CONDITIONING UNITS								
TOTAL AIRCOND	EA	21336.00	0	.00	.00	21336.00	21336.00	.00
APPLIAN - KITCHEN APPLIANCES								
TOTAL APPLIAN	LS	76800.00	0	.00	.00	76800.00	76800.00	.00
CABINETS - CABINETWORK								
TOTAL CABINETS	EA	9709.30	0	.00	.00	9709.30	9709.30	.00
CABLE - CABLE								
TOTAL CABLE	LF	93.05	0	.00	.00	93.05	93.05	.00
CARPENTR - CARPENTERS								
TOTAL CARPENTR	PDAY	136087.61	0	.00	.00	136087.61	136087.61	.00
CEM FIN - CEMENT FINISHERS								
TOTAL CEM FIN	PDAY	448.00	0	.00	.00	448.00	448.00	.00
CONCRETE - CONCRETE								
TOTAL CONCRETE	CY	6348.00	0	.00	.00	6348.00	6348.00	.00
CRANE - CRANE								
TOTAL CRANE	EA	49664.00	0	.00	.00	49664.00	49664.00	.00
*** REPORT TOTAL ***		300485.96	0	.00	.00	300485.96	300485.96	.00

Table 12-13   Monthly Tabular Cost Report

```
----------------------------------------------------------------------------------------------------
AMERICAN COMMUNITY DEVELOPERS, INC.          PRIMAVERA PROJECT PLANNER          BRIAN'S DUPLICATE OF PROJECT "HOME"

REPORT DATE  12FEB83  RUN NO.   21         TABULAR  COST  REPORT - MONTHLY      START DATE 13DEC82  FIN DATE  6SEP84

MONTHLY CASH FLOW USAGE AND FORECAST BY SCHEDULE                                DATA DATE   1FEB83  PAGE NO.   1
----------------------------------------------------------------------------------------------------
```

PERIOD BEGINNING	-----EARLY SCHEDULE-----		------LATE SCHEDULE-----		-----EARLY/LATE AVG.---	
	USAGE	CUMULATIVE	USAGE	CUMULATIVE	USAGE	CUMULATIVE
	UNIT OF MEASURE = COST					
1DEC82	.00	.00	.00	.00	.00	.00
1JAN83	.00	.00	.00	.00	.00	.00
DATA DATE						
1FEB83	.00	.00	.00	.00	.00	.00
1MAR83	.00	.00	980.00	980.00	490.00	490.00
1APR83	1102.50	1102.50	2572.50	3552.50	1837.50	2327.50
1MAY83	2572.50	3675.00	2572.50	6125.00	2572.50	4900.00
1JUN83	4699.04	8374.04	24739.48	30864.48	14719.26	19619.26
1JUL83	22490.43	30864.48	1124.52	31989.00	11807.48	31426.74
1AUG83	1124.52	31989.00	9652.45	41641.45	5388.49	36815.22
1SEP83	9652.45	41641.45	.00	41641.45	4826.23	41641.45
1OCT83	3469.82	45111.27	.00	41641.45	1734.91	43376.36
1NOV83	.00	45111.27	.00	41641.45	.00	43376.36
1DEC83	.00	45111.27	.00	41641.45	.00	43376.36
1JAN84	.00	45111.27	.00	41641.45	.00	43376.36
1FEB84	.00	45111.27	.00	41641.45	.00	43376.36
1MAR84	408.00	45519.27	3264.00	44905.45	1836.00	45212.36
1APR84	2856.00	48375.27	.00	44905.45	1428.00	46640.36
1MAY84	.00	48375.27	.00	44905.45	.00	46640.36
1JUN84	.00	48375.27	3469.82	48375.27	1734.91	48375.27
1JUL84	13966.60	62341.87	13966.60	62341.87	13966.60	62341.87
1AUG84	936.40	63278.27	936.40	63278.27	936.40	63278.27
1SEP84	.00	63278.27	.00	63278.27	.00	63278.27

Earned Value Report—Cost

This highly useful report (Table 12-14) provides earned-value cost information by cost account, by resource, and by activity (this order could easily be changed). The following information is also given:

- Percent complete
- Cumulative ACWP, BCWP, and BCWS
- Cost and schedule variances
- At-completion budgets and estimates
- Group and report totals

Earned Value Report—Quantity

This highly-useful report (Table 12-15) provides earned-value resource-quantity information by resource, by cost account, and by activity (this order could easily be changed). It gives the same information as the above report, but measured in resource units rather than monetary cost values.

Labor Rate Analysis Report

This report (Table 12-16) is organized by cost account. Within each of these, the budgeted amount, the actual amount

experienced to date, and the forecasted value are provided for each of the actual quantity, the labor amount, and the quantity-per-unit-labor cost factor. Report totals (not shown) are also included.

Price Rate Analysis Report

This report (Table 12-17) is organized exactly the same as above, but along monetary lines. The latter two values listed above are replaced by "cost amount" and "cost-per-unit-quantity" cost factor, respectively. Report totals are also provided.

Project Schedule with Budgets and Earned-Value Amounts by Worker Category

This extremely-valuable report (Table 12-18) is precisely the same as the schedules we saw a long time ago, but additionally includes the budgeted BCWS and the earned value BCWP amounts. The complete schedule may be pre-

Table 12-14   Earned Value Report—Cost

```
--------------------------------------------------------------------------------------------------
AMERICAN COMMUNITY DEVELOPERS, INC.        PRIMAVERA PROJECT PLANNER        BRIAN'S DUPLICATE OF PROJECT "HOME"

REPORT DATE 12FEB83 RUN NO.  22            EARNED VALUE REPORT - COST        START DATE 13DEC82 FIN DATE  6SEP84

EARNED VALUE COST REPORT BY COST ACCOUNT, RESOURCE, AND ACTIVITY WITH SUMMARIES    DATA DATE  1FEB83  PAGE NO.   1
--------------------------------------------------------------------------------------------------
```

COST ACCOUNT	RESOURCE	ACTIVITY ID	PCT CMP	ACWP	BCWP	BCWS	COST	SCHEDULE	BUDGET	ESTIMATE
					CUMULATIVE TO DATE		VARIANCE		AT COMPLETION	

```
                  101  -  EXCAVATION

   101L LABORERS      1  100    .00   1224.00   1224.00   1224.00      .00    1224.00   1224.00

   101L SURVEYOR      1  100    .00    852.00    852.00    852.00      .00     852.00    852.00

                          ---
   101         TOTAL   100    .00   2076.00   2076.00   2076.00      .00    2076.00   2076.00
==================================================================================================

                  102  -  SOIL STABILIZATION

   102L LABORERS      3  100    .00   1632.00   1632.00   1632.00      .00    1632.00   1632.00

                          ---
   102         TOTAL   100    .00   1632.00   1632.00   1632.00      .00    1632.00   1632.00
==================================================================================================

                  105  -  CONCRETE WORK

   105E DOZER         7   60    .00   5826.00   9710.00   5826.00  -3884.00   9710.00   9710.00

   105L CEM FIN      22    0    .00      .00      .00      .00      .00     448.00    448.00

   105L LABORERS      7   60    .00    979.20   1632.00    979.20   -652.80   1632.00   1632.00
   105L LABORERS      9    0    .00      .00    407.98      .00   -407.98   2856.00   2856.00
   105L LABORERS     22    0    .00      .00      .00      .00      .00    2040.00   2040.00
                          ---
   105L LABORERS TOTAL 15   .00    979.20   2039.98    979.20  -1060.78   6528.00   6528.00

   105L OP ENG        7   60    .00    720.00   1200.00    720.00   -480.00   1200.00   1200.00
   105L OP ENG       22    0    .00      .00      .00      .00      .00    1200.00   1200.00
                          ---
   105L OP ENG  TOTAL  30    .00    720.00   1200.00    720.00   -480.00   2400.00   2400.00

   105L SURVEYOR     67    0    .00      .00      .00      .00      .00    1654.56   1654.56

   105M CONCRETE     22    0    .00      .00      .00      .00      .00    5148.00   5148.00
   105M CONCRETE     67    0    .00      .00      .00      .00      .00    1200.00   1200.00
                          ---
   105M CONCRETE TOTAL  0    .00      .00      .00      .00      .00    6348.00   6348.00

   105M LUMBER       22    0    .00      .00      .00      .00      .00      92.00     92.00

   105M STONE         9    0    .00      .00     55.71      .00    -55.71    390.00    390.00

                          ---
   105         TOTAL   27    .00   7525.20  13005.69   7525.20  -5480.49  27570.56  27570.56
==================================================================================================


   *** REPORT TOTAL ***    1    .00  11233.20  16713.69  11233.20  -5480.49 903105.13 903105.13
==================================================================================================
```

Table 12-15   Earned Value Report—Quantity

```
--------------------------------------------------------------------------------------------------------------
AMERICAN COMMUNITY DEVELOPERS, INC.          PRIMAVERA PROJECT PLANNER           BRIAN'S DUPLICATE OF PROJECT "HOME"

REPORT DATE  12FEB83  RUN NO.   23              EARNED VALUE REPORT - QUANTITY        START DATE 13DEC82  FIN DATE  6SEP84

EARNED VALUE REPORT BY RESOURCE, BY COST ACCOUNT, BY ACTIVITY NUMBER                 DATA DATE   1FEB83  PAGE NO.    1
--------------------------------------------------------------------------------------------------------------
```

COST ACCOUNT	RESOURCE	ACTIVITY ID	PCT CMP	ACWP	BCWP	BCWS	COST	SCHEDULE	BUDGET	ESTIMATE
					CUMULATIVE TO DATE		VARIANCE		AT COMPLETION	
	CARPENTERS									
1	L CARPENTR	43	62	0	5	0	5	5	8	8
1	L CARPENTR	107	0	0	0	0	0	0	10	10
1	L CARPENTR	128	0	0	0	0	0	0	30	30
1	L CARPENTR	144	0	0	0	0	0	0	40	40
110	L CARPENTR	34	0	0	0	0	0	0	25	25
110	L CARPENTR	45	0	0	0	0	0	0	15	15
110	L CARPENTR	49	0	0	0	0	0	0	32	32
112	L CARPENTR	41	0	0	0	0	0	0	40	40
112	L CARPENTR	70	0	0	0	0	0	0	150	150
112	L CARPENTR	72	0	0	0	0	0	0	340	340
112	L CARPENTR	80	0	0	0	0	0	0	16	16
112	L CARPENTR	87	0	0	0	0	0	0	72	72
115	L CARPENTR	50	0	0	0	0	0	0	80	80
115	L CARPENTR	93	0	0	0	0	0	0	20	20
116	L CARPENTR	66	0	0	0	0	0	0	20	20
116	L CARPENTR	76	0	0	0	0	0	0	42	42
125	L CARPENTR	99	0	0	0	0	0	0	32	32
130	L CARPENTR	115	0	0	0	0	0	0	154	154
131	L CARPENTR	112	0	0	0	0	0	0	0	0
132	L CARPENTR	123	0	0	0	0	0	0	20	20
303	L CARPENTR	117	0	0	0	0	0	0	20	20
	CARPENTR	TOTAL	0	0	5	0	5	5	1166	1166

```
===============================================================================================================
```

	LABORERS									
1	L LABORERS	43	62	0	6	0	6	6	10	10
1	L LABORERS	107	0	0	0	0	0	0	15	15
1	L LABORERS	128	0	0	0	0	0	0	22	22
1	L LABORERS	142	0	0	0	0	0	0	80	80
1	L LABORERS	144	0	0	0	0	0	0	50	50
101	L LABORERS	1	100	0	15	15	15	0	15	15
102	L LABORERS	3	100	0	20	20	20	0	20	20
105	L LABORERS	7	60	0	12	20	12	-8	20	20
105	L LABORERS	9	0	0	0	5	0	-5	35	35
105	L LABORERS	22	0	0	0	0	0	0	25	25
107	L LABORERS	26	0	0	0	0	0	0	35	35
107	L LABORERS	27	0	0	0	0	0	0	20	20
116	L LABORERS	74	0	0	0	0	0	0	72	72
301	L LABORERS	5	62	0	20	32	20	-12	32	32
	LABORERS	TOTAL	16	0	73	92	73	-19	451	451

```
===============================================================================================================
```

| | *** REPORT TOTAL *** | | 5 | 0 | 78 | 92 | 78 | -14 | 1617 | 1617 |

```
===============================================================================================================
```

Table 12-16   Labor Rate Analysis Report

```
----------------------------------------------------------------------------------------------------
AMERICAN COMMUNITY DEVELOPERS, INC.          PRIMAVERA PROJECT PLANNER          BRIAN'S DUPLICATE OF PROJECT "HOME"

REPORT DATE  12FEB83  RUN NO.  24            LABOR RATE ANALYSIS REPORT         START DATE 13DEC82  FIN DATE  6SEP84

LABOR RATE ANALYSIS BY (SELECTED) ACCOUNT NUMBER                               DATA DATE   1FEB83  PAGE NO.    1
----------------------------------------------------------------------------------------------------
```

COST ACCOUNT	..............QUANTITY..................			..................LABOR.................			......QUANTITY PER UNIT LABOR.........		
	BUDGET	TO DATE	FORECAST	BUDGET	TO DATE	FORECAST	BUDGET	TO DATE	FORECAST
WR CARPENTR 1 - 503									
	0	0	0	2596	0	2596	.00000	.00000	.00000
105 - CONCRETE WORK CONCRETE (CY) PER LABOR UNIT									
	0	0	0	123	0	123	.00000	.00000	.00000
WR ELECTRCN 502 - 503									
	0	0	0	180	0	180	.00000	.00000	.00000
116 - INSULATION INSULTN (SF) PER LABOR UNIT									
	0	0	0	134	0	134	.00000	.00000	.00000
WR LABORERS 1 - 134									
	0	0	0	2006	0	2006	.00000	.00000	.00000
120 - PAINTING PAINT (SF) PER LABOR UNIT									
	0	0	0	215	0	215	.00000	.00000	.00000
120 - PAINTING PAINTERS (PDAY) PER LABOR UNIT									
	0	0	0	215	0	215	.00000	.00000	.00000
107 - PRECAST CONCRETE PRECAST (EA) PER LABOR UNIT									
	0	0	0	83	0	83	.00000	.00000	.00000

Table 12-17 Price Rate Analysis Report

```
-----------------------------------------------------------------------------------------------
AMERICAN COMMUNITY DEVELOPERS, INC.        PRIMAVERA PROJECT PLANNER        BRIAN'S DUPLICATE OF PROJECT "HOME"

REPORT DATE  12FEB83  RUN NO.  25          PRICE RATE ANALYSIS REPORT       START DATE 13DEC82  FIN DATE  6SEP84

PRICE RATE ANALYSIS BY (SELECTED) ACCOUNT NUMBER                           DATA DATE   1FEB83  PAGE NO.   1
-----------------------------------------------------------------------------------------------
```

COST ACCOUNT	..............QUANTITY.................			................COST.................			........COST PER UNIT QUANTITY........		
	BUDGET	TO DATE	FORECAST	BUDGET	TO DATE	FORECAST	BUDGET	TO DATE	FORECAST
WR CARPENTR	1	-	503						
	0	0	0	.00	.00	.00	.000	.000	.000
105 - CONCRETE WORK				COST PER CONCRETE (CY)					
	0	0	0	.00	.00	.00	.000	.000	.000
WR ELECTRCN	502	-	503						
	0	0	0	.00	.00	.00	.000	.000	.000
116 - INSULATION				COST PER INSULTN (SF)					
	0	0	0	.00	.00	.00	.000	.000	.000
WR LABORERS	1	-	134						
	0	0	0	.00	.00	.00	.000	.000	.000
120 - PAINTING				COST PER PAINT (SF)					
	0	0	0	.00	.00	.00	.000	.000	.000
120 - PAINTING				COST PER PAINTERS (PDAY)					
	0	0	0	.00	.00	.00	.000	.000	.000
107 - PRECAST CONCRETE				COST PER PRECAST (EA)					
	0	0	0	.00	.00	.00	.000	.000	.000
				=========	========				
*** REPORT TOTAL ***				130858.93	19142.23				

Table 12-18   Project Schedule, with BCWS and BCWP

```
------------------------------------------------------------------------------------------------------------------------
AMERICAN COMMUNITY DEVELOPERS, INC.          PRIMAVERA PROJECT PLANNER          BRIAN'S DUPLICATE OF PROJECT "HOME"

REPORT DATE  12FEB83  RUN NO.   26              PROJECT SCHEDULE                 START DATE 13DEC82  FIN DATE  6SEP84

PROJECT SCHEDULE (W/ BUDGET AND EARNED-VALUE AMOUNTS) BY WORKER CATEGORY AND EARLY START      DATA DATE   1FEB83  PAGE NO.    1
```

CARPENTER

ACTIVITY ID	ORIG DUR	REM DUR	%	ACTIVITY DESCRIPTION / BUDGET	EARNED	EARLY START	EARLY FINISH	LATE START	LATE FINISH	TOTAL FLOAT
50	20	20	0	FRAME INTERIOR WALLS		19APR83	16MAY83	8JUL83	4AUG83	56
				8738.64	.00					
34	20	20	0	REDWOOD FASCIA,SOFFIT AND PLYWOOD DECKING		2AUG83	29AUG83	5JUL83	1AUG83	-20
				3566.01	.00					
41	5	5	0	DRY SHEETING		30AUG83	5SEP83	2AUG83	8AUG83	-20
				5050.00	.00					
43	4	1	62	STOCK BULK MATERIAL INSIDE BUILDING		6SEP83	6SEP83	9AUG83	9AUG83	-20
				4706.50	2918.03					
58	15	15	0	ROOF SHINGLES		6SEP83	27SEP83	11AUG83	31AUG83*	-18
				585793.10	.00					
45	3	3	0	SET INFILL PANEL FRAMING		7SEP83	9SEP83	10AUG83	12AUG83	-20
				2489.10	.00					
47	5	5	0	WINDOWS		13SEP83	19SEP83	15AUG83	19AUG83	-20
				9652.45	.00					
49	8	8	0	WOOD SIDING		20SEP83	29SEP83	22AUG83	31AUG83	-20
				4308.51	.00					
66	5	5	0	WALL INSULATION		30SEP83*	6OCT83	1SEP83*	7SEP83	-20
				2844.84	.00					
70	25	25	0	SHEETROCK WALLS		7OCT83	10NOV83	20SEP83	24OCT83	-13
				18753.90	.00					
72	20	20	0	TAPE AND BED		11NOV83	9DEC83	25OCT83	21NOV83	-13
				39525.00	.00					
76	5	5	0	FUR DOWN FOR CEILING AIR CONDITIONER		12DEC83	16DEC83	22NOV83	29NOV83	-13
				5143.32	.00					
74	10	10	0	BLOW ON CEILING INSULATION		12DEC83	23DEC83	31MAY84	13JUN84	121
				7196.40	.00					
80	4	4	0	SHEETROCK FUR DOWNS		4JAN84	9JAN84	14DEC83	19DEC83	-13
				2177.94	.00					
87	15	15	0	TAPE AND BED FUR DOWNS		10JAN84	30JAN84	20DEC83	11JAN84	-13
				8370.00	.00					
93	10	10	0	DOORS AND TRIM		17FEB84	1MAR84	31JAN84	13FEB84	-13
				3287.20	.00					
99	5	5	0	HARDWARE		30MAR84	5APR84	7JUN84	13JUN84	49
				4538.40	.00					
115	13	13	0	INSTALL CABINETS		2MAY84	18MAY84	13APR84*	1MAY84	-13
				27611.80	.00					
112	14	14	0	PANELING, FINISH CARPENTRY AND MILLWORK		2MAY84	21MAY84	25MAY84	13JUN84	17
				1113.30	.00					
123	5	5	0	BATHROOM ACCESSORIES		7JUN84	13JUN84	7JUN84	13JUN84	0
				2325.00	.00					
128	10	10	0	CLEAN UP		14JUN84	27JUN84	14JUN84	27JUN84	0
				5477.40	.00					
142	10	10	0	CLEAN UP		3AUG84	16AUG84	3AUG84	16AUG84	0
				7236.00	.00					
144	10	10	0	PUNCH LIST		17AUG84	30AUG84	17AUG84	30AUG84	0
				15779.50	.00					
SUBTOTAL				CARP 775684.31	2918.03					
*** REPORT TOTAL ***				1130858.93	19142.23					

sented, or (as before) it may be distributed by resource, by responsible manager, by area, by phase, and so on. It may also be summarized by various categories. In the sample report shown, resource categories are summarized by total remaining duration, percentage complete, budgeted amount (BCWS), earned value (BCWP), Early Start, Early Finish, Late Start, Late Finish, and by total float. BCWS and BCWP values are totaled at the bottom. For Project HOME car-

penters, only Activity 43 claims any earned value because no other activity has started.

Summary Project Schedule with Budgets and Earned-Value Amounts by Worker Category

This report (Table 12-19) summarizes the above information by resource category. For each resource, it presents total

Table 12-19   Summary Project Schedule, with BCWS and BCWP

```
----------------------------------------------------------------------------------------------------------------
AMERICAN COMMUNITY DEVELOPERS, INC.          PRIMAVERA PROJECT PLANNER            BRIAN'S DUPLICATE OF PROJECT "HOME"

REPORT DATE  12FEB83  RUN NO.   27           PROJECT SCHEDULE                     START DATE 13DEC82  FIN DATE  6SEP84

SUMMARY PROJECT SCHEDULE (WITH BUDGET AND EARNED-VALUE AMOUNTS) SORTED BY RESOURCE CATEGORY    DATA DATE   1FEB83  PAGE NO.   1
----- -----  ---- ---- - ---  ----------  ------------------------------------------------  --------  --------  --------  --------  -----
```

	DUR	%	CODE	SUMMARY DESCRIPTION BUDGET	EARNED	EARLY START	EARLY FINISH	LATE START	LATE FINISH	TOTAL FLOAT
	5	0		.00	.00	31AUG84	6SEP84	31AUG84	6SEP84	0
CARP	351	1	CARP CARPENTER	775684.31	2918.03	19APR83	30AUG84	5JUL83	30AUG84	0
CONC	173	6	CONC CONCRETE WORKER	78426.06	7525.20	4FEB83	10OCT83	7JAN83	13JUN84	174
CRPT	15	0	CRPT CARPET LAYER	12562.00	.00	6JUL84	26JUL84	6JUL84	26JUL84	0
DRPS	5	0	DRPS DRAPE HANGER	2341.00	.00	27JUL84	2AUG84	27JUL84	2AUG84	0
ELEC	330	0	ELEC ELECTRICIAN	22677.05	.00	17FEB83	1JUN84	28JAN83	13JUN84	8
EXCA	25	61	EXCA EXCAVATOR	3708.00	3708.00	14DEC82A	8MAR83		7FEB83	-20
HVAC	317	0	HVAC HEATING VENTILATING AND AIR CONDITIONING	40301.60	.00	17FEB83	15MAY84	1FEB83	13JUN84	21
IWKR	124	0	IWKR IRON WORKER	35458.82	.00	19APR83	12OCT83	22MAR83	13JUN84	172
PLBG	345	17	PLBG PLUMBER	129056.50	4991.00	24JAN83A	6JUN84		6JUN84	0
PNTR	112	0	PNTR PAINTER	30643.59	.00	31JAN84	5JUL84	12JAN84	5JUL84	0
TILE	53	0	TILE TILE SETTER	.00	.00	17FEB84	1MAY84	7FEB84	12APR84	-13

person-days duration, percentage complete, resource code, BCWS, BCWP, earliest start dates, latest finish dates, and total float available to this resource. As shown in this report, Excavators and Tile Setters are, taken as a group, in negative-float mode. Other resources, of course, may be unavailable for certain time periods but still indicate zero or positive float for the entire project.

Whatever-Information-You-Need-Now-Is-Easily-Available-Now

As seen before, *Primavera* provides 16 user-customizable information groups, from which may be produced hundreds of useful reports:

I. Tabular schedules
II. Bar charts
III. Network logic diagrams
IV. Resources
    A. Resource usage
    B. Cumulative resource usage
    C. Resource control
    D. Productivity
    E. Earned value (units)
    F. Tabular resource usage
V. Costs
    A. Resource cost
    B. Cumulative cost profile
    C. Cost control
    D. Cost, price, and rates control
    E. Earned value (costs)
    F. Tabular costs
VI. Resource loading

Building a new *P3* report is like eating in a cafeteria—select one thing from this group, two from that, and so on. Be creative! But don't:

- Be a pig in the cafeteria
- Go "hog wild" on these reports!

The above advice notwithstanding, *never* set needless, arbitrary, or artificial constraints on your:

- Mind
- Options
- Insight
- Ability to do things correctly

The term *paradigm paralysis* describes how even well-meaning persons can be oblivious to good ideas simply because they do not conform to:

- Present knowledge
- Current methodologies
- Expectations of how even new things should look

FINAL THOUGHTS

Almost twelve chapters ago we began with these thoughts:

- *Everyone* is a project manager.
- Project management offers the best available technique to plan, operate, and control a firm's operation.
- For many companies, the competitive battle will be won by whomever has the sharpest pencil and the sharpest knife—the most careful project scheduling and the most exact cost controls. The instrument putting the point to the pencil and the edge to the knife is a new generation of project management software. Beating competitors calls for sharp pencils and sharp knives. Integrated software is the cutting edge.

It would be most appropriate to close with selected thoughts from those world-class project management authors on whom I especially relied to write this book, and to whom I am most grateful:

Levine (special to Computer Associates Summer 1988 newsletter *CA-INSIGHT*, p. 48):

"At least part of the solution lies in the commitment of the user to make the full investment necessary to assure the adequate preparation and support for a project management software installation. It is highly advisable that the new software owner strive to observe a prescribed set of *Owner Obligations . . .*"

These are summarized as follows:

1. Perform a formal system study prior to preparing the final software specification and making the software selection. Identify all needs, *both current and future,* before selecting the software tool.
2. Identify the "stakeholders" involved in the success of company projects.
3. Provide appropriate training for these stakeholders and maintain their competency in project management methodologies and software usage. Provide appropriate training, of suitable content, to users and involved management. Note well: "Lack of understanding of basic project management principles" coupled with the fact that project management software "typically requires knowledge of a major portion of the program's features in order to use it effectively" makes education and training absolutely essential to project management success.
4. Identify one or more key persons as central contact points for system users and the software vendor. These persons should be provided the maximum training (in both principles and the software tool) available and be accessible to other company personnel for assistance when needed.
5. Contract for continued software maintenance, so that vendor support (hot-line service) and software upgrades are available to the users.
6. Encourage participation of key persons and other interested users in the vendor's user groups, where available.
7. Enhance awareness of state-of-the-art methodologies

through active participation in, and support of, professional organizations, such as the Project Management Institute (Box 43, Drexel Hill, Pennsylvania 19026; 215-622-1796).

"The promise of project management software is as strong as ever. As users become more demanding and vendors respond with sophisticated programs, I am equally convinced that this promise will not be realized without a commitment on the part of the owner to be fully involved in the process. This commitment starts with a thorough understanding of the user environment, methodology, and personnel, and continues through the training and support necessary to its successful implementation. A continued partnership of both enlightened users and responsive vendor is the key to this success."

Armstrong-Wright (p. 3): "The present-day widespread use of network analysis techniques stems from the growing importance of the time element in commerce, industry, public works, and defence commitments. High overheads resulting from mechanization and the need to achieve maximum utilization of expensive plant, equipment, and other resources has made it essential that the planning and control of projects is precise and provides ample warning of difficulties that may lie ahead, in sufficient time to permit any replanning that might be necessary."

Kerzner (p. 886): "Project management and the 'systems approach' to human enterprise today constitute an extremely flexible and highly effective approach to multidisciplinary program management. This approach is likely to be even more important in the future, as less flexible or less creative methods are executed by computers or robots.

"Successful future enterprises will be differentiated by the quality of management planning and decision making. By virtue of broad experience, flexible approach, and a "people-oriented" leadership style, tomorrow's project managers should be able to cope in the year 2000."

Randolph and Posner (pp. 137–138): "The key to going fast later is to go slow early. Take the time to build solid "GO-CARTS." For every one of your projects, remember what is summarized in Table 12-20.

Develop your abilities as a "DRIVER" so that project implementation goes smoothly. This is facilitated when you perform all the actions noted in Table 12-21.

These are the rules that successful project managers follow. Now that you know and understand how to apply these rules, the only thing left for you to do is to begin using them."

Table 12-20   "GO-CARTS"

```
Goals for the project
Objectives for the project
Checkpoints to monitor progress
Activities to be completed
Relationships among the activities
Time estimates for the activities
Schedule for the project.
```

Table 12-21   "DRIVER"

```
Direct people, both individually and as a team
Reinforce project team members' excitement and commitment
Inform all people connected with the project
Vitalize participants by building agreements
Empower yourself and others
Risk approaching problems creatively.
```

Glossary

Important Note

This glossary contains both CPM and PERT definitions from multiple sources. Consequently, the same general concept may be expressed using several different words or phrases. By including alternative definitions, it is hoped that the reader may better understand other writings on the subject.

20/20. High-end integrated electronic spreadsheet and database query language.

5 Ps. *Proper Preparation Prevents Poor Performance.*

90% Syndrome. Common malady among project management team members who, when measuring progress, always feel themselves to be "90% done" with the project.

a. Optimistic time estimate for an activity when three time estimates are used, as in PERT. This duration should occur only 1 percent of the time.

A. Abbreviation for TA used in PERT graphic reports.

Account Code Structure. Numbering system used to assign summary numbers to elements of the Work Breakdown Structure (WBS) and charge numbers to individual work packages for accounting data-collection and reporting purposes.

Activity. Specific action that must be done to complete a project, that consumes time and resources, and whose endpoints are represented by a node in activity-on-arrow (ADM) format and by node walls in activity-on-node (AON/PDM) format. Application of time and resources necessary to progress from one project event to the next. Can be a process, job, task, procurement, or deliverable production routine.

Activity Codes. Used to organize project activities into manageable groups for updating, analyzing, reporting, plotting, and summarizing. Examples include RESP (responsibility), AREA (area/department), and MILE (milestone). Defined and maintained in an activity codes dictionary.

Activity Codes Dictionary. Defines an activity coding structure.

Activity Direct Costs. Costs associated with expediting activities.

Activity ID. A unique alphanumeric string assigned for identification purposes to each activity in any network format. In a PERT or activity-on-arrow network, the activity ID is made up of the combined start and end events, joined together by a dash. Activity IDs should follow an intelligent coding scheme. They need not be sequential, but by convention larger values generally refer to later activities.

Activity-on-Arrow (AOA). A Critical Path diagramming technique in which activities and their sequence are represented by arrows, with a node at the end of each arrow representing an event, or by the activity start and finish points. Cannot support more advanced relationships and often requires the use of dummy activities. See "Precedence Diagram Method."

Activity-on-Node (AON). A Critical Path diagramming technique in which activities and their sequence are graphically represented by boxes or nodes and in which connecting arrows, called precedences, show the sequence in which the activities are performed. See "Precedence Diagram Method."

Actual Cost. Incurred expenditures plus any prespecified types of unliquidated commitments charged or assigned to a work effort.

Actual Cost for Work Performed (ACWP). Represents the costs actually incurred for the work accomplished during a specific time period, or the costs accumulated through a certain point in time (the same as the "percent complete" mark). The cost of the work is independent of both its value and its planned (expected) amount.

Actual Cost This Period (TPC). Represents project expenditures for a particular resource and cost account for the current period.

Actual Cost To Date (TDC). Represents cumulative project expenditures for a particular resource and cost account to date.

Actual Dates.   Dates recorded for an activity with progress; consists of Actual Start (AS) and Actual Finish (AF).

Actual Finish (AF).   Time at which an activity actually completes.

Actual Quantity This Period (TPQ).   Represents resource usage during the current period.

Actual Quantity To Date (TDQ).   Represents cumulative resource usage to date.

Actual Start (AS).   Time at which an activity actually begins.

Actual Time (AT).   Time at which an activity actually occurred.

ACWP.   See "Actual Cost for Work Performed."

ADM.   Arrow Diagram Method. See "Activity-on-Arrow."

ALAP.   As long as possible.

All-Crash Cost.   Project cost when all activities are reduced to all-crash times. Project length is no shorter, however, than its crash cost/time point.

AOA.   See "Activity-on-Arrow."

AON.   See "Activity-on-Node."

Arrow Diagram Method (ADM).   See "Activity-on-Arrow."

ASAP.   As soon as possible. In project management, must specify:

- How soon is soon
- How possible is possible

Autocost.   *P3* feature which automatically, by user-specified rules, calculates costs and estimates resource usage after activity progress updates.

b.   Pessimistic time estimate for an activity when three time estimates are used, as in PERT. This duration should occur only 1 percent of the time.

BAC.   Budget at completion. The budget for an entire item or group of items, or a roll-up (summary) of the entire project.

Backward Pass.   Scheduling step in which network late dates are computed from right to left (finish to start) (see Table 4-38).

Calculation of Late Start and Late Finish Times (Backward Pass)

Activity	Relationship	Late Start (LS)	Late Finish (LF)
Last	Any	LF − activity duration	EF (always)
All prior: select earliest of (1), (2), and (3)	(1) SS	LS of following activity	LS of following activity, + own duration
	(2) FS	LF − activity duration	LS of following activity
	(3) FF	LF − nactivity duration	LF of following activity
First	Any	Zero (always)	

Bar Chart.   See "Gantt Chart."

Baseline (target).   Original project plan, including time schedule and resource/cost allocations; used to compare actuals with planned in order to determine a project's time, cost, and value progress, and its variances.

BCWP.   See "Budgeted Cost for Work Performed."

BCWS.   See "Budgeted Cost for Work Scheduled."

BE.   Beginning event in a PERT network.

Boss.   1. Loathsome, contemptible person whose greatest joy in life is to cause misery in yours. 2. Someone Will Rogers never met. The boss-employee relationship is shown in Fig. G-1.

FIGURE G-1

Budget.   Planned expenditures (costs) and commitments (resources) by time periods. Also called "Budgeted Cost."

Budget Quantity.   An estimate of the total resource units required by an activity.

Budgeted Cost.   See "Budget."

Budgeted Cost for Work Performed (BCWP).   Also known as "Earned Value." Represents the actual fair-market value of work performed, rather than its cost. The BCWP excludes both schedule and unit price variances. It equals the product of resource percent complete and resource budget; or, if resource percent complete is unknown, the product of schedule percent complete and resource budget. It is measured in monetary units.

Budgeted Cost for Work Scheduled (BCWS).   Represents the planned amount of work that should have been accomplished by the data date had the project proceeded according to target plan. It equals the product of budget and percent complete the target activity should be on the data date and is measured in monetary units.

Burst Point.   Activity with multiple parallel successors. See "Sink Point."

C/SCSC.   Cost/Schedule Control Systems Criteria. Department of Defense project measurement system whose basis is the fair market value of actual progress (called the earned value or BCWP) measured against the costs and time incurred to produce this progress. Represents the most accurate and useful progress metric.

CAC.   See "Cost at Completion."

Calendar.   Mechanism by which project worker time schedule is mapped to the project to reflect the typical workweek, days off, holidays, and so on; determines when an activity can be scheduled or resources applied.

Calendar Catch-up.   Situation in which an activity assigned to one calendar in a multiple-calendar project must wait—only because of differences between the calendars that would disappear with a common calendar—until another activity, assigned to a different calendar, is completed.

Calendar ID.   Identifies an individual project calendar.

Charge Number.   Number used to identify labor/material costs charged to a work package.

Commitment.   Obligation within a company or government organization to charge costs against a specific work package, perhaps in advance of a legal obligation against a contract.

Constraint.   Restriction placed on when an activity may begin or end—or how long it may last—to reflect real project requirements; see "Date Constraints" and "Duration Constraints" for further details. Examples include:

- Expected Finish
- Finish No Earlier/Later Than
- Hammock Activity
- Mandatory Start/Finish
- Start No Earlier/Later Than
- Start On
- Zero Free/Total Float

Contiguous.   Activity that must, once started, progress without interruption until finished; compare "Interruptible."

Contingency Analysis.   See "What If Analysis."

Control.   To direct the progress of a plan.

Conventional Relationship.   See "Finish-to-Start."

Cost Account.   Identifies, organizes, and accumulates costs for a resource or activity; used for summary (roll-up) or drill down purposes. Defined and maintained in a "Cost Accounts Dictionary."

Cost Accounts Dictionary.   Defines an accounting structure using cost accounts and cost categories.

Cost Activity.   Activity that consumes resources, the cost of which is a direct charge to the project (except where indirect costs are required).

Cost at Completion (CAC).   Represents the accumulated costs of the resource/cost account at the completion of the associated activity.

Cost/Benefit Analysis.   Time-discounted quantification of investment costs and benefits; used to evaluate and compare competing investment alternatives.

Cost Category.   Code that identifies significant groups of similar costs to be summarized; for example, E–equipment, L–labor, M–material. Categories may be the same as, or different from, corresponding resource categories.

Cost Optimization.   Utilization of normal and crash cost estimates for each activity to make time–cost tradeoff computations and to select least-cost project duration schedule.

Cost Performance Index (CPI).   Measures contract (or a given item) cost efficiency as a percentage of actual costs; is equal to: (BCWP/ACWP) * 100 percent.

Cost/Schedule Control Systems Criteria.   See "C/SCSC."

Cost to Complete (CTC).   An estimate of the cost remaining to complete a particular resource or account.

Cost Variance (CV).   The difference, expressed in monetary units, between the work accomplished and its actual cost, or earned value and actual cost:

> Budgeted Cost for Work Performed (BCWP)
> − Actual Cost for Work Performed (ACWP)

CPM.   See "Critical Path Method."

Crash Cost (CC).   Cost associated with crash time of an activity.

Crash Time (CT).   Shortest possible time required to complete an activity.

Critical Activity.   Activity on the Critical Path with zero (in multiple-calendar environments, occasionally positive) float.

Critical Path.   Longest sequence(s) of connected activities through the network, defined as the path(s) with zero (or negative, if applicable) float, or slack time. Activities on the Critical Path are those activities for which (assuming no negative float values):

1. ES = LS,
2. EF = LF,
3. EF − ES = activity duration, and
4. Any delay in the activity causes a similar delay in the project—perhaps even greater than the delay experienced by the individual activity.

Critical Path Method (CPM).   Scheduling method in which activities are organized to determine the longest sequence(s) of connected activities through the network.

Critical Predecessor.   Activity/event that immediately precedes the activity under consideration in the most time-consuming path leading to that activity.

Critical Successor.   Activity/event that immediately succeeds the activity under consideration in the most time-consuming path leading from that activity.

Criticality Index.   Ratio of required resources to available resources, which is a rough measure of resource "tightness" or criticality; an approach for estimating the impact of resource constraints:

$$\text{Criticality Index} = \frac{\text{Average daily units required}}{\text{Maximum daily amount available.}}$$

CTC.   See "Cost to Complete."

Current Assets.   Cash, inventory, accounts receivable, and other assets that are reasonably expected to be converted into cash, or sold, or consumed during the normal operating cycle of the organization (usually one year).

Current Liabilities.   Accounts payable, notes payable, estimated taxes, accrued expenses payable, and other liabilities that are expected to be satisfied either by the use of current assets or by the creation of other current liabilities during the normal operating cycle of the organization (usually one year).

CV.   See "Cost Variance."

Dangling Activity/Event.   Any activity (or PERT/activity-on-arrow event), other than the start or end activities, that has either no predecessor or no successor; open end. A no-no in good scheduling.

Data Date.   Date as of which project status is measured; status, report, or "as of" date. It can be *any* date—past, present, or future—not just today's date.

Date Constraints.   Restriction(s) placed on when activity may begin or end:

1. Start No Earlier Than (constrained Early Start). This will not affect Late Start because it is applied only during forward scheduling pass.
2. Finish No Earlier Than (constrained Early Finish). This will not affect Late Finish because it is applied only during forward scheduling pass.
3. Start No Later Than (constrained Late Start). This will not affect Early Start because it is applied only during backward scheduling pass.
4. Finish No Later Than (constrained Late Finish). This will not affect Early Finish because it is applied only during backward scheduling pass.
5. Start On (constrained Early and Late Start).
6. Mandatory Start: $ES = LS =$ Mandatory date.
7. Mandatory Finish: $EF = LF =$ Mandatory date.

Decision Support System (DSS).   Software information system that models business information and helps solve business problems, especially structured and semi-structured. More capable tools, such as Comshare *IFPS/Plus*, are based on artificial intelligence rule sets.

Dictionary.   Used to classify, define, and maintain codes, resources, and cost account information.

Directed Date (TD).   Date for specific activity accomplishment formally directed by contracting or organizational authority; imposed date.

Discount Factor.   Percent, often representing the current cost of new capital, by which future monetary values are reduced in time to arrive at their equivalent current economic cost/utility. See "Present Value."

Drill Down.   The opposite of summarization or roll-up. Digging deeper into the data structure for greater detail, to find and explain why the results at the current level happened.

Driving Predecessor.   Activity predecessor that determines the current activity dates.

DSS.   See "Decision Support System."

Dummy Activity.   Fictitious activity used for denoting proper sequencing and unique activity identification in a PERT or activity-on-arrow CPM network. Its time duration is zero; it consumes no resources; and it is typically depicted as a dashed arrow.

Duration.   Amount of time needed to complete an activity. Original duration is the planned estimate and is equal to $|(EF - ES)|$, or $|(LF - LS)|$; remaining duration indicates how much longer is actually left to finish an activity.

Duration Constraints.   Restriction placed on activity length:

1. Expected Finish (XF): Updates schedule and activity duration based on expected activity finish date.
2. Hammock Activity (HA): Summarizes a group of detailed activities; however, only under ideal conditions (no out-of-sequence progress and no imposed constraints on any contained activities) will the hammock start and end dates precisely correspond to the earliest ES and latest EF of the spanned activities.

3. Zero Free Float (ZFF): Allows an activity with positive float to turn critical and start as late as possible, without delaying its successors, by setting its early dates equal to its late.
4. Zero Total Float (ZTF): Allows an activity with positive float to turn critical and start as early as possible by setting its late dates equal to its early. It can also reduce predecessor-activity float to zero.

E.   Abbreviation for TE used in PERT graphic reports.

EAC.   See "Estimate at Completion."

Earliest Expected Date (TE).   Earliest calendar date on which an activity/event can be expected to occur, based on a summation of the Te's on the longest path leading to the activity/event.

Early Dates (or Schedule).   See "Early Start" (ES) and "Early Finish" (EF).

Early Finish (EF).   Earliest possible time an activity (or the entire project) can complete; does *not* mean "finishing early"!

Early Start (ES).   Earliest possible time an activity (or the entire project) can begin; does *not* mean "starting early"!

Earned Value.   See "C/SCSC" and "Budgeted Cost for Work Performed (BCWP)."

EE.   Ending event in a PERT network.

EF.   See "Early Finish."

Elapsed Time.   Total time, either actual or estimated, to complete an activity, including time required for delays, waiting periods, and the like.

Equivalent Persons.   Total hours expended (including overtime) divided by average hours worked per week per employee.

ES.   See "Early Start."

Estimate at Completion (EAC).   Total estimated person-hours, costs, and time required to complete a work package or summary item; sum of ACWP actuals to date plus ETC (defined below). Includes applicable overhead except where only direct costs are specified.

Estimate to Complete (ETC).   Estimated person-hours, costs, and time required to complete work remaining on a work package or summary item. Includes applicable overhead except where only direct costs are specified.

ETC.   See "Estimate to Complete."

Event.   Start or completion of an activity, represented by a node in a PERT or activity-on-arrow network or, conceptually, by node walls in a PDM or activity-on-node network. An event never consumes either time or resources.

Event Number.   A unique number assigned to each event in a PERT or activity-on-arrow network. Not applicable to a PDM or activity-on-node network.

Exception.   1. Value out of tolerance or desired range. 2. A period when work must occur that was originally designated as nonworktime.

Expected Duration (e).   Expected time necessary to complete one activity; PERT activity duration. Is computed as: $[(a + 4m + b)/6]$.

Expected Finish (XF).   Duration constraint that estimates an activity's anticipated or estimated finish date.

Expected Value.   See "Mean."

Expenditure.   Actual disbursement of funds.

Expense.   Cost items that are subtracted from revenue in that accounting period in which the corresponding revenue is realized, resulting in a decrease to Owners' Equity. Expenses are *not* to be confused with asset acquisition (such as the investment in software), which is a cost, and perhaps also an expenditure—but is *not* an *expense* unless the asset is entirely consumed during the same year. Expenses also include inventories (which are assets that become expenses when products are sold); prepaid expenses (which represent assets purchased, but not yet consumed, prior to this year); and depreciation (defined below under "Fixed Assets").

Asset Acquisition	Expense
• Is NOT subtracted from revenue	• Is ALWAYS subtracted from revenue
• Does NOT affect Net Income	• Reduces Net Income
• Does NOT affect Owners' Equity	• Reduces Owners' Equity
• Exchanges one asset for another	• Usually reduces Current Assets
• *Example:* software acquisition dr. Software .. 1,000 cr. Cash .... 1,000 (Revenue unaffected)	• *Example:* pay power & light bill dr. Accts Payable ..500 cr. Cash ....500 (Charged against revenue)

Facility.   Plant location.

FF.   See "Finish-to-Finish."

Finish Activity (Event).   Final network activity (event).

Finish Date.   Date on which project is scheduled to be completed.

Finish Flag/Milestone (FM).   Zero-duration activity marking the end of an activity or set of activities.

Finish Float.   Workperiod difference between Early Finish and Late Finish.

Finish No Earlier Than (FNET).   Date constraint affecting Early Finish that limits the earliest time an activity can be completed. It is usually applied to activities with few predecessors that must be finished just in time for the next project phase. It is applied only when later than the calculated Early Finish.

Finish No Later Than (FNLT).   Date constraint affecting Late Finish that limits the latest time by which an activity must be completed. It affects only late dates and is used to ensure activity Late Finish is not later than the imposed deadline. The constraint may also be applied to the entire project to indicate the project deadline. It is applied only when earlier than the calculated Late Finish.

Finish-to-Finish (FF).   PDM relationship in which a successor activity's finish depends on its predecessor activity's finish.

Finish-to-Start (FS or F/S).   PDM relationship in which a successor activity can begin only when its predecessor activity finishes. Sometimes called a "Conventional Relationship."

Fixed Assets.   Real property (land), plant, and equipment. The current net value of plant and equipment is its original cost less all accumulated depreciation (which is that fraction of an asset's cost converted during the current accounting period into an expense to reflect asset consumption through both deterioration and obsolescence) that may in turn be computed by a variety of ways, of which the straight-line, the double-declining balance, and the sum-of-years-digits methods are the most common.

Flag Activity.   An activity that signals the start or completion of an activity or set of activities.

Float.   In a CPM network, the amount of time by which a given activity may be delayed without delaying the completion of another activity, or of the project, i.e., (LS − ES) or (LF − EF). The difference between the time available and the time necessary for an activity. Zero float denotes a critical activity; negative float denotes a super-critical activity behind before it even starts by the number of days indicated (assuming full resource availability).

FM.   See "Finish Flag/Milestone."

FNET.   See "Finish No Earlier Than."

FNLT.   See "Finish No Later Than."

Forward Pass.   Scheduling step in which network early dates are computed from left to right (start to finish) (See Table 4-37).

Calculation of Early Start and Early Finish Times (Forward Pass)

Activity	Relationship	Early Start (ES)	Early Finish (EF)
First	Any	Zero (always)	Activity duration
All subsequent: select latest	(1) SS	ES of preceding activity	ES + activity duration
of (1), (2), and (3)	(2) FS	EF of preceding activity	ES + activity duration
	(3) FF	EF of preceding activity, less own duration	EF of preceding activity

Free Float.   Float owned by an activity that, if used, will not delay successor Early Start (or therefore change the float in later activities); can never be less than zero. It is the relative difference in the amount of total float between the activity with the least total float value entering into a given activity and the total float values of all activities entering into that same activity. See "Total Float."

FS (or F/S).   See "Finish-to-Start."

FUBAR.   *F*ouled *U*p *B*eyond *A*ll *R*epair.

FUBAR-Factor.   Degree to which project is Fouled Up Beyond All Repair.

Function Point.   One (information system) end-user business function.

Function Point Analysis.   State-of-the-art methodology by which information system value, size, cost, development time, and quality may be accurately determined.

GAAP.   *G*enerally *A*ccepted *A*ccounting *P*rinciples (the ideal objective); *G*enerally *A*wful *A*ccounting *P*ractices (the usual situation).

Gantt Chart.   A graphic representation of a project schedule that shows each task as a bar whose length is proportional to its duration; the bars appear in rows on a timeline chart that covers the time frame in which the project occurs. Named for Henry Gantt, early scheduling practitioner and its inventor.

GIGO.   "Garbage in, garbage out." An output is only as good as the quality of the input and the quality of the processing transactions.

Goal-seek.   "Back-solve" a model or equation such that certain variables are allowed to change in order that a specified goal may be achieved. A feature included in the more capable spreadsheets and other modeling tools. Solution produced is viable but not optimal.

HA.   See "Hammock Activity."

Hammock Activity (HA).   Summary activity that represents a set of activities. Always SSO-related to its predecessor and FFO-related to its successor, a hammock activity calculates its duration from predecessor start dates through successor finish dates only after the rest of the network has been scheduled. It does not include or change the schedule dates for the activities it spans; it includes only predecessor start and successor finish times. It may be considered a special type of duration constraint. Hammock activities may summarize regular activities, other hammock activities, or both. *Primavera* does not limit the number of times a hammock may be used.

Headcount.   Total hours expended (excluding overtime) divided by average hours worked per week per employee.

IFPS/Plus.   *Interactive Financial Planning System*; high-end integrated business modeling software and AI-based decision support system.

Imposed Dates.   Dates that constrain or override calculated early or late schedule dates. Examples include:

- Expected Finish
- Finish No Earlier/Later Than
- Mandatory Start/Finish
- Start No Earlier/Later Than
- Start On

Individual Cost Activity.   Cost activity that by itself constitutes a work package with identifiable resources.

Interruptible.   Activity whose progress need not be contiguous but instead may start and stop as needed—including to balance resource demands; compare with "Contiguous."

Joint Cost Activity.   Group of cost activities that share resources jointly in so tightly coupled a way that it is impractical to further allocate them to individual activities.

L.   Abbreviation for TL used in PERT graphic reports.

Labor.   Direct person-hours and/or monetary units expended by personnel involved in direct labor activities.

Laddering.   A method for showing the logical precedence relationship of a set of several activities that is repeated multiple times.

Lag.   An offset (either positive or negative) or delay from an activity to its successor, measured in the project's time planning unit. Lag decreases as progress is recorded and often affects nonconventional PDM relationships. Lag can also represent a delay in resource need or availability from its assigned activity start.

Late Dates (or Schedule).   See "Late Start" (LS) and "Late Finish" (LF).

Late Finish (LF).   Latest time an activity (or the entire project) can complete without delaying the project; does *not* mean "finishing late"!

Late Start (LS).   Latest time an activity (or the entire project) can begin without delaying the project; does *not* mean "starting late"!

Latest Allowable Date (TL).   Latest time on which a PERT event can start without delaying project completion; similar to CPM Late Start.

Latest Completion Date (SL).   Latest time on which a PERT event can finish without delaying project completion; similar to CPM Late Finish.

Latest Revised Estimate.   Current sum of the actual costs plus the latest estimate-to-complete for a work package or summary item (including applicable overhead, except where direct costs are specified).

LC.   Level code.

Lead Time.   The waiting time that must occur between two activities, regardless of any other activities that occur between them; lag in reverse perspective.

Level.   1. Work Breakdown Structure (WBS) level at which a charge or summary number appears. 2. Apply maximum resources to those activities for which the normal limit is insufficient to schedule the activity.

LF.   See "Late Finish."

Loop.   Circular logic, representing an impossible backward passage of time within a network. A path of activities that goes in a continuous circle and is not allowed.

Lost Progress.   How far behind the project is in time; schedule slippage.

LS.   See "Late Start."

m.   Most likely time estimate, which should occur about 50 percent of the time, for an activity when three time estimates are used, as in PERT.

Management.   Plan, staff, organize, direct, and control business processes.

Management by Exception.   Managing a project (or ongoing operation) by directing primary attention to critical (out of tolerance) project areas.

Mandatory Finish (MF).   Date constraint that sets both Early Finish and Late Finish to the date specified.

Mandatory Start (MS).   Date constraint that sets both Early Start and Late Start to the date specified.

Material Costs.   Cost of materials and purchased parts used in development or manufacturing as a direct charge.

Maximum Limit.   The highest rate of resource availability—including overtime, loan-ins, and temporary help/equipment—within a specified time interval. Compare "Normal Limit."

Mean.   1. Your boss's usual nature. 2. A measure of central tendency that divides the area under the probability distribution curve into two equal parts. Also called the "Expected Value."

Merge Point.   Non-critical activity whose successor is on the Critical Path; so named because the (non-critical) path on which this activity lies will at completion of this activity merge with the Critical Path. It is generally the only type of activity against which a Zero Free Float constraint is applied. Also called "Sink Point."

MF. See "Mandatory Finish."

Milestone. Zero-duration, no-resource activity that represents:

- A significant point in time
- A motivator toward which project staff can direct efforts
- Overall progress via a checkpoint
- A major accomplishment
- Notable deliverable result
- Critical event or approval/decision point in a time-logic network.

Milestones can indicate the start or end of a series of related activities (including project phases) or an accomplishment in the course of a project. Finish dates are blank for start milestones, and start dates are blank for finish. Milestones are sometimes erroneously equated to resource-consuming activities.

Milestone Manipulation. Unauthorized alteration of project milestones for reporting purposes; monkey business.

Most Critical Float. The lower value of start float and finish float.

Most Likely Time Estimate (m). Most realistic estimate of the time an activity might consume; the mean time of one hundred actual or imaginary performances resulting in a 50 percent probability that the activity will take exactly this much time.

MS. See "Mandatory Start."

Multiple-calendar. Refers to a project whose schedule is computed under more than one work calendar.

Multiple Finish Network. A(n improper) network with more than one finish activity.

Multiple Start Network. A(n improper) network with more than one start activity.

Net Present Value (NPV). Investment measurement standard that includes the time value of money and equals the sum of the present values of the benefits (returns) less the sum of the present values of the investments (costs). The resulting value can be positive, zero, or negative. The algebraic sign of the value reflects the rate of return of the investment with respect to a given discount rate.

Network. Visual or graphical representation of a project plan made up of one or more series of activities joined by lines to depict sequences and logical interdependencies. Also called "Network Diagram."

Network Analysis. Investigating all parts of a schedule to determine project and individual activity status, the causes of schedule changes, and the most effective ways to replan.

Network Diagram. See "Network."

Network Finish. Activity with no successors representing project completion.

Network Integration. Joining subnetworks together to produce a master network reflecting the total project.

Network Planning. Any project planning and scheduling technique that uses a network diagram.

Network Start. Activity with no predecessors representing project start.

Network Type. Designates how network activities are represented and related to each other; may be activity-on-arrow (AOA or ADM), activity-on-node (AON), or (preferred) Precedence Diagram Method (PDM).

Node. Network connecting point that graphically represents both activities and events in AON and PDM formats, and only events in AOA format.

Noncritical Activity. Activity off the Critical Path with positive float.

Noncritical Path. Any network path with positive float that does not affect project length.

Noncurrent Liabilities. Long-term debt and other liabilities due beyond the end of the normal operating cycle of the organization (usually one year).

Nonworkperiod. Time period in which no work is normally scheduled—weekends, holidays, and the like. Each project calendar may have its own set of nonworkperiods.

Normal Cost (NC). Lowest expected activity cost, using standard methodologies and resources, that produces an activity's Normal Time.

Normal Limit. The usual extent of resource availability—without overtime, loan-ins, or temporary help/equipment—within a specified time interval. Compare "Maximum Limit."

Normal Time (NT). Time associated with Normal Cost of an activity.

NPV. See "Net Present Value."

NPV Coefficient. The ratio between the project net present value and its required investment. The coefficient is a percentage value that can be used to compare the financial worth of various projects.

Open End. An activity, other than project start or finish, without both predecessor and successor relationships; its presence produces a(n improper) network with more than one start or finish activity. A no-no in good scheduling.

Optimistic Time Estimate (a). Minimum reasonable time in which an activity can be completed if everything goes exceptionally well—the best time possible given one hundred actual or imaginary performances. Optimistic time should occur about 1 percent of the time; faster times than this should occur less than 1 percent of the time.

Optimize. Perfectly assign resources to the project schedule such that no other possible solution is better than the chosen solution.

Original Duration (OD). Planned estimate of time required to complete an activity.

Other Assets. Intangible assets and assets not easily categorized as either current or fixed.

Out-of-Sequence Progress. Work completed on an activity before it is logically scheduled to occur. If an activity starts before its predecessor is complete, then it is said to have out-of-sequence progress. It may either be recognized (see "Progress Override") or disregarded (see "Retained Logic").

Overrun. Amount by which actual costs plus estimates-to-complete exceed the current approved contract price.

Owners' Equity. Excess (deficit) of "Total Assets" over "Total Liabilities."

P3. *Primavera Project Planner;* high-end integrated project planning, scheduling, management, and control software.

Paid-in Capital. Capital stock and other moneys invested by the owners in the organization.

Paradigm. Set of rules and filters through which we accept (or reject) and interpret information.

Paradigm Paralysis. Human tendency to reject or ignore information that is contrary to expectations or desired outcome.

Parallel Activities. Unrelated activities that may take place concurrently (simultaneously); they often compete for the same resources.

Parallel Resource Allocation Method. Resource allocation method that does not allow partial loading when sufficient resources are unavailable; activities are delayed until all needed resources become available. More complex, and produces a longer schedule, but does not violate network logic. Compare with "Serial Resource Allocation Method."

Path. A set or chain of connected activities in a network.

Payment Lag. Amount of time delay between work completion and payment for the effort.

PCT. See "Percent Complete."

PDM. See "Precedence Diagram Method."

Percent Complete (PCT). Proportion of an activity (or, alternately, its resource requirement) that has been completed; is equal to $100 * (OD - RD)/OD$.

Percent Expended. A calculated value, based on the actual cost to date and the original budgeted cost, that represents the proportion of the cost budget that has been spent. It differs from percent complete, which reflects how much has been accomplished rather than the proportion expended.

PERT. *Program Evaluation and Review Technique*. A scheduling methodology that uses three time estimates as the basis by which activities are placed in proper relationship and order; includes a statistical estimate of project on-time completion.

Pessimistic Time Estimate (b). Maximum reasonable time in which an activity would be completed if everyting goes exceptionally poorly—the worst time possible given one hundred actual or imaginary performances. It should occur about 1 percent of the time; slower times than this should occur less than 1 percent of the time.

Plan. A sequence of activities designed to accomplish a set of project objectives.

Planned Cost. Approved future cost for a work package or summary item.

Planning Unit. The increment of time (day, week, month, and so on) used to schedule a project.

Precedence Diagram Method (PDM). State-of-the-art Critical Path diagramming technique that expands the Activity-on-Node method to include the advanced relationships Start-to-Start, Finish-to-Finish, and Start-to-Finish.

Precedence Relationship. The ordered relationship requiring certain activities to finish (or at least start) before others can be started.

Predecessor. Activity that must finish (or, in certain special cases, at least start) before current activity can start; prerequisite. An activity can have many predecessors, each with a different relationship to the current activity.

Present Value (PV). Economic evaluation methodology that recognizes the time value of money by discounting future monetary values back in time at given rates (the discount factor) to arrive at their equivalent current economic cost/utility. It equates different investment opportunities with dissimilar costs, benefits, discount rates, and lengths to a common measurement standard—current monetary units.

Price/Unit. Cost to use one unit of a given resource within a specified time interval.

Primavera Project Planner (P3). High-end integrated project planning, scheduling, management, and control software.

Prioritized Resource Leveling/Smoothing. Resource leveling, and perhaps smoothing, ordered by user-specified criteria

when two or more activities compete for the same resource at the same time.

Probability. The likelihood of occurrence; used in PERT networks to calculate the chance of on-time milestone or project completion.

Production Rate. See "Schedule Performance Index."

Program. Proposed work, usually quite large and which may take years to complete, whose purpose is to accomplish a stated nonrecurring set of objectives; is also:

- Complex
- Comprised of several or many interrelated projects
- Part of the ongoing long-term business objectives: "the system."

Program Evaluation and Review Technique. See "PERT."

Progress. Work accomplished on an activity or a project in support of stated objectives.

Progress Override. An activity with out-of-sequence progress may recognize same (and continue to progress without delay), regardless of incomplete predecessors. Compare with "Retained Logic."

Project. Series of activities usually directed toward some major objective and requiring resources and an extended period of time to perform; sometimes one-time processes. A project must also have a well-defined start and end time. A collection of related projects is called a "Program."

Project Direct Costs. Personnel, materials, facilities, plant, and equipment costs used to expedite an activity; increase as project length is reduced. Compare "Project Indirect Costs."

Project Indirect Costs. Costs associated with sustaining (lengthening) a project; general business and overhead costs. Compare "Project Direct Costs."

Project Management. Planning, organizing, directing, and controlling resources for a specific time period to meet a specific set of one-time objectives:

- On time
- On budget
- At the desired performance level
- All with good customer and employee relations

Project management is used to provide a product or service that conforms to valid customer requirements and in some way improves the customer's life. Furthermore, project management utilizes the systems approach to management by having functional (line) personnel (the vertical hierarchy) assigned to a specific project (the horizontal hierarchy).

Project Objective. The purpose or underlying reason for undertaking the project; should consist of "*SMART*" goals that represent valid customer requirements.

Pure-logic Plot. Network logic diagram in which only the activities' predecessor/successor relationships and not their time duration or schedule determines its layout; compare "Time-Logic Plot," in which both factors are included.

PV. See "Present Value."

QAC. See "Quantity at Completion."

Quantity at Completion (QAC). Total amount of resource units required to complete an activity; is equal to the actual quantity to date plus the "Quantity to Complete."

Quantity to Complete (QTC).   Amount of additional resource units required to finish an underway activity; is equal to the difference between "Quantity at Completion" and actual quantity to date.

QTC.   See "Quantity to Complete."

Relationship.   Defines the logical order between a given activity and its predecessors or successors. May be one of four types:

1. Finish-to-Start: normal (conventional)
2. Start-to-Start: common start
3. Finish-to-Finish: common end
4. Start-to-Finish: successor cannot complete until predecessor starts.

Remaining Duration (RD).   Indicates how much longer is actually left to finish an activity.

Replan.   To revise or alter the project plan due to schedule changes or further analysis.

Report.   Logically-organized set of information summarizing or detailing specified aspects of project status.

Report Specification.   Defines the content and format of a report and specifies the selection and order of data.

Report Time.   Time or date when a schedule is calculated; data date.

Resource.   Personnel, equipment, material, or facility (other than time) required to complete a project task or activity.

Resource Allocation.   Process of assigning resources to project activities; is usually prioritized by activity Late Start and float value to minimize both project duration and resource requirements.

Resource Category.   Code that identifies significant group of similar resources to be summarized, for example, E–equipment, L–labor, M–material. Categories may be the same as or different from corresponding cost categories.

Resource Code.   Code to indicate the type of resource applied to the work package and by which resource types may be grouped and categorized.

Resource Dictionary.   Defines a resource coding structure, associated unit prices, and resource time/quantity availability limits.

Resource Duration.   The length of time a resource is used by an activity. Together with "Resource Lag," resource duration defines the application of a resource to an activity.

Resource Lag.   Amount of time delay between the start of a given activity and when resources are applied to that activity. Together with "Resource Duration," resource lag defines the application of a resource to an activity.

Resource Leveling.   Balancing resource usage to meet set limits or to reduce conflicts in availability. Apply maximum resources to those activities for which the normal limit is insufficient to schedule the activity.

Resource Leveling Analysis Report.   Report that details the cause(s) of activity delay during resource leveling. These delays are caused by late predecessors, by insufficient resources, or both.

Resource Smoothing.   Refinement of resource leveling in which the resource availability limits are gradually increased, from normal to maximum, for positive-float activities until the activity can (if possible) be scheduled without the application of excess resources. The objective is to resolve resource conflicts by delaying activities with positive float, but without claiming resources unnecessarily.

Resume Date.   Date on which activity work starts up again after a period of inactivity. Compare "Suspend Date."

Retained Earnings.   Difference between the organization's total earnings to date and the total amount of dividends paid to date to the shareholders; retained earnings represent that part of the total earnings that have been retained by the organization for its own use.

Retained Logic.   An out-of-sequence activity cannot be reported as having been completed until all its predecessors (back to the network beginning) have also been fully completed. Compare "Progress Override."

Return on Investment (ROI).   Same as "NPV Coefficient."

Rev Mode.   Breakneck work effort, with velocity approaching the speed of light and staff morale approaching zero, ordered by the boss to recover lost progress and counteract project *mis*management.

Revenues.   Increases in "Owners' Equity" resulting from operation of the entity (including, especially, providing goods and services to customers), recognized in the period in which these goods are shipped or services are rendered and against which accompanying costs are matched.

ROI.   See "Return on Investment."

RS/1.   High-end statistical analysis tool.

S.   Abbreviation for TS used in PERT graphic reports.

Schedule.   A timetable for a project plan listing required activities, the time at which they must start, and the time at which they must finish.

Schedule Calculation Logic.   Controls how out-of-sequence progress is treated (see "Retained Logic" and "Progress Override") and whether or not activities may be interrupted as they progress (see "Contiguous" and "Interruptible").

Schedule Parameter Codes.   Specific values by which activities may be selected, ordered, grouped, and summarized.

Schedule Performance Index (SPI).   Measures contract (or a given item) schedule efficiency as a percentage of the planned earned value. It is equal to: (BCWP/BCWS) ∗ 100 percent.

Schedule Variance (SV).   The difference, expressed in monetary units, between the work accomplished and the work planned, or earned value and planned effort:

Budgeted Cost for Work Performed (BCWP)
− Budgeted Cost For Work Scheduled (BCWS)

Scheduled Time (ST).   Time chosen for the earliest expected occurrence of a network start activity, or the latest allowable occurrence of a network finish activity or milestone.

SE.   Earliest completion date for a PERT activity.

Selection Criteria.   Mathematical filters that choose or reject data according to the following criteria:

EQ   Equal to
NE   Not equal to
GT   Greater than
GE   Greater than or equal to
LT   Less than
LE   Less than or equal to
WR   Within specified range
NR   Not within specified range

Serial Resource Allocation Method.   Resource allocation method that allows partial loading when sufficient resources are unavailable; activities are not delayed until all needed resources become available. Often results in a shorter schedule that violates network logic. Compare "Parallel Resource Allocation Method."

SF.   See "Start-to-Finish."

Simulation.   Processing alternative actions to determine effect such actions would have on the project; "What if" contingency analysis.

Single-calendar.   Refers to a project whose entire schedule is computed under one work calendar.

Sink Point.   Activity with multiple converging predecessors. Also called "Merge Point." See "Burst Point."

SL.   Latest completion date for a PERT activity.

Slack Time.   In a PERT network, the difference between latest allowable date and the expected date, or TL − TE. Slack may be positive, zero, or negative. See "Float."

Slide.   Delay of an unstarted activity measured as the difference between original Early Start and current Early Start. Also called "Slippage."

Slip Buffer.   The maximum value of free float for an activity after it has been slipped.

Slippage.   Delay of an unstarted activity measured as the difference between original Early Start and current Early Start. Also called "Slide."

SM.   See "Start Flag/Milestone."

SMART goals.   Mandatory project success criteria:
*S*pecific
   *M*easurable
      *A*greed upon
         *R*ealistic
            *T*ime-framed

Smoothing.   Type of resource leveling. Apply resources in incremental steps between normal and maximum limits to those activities for which the normal limit is insufficient to schedule the activity.

SNET.   See "Start No Earlier Than."

SNLT.   See "Start No Later Than."

SO.   See "Start On."

SS.   See "Start-to-Start."

Standard Deviation.   A measure of the dispersion or spread of a probability distribution; is equal to the square root of "Variance."

Start Activity (Event).   Leadoff network activity (event).

Start Date.   Date on which project is scheduled to begin.

Start Flag/Milestone (SM).   Zero-duration activity marking the beginning of an activity or set of activities.

Start Float.   Workperiod difference between Early Start and Late Start.

Start No Earlier Than (SNET).   Date constraint affecting Early Start that limits the earliest time an activity can begin; applied only when later than the calculated Early Start.

Start No Later Than (SNLT).   Date constraint affecting Late Start that limits the latest time an activity can begin; applied only when earlier than the calculated Late Start.

Start On (SO).   Date constraint affecting both Early Start and Late Start that sets each date equal to the imposed date, just as though an SNET and SNLT constraint were simultaneously applied. This constraint does not violate network logic, as sometimes can the Mandatory Start (MS).

Start-to-Finish (SF).   PDM relationship in which a successor activity cannot be completed until its predecessor activity starts; is usually better represented by other PDM logic.

Start-to-Start (SS).   PDM relationship in which a successor activity's start depends on the start of its predecessor.

Stochastic.   Takes into account the probability of occurrence of many values.

Subnetwork.   A network for a particular portion or phase of the entire plan.

Subtask.   A portion of a task.

Successor.   Activity that cannot start until current activity finishes (or, in certain special cases, at least starts); postrequisite. An activity can have many successors, each with a different relationship to the current activity.

Summary Activity Data.   Activity data that is totaled and summarized based on some specified criteria—by cost account, by resource, by time period, for example.

Summary Item.   Item appearing in Work Breakdown Structure (WBS) and consisting of groups of work packages.

Summary Network.   A network that contains a small number of high-level, summarizing activities rather than a large number of detailed activities.

Summary Number.   Number that identifies an item in Work Breakdown Structure (WBS).

Super-Critical Activity.   Activity on the Critical Path with negative float.

Suspend Date.   Date on which activity work stops for a period of inactivity. Compare "Resume Date."

Suspended Activity.   An activity on which work has temporarily stopped. The time between the suspend and the resume dates is not applied to activity duration.

SV.   See "Schedule Variance."

SWAG.   *S*cientific *W*ild-*A*ss *G*uess.

Systems Approach.   Seven-step problem-solving methodology:

1. Define the true problem.
2. Gather data and information describing the problem.
3. Identify alternate solutions.
4. Evaluate the alternatives.
5. Select the best alternative.
6. Implement the solution.
7. Follow-up to ensure that the solution is effective.

TA.   1. Actual date on which a PERT event occurs or an activity is completed.   2. Total assets.

Target Schedule.   Objective, baseline (not necessarily the original plan) schedule against which actual progress and cost performance will be measured.

Task.   Work effort, a portion of a project activity, designed to detail and clarify the process and resources required.

TD.   1. What the Denver Broncos need to score more of, and allow fewer. 2. Directed date for a PERT event.

TDC.   See "Actual Cost To Date."

TDQ.   See "Actual Quantity To Date."

Te.   Expected elapsed time for a PERT activity. Is equal to $(a + 4m + b)/6$, and represents a 50 percent probability that the PERT activity will be completed within that amount of time.

TE.   Expected date on which a PERT event will occur.

TF.   See "Total Float."

Through Date.   Point in time that specifies the last date on which a resource is available in a stated quantity (both normal and maximum) or when a resource price per unit is effective.

Time Estimate.   Approximate value for activity duration.

Time-logic Plot.   Network logic diagram in which both relationships and activity time duration/schedule determine its layout; compare "Pure-logic Plot," which includes only relationships and not time considerations.

Time Units.   Activity duration in standard time units, usually hours, days (currently most common), weeks (formerly most common), months, and the like.

Time Value of Money.   The understanding that the value of a sum of money today is different from the value of the same nominal sum tomorrow—or yesterday.

TL.   1. Latest allowable date for a PERT event. 2. Total liabilities.

Topological Sequence.   Integrated, global collection of activities merged from several subprojects all requiring resources from the resource pool.

Total Assets.   Total monetary value of all economic resources controlled by an organization whose cost at the time of acquisition could be objectively measured. By definition, must always equal the sum of Total Liabilities and Owners' Equity.

Total Float (TF).   The total number of workperiods that the start or finish of an activity can be delayed without affecting the project finish date; equal to (LS − ES) or (LF − EF). See "Free Float."

Total Liabilities.   Total monetary value of all claims against the organization's assets.

Total Slack.   See "Total Float."

TPC.   See "Actual Cost This Period."

TPQ.   See "Actual Quantity This Period."

Ts.   Scheduled elapsed time for a PERT activity.

TS.   Scheduled completion date for a PERT activity or event.

Underrun.   Amount by which current expenditures are lower than approved amounts.

Units.   The measure used for each resource—pounds, kilograms, linear feet, square feet, yards, meters, person-days, and so on.

Units per Time Period.   The amount of resource units per workperiod that can be applied to a particular activity.

Update.   To revise the project schedule and plan based on progress recording and replanning.

Variance.   1. Any schedule, technical performance, or cost deviation from a specific plan. 2. Measure of uncertainty, dispersion, or spread associated with statistical expected time in a PERT network; equal to the square of the Standard Deviation, or $[(b - a)/6]^2$.

(Note: ACWP = actual cost to date;

BCWP = earned value to date;

BCWS = scheduled budget to date.)

1. Schedule:
   Budgeted Cost for Work Performed (BCWP)
   − Budgeted Cost for Work Scheduled (BCWS)
   (Positive number indicates favorable variance.)
2. Cost:
   Budgeted Cost for Work Performed (BCWP)
   − Actual Cost for Work Performed (ACWP).
   (Positive number indicates favorable variance.)
3. Total:
   Actual Cost for Work Performed (ACWP)
   − Budgeted Cost for Work Scheduled (BCWS).
   (Has little or no analytical value.)

WBS.   See "Work Breakdown Structure."

What-if Analysis.   Processing alternative actions to determine effect such actions would have on the project; simulation, contingency analysis.

"Wheels in Motion" Person (WIMP).   A person who confuses activity and effort with actual progress.

Work Breakdown Structure (WBS).   A graphic technique that subdivides a project into phases, functions, areas, and the like. Specifies which organizational units are responsible for each activity required by the project; broken down like an organization chart into levels beginning with the end objectives and subdividing these into successively smaller end-item subdivisions: program, project, task, subtask, work package. Often code numbers organized and assigned to specific activities in order to facilitate reporting, tracking, and control.

Work Package.   Lowest level of cost significance in project Work Breakdown Structure (WBS) arrangement; consists of one or more cost-significant activities all charged to a single cost account. The Work Package corresponds to responsibility assignments as well as project time and cost elements.

Workday.   Any day of the week when work can be scheduled.

Workperiod.   Indicates when an activity begins or ends relative to the project calendar.

XF.   See "Expected Finish."

Zero Free Float (ZFF).   Duration constraint that allows an activity with positive float to turn critical and start as late as possible, without delaying its successors, by setting its early dates equal to its late.

Zero Total Float (ZTF).   Duration constraint that allows an activity with positive float to turn critical and start as early as possible by setting its late dates equal to its early. It can also reduce predecessor-activity float to zero.

ZFF.   See "Zero Free Float."

ZTF.   See "Zero Total Float."

Appendix A:
Project CARS Plant Expansion Exercise

Pat Andersen, a project manager for XYZ Construction Company, is responsible for expanding and modernizing the Acme Motors car manufacturing plant. This project involves three subprojects, listed as follows:

A—Designing, installing, and testing a new **a**utomation system

B—Building an addition to the maintenance and tooling **b**uilding to house the new conveyor system

C—Designing and installing a new **c**onveyor system.

Activity identifiers begin with the appropriate subsystem letter. The 58-activity project began 24 July 1989 and must complete by 5 September 1990. Following are some of the possible *P3* reports that can be produced for this project.

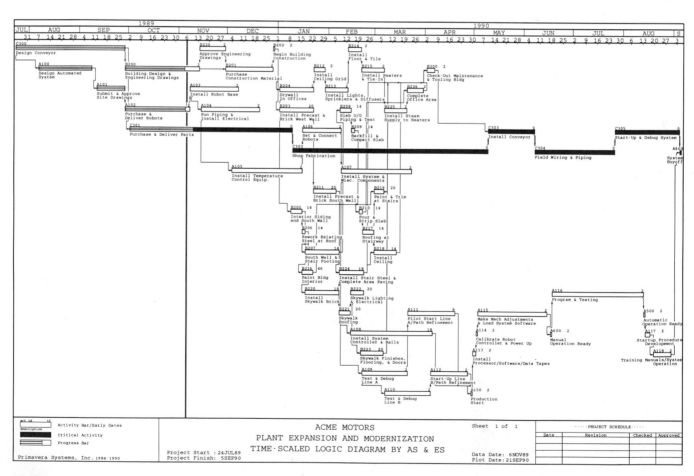

FIGURE A-1.   Project CARS time-logic plot.

314

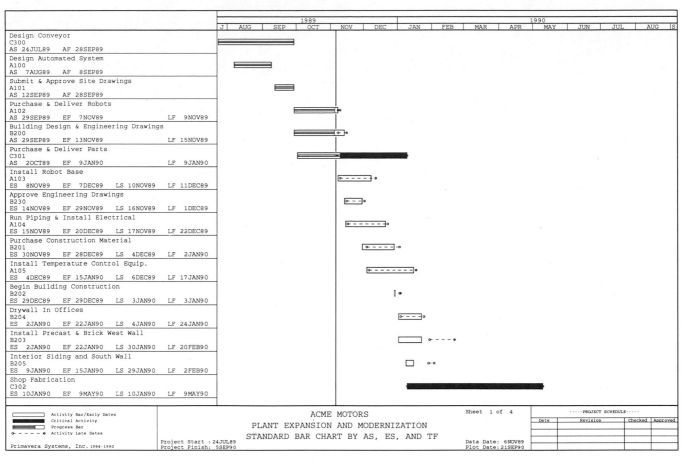

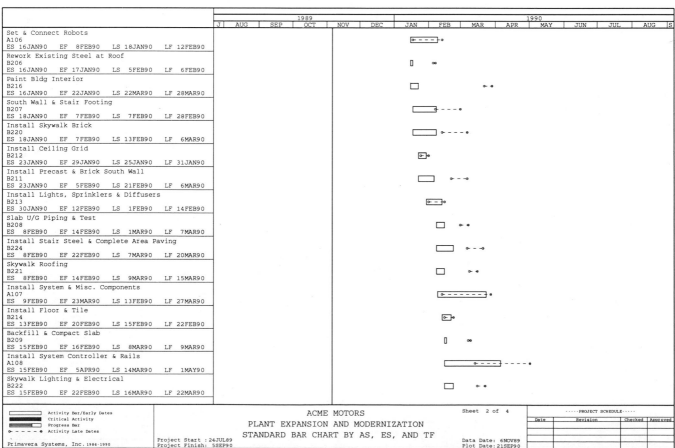

FIGURE A-2. Project CARS Gantt Chart.

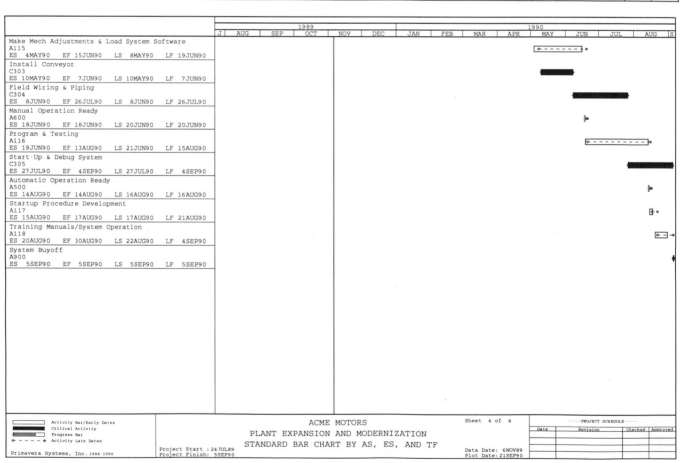

Sheet 3 of 4 — ACME MOTORS — PLANT EXPANSION AND MODERNIZATION — STANDARD BAR CHART BY AS, ES, AND TF

Pour & Strip Slab
B210
ES 20FEB90   EF 21FEB90   LS 12MAR90   LF 13MAR90

Install Heaters & Tie-In
B215
ES 21FEB90   EF 6MAR90   LS 23FEB90   LF 8MAR90

Skywalk Finishes, Flooring, & Doors
B223
ES 21FEB90   EF 6MAR90   LS 21MAR90   LF 3APR90

Test & Debug Line A
A109
ES 22FEB90   EF 21MAR90   LS 26FEB90   LF 23MAR90

Roofing at Stairway
B217
ES 22FEB90   EF 28FEB90   LS 14MAR90   LF 20MAR90

Install Ceiling
B218
ES 1MAR90   EF 14MAR90   LS 21MAR90   LF 3APR90

Paint & Trim at Stairs
B219
ES 1MAR90   EF 6MAR90   LS 29MAR90   LF 3APR90

Install Steam Supply to Heaters
B225
ES 7MAR90   EF 20MAR90   LS 9MAR90   LF 22MAR90

Test & Debug Line B
A110
ES 8MAR90   EF 4APR90   LS 12MAR90   LF 6APR90

Complete Office Area
B226
ES 21MAR90   EF 30MAR90   LS 23MAR90   LF 3APR90

Pilot Start Line A/Path Refinement
A111
ES 22MAR90   EF 19APR90   LS 3APR90   LF 1MAY90

Check-Out Maintenance & Tooling Bldg
B300
ES 2APR90   EF 6APR90   LS 4APR90   LF 10APR90

Start-Up Line B/Path Refinement
A112
ES 5APR90   EF 27APR90   LS 9APR90   LF 1MAY90

Production Start
A150
ES 30APR90   EF 30APR90   LS 2MAY90   LF 2MAY90

Install Processor/Software/Data Tapes
A113
ES 1MAY90   EF 2MAY90   LS 3MAY90   LF 4MAY90

Calibrate Robot Controller & Power Up
A114
ES 3MAY90   EF 3MAY90   LS 7MAY90   LF 7MAY90

Legend:
☐ Activity Bar/Early Dates
▬ Critical Activity
▭ Progress Bar
o – – – – ● Activity Late Dates

Primavera Systems, Inc. 1984-1990
Project Start : 24JUL89
Project Finish: 5SEP90
Data Date: 6NOV89
Plot Date: 21SEP90

Sheet 4 of 4 — ACME MOTORS — PLANT EXPANSION AND MODERNIZATION — STANDARD BAR CHART BY AS, ES, AND TF

Make Mech Adjustments & Load System Software
A115
ES 4MAY90   EF 15JUN90   LS 8MAY90   LF 19JUN90

Install Conveyor
C303
ES 10MAY90   EF 7JUN90   LS 10MAY90   LF 7JUN90

Field Wiring & Piping
C304
ES 8JUN90   EF 26JUL90   LS 8JUN90   LF 26JUL90

Manual Operation Ready
A600
ES 18JUN90   EF 18JUN90   LS 20JUN90   LF 20JUN90

Program & Testing
A116
ES 19JUN90   EF 13AUG90   LS 21JUN90   LF 15AUG90

Start-Up & Debug System
C305
ES 27JUL90   EF 4SEP90   LS 27JUL90   LF 4SEP90

Automatic Operation Ready
A500
ES 14AUG90   EF 14AUG90   LS 16AUG90   LF 16AUG90

Startup Procedure Development
A117
ES 15AUG90   EF 17AUG90   LS 17AUG90   LF 21AUG90

Training Manuals/System Operation
A118
ES 20AUG90   EF 30AUG90   LS 22AUG90   LF 4SEP90

System Buyoff
A900
ES 5SEP90   EF 5SEP90   LS 5SEP90   LF 5SEP90

Legend:
☐ Activity Bar/Early Dates
▬ Critical Activity
▭ Progress Bar
o – – – – ● Activity Late Dates

Primavera Systems, Inc. 1984-1990
Project Start : 24JUL89
Project Finish: 5SEP90
Data Date: 6NOV89
Plot Date: 21SEP90

FIGURE A-2. Continued.

316

Table A-1. Project Schedule Sorted by Early Start and Total Float

ACTIVITY ID	ORIG DUR	REM DUR	%	CODE	ACTIVITY DESCRIPTION	EARLY START	EARLY FINISH	LATE START	LATE FINISH	TOTAL FLOAT
C300	45	0	100	ENG	Design Conveyor	24JUL89A	28SEP89A			
A100	20	0	100	ENG	Design Automated System	7AUG89A	8SEP89A			
A101	14	0	100	ENG	Submit & Approve Site Drawings	12SEP89A	28SEP89A			
A102	30	2	93	PCH	Purchase & Deliver Robots	29SEP89A	7NOV89		9NOV89	2
B200	30	6	80	ENG	Building Design & Engineering Drawings	29SEP89A	13NOV89		15NOV89	2
C301	70	43	39	PCH	Purchase & Deliver Parts	20OCT89A	9JAN90		9JAN90	0
A103	20	20	0	ENG	Install Robot Base	8NOV89	7DEC89	10NOV89	11DEC89	2
B230	10	10	0	ENG	Approve Engineering Drawings	14NOV89	29NOV89	16NOV89	1DEC89	2
A104	24	24	0	ENG	Run Piping & Install Electrical	15NOV89	20DEC89	17NOV89	22DEC89	2
B201	20	20	0	PCH	Purchase Construction Material	30NOV89	28DEC89	4DEC89	2JAN90	2
A105	29	29	0	ENG	Install Temperature Control Equip.	4DEC89	15JAN90	6DEC89	17JAN90	2
B202	1	1	0	CON	Begin Building Construction	29DEC89	29DEC89	3JAN90	3JAN90	2
B204	15	15	0	CON	Drywall In Offices	2JAN90	22JAN90	4JAN90	24JAN90	2
B203	15	15	0	CON	Install Precast & Brick West Wall	2JAN90	22JAN90	30JAN90	20FEB90	20
B205	5	5	0	CON	Interior Siding and South Wall	9JAN90	15JAN90	29JAN90	2FEB90	14
C302	85	85	0	CON	Shop Fabrication	10JAN90	9MAY90	10JAN90	9MAY90	0
A106	18	18	0	ENG	Set & Connect Robots	16JAN90	8FEB90	18JAN90	12FEB90	2
B206	2	2	0	CON	Rework Existing Steel at Roof	16JAN90	17JAN90	5FEB90	6FEB90	14
B216	5	5	0	CON	Paint Bldg Interior	16JAN90	22JAN90	22MAR90	28MAR90	46
B207	15	15	0	CON	South Wall & Stair Footing	18JAN90	7FEB90	7FEB90	28FEB90	14
B220	15	15	0	CON	Install Skywalk Brick	18JAN90	7FEB90	13FEB90	6MAR90	18
B212	5	5	0	CON	Install Ceiling Grid	23JAN90	29JAN90	25JAN90	31JAN90	2
B211	10	10	0	CON	Install Precast & Brick South Wall	23JAN90	5FEB90	21FEB90	6MAR90	20
B213	10	10	0	CON	Install Lights, Sprinklers & Diffusers	30JAN90	12FEB90	1FEB90	14FEB90	2
B208	5	5	0	CON	Slab U/G Piping & Test	8FEB90	14FEB90	1MAR90	7MAR90	14
B224	10	10	0	CON	Install Stair Steel & Complete Area Paving	8FEB90	22FEB90	7MAR90	20MAR90	18
B221	5	5	0	CON	Skywalk Roofing	8FEB90	14FEB90	9MAR90	15MAR90	20
A107	30	30	0	ENG	Install System & Misc. Components	9FEB90	23MAR90	13FEB90	27MAR90	2
B214	5	5	0	CON	Install Floor & Tile	13FEB90	20FEB90	15FEB90	22FEB90	2
B209	2	2	0	CON	Backfill & Compact Slab	15FEB90	16FEB90	8MAR90	9MAR90	14
A108	35	35	0	ENG	Install System Controller & Rails	15FEB90	5APR90	14MAR90	1MAY90	18
B222	5	5	0	CON	Skywalk Lighting & Electrical	15FEB90	22FEB90	16MAR90	22MAR90	20
B210	2	2	0	CON	Pour & Strip Slab	20FEB90	21FEB90	12MAR90	13MAR90	14
B215	10	10	0	CON	Install Heaters & Tie-In	21FEB90	6MAR90	23FEB90	8MAR90	2
B223	10	10	0	CON	Skywalk Finishes, Flooring, & Doors	21FEB90	6MAR90	21MAR90	3APR90	20
A109	20	20	0	ENG	Test & Debug Line A	22FEB90	21MAR90	26FEB90	23MAR90	2
B217	5	5	0	CON	Roofing at Stairway	22FEB90	28FEB90	14MAR90	20MAR90	14
B218	10	10	0	CON	Install Ceiling	1MAR90	14MAR90	21MAR90	3APR90	14
B219	4	4	0	CON	Paint & Trim at Stairs	1MAR90	6MAR90	29MAR90	3APR90	20
B225	10	10	0	CON	Install Steam Supply to Heaters	7MAR90	20MAR90	9MAR90	22MAR90	2
A110	20	20	0	ENG	Test & Debug Line B	8MAR90	4APR90	12MAR90	6APR90	2
B226	8	8	0	CON	Complete Office Area	21MAR90	30MAR90	23MAR90	3APR90	2
A111	21	21	0	ENG	Pilot Start Line A/Path Refinement	22MAR90	19APR90	3APR90	1MAY90	8
B300	5	5	0	ENG	Check-Out Maintenance & Tooling Bldg	2APR90	6APR90	4APR90	10APR90*	2
A112	17	17	0	ENG	Start-Up Line B/Path Refinement	5APR90	27APR90	9APR90	1MAY90	2
A150	1	1	0	PRG	Production Start	30APR90	30APR90	2MAY90	2MAY90	2
A113	2	2	0	ENG	Install Processor/Software/Data Tapes	1MAY90	2MAY90	3MAY90	4MAY90	2
A114	1	1	0	ENG	Calibrate Robot Controller & Power Up	3MAY90	3MAY90	7MAY90	7MAY90	2
A115	30	30	0	ENG	Make Mech Adjustments & Load System Software	4MAY90	15JUN90	8MAY90	19JUN90	2
C303	20	20	0	ENG	Install Conveyor	10MAY90	7JUN90	10MAY90	7JUN90	0
C304	35	35	0	ENG	Field Wiring & Piping	8JUN90	26JUL90	8JUN90	26JUL90	0
A600	1	1	0	ENG	Manual Operation Ready	18JUN90	18JUN90	20JUN90	20JUN90	2
A116	40	40	0	PRG	Program & Testing	19JUN90	13AUG90	21JUN90	15AUG90	2
C305	27	27	0	ENG	Start-Up & Debug System	27JUL90	4SEP90	27JUL90	4SEP90	0
A500	1	1	0	PRG	Automatic Operation Ready	14AUG90	14AUG90	16AUG90	16AUG90	2
A117	3	3	0	ENG	Startup Procedure Development	15AUG90	17AUG90	17AUG90	21AUG90	2
A118	9	9	0	ENG	Training Manuals/System Operation	20AUG90	30AUG90	22AUG90	4SEP90	2
A900	1	1	0	ENG	System Buyoff	5SEP90	5SEP90	5SEP90	5SEP90	0

Table A-2. Project Schedule Sorted by Total Float and Early Start

---

PROJECT SCHEDULE SORTED BY TOTAL FLOAT AND EARLY START   DATA DATE   6NOV89   PAGE NO.   1

ACTIVITY ID	ORIG DUR	REM DUR	%	CODE	ACTIVITY DESCRIPTION	EARLY START	EARLY FINISH	LATE START	LATE FINISH	TOTAL FLOAT
C300	45	0	100	MASON	Design Conveyor	24JUL89A	28SEP89A			
A100	20	0	100	MASON	Design Automated System	7AUG89A	8SEP89A			
A101	14	0	100	ACME	Submit & Approve Site Drawings	12SEP89A	28SEP89A			
C301	70	43	39	FOLEY	Purchase & Deliver Parts	2OCT89A	9JAN90		9JAN90	0
C302	85	85	0	UCCI	Shop Fabrication	10JAN90	9MAY90	10JAN90	9MAY90	0
C303	20	20	0	MILLS	Install Conveyor	10MAY90	7JUN90	10MAY90	7JUN90	0
C304	35	35	0	MILLS	Field Wiring & Piping	8JUN90	26JUL90	8JUN90	26JUL90	0
C305	27	27	0	EVANS	Start-Up & Debug System	27JUL90	4SEP90	27JUL90	4SEP90	0
A900	1	1	0	EVANS	System Buyoff	5SEP90	5SEP90	5SEP90	5SEP90	0
A102	30	2	93	FOLEY	Purchase & Deliver Robots	29SEP89A	7NOV89		9NOV89	2
B200	30	6	80	MASON	Building Design & Engineering Drawings	29SEP89A	13NOV89		15NOV89	2
A103	20	20	0	MILLS	Install Robot Base	8NOV89	7DEC89	10NOV89	11DEC89	2
B230	10	10	0	ACME	Approve Engineering Drawings	14NOV89	29NOV89	16NOV89	1DEC89	2
A104	24	24	0	MILLS	Run Piping & Install Electrical	15NOV89	20DEC89	17NOV89	22DEC89	2
B201	20	20	0	FOLEY	Purchase Construction Material	30NOV89	28DEC89	4DEC89	2JAN90	2
A105	29	29	0	MILLS	Install Temperature Control Equip.	4DEC89	15JAN90	6DEC89	17JAN90	2
B202	1	1	0	SMITH	Begin Building Construction	29DEC89	29DEC89	3JAN90	3JAN90	2
B204	15	15	0	NOLAN	Drywall In Offices	2JAN90	22JAN90	4JAN90	24JAN90	2
A106	18	18	0	MILLS	Set & Connect Robots	16JAN90	8FEB90	18JAN90	12FEB90	2
B212	5	5	0	NOLAN	Install Ceiling Grid	23JAN90	29JAN90	25JAN90	31JAN90	2
B213	10	10	0	NOLAN	Install Lights, Sprinklers & Diffusers	30JAN90	12FEB90	1FEB90	14FEB90	2
A107	30	30	0	MILLS	Install System & Misc. Components	9FEB90	23MAR90	13FEB90	27MAR90	2
B214	5	5	0	NOLAN	Install Floor & Tile	13FEB90	20FEB90	15FEB90	22FEB90	2
B215	10	10	0	NOLAN	Install Heaters & Tie-In	21FEB90	6MAR90	23FEB90	8MAR90	2
A109	20	20	0	MILLS	Test & Debug Line A	22FEB90	21MAR90	26FEB90	23MAR90	2
B225	10	10	0	NOLAN	Install Steam Supply to Heaters	7MAR90	20MAR90	9MAR90	22MAR90	2
A110	20	20	0	MILLS	Test & Debug Line B	8MAR90	4APR90	12MAR90	6APR90	2
B226	8	8	0	SMITH	Complete Office Area	21MAR90	30MAR90	23MAR90	3APR90	2
B300	5	5	0	ACME	Check-Out Maintenance & Tooling Bldg	2APR90	6APR90	4APR90	10APR90*	2
A112	17	17	0	MILLS	Start-Up Line B/Path Refinement	5APR90	27APR90	9APR90	1MAY90	2
A150	1	1	0	HARIS	Production Start	30APR90	30APR90	2MAY90	2MAY90	2
A113	2	2	0	MILLS	Install Processor/Software/Data Tapes	1MAY90	2MAY90	3MAY90	4MAY90	2
A114	1	1	0	MILLS	Calibrate Robot Controller & Power Up	3MAY90	3MAY90	7MAY90	7MAY90	2
A115	30	30	0	MILLS	Make Mech Adjustments & Load System Software	4MAY90	15JUN90	8MAY90	19JUN90	2
A600	1	1	0	MILLS	Manual Operation Ready	18JUN90	18JUN90	20JUN90	20JUN90	2
A116	40	40	0	HARIS	Program & Testing	19JUN90	13AUG90	21JUN90	15AUG90	2
A500	1	1	0	HARIS	Automatic Operation Ready	14AUG90	14AUG90	16AUG90	16AUG90	2
A117	3	3	0	EVANS	Startup Procedure Development	15AUG90	17AUG90	17AUG90	21AUG90	2
A118	9	9	0	EVANS	Training Manuals/System Operation	20AUG90	30AUG90	22AUG90	4SEP90	2
A111	21	21	0	MILLS	Pilot Start Line A/Path Refinement	22MAR90	19APR90	3APR90	1MAY90	8
B205	5	5	0	NOLAN	Interior Siding and South Wall	9JAN90	15JAN90	29JAN90	2FEB90	14
B206	2	2	0	NOLAN	Rework Existing Steel at Roof	16JAN90	17JAN90	5FEB90	6FEB90	14
B207	15	15	0	NOLAN	South Wall & Stair Footing	18JAN90	7FEB90	7FEB90	28FEB90	14
B208	5	5	0	NOLAN	Slab U/G Piping & Test	8FEB90	14FEB90	1MAR90	7MAR90	14
B209	2	2	0	SMITH	Backfill & Compact Slab	15FEB90	16FEB90	8MAR90	9MAR90	14
B210	2	2	0	SMITH	Pour & Strip Slab	20FEB90	21FEB90	12MAR90	13MAR90	14
B217	5	5	0	NOLAN	Roofing at Stairway	22FEB90	28FEB90	14MAR90	20MAR90	14
B218	10	10	0	NOLAN	Install Ceiling	1MAR90	14MAR90	21MAR90	3APR90	14
B220	15	15	0	NOLAN	Install Skywalk Brick	18JAN90	7FEB90	13FEB90	6MAR90	18
B224	10	10	0	NOLAN	Install Stair Steel & Complete Area Paving	8FEB90	22FEB90	7MAR90	20MAR90	18
A108	35	35	0	MILLS	Install System Controller & Rails	15FEB90	5APR90	14MAR90	1MAY90	18
B203	15	15	0	SMITH	Install Precast & Brick West Wall	2JAN90	22JAN90	30JAN90	20FEB90	20
B211	10	10	0	SMITH	Install Precast & Brick South Wall	23JAN90	5FEB90	21FEB90	6MAR90	20
B221	5	5	0	NOLAN	Skywalk Roofing	8FEB90	14FEB90	9MAR90	15MAR90	20
B222	5	5	0	NOLAN	Skywalk Lighting & Electrical	15FEB90	22FEB90	16MAR90	22MAR90	20
B223	10	10	0	NOLAN	Skywalk Finishes, Flooring, & Doors	21FEB90	6MAR90	21MAR90	3APR90	20
B219	4	4	0	NOLAN	Paint & Trim at Stairs	1MAR90	6MAR90	29MAR90	3APR90	20
B216	5	5	0	NOLAN	Paint Bldg Interior	16JAN90	22JAN90	22MAR90	28MAR90	46

Table A-3. Summary Project Schedule, by Responsibility, with BCWS and BCWP

```
-----------------------------------------------------------------------------------------------------------
ACME MOTORS, INC.                      PRIMAVERA PROJECT PLANNER          PLANT EXPANSION AND MODERNIZATION

REPORT DATE 23OCT89   RUN NO.   3        PROJECT SCHEDULE                  START DATE 24JUL89  FIN DATE  5SEP90

PROJECT SCHEDULE (WITH BUDGET AND EARNED-VALUE AMOUNTS)                    DATA DATE   6NOV89  PAGE NO.    1
            SORTED BY RESPONSIBLE PERSON AND ACTIVITY ID
ACME MOTORS - OWNER
----- -----  ---- ---- - ---  -----------  -----------------------------------  ---------  --------  --------  --------  --------  -----
```

ACME MOTORS - OWNER

ACTIVITY ID	ORIG DUR	REM DUR	%	ACTIVITY DESCRIPTION	BUDGET	EARNED	EARLY START	EARLY FINISH	LATE START	LATE FINISH	TOTAL FLOAT
A101	14	0	100	Submit & Approve Site Drawings	.00	.00	12SEP89A	28SEP89A			
B230	10	10	0	Approve Engineering Drawings	1360.00	.00	14NOV89	29NOV89	16NOV89	1DEC89	2
B300	5	5	0	Check-Out Maintenance & Tooling Bldg	700.00	.00	2APR90	6APR90	4APR90	10APR90*	2
SUBTOTAL				ACME	2060.00	.00					

```
-----------------------------------------------------------------------------------------------------------
ACME MOTORS, INC.                      PRIMAVERA PROJECT PLANNER          PLANT EXPANSION AND MODERNIZATION

REPORT DATE 23OCT89   RUN NO.   3        PROJECT SCHEDULE                  START DATE 24JUL89  FIN DATE  5SEP90

PROJECT SCHEDULE (WITH BUDGET AND EARNED-VALUE AMOUNTS)                    DATA DATE   6NOV89  PAGE NO.    1
            SORTED BY RESPONSIBLE PERSON AND ACTIVITY ID
```

TIM EVANS - SYSTEMS ENGINEER

ACTIVITY ID	ORIG DUR	REM DUR	%	ACTIVITY DESCRIPTION	BUDGET	EARNED	EARLY START	EARLY FINISH	LATE START	LATE FINISH	TOTAL FLOAT
A117	3	3	0	Startup Procedure Development	780.00	.00	15AUG90	17AUG90	17AUG90	21AUG90	2
A118	9	9	0	Training Manuals/System Operation	1170.00	.00	20AUG90	30AUG90	22AUG90	4SEP90	2
A900	1	1	0	System Buyoff	.00	.00	5SEP90	5SEP90	5SEP90	5SEP90	0
C305	27	27	0	Start-Up & Debug System	7020.00	.00	27JUL90	4SEP90	27JUL90	4SEP90	0
SUBTOTAL				EVANS	8970.00	.00					

```
-----------------------------------------------------------------------------------------------------------
ACME MOTORS, INC.                      PRIMAVERA PROJECT PLANNER          PLANT EXPANSION AND MODERNIZATION

REPORT DATE 23OCT89   RUN NO.   3        PROJECT SCHEDULE                  START DATE 24JUL89  FIN DATE  5SEP90

PROJECT SCHEDULE (WITH BUDGET AND EARNED-VALUE AMOUNTS)                    DATA DATE   6NOV89  PAGE NO.    1
            SORTED BY RESPONSIBLE PERSON AND ACTIVITY ID
```

MEG FOLEY - PURCHASING MANAGER

ACTIVITY ID	ORIG DUR	REM DUR	%	ACTIVITY DESCRIPTION	BUDGET	EARNED	EARLY START	EARLY FINISH	LATE START	LATE FINISH	TOTAL FLOAT
A102	30	2	93	Purchase & Deliver Robots	200000.00	186000.00	29SEP89A	7NOV89		9NOV89	2
B201	20	20	0	Purchase Construction Material	225000.00	.00	30NOV89	28DEC89	4DEC89	2JAN90	2
C301	70	43	39	Purchase & Deliver Parts	75000.00	29250.00	2OCT89A	9JAN90		9JAN90	0
SUBTOTAL				FOLEY	500000.00	215250.00					

(continued)

Table A-3.   Continued.

```
-------------------------------------------------------------------------------------------
ACME MOTORS, INC.                      PRIMAVERA PROJECT PLANNER         PLANT EXPANSION AND MODERNIZATION

REPORT DATE 23OCT89  RUN NO.   3         PROJECT SCHEDULE               START DATE 24JUL89  FIN DATE  5SEP90

PROJECT SCHEDULE (WITH BUDGET AND EARNED-VALUE AMOUNTS)                 DATA DATE   6NOV89  PAGE NO.    1
           SORTED BY RESPONSIBLE PERSON AND ACTIVITY ID
```

LINDA HARIS - SENIOR PROGRAMMER

ACTIVITY ID	ORIG DUR	REM DUR	%	ACTIVITY DESCRIPTION BUDGET	EARNED	EARLY START	EARLY FINISH	LATE START	LATE FINISH	TOTAL FLOAT
A116	40	40	0	Program & Testing		19JUN90	13AUG90	21JUN90	15AUG90	2
				11600.00	.00					
A150	1	1	0	Production Start		30APR90	30APR90	2MAY90	2MAY90	2
				.00	.00					
A500	1	1	0	Automatic Operation Ready		14AUG90	14AUG90	16AUG90	16AUG90	2
				.00	.00					
SUBTOTAL				HARIS 11600.00	.00					

```
-------------------------------------------------------------------------------------------
ACME MOTORS, INC.                      PRIMAVERA PROJECT PLANNER         PLANT EXPANSION AND MODERNIZATION

REPORT DATE 23OCT89  RUN NO.   3         PROJECT SCHEDULE               START DATE 24JUL89  FIN DATE  5SEP90

PROJECT SCHEDULE (WITH BUDGET AND EARNED-VALUE AMOUNTS)                 DATA DATE   6NOV89  PAGE NO.    1
           SORTED BY RESPONSIBLE PERSON AND ACTIVITY ID
```

ANDY MASON - SENIOR DESIGN ENGINEER

ACTIVITY ID	ORIG DUR	REM DUR	%	ACTIVITY DESCRIPTION BUDGET	EARNED	EARLY START	EARLY FINISH	LATE START	LATE FINISH	TOTAL FLOAT
A100	20	0	100	Design Automated System		7AUG89A	8SEP89A			
				8160.00	8160.00					
B200	30	6	80	Building Design & Engineering Drawings		29SEP89A	13NOV89		15NOV89	2
				12240.00	9792.00					
C300	45	0	100	Design Conveyor		24JUL89A	28SEP89A			
				12240.00	12240.00					
SUBTOTAL				MASON 32640.00	30192.00					

(continued)

Table A-3.   Continued.

ACME MOTORS, INC.   PRIMAVERA PROJECT PLANNER   PLANT EXPANSION AND MODERNIZATION

REPORT DATE 23OCT89   RUN NO.   3   PROJECT SCHEDULE   START DATE 24JUL89 FIN DATE 5SEP90

PROJECT SCHEDULE (WITH BUDGET AND EARNED-VALUE AMOUNTS)   DATA DATE   6NOV89 PAGE NO.   1
        SORTED BY RESPONSIBLE PERSON AND ACTIVITY ID

TOM MILLS - FIELD SERVICE ENGINEER

ACTIVITY ID	ORIG DUR	REM DUR	%	ACTIVITY DESCRIPTION BUDGET	EARNED	EARLY START	EARLY FINISH	LATE START	LATE FINISH	TOTAL FLOAT
A103	20	20	0	Install Robot Base		8NOV89	7DEC89	10NOV89	11DEC89	2
				1600.00	.00					
A104	24	24	0	Run Piping & Install Electrical		15NOV89	20DEC89	17NOV89	22DEC89	2
				7930.00	.00					
A105	29	29	0	Install Temperature Control Equip.		4DEC89	15JAN90	6DEC89	17JAN90	2
				4640.00	.00					
A106	18	18	0	Set & Connect Robots		16JAN90	8FEB90	18JAN90	12FEB90	2
				1440.00	.00					
A107	30	30	0	Install System & Misc. Components		9FEB90	23MAR90	13FEB90	27MAR90	2
				2400.00	.00					
A108	35	35	0	Install System Controller & Rails		15FEB90	5APR90	14MAR90	1MAY90	18
				5600.00	.00					
A109	20	20	0	Test & Debug Line A		22FEB90	21MAR90	26FEB90	23MAR90	2
				4000.00	.00					
A110	20	20	0	Test & Debug Line B		8MAR90	4APR90	12MAR90	6APR90	2
				4000.00	.00					
A111	21	21	0	Pilot Start Line A/Path Refinement		22MAR90	19APR90	3APR90	1MAY90	8
				1680.00	.00					
A112	17	17	0	Start-Up Line B/Path Refinement		5APR90	27APR90	9APR90	1MAY90	2
				1360.00	.00					
A113	2	2	0	Install Processor/Software/Data Tapes		1MAY90	2MAY90	3MAY90	4MAY90	2
				480.00	.00					
A114	1	1	0	Calibrate Robot Controller & Power Up		3MAY90	3MAY90	7MAY90	7MAY90	2
				160.00	.00					
A115	30	30	0	Make Mech Adjustments & Load System Software		4MAY90	15JUN90	8MAY90	19JUN90	2
				6844.00	.00					
A600	1	1	0	Manual Operation Ready		18JUN90	18JUN90	20JUN90	20JUN90	2
				.00	.00					
C303	20	20	0	Install Conveyor		10MAY90	7JUN90	10MAY90	7JUN90	0
				9600.00	.00					
C304	35	35	0	Field Wiring & Piping		8JUN90	26JUL90	8JUN90	26JUL90	0
				18550.00	.00					
				----------- -----------						
SUBTOTAL				MILLS 70284.00	.00					

(continued)

Table A-3.   Continued.

```
-------------------------------------------------------------------------------------
ACME MOTORS, INC.                    PRIMAVERA PROJECT PLANNER       PLANT EXPANSION AND MODERNIZATION

REPORT DATE 23OCT89  RUN NO.   3        PROJECT SCHEDULE             START DATE 24JUL89  FIN DATE  5SEP90

PROJECT SCHEDULE (WITH BUDGET AND EARNED-VALUE AMOUNTS)             DATA DATE   6NOV89  PAGE NO.    1
         SORTED BY RESPONSIBLE PERSON AND ACTIVITY ID
```

JOE NOLAN - CONSTRUCTION MANAGER

ACTIVITY ID	ORIG DUR	REM DUR	%	ACTIVITY DESCRIPTION / BUDGET	EARNED	EARLY START	EARLY FINISH	LATE START	LATE FINISH	TOTAL FLOAT
B204	15	15	0	Drywall In Offices		2JAN90	22JAN90	4JAN90	24JAN90	2
				6187.50	.00					
B205	5	5	0	Interior Siding and South Wall		9JAN90	15JAN90	29JAN90	2FEB90	14
				5950.00	.00					
B206	2	2	0	Rework Existing Steel at Roof		16JAN90	17JAN90	5FEB90	6FEB90	14
				1040.00	.00					
B207	15	15	0	South Wall & Stair Footing		18JAN90	7FEB90	7FEB90	28FEB90	14
				8550.00	.00					
B208	5	5	0	Slab U/G Piping & Test		8FEB90	14FEB90	1MAR90	7MAR90	14
				16313.75	.00					
B212	5	5	0	Install Ceiling Grid		23JAN90	29JAN90	25JAN90	31JAN90	2
				3435.00	.00					
B213	10	10	0	Install Lights, Sprinklers & Diffusers		30JAN90	12FEB90	1FEB90	14FEB90	2
				8150.00	.00					
B214	5	5	0	Install Floor & Tile		13FEB90	20FEB90	15FEB90	22FEB90	2
				3800.00	.00					
B215	10	10	0	Install Heaters & Tie-In		21FEB90	6MAR90	23FEB90	8MAR90	2
				3450.00	.00					
B216	5	5	0	Paint Bldg Interior		16JAN90	22JAN90	22MAR90	28MAR90	46
				2280.00	.00					
B217	5	5	0	Roofing at Stairway		22FEB90	28FEB90	14MAR90	20MAR90	14
				2600.00	.00					
B218	10	10	0	Install Ceiling		1MAR90	14MAR90	21MAR90	3APR90	14
				4750.00	.00					
B219	4	4	0	Paint & Trim at Stairs		1MAR90	6MAR90	29MAR90	3APR90	20
				1682.00	.00					
B220	15	15	0	Install Skywalk Brick		18JAN90	7FEB90	13FEB90	6MAR90	18
				5700.00	.00					
B221	5	5	0	Skywalk Roofing		8FEB90	14FEB90	9MAR90	15MAR90	20
				1650.00	.00					
B222	5	5	0	Skywalk Lighting & Electrical		15FEB90	22FEB90	16MAR90	22MAR90	20
				1450.00	.00					
B223	10	10	0	Skywalk Finishes, Flooring, & Doors		21FEB90	6MAR90	21MAR90	3APR90	20
				5725.00	.00					
B224	10	10	0	Install Stair Steel & Complete Area Paving		8FEB90	22FEB90	7MAR90	20MAR90	18
				1900.00	.00					
B225	10	10	0	Install Steam Supply to Heaters		7MAR90	20MAR90	9MAR90	22MAR90	2
				1150.00	.00					
SUBTOTAL				NOLAN 85733.25	.00					

(continued)

Table A-3.   Continued.

```
--------------------------------------------------------------------------------------------
ACME MOTORS, INC.                    PRIMAVERA PROJECT PLANNER            PLANT EXPANSION AND MODERNIZATION

REPORT DATE 23OCT89  RUN NO.   3        PROJECT SCHEDULE              START DATE 24JUL89 FIN DATE  5SEP90

PROJECT SCHEDULE (WITH BUDGET AND EARNED-VALUE AMOUNTS)                 DATA DATE   6NOV89  PAGE NO.    1
              SORTED BY RESPONSIBLE PERSON AND ACTIVITY ID


MIKE SMITH - OPERATING ENGINEER
----- -----  ---- ---- - ---  ----------  ------------------------------------   --------  --------  --------  --------  -----
ACTIVITY     ORIG REM                       ACTIVITY DESCRIPTION          EARLY     EARLY     LATE      LATE     TOTAL
   ID        DUR  DUR   %                         BUDGET      EARNED      START    FINISH    START    FINISH    FLOAT
----- -----  ---- ---- - ---               ------------------------------------   --------  --------  --------  --------  -----

B202           1    1   0     Begin Building Construction                        29DEC89   29DEC89    3JAN90    3JAN90      2
                                                      .00        .00

B203          15   15   0     Install Precast & Brick West Wall                   2JAN90   22JAN90   30JAN90   20FEB90     20
                                                 66806.00        .00

B209           2    2   0     Backfill & Compact Slab                            15FEB90   16FEB90    8MAR90    9MAR90     14
                                                  1130.00        .00

B210           2    2   0     Pour & Strip Slab                                  20FEB90   21FEB90   12MAR90   13MAR90     14
                                                  4158.40        .00

B211          10   10   0     Install Precast & Brick South Wall                 23JAN90    5FEB90   21FEB90    6MAR90     20
                                                363800.00        .00

B226           8    8   0     Complete Office Area                               21MAR90   30MAR90   23MAR90    3APR90      2
                                                  2200.00        .00
                                             ------------ ------------
   SUBTOTAL               SMITH                 438094.40        .00


--------------------------------------------------------------------------------------------
ACME MOTORS, INC.                    PRIMAVERA PROJECT PLANNER            PLANT EXPANSION AND MODERNIZATION

REPORT DATE 23OCT89  RUN NO.   3        PROJECT SCHEDULE              START DATE 24JUL89 FIN DATE  5SEP90

PROJECT SCHEDULE (WITH BUDGET AND EARNED-VALUE AMOUNTS)                 DATA DATE   6NOV89  PAGE NO.    1
              SORTED BY RESPONSIBLE PERSON AND ACTIVITY ID


STEVE UCCI - MACHINIST
----- -----  ---- ---- - ---  ----------  ------------------------------------   --------  --------  --------  --------  -----
ACTIVITY     ORIG REM                       ACTIVITY DESCRIPTION          EARLY     EARLY     LATE      LATE     TOTAL
   ID        DUR  DUR   %                         BUDGET      EARNED      START    FINISH    START    FINISH    FLOAT
----- -----  ---- ---- - ---               ------------------------------------   --------  --------  --------  --------  -----

C302          85   85   0     Shop Fabrication                                   10JAN90    9MAY90   10JAN90    9MAY90      0
                                                 31450.00        .00
                                             ------------ ------------
   SUBTOTAL               UCCI                   31450.00        .00

                                             ============ ============
   REPORT TOTAL                               1180831.65   245442.00
```

(continued)

Table A-4.   Single-Bar Monthly Gantt Chart, by Department and Early Start

```
----------------------------------------------------------------------------------------------------------
ACME MOTORS, INC.                        PRIMAVERA PROJECT PLANNER          PLANT EXPANSION AND MODERNIZATION

REPORT DATE 23OCT89   RUN NO.   4        PROJECT SCHEDULE                   START DATE 24JUL89 FIN DATE  5SEP90

PROJECT SCHEDULE: SINGLE-BAR MONTHLY GANTT CHART                  DATA DATE   6NOV89  PAGE NO.   1
                SORTED BY DEPARTMENT, BY EARLY START, AND BY TOTAL FLOAT
CONSTRUCTION                                                      WEEKLY-TIME PER.   1
----------------------------------------------------------------------------------------------------------
```

............ACTIVITY DESCRIPTION.............					FLOAT	SCHEDULE	07 AUG 89	04 SEP 89	02 OCT 89	06 NOV 89	04 DEC 89	01 JAN 90	05 FEB 90	05 MAR 90	02 APR 90	07 MAY 90	04 JUN 90	02 JUL 90	06 AUG 90	03 SEP 90	01 OCT 90	05 NOV 90
ACTIVITY ID	OD	RD	PCT	CODES																		

```
PHASE II - RESPONSIBILITY OF M.J. SMITH
Begin Building Construction              CURRENT       .   .   .   *   .  EL   .   .   .   .   .   .   .   .   .   .
B202         1    1    0           2                   .   .   .   *   .   .   .   .   .   .   .   .   .   .   .   .

PHASE II - RESPONSIBILITY OF J.P. NOLAN
Drywall In Offices                       CURRENT       .   .   .   *   .  /EEE .   .   .   .   .   .   .   .   .   .
B204        15   15    0           2                   .   .   .   *   .   .   .   .   .   .   .   .   .   .   .   .

PHASE II - RESPONSIBILITY OF M.J. SMITH
Install Precast & Brick West Wall        CURRENT       .   .   .   *   .  EEEELLLL .   .   .   .   .   .   .   .   .
B203        15   15    0          20                   .   .   .   *   .   .   .   .   .   .   .   .   .   .   .   .

PHASE II - RESPONSIBILITY OF J.P. NOLAN
Interior Siding and South Wall           CURRENT       .   .   .   *   .  .EE+L.   .   .   .   .   .   .   .   .   .
B205         5    5    0          14                   .   .   .   *   .   .   .   .   .   .   .   .   .   .   .   .

PHASE II - RESPONSIBILITY OF S.J. UCCI
Shop Fabrication                         CURRENT       .   .   .   *   .  ./EEEEEEEEEEEEEEEE   .   .   .   .   .
C302        85   85    0           0                   .   .   .   *   .   .   .   .   .   .   .   .   .   .   .   .

PHASE II - RESPONSIBILITY OF J.P. NOLAN
Rework Existing Steel at Roof            CURRENT       .   .   .   *   .  . E++L   .   .   .   .   .   .   .   .   .
B206         2    2    0          14                   .   .   .   *   .   .   .   .   .   .   .   .   .   .   .   .

Paint Bldg Interior                      CURRENT       .   .   .   *   .  . EE+++++++LL.   .   .   .   .   .   .   .
B216         5    5    0          46                   .   .   .   *   .   .   .   .   .   .   .   .   .   .   .   .

South Wall & Stair Footing               CURRENT       .   .   .   *   .  . EEE/LLL.   .   .   .   .   .   .   .   .
B207        15   15    0          14                   .   .   .   *   .   .   .   .   .   .   .   .   .   .   .   .

Install Skywalk Brick                    CURRENT       .   .   .   *   .  . EEEELLLL   .   .   .   .   .   .   .   .
B220        15   15    0          18                   .   .   .   *   .   .   .   .   .   .   .   .   .   .   .   .

Install Ceiling Grid                     CURRENT       .   .   .   *   .  . /E.   .   .   .   .   .   .   .   .   .
B212         5    5    0           2                   .   .   .   *   .   .   .   .   .   .   .   .   .   .   .   .

PHASE II - RESPONSIBILITY OF M.J. SMITH
Install Precast & Brick South Wall       CURRENT       .   .   .   *   .  . EEE+LLL   .   .   .   .   .   .   .   .
B211        10   10    0          20                   .   .   .   *   .   .   .   .   .   .   .   .   .   .   .   .

PHASE II - RESPONSIBILITY OF J.P. NOLAN
Install Lights, Sprinklers & Diffusers   CURRENT       .   .   .   *   .  . /EE .   .   .   .   .   .   .   .   .
B213        10   10    0           2                   .   .   .   *   .   .   .   .   .   .   .   .   .   .   .   .
```

Table A-4. Continued.

```
--------------------------------------------------------------------------------------------------------
ACME MOTORS, INC.                    PRIMAVERA PROJECT PLANNER           PLANT EXPANSION AND MODERNIZATION

REPORT DATE 23OCT89   RUN NO.   4    PROJECT SCHEDULE                    START DATE 24JUL89 FIN DATE  5SEP90

PROJECT SCHEDULE: SINGLE-BAR MONTHLY GANTT CHART                         DATA DATE    6NOV89  PAGE NO.   2
                 SORTED BY DEPARTMENT, BY EARLY START, AND BY TOTAL FLOAT
CONSTRUCTION                                                             WEEKLY-TIME PER.   1
--------------------------------------------------------------------------------------------------------
```

...........ACTIVITY DESCRIPTION.............					FLOAT	SCHEDULE	07 AUG 89	04 SEP 89	02 OCT 89	06 NOV 89	04 DEC 89	01 JAN 90	05 FEB 90	05 MAR 90	02 APR 90	07 MAY 90	04 JUN 90	02 JUL 90	06 AUG 90	03 SEP 90	01 OCT 90	05 NOV 90
ACTIVITY ID	OD	RD	PCT	CODES																		
PHASE II - RESPONSIBILITY OF J.P. NOLAN																						
Slab U/G Piping & Test						CURRENT	.	.	.	*	.	.	EE+LL	.	.	.	.	.	.	.	.	.
B208	5	5	0		14		.	.	.	*	.	.	.	.	.	.	.	.	.	.	.	.
Install Stair Steel & Complete Area Paving						CURRENT	.	.	.	*	.	.	EEE+LLL	.	.	.	.	.	.	.	.	.
B224	10	10	0		18		.	.	.	*	.	.	.	.	.	.	.	.	.	.	.	.
Skywalk Roofing						CURRENT	.	.	.	*	.	.	EE++LL	.	.	.	.	.	.	.	.	.
B221	5	5	0		20		.	.	.	*	.	.	.	.	.	.	.	.	.	.	.	.
Install Floor & Tile						CURRENT	.	.	.	*	.	.	./E	.	.	.	.	.	.	.	.	.
B214	5	5	0		2		.	.	.	*	.	.	.	.	.	.	.	.	.	.	.	.
PHASE II - RESPONSIBILITY OF M.J. SMITH																						
Backfill & Compact Slab						CURRENT	.	.	.	*	.	.	.E++L	.	.	.	.	.	.	.	.	.
B209	2	2	0		14		.	.	.	*	.	.	.	.	.	.	.	.	.	.	.	.
PHASE II - RESPONSIBILITY OF J.P. NOLAN																						
Skywalk Lighting & Electrical						CURRENT	.	.	.	*	.	.	.EE++LL	.	.	.	.	.	.	.	.	.
B222	5	5	0		20		.	.	.	*	.	.	.	.	.	.	.	.	.	.	.	.
PHASE II - RESPONSIBILITY OF M.J. SMITH																						
Pour & Strip Slab						CURRENT	.	.	.	*	.	.	. E++L	.	.	.	.	.	.	.	.	.
B210	2	2	0		14		.	.	.	*	.	.	.	.	.	.	.	.	.	.	.	.
PHASE II - RESPONSIBILITY OF J.P. NOLAN																						
Install Heaters & Tie-In						CURRENT	.	.	.	*	.	.	./EE	.	.	.	.	.	.	.	.	.
B215	10	10	0		2		.	.	.	*	.	.	.	.	.	.	.	.	.	.	.	.
Skywalk Finishes, Flooring, & Doors						CURRENT	.	.	.	*	.	.	. EEE+LLL	.	.	.	.	.	.	.	.	.
B223	10	10	0		20		.	.	.	*	.	.	.	.	.	.	.	.	.	.	.	.
Roofing at Stairway						CURRENT	.	.	.	*	.	.	. EE+LL	.	.	.	.	.	.	.	.	.
B217	5	5	0		14		.	.	.	*	.	.	.	.	.	.	.	.	.	.	.	.
Install Ceiling						CURRENT	.	.	.	*	.	.	. EEELLL	.	.	.	.	.	.	.	.	.
B218	10	10	0		14		.	.	.	*	.	.	.	.	.	.	.	.	.	.	.	.
Paint & Trim at Stairs						CURRENT	.	.	.	*	.	.	. EE++LL	.	.	.	.	.	.	.	.	.
B219	4	4	0		20		.	.	.	*	.	.	.	.	.	.	.	.	.	.	.	.
Install Steam Supply to Heaters						CURRENT	.	.	.	*	.	.	. /EE	.	.	.	.	.	.	.	.	.
B225	10	10	0		2		.	.	.	*	.	.	.	.	.	.	.	.	.	.	.	.
PHASE II - RESPONSIBILITY OF M.J. SMITH																						
Complete Office Area						CURRENT	.	.	.	*	.	.	.	. /EL	.	.	.	.	.	.	.	.
B226	8	8	0		2		.	.	.	*	.	.	.	.	.	.	.	.	.	.	.	.

(continued)

Table A-4.   Continued.

```
------------------------------------------------------------------------------------------
ACME MOTORS, INC.                    PRIMAVERA PROJECT PLANNER         PLANT EXPANSION AND MODERNIZATION

REPORT DATE 23OCT89   RUN NO.   4    PROJECT SCHEDULE                  START DATE 24JUL89 FIN DATE  5SEP90

PROJECT SCHEDULE: SINGLE-BAR MONTHLY GANTT CHART                       DATA DATE   6NOV89  PAGE NO.   1
              SORTED BY DEPARTMENT, BY EARLY START, AND BY TOTAL FLOAT
ENGINEERING                                                           WEEKLY-TIME PER.   1
------------------------------------------------------------------------------------------
...........ACTIVITY DESCRIPTION.............      07  04  02  06  04  01  05  05  02  07  04  02  06  03  01  05
ACTIVITY ID  OD  RD  PCT   CODES    FLOAT  SCHEDULE  AUG SEP OCT NOV DEC JAN FEB MAR APR MAY JUN JUL AUG SEP OCT NOV
----------- ---- ---- --- ----------- ----- --------  89  89  89  89  89  90  90  90  90  90  90  90  90  90  90  90
                                                     ------------------------------------------------------------

PHASE I - RESPONSIBILITY OF A.J. MASON
Design Conveyor                            CURRENT  AAAAAAAAAA.     *   .   .   .   .   .   .   .   .   .   .   .   .
  C300        45   0 100                            .   .   .      *   .   .   .   .   .   .   .   .   .   .   .   .

Design Automated System                    CURRENT  AAAAA   .      *   .   .   .   .   .   .   .   .   .   .   .   .
  A100        20   0 100                            .   .   .      *   .   .   .   .   .   .   .   .   .   .   .   .

PHASE I - RESPONSIBILITY OF ACME MOTORS
Submit & Approve Site Drawings             CURRENT  .   .AAA.      *   .   .   .   .   .   .   .   .   .   .   .   .
  A101        14   0 100                            .   .   .      *   .   .   .   .   .   .   .   .   .   .   .   .

PHASE I - RESPONSIBILITY OF A.J. MASON
Building Design & Engineering Drawings     CURRENT  .   . AAAAAA/E .   .   .   .   .   .   .   .   .   .   .   .   .
  B200        30   6  80         2                  .   .   .      *   .   .   .   .   .   .   .   .   .   .   .   .

PHASE II - RESPONSIBILITY OF T.M. MILLS
Install Robot Base                         CURRENT  .   .   .  /EEEEL .   .   .   .   .   .   .   .   .   .   .   .
  A103        20  20   0         2                  .   .   .      *   .   .   .   .   .   .   .   .   .   .   .   .

PHASE I - RESPONSIBILITY OF ACME MOTORS
Approve Engineering Drawings               CURRENT  .   .   .  */EE. .   .   .   .   .   .   .   .   .   .   .   .
  B230        10  10   0         2                  .   .   .      *   .   .   .   .   .   .   .   .   .   .   .   .

PHASE II - RESPONSIBILITY OF T.M. MILLS
Run Piping & Install Electrical            CURRENT  .   .   .  */EEEEE .  .   .   .   .   .   .   .   .   .   .   .
  A104        24  24   0         2                  .   .   .      *   .   .   .   .   .   .   .   .   .   .   .   .

Install Temperature Control Equip.         CURRENT  .   .   .      * /EEEEEE .  .   .   .   .   .   .   .   .   .   .
  A105        29  29   0         2                  .   .   .      *   .   .   .   .   .   .   .   .   .   .   .   .

Set & Connect Robots                       CURRENT  .   .   .      *   . /EEEL .   .   .   .   .   .   .   .   .   .
  A106        18  18   0         2                  .   .   .      *   .   .   .   .   .   .   .   .   .   .   .   .

Install System & Misc. Components          CURRENT  .   .   .      *   .   . E/EEEEEL. .   .   .   .   .   .   .   .
  A107        30  30   0         2                  .   .   .      *   .   .   .   .   .   .   .   .   .   .   .   .

Install System Controller & Rails          CURRENT  .   .   .      *   .   .  .EEEE/EEELLLL. .   .   .   .   .   .
  A108        35  35   0        18                  .   .   .      *   .   .   .   .   .   .   .   .   .   .   .   .

Test & Debug Line A                        CURRENT  .   .   .      *   .   .  . E/EEE .   .   .   .   .   .   .   .
  A109        20  20   0         2                  .   .   .      *   .   .   .   .   .   .   .   .   .   .   .   .

Test & Debug Line B                        CURRENT  .   .   .      *   .   .  . E/EEE  .   .   .   .   .   .   .   .
  A110        20  20   0         2                  .   .   .      *   .   .   .   .   .   .   .   .   .   .   .   .
```

(continued)

Table A-4.   Continued.

```
-------------------------------------------------------------------------------------------
ACME MOTORS, INC.                    PRIMAVERA PROJECT PLANNER         PLANT EXPANSION AND MODERNIZATION

REPORT DATE 23OCT89   RUN NO.   4    PROJECT SCHEDULE                  START DATE 24JUL89 FIN DATE  5SEP90

PROJECT SCHEDULE: SINGLE-BAR MONTHLY GANTT CHART                       DATA DATE   6NOV89  PAGE NO.   2
                 SORTED BY DEPARTMENT, BY EARLY START, AND BY TOTAL FLOAT
ENGINEERING                                                           WEEKLY-TIME PER.   1
-------------------------------------------------------------------------------------------
.............ACTIVITY DESCRIPTION.............   07  04  02  06  04  01  05  05  02  07  04  02  06  03  01  05
ACTIVITY ID  OD   RD   PCT    CODES    FLOAT   SCHEDULE  AUG SEP OCT NOV DEC JAN FEB MAR APR MAY JUN JUL AUG SEP OCT NOV
-----------  ---- ---- --- ------------ -----  --------  89  89  89  89  89  90  90  90  90  90  90  90  90  90  90  90
                                                         ---------------------------------------------------------------

PHASE II - RESPONSIBILITY OF T.M. MILLS
Pilot Start Line A/Path Refinement              CURRENT    .   .   .   *   .   .   .   . EE/EELL.   .   .   .   .   .
A111         21   21   0                    8              .   .   .   *   .   .   .   .   .   .   .   .   .   .   .   .

PHASE II - RESPONSIBILITY OF ACME MOTORS
Check-Out Maintenance & Tooling Bldg            CURRENT    .   .   .   *   .   .   .   . /L  .   .   .   .   .   .   .
B300          5    5   0                    2              .   .   .   *   .   .   .   .   .   .   .   .   .   .   .   .

PHASE II - RESPONSIBILITY OF T.M. MILLS
Start-Up Line B/Path Refinement                 CURRENT    .   .   .   *   .   .   .   . E/EEL.   .   .   .   .   .   .
A112         17   17   0                    2              .   .   .   *   .   .   .   .   .   .   .   .   .   .   .   .

Install Processor/Software/Data Tapes           CURRENT    .   .   .   *   .   .   .   .   . /.  .   .   .   .   .   .
A113          2    2   0                    2              .   .   .   *   .   .   .   .   .   .   .   .   .   .   .   .

Calibrate Robot Controller & Power Up           CURRENT    .   .   .   *   .   .   .   .   . EL  .   .   .   .   .   .
A114          1    1   0                    2              .   .   .   *   .   .   .   .   .   .   .   .   .   .   .   .

Make Mech Adjustments & Load System Software    CURRENT    .   .   .   *   .   .   .   .   . E/EEEEEL .   .   .   .   .
A115         30   30   0                    2              .   .   .   *   .   .   .   .   .   .   .   .   .   .   .   .

Install Conveyor                                CURRENT    .   .   .   *   .   .   .   .   .   . /EEEE  .   .   .   .
C303         20   20   0                    0              .   .   .   *   .   .   .   .   .   .   .   .   .   .   .   .

Field Wiring & Piping                           CURRENT    .   .   .   *   .   .   .   .   .   .   . /EEEEEEE .   .   .
C304         35   35   0                    0              .   .   .   *   .   .   .   .   .   .   .   .   .   .   .   .

Manual Operation Ready                          CURRENT    .   .   .   *   .   .   .   .   .   .   .   . /  .   .   .
A600          1    1   0                    2              .   .   .   *   .   .   .   .   .   .   .   .   .   .   .   .

PHASE II - RESPONSIBILITY OF T.H. EVANS
Start-Up & Debug System                         CURRENT    .   .   .   *   .   .   .   .   .   .   .   . /EEEEE  .   .
C305         27   27   0                    0              .   .   .   *   .   .   .   .   .   .   .   .   .   .   .   .

Startup Procedure Development                   CURRENT    .   .   .   *   .   .   .   .   .   .   .   .   . ./L  .   .
A117          3    3   0                    2              .   .   .   *   .   .   .   .   .   .   .   .   .   .   .   .

Training Manuals/System Operation               CURRENT    .   .   .   *   .   .   .   .   .   .   .   .   . /EL  .   .
A118          9    9   0                    2              .   .   .   *   .   .   .   .   .   .   .   .   .   .   .   .

System Buyoff                                   CURRENT    .   .   .   *   .   .   .   .   .   .   .   .   . /  .   .
A900          1    1   0                    0              .   .   .   *   .   .   .   .   .   .   .   .   .   .   .   .
```

(continued)

Table A-4.   Continued.

```
-------------------------------------------------------------------------------------------------
ACME MOTORS, INC.                    PRIMAVERA PROJECT PLANNER          PLANT EXPANSION AND MODERNIZATION

REPORT DATE 23OCT89  RUN NO.   4     PROJECT SCHEDULE                   START DATE 24JUL89 FIN DATE  5SEP90

PROJECT SCHEDULE: SINGLE-BAR MONTHLY GANTT CHART                        DATA DATE   6NOV89  PAGE NO.   1
                 SORTED BY DEPARTMENT, BY EARLY START, AND BY TOTAL FLOAT
PROGRAMMING                                                            WEEKLY-TIME PER.   1
-------------------------------------------------------------------------------------------------
.............ACTIVITY DESCRIPTION.............    07  04  02  06  04  01  05  05  02  07  04  02  06  03  01  05
ACTIVITY ID  OD   RD  PCT   CODES   FLOAT  SCHEDULE  AUG SEP OCT NOV DEC JAN FEB MAR APR MAY JUN JUL AUG SEP OCT NOV
------------ ---- ---- --- ----------- -----  --------  89  89  89  89  89  90  90  90  90  90  90  90  90  90  90  90
                                                 -------------------------------------------------------
PHASE II - RESPONSIBILITY OF L.A. HARIS
Production Start                           CURRENT   .   .   .   *   .   .   .   .   .   /.  .   .   .   .   .   .
 A150      1    1   0            2                   .   .   .   *   .   .   .   .   .   .   .   .   .   .   .   .

Program & Testing                         CURRENT   .   .   .   *   .   .   .   .   .   .   ./EEEEEEEE  .   .   .
 A116     40   40   0            2                   .   .   .   *   .   .   .   .   .   .   .   .   .   .   .   .

Automatic Operation Ready                 CURRENT   .   .   .   *   .   .   .   .   .   .   .   ./  .   .   .
 A500      1    1   0            2                   .   .   .   *   .   .   .   .   .   .   .   .   .   .   .   .
```

```
-------------------------------------------------------------------------------------------------
ACME MOTORS, INC.                    PRIMAVERA PROJECT PLANNER          PLANT EXPANSION AND MODERNIZATION

REPORT DATE 23OCT89   RUN NO.   4    PROJECT SCHEDULE                   START DATE 24JUL89 FIN DATE  5SEP90

PROJECT SCHEDULE: SINGLE-BAR MONTHLY GANTT CHART                        DATA DATE   6NOV89  PAGE NO.   1
                 SORTED BY DEPARTMENT, BY EARLY START, AND BY TOTAL FLOAT
PURCHASING                                                             WEEKLY-TIME PER.   1
-------------------------------------------------------------------------------------------------
.............ACTIVITY DESCRIPTION.............    07  04  02  06  04  01  05  05  02  07  04  02  06  03  01  05
ACTIVITY ID  OD   RD  PCT   CODES   FLOAT  SCHEDULE  AUG SEP OCT NOV DEC JAN FEB MAR APR MAY JUN JUL AUG SEP OCT NOV
------------ ---- ---- --- ----------- -----  --------  89  89  89  89  89  90  90  90  90  90  90  90  90  90  90  90
                                                 -------------------------------------------------------
```

```
PHASE I - RESPONSIBILITY OF M.C. FOLEY
Purchase & Deliver Robots                 CURRENT   .   . AAAAAA/ .   .   .   .   .   .   .   .   .   .   .   .
 A102     30    2  93            2                   .   .   .   *   .   .   .   .   .   .   .   .   .   .   .   .

Purchase & Deliver Parts                  CURRENT   .   . AAAAA/EEEEEEEEEE .   .   .   .   .   .   .   .   .   .
 C301     70   43  39            0                   .   .   .   *   .   .   .   .   .   .   .   .   .   .   .   .

Purchase Construction Material            CURRENT   .   .   .   * E/EEEL .   .   .   .   .   .   .   .   .   .
 B201     20   20   0            2                   .   .   .   *   .   .   .   .   .   .   .   .   .   .   .   .
```

Appendix B:
Weekly Activity Planner

SCHEDULE FOR: _____ WEEK OF: _____

TIME	MON	TUE	WED	THU	FRI
6:00AM 6:30AM					
7:00AM 7:30AM					
8:00AM 8:30AM					
9:00AM 9:30AM					
10:00AM 10:30AM					
11:00AM 11:30AM					
12:00PM 12:30PM					
1:00PM 1:30PM					
2:00PM 2:30PM					
3:00PM 3:30PM					
4:00PM 4:30PM					
5:00PM 5:30PM					
6:00PM 6:30PM					
7:00PM 7:30PM					
8:00PM 8:30PM					
9:00PM 9:30PM					

FIGURE B-1. Weekly planning guide. Dreger, *Project Management: Effective Scheduling* © Van Nostrand Reinhold, 1992.

BIBLIOGRAPHY

20/20 VAX/VMS and MS-DOS *Reference Manual* and electronic spreadsheet software, Natick, Massachusetts: Access Technology, Inc., 1991.

Anthony, Robert N., and James S. Reece. *Accounting: Text and Cases*. Homewood, Illinois: Richard D. Irwin, 1983.

Armstrong-Wright, A.T. *Critical Path Method*. London: Longman Group, 1969.

Barker, Joel A. *Discovering the Future: The Business of Paradigms* (2nd edition). Charthouse Learning Corporation, 1989. Video.

Betts, Mitch. "Risk Management: As Easy as 1 Through 10." *Computerworld,* 19 November 1990: 77.

Burman, P.J. *Precedence Networks for Project Planning and Control*. London: McGraw-Hill (UK), 1972.

Chase, Richard B., and Nicholas J. Aquilano. *Production and Operations Management: A Life Cycle Approach*. Chapter 9. Homewood, Illinois: Richard D. Irwin, Inc., 1985.

Chesnut, D.R. *Program Management*. Wichita, Kansas: The Boeing Company, 1988.

Cleland, David I. *A Project Management Dictionary of Terms*. New York: Van Nostrand Reinhold, 1985.

Cleland, David I. *Project Management: Strategic Design and Implementation,* Blue Ridge Summit, Pennsylvania: TAB Books, Inc., 1990.

Comshare, Inc. *Interactive Financial Planning System (IFPS/Plus) User's Manual* and decision support system software, Austin, Texas: Comshare. 1989.

Cox, John. "VAX Project Management." *Digital News,* 16 May 1988: 58.

Customer Oriented Selling II Workshop. Los Angeles: Tratec/McGraw-Hill, 1983.

Diagraph Symbol Handbook. Dallas, Texas: Computer Support Corporation, 1988.

Dinsmore, Paul C. *Human Factors in Project Management*. New York: AMACOM, 1990.

DOD/NASA PERT Cost Systems Design. Washington, D.C.: U.S. Government Printing Office, 1962.

Dreger, J. Brian. "The CASE for Business Strategy and Performance." Paper presented at seminar, *Managing Change—The Strategic Information Advantage*. Unisys Australia Limited, Gold Coast, Queensland, Australia, 25–28 April 1990.

Dreger, J. Brian. *Function Point Analysis*. Englewood Cliffs, New Jersey: Prentice-Hall, 1989.

Dreger, J. Brian. Lesson plan lecture notes for seminar, *Program Management for the Boeing Executive*. The Boeing Company, Wichita, Kansas, 22–26 February and 20–24 June 1988.

Dreger, J. Brian. Lesson plan lecture notes for seminar, *Project Management: Basic Scheduling Principles*. The Boeing Company, Wichita, Kansas, September 1991.

Dreger, J. Brian. Lesson plan lecture notes, BUS 608 "Business Information Systems." Webster University Graduate School of Business Administration, 1988.

Dreger, J. Brian. Lesson plan lecture notes, Wichita State University Graduate School of Computer Science, CS 684 "Structured Applications Systems Analysis and Design." 1987.

Dreger, J. Brian. *Total Quality Management*. New York: Van Nostrand Reinhold. Under development.

Dreger, J. Brian. "VAX Project Management: Evaluating Project Management Software," Interview by John Cox, *Digital News,* 16 May 1988: 58–59.

Evarts, Harry F. *Introduction to PERT*. Boston: Allyn and Bacon, 1964.

FitzGerald, Jerry, and Ardra F. FitzGerald. *Fundamentals of Systems Analysis*. New York: John Wiley & Sons, 1987.

Frame, J. Davidson. *Managing Projects in Organizations*. Silver Spring, Maryland: U.S. Professional Development Institute, 1987.

Fujikawa, Gyo. *Let's Play*. Japan: Zokeisha Publications, Ltd., 1975.

Gaither, Norman. *Production and Operations Management: A Problem-Solving and Decision-Making Approach*. Hinsdale, Illinois: Dryden Press, 1980.

Getting to Know P3. Bala Cynwyd, Pennsylvania: Primavera Systems, Inc., 1991.

Gido, Jack. *An Introduction to Project Planning*. New York: Industrial Press, 1985.

Hansen, B.J. *Practical PERT*. Washington, D.C.: America House, 1964.

Instruction Manual and Systems and Procedures for PERT. Washington, D.C.: Special Projects Office, Bureau of Naval Weapons, Department of the Navy, 1960.

Jones, Capers. Foreword to *Function Point Analysis,* by Dreger, J. Brian. Englewood Cliffs, New Jersey: Prentice-Hall, 1989.

Kerzner, Harold. *Project Management for Executives*. New York: Van Nostrand Reinhold, 1982.

Kerzner, Harold. *Project Management: A Systems Approach*. New York: Van Nostrand Reinhold, 1984.

Kliem, Ralph L. "10 Ways to Keep Your Project on Track." *System Builder,* October/November 1990: 42–43.

Kopitowsky, Ronald. "Telecom Project Management Tips." *Computerworld,* 4 May 1988: 51.

Krakow, Ira H. *Project Management with the IBM PC*. Bowie, Maryland: Brady Communications Company (Prentice-Hall), 1985.

Lang, Douglas W. *Critical Path Analysis*. London: St. Paul's House, 1970.

Levine, Harvey A. "Project Management Software: Different [from] Others." *CA-INSIGHT,* Summer 1988: 45–48.

Levine, Harvey A. *Project Management Using Microcomputers*. Berkeley, California: Osborne/McGraw-Hill, 1986.

Maher, Robert, and Constance Alexander. "Happy Ending for Your Systems Project." *Computerworld,* 7 July 1986: 63–65.

Making It Happen. Bala Cynwyd, Pennsylvania: Primavera Systems, Inc., 1989.

"Managing the Variables of Project Management." *Digital Review,* 3 June 1991: 21–23.

Martin, Charles C., *Project Management: How to Make it Work*. New York: American Management Associations, 1976.

Martin, James. *Managing the Data-Base Environment*. Englewood Cliffs, New Jersey: Prentice-Hall, 1983.

McLeod, Raymond, Jr. *Management Information Systems*. Chicago: Science Research Associates, 1986.

Metzger, Philip W. *Managing a Programming Project*. Englewood Cliffs, New Jersey: Prentice-Hall, 1981.

Moder, Joseph J., Cecil R. Phillips, and Edward W. Davis. *Project Management With CPM, PERT, and Precedence Diagramming*. New York: Van Nostrand Reinhold, 1983.

Monks, Joseph G. "Project Management." Chapter 16 in *Operations Management*. New York: Schaum/McGraw-Hill, 1985.

"Murphy's Law Desk Calendar: 365 Reasons Why Things Continue to Go Wrong." Los Angeles: Price Stern Sloan, Inc., Published annually since 1981.

O'Brien, James J. *Scheduling Handbook.* New York: McGraw-Hill, 1969.

PERT Summary Report, Phases I and II. Washington, D.C.: Special Projects Office, Bureau of Naval Weapons, Department of the Navy, 1958.

Powers, Michael J., David R. Adams, and Harlan D. Mills. *Corporate Information Systems Development: Analysis and Design.* Cincinnati; South-Western Publishing Company, 1984.

Primavera Systems, Inc. *Expedition: Construction Contract Control Software User Reference Guide* and (MS-DOS) project management software, Bala Cynwyd, Pennsylvania; Primavera Systems, Inc., 1991.

Primavera Systems, Inc. *Finest Hour: Project Management and Control Software User Reference Guide* and (MS-DOS) project management software, Bala Cynwyd, Pennsylvania; Primavera Systems, Inc., 1992.

Primavera Systems, Inc. *Parade: Performance Measurement Software User Reference Guide* and (MS-DOS/VAX) project management software, Bala Cynwyd, Pennsylvania; Primavera Systems, Inc., 1991.

Primavera Systems, Inc. *Primavera Project Planner: Project Management and Control Software User Reference Guide* and (MS-DOS/VAX) project management software, Bala Cynwyd, Pennsylvania; Primavera Systems, Inc., 1992.

Program Planning and Control System. Washington, D.C.: Special Projects Office, Bureau of Naval Weapons, Department of the Navy, 1960.

Randolph, W. Alan, and Barry Z. Posner. *Effective Project Planning and Management.* New Jersey: Prentice-Hall, Englewood Cliffs, 1988.

Sackman, Harold, and Ronald Critenbaum. *On-line Planning.* Englewood Cliffs, New Jersey: Prentice-Hall, 1972.

Sandler, Corey. "Project Management Goes Mainstream." *Digital News,* 21 August 1989: 45ff.

Schlesinger, Lee. "Using Project Management for Applications." *Digital Review,* 12 November 1990.

Shaffer, Louis R. *The Critical Path Method.* New York: McGraw-Hill, Inc., 1965.

Shelly, Gary B., and Thomas J. Cashman. *Business Systems Analysis and Design.* Boston: Boyd and Fraser Publishing Company, 1975.

Skelton, Ron. "Projects Take Teamwork." *Computerworld,* 8 February 1988: 67ff.

Spirer, Herbert F. "The Basic Analytical Principles of Project Management" *Project Management Journal,* December 1984: 77–81.

Steiner, George, and William G. Ryan, *Industrial Project Management.* New York: Macmillan, 1968.

Stilian, Gabriel N. *PERT.* New York: American Management Association, 1962.

"Structuring Project Plans to Cash in on Innovation." *Digital Review,* 11 December 1989: 35–45.

Turban, Efraim, and N. Paul Loomba. "Networks," Chapter 4 in *Readings in Management Science.* Dallas: Business Publications, Inc., 1976.

Ullman, John E. "Network Analysis." Chapter 5 in *Quantitative Methods in Management.* New York: Schaum/McGraw-Hill, 1976.

Weston, J. Fred, and Eugene F. Brigham. *Managerial Finance.* Hinsdale, Illinois: The Dryden Press, 1975.

Wiest, Jerome D., and Ferdinand K. Levy. *A Management Guide to PERT/CPM.* New Jersey: Prentice-Hall, Englewood Cliffs, 1977.

Index